THE HOLY BIBLE AND THE LAW

By

J. W. EHRLICH

OCEANA PUBLICATIONS, INC.

NEW YORK, N. Y.

Library of Congress Catalog Card Number: 61-14004

MANUFACTURED IN THE UNITED STATES OF AMERICA

But as for thee, stand thou here by me, and I will speak unto thee all the commandments, . . . which thou shalt teach them, that they may do them. . . .

Deuteronomy 5:31

PURPOSE

THE HOLY BIBLE AND THE LAW is intended as a quick-finder for the literate citizen, the student, the men of cloth, the lawyer, the social worker, the doctor, the judge, the orator, the law office, the library, and the teacher. Each legal subject has been, wherever possible, set out in plain, non-technical language, and the Holy Bible has been quoted without comment except citation to the source book. No distinction is made between the various and varied biblical translations, but all quotations are found in the Hebrew, Catholic and Protestant Bibles most commonly used today.

TABLE OF CONTENTS

INTRODUCTION

The Bible (Greek-biblos, book) consists of sixty-six books aside from those of the Apocrypha. The word Bible was first applied to the Hebrew Scripture in the second century A.D. (Second Epistle to Corinth) and has been used for the combined Old and New Testaments since the fifth century A.D. The word Bible does not occur in the text of the Scriptures.

The so-called Books of Moses are also known as the Pentateuch (Greek, five scrolls), or the Law. Much of the Pentateuch goes back to the remote past, and other parts of it may have been written as late as the Fifth Century B.C. It came to be regarded as authoritative about 400 B.C.

It is impossible to determine exactly when the first collection of sacred books was made. It is uncertain at what date the Hebrews, under the leadership of Esdras, bound themselves to the observance of the Torah, or Law of Moses. From the prologue of Ecclesiasticus, it appears that a collection which included 'the Law, the Prophets, and the Writings' was in existence in 130 B.C. It is unknown by what authority it was determined which books should be included in the collection. In all probability the books were in the custody of the priesthood. It is reasonable to assume that the Scribes subsequently asserted their authority to exclude books from the collection. However, the vagueness of this determination is seen in the existence of two canons. The Palestinian canon, represented by the Old Testament in Hebrew, and the Alexandrine canon, represented by the Old Testament in

Greek, which contained books not admitted into the Palestinian collection.

These five books of Moses were the most highly venerated of the sacred books. Torah actually means 'instruction' or 'doctrine,' rather than 'law'; and a large portion of the books of Moses is narrative. From the narrative portions as well as from the legal portions were deduced conclusions about God, His providence, and human conduct. 'Law,' however, expresses accurately the attitude of the Hebrews toward these books. The basis of legal observance was faith in the covenant of God with Israel and in divine retribution.

The Law, however, was more than a series of regulations of external conduct. It was possible for Hillel to sum it up in the rule, 'Do not to another what you would not have him do to you,' and for Jesus to point out as its greatest and first commandment, 'Thou shalt love the Lord thy God with thy whole heart,' and as the second, 'Thou shalt love thy neighbor as thyself.'

Mosaic law was studied carefully for generations. Extensions and refinements in that law were made by scholars and orally transmitted to their students.

Many interpretations of the Bible developed, and in the Third Century A.D. these were codified in written form called the Mishnah. Later, scholars commented and elaborated upon the Mishnah and thus created a new work called the Gemara. Thus, the Mishnah and Gemara resulted in two compilations each known as the Talmud, one in Palestine in the Fourth Century; the other in Babylon in the Fifth.

The Talmud treats of civil and religious law, history, mathematics, astronomy, medicine, metaphysics, and theosophy. It passes from law to myth, from jest to earnest. It is replete with chaste diction, legendary illustration, touches of pathos, bursts of genuine eloquence, finished rhetoric, and flashes of wit and sarcasm.

By 200 A.D. the New Testament was generally accepted as Scripture. In 367 A.D. Athanasius, Bishop of Alexandria, in a public letter, listed the twenty-seven books which have been held as authoritative to this day.

The fourteen books of the Apocrypha (Greek, for "hidden" or "obscure") have not been included in the Protestant Bible since the beginning of the Ninteenth Century. There are editions of the Bible containing the Apocrypha, but since the books are rejected as non-inspired, although of Hebrew origin, most Hebrew and Protestant religious leaders have ignored their beauty and value. The Catholic Bible contains some of the Apocrypha.

Blackstone, in his commentaries on the Laws of England, wrote that Divine Providence has been pleased at sundry times and in divers manners to discover and enforce its laws by an immediate and direct revelation. And that the doctrines thus discovered are called the revealed or divine law, and are to be found only in the Holy Scriptures.

Mosaic law is a law of principles, directing man in the ways of righteousness, happiness and tranquility. The principles were not of immediate creation, but grew through thousands of years of human experience.

Research has established that much of the Five Books of Moses gradually built up during some eight or ten centuries of development. It is believed that Moses codified the laws which had long been known. In Genesis 26:5,

God said of Abraham that he "kept my charge, my commandments, my statutes, and my laws," which indicates that the laws of Moses must have been promulgated long before.

The translations and the various versions of the Bible are: 1. The "Septuagint," (seventy) so called because the translation from the Hebrew to the Greek language in 285 B.D. was allegedly made by seventy men. 2. The "Peshito" (literal) translation, embracing the Old and New Testaments was made about 200 A.D. for the Syrian Christians. 3. The "Vulgate" (vulgus—for the common people) translation of the Old and New Testament into Latin was made about 400 A.D. It is the standard Bible of the Roman Catholic Church. 4. The "King James Version" of the Holy Scriptures—the English translation—was first published in 1611.

In 1250 A.D. the Holy Scriptures were divided into chapters by Cardinal Hugo de Sancto Caro. The division into verses was made about 1550 A.D. The first versified New Testament in English was published in 1557, and in 1560 A.D. the entire Bible was printed in versified form.

It should be noted that in the versification there is much repetition as evidenced in the Seventh Chapter of Numbers which has 89 verses. Of these, verses 15, 21, 27, 33, 39, 45, 51, 57, 63, 69 and 75 are alike.

Verses 16, 22, 28, 34, 40, 46, 52, 58, 64, 70, 76 and 82 are the same.

Verses 26, 32, 38, 44, 50, 56, 62, 68, 74 and 80 are identical.

Verses 25, 37, 49, 61, 67, 73 and 98 are worded the same.

Verses 38 and 55 are alike.

Verse 43 differs from verses 31 and 55 in only one word: where verse 43 reads "a," verses 31 and 55 read "one."

The oldest available manuscripts of substantial parts of the Old Testament in Hebrew are dated 897 and 916 A.D. The oldest manuscript of the entire Old Testament in Hebrew is dated 1008 A.D. The oldest manuscript of the Bible in Greek is the Codex Vaticanus dated in the Fourth Century, a possession of the Vatican Library. The Septuagint Bible (Greek) is the version of the Bible most quoted in the New Testament.

Martin Luther translated the Bible into German in 1534 A.D.

At the end of the Fourteenth Century, John Wyclif made his translation of the Bible from Latin to English, and those who dared to read his work were persecuted. The English law in 1414 provided that those who read the Scriptures in English should "forfeit land, cattle, life and goods from their heirs forever." Some were burned at the stake for the offense, with copies of the Bible dangling from their necks.

For the English-speaking world, the name of William Tyndale is synonymous with the story of the Bible in English. Because of the prohibition against translating the Bible into language readable by the so-called average man, his work in translating the Bible from Hebrew and Greek made him a fugivitive from the England of Henry VIII. Hunted like a wild beast by the Inquisition, he was finally caught in 1536, was imprisoned, strangled, and burned at the stake in Velvorde, Belgium.

The Five Books of Moses contain all the law, and while the laws in Exodus presumably date from the 15th Century B.C., those in Deuteronomy probably were not proclaimed until about the 5th Century B.C. The best known are, of course, the Ten Commandments.

There are two versions of the Ten Commandments; one in Exodus, which is the most commonly accepted version, the other in Deuteronomy. It is assumed that both versions were in exsitence hundreds of years before the five Books of Moses were reduced to writing.

The Ten Commandments begin with the declaration that Israel's God brought him out of Egypt and bondage. Israel shall have no other gods, and shall not make any graven image or representation of anything as an idol to bow down to and serve. The sin of idolatry is proscribed by the admonition that God will punish the children for the sins of their fathers unto the third and fourth generation, and that God is merciful to those who love Him and keep His commandments. Next comes the prohibition against taking His name in vain, and is followed by the directive to keep the Sabbath holy as a rest day from all work for man, beast, and for the stranger. Honoring father and mother is the next commandment. Forbidden are murder, adultery, theft, and false testimony. The Commandments conclude with a prohibition of covetousness of anything belonging to one's neighbor.

The differences in the two versions of the Commandments form an interesting study. While there is no essential variation so far as vital obligations are concerned, verbal changes occur, and in one instance, that of the Sabbath, an entirely different reason is adduced for its observance. The slight variants in the Masoretic text, occasional differences in words, as for instance "covet" for "desire," "Remember the Sabbath," in one case, and "Keep" in the other, and "false witness" in one, and "a witness of deceit" in the other; some additions and amplifications, all this is sought to be explained as due to carelessness on the part of the transcribers. But the variation in the reason alleged for the Sabbath cannot be so readily explained. The Exodus Version connects it with creation; that of Deuteronomy associates it with Israel's release from Egyptian slavery.

The division of the Ten Commandments is another matter of inquiry. As it was written on two tablets of stone and on both sides, its arrangement would have been naturally one group of five "words," each on one stone. So, in fact, is the statement as to the original division made by Josephus ('Antiquitates' Vol. III, 5, 4) and by Phil ('De Decalogo' 12) the first group of five, including the commandments referring to our conduct toward our neighbors.

Another variation is the sequence of certain of the "words" which differ in various versions. The Masoretic text, Josephus, the Syrian Hexapla agree as to the order of the prohibitions against murder, adultery, and theft, but the Septuagint, Codex Alexandrinus and Abrosianus have the sequence of "murder, theft and adultery," while Philo ('De Decalogo' 12) the first group of five, including Codex Vaticanus "adultery, theft, murder"—slight variations, it is true; but in so fundamental a code as the Commandments one would expect uniformity throughout. No less peculiar is the diversity in the numbering of the different commandments.

According to the Jewish tradition, Ex 20:2, forms the first, while Verses 3-6, constitute the second. The Codex Vaticanus of the Septuagint and the Deuteronomy of Ambrosianus have a similar arrangement. Josephus and Philo regard Verse 3 as first, Verses 4-6 as second, Verse 7 as third, Verses 8-11 as fourth, Verse 12 as fifth, Verse 13 as sixth, Verse 14 as seventh, Verse 15 as eighth, Verse 16 as ninth, and Verse 17 as the tenth Commandment. The Roman Catholic and Lutheran combine Verses 3-6 into the first, and every commandment is advanced by one to the last, the traditional Jewish "tenth" being divided into ninth and tenth, to maintain the traditional number.

Most view the Ten Commandments solely as religious rules, but our courts have predicated decisions on much that is in the Bible. In 1899, the West Virginia Supreme Court said: "These Commandments, which, like a collection of diamonds, bear testimony to their own intrinsic worth, in themselves appeal to us as coming from a superhuman or divine source, and no conscientious or reasonable man has yet been able to find a flaw in them. Absolutely flawless, negative in terms, but positive in meaning, they easily stand at the head of our whole moral system, and no nation or people can long continue a happy existence in open violation of them."

Law, generally, is defined as a rule of human action or conduct. Laws are meant to regulate and direct the acts and rights of man. Every man belongs to himself, and has the right to do as he pleases with himself so long as he accords the same right to others, and, further, that he does not do unto others what he would not have them do unto him. This principle is the foundation of English and American law. The Bible embodies these fundamentals which have attained legal effectiveness among nearly all peoples. Much of the law of England and America is founded upon Mosaic Law.

Without law, man would be plunged back into the chaos from which he emerged at the dawn of civilization. Law creates an orderly society, where mankind may follow his pursuits, secure in the knowledge that his rights will be protected and his obligations enforced. The law is so powerful that it is the only protection the individual has against the tyranny of his government. Man searching for the foundation of our law can find no firmer ground than the Bible.

No attempt is made herein to explain every refinement and technicality of our present laws. Enough is stated in general to give the reader a base for comparison of today's law with that in the Bible, though thousands of years separate the two.

Different? We will see.

San Francisco, California, 1961. J. W. EHRLICH

CONTENTS AND ORDER OF THE BOOKS

OF

THE HOLY SCRIPTURES (HEBREW)

THE MASORETIC TEXT

CONTENTS AND ORDER OF THE BOOKS

OF

THE KING JAMES VERSION

(PROTESTANT)

THE OLD TESTAMENT

Genesis
Exodus
Leviticus
Numbers
Deuteronomy
Joshua
Judges
Ruth
1 Samuel
2 Samuel
1 Kings
2 Kings
1 Chronicles
2 Chronicles
Ezra
Nehemiah
Esther
Job
Psalms
Proverbs
Ecclesiastes
The Song of Solomon
Isaiah
Jeremiah
Lamentations
Ezekiel
Daniel
Hosea
Joel
Amos
Obadiah
Jonah
Micah
Nahum
Habakkuk
Zephaniah
Haggai
Zechariah
Malachi

THE NEW TESTAMENT

Matthew
Mark
Luke
John
The Acts
Romans
1 Corinthians
2 Corinthians
Galatians
Ephesians
Philippians
Colossians
1 Thessalonians
2 Thessalonians
1 Timothy
2 Timothy
Titus
Philemon
To the Hebrews
James
1 Peter
2 Peter
1 John
2 John
3 John
Jude
Revelation

CONTENTS AND ORDER OF THE BOOKS

OF

THE DOUAY VERSION

(CATHOLIC)

THE OLD TESTAMENT

THE NEW TESTAMENT

CONTENTS AND ORDER OF THE BOOKS

OF

THE APOCRYPHA

THE TEN COMMANDMENTS

A Comparison

THE FIRST COMMANDMENT

Hebrew Version	Catholic Version	Protestant Version
I am the Lord thy God, who brought thee out of the land of Egypt, out of the house of bondage.	I am the Lord thy God. Thou shalt not have strange Gods before me.	I am the Lord thy God. Thou shalt have no other Gods before me.

THE SECOND COMMANDMENT

Thou shalt have no other Gods before me. Thou shalt not make unto thee a graven image, not any manner of likeness, of any thing that is in heaven above, or that is in the earth beneath, or that is in the water under the earth; Thou shalt not bow down unto them, nor serve them; for I the Lord thy God am a jealous God, visiting the iniquity of the fathers upon the children unto the third and fourth generation of them that hate Me; And showing mercy unto the thousandth generation of them that love Me and keep My commandments.	Thou shalt not take the name of the Lord thy God in vain.	Thou shalt not make unto thee any graven image, or any likeness of any thing that is in heaven above, or that is in the earth beneath, or that is in the water under the earth; Thou shalt now bow down thyself to them, nor serve them; for I the Lord thy God am a jealous God, visiting the iniquity of the fathers upon the children unto the third and fourth generation of them that hate Me; And showing mercy unto thousands of them that love Me, and keep my commandments.

THE THIRD COMMANDMENT

Thou shalt not take the name of the Lord thy God in vain; for the Lord will not hold him guiltless that taketh his name in vain.

Remember thou keep holy the Sabbath Day.

Thou shalt not take the name of the Lord thy God in vain; for the Lord will not hold him guiltless that taketh his name in vain.

THE FOURTH COMMANDMENT

Remember the Sabbath Day to keep it holy. Six days shalt thou labor and do all thy work; but the seventh day is a sabbath unto the Lord thy God, in it thou shalt not do any manner of work, thou, nor thy son, nor thy daughter, nor thy manservant, nor thy maidservant, nor thy cattle, nor thy stranger that is within thy gates; for in six days the Lord made heaven and earth, the sea, and all that in them is, and rested on the seventh day; Wherefore the Lord blessed the sabbath day, and hallowed it.

Honor thy father and mother.

Remember the sabbath day, to keep it holy. Six days shalt thou labor, and do all thy work; But the seventh day is the sabbath of the Lord thy God: in it thou shalt not do any work, thou, nor thy son, nor thy daughter, thy manservant, nor thy maidservant, nor thy cattle, nor thy stranger that is within thy gates: For in six days the Lord made Heaven and Earth, the sea, and all that in them is, and rested the seventh day; wherefore the Lord blessed the sabbath day, and hallowed it.

THE FIFTH COMMANDMENT

Honor thy father and thy mother; that thy days may be long upon the land which the Lord thy God giveth thee.

Thou shalt not kill.

Honor thy father and thy mother; that thy days may be long upon the land which the Lord thy God giveth thee.

THE SIXTH COMMANDMENT

Thou shalt not murder.

Thou shalt not commit adultery.

Thou shalt not kill.

THE SEVENTH COMMANDMENT

Thou shalt not commit adultery.

Thou shalt not steal.

Thou shalt not commit adultery.

THE EIGHTH COMMANDMENT

Thou shalt not steal.

Thou shalt not bear false witness against thy neighbor.

Thou shalt not steal.

THE NINTH COMMANDMENT

Thou shalt not bear false witness against thy neighbor.

Thou shalt not covet thy neighbor's wife.

Thou shalt not bear false witness against thy neighbor.

THE TENTH COMMANDMENT

Thou shalt not covet thy neighbor's house; thou shalt not covet thy neighbor's wife, nor his manservant, nor his maidservant, nor his ox, nor his ass, nor any thing that is thy neighbor's.

Thou shalt not covet thy neighbor's goods.

Thou shalt not covet thy neighbor's house, thou shalt not covet thy neighbor's wife, nor his manservant, nor his maidservant, nor his ox, nor his ass, nor any thing that is thy neighbor's.

THE TEN COMMANDMENTS

As They Appear in "Antiquities of the Jews"

BY

Flavius Josephus

(One of the World's greatest histories, it was written in 93 A.D. when much of the New Testament was being created.)

"The First Commandment teaches us that there is but one God, and that we ought to worship Him only.

"The Second commands us not to make the image of any living creature to worship it.

"The Third, that we must not swear by God in a false matter.

"The Fourth, that we must keep the seventh day, by resting from all sorts of work.

"The Fifth, that we must honour our parents.

"The Sixth, that we must abstain from murder.

"The Seventh, that we must not commit adultery.

"The Eighth, that we must not be guilty of theft.

"The Ninth, that we must not bear false witness.

"The Tenth, that we must not admit of the desire of any thing that is another's."

BIBLICAL CHAPTER AND VERSE ARRANGEMENTS

THE BIBLICAL quotations in this book are from the three accepted Bibles. The chaptering and the versing of the original Hebrew Version were placed where the translator, in his opinion, judged they belonged. The reader will do well to compare the Hebrew Bible, the King James Version, and the Douay Version.

LEVITICUS 5 (HEBREW)	LEVITICUS 6 (CATHOLIC)	LEVITICUS 6 (PROTESTANT)
20. And the Lord spoke unto Moses, saying:	1. The Lord spoke to Moses, saying:	1. And the Lord spake unto Moses, saying:
21. If any one sin, and commit a trespass against the Lord, and deal falsely with his neighbor in a matter of deposit, or of pledge, or of robbery, or have oppressed his neighbor;	2. Whosoever shall sin and despising the Lord, shall deny to his neighbor the thing delivered to his keeping, which was committed to his trust; or shall by force extort any thing, or commit oppression;	2. If a soul sin, and commit a trespass against the Lord, and lie unto his neighbour in that which was delivered to him to keep, or in fellowship, or in a thing taken away by violence, or hath deceived his neighbour;
22. Or have found that which was lost, and deal falsely therein, and swear to a lie; in any of all these that a man doeth, sinning therein;	3. Or shall find a thing lost, and denying it shall also swear falsely, or shall do any other of the many things, wherein men are wont to sin;	3. Or have found that which was lost, and lieth concerning it, and sweareth falsely; in any of all these that a man doeth sinning therein:

LEVITICUS 5 (HEBREW)	LEVITICUS 6 (CATHOLIC)	LEVITICUS 6 (PROTESTANT)
23. Then it shall be, if he hath sinned, and is guilty, that he shall restore that which he took by robbery, or the thing which he hath gotten by oppression, or the deposit which was deposited with him, or the lost thing which he found,	4. Being convicted of the offence, he shall restore	4. Then it shall be, because he hath sinned, and is guilty, that he shall restore that which he took violently away, or the thing which he hath deceitfully gotten, or that which was delivered to him to keep, or the lost thing which he found
24. Or anything about which he hath sworn falsely, he shall even restore it in full, and shall add the fifth part more thereunto; unto him to whom it appertaineth shall he give it, in the day of his being guilty.	5. All that he would have gotten by fraud, in the principal, and the fifth part besides to the owner, whom he wronged.	5. Or all that about which he hath sworn falsely; he shall even restore it in the principal, and shall add the fifth part more thereto, *and* give it unto him to whom it appertaineth, in the day of his trespass offering.

ABRIDGMENT OF BIBLICAL LAW

2 Maccabees 2

25. We have been careful, that they that will read may have delight, and that they that are desirous to commit to memory might have ease, and that all into whose hands it comes might profit.
26. Therefore to us, that have taken upon us this painful labor of abridging, it was not easy, but a matter of sweat and watching;
27. Even as it is no ease unto him that prepareth a banquet, and seeketh the benefit of others; yet for the pleasuring of many will undertake gladly this great pains;
28. Leaving to the author the exact handling of every particular, and labouring to follow the rules of abridgment.
29. For as the master builder of a new house must care for the whole building; be he that undertaketh to set it out, and paint it, must seek out fit things for the adorning thereof: even so I think it is with us.
30. To stand upon every point, and go over things at large, and to be curious in particulars, belongeth to the first author of the story:
31. But to use brevity, and avoid much laboring of the work, is to be granted to him that will make an abridgment.
32. Here then will we begin the story: only adding thus much to that which hath been said, that it is a foolish thing to make a long prologue, and to be short in the story itself.

ADOPTION

Adoption, in the legal sense, is the taking of a stranger into one's family, as a son or daughter. By such action, the adopted person became one's heir. Legal adoption is not recognized by the Common Law of England, and exists in our country by statute.

The various States have adoption laws which generally provide that the person or persons adopting a child or children shall thereafter stand in the place of parent to such as are adopted, and be liable to all the duties and entitled to all the rights of parents. The adopted child becomes an heir-at-law of such persons, the same as if he or she were in fact the natural child of such person.

The right of adoption was known to the ancients of Greece and Rome and was practiced among many nations and peoples from the remotest antiquity.

In Biblical days Mordecai, "when her (Esther) father and mother were dead took her for his own daughter."

It is apparent that in Biblical times there was no formal or so-called legal procedure to be followed in adoption proceedings. It was the intent and act of the person adopting as well as the assent of the person adopted which brought the relationship into existence.

Bible history tells us that where no children were born to a husband and his wife, the wife would direct the husband to cohabit with another woman so that the children of such union would become and be the children of the husband and wife.

THE BIBLICAL LAW

And Jacob said unto Joseph . . . thy two sons Ephraim and Manassah, which were born unto thee . . . are mine; as Reuben and Simeon, they shall be mine. *Genesis 48:3, 5*

Now Sarai Abrams wife bore him no chidren . . . and Sarai . . . took Hagar her maid . . . and gave her to her husband Abram to be his wife . . . it may be that I may obtain children by her. And he went in unto Hagar and she conceived. . . .

Genesis 16:1, 2, 3, 4

And when Rachel saw that she bore Jacob no children . . . Rachel said unto Jacob give me children or I die . . . and he said, am I . . . who hath withheld from thee the fruit of the womb? And she said behold my maid Bilhah, go in unto her; and she shall bear upon my knees, that I may also have children by her. And Bilhah conceived, and bore Jacob a son. And Rachel said God hath given me a son. *Genesis 30:1, 2, 3, 6*

And the daughter of Pharoah came down to wash herself at the river . . . she saw the ark . . . among the flags . . . and she opened it, she saw a child . . . and the child grew . . . and he became her son. And she called his name Moses. . . .

Exodus 2:5, 6, 10

And he brought up Hadassah, that is, Esther . . . for she had neither father nor mother . . . (for) Mordecai . . . had taken her for his daughter. . . . *Esther 2: 7, 15*

AGRICULTURE

Our States and the National Government have created codes of law for the guidance of the farming industry.

When our country was young, its leaders recognized the necessity of education in agriculture. It was evident that more had to be known by the farmer than merely tilling the soil and planting the seed.

In America during the early years of our Government, societies for promoting agriculture were organized in many of the states. These played an important role in the establishment of agricultural colleges. One of the first to be organized was the Philadelphia Society for Promoting Agriculture in 1785. Among its members were George Washington, Noah Webster, and Benjamin Franklin.

It is an accepted practice today to give land a rest from the growing of crops. To many this is a new theory in scientific agricultural development. The Bible anticipated the need for resting the land, and provided in Exodus 23 that all land, producing crops of any kind, be not farmed during every seventh year, thus giving nature an opportunity to replenish the mineral content of the soil. Some writers have thought that this Sabbath year had religious overtones.

Biblical directives and laws dealing with agriculture are even today of basic value. Since food production was of importance to the nomadic Hebrew tribes, it is not surprising that the Bible gives advice and guidance.

THE BIBLICAL LAW

He that tilleth his land shall have plenty of bread. . . .
Proverbs 28:19

Hate not husbandry. . . . *Ecclesiasticus 7:15*

God sent him (Adam) forth from the Garden of Eden, to till the ground from whence he was taken. *Genesis 3:23*

He that observeth the wind shall not sow; and he that regardeth the clouds shall not reap. *Ecclesiastes 11:4*

The sluggard will not plow by reason of the cold; therefore shall he beg in harvest, and have nothing. *Proverbs 20:4*

Thou shalt not plow with an ox and an ass together.
Deuteronomy 22:10

. . . he which soweth sparingly shall realp also sparingly; and he which soweth bountifully shall reap also bountifully.
2 Corinthians 9:6

And six years thou shalt sow thy land, and shalt gather in the fruits thereof; but the seventh year thou shalt let it rest and lie still; that the poor of thy people may eat; and what they leave the beasts of the field shall eat. In like manner thou shalt deal with thy vineyard, and with thy oliveyard. *Exodus 23:10, 11*

Thou shalt not sow thy vineyard with divers seeds: lest the fruit of thy seed which thou hast sown, and the fruit of thy vineyard, be defiled. *Deuteronomy 22:9*

Six years thou shalt sow thy field, and six years thou shalt prune thy vineyard, and gather in the fruit thereof; But in the seventh year shall be a sabbath of rest unto the land . . . thou shalt neither sow thy field, nor prune thy vineyard.
Leviticus 25:3, 4

And when ye reap the harvest of your land, thou shalt not wholly reap the corners of thy field, neither shall thou gather the gleanings of thy harvest. And thou shalt not glean thy vineyard, neither shall thou gather every grape of thy vineyard; thou shalt leave them for the poor and stranger. . . . *Leviticus 19:9, 10*

In the morning sow thy seed, and in the evening withhold not thine hand: for thou knowest not whether shall prosper, either this or that, or whether they both shall be alike good.

Ecclesiastes 11:6

. . . thou shalt not sow thy field with mingled seed. . . .

Leviticus 19:19

Look that thou hedge thy possession about with thorns. . . .

Ecclesiasticus 28:24

Be thou diligent to know the state of thy flocks, and look well to thy herds. *Proverbs 27:23*

ALIENS

An alien is any person to whom the rights of citizenship have not been granted by the State in which he resides or sojourns. Aliens in a political sense, are not members of the State although they are subject to the jurisdiction and in a sense clothed with its national character. They are held to owe the State in which they reside allegiance and are bound to obey the laws equally with citizens as well as to carry their share of the public burden.

Being subject to certain obligations and duties, aliens are equally entitled to certain rights and privileges, the most important of which is the right to protection in their persons and property.

The term "citizen" is a different status entirely. In its legal sense it signifies a person who is vested with the freedom and privileges of a city, state or nation as distinguished from a foreigner. The term also signifies one who owes allegiance to, and claims protection from, the city, state, or Government.

The Alien Registration Act of 1940 is said to be the most far-reaching legislation affecting aliens ever enacted in the United States. It requires the registration and fingerprinting of all aliens in the country. When this law was passed by Congress it caused a great furore. Newspapers, magazines and books attacked the unfairness of the legislation. However, it is of moment to note that thousands of years ago, King David and King Solomon did the same thing and required all "foreigners" to be numbered, and thereafter King Solomon "set threescore and ten thousand of them to be bearers of burden, and fourscore thousand to be hewers in the mountain, and three thousand and six hundred overseers to set the people to work."

Mosaic law was created to meet then existing conditions. In every country today like conditions exist. The relationship of Israel with the Phillistines, and other peoples and governments was strained from time to time. The special attention given to aliens was a necessary defense measure. Biblical law, however, directs that strangers, i.e., aliens, are to be treated decently.

THE BIBLICAL LAW

Love ye therefore the stranger: for ye were strangers in the land of Egypt. *Deuteronomy 10:19*

The Lord preserveth the strangers. . . . *Psalms 146:9*

But the stranger that dwelleth with you shall be unto you as one born among you, and thou shalt love him as thyself. . . .
Leviticus 19:34

. . . the sons of the stranger shall not drink thy wine, for which thou hast labored: but they that have gathered it shall eat it . . . and they that brought it together shall drink it. . . .
Isaiah 62:8, 9

Receive a stranger into thine house, and he will disturb thee, and turn thee out of thine own. *Ecclesiasticus 11:34*

And David commanded to gather together the strangers that were in the land of Israel; and he set masons to hew wrought stones to build the house of God. *1 Chronicles 22:2*

. . . your land, strangers devour it in your presence, and it is desolate. . . . *Isaiah 1:7*

Strangers have devoured his strength, and he knoweth it not. . . . *Hosea 7:9*

Lest strangers be filled with thy wealth; and thy labors be in the house of a stranger. *Proverbs 5:10*

And the sons of strangers shall build up thy walls. . . .
Isaiah 60:10

And strangers shall stand and feed your flocks, and the sons of the alien shall be your plowman and your vinedressers.
Isaiah 61:5

And he (Solomon) set threescore and ten thousand of them (aliens) to be bearers of burden, and fourscore thousand to be hewers in the mountain, and three thousand and six hundred overseers to set the people to work. *2 Chronicles 2:18*

And Solomon numbered all the strangers that were . . . in Israel . . . and they were found an hundred and fifty thousand and three thousand and six hundred. *2 Chronicles 2:17*

When a stranger shall sojourn with thee, and will keep the passover to the Lord, let all his males be circumcized . . . and he shall be as one that is born in the land. . . . *Exodus 12:48*

The children that are begotten of them (foreigners) shall enter into the congregation of the Lord in their third generation.
Deuteronomy 23:8

One law shall be to him that is homeborn, and unto the stranger that sojourneth among you. *Exodus 12:49*

ANIMALS

MUCH ATTENTION was paid to animals during Biblical days. It was commanded that "Thou shalt not let thy cattle gender with a diverse kind," presumably to retain the characteristics of the individual type. On the Sabbath Day the domestic animals must be permitted to rest.

The Bible directs that every man must give assistance to an animal in distress, regardless of whether it belongs to him or to a stranger. One of the unexplained Biblical directives is for the methods of punishing animals for injury done to man. Even as today, the owner is liable for any injury done by an animal, if he has knowledge of the animal's viciousness.

Animal worship prevailed in many parts of the world. In India where it is a consequence of the belief in the transmigration of the soul of a god into the body of an animal. In South America instances of it were met with by the early Spanish conquerors. Its most extraordinary developments were in ancient Egypt, where animals in some parts of the country were regarded as sacred throughout the whole land, and in many cases animals enjoyed a local reverence.

The degree of reverence paid to the sacred animals was such that the voluntary killing of one was punishable with death. It is, therefore, understandable why the Bible in so many instances calls for protection and aid to animals.

The Society for Prevention of Cruelty to Animals in the United States was chartered in 1866 and agitation by similar societies has resulted in laws in almost every state providing for the punishment of cruelty to domestic animals.

THE BIBLICAL LAW

A righteous man regardeth the life of his beast. . . .
Proverbs 12:10

Thou shalt not let the cattle gender with a diverse kind. . . .
Leviticus 19:19

Thou shalt not muzzle the ox when he treadeth out the corn.
Deuteronomy 25:4

But on the seventh day . . . thou shalt not do any work, thou nor . . . thy cattle. . . . *Exodus 20:8,10*

If thou see the ass of him that hateth thee lying under his burden . . . thou shalt surely help with him. *Exodus 23:5*

If thou meet thine enemy's ox or his ass going astray, thou shalt surely bring it back to him again. *Exodus 23:4*

Thou shalt not see thy brother's ass or his ox fall down by the way, and hide thyself from them: thou shalt surely help him to lift them up again. *Deuteronomy 22:4*

If an ox gore a man or a woman that they die; then the ox shall be surely stoned, and his flesh shall not be eaten: but the owner of the ox shall be quit. *Exodus 21:28*

But if the ox were wont to push with his horn in time past, and it hath been testified to his owner, and he hath not kept him in, but that he hath killed a man or a woman; the ox shall be stoned, and his owner also shall be put to death. If there be laid on him a sum of money, then he shall give for the ransom of his life whatsoever is laid upon him. *Exodus 21:29, 30*

If the ox shall push a manservant or a maidservant; he shall give unto their master thirty shekels of silver, and the ox shall be stoned. *Exodus 21:32*

And if one man's ox hurt another's that he die; then they shall sell the live ox, and divide the money of it; and the dead ox also they shall divide. *Exodus 21:35*

Or if it be known that the ox hath used to push in time past, and his owner hath not kept him in; he shall surely pay ox for ox, and the dead shall be his own. *Exodus 21:36*

If a man shall cause a field or vineyard to be eaten, and shall put in his beast, and shall feed in another man's field; of the best of his own field, and of the best of his own vineyard, shall he make restitution. *Exodus 22:5*

And he that killeth a beast shall make it good; beast for beast. And he that killeth a beast, he shall restore it. . . .
Leviticus 24:18, 21

And if a man shall open a pit, or if a man shall dig a pit, and not cover it, and an ox or an ass fall therein; the owner of the pit shall make it good, and give money unto the owner of them, and the dead beast shall be his. *Exodus 21:33, 34*

Thou shalt not plow with an ox and an ass together.
Deuteronomy 22:10

Thou shalt not muzzle the ox when he treadeth out the corn.
Deuteronomy 25:4

. . . the good shepherd giveth his life for the sheep.
John 10:11

If a man shall steal an ox, or a sheep, and kill it, or sell it; he shall restore five oxen for an ox, and four sheep for a sheep.
Exodus 22:1

If the theft be certainly found in his hand alive, whether it be ox, or ass, or sheep; he shall restore double. *Exodus 22:4*

BAILMENTS

In the law today, Bailment, generally, is the delivery of personal property by one person to another for a specific purpose with an agreement that the property be returned or accounted for when the purpose for which it was delivered is accomplished, or until the bailor reclaims it.

When a person receives the goods of another, to keep without recompense, and he acts in good faith, keeping them as his own, he is not answerable for their loss or injury. As he derives no benefit from the bailment, he is responsible only for bad faith or gross negligence.

In bailments for storage or for hire, the bailee acquires a right to defend the property as against third parties and strangers, and is answerable for loss or injury occasioned through his failure to exercise ordinary care.

In the case where cloth is delivered to a tailor to be made up into a garment, the owner does not part with his title, and he may come and take his property after the work has been done, but the workman who has made the garment has a lien upon it for his compensation which, of course, must be reasonable.

There is much similarity in the law today and the law of the Bible.

A people who were constantly on the move had need of laws protecting goods left with and entrusted to those who had a permanent or fixed domicile.

Failure to return property which is entrusted to one's keeping was, under Biblical law, punishable by death.

One who ". . . hath not restored the pledge . . . he shall surely die. . . ." *Ezekiel 18:12, 13*

Today's law is not as severe, providing only for the return of the property, and for damages for the detention; each case, of course, being under the laws made and provided in the several states.

THE BIBLICAL LAW

If a man shall deliver unto his neighbor money or stuff to keep, and it be stolen out of the man's house; if the thief be found, then the master of the house shall be brought unto the judges to see whether he have put his hand unto his neighbor's goods.

. . . so when the judges shall condemn, he shall pay double unto his neighbor. *Exodus 22:7, 8, 9*

If a man deliver unto his neighbor an ass, or an ox, or a sheep, or any beast, to keep; and it die, or be hurt, or driven away, no man seeing it: Then shall an oath of the Lord be between them both, that he hath not put his hand unto his neighbor's goods; and the owner of it shall accept thereof, and he shall not make it good. And if it be stolen from him, he shall make restitution unto the owner thereof. If it be torn to pieces, then let him bring it for witness, and he shall not make good that which is torn.

Exodus 22:10, 11, 12, 13

And if a soul . . . lie unto his neighbor in that which was delivered him to keep . . . he shall restore it in the principal, and shall add the fifth part more thereto. . . . *Leviticus 6:2, 5*

BRIBERY

IN OUR LAWS, the receiving or giving of a reward to influence the actions of a person in judicial office or in any other office or place of decision is prohibited; particularly, the taking or giving a reward or a bribe to hinder, delay or avoid justice. The accepting of a gift is prohibited not only in our law, but also in the Bible because "the gift blindeth the wise."

Bribery generally is the offering, giving, receiving or soliciting of anything of value with intent to influence the recipient's action as a public official, whether executive, legislative or judicial. The crime includes the acts of soliciting a bribe and attempts to bribe.

Bribery is also the receiving or offering of any undue reward by or to any person whose ordinary profession or business relates to the administration of public affairs in order to incline him to act contrary to the rules of honesty and integrity.

Among ancient peoples, and even as late as the time of the Romans the giving of rewards and emoluments to public officers, especially judicial officers, was tolerated and even encouraged. A later age apprehended the danger, and in modern times the heinousness of the offense became so apparent that the crime has been made punishable as a felony.

Bribery tends to corrupt, and as the law abhors the least tendency to corruption it punishes the act which is calculated to debase and which may affect prejudicially the morals of the community. A public official is the servant of the people. It is his duty impartially to represent the people, and he is not permitted to profit through the performance of his public functions.

In Ecclesiasticus there is the direct admonition that "all bribery shall be blotted out," and the Bible directs:

THE BIBLICAL LAW

Gather not my soul with sinners . . . in whose hands is mischief, and their right hand is full of bribes *Psalms 26:9, 10*

For I know . . . they take a bribe, and they turn aside the poor . . . *Amos 5:12*

All bribery . . . shall be blotted out; but true dealing shall endure forever. *Ecclesiasticus 40:12*

A wicked man taketh a gift . . . to pervert the laws of judgment. *Proverbs 17:23*

The king by judgment establishes the land: but he that receiveth gifts overthroweth it. *Proverbs 29:4*

And thou shalt take no gift; for the gift blindeth the wise, and perverteth the words of the righteous. *Exodus 23:8*

Then . . . Judas Iscariot went unto the chief priests, and said unto them, What will ye give me, and I will deliver him unto you? And they covenanted with him for thirty pieces of silver. And from that time he sought opportunity to betray him.
Matthew 26:14, 15, 16

And his sons . . . turned aside after lucre, and took bribes, and perverted judgment. *1 Samuel 8:3*

CONTRACTS

In American law, a contract is defined as an agreement by which a person undertakes to do or not to do a particular thing, for a valuable consideration.

In a contract there must be a promise and this promise binds the maker for a future happening, intention or desire.

To create a promise, all that is necessary is that a fair interpretation of the words used shall make it appear that a promise was intended.

Many contracts are mentioned in the Scriptures. One wherein Labin employed Jacob. Jacob by contract offered to work for Labin, and thus buy Labin's younger daughter. Labin accepted the offer saying "it is better that I give her to thee than I give her to another man." After Jacob had served Labin seven years and the agreed time of payment arrived, Labin substituted Leah in place of the younger Rachel, contending that custom required the elder daughter to first be given in marriage. Jacob accepted the substitution and made a second contract to serve seven more years for Rachel, but exacted delivery of Rachel in advance. At the end of this period, he made a third contract to serve Labin for a share of his livestock so that he could get started in his own home and enterprises.

Another contract is that between Pharoh's daughter with the natural mother of Moses to nurse him after he was found in the bulrushes.

The Bible contains many rules, regulations and laws for the creation, maintenance and enforcement of contractual obligations. While it may appear strange that a country of shepherds paid so much attention to contractual liabilities and rights, it was necessary because as Biblical history moved on, the children of Israel became city dwellers and merchants, and acted as middlemen between the nations to the north and those to the south.

A contract for timber (1 Kings 5) between Solomon, King of Israel, and Hyram, King of Tyre, would be by its terms as legally binding today as it was in Biblical times.

Primitive society held that one who was undertaken a duty, in legal form, must fully and exactly perform it, at all events. That a man of full age must take care of himself, and if he has made a foolish bargain he must perform for he had himself to blame. If a man acted, he did so at his own risk. It was his duty to keep his eyes open and abide by the consequences of his agreement.

Laws generally are not now so severe and uncompromising. There are, today, many factors entering into the law of contracts which permit non-performance for fraudulent representation, misrepresentation, inequities, failure of consideration, minority of the person entering into the contract, and many other legal excuses for avoiding the agreement.

THE BIBLICAL LAW

If a man vow a vow . . . or swear an oath to bind his soul with a bond; he shall not break his word, he shall do according to all that proceedeth out of his mouth. *Numbers 30:2*

And Hiram sent to Solomon, saying, I have considered the things which thou sentest to me for; and I will do all thy desire concerning timber of cedar, and concerning timber of fir. My servants shall bring them down from Lebanon unto the sea: and I will convey them by sea in floats unto the place that thou shall appoint me, and will cause them to be discharged there, and thou shall receive them and thou shalt accomplish my desire, in giving food for my household. So Hiram gave Solomon . . . trees . . . and Solomon gave Hiram twenty thousand measures of wheat for food. . . . *1 Kings 5:8, 9, 10, 11*

Keep thy word, and deal faithfully. . . . *Ecclesiasticus 40:12*

For if thy deal truly, thy doings shall prosperously succeed to thee. . . . *Tobit 4:6*

. . . ye should do that which is honest. . . . *II Corinthians 13:7*

. . . do uprightly all thy life. . . . *Tobit 4:5*

He that worketh deceit shall not dwell within my house. . . . *Psalms 101:7*

. . . ye shall not . . . deal falsely. . . . *Leviticus 19:11*

Woe to thee that . . . dealest treacherously and they dealt not treacherously with thee. . . . *Isaiah 33:1*

Have we not all one father? Hath not one God created us? Why do we deal treacherously every man against his brother?. . . . *Malachi 2:10*

Be steadfast in thy understanding; and let thy word be the same. *Ecclesiasticus 5:20*

That which is gone out of thy lips, thou shalt keep and perform. *Deuteronomy 23:23*

CRIME AND PUNISHMENT

THROUGHOUT Biblical literature there are Hebrew words for sin, iniquity, and other synonymous expressions, but no words or phrases such as crime and criminal law in their accepted legal sense. There are only two general classifications: civil cases and cases involving capital punishment. Every offense is termed: transgression.

The absence of the term crime indicates that the will of God is the sole source of all the law, and thus all punishable acts constitute sins which are in violation of God's will.

The Law of Moses contains six hundred and thirteen commandments. Of these, two hundred and forty-eight make the performance of certain acts compulsory. The remaining three hundred and sixty-five prohibit the performance of certain acts.

From the earliest days of recorded history, law-makers and rules appeased the wrath of the Deity by wreaking vengeance not only upon the perpetrator of the crime, but also upon his entire family, parents as well as children.

The Mosaic Law does away with this barbaric practice for in Deuteronomy 24:16—"The fathers shall not be put to death for the children, neither shall the children be put to death for the fathers; every man shall be put to death for his own sin."

In Biblical law, capital punishment has two definitive purposes: (1) retributive, which concerns itself chiefly with rooting out evil by punishing the sinner for his wrong-doing; and (2) deterrent, which makes the punishment so severe that it cannot escape the attention of the public, thereby preventing others from committing a similar act.

Mosaic law provides for thirty-six capital offenses in which number is included adultery, sex perversion, incest, homosexuality, blasphemy, idolatry, false prophecy, profaning the Sabbath, witchcraft, pythonism, sins against parents, kidnapping, treason and murder.

When Ezra, the Scribe, obtained permission from Artaxerxes, King of Babylon, to return with some of the exiled Jews (about 450 B.C.) to the site of old Judea, and there form a new state to be governed by the Law of his God, the authority given by the King to him, permitted only four methods of punishment: death, banishment, confiscation of goods, and imprisonment. The Mosaic law with reference to sin (crime) was unforgiving and harsh.

THE BIBLICAL LAW

. . . there is no man that sinneth not. . . . *1 Kings 8:46*

Because the law worketh wrath: for where no law is, there is no transgression. *Romans 4:15*

. . . sin is not imputed when there is no law. *Romans 5:13*

Woe unto the world because of offences! For it must needs be that offences come; but woe to that man by whom the offence cometh. *Matthew 18:7*

How shall I pardon thee for this? Thy children have forsaken me . . . when I had fed them to the full, they them committed adultery, and assembled themselves by troops in the harlots' houses. They were as fed horses in the morning: every one neighed after his neighbor's wife. *Jeremiah 5:7, 8*

(The Lord) hath commanded no man to do wickedly, neither hath he given any man license to sin. *Ecclesiasticus 15:20*

Keep thou far from a false matter . . . for I will not justify the wicked. *Exodus 23:7*

If one be found slain in the land . . . lying in the field, and it be known who hath slain him: Then the elders and thy judges . . . shall measure unto the cities which are found about him that is slain . . . and all the elders of that city, that are next unto the slain man . . . shall answer and say, our hands have not shed this blood, neither have our eyes seen it. *Deuteronomy 21:1, 2, 6*

When, Pilate . . . asked wether the man (Christ) were a Galilean . . . he knew that he belonged unto Herod's jurisdiction. . . . *Luke 23:6, 7*

For it seemeth to me unreasonable to send a prisoner, and not withal to signify the crimes laid against him. *Acts 25:27*

For it is a token of his great goodness, when wicked doers are not suffered any long time, but forthwith punished.

2 Maccabees 6:13

Let me be weighed in an even balance, that God may know mine integrity. *Job 31:6*

He that answereth a matter before he heareth it, it is folly and shame unto him. *Proverbs 18:13*

Doth our law judge any man, before it hear him, and know what he doeth? *John 7:51*

I will hear thee (Paul) when thine accusers are also come. . . .

Acts 23:35

. . . It is not the manner of the Romans to deliver any man to die, before that he which is accused have the accusers face to face, and have license to answer for himself concerning the crime laid against him. *Acts 25:16*

And whosoever will not do the law . . . let judgment be executed speedily upon him. . . . *Ezra 7:26*

Whoso killeth any person, the murderer shall be put to death by the mouth of witnesses: but one witness shall not testify against any person to cause him to die. *Numbers 35:30*

And the judges shall make diligent inquisition; and behold if the witness be a false witness . . . Then shall ye do unto him, as he had thought to have done unto his brother. . . .

Deuteronomy 19:18, 19

If therefore be any pestilent fellows, that have fled from their country unto you, deliver them unto Simon the High Priest, that he may punish them according to their own law.

1 Maccabees 15:21

DAMAGES

WHERE ONE wrongfully or negligently does an act which in its consequences is injurious to another, he is liable for the damage caused by such wrongful act. Damages to be recovered by the claimant must result from a wrong inflicted.

Generally the term "damages" is the sum of money which the law awards or imposes as compensation for an injury done or a wrong sustained. The idea of compensation is fundamental in the conception of damages and the term is used synonymously with compensation.

Ordinarily, nominal damages are recoverable where a right is to be vindicated or where some injury has been done. It is inferred by the law that when there is a breach of an agreement, nominal damages should be awarded plaintiff for an infraction or breach of a contract into which he has entered in good faith.

Biblical law provides for payment of damages. Even as today, Mosaic laws provide for payment of wages lost due to injury, and for the cost of doctors and medication.

If one sustains an injury, either in his person, property or rights, through the act or default of another, he is entitled to receive damages in payment. Punitive damages are levied where injuries are maliciously, recklessly or wantonly inflicted. To constitute the right to recover damages, there must be a loss sustained by the claimant; the defendant must be chargeable with the wrong done, and the loss must be the natural and proximate result of the wrong done.

In the Bible, damages are specifically fixed for each wrong, and are not left to the discretion or judgment of the judge, or as today, the judgment of a jury.

The Bible is mandatory in its laws concerning damages.

THE BIBLICAL LAW

If a man shall steal an ox, or a sheep, and kill it, or sell it; he shall restore five oxen for an ox, and four sheep for a sheep.
Exodus 22:1

If a thief be found . . . he should make full restitution; if he have nohting, then he shall be sold for his theft. *Exodus 22:2, 3*

If the theft be found in his hand alive, whether it be ox, or ass, or sheep, he shall restore double. *Exodus 22:4*

And if a man entice a maid that is not betrothed, and lie with her, he shall surely endow her to be his wife. If her father utterly refuse to give her unto him, he shall pay money according to the doury of virgins. *Exodus 22:16, 17*

And if men strive together, and one smite another with a stone, or with his fist, and he die not, but keepeth his bed: If he rise again, and walk abroad upon his staff, then shall he that smote him be quit; only he shall pay for the loss of his time, and shall cause him to be thoroughly healed.
Exodus 21:18, 19

If a soul . . . commit a trespass . . . and lie unto his neighbor in that which was delivered him to keep, or in fellowship, or a thing taken away by violence, or hath deceived his neighbor;
Or have found that which was lost, and lieth concerning it, and sweareth falsely . . . he shall restore that which he took violently away, or the thing which he hath deceitfully gotten, or that which was delivered to him to keep, or the lost thing which he found.

Or all that about which he hath sworn falsely; he shall even restore it in the principal, and shall add the fifth part more thereto, and give it unto him to whom it appertaineth. . . .
Leviticus 6:2, 3, 4, 5

If a man shall deliver unto his neighbor money or stuff to keep, and it be stolen out of the man's house; if the thief be found, let him pay double. If the thief be not found, then the master of the house shall be brought into the judges, to see whether he have put his hand unto his neighbor's goods.

Exodus 22:7, 8

Men do not despise a thief, if he steal to satisfy his soul when he is hungry; but if he be found, he shall restore sevenfold. . . .

Proverbs 6:30, 31

DEBTORS

BRIEFLY, a debtor is a person who owes something to another, or to others. Debt is an obligation to pay or return something.

Debt denotes not only the obligation to pay, but also the right of the creditor to receive as well as enforce payment. Everything is a debt which is an obligation on the person to perform. Debt is synonymous with due; both are derived from the same verb.

Becoming a debtor has, through the history of man, been easy of accomplishment and therefore the law has taken into consideration the wilfulness of those who are holders of obligations of others and has provided that the lender shall not burden the debtor beyond what is reasonable for the use of the money or property involved.

Usury is defined as an unlawful contract upon the loan of money to receive the same again with exorbitant increase, but generally, usury is actually the receiving, securing or taking of a greater sum or value for the loan of money, goods or things in action than is allowed by the existing law. Many states have enacted laws limiting the highest rate of interest to be charged.

In those places where a usury law has been adopted, a limitation is set on the amount of interest to be paid and in the cases where there is a greater amount exacted than the law allows, punitive penalties have been attached to the receiving of exorbitant amounts.

The common law of England which is basically followed in this country, did not have a law against usurious interest on money or things loaned; even though most of the common law is predicated on the Mosaic law, which prohibits usurious interest.

Deuteronomy 15:6 easily solves the problem of debt: "Thou shalt not borrow."

. . . thou shalt not borrow. . . . *Deuteronomy 15:6*

Be not made a begger by banqueting upon borrowing, when thou hast nothing in thy purse. . . . *Ecclesiasticus 18:33*

He that buildeth his house with other men's money is like one that gathered himself stones for the tomb of his burial. *Ecclesiasticus 21:8*

. . . the borrower is servant to the lender. *Proverbs 22:7*

. . . from him that would borrow of thee turn not thou away. *Matthew 5:42*

Lose thy money for thy brother and thy friend, and let it not rust under a stone to be lost. *Ecclesiasticus 29:10*

Lend not unto him that is mightier than thyself; for if thou lendest him, count it but lost. *Ecclesiasticus 8:12*

Owe no man anything. . . . *Romans 13:8*

Usury

If thou lend money to any of my people that is poor by thee, thou shalt not be to him as an usurer, neither shall thou lay upon him usury. *Exodus 22:25*

(He that) hath given forth upon usury, and hath taken increase . . . shall surely die. . . . *Ezekiel 18:13*

Thou shalt not lend upon usury to thy brother; usury of money, usury of victuals, usury of anything that is lent upon usury:

Unto a stranger thou mayest lend upon usury; but unto thy brother thou shalt not lend upon usury. . . . *Deuteronomy 23:19, 20*

Repayment

He that is hasty to give credit is lightminded. . . .

Ecclesiasticus 19:4

Let not thine hand be stretched out to receive, and shut when thou shouldest repay. *Ecclesiasticus 4:31*

And forgive us our debts, as we forgive our debtors.

Matthew 6:12

. . . for we also forgive everyone that is indebted to us.

Luke 11:4

Greed

. . . thou hast taken usury and increase, and thou hast greedily gained of thy neighbors by extortion. . . . *Ezekiel 22:12*

. . . he that maketh haste to be rich shall not be innocent.

Proverbs 28:20

For the love of money is the root of all evil. . . .

1 Timothy 6:10

Be not greedy to add money to money. . . . *Tobit 5:18*

Statute of Limitations

At the end of every seven years thou shalt make a release . . . Every creditor that lendeth ought unto his neighbor shall release it; he shall not exact it of his neighbor, or of his brother. . . .

Deuteronomy 15:1, 2

Banks

Wherefore then gavest not thou my money into the bank, that at my coming I might have required mine own with usury?

Luke 19:23

DEFENSES

THE VARIOUS DEFENSES for the almost limitless number of subjects in the law cannot be discussed in a book of this kind. It is sufficient that under the various headings hereinafter found there will be discussed many general, special, and specific defenses to various sins which we term crimes.

In Genesis, Adam defends himself from the sin of eating of the Tree of Life, by blaming the woman whom God gave to him, and the woman, in turn, blamed the serpent.

It is interesting to observe that in Biblical times too man sought to avoid responsibility for crime or for the commission of an act which was not in accordance with the accepted standards of the community.

Law makers from time immemorial have not only created crimes and punishments, but realized the weakness and frailty of mankind and set standards of defense to excuse, justify or vindicate.

Among defenses permitted by Biblical law is, committing an act through ignorance "but the soul that doeth aught presumptuously shall be cut off from his people."

The defense of mental inadequacy was not known to the Bible, nor is any mental deficiency recognized. There was, however, the right to be confronted by an accuser before it was necessary to defend. Basically, the law today is a repetition and refinement of Mosaic law.

THE BIBLICAL LAW

The woman whom thou gavest to be with me, she gave me of the tree, and I did eat. *Genesis 3:12*

And the woman said, the serpent beguiled me, and I did eat. *Genesis 3:13*

And if any soul sin through ignorance . . . the priest shall make an atonement . . . and it shall be forgiven him. But the soul that doeth ought presumptuously . . shall be cut off from among his people. *Numbers 15:27, 28, 30*

And that servant, which knew his Lord's will, and . . . neither did according to his will, shall be beaten with many stripes. But he that knew not . . . shall be beaten with few stripes. *Luke 12:47, 48*

. . . Our hands have not shed this blood, neither have our eyes seen it. . . . *Deuteronomy 21:7*

. . . if ye put me to death, ye shall surely bring innocent blood upon yourselves. . . . *Jeremiah 26:15*

. . . hear ye my defence, which I make now unto you. *Acts 22:1*

What have I offended against thee, or against thy servants, or against this people, that ye have put me in prison? *Jeremiah 37:18*

Save me from all them that persecute me, and deliver me. *Psalms 7:1*

. . . deliver me from the hand of mine enemies, and from them that persecute me. *Psalms 31:15*

. . . he remembered not to show mercy, but persecuted the poor and needy man, that he might even slay the broken in heart. *Psalms 109:16*

Persecuted, but not forsaken; cast down, but not destroyed.
2 Corinthians 4:9

Blessed are they which are persecuted for righteousness' sake: for theirs is the kingdom of heaven. *Matthew 5:10*

. . . my persecutors shall stumble, and they shall not prevail. . . .
Jeremiah 20:11

And Samuel said unto all Israel . . . Behold here I am: witness against me before the Lord . . . whose ox have I taken? Or whose ass have I taken? Or whom have I defrauded? Whom have I oppressed? Or of whose hand have I received any bribe to blind my eyes therewith? And I will restore it to you.
1 Samuel 12:1, 3

And the scribes and Pharisees brought unto him (Jesus) a woman taken in adultery . . . They say to him . . . Moses in the law commanded us, that such be stoned: but what sayest thou? . . . and [Jesus] said unto them, He that is without sin among you, let him first cast a stone at her. *John 8:3, 4, 5, 7*

Former Jeopardy

And the righteous [i.e. he that was once declared to be righteous] slay thou not. *Exodus 23:7*

DIVORCE

UNDER MOSAIC LAW, a husband could divorce his wife by giving her a Bill of Divorcement and sending her out of his house whenever he found some uncleanness in her. The dissolution of the marriage thus brought about was absolutely final so that even the wife was free to marry again.

The teachings of the Christian faith, however, have led to restrictions concerning divorce, but by the general civil law, either party could abrogate the marriage contract, first at the pleasure of the one desiring to do so, and later for reasons granted by the law.

Denying of divorce under certain circumstances and conditions creates hatreds, miseries and crimes which result and flow from indissoluable marital connections, but no law has ever gone so far as to subject marriage to dissolution by the mutual will of the parties.

Sir William Blackstone in his Commentaries on the Common Law said that divorces were within the cognizance of the Ecclesiastical courts only, and were of two kinds—the one total and the other partial. The total divorce was always for some one of the cannonical causes such as consanguinity or affinity. The partial divorce was allowed when for some cause it became improper or impossible for the parties to live together.

The Common Law of England and the Ecclesiastical law of that country were never adopted in this country. Here it is the province of the legislature of the several states to regulate the subject of divorce as applied to their citizens and persons domiciled within their jurisdiction. The power of the Legislature over the subject of marriage and over the matter of its dissolution is unlimited and supreme, subject of course, to the constitutional restriction that each community shall not pass any local or special law granting divorces.

Every person has the right to seek and obtain a divorce, but must do so under the statutes of the several states. Divorce is not a right, but is solely granted by general laws enacted for that purpose.

Divorce is the ending of the marriage relation other than by death. An annulment differs from a divorce; it may be had for causes existing before or at the time of marriage and which go to the very essence of the marital relation, such as the wife committed fornication and was pregnant by another, or that she concealed her sterility, or that one or both of the parties was not legally capable of marrying, or that the husband was impotent.

Biblical law is without equivocation in matters of divorce. It can be accepted as fact that the tribal laws and regulations of the Hebrews were directed toward the permanency of the family and its necessity in the life of the nation.

Since Biblical days, cause for divorce has been enlarged. Today the most often used is "extreme cruelty"; a term which may mean almost anything.

Generally it is the wrongful infliction of grievous bodily injury, or grievous mental suffering by one spouse on the other. Each case must be determined on its own facts and circumstances. Since the disposition, habit and custom varies from person to person, it is not possible for the legislature or the courts to precisely define a universal rule. A decision by the court must depend on the sound judgment and "common sense" of the trial court.

What is cruelty, is difficult to state comprehensively; some courts are far more lenient than others, but the reason of the difference lies in the varying views the courts take of the marital relation and of its place in the social polity. Cruelty is such conduct in one of the married parties as, to the reasonable apprehension of the other, or in fact, renders cohabitation physically unsafe, to a degree justifying a withdrawal therefrom. The actual use or the apprehension of violence is considered necessary; or perhaps it would more faithfully represent the position of some of our conservative courts to say, that although violence be pronounced essential, yet acts are now placed under the head of violence which were not so regarded by the earlier judges. The reason for granting a divorce for this cause at all is in the fact that courts of law will not compel a person to live with one from whom injury is to be feared. It is not so much to punish an offense already committed as to relieve the complaining party from apprehended danger.

A classical discussion of this subject is found in an 1836 decision of a New Hampshire court:

"The parties in this case were married in March, 1816. They have no children. The husband is proved to be a man in easy circumstances, and of a hasty and irritable temper. The wife is shown to be a very active and efficient manager of her household affairs, and of a high, bold, masculine spirit; somewhat impatient of control; in a high degree jealous of the liberty that belongs to her as a wife, and not always ready to submit, even to the legitimate authority of her husband. For aught that appears in this case, they lived in peace and harmony until some time since the year 1830, when the wife, having become a professor of religion, united herself to a church whose doctrines and opinions the husband did not approve.

This diversity of sentiments in religious matters seems to have been the original fountain whence has flowed all the bitterness which has since existed between them, and which has driven them into quarrels, squabbles and encounters, that certainly do no credit to either party. The result of these broils was, that the wife left the house of the husband, and has since resided separate and apart from him; and she now seeks to have the bonds of matrimony dissolved, on the ground that in the contest which ended in their separation, he exercised a tyranny over her which amounted to extreme cruelty.

In a contest about religion between two persons standing in the relation, and having the dispositions and tempers of these parties, it is hardly to be conceived that the blame could have been all on one side. Mere profession of religion weighs nothing in such a case If the spirit of the gospel abide with one of the parties, not in word only but in its power, there can be no contest; whatever wrong or injury there may be on the one side—all will be patience and suffering on the other. Where strife is, there is every evil work. But that wisdom which is from above is first pure, then peaceable, gentle, and easy to be entreated, full of mercy and good fruits. This is the language of inspiration.

The evidence in this case shows much strife between these parties; and an attentive examination of that evidence will enable us to see who has been to blame.

One of the complaints of the wife in this case is that the husband has often addressed her in harsh, abusive, and profane language. This charge is sustained by the evidence, and his conduct in this respect can be viewed in no other light than as unmanly, indecorous, and in the highest degree reprehensible. And in the case of a woman of a meek and quiet spirit, incapable of rendering evil for evil, or railing for railing, but patient in all her tribulations, such language on the part of a husband, often repeated, wantonly and unprovoked, would go a great way, and be a circumstance of much weight, in making out a case of extreme cruelty.

But here much of the evidence on both sides, and even the tone and temper of the affidavit which she has drawn up herself and filed in the case, indicate in the wife anything rather than a meek and quiet spirit. And one of her own witnesses says that her conduct was often provoking and vexatious. She herself admits, in her affidavit, that she sometimes used passionate language, but says she used it only when he gave her occasion. It is very likely that she may think she had always an occasion for the passionate language she used; and it is equally likely that he may think he had an occasion for the harsh and abusive language he used towards here. It is not proved that he used such language wantonly and unprovoked on any occasion. And if a wife chooses so to act and to talk as to raise a storm in the temper of an irritable husband, it is doing her no injustice to say to her, when it has come attended only with harsh and abusive language, that she has had in its peltings her just and merited reward. However reprehensible his conduct may have been in this respect, she is not to be heard, when she would complain of it. She ought not to be heard to complain of abuse which she has wantonly provoked.

Her next complaint grows out of a contest between them with respect to some wood, in August, 1833. Her story is that she sent a little girl out to procure some wood—that the husband met the girl at the door and told her "she should not"—that she then went herself for the wood, and as she went out, he went into the house. When she returned she found the door fastened—upon which she threw her wood into the house through the window, and took a crowbar and knocked at the door; that he came out in a great passion, and using very profane language, which she repeats, but which we shall not, took the crowbar from her by force; that she screamed murder, and he stopped her mouth. But at length she escaped, and soon after deserted the house.

Now in this account it is virtually admitted that she went out in open rebellion against the known will of her husband. And the throwing of the wood into the house by the window, the use she made of the crowbar, and her screams of murder when he took the bar from her, indicate a spirit and temper quite too belligerent, when indulged against a husband, to be becoming in a lady. But her witness adds other material circumstances, which she has omitted, and says that the husband told the girl not to take the wood that was on the other side of the road, but to take it from the mill-house, because he wanted to clear that—that upon this the wife came out and said that she sent the girl, and intended to have the wood. He further says, that she struck the door with the crowbar and made several dents in it, which are still visible; and that after the husband took the bar from her she threatened to go to a magistrate and compel him to give sureties of the peace, and that he told her that she had better go into the house.

Such is the transaction, as it stands disclosed in the evidence. There seems to have been nothing unreasonable or improper in the direction which the husband gave to the little girl. And the temper in which the wife went forth from the house, and her declared intention of having her own will and her own way, in defiance of him, which was immediately carried into overt acts of rebellion against his authority, show her to have been entirely in the wrong on that occasion. She was to blame in the beginning: and she carried out the quarrel in a manner which all candid and impartial minds must pronounce to have been equally inconsistent with her connubial duties and her religious professions. In the skirmish which ended in his taking the crowbar from her, she seems to have been rather roughly handled. But considering the irritable temper of the husband, it seems to us that she escaped with quite as little injury as she could have had any right to expect, in such an attempt to take his castle by storm.

Her next complaint is founded upon a quarrel between her and her husband which took place upon the Sabbath. The account which she gives of the matter in her affidavit is, that she asked him to let her have the horse and chaise to go to church. This he refused, because he did not like the minister. She then ordered the boy to put the horse to the chaise, and went out herself to the chaise-house to assist the boy. Finding the chaise-house locked, she requested him to let her have the key, which he refused. She thereupon took hold of the door, "and made as though she would open it." Upon this, the husband came out and struck her upon the head, and made her head ache for several days. Such is her account of the affair. But her witness states other material circumstances, which she omits. He says that she went out to the chaise-house and attempted to force the lock with a wedge; that the husband came out, and took the wedge from her, and ordered her to go into the house. She, however, still persisted in her attempt to obtain the chaise, until he struck her.

Now, in this instance, the quarrel had its origin in the misconduct of the husband. No good reason is shown why the use of the horse and chaise should not have been freely accorded to her. And his refusal of her reasonable request, not only has the appearance of great unkindness, but of a tyrannical attempt to embarrass her in the enjoyment of that religious liberty which belongs to every wife.

But it was the Sabbath—and, under the circumstances, what course of conduct did duty prescribe to a Christian wife and to a member of the church? The very essence of the religion she professes is, that charity suffereth long and is kind, which vaunteth not itself, doth not behave unseemly, is not easily provoked, and not only believeth and hopeth, but beareth and endureth all things. What course of conduct, then, did duty prescribe to one who professed to have adopted that religion as the guide of her life? If when ye do well and suffer for it, yet take it patiently, this is acceptable with God, says the Bible. What course of conduct did duty then prescribe to one who professes to believe the Bible to be the word of God? In my judgment, there cannot be any diversity of opinion on these questions. It was due to the day, it was due to the religion she professes, it was due to the relation in which she stood to her oppressor, that, if she could not obtain his consent by kindness and condescension, she should have submitted in silence to the wrong he was doing her. But instead of this, regardless of the day and of the modesty and of all the sober virtues that belong to the character of a pious matron, at the head of a respectable family, and setting her husband completely at defiance, she at once undertook to accomplish her purpose by force and violence; and in this course she persisted, until, provoked by her perverse obstinacy, the husband was led so far to forget himself as to strike her.

Whatever the old books may say upon the subject, there never was, in my opinion, in the relation between husband and wife, when rightly understood, anything that gave to a husband the right to reduce a refractory wife to obedience by blows. And at this day the moral sense of the community revolts at the idea that a husband may inflict personal chastisement upon his wife, even for the most outrageous conduct. The blow given by the husband in this case deserved the severest censure. All must condemn it. But I am much mistaken if the stubborn obstinacy with which the wife set him at defiance, and the violence she used in her rebellion against his authority, will not, under all the circumstances, be quite as revolting to the moral sense of an enlightened and a religious community as the unmanly conduct of the husband.

She further complains of personal violence, inflicted by the husband in the quarrel about making matches. The account she gives of the transaction in her affidavit is, that while she was making the matches, according to his directions, and obeying him in all things, he, without any provocation, became violently enraged, and having beaten her cruelly with a horsewhip, imprisoned her in the cellar. The story is confirmed in some particulars by one witness who says he heard a dispute between the parties, and two blows of a whip, and saw her come up from the cellar, and by another witness who says he saw the husband strike her two or three times with a whip, but not very heavily. He also saw him carry her into the cellar. This witness further says that the parties talked very angrily. Still another witness says she heard blows of a whip and afterwards saw marks of violence upon the person of plaintiff.

She has another complaint of personal chastisement, inflicted by the husband, in the dispute about certain papers belonging to the society for educating pious young men, of which society she was treasurer. Her account of this affair is, that the husband took the papers from her drawer and put them into his desk; that she demanded them, and he refused to restore them; that a few days afterwards she had an opportunity to obtain possession of them, in his absence, and took them away. When he came home and was informed of this, he flew into a violent passion, and using very profane and abusive language, finally horsewhipped her. Her account is, in some reports, confirmed by the testimony of a witness.

Such is the case presented by the evidence laid before us on the part of the wife. And I shall, in the first place, consider whether, upon the case thus presented, she is entitled to the decree she asks. It then becomes necessary to consider the true nature of the relation between husband and wife, and what is to be deemed extreme cruelty, within the meaning and intent of the statute.

In scripture the wife is represented as standing, in some respects, in the same relation to the husband as the husband stands to the Redeemer, and the Redeemer to God. The words are: The head of every man is Christ, and the head of the woman is the man, and the head of Christ is God. And in our law the wife is considered as being, in some respects, subordinate to the husband, who is the head of the house. The husband and wife are, in the contemplation of the law, one. Her legal existence and authority are suspended during the continuance of the matrimonial union. He is bound to support and maintain her in a manner suitable to her situation and his condition. He is made answerable for her debts contracted before the marriage. And during the continuance of the union he alone is responsible for crimes committed by her in his presence—the law not considering her, in such a case, as acting by her own will, but by his compulsion. He is answerable for all torts and frauds committed by her; and if committed in his company he alone is answerable. And she is wisely made subject in many thing to his authority, as he is subject to the laws under which he lives. But a wife is neither the slave nor the servant of a husband. He is the head of the house, to whom as such she is subordinate. But she is at the same time his companion, the partner and sharer of his fortune, in many respects his equal; who in her appropriate sphere is entitled to share largely in his authority.

He is bound, not only to honor and support her, but to accord to her freely and liberally all her rights, and to guarantee to her the full and free enjoyment of all her just privileges and prerogatives as the mistress of the family.

He is bound to leave her free to enjoy her own religious opinions, and worship God according to the dictates of her own reason and conscience; and not to molest or restrain her in this respect, provided she does not in her zeal disturb the public peace, nor rebel against his lawful authority. Such is the equality and dignity which our laws confer upon the female character; and such the relation in which husband and wife stand to one another.

What then is extreme cruelty? It is not mere austerity of temper, petulance of manners, rudeness of language, a want of civil attention, or even occasional sallies of temper, if there be no threat of bodily harm. It is not the denial of little indulgencies or particular accommodations. Such denial may in many cases be extremely unkind and unhandsome, and disgraceful to the character of a husband, and yet not amount to the cruelty intended by the statute. To constitute extreme cruelty in a husband, his misconduct must be such as to show that the inward knot of marriage, which is peace and love, is untied, and that he exercises over his wife, not the mild and salutary authority of a husband, but a harsh and cruel tyranny. In the judgment of the law, any willful misconduct of the husband, which endangers the life or the health of the wife; which exposes her to bodily hazard and intolerable hardship, and renders cohabitation unsafe, is extreme cruelty.

In order to amount to such cruelty it is not necessary that there should be many acts. Whenever force and violence, preceded by deliberate insult and abuse, have been once wantonly and without provocation used, the wife can hardly be considered as safe. But it is a well-settled rule, that a wife is not entitled to be divorced on the ground of ill treatment received from her husband, if that ill treatment has been drawn upon her by her own misconduct. The cruelty which lays a just and legal foundation for a divorce, must be unmerited and unprovoked. When she is ill treated on account of her own misconduct, her remedy is in a reform of her manners, unless the return from the husband is wholly unjustified by the provocation, and quite out of proportion to the offense.

Such are the rules of law that are to govern this decision; and there is very little difficulty in the application of them to the facts in this case. With respect to the quarrels and contests between the parties about the wood, and about the horse and chaise, there is no doubt. Whatever may have been the ill treatment which the wife received on those occasions it is very manifest she drew it down upon herself by her obstinacy and ill conduct. Nor does the return made by the husband appear to have been much out of proportion to the offense.

With regard to the quarrel about the matches, it is very clear that such was the conduct of the husband on that occasion, that if it is to be considered as altogether wanton and unprovoked, it entitles the libelant to the decree she asks. To beat a wife with a whip, and then put her into the cellar without any provocation, is both unjust and tyrannical; and, even in a case of great provocation, it could hardly be considered as manly conduct. It is not denied that he struck her with a whip, or that he put her into the cellar; and she states in her affidavit that she gave him no provocation whatever. This, however, is denied by him in his affidavit. The parties were alone when the quarrel began, and no other person knows in what it originated. It is proved that both very soon became very angry. It is not at all probable that all the fault was on one side. Nor is it likely that he would have proceeded to blows if there was no provocation, but all was submission on her part. The proofs which are in the case of her conduct and spirit on other occasions, render it quite improbable that she was at this time beaten and abused for her meekness and condescension. Besides, we have had an opportunity to compare her accounts of other transactions between herself and her husband, with the accounts which her witnesses give of the same transactions; and this comparison shows very clearly, that however fair her general character for truth and veracity may be, very little reliance can be placed upon her statements, when they relate to her disputes with her husband.

Perhaps it would be too much to expect that she should, under the circumstances, give a full and fair account of those transactions. It is certain, if her witnesses are to be believed, her accounts are neither full nor fair; and we cannot presume that her account of the occurrence we are now considering, is perfectly correct. We entirely condemn the use of the whip by the husband, as unlawful and unmanly. But no very serious injury was done to her person; and her own affidavit, unsupported as it is by any other testimony, has failed to satisfy us that the conduct of the husband was wanton, unprovoked, and unmerited, which is essential, to make it a legal ground of a divorce.

Indeed, taking all the testimony together, it seems to us to be rather more probable, on the whole, that she may have designedly used means to provoke him to acts of violence, in order that she might have a pretense for leaving him, than that, wantonly and unprovoked, he inflicted personal chastisement upon her. The same remarks, to a very great extent, are applicable in all their force to the quarrel between the parties about the papers belonging to the society for educating pious young men. The parties were alone during the whole contest, and they alone know the spirit and temper in which it proceeded. There are, however, two circumstances to be considered in this instance, which did not exist in the contest about the matches. The wife was the treasurer of the society, and to take the papers from her without her consent and lock them up in his desk, certainly had the appearance, not only of unkindness, but of an unmanly meddling in a concern which was exclusively under the management of the ladies who belonged to the society, and must have been calculated to vex and irritate the wife. On the other hand, her taking advantage of his absence to open the desk and take away the papers, has in it too much of a disposition to have her own will, and her own way, by foul means if not by fair, to be commended in a wife, and was calculated to exasperate her husband.

Now, considering the temper and disposition this lady is proved to have exhibited on other occasions, what is the probability as to her course of conduct when the husband came to reproach her for taking away the papers from his desk in his absence? Did she endeavor to avert the gathering storm by meek and submissive behavior, or did she retort upon him as unmanly interference in the concerns of a female society, with which he had nothing to do? It seems to us much more probable that he was driven to violence by her provoking taunts—taunts which may have been the more provoking, because he felt in them the sting of truth and justice—than that he should have resorted to blows without any new provocation on her part at that time. And this presumption is much strengthened by the consideration that the husband although quick and hasty in his temper, does not seem to be naturally vindictive; while the wife is shown to have been at other times quite as busy and active in a quarrel with her husband, as in the management of her ordinary household affairs. And we are of opinion, on the whole, that however obnoxious to censure the conduct of the husband may have been on any, or on all the occasions to which we have averted, the wife has no right to complain; because it is in the highest degree probable that in every instance she drew upon herself the chastisement she received, by her own improper conduct. And it does not appear that on any occasion the injury she received was much out of proportion to her offense.

Her remedy is to be sought, then, not in this court, but in a reformation of her own manners. Let her return to the path of duty; and if to a discreet and prudent exercise of her just rights and privileges as a wife, she will join that meekness, patience, and kindness which the religion she professes inculcates, and temper all her conduct towards her husband with that sweetness and goodness which belong to the true character of a wife, we think she will have no reasonable ground to apprehend any further injury to her person. Let her submit to the authority of her husband, and remember that the dignity of a wife cannot be violated by such submission. Let her return to the path of duty; and by displaying in all her conduct the mild and gentle spirit of the gospel, make that path a path of peace and safety.

And let the husband recollect that the first duty of the head of a family is to be master of himself, and to have his temper and feelings in due subjection to his reason and understanding, so that no provocation shall drive him, on any occasion, to unjust and unmanly acts of violence, or even to the use of profane and abusive language. And remembering his own infirmities let him generously go forward, and not only invite but encourage his wife to return to her duty, by satisfactory assurances, not only that her person shall be safe, but that her feeling shall not be insulted again by profane or abusive language, and that her religious rights shall not be in any way abridged. And let all those who attempt to advise them, consider who it is that has said, "Blessed are the peacemakers, for they shall be called the children of God.

Between these parties there is much to be forgotten and forgiven on both sides. But if they shall be disposed to retrace their steps; and if those who are around them shall aid and encourage them in all their attempts at reconcilation, it is to be hoped that they will encounter no serious obstacle in finding their way back to domestic peace and happiness."

THE BIBLICAL LAW

. . . let none deal treacherously against the wife of his youth.
Malachi 2:15

When a man hath taken a wife, and married her, and it come to pass that she find no favor in his eyes, because he hath found some uncleanness in her; then let him write her a bill of divorcement, and give it in her hand, and send her out of his house. *Deuteronomy 24:1*

And when she is departed . . . she may go and be another man's wife. And if the latter husband write her a bill of divorcement . . . or if the latter husband die . . . her former husband . . . may not take her again to be his wife.
Deuteronomy 24:1, 2, 3, 4

If she go not as thou wouldest have her, cut her off from thy flesh, and give her a bill of divorce, and let her go.
Ecclesiasticus 25:26

But I say unto you, that whosoever shall put away his wife, saving for the cause of fornication, causeth her to commit adultery: and whosover shall marry her that is divorced commiteth adultery. *Matthew 5:32*

. . . What therefore God hath joined together, let no man put asunder. *Matthew 19:6*

An evil wife is a yoke shaken to and fro: he that hath hold of her is as though he held a scorpion *Ecclesiasticus 26:7*

Let not the wife depart from her husband. *1 Corinthian 7:10*
For the woman which hath an husband is bound by the law to her husband as long as he liveth. . . . *Romans 7:2*

If any brother hath a wife that believeth not, and she be pleased to dwell with him, let him not put her away. And the woman which hath an husband that believeth not, and if he be pleased to dwell with her, let her not leave him.
1 Corinthians 7:13, 14

Whosoever putteth away his wife, and marrieth another, committeth adultery: and whosoever marrieth her that is put away from her husband committeth adultery. *Luke 16:18*

. . . where is the bill of your mother's divorcement, whom I have put away? *Isaiah 50:1*

I had rather dwell with a lion and a dragon, than to keep house with a wicked woman. *Ecclesiasticus 25:16*

DRINKING

The origin of the word "alcohol" is somewhat obscure. However, the drinking problem has been of importance in every organized society. From time to time prohibition movements against the use of intoxicating liquors have been enacted and repealed. In some countries organizations commonly known as the Prohohibition Party, and in some as the Anti-Saloon League, and like organizations, have been urging national prohibition.

There has always been concern about drinking of alcoholic beverages to excess. The Bible is replete with references to the drinking of wine, and reminds constantly that wine is as good as life to a man if it be drunk moderately. In Proverbs it is written "give strong drink unto him that is ready to perish and wine unto those that be of heavy hearts."

It is not understandable how laws forcing men to refrain from drinking can be enforced any more than laws which direct man to drink. Moderation is a matter of personal choice, and whether it is the law of the Bible, or the law today, no regulation can accomplish that which the human will does not desire.

Moderation is what the Bible seeks in its mandates, and its cautionary advice is best said in Proverbs 23: "look not thou upon the wine when it is red . . . it biteth like a serpent and stingeth like an adder."

Wine is as good as life to a man, if it be drunk moderately. . . .
Ecclesiasticus 31:27

Give strong drink unto him that is ready to perish, and wine unto those that be of heavy hearts. Let him drink, and forget poverty, and remember his misery no more. *Proverbs 31:6, 7*

Drink no longer water, but use a little wine for thy stomach's sake and thine often infirmities. *1 Timothy 5:23*

. . . it is hurtful to drink wine or water alone; wine mingled with water is pleasant, and delighteth the taste. . . .
2 Maccabees 15:39

It is good neither . . . to drink wine . . . whereby thy brother tumbleth, or is offended, or is made weak. *Romans 14:21*

. . . it is not for kings to drink wine; nor for princes strong drink: lest they drink and forget the law, and pervert the judgement of any of the afflicted. *Proverbs 31:4, 5*

Shew not thy valiantness in wine; for wine has destroyed many.
Ecclesiasticus 31:25

And he drank of the wine, and was drunken; and he was uncovered (indecent exposure) within his tent. *Genesis 9:21*

For a bishop must be blameless . . . a lover of . . . good men, sober . . . temperate. *Titus 1:7, 8*

Wherefore gird up the loins of your mind, be sober.
1 Peter 1:13

Meekness, temperance: against such there is no law.
Galatians 5:23

. . . drink not wine to make thee drunken: neither let drunkenness go with thee in thy journey. *Tobit 4:15*

Drunkenness increaseth the rage of a fool till he offend: it diminisheth strength, and maketh wounds.

Ecclesiasticus 31:30

Woe unto them that rise up early in the morning that they may follow strong drink; that continue till night, till wine inflame them. *Isaiah 5:11*

Do not drink wine nor strong drink . . . when ye go into the tabernacle of the congregation. . . . *Leviticus 10:9*

Look not thou upon the wine when it is red . . . it biteth like a serpent, and stingeth like an adder. *Proverbs 23:31, 32*

A laboring man that is given to drunkeness shall not be rich. . . . *Ecclesiasticus 19:1*

Woe unto him that giveth his neighbor drink . . . and makest him drunken also. . . . *Habakkuk 2:15*

. . . the priest and the prophet have erred through strong drink. . . . *Isaiah 28:7*

And every man that striveth for the mastery is temperate in all things. *1 Corinthians 9:25*

ECONOMICS

THE BIBLE contains law concerning possessions and their acquisition. In one of the ten commandments . . . "thou shalt not covet thy neighbor's house"—unlawful acquisition is prohibited.

Isaiah says "Woe unto them that join house to house, that lay field to field until there be no place, that they may be placed alone in the midst of the earth." It must be assumed that this is the first law against the appropriation of large grants of land to the exclusion of the general public.

England, France and Canada divided most of the land among the powerful families who financed the expeditions to the so-called "new world." Times have changed since then, and now the average man is able to acquire land in his own right.

Biblical law provides for the division of land among the twelve tribes of Israel, but whether it was apportioned to each family is not clear.

Exodus 23:10, 11 provides for a Sabbath year. Its object was not economic, to increase the fertility of the soil, but religious, to acknowledge God's ownership of the land by renouncing its use every seventh year.

In accordance with the directive in Exodus 23:19—"The first of the first fruits of thy land thou shalt bring unto the house of the Lord thy God," which may indicate that all ownership was subject to the will of God, and that the management of the affairs of government as well as the needs of the individual were religious rather than legal or political.

There were only two classes in the Holy Land; the rich, and the poor. It is assumed that much of the economy was controlled by but a few and therefore great stress was placed on the necessity to care for those in need.

Both wealth and poverty were extreme in Biblical Israel since there were no middle classes between the wealthy and the poor. Jerusalem was the center of Hebrew learning, and the residence of the priestly aristocracy who were the wealthy merchants and landlords and whose wealth was built upon the laborers and the peasants.

Slavery was commonplace in the Near East, but there was little or no slavery in Israel because Hebrew sentiment was opposed to the enslavement of one Hebrew by another. Since the Bible and the rabbis praised the dignity of manual labor, the fact that a man earned his living by working was not a social stigma. Not only Jesus and Paul, but many of the great rabbis practiced a trade; and they were accepted in the homes of the great because of their knowledge of the law.

The economic system of the Hebrews in Biblical days was agrarian since nearly all the people lived upon the land, and it was the Mosaic plan that all should be equal in possessions and position.

Luke 19 condemns man for "taking up that (which he) laid not down, and reaping that (which he) did not sow."

THE BIBLICAL LAW

He that hath two coats, let him impart to him that hath none; and he that hath meat, let him do likewise. *Luke 3:11*

. . . thou takest up that thou layedst not down, and reapest that thou didst not sow. *Luke 19:21*

. . . . I reap where I sowed not, and gather where I have not strawed. *Matthew 25:26*

They helped everyone his neighbor; and everyone said to his brother, be of good courage. *Isaiah 41:16*

Thou shalt not covet thy neighbor's house. *Exodus 20:17*

As the wild ass is the lion's prey in the wilderness: so the rich eat up the poor. *Ecclesiasticus 13:19*

. . . There is not a more wicked thing than a covetous man. . . .
Ecclesiasticus 10:9

Woe unto them that join house to house, that lay field to field, till there be no place, that they may be placed alone in the midst of the earth. *Isaiah 5:8*

The life of him that dependeth on another man's table is not to be counted for a life; for he polluteth himself with other men's meat. . . . *Ecclesiasticus 40:29*

. . . eat ye every one of his vine, and every one of his fig tree, and drink ye every one the waters of his own cistern.
Isaiah 36:16

. . . in all things I have kept myself from being burdensome unto you, and so will I keep myself. *2 Corinthians 11:9*

He that tilleth his land shall have plenty of bread. . . .
Proverbs 28:19

For thou shall eat the labor of thine hands: happy shall thou be, and it shall be well with thee. *Psalms 128:2*

. . . to be content with that a man hath, is a sweet life. *Ecclesiasticus 40:18*

For we brought nothing into this world, and it is certain we can carry nothing out. And having food and raiment let us be therewith content. *1 Timothy 6:7, 8*

He that loveth gold shall not be justified . . . Gold hath been the ruin of many, and . . . it is a stumbling block unto them that sacrifice unto it. . . . *Ecclesiasticus 31:5, 6, 7*

For I [Christ] say unto you, That unto every one which hath shall be given; and from him that hath not, even that he hath shall be taken away from him. *Luke 19:26*

And he [Christ] went into the temple, and began to cast out them that sold therein, and them that bought; Saying unto them, It is written, My house is the house of prayer: but ye have made it a den of thieves. *Luke 19:45, 46*

EDUCATION

THROUGHOUT the Bible there is repetitive direction to educate the young, to learn the words of knowledge, and not only to receive instruction, but to hear counsel. To absorb wisdom, to get understanding, and that the mind should be filled with pleasures and riches, resulting only from education and learning. The Mosaic law does caution that wisdom is much grief and that a man who has great knowledge increaseth sorrow.

Biblical law directs that children shall receive their instruction from the father. There is no record of a school system. Each family taught their children the laws, and it was the head of the family who was charged with the responsibility of educating the children so that in due time they might take the place of the parents as heads of the family.

The Levites, who assisted the priests administering to the religious needs of Israel, were not required to attend a school, but were educated by their family elders in the knowledge of the requirements of their special position.

"Receive my instruction, and not silver; and knowledge rather than choice gold" is sufficient to show the high plane on which education was placed, and the importance of its acquisition.

Mandatory school attendance for children has made the United States the leader in education and progress.

THE BIBLICAL LAW

Apply thine heart unto instruction, and thine ears to the words of knowledge. *Proverbs 23:12*

Receive my instruction, and not silver; and knowledge rather than choice gold. *Proverbs 8:10*

Hear counsel, and receive instruction, that thou mayest be wise in thy latter end. *Proverbs 19:20*

Wisdom is the principal thing; therefore get wisdom; and with all thy getting get understanding. *Proverbs 4:7*

. . . The Lord is a God of knowledge. *1 Samuel 2:3*

And by knowledge shall the chambers of the mind be filled with all precious and pleasant riches. *Proverbs 24:4*

. . . that the soul be without knowledge . . . is not good. *Proverbs 19:2*

. . . a man of understanding walketh uprightly. *Proverbs 15:21*

. . . gather instruction from thy youth up: so shalt thou find wisdom till thine old age. *Ecclesiasticus 6:18*

For in much wisdom is much grief: and he that increaseth knowledge increaseth sorrow. *Ecclesiastes 1:18*

. . . be admonished; of making many books there is no end; and much study is a weariness of the flesh. *Ecclesiastes 12:12*

Thy wisdom and thy knowledge, it hath perverted thee; and thou hast said in thine heart, I am, and none else beside me. *Isaiah 47:10*

Hast thou children? Instruct them, and bow down their neck from their youth. *Ecclesiasticus 7:23*

My son, hear the instruction of thy father, and foresake not the law of thy mother. *Proverbs 1:8*

Hear, ye children, the instruction of a father, and attend to know understanding. *Proverbs 4:1*

Oh that my words . . . were printed in a book! *Job 19:23*

. . . of making books there is no end; and much study is a weariness of the flesh. *Ecclesiastes 12:12*

EMBEZZLEMENT, FRAUD AND DEECEIT

THE BIBLE likens the man who deceiveth his neighbor, to a mad man. Our laws prohibit deceitful dealing and taking advantage of another. Penalties are fixed for every deceitful act. One who obtains the promise of another by fraud is estopped from receiving any gain.

The law requires honest dealing, and that one who enters into an agreement with his fellow man must do so justly and honestly.

Embezzlement today is a statutory crime, and there must be proof of the taking of some specific property mentioned in the statute.

It is difficult to compare Biblical sins with statutory crimes since in the former all are based on moral and spiritual values whereas in the latter only that is a crime which fits into the structure of the statute sought to be enforced.

Man's desire to have the possessions of others has been the subject of much legal legislation. Gaining property, whether real or personal, by fraud and deceit has been a curse of man from time immemorial.

The Mosaic law condemns deceit, fraud, and all unrighteous dealings between men. Centuries have changed many things, but man's greed is still the subject of our punitive legal system.

THE BIBLICAL LAW

If a soul . . . lie unto his neighbor in that which was delivered him to keep, or in a thing taken away by violence, or hath deceived his neighbor . . . or have found that which was lost, and lieth concerning it, and sweareth falsely . . . then . . . he shall restore that which he took violently away, or the thing which he hath deceitfully gotten, or that which was delivered him to keep, or the lost thing which he found . . . or all that about which he has sworn falsely; he shall restore it in the principal, and shall add a fifth part more thereto. . . .

Leviticus 6:1, 2, 3, 4, 5

The getting of treasures by a lying tongue is a vanity. . . .

Proverbs 20:6

. . . defraud not. . . . *Mark 10:19*

Defraud ye not one another. . . . *1 Corinthians 7:5*

. . . we have wronged no man, we have corrupted no man, we have defrauded no man. *2 Corinthians 7:2*

For ye know what commandments we gave you . . . that no man go beyond and defraud his brother in any matter. . . .

1 Thessalonians 4:2, 6

. . . he that getteth riches, and not by right, shall leave them in the midst of his days and at his end shall be a fool.

Jeremiah 17:11

Thou shalt not defraud thy neighbor. . . .

Leviticus 19:13

He that worketh deceit shall not dwell within my house. . . .

Psalms 101:7

EVIDENCE AND WITNESSES

In the conduct of a trial each litigant is required to produce evidence to prove his claim, or to disprove the claim of his opposition. The history of evidence has from the beginning put the burden on him who contends for his position and he is required to prove his case by producing his evidence first. He must bring forth his witnesses who must give honest and truthful evidence of the facts, known to them of their own knowledge, or they may relate that which they have seen, and under some circumstances and conditions, that which they have heard.

Each witness must testify concerning actual facts and not what he thinks or infers. It is for the judge, or the jury to resolve the testimony given, and to conclude which is or is not to be believed.

Mosaic law did not require, as today, that before a witness testified in a court of law, he take an oath before God to tell the truth. Through the ages some form of oath-taking has been mandatory before a witness could be heard. Since in our practice no inquiry is made of the person taking such oath as to his belief in God or his belief in immortality, or his belief in punishment after death, in the event he has sworn falsely, it seems useless to administer an oath to one who disregards its moral as well as legal obligation.

The giving of testimony, and the taking of evidence from witnesses, is one of the most important events in man's juridical systems.

When testimony is being given by an honest witness who testifies to something he saw, he represents under oath that he accurately saw or heard some past events; that now he accurately remembers what he saw or heard; and that he is now accurately reporting his memory. Into each of these three, error can enter, and often does. Observation is not a mechanical process. While part of what man perceives comes from the object before him, another part—and it may be the greater part—always comes out of his mind.

A reading of Ruth 4:7 indicates that evidence of sale and purchase, and perhaps evidence of the completion of any transaction, was by manual and physical acts: "Now this was the manner in former time in Israel concerning redeeming and concerning changing, for to confirm all things; a man plucked off his shoe, and gave it to his neighbor: and this was testimony in Israel."

What is meant by "now this was the manner in former time in Israel" is not clear. It can mean that this "manner" of evidence was the existing rule, or it may be the statement of an earlier custom. However, when read together with all that precedes and follows the above quotation it is safe to assume that reference is made to an existing rule of evidence.

Cross-Examination

Two chapters of the Book of Daniel appear only in the Apocrypha because neither was written in Hebrew. Had they been in Hebrew they would have been Chapters 13 and 14 of Daniel.

The second of these chapters is the history of the Destruction of Bel and the Dragon. It deals with Daniel in the lions' den. The other is called The History of Susanna, and treats of Daniel's defense of a woman accused of adultery and against whom there were two witnesses who testified they saw her in the act. She was, as a result, sentenced to death. Daniel, in effect, asked that a new trial be granted her. This was done and Daniel, acting as defense counsel, cross-examined the two accusers and established the falsity of their testimony. The book closes with the punishment decreed for the two perjurers: "And they arose against the two elders (for Daniel had convicted them of false witness by their own mouth) and according to the law of Moses they did unto them in such sort as they maliciously intended to do their neighbor: and they put them to death."

Trial

There was no manner of jury trial known to the Mosaic law. The procedure was for the judges who tried the case to examine all witnesses and afterward in their deliberations to first advance all the arguments available in favor of the defense. Their opening argument or discussion must be for acquittal. It is from this Mosaic principle that we have inherited the legal premise that all men are presumed to be innocent, and cannot be convicted until the contrary is proved to a moral certainty and beyond a reasonable doubt.

Self-Incrimination

In our law the privilege against self-incrimination doubtless had its birth in the abhorrence with which confessions coerced by inquisitorial means were regarded by all men. The rule is that no defendant in a criminal case may be compelled to be a witness against himself.

The accused was never compelled to testify against himself. A confession of guilt was accepted in evidence and considered in connection with other facts of the case, but standing alone it could not be the basis of a conviction. Maimonides in his commentaries on the Mishna discusses this rule: "We have it as a fundamental principle of our jurisprudence that no one can bring an accusation against himself. Should a man make a confession of guilt before a legally constituted tribunal, such confession is not to be used against him, unless properly attested by two other witnesses. It is, however, well to remark that the death sentence issued against Achan (Joshua 7:19, 20, 24, 25) was an exceptional case, brought about by the nature of the circumstances attending it, for our law never condemns on the single confession of an accused part."

During the military leadership of Joshua, self-incrimination was an accepted legal procedure as more fully appears in the biblical description of the case of Achan.

Circumstantial Evidence

Only direct evidence was permitted under biblical law. The strongest chain of circumstantial evidence would not suffice for conviction. Witnesses were instructed that hearsay evidence was not admissible. The witness, to testify in a trial, must give evidence only of that which he actually heard or had seen. As directed in Deuteronomy 17:6 "at the mouth of two witnesses, or three witnesses, shall he that is worthy of death be put to death."

Most of the procedural rules are found only in the Mishna and the Gemara, which are books of the decisions construing the Mosaic law.

Qualification of Witnesses

Women, because of the "levity and boldness of the sex" were not permitted to testify. This was particularly true in capital cases, since the law required the witness to be the executioner.

Minors were competent witnesses if passed their thirteenth birthday.

Those who were "wicked", or those known as immoral or irreligious people were not accepted as witnesses.

In the list of incompetent witnesses there is included: slaves, idiots, deaf mutes, lunatics, gamblers, blind men, usurers, the immodest, and the illiterate.

All witnesses presented in a case were required to agree in all essential details. If one contradicted another in any material matter, their entire testimony was disregarded. This rule applied in criminal cases only; it was not the rule in civil cases.

It was mandatory that witnesses give their testimony separately, but always in the presence of defendant.

Pretrial and Discovery Proceedings

Our law has but recently adopted a pretrial and discovery procedure intended to limit the issues and facts in each case, and to discard immaterial or irrelevant evidence. Our procedure contemplates a hearing before the judge prior to the scheduled trial to simplify the issues in controversy, and avoid unnecessary proof of facts. The Biblical law provided for, and used this procedure thousands of years ago.

To prevent the admission of irrelevant testimony, a preliminary examination of witnesses was conducted in private by a committee of the members of the Sanhedrin. All irrelevant testimony developed at this private examination was cast aside. The result of this proceeding was the discovery of discrepancies in statements of witnesses. The full court sitting in regular session was not, therefore, exposed to or prejudiced by facts that had no legal connection with the case, since every impression, legal or illegal, received at a trial, affects the judgment of the court or jury and enters into the resulting verdict.

THE BIBLICAL LAW

Thou shalt not bear false witness against thy neighbor.
Exodus 20:16

For a man's mind is sometime want to tell him more than seven watchmen, that sit above in an high tower.
Ecclesiasticus 37:14

And Joshua said unto Achan . . . make confession . . . and tell me now what thou has done: and Achan . . . said, Indeed I have sinned . . . and thus and thus have I done. And Joshua and all Israel took Achan . . . and his sons and his daughters . . . and all that he had . . . and all Israel stoned him . . . and burned them with fire. . . . *Joshua 7:19, 20, 24, 25*

Let them bring them forth, and shew us what shall happen: let them show the former things, what they be, that we may consider them, and know the latter end of them; or declare us things for to come. *Isaiah 41:22*

. . . Let them bring forth their witnesses, that they may be justified: or let them hear, and say, It is truth. *Isaiah 43:9*

A faithful witness will not lie: but a false witness will utter lies. *Proverbs 14:5*

. . . one witness shall not testify against any person to cause him to die. *Numbers 35:30*

One witness shall not rise up against a man for any iniquity, or for any sin that he sinneth: at the mouth of two witnesses, or at the mouth of three witnesses, shall the matter be established.
Deuteronomy 20:15

. . . Thy blood be upon thy head; for thy mouth hath testified against thee. . . . *2 Samuel 1:16*

The hands of the witnesses shall be first upon him to put him to death, and afterward the hands of all the people.
Deuteronomy 17:7

Be not a witness against thy neighbor without cause. . . .
Proverbs 24:28

Do not bear false witness against thy neighbor. *Exodus 20:16*

For children begotten of unlawful beds are witnesses of wickedness against their parents in their trial. *Wisdom of Solomon 4:6*

Thine own mouth condemneth thee, and not I. Yea, thine own lips testify aaginst thee. *Job 15:6*

If I justify myself, mine own mouth shall condemn me. . . .
Job 9:20

For by thy words thou shalt be justified, and by thy words thou shalt be condemned. *Matthew 12:37*

Blame not before thou hast examined the truth: understand first, and then rebuke. *Ecclesiasticus 11:7*

Answer not before thou hast heard the cause: neither interrupt men in the midst of their talk. *Ecclesiasticus 11:8*

FOOD

"There is nothing better for a man, than that he should eat and drink, and that he should make his soul enjoy good in his labor." However, by Biblical law man was cautioned to use discretion and moderation and to be temperate in all eating and drinking. Ecclesiasticus cautions that man "should have a care of his meat and diet."

While the Bible says that every man that strives for mastery is temperate in all things it also provides that no one "be unsatiable in any dainty thing, nor too greedy upon meats" and that "excess of meats bringeth sickness, and surfeiting will turn into choler. By surfeiting many have perished; but he that taketh heed prolongeth his life."

Leviticus II and Deuteronomy 14 contain the laws and directives concerning the foods which may be eaten. Each animal, fowl, and fish is "clean" which may be eaten, or "unclean" which may not be eaten.

Prohibition prevails against eating anything with blood, and that one shall "pour it upon the ground as water."

Table manners too are given consideration, and suggestions for man's conduct when visiting and dining are suggested. It may be assumed that the culture of Biblical times demanded a high degree of decorum and decent conduct. That proper etiquette is discussed is evidence of a life of social amenities and that all life was not herding of sheep and tilling of fields.

THE BIBLICAL LAW

Let your moderation be known unto all men.
Philippians 4:5

Sound sleep cometh of moderate eating: he riseth early, and his wits are with him. *Ecclesiasticus 31:20*

. . . temperance: against such there is no law.
Galatians 5:23

There is nothing better for a man, than that he should eat and drink, and that he should make his soul enjoy good in his labor. *Ecclesiastes 2:24*

. . . every man should eat and drink, and enjoy the good of his labor. . . . *Ecclesiastes 3:13*

. . . it is good and comely for one to eat and to drink and to enjoy the good of all his labor that he taketh under the sun all the days of his life. *Ecclesiastes 5:18*

A cheerful and good heart will have a care of his meat and diet. *Ecclesiasticus 30:25*

Be not unsatiable in any dainty thing, nor too greedy upon meats. *Ecclesiasticus 37:29*

For excess of meats bringeth sickness, and surfeiting will turn into choler. *Ecclesiasticus 37:30*

By surfeiting many have perished; but he that taketh heed prolongeth his life. *Ecclesiasticus 37:31*

And every man that striveth for the mastery is temperate in all things. *1 Corinthians 9:25*

. . . of every tree of the garden thou mayest freely eat; but of the tree of knowledge of good and evil, thou shalt not eat of it. . . . *Genesis 2:16, 17*

It is good neither to eat flesh, nor to drink wine, nor anything whereby thy brother stumbleth, or is offended or is made weak.
Romans 14:21

Every moving thing that liveth shall be meat for you; even as the green herb. . . . *Genesis 9:3*

Thou shalt not eat any abominable thing. *Deuteronomy 14:3*

. . . These are the beasts which ye shall eat among all the beasts that are on the earth. Whatever parteth the hoof and is clovenfooted, and cheweth the cud . . . nevertheless these shall ye not eat of them that chew the cud, or of them that divide the hoof; as a camel, because he cheweth the cud, but divideth not the hoof; he is unclean unto you. *Leviticus 11:2, 3, 4*

Ye shall not eat of anything that dieth of itself. . . .
Deuteronomy 14:21

. . . neither shall ye eat any flesh that is torn of beasts in the field; ye shall cast it to the dogs. *Exodus 22:31*

. . . ye shall eat no manner of blood, whether it be of fowl or of beast. . . . *Leviticus 7:26*

Ye shall not eat anything with the blood. . . .
Leviticus 19:26

And whatever man there be of the House of Israel, or of the strangers that soujourn among you that eateth any manner of blood; . . . cut him off from his people. *Leviticus 17:10*

No soul of you shall eat blood, neither shall any stranger that sojourneth among you eat blood. *Leviticus 17:12*

Ye shall eat the blood of no manner of flesh; for the life of all flesh is the blood thereof. . . . *Leviticus 17:14*

Ye shall eat no manner of fat, of ox, or of sheep or of goat.
Leviticus 7:23

It shall be a perpetual statute for your generations throughout all your dwellings, that ye eat neither fat nor blood.
Leviticus 3:17

GENERAL LAWS

Consideration is given the many laws and statutes proclaimed in the Bible dealing with general conditions affecting the every day living of the Hebrew people.

The routine of living then was not much different than it is today. Prohibition against man wearing women's clothing and juvenile delinquency receive attention. Equality before the law, begging, kidnapping, mortgages, insane persons, and all forms of general subjects arising in community living are provided for. It is clear in Biblical history that life in the cities and on the farms required regulation as much then as it does today.

Interesting comparisons can be made. For cleanliness, man was required to cut his hair short. This was necessary in a country of heat, sand, and where the supply of water was limited.

Much of the law in the Bible is the law today, and which our legislatures enact and repeat and re-enact from time to time. Could we but transfer ourselves from our street to a street in the Holy Land as it existed then, it seems there would be little difference insofar as the laws are concerned.

The many Biblical laws for the treatment of indigents and the poor generally, indicate the great poverty of the lower classes. Whether this was due to the economy of the Holy Land or to the caste system is not clear.

Application of Laws

One law shall be to him that is homeborn, and unto the stranger that sojourneth among you. *Exodus 12:49*

. . . he [the King] shall write him a copy of this law in a book out of that which is before the priests . . . and he shall read therein . . . that he may learn . . . to keep all the words of this law and these statutes, to do them.

Deuteronomy 17:18, 19

A wise man hateth not the law . . . a man of understanding trusteth in the law; and the law is faithful unto him. . . .

Ecclesiasticus 33:2, 3

It is easier for heaven and earth to pass, than one tittle of the law to fail. *Luke 16:17*

Where no law is, there is no transgression. *Romans 4:15*

. . . the law is not made for a righteous man, but for the lawless and disobedient. *1 Timothy 1:8, 9*

Avoid . . . strivings about the law; for they are unprofitable and vain. *Titus 3:9*

Bastards

A bastard shall not enter unto the congregation of the Lord; even to his tenth generation shall he not enter into the congregation of the Lord. *Deuteronomy 23:2*

Begging

Be not a beggar by banqueting upon borrowing, when thou hast nothing in thy purse. . . . *Ecclesiasticus 18:33*

. . . lead not a begger's life: for better it is to die than to beg. The life of him that dependeth on another man's table is not to be counted for a life; for he polluteth himself with other men's meat. *Ecclesiasticus 40:28*

Better is the life of a poor man in a mean cottage, than delicate fare in another man's house. *Ecclesiasticus 29:22*

Birds and Bees

If a bird's nest chance to be before thee . . . in any tree or on the ground, whether they be young ones, or eggs, and the dam setting upon the young, or upon the eggs, thou shalt not take the dam with the young. But thou shalt in any wise let the dam go, and take the young to thee. . . .
Deuteronomy 22:6, 7

The bee is little among such as fly; but her fruit is the chief of sweet things. *Ecclesiasticus 11:3*

Building Code

For which of you, intending to build a tower, sitteth not down first, and counteth the cost, whether he have sufficient to finish it? *Luke 14:28*

When thou buildest a new house, then thou shalt make a battlement for thy roof, that thou bring not blood upon thy house, if any man fall from thence. *Deuteronomy 22:8*

He that buildeth his house with other men's money is like one that gathereth himself stones for the tomb of his burial.
Ecclesiasticus 21:8

Clothes

The woman shall not wear that which pertaineth unto a man, neither shall a man put on a woman's garment: for all that do so are abomination. . . . *Deuteronomy 22:5*

Thou shalt not wear a garment of a divers sorts, as of woolen and linen together. *Deuteronomy 22:11*

Diet

Ye shall eat no manner of fat, or ox, or of sheep, or of goat. *Leviticus 7:23*

Equality Before the Law

One law shall be to him that is homeborn, and unto the stranger that sojourneth among you. *Exodus 12:49*

Flight

The wicked flee when no man pursueth: but the righteous are bold as a lion. *Proverbs 28:1*

Fortune-Tellers and Magicians

Ye shall not . . . use enchantment, nor observe times. *Leviticus 19:26*

Regard not them that have familiar spirits, neither seek after wizards, to be defiled by them. *Leviticus 19:31*

Divinations, and soothsayings, and dreams, are vain: for dreams have deceived many, and they have failed that put their trust in them. *Ecclesiasticus 34:5, 7*

And when they say unto you, Seek unto them that have familiar spirits, and unto wizards that peep, and that mutter: should not a people seek unto their God? *Isaiah 8:19*

And the soul that turneth after such as have familiar spiritis, and after wizards, to go a whoring after them . . . I will cut him off from among his people. *Leviticus 20:6*

There shall not be found among you anyone that maketh his son or his daughter to pass through the fire, or that useth divination, or an observer of times, or an enchanter, or a witch, or a charmer, or a consulter with familiar spirits, or a wizard, or a necromancer. *Deuteronomy 18:10, 11*

Gambling

And Aaron . . . shall take . . . two goats . . . and shall cast lots upon the two goats; one lot for the Lord, and the other lot for the scapegoat . . . to let him go for a scapegoat unto the wilderness. . . . *Leviticus 16:7, 8, 9, 10*

. . . the land shall be divided by lot. . . . *Numbers 26:55*

The lot causes contentions to cease. . . . *Proverbs 18:18*

Guests

. . . I opened my doors to the traveller. *Job 31:32*

Bring not every man unto thine house: for the deceitful man hath many trains (paths). *Ecclesiasticus 11:29*

Who will trust a thief . . . that skippeth from city to city? so [who will believe] a man that hath no house, and lodgeth wheresoever the night taketh him? *Ecclesiasticus 36:26*

. . . howsoever let all thy wants lie upon me; only lodge not in the street. *Judges 19:20*

If any . . . bid you to a feast, and ye be disposed to go, whatsoever is set before you, eat, asking no questions.
1 Corinthians 10:27

Hair

. . . If a man have long hair, it is a shame unto him, but if a woman have long hair, it is a glory to her. . . .
1 Corinthians 11: 14, 15

Indigents

Give alms of thy substance; and when thou givest alms, let not thine eye be envious, neither turn thy face from any poor. . . .
Tobit 4:7

If thou hast abundance, give alms accordingly; if thou have but a little, be not afraid to give accordingly to that little.
Tobit 4:8

. . . relieve the oppressed. . . . *Isaiah 1:17*

Strengthen ye the weak hands, and confirm the feeble knees.
Isaiah 35:3

Rob not the poor, because he is poor: neither oppress the afflicted. . . . *Proverbs 22: 22*

. . . Go and bring the poor, and the maimed, and the halt, and the blind. *Luke 14:21*

Thou shalt not curse the deaf, nor put a stumbling block before the blind. . . . *Leviticus 19:14*

Cursed be he that maketh the blind to wander out of the way.
Deuteronomy 27:18

Dishonor not a man in his old age: even some of us wax old.
Ecclesiasticus 8:6

Rebuke not an elder, but intreat him as a father . . . the elder women as mothers. . . . *1 Timothy 5:1, 2*

Thou shalt open thine hand wide unto thy brother, to thy poor, to thy needy, in thy land. *Deuteronomy 15:11*

And when ye reap the harvest of your land, thou shalt not make clean riddance of the corners of thy field when thou reapest; neither shalt thou gather any gleaning of thy harvest: thou shalt leave them unto the poor, and to the stranger. . . .
Leviticus 23:22

For the poor shall never cease out of the land. . . .
Deuteronomy 15:11

Thou shalt rise up before the hoary head, and honor the face of the old man. *Leviticus 19:32*

That the aged man be sober, grave, temperate, sound in faith, in charity, in patience. The aged woman likewise, that they be in behavior as becometh holiness, not false accusers, not given to much wine, teachers of good things. *Titus 2:2, 3*

For the poor shall never cease out of the land: therefore I command thee, saying Thou shalt open thine hand wide unto thy brother, to thy poor, and to thy needy. . . .
Deuteronomy 15:11

And oppress not the widow, nor the fatherless, the stranger, nor the poor. . . . *Zechariah 7:10*

Blessed is he that considereth the poor. *Psalms 41:1*

And if thy brother be waxen poor, and fallen in decay with thee; then thou shalt relieve him: yea, though he be a stranger, or a sojourner; that he may live with thee. *Leviticus 25:35*

. . . thou . . . shalt surely lend him sufficient for his need . . .
Deuteronomy 15:8

And if thy brother that dwelleth by thee be waxen poor, and be sold unto thee; thou shalt not compel him to serve as a bond-servant: but as an hired servant, and as a sojourner, he shall be with thee . . . and then shall he depart from thee, both he and his children with him. . . . *Leviticus 25:39, 40, 41*

I have been young, and now am old; yet have I not seen the righteous forsaken, nor his seed begging bread. *Psalms 37:25*

. . . if any would not work, neither should he eat.
2 Thesalonians 3:10

. . . when ye reap the harvest of your land, thou shalt not wholly reap the corners of thy field . . . and thou shalt not . . . gather every grape of thy vineyard; thou shalt leave them for the poor and stranger. . . . *Leviticus 19:9, 10*

When thou cuttest down thine harvest in thy field, and hast forgot a shief in the field, thou shalt not go again to fetch it . . . When thou beatest thine olive tree, thou shalt not go over the boughs again, and it shall be for the stranger, for the fatherless, and for the widow. *Deuteronomy 24:19, 20*

Be as a father unto the fatherless, and instead of an husband unto their mother. . . . *Ecclesiasticus 4:10*

Ye shall not afflict any widow, or fatherless child.
Exodus 22: 22

Insane Persons

. . . have mercy on my son: for he is a lunatic, and sore vexed. . . . *Matthew 17:15*

. . . comfort the feebleminded, support the weak, be patient to all men. *1 Thessalonians 5:14*

Juvenile Delinquency

Do not sin against the child. . . . *Genesis 42:22*

If a man have a stubborn and rebelious son, which will not obey the voice of his father, or the voice of his mother, and that, when they have chastened him, will not hearken unto them . . . [then] all the men of the city shall stone him with stones, that he die. *Deuteronomy 21:18, 19, 20, 21*

Chasten thy son while there is hope, and let not thy soul spare for his crying. *Proverbs 19:18*

Withhold not correction from the child: for if thou beatest him with the rod, he shall not die. *Proverbs 23:13*

Hast thou children? instruct them, and bow down their neck from their youth. *Ecclesiasticus 7:23*

Children, obey your parents in all things: for this is well pleasing to the Lord. *Colossians 3:20*

An horse not broken becometh headstrong: and a child left to himself will be wilful. *Ecclesiasticus 30:8*

Knowledge of the Law

At the end of every seven years, in the solemnity of the year of release, thou shalt read this law before all Israel in their hearing. Gather the people, together, men and women, and children, and thy stranger that is within thy gates, that they may hear and that they may learn . . . and observe to do all the words of this law. *Deuteronomy 31:10-12*

Thou shalt teach them (The Commandments) dilligently unto thy children, and shalt talk of them when thou sittest in thine house and when thy walkest by the way, and when thy liest down, and when risest up . . . and thou shalt write them upon the posts of thy house, and on thy gates.

Deuteronomy 6:7-9

Lost or Found Property

Thou shalt not see thy brother's ox or his sheep go astray . . . thou shalt in any case bring them again unto thy brother. And if thy brother be no nigh unto thee, or if thou know him not, then thou shalt bring it unto thine own house, and it shall be with thee until thy brother seek after it, and thou shalt restore it to him again . . . and with all lost things of thy brother's, which he has lost and thou hast found, shalt thou do likewise; thou mayest not hide thyself.

Deuteronomy 22:1, 2, 3

If a soul . . . have found that which was lost and lieth concerning it, and sweareth falsely . . . he shall restore . . . the lost thing which he found . . . and shall add the fifth part more thereto. *Leviticus 6:25*

Mourning and Burial

Seven days do men mourn for him that is dead. . . .

Ecclesiasticus 22:12

. . . let tears fall down over the dead, and begin to lament, as if thou hadst suffered great harm thyself; and then cover his body according to the custom, and neglect not his burial.
Ecclesiasticus 38:15

Mortgages

. . . We have mortgaged our lands, vineyards, and houses, so that we might buy corn. . . . *Nehemiah 5:3*

Offenses Against the Person

If men strive and hurt a woman with child, so that her fruit depart from her, and yet no mischief follow . . . he shall pay as the judges determine. *Exodus 21:22*

And if any mischief follow, then thou shalt give life for life. Eye for eye, tooth for tooth, hand for hand, foot for foot.
Exodus 21:23, 24

And if a man cause a blemish in his neighbor; as he has done, so shall it be done to him. *Leviticus 24:19*

When men strive together one with another, and the wife of the one draweth near for to deliver her husband out of the hand of him that smiteth him, and putteth forth her hand and taketh him by the secrets: then thou shalt cut off her hand. . . .
Deuteronomy 25:11, 12

Removing Landmarks

Thou shalt not remove thy neighbor's landmarks, which they of old time have set. *Deuteronomy 19:14*

Cursed be he that removeth his neighbor's landmark.
Deuteronomy 27:17

Remove not the ancient landmark, which thy fathers have set.
Proverbs 22:28

Social Behavior

If thou sit at a bountiful table, be not greedy upon it, and say not, there is much meat on it. *Ecclesiasticus 31:12*

Eat as it becometh a man, those things which are set before before thee; and devour not, lest thou be hated.
Ecclesiasticus 31:16

Leave off first for manners' sake; and be not unsatiable, lest thou offend. *Ecclesiasticus 31:17*

The greater thou art, the more humble thyself. . . .
Ecclesiasticus 3:18

Some man holdeth his tongue, because he hath not to answer: and some keepeth silence, knowing his time.
Ecclesiasticus 20:6

Let your speech be always with grace, seasoned with salt, that ye may know how ye ought to answer every man.
Colossians 4:6

Without eyes thou shalt want light: profess not the knowledge therefore that thou hast not. *Ecclesiasticus 3:25*

He that hath no experience knoweth little. . . .
Ecclesiasticus 34:10

When thou sittest among many, reach not thine hand out first of all. *Ecclesiasticus 31:18*

A very little is sufficient for a man well nurtured, and he fetcheth not his wind short . . . sound sleep cometh of moderate eating. . . . *Ecclesiasticus 31:19, 20*

For the wages of sin is death. . . . *Romans 6:23*

[He] loved the wages of unrighteousness. *2 Peter 2:15*
If any of them that believe not bid you to a feast, and ye be disposed to go; whatsoever is set before you, eat, asking no question for conscience sake. *1 Corinthians 10:27*

, . . him that hath an high look and a proud heart will not I suffer. *Psalms 101:5*

Put not forth thyself . . . and stand not in the place of great men. For better it is that it be said unto thee, come up hither; then that thou shouldest be put lower. . . . *Proverbs 25:6, 7*

Swearing

Thou shalt not take the name of the Lord thy God in vain. . . . *Exodus 20:7*

And ye shall not swear by my name falsely. *Leviticus 19:12*

Use not thy mouth to intemperate swearing, for therein is the word of sin. *Ecclesiasticus 23:13*

But I say unto you, swear not at all. . . . *Matthew 5:34*

. . . swear not, neither by heaven, neither by the earth, neither by any other oath. . . . *James 5:12*

The talk of him that sweareth much maketh the hair stand upright. . . . *Ecclesiasticus 27:14*

Tatooing

. . . [do not] print any marks upon you. . . . *Leviticus 19:28*

Widows and Orphans Pensions

Then the high priest told him that there was . . . money laid up for the relief of widows and fatherless children. *2 Maccabees 3:10*

Ye shall not afflict any widow, or fatherless child. If thou afflict them in any wise, and they cry at all unto me . . . I will kill you with the sword; and your wives shall be widows and your children fatherless. *Exodus 22:22, 23, 24*

Witchcraft

And I will cut off witchcrafts out of thine hand; and thou shalt have no more soothsayers. *Micah 5:12*

A man also or a woman that hath a familiar spirit, or that is a wizard, shall surely be put to death: they shall stone them. *Leviticus 20:27*

Thou shalt not suffer a witch to live. *Exodus 22:18*

GIFTS

A GIFT is a transfer of property, made voluntarily and without consideration. In order for a gift to be valid, there must be a complete delivery and transfer of dominion within the donor's lifetime. Acceptance by the donee is an essential element of a completed gift. To create a valid and enforceable gift there must be a donative intent by the donor, an effectual transfer of title and delivery, and an actual or imputed acceptance by the donee. A clear intention on the part of the donor to make a gift is essential to a valid gift and it is sufficient if the donor uses words clearly importing an intention to give.

The Bible understands man: "every one loveth gifts, and followeth after rewards."

. . . it is more blessed to give than to receive. *Acts 20:35*

. . . let him labor, working with his hands . . . that he may have to give him that needeth. *Ephesians 5:28*

And thou shalt take no gift: for the gift blindeth the wise, and perverteth the words of the righteous. *Exodus 23:8*

He that is greedy of gain troubleth his own house; but he that hateth gifts shall live. *Proverbs 15:27*

Unto the sons of the (his) concubines . . . Abraham gave gifts . . . and sent them away. . . . *Genesis 25:6*

Take, I pray thee, my blessing (gift) that is brought to thee; because God hath dealt graciously with me, and because I have enough . . . *Genesis 33:11*

. . . a gift destroyeth the heart (understanding). *Ecclesiastes 7:7*

. . . and he that giveth to the rich, shall surely come to want. *Proverbs 22:16*

Give to him that asketh thee, and from him that would borrow of thee turn not thou away. *Matthew 5:42*

. . . sell whatever thou hast, and give to the poor . . . *Mark 10:21*

. . . Say not unto thy neighbor, Go, and come again, and tomorrow I will give; when thou hast it by thee. *Proverbs 3:28*

. . . Give unto the good and help not the sinner. *Ecclesiasticus 12:7*

Give not thy son and wife, thy brother and friend, power over thee while thou livest, and give not thy goods to another: lest it repent thee, and though intreat for the same again.

As long as thou livest and hast breath in thee, give not thyself over to any. *Ecclesiasticus 33:19, 20*

GOVERNMENT AND CRIMES AGAINST THE STATE

After the Return from Babylonian captivity, the influence of the priesthood so grew that when, for a period under the Maccabees, the Hebrews won their political liberty, both spiritual and temporal power were in its hands. The Mosaic institutions, too, received several additions: writers, many of them laymen, devoted to the study and explanation of the law, and the Sanhedrin or council of elders, which, during the Greek domination was the chief administrative authority.

The duties of the priests were not confined to religious matters. They were the governing class, and performed political functions. Provisions for their support took the place of taxes.

The priesthood was a distinct hereditary order, and while priests might marry women of non-priestly families, they had to be undefiled virgins or widows of pure Israelite extraction. The high-priest might marry only an undefiled Israelite virgin.

The Levites, like the priests, were a hereditary order and were entrusted with duties such as singers, janitors, servants of the priests, and the carrying on of the menial conduct of the temple and the work performed by the priests.

The separation of church and state is a modern development. In ancient states and communities, the priest was not only the king, but also the judge. This government of and by priests is known as theocracy, but Constantine the Great adopted the principle that the church was subservient to the state, and so it is to this day.

THE BIBLICAL LAW

When the righteous are in authority, the people rejoice; but when the wicked beareth rule, the people mourn.

Proverbs 29:2

. . . He that ruleth over men must be just, ruling in the fear of God. *II Samuel 23:3*

Thou shalt in any wise set him King over thee, whom the Lord thy God shall choose; one from among thy brethren shalt thou set king over thee: thou mayest not set a stranger over thee, which is not thy brother. *Deuteronomy 17:15*

Woe to thee, O land, when thy King is a child . . .

Ecclesiastes 10:16

O King of Judah . . . execute ye judgment and righteousness, and deliver the spoiled out of the hand of the oppressor: and do no wrong, do no violence to the stranger, the fatherless, nor the widow, neither shed innocent blood. . . .

Jeremiah 22:3

. . . and my princes shall no more oppress my people. . . .

Ezekiel 45:8

Thou shalt not . . . curse the ruler of thy people.

Exodus 22:28

Obey them that hath rule over you, and submit yourselves . . .

Hebrews 13:17

Moreover thou shalt provide . . . men of truth . . . to be rulers of thousands, and rulers of hundreds, rulers of fifties, and rulers of tens. *Exodus 18:21*

. . . what manner of man the ruler of the city is, such are all they that dwell therein. *Ecclesiasticus 10:2*

. . . proclaim liberty throughout all the land unto all the inhabitants thereof. *Leviticus 25:10*

[Do not use] your liberty for a cloak of maliciousness.
1 Peter 2:16

Breach of the Peace

. . . seek peace and pursue it. *Psalms 34:14*

. . . but that thou thyself also walkest orderly, and keepest the law. *Acts 21:24*

And be at peace among yourselves. *1 Thessalonians 5:13*

Let us therefore follow after the things which make for peace . . . *Romans 14:19*

If it be possible, as much as lieth in you, live peaceably with all men. *Romans 12:18*

Abstain from strife . . . for a furious man will kindle strife.
Ecclesiasticus 28:8

Strive not with a man without cause, if he hath done thee no harm. *Proverbs 3:30*

Strive not in a matter that concerneth thee not . . .
Ecclesiasticus 11:9

Thou shalt not follow a multitude to do evil . . .
Exodus 23:2

Petty Treason

And he that smiteth his father, or his mother, shall be surely put to death. *Exodus 21:15*

Rumor Mongers

Thou shalt not raise a false report . . . *Exodus 23:1*

Thou shalt not go up and down as a talebearer among thy people . . . *Leviticus 19:16*

A talebearer revealeth secrets: but he that is of a faithful spirit concealeth the matter. *Proverbs 11:13*

Rehearse not unto another that which is told unto thee. . . .
Ecclesiasticus 19:7

Be not a whisperer, and lie not in wait with thy tongue. . . .
Ecclesiasticus 5:14

These . . . things doth the Lord hate . . . he that soweth discord among brethren. *Proverbs 6:16, 19*

Treason

Whosoever . . . doth rebel against thy commandment, and will not hearken unto thy words in all that thou commandest him, he shall be put to death . . . *Joshua 1:18*

And the man that will do presumptuously, and will not harken . . . unto the judge, even that man shall die.
Deuteronomy 17:12

Then Athaliah rent her clothes, and cried, Treason, Treason.
2 Chronicles 23:13

. . . bow down your shoulders to serve the King of Babylon: so shall ye remain in the land that I gave unto your fathers.
2 Baruch 2:21

I counsel thee to keep the king's commandment . . .
Ecclesiastes 8:2

We will not hearken to the king's words, to go from our religion, either on the right hand, or the left.
1 Maccabees 2:22

HEALTH

THE REPUBLIC of Venice established the first Board of Health. It consisted of three nobles, and was called the "Council of Health." It was ordered to investigate the best means of preserving health, and of preventing the introduction of disease from abroad. Its efforts not having been entirely successful, its powers were enlarged in 1504, so as to grant it "the power of life and death over those who violated the regulations for health." No appeal was allowed from the sentence of this tribunal.

During the plague in London in 1665, the magistrates consulted to devise means for stopping, or at least impeding, the progress of the disease, and the result of their deliberations was a series of orders which appointed commissioners, searchers, and buriers to each district. Every house which was visited, as it was called, was by those orders marked with a red cross of a foot long in the middle of the door, evident to be seen.

Under Biblical law, health regulations were administered and enforced by the priests, who were thus the forerunners of modern health officers and boards of health.

The Mosaic law also required personal cleanliness as well as moral and spiritual cleanliness. The Bible provides for the isolation and segregation of the diseased and for their being quarantined particularly where communicable diseases are involved.

THE BIBLICAL LAW

Better is the poor, being sound and strong of constitution, than a rich man that is afflicted in his body. Health and good estate of body are above all gold, and a strong body above infinite wealth. *Ecclesiasticus 30:14, 15*

There is no riches above a sound body, and no joy above the joy of heart. *Ecclesiasticus 30:16*

Death is better than a bitter life or continual sickness. *Ecclesiasticus 30:17*

Beloved, I wish above all things thou mayest . . . be in health. *3 John 2*

Woe unto you . . . Hypocrites! For ye make clean the outside of the cup and of the platter, but within they are full of extortion and excess. *Matthew 23:25*

O Jerusalem, wash thine heart . . . *Jeremiah 4:14*
. . . let us cleanse ourselves from all filthiness of the flesh . . . *2 Corinthians 7:1*

And when they come from the market, except they wash, they eat not. *Mark 7:4*

And if any man's seed of copulation go out from him, then he shall wash all his flesh in water . . . *Leviticus 15:16*

The woman also with whom a man shall lie with seed of copulation, they shall both bathe themselves in water . . . *Leviticus 15:18*

Be not overmuch wicked, neither be thou foolish: why shouldest thou die before thy time? *Ecclesiastes 7:17*

The days of our years are threescore years and ten. *Psalms 90:10*

Quarantine

Command the children of Israel, that they put out of the camp every leper, and every one that hath an issue . . .

Numbers 5:2

All the days wherein the plague shall be in him . . . he shall dwell alone; without the camp shall his habitation be.

Leviticus 13:46

He shall therefore burn that garment, whether warp or woof, in woolen or in linen, or anything of skin, wherein the plague is . . .

Leviticus 13:52

HOMICIDE

HOMICIDE is either felonious, excusable or justifiable.

The law arms every private citizen in the community with the power of life and death for the prevention of atrocious felonies accompanied with violence and personal danger to others, as in case of an attempt to murder or rob, or commit burglary or arson, the person making the attempt may, if he cannot be otherwise prevented, be killed on the spot, and the law will not recognize the act as a crime. In cases of this sort, in order to justify the homicide, it must appear that there were good grounds for a suspicion that the person killed has a felonious intent. A woman is justifiable in killing one who attempts to ravish her, and the husband or father may be justified in killing a man who attempts a rape on his wife or daughter.

The cases of justifiable homicide are those in which the public authority and laws are directly concerned. The laws of society, however, leave every individual a portion of that right of personal defense with which he is invested by nature. As one may interpose to prevent an atrocious crime against society, where he is not himself in any personal danger, the laws will permit him to defend himself against attacks upon his own person.

Murder is the killing of a person with malice aforethought, either express or implied. It is not necessary in order to constitute the crime of murder that the slayer should have the direct intention of killing. If the act be done with a wicked, depraved, malignant spirit, a heart regardless of social duty, and deliberately bent upon mischief it is characterized by what the law denominates malice though it may not result from any enmity or grudge against the particular victim. So if a man wantonly discharges a gun among a group of people, whereby any one is killed, the act will be done with that depravity of disposition which the law considers malice.

Murder can be committed only by a free agent, for the crime presupposed a will, or disposition on the part of the perpetrator. An idiot or insane person cannot commit this crime, and drunkenness is in general no excuse for homicide, though the act be done under its immediate influence.

The manner of killing is not material. Whether it be by shooting, poison, beating, imprisonment, starvation or exposure to the inclemency of the atmosphere, it will be equally murder. This crime may be committed by mere advice and encouragement.

The lines of distinction between felonious and excusable or justifiable homicide, and between manslaughter and murder, are in many cases difficult to define with precision. The characteristic distinction between murder and manslaughter is the absence of malice in the latter. Sudden provocation may be an excuse for striking another without the intention to give a deadly blow; and though death ensue, the party may not be guilty of murder. One circumstance, showing the degree of malice, or rather showing its presence or absence, is the kind of weapon used in giving a wound on a sudden provocation; and another circumstance of importance is the fact of the weapon's being already in the hand or not, for going to seek a weapon gives time for deliberation. The ground of excuse for homicide, in case of provocation merely, is the supposed sudden passion, some influence of which the law concedes to the frailty of human nature. But the excuse of self-defense goes still further; and where a man is attacked, so that his own life is endangered, or in such way that he may reasonably suppose it to be so, he may repel the attack with mortal weapons.

The crime of murder in its most aggravated degree is punished with death in most parts of the civilized world.

THE BIBLICAL LAW

Thou shalt not commit murder. (Hebrew Version)
Exodus 20:13

Thou shalt not kill. (Protestant and Catholic Version)
Exodus 20:13

Whose sheddeth man's blood, by man shall his blood be shed.
Genesis 9:6

. . . Thou shalt do no murder . . . *Matthew 19:18*

. . . the innocent and righteous slay thou not . . .
Exodus 23:7

Cursed be he that taketh reward to slay an innocent person.
Deuteronomy 27:25

And he that killeth any man shall surely be put to death.
Leviticus 24:17

He that smiteth a man so that he die, shall be surely put to death. *Exodus 21:12*

And if a man lie not in wait, but God deliver him (the victim) unto his hand; then I will appoint thee a place whither he shall flee. But if a man come presumptuously upon his neighbor to slay with guile; thou shalt take him from mine alter, that he may die. *Exodus 21:13, 14*

If a thief be found breaking up, and be smitten that he die, there shall no blood be shed from him. If the sun be risen upon him there shall be blood shed for him; for he should make full restitution: if he have nothing, then he shall be sold for his theft. *Exodus 22:2, 3*

. . . blood . . . defileth the land: and the land cannot be cleansed of the blood that is shed therein, but by the blood of him that shed it. *Numbers 35:33*

. . . when wicked men have slain a righteous person in his own house upon his bed, shall I not therefore now require his blood of your hand? . . . *2 Samuel 4:11*

HUSBAND AND WIFE

THE FAMILY is the most important element in human society, and the destruction of the family would destroy the state and nation. The primitive family was an independent unit and the simplest form of society. The oldest male was ordinarily the Chief and was the law. As man progressed from the single family unit to tribal groups, and then nations, laws replaced the directives of the family heads. Most of these general laws were directed toward and defined the relationship of husband and wife.

It is the duty of husband and wife to adhere to the marriage contract and cohabit; the husband having the right to determine the place of domicile. If he changes the same the wife must go with him; though there are times when the husband is obliged to show a reasonable cause for removing to another abide in order to obligate the wife to follow him. The unreasonable refusal of the wife to follow would be an act of desertion. There is a duty that the spouses by mutual forbearance make living together tolerable. The Common Law of England would find few supporters today. It provided that a husband may correct his wife by subjecting her to restraint and even to "moderate" corporeal punishment. Such restraint and chastisement would have to be very moderate to satisfy modern ideas of ethical or legal propriety.

If the husband drives his wife from his house by "conduct so abominable that no decent woman would live under the same roof with him," her departure would not be desertion. Incontinence, of course, would justify the innocent party in leaving the guilty one, and no legal right would be forfeited in consequence.

The duty of the husband to protect implies his right to defend the wife from personal injury; and a battery committed by either in defense of the other is justifiable and lawful.

The husband must support and maintain the wife as long as she lives with him. He is not relieved from this duty even though the wife have independent means adequate to her needs. The obligation of the husband is to provide "necessaries", and to obtain these the wife may contract debts which the husband, by law, is bound to pay.

When husband and wife are living together there is a presumption that the wife has the husband's authority to enter into contracts, binding on the latter, in relation to all domestic matters ordinarily entrusted to the woman of the house, and to obtain on the husband's credit the things necessary to the conduct of the household. The term "necessaries" means a reasonable supply of such goods and services as are suitable in kind, sufficient in quantity and required in fact, for the use of the husband, the wife, the children and other members of the household, according to the conditions in which they live

Marriage is considered a sacred obligation, but in most nations it is created by a civil contract regulated by law. Polygamy is not prohibited by the Bible and Biblical law provides no punishment. It was an accepted institution and depended on the economic ability of the man to provide for his wives. Polygamy was practiced in ancient Israel and until outlawed, in the State of Utah.

Shakespeare in the Taming of the Shrew (Act 3, Scene

2) has Petruchio restate the Biblical relation of husband and wife: "I will be master of what is my own: she is my goods, my chattels; she is my house, my household stuff, my field, my barn, my horse, my ox, my ass, my anything." The wife was the property of her husband.

THE BIBLICAL LAW

Thou shalt not commit adultery. *Exodus 20:14*

Therefore shall a man leave his father and his mother, and shall cleave unto his wife: and they shall be one flesh.
Genesis 2:24

For the husband is the head of the wife . . .
Ephesians 5:23

And God blessed them (Adam and Eve), and God said . . . be fruitful and multiply . . . *Genesis 1:28*

Take ye wives, and beget sons and daughters; and take wives for your sons, and give your daughters to husbands, that they may bear sons and daughters . . . *Jeremiah 29:6*

Lo, children are a heritage of the Lord and the fruit of the womb is his reward. *Psalms 127:3*

. . . every man should bear rule in his own house . . .
Esther 1:22

Hast thou a wife after thy own mind? Foresake her not: but give not thyself over to a light woman. *Ecclesiasticus 7:26*

Husbands, love your wives . . .let every one of you in particular so love his wife even as himself. *Ephesians 5:33*

Likewise, ye husbands, dwell with them (wives) according to knowledge, giving honor unto the wife, as unto the weaker vessel . . . *1 Peter 3:7*

Wives, submit yourselves unto your own husbands . . .
Colossians 3:18

Husbands, love your wives, be not bitter against them.
Colossians 3:19

Let the husband render unto the wife due benevolence: and likewise also the wife unto the husband. *1 Corinthians 7:3*

Be not jealous over the wife of thy bosom, and teach her not an evil lesson against thyself. *Ecclesiasticus 9:1*

But if any provide not for his own, and specially for those of his own house, he hath denied the faith, and is worse than an infidel. *1 Timothy 5:8*

. . . teach the young women to be sober, to love their husbands, to love their children, to be discreet, chaste, keepers (workers) at home, good, obedient to their husbands.
Titus 2:4, 5

. . . the wives shall give to their husbands honor, both to great and small. *Esther 1:20*

An honest woman will reverence her husband.
Ecclesiasticus 26:24

. . . women . . . are commanded to be under obedience . . .
1 Corinthians 14:34

Who can find a virtuous woman? . . . The heart of her husband doth safely trust in her . . . She will do him good and not evil . . . *Proverbs 31:10, 11, 12*

. . . she that is married careth . . . how she may please her husband . . . *1 Corinthians 7:34*

. . . Thou shalt not covet thy neighbor's wife . . .
Exodus 20:17

. . . thy desire shall be to thy husband, and he shall rule over thee. *Genesis 3:16*

A virtuous woman is a crown to her husband . . .
Proverbs 12:4

An evil wife is a yoke shaken to and fro: he that hath hold of her is as though he held a scorpion. *Ecclesiasticus 26:7*

Desire not a multitude of unprofitable children, neither delight in ungodly sons. *Ecclesiasticus 16:1*

. . . let them marry to whom they think best; only to the family of the tribe of their father shall they marry. *Numbers 36:6*

. . . to avoid fornication, let every man have his own wife, and let every woman have her own husband. *1 Corinthians 7:1, 2*

I say . . . to the unmarried and widows, it is good for them if they abide even as I. But if they cannot contain, let them marry: for it is better to marry than to burn. *1 Corinthians 7:8, 9*

The wife is bound by the law as long as her husband liveth; but if her husband be dead, she is at liberty to be married to whom she will . . . *1 Corinthians 7:39*

If brethren dwell together, and one of them die, and have no child, the wife of the dead shall not marry without unto a stranger: her husband's brother shall go unto her, and take her to him to wife and perform the duty of a husband's brother unto her. And it shall be, that the firstborn which she beareth him shall succeed in the name of his brother which is dead, that his name be not put out of Israel. *Deuteronomy 25:5, 6*

Ask me never so much dowry and gift, and I will give according as ye shall say unto me: but give me the damsel to wife. *Genesis 34:12*

A wise daughter shall bring an inheritance (dowry) to her husband . . . *Ecclesiasticus 22:4*

And Boaz said unto the elders and unto all the people, Ye are witnesses this day, that . . . Ruth the Moabitess . . . have I purchased to be my wife . . . and all the people . . . and the elders . . . said, we are witnesses. So Boaz took Ruth, and she was his wife. *Ruth 4:9, 10, 11, 13*

Then he called his daughter, Sara, and she came to her father, and he . . . gave her to be wife to Tobias . . . and called Edna his wife, and took paper and did write an instrument of covenants, and sealed it. *Tobit 7:13, 14*

When a man hath taken a new wife, he shall not go out to war, neither shall he be charged with any business: but he shall be free at home one year, and shall cheer up his wife which he has taken. *Deuteronomy 24:5*

Rejoice with the wife of thy youth. *Proverbs 5:18*

Live joyfully with the wife whom thou lovest all the days of life of thy vanity . . . for that is thy portion in this life. *Ecclesiastes 9:9*

Let every one of you . . . love his wife even as himself. *Ephesians 5:33*

A man shall leave his father and his mother, and shall cleave unto his wife: and they shall be one flesh. *Genesis 2:24*

. . . let every man have his own wife, and let every woman have her own husband. *1 Corinthians 7:2*

Let the husband render unto the wife due benevolence: and likewise also the wife unto the husband. *1 Corinthians 7:3*

A bishop then must be . . . the husband of one wife . . . Even so must their wives be grave, not slanderers, sober, faithful in all things. *1 Timothy 3:2, 11*

They (the priests) shall not take a wife, that is a wrote, or profane; neither shall they take a woman put away from her husband . . . *Leviticus 21:7*

A widow, or a divorced woman, or profane (godless) or an harlot, these shall he (the priests) not take: but he shall take a virgin of his own people to wife. *Leviticus 21:14*

Neither shalt thou make marriages with them (foreigners); thy daughter thou shalt not give unto his son, nor his daughter shalt thou take unto thy son. *Deuteronomy 7:3*

. . . take a wife of the seed of thy fathers, and take not a strange woman to wife, which is not of thy father's tribe.

Tobit 4:12

A silent and loving woman is a gift of the Lord . . .

Ecclesiasticus 26:14

LABOR

In Biblical times, as today, manual labor was an honorable calling. It was not unusual for the worker to be educated in the law and to sit with the wealthy in discussion of the Mosaic writings.

Labor laws have been part of every judicial system in history, and since early in the twentieth century the working man has been protected by legislation to guarantee him equality of living conditions and opportunities for education and advancement.

In modern industry brains are needed as well as muscle. Men are educated and trained to do jobs that were in the last century thought fit for only the unlearned. Organized productive forces depend upon the ability quite as much as upon the skill and strength of the manual worker.

The economic system of the Bible is based on the fact that nearly all of Israel lived upon the land. Every man was directed to "eat the labor of thine hands and happy shalt thou be."

The unwillingness to work and to live by means other than by honest effort is condemned: "Go to the ant thou sluggard; consider her ways, and be wise: which having no guide, overseer or ruler, provideth her meat in the summer, and gathereth her food in the harvest. How long wilt thou sleep, a little slumber, a little folding of the hands to sleep: so shall thy poverty come as one that travelleth, and thy want as an armed man." This advice in 6 Proverbs may be the forerunner of our laws against idle loiterers and those who wander around without occupation or visible means of support.

Dignity of man, liberty of the individual, and freedom from oppression are all basic in Mosaic jurisprudence. Liberty in its broad sense is the right, not only of freedom from actual servitude, but the right of one to use his faculties in all lawful ways, to live, to work and to earn a livelihood in any lawful manner.

The matter of retirement age was of concern in Biblical days as now. The Mosaic law in reference to the Levites fixes the term of years to be worked before retirement: "from twenty and five years old and upward they (the Levites) shalt go in to wait upon the service of the Tabernacle of the congregation; and from the age of fifty years they shall cease waiting upon the service thereof, and shall serve no more: but shall minister with their brethren in the Tabernacle of the congregation, to keep the charge, and shall do no service." While 8 Numbers fixes this rule as to the Levites, there is no general law in the Mosaic code covering length of service or retirement.

Deuteronomy prohibits unfair dealing with labor: "thou shalt not oppress an hired servant that is poor and needy, whether he be of thy brethren, or of thy strangers," and "at his day thou shalt give him his hire." And Jeremiah "woe unto him that useth his neighbor's service without wages, and giveth him not for his work."

All was not perfect, and relation between employer and employee was not always satisfactory to both sides in Biblical days. As today, wage and hour disputes arose:

. . . an householder, which went out early in the morning to hire laborers unto his vineyard . . . he agreed with the laborers for a penny a day . . . and about the eleventh hour he went out, and found others (laborers) and said to them, go ye also into the vineyard; and whatever is right, that shall ye receive. So when even was come . . . they received every man a penny. But when the first came, they supposed that they should have received more; and they likewise received every man a penny . . . they murmured . . . saying, these last have wrought but one hour, and thou hast made them equal unto us, which have borne the burden and heat of the day. But he answered . . . and said friend, I do thee no wrong: didst thou not agree with me for a penny? Take that thine is, and go thy way. . . . *Matthew 20:1, 2, 7, 8, 9, 10, 11, 12, 13, 14*

THE BIBLICAL LAW

The soul of the sluggard desireth, and hath nothing . . .
Proverbs 13:4

Whatsoever thy hand findeth to do, do it with thy might.
Ecclesiastes 9:10

In all labor there is profit *Proverbs 14:23*

Better is he that laboreth, and aboundeth in all things, than he that boasteth himself, and wanteth bread.
Ecclesiastes 10:27

The sluggard will not plow by reasons of the cold; therefore shall he begin harvest, and have nothing. *Proverbs 20:4*

Go to the ant thou sluggard; consider her ways and be wise: which having no guide, overseer, or ruler, provideth her meat in the summer, and gathereth her food in the harvest. How long wilt thou sleep, O sluggard? When wilt thou arise . . . ?
Proverbs 6:6, 7, 8, 9

In the sweat of thy face shalt thou eat bread . . .
Genesis 3:19

But let every man prove his own work, and then shall he have rejoicing in himself alone . . . For every man shall bear his own burden. *Galatians 6:4, 5*

. . . that with quietness they work, and eat their own bread.
2 Thessalonians 3:12

Let him who stole steal no more: but rather let him labor, working with his hands . . . *Ephesians 4:28*

To labor, and to be content with that a man hath, is a sweet life . . . *Ecclesiasticus 40:18*

He that tilleth his land shall have plenty of bread . . .
Proverbs 28:19

. . . thou shalt eat the labor of thine hands: happy shalt thou be, and it shall be well with thee. *Psalms 128:2*

. . . every man should eat and drink, and enjoy the good of all his labor . . . *Ecclesiastes 3:13*

The husbandman that laboreth must be first partaker of the fruits. *2 Timothy 2:6*

For we brought nothing into this world, and it is certain we can carry nothing out. And having food and raiment let us be therewith content. *Timothy 6:7, 8*

Do violence to no man, neither accuse any falsely; and be content with your wages. *Luke 3:14*

Hate not laborious work . . . *Ecclesiasticus 7:15*

He that laboreth, laboreth for himself; for his mouth craveth it of him. *Proverbs 16:26*

The hand of the diligent shall bear rule: but the slothful shall be under tribute. *Proverbs 12:24*

. . . if any would not work, neither should he eat.
2 Thessalonians 3:10

. . . an idle soul shall suffer hunger. *Proverbs 18:15*

I therefore . . . beseech you that ye walk worthy of the vocation wherewith ye are called. *Ephesians 4:1*

. . . we have done that which was our duty to do.
Luke 17:10

And Pharoah's daughter said unto her, take this child away, and nurse it for me, and I will give thee thy wages . . .
Exodus 2:9

. . . and he rested on the seventh day from all his work . . .
Genesis 2:2

Six days may work be done; but in the seventh is the sabbath of rest . . . *Exodus 31:15*

Six days shalt thou labor, and do all thy work . . .
Exodus 20:9

Thou hypocrite, doth not each one of you on the sabbath loose his ox . . . from the stall, and lead him to watering?
Luke 13:15

Thou shalt not oppress an hired servant that is poor and needy, whether he be of thy brethren, or of thy strangers that are in thy land within thy gates. *Deuteronomy 24:14*

. . . every man shall receive his own reward according to his own labor. , *1 Corinthians 3:8*

. . . he that defraudeth the laborer of his hire is a blood-shedder. *Ecclesiasticus 34:22*

Woe unto him . . . that useth his neighbor's service without wages, and giveth him not for his work. *Jeremiah 22:13*

. . . the laborer is worthy of his hire. *Luke 10:7*

. . . the laborer is worthy of his reward. *1 Timothy 5:18*

Now to him that worketh is the reward not reckoned of grace, but of debt. *Romans 4:4*

. . . the recompense of a man's hands shall be rendered unto him. *Proverbs 12:14*

Let not the wages of any man, which hath wrought for thee, tarry with thee, but give him it out of hand . . . *Tobit 4:14*

. . . the wages of him that is hired shall not abide with thee all night until the morning. *Leviticus 19:13*

At his day thou shalt give him his hire, neither shall the sun go down upon it; for he is poor, and sitteth his heart upon it . . .

Deuteronomy 24:15

Woe unto him that buildeth his house by unrighteousness, and his chambers by wrong; that useth his neighbor's service without wages, and giveth him not for his work.

Jeremiah 22:13

. . . and he that earneth wages earneth wages to put it into a bag with holes. *Haggai 1:6*

. . . Thou shalt not covet . . . thy neighbor's man-servant, nor his maidservant . . . *Exodus 20:17*

Because thou art my brother, shouldst thou therefore serve me for naught? Tell me, what shall thy wages be? *Genesis 29:15*

A laboring man that is given to drunkenness shall not be rich . . . *Ecclesiasticus 19:1*

LAW, LAWYERS AND JUDGES

LAWYERS were unknown to the Mosaic judicial system. The judges who tried the accused were also his defenders. In such legal system lawyers were unnecessary, and in the early Biblical days, litigants pleaded their own cases, as appears in the case of the two women who appeared before King Solomon, and argued their respective claims to a child (I Kings 3:16-28). Not until the New Testament is there mention of lawyers.

There was no accusatory body such as our Grand Jury. The witnesses were the accusers; their testimony constituting both the indictment and the evidence.

There was no attorney general, district attorney or state prosecutor. In capital cases the witnesses were not only the prosecutors, and givers of evidence, but executioners as well.

The highest court in Israel was the Sanhedrin. This Aramaic word Sanhedrin is identical with the Greek synedrion; assembly or council. When this institution arose cannot be definitely determined, but from the earliest times local government had been conducted by a council of the elders, men whose age, rank and wealth gave weight to their decisions. It is possible that it was established by Moses in the wilderness in accordance with the command in Numbers 11:16, 17: "Gather unto me seventy men . . . whom thou knowest to be the elders of the people . . . and bring them unto the tabernacle of the congregation, that they may stand there with thee. And I will come down and talk with thee there . . . and they shall bear the burden of the people with thee, that thou bear it not thyself alone."

The presidency of the Sanhedrin was vested in the high-priest, who was the supreme magistrate. The original composition of the Sanhedrin was exclusively aristocratic: members of the high-priestly families, and the 'elders' of the lay aristocracy. At one period scribes were admitted. These classes are the 'chief priests, elders and scribes' of the Gospels.

No court could consist of a single judge. There were three courts which were charged with the trial of cases; the Great Sanhedrin, seventy-one judges; the Minor Sanhedrin, twenty-three; the Lower Tribunal, or the Court of Three. The Great Sanhedrin sat in Jerusalem. It had original jurisdiction of all offenses committed by those in public office, and of offenses affecting the security of the country.

The jurisdiction of the Sanhedrin was originally very broad, including all religious questions, and all civil and criminal cases. It was the supreme authority in determining the interpretation of the law, both oral and written. It had its own police force.

The Criminal Procedure of the Sanhedrin favored the accused. In capital cases, the arguments of the defense were heard first, and favorable testimony was irreversible. Unfavorable testimony could be reversed. It was mandatory that a delay of one day intervene between the trial and sentence. A majority of one sufficed for acquittal; a majority of two was required for conviction.

According to the Mishna, a guilty vote by thirty-seven of the seventy-one members of the Sanhedrin was needed to convict. The procedure in Biblical trial law provided that a unanimous verdict of guilty rendered on the day of trial, had the effect of an acquittal. Such unanimous verdict was thought to result more from a group hatred conspiracy rather than from mature deliberation.

The study and interpretation of the law was in the hands of those who are called scribes and doctors of law in the Gospels. Originally the interpretation of the Torah (law) was the function of the priests; but the scribes as such were not priests, although priests were included in their number. Once the Law was accepted as the basis of Hebrew life, it was necessary to determine its meaning, and to apply it, as far as possible, to situations that might arise. Hence, the scribes. The name is first given to Esdras, 'a ready scribe in the law of Moses.'

The scribes had no official position; and their opinions had no authority except that of personal influence and public opinion. But this authority was enough. They were legislators, teachers and judges. They sat 'in the chair of Moses,' and were addressed by the title of Rabbi (master). The study of the law was, in the eyes of the devout, the highest occupation. It was not remunerative; many of the scribes, who did not enjoy an independent income, were quite poor and supported themselves by a trade.

THE BIBLICAL LAW

And he [Christ] said, Woe unto you also, ye lawyers! for ye lade men with burdens grievous to be borne, and ye yourselves touch not the burdens with one of your fingers. *Luke 11:46*

. . . neither shalt thou speak in a cause to decline after many to wrest judgment. *Exodus 23:2*

Thou shalt not wrest the judgment of thy poor in his cause. *Exodus 23:6*

Thou shalt not pervert the judgment of the stranger, nor of the fatherless; nor take a widow's raiment to pledge.
Deuteronomy 24:17

I charge thee . . . that thou observe these things without prefering one before another, doing nothing by partiality.
1 Timothy 5:21

Then stood there up one in the council . . . a doctor of the law, had in reputation among all the people, and commanded to put the apostles forth . . . and said . . . take heed to yourselves what ye intend to do as touching these men.
Acts 5:34, 35

The one of them, which was a lawyer asked him a question . . . saying Master which is the best commandment in the law?
Matthew 22:35, 36

But the Pharisees and lawyers rejected the counsel of God . . .
Luke 7:30

Judges and officers shalt thou make . . . throughout thy tribes: and they shall judge the people with just judgment.
Deuteronomy 16:18

Thou shalt not wrest judgment; thou shalt not respect persons, neither take a gift: for a gift doth blind the eyes of the wise, and pervert the words of the righteous. *Deuteronomy 16:19*

If one man sin against another, the judge shall judge him. . . .
1 Samuel 2:25

Many seek the ruler's favor; but every man's judgment cometh from the Lord. *Proverbs 29:26*

Mercy is seasonable in the time of affliction, as clouds of rain in the time of drought. *Ecclesiasticus 35:20*

And Moses chose able men out of all Israel . . . and they judged the people at all season; the hard causes they brought unto Moses, but every small matter they judged themselves.
Exodus 18:25, 26

Thus saith the Lord . . . do justice. *Isaiah 56:1*

And thou, Ezra . . . set magistrates and judges, which may judge all the people that are beyond the river, all such as know the laws . . . and teach ye them that know them not. *Ezra 7:25*

Judge not that ye be not judged. *Matthew 7:1*

For with what judgment ye judge, ye shall be judged: and with what measure ye mete, it shall be measured to you again.
Matthew 7:2

. . . and he (Moses) said to him that did the wrong, wherefore smitest thou thy fellow? And he said, who made thee a judge over us? . . . *Exodus 2:13, 14*

And he (Samuel) went from year to year in circuit to Beth-el and Gilgal, and Mizpeh, and judged Israel in all those places. And his return was to Ramah; for there was his house; and there he judged Israel. . . . *1 Samuel 7:16, 17*

A man of understanding trusteth in the law; and the law is faithful unto him. . . . *Ecclesiasticus 33:3*

And I (Moses) charged your judges . . . saying, Hear the causes between your brethren, and judge righteously between every man and his brother, and the stranger that is with him.
Deuteronomy 1:16

Ye shall not respect persons in judgment; but ye shall hear the small as well as the great; ye shall not be afraid of the face of man . . . and the cause that is too hard for you, bring it unto me, and I will hear it. *Deuteronomy 1:17*

Ye shall do no unrighteousness in judgment; thou shalt not respect the person of the poor, nor honour the person of the mighty: but in righteousness shalt thou judge thy neighbor.
Leviticus 19:15

And he (Jehosphaphat, King of Judah) set judges in the land throughout all the fenced cities of Judah . . . and said to the judges, take heed what ye do: for ye judge not for man, but for the Lord, who is with you in judgment.
2 Chronicles 19:5, 6

And what cause soever shall come to you for your brethren . . . . between blood and blood, between law and commandment, statutes and judgments, ye shall even warn them that they trespass not against the Lord . . . *2 Chronicles 19:10*

Ye shall do no unrighteousness in judgment . . .
Leviticus 19:35

Woe unto them that decree unrighteous decrees, and that write grievousness which they have prescribed; to turn aside the needy from judgment, and to take away the right from the poor of my people . . . *Isaiah 10:1, 2*

Absolom said moreover, Oh that I were made judge in the land, that every man which hath any suit or cause might come unto me, and I would do him justice! *2 Samuel 15:4*

He (the King) shall judge thy people with righteousness, and thy poor with judgment. *Psalms 72:2*

. . . execute the judgment of truth and peace in your gates (courts). *Zechariah 8:16*

Judge not according to the appearance, but judge righteous judgment. *John 7:24*

Then said Pilate unto them, Take ye him (Christ) and judge him according to your law. The Jews therefore said unto him, it is not lawful for us to put any man to death. *John 18:31*

And in controversy they shall stand in judgment; and they shall judge it according to my judgments. *Ezekiel 44:24*

If there be a controversy between men, and they come unto judgment, that the judges may judge them; then they shall justify the righteous and condemn the wicked.
Deuteronomy 25:1

How long will ye judge unjustly, and accept the persons of the wicked? . . . Defend the poor and fatherless: do justice to the afflicted and needy. *Psalms 82:2, 3*

For this is a heinous crime; yea, it is an iniquity, to be punished by the judges. *Job 31:11*

And the judges shall make diligent inquisition: and, behold, if the witness be a false witness, and hath testified falsely against his brother; then shall ye do unto him, as he had thought to have done unto his brother . . . *Deuteronomy 19:18, 19*

Love righteousness, ye that be judges of the earth . . .
Wisdom of Solomon 1:1

A wise judge will instruct his people . . . *Ecclesiasticus 10:1*

. . . be not fainthearted when thou sittest in judgment.
Ecclesiasticus 4:9

For all manner of trespass, whether it be for ox, for ass, for sheep, for raiment, or for any manner of lost thing, which another challengeth to be his, the cause of both parties shall come before the judges; and whom the judges shall condemn, he shall pay double unto his neighbor. *Exodus 22:9*

So shall I keep thy law continually forever and ever. And I will walk at liberty: for I seek thy precepts. *Psalms 119:44, 45*

. . . where the spirit of the Lord is, there is liberty.
2 Corinthians 3:17

But we know that the law is good, if a man use it lawfully.
1 Timothy 1:8

. . . the law is not made for a righteous man, but for the lawless and disobedient . . . *1 Timothy 1:9*

Let thy tender mercies come unto me, that I may live: for thy law is my delight. *Psalms 119:77*

I hate and abhor lying: but thy law do I love.
Psalms 119:163

Now we know that what things soever the law saith, it saith to them who are under the law . . . *Romans 3:19*

But whoso looketh into the perfect law of liberty, and continueth therein . . . shall be blessed in his deed. *James 1:25*

Then spake Jesus . . . saying . . . all therefore whatsoever they bid you observe, that observe and do. *Matthew 23:1, 2, 3*

Submit yourselves to every ordinance of man for the Lord's sake: whether it be of the King . . . or unto governors, as unto them that are sent by him for the punishment of evildoers . . . *1 Peter 2:13, 14*

And he said unto them, Render therefore unto Caeser the things which be Caeser's, and unto God the things which be God's. *Luke 20:25*

Law Suits

Go not to law with a judge; for they will judge for him according to his honor. *Ecclesiasticus 8:14*

. . . he that undertaketh and followeth other men's business for gain shall fall into suits. *Ecclesiasticus 29:19*

And if a man will sue thee at the law, and take away thy coat, let him have thy cloke also. *Matthew 5:40*

But we know that the law is good, if a man use it lawfully.
1 Timothy 1:8

Moreover if thy brother shall trespass against thee, go and tell him his fault between thee and him alone . . . But if he will not hear thee . . . tell it unto the church.
Matthew 18:15, 16, 17

Dare any of you, having a matter against another, go to law . . . it is so, that there is not a wise man among you? No, not one that shall be able to judge between his brethren?
1 Corinthians 6:1, 5

. . . If thy brother trespass against thee, rebuke him; and if he repent, forgive him. And if he trespass against thee seven times in a day, and seven times in a day turn again to thee, saying, I repent; thou shalt forgive him. *Luke 17:3, 4*

Appeals

And they (the judges) judged the people at all season: the hard causes they brought unto Moses, but every small matter they judged themselves. *Exodus 18:26*

If there arise a matter too hard for thee in judgment . . . then shalt thou . . . come unto the priests the Levites, and unto the judge that shall be in those days, and enquire; and they shall show thee the sentence of judgment . . . and according to the judgment . . . thou shalt do . . . thou shalt not decline . . . to the right hand, nor to the left.
Deuteronomy 17:8, 9, 10, 11

LIBEL AND SLANDER

SLANDER in general is the defaming of a man in his reputation by speaking words from whence any injury to his character or property arises, or may arise. It is generally limited in the legal sense to defamation by words spoken, and which words tend to the prejudice of the reputation, office, trade, business, or means of getting a living. This definition is subject to many legal changes and additions, and is used only to establish the general subject as it pertains to Biblical law.

The various books of the bible deal with the prohibition against slander, and is indicative of the existence of much social intercourse among the wandering Hebrew tribes. Then as now a man's reputation was a valuable asset and was protected by law.

Today as in biblical times the utterance of defamatory words injuring another's reputation or suggesting that he has an "evil disease" is slander.

Defamation of persons or property is actionable by either criminal or civil process.

Libel as known in our law today, is not mentioned as such in the Bible. Alexander Hamilton defined libel as a censorious or ridiculing writing, picture, or sign, made with malicious intent towards individuals. Since biblical and general history indicates that only a few knew how to read and write, it is not strange that Mosaic law should not mention libel.

Set a watch, O Lord, before my mouth; and a door round about my lips. *Psalms 141:3*

An hypocrite with his mouth destroyeth his neighbor. . . . *Proverbs 11:9*

Put them in mind . . . to speak evil of no man. *Titus 3:1, 2*

Let no corrupt communication proceed out of your mouth... *Ephesians 4:29*

Speak not evil one of another . . . *James 4:11*

If a man take a wife, and go in into her, and hate her, and give occasions of speech against her, and bring up an evil name upon her, and say, I took this woman, and when I came to her, I found her not a maid . . . the elders of that city shall take that man and chastise him; but if this thing be true . . . then . . . the men of the city shall stone her . . . that she die . . . *Deuteronomy 22:13, 14, 18, 20, 21*

he that uttereth a slander, is a fool. *Proverbs 10:18*

All that hate me whisper together against me . . . an evil disease say they, cleaveth fast unto him . . . *Psalms 41:7, 8*

Whoso privily slandereth his neighbor, him will I cut off.... *Psalms 101:5*

LOANS AND PLEDGES

A LOAN is a contract wherein one party agrees to let another party have the use of a sum of money, or of a particular thing, for a definite period of time in consideration of a promise by the borrower to repay it with or without interest. It is the delivery of a sum of money to another under a contract to return it at some future time with or wihout an additional sum agreed on for its use. This contract or agreement may be expressed or it may be implied. It needs no particular form, but something must be lent, and there must be a lender and a borrower.

An important element of a loan is delivery, that is, delivery to another for use. While this does not mean a manual delivery by the lender to the borrower, it does mean a parting with the thing lent by the lender and its acquisition by the borrower. The borrower is bound to take good care of the thing borrowed, and to use it only according to the intention of the lender. It is an essential and characteristic feature of a loan that it be returnable. The borrower expressly or impliedly promises to return the thing lent. This promise to repay is absolute.

A transaction of this kind may be without reward or compensation. Ordinarily, the compensation for the use of money is called interest.

A pledge is a transfer of personal property. It can be as security for a debt, or other obligation. It is a delivery of goods by a debtor to his creditor to be kept until the debtor's obligation is discharged. It is in the form of a lien created by the owner of personal property by the mere delivery to another on an express or implied understanding that it shall be retained as security for a debt. A pledge differs from a sale; in the case of a pledge, only the possession of the property passes, and not the title thereto, while in the case of a sale, transfer of possession may or may not be made.

The philosopher of the Bible, Ecclesiasticus, sums up the general weaknesses of man concerning loans "till he hath received, he will kiss a man's hand; and for his neighbor's money he will speak submissly: but when he should repay, he will prolong the time, and return words of grief, and complaint of the time."

And if a man borrow ought of his neighbor, and it be hurt, or die, the owner thereof being not with it, he shall surely make it good. But if the owner thereof be with it, he shall not make it good: if it be an hired thing, it came for his hire.

Exodus 22:14, 15

A good man sheweth favour, and lendeth . . .

Psalms 112:5

. . . Love ye your enemies, and do good, and lend for nothing . . . *Luke 6:35*

He that hath pity upon the poor lendeth unto the Lord; and that which he has given will he pay him again.

Proverbs 19:17

. . . and lend, hoping for nothing again. . . . *Luke 6:35*

Many, when a thing was lent them, reckoned it to be found, and put them to trouble that helped them . . . many therefore have refused to lend for other men's ill dealing, fearing to be defrauded . . . yet have thou patience with a man in poor estate, and delay not to show him mercy. *Ecclesiasticus 29:4, 7, 8*

Till he hath received, he will kiss a man's hand; and for his neighbors money he will speak submissly: but when he should repay, he will prolong the time, and return words of grief, and complain of the time. *Ecclesiasticus 29:5*

Lend to thy neighbor in time of his need, and pay thou thy neighbor again in due season. *Ecclesiasticus 29:2*

The wicked borroweth, and payeth not again . . .

Psalms 37:21

No man shall take the nether or the upper millstone to pledge: for he taketh a man's life to pledge.

Deuteronomy 24:6

Thou shalt not . . . take a widow's raimant to pledge.
Deuteronomy 24:17

When thou doest lend thy brother anything, thou shalt not go unto his house to fetch his pledge. Thou shalt stand abroad, and the man to whom thou doest lend shall bring out the pledge abroad unto thee. And if man be poor, thou shalt not sleep with his pledge; in any case thou shalt deliver him the pledge again when the sun goeth down that he may sleep in his own raiment . . . *Deuteronomy 24:10, 11, 12, 13*

. . . he that hath not restored the pledge . . . shall surely die . . . *Ezekiel 18:12, 13*

Lend not unto him that is mightier than thyself; for if thou lendest him, count it but lost. *Ecclesiasticus 8:12*

He that is hasty to give credit is lightminded . . .
Ecclesiasticus 19:4

For the love of money is the root of all evil . . .
1 Timothy 6:10

He that buildeth his house with other men's money is like one that gathereth himself stones for the tomb of his burial.
Ecclesiasticus 21:8

Be not made a beggar by banqueting upon borrowing, when thou hast nothing in thy purse. *Ecclesiasticus 18:33*

MASTER AND SERVANT

BLACKSTONE in his Commentaries on the Law points out that there are three great relationships in private life:

1. That of master and servant; which is founded in convenience, whereby a man is directed to call in the assistance of others, where his own skill and labor will not be sufficient to answer the duties incumbent upon him.

2. That of husband and wife, which is founded in nature, but modified by society: the one directing man to continue and multiply his species, the other prescribing the manner in which that natural impulse must be confined and regulated.

3. That of parent and child, which is consequential to that of marriage being its principle and design; and it is by virtue of this relationship that infants are protected, maintained and educated.

He further comments on the several sorts of servants: (1) that of pure slavery, and (2) menial servants; so-called from being within the walls, or domestics.

The contract between them and their master arises upon the hiring. If the hiring be general without any particular time limited, the law construes it to be a hiring for one year; upon a principle of natural equity, that the servant shall serve, and master maintain him, as well when there is work to be done and when there is not: but the contract may be made for any longer or shorter term.

There is little difference between the common law and

the present-day law. While today the relationship of master and servant is not capable of exact definition, it may nevertheless be stated broadly that the relationship is that which arises under a contract of employment between a master or employer, on the one hand, and his servant or employee, on the other. The master is deemed to have the superior choice, control and direction of the servant, and whose will the servant represents in the detail as well as the ultimate result of the work.

Servant in its broadest sense includes any person over whom personal authority is exercised, or who asserts himself or labors for the benefit of a master or employer. In more recent times, the words employer and employee have merely supplanted the older term of master and servant. This shift has been due no doubt to the vast increase of employment of skilled persons in industry.

In Biblical times the servant was subject to absolute control of the master, and the servant's labors were solely for the benefit of the master, who had to answer to no one for the treatment accorded the servant, except to God.

"No man can serve two masters" are the words of Matthew, and they are a basic rule of man's guidance.

Escaping servants (slaves) are not to be returned to their master is a provision of Deuteronomy 23 and this was, thousands of years later, rewritten into our various state laws prior to the Civil War.

THE BIBLICAL LAW

No man can serve two masters: for either he will hate the one and love the other; or else he will hold to the one, and despise the other. . . . *Matthew 6:24*

Accuse not a servant unto his master, lest he curse thee, and thou be found guilty. *Proverbs 30:10*

. . . and they drew and lifted up Joseph out of the pit, and sold Joseph to the Ishmeelites for twenty pieces of silver. *Genesis 37:28*

If thy buy a Hebrew servant, six years he shall serve: and in the seventh he shall go out free for nothing.

If he come in by himself, he shall go out by himself; if he were married, then his wife shall go out with him.

If his master have given him a wife, and she have born him sons or daughters; the wife and her children shall be her master's . . . and if the servant shall plainly say I love my master, my wife, and my children; I will not go out free;

Then his master shall bring him unto the judges; . . . and he (the servant) shall serve him forever. *Exodus 21:2, 3, 4, 5, 6*

And if thy brother, an Hebrew man, or an Hebrew woman, be sold unto thee, and serve thee six years; then in the seventh year thou shall let him go free from thee . . . though shalt not let him go away empty: thou shalt furnish him liberally out of thy flock and out of thy floor, and out of thy winepress. . . . *Deuteronomy 15:12, 13*

If a man sell his daughter to be a maidservant, she shall not go out as the menservants do. If she please not her master, who hath betrothed her to himself, then shall he let her be redeemed: to sell her unto a strange nation he shall have no power, seeing he hath dealt deceitfully with her. And if he have betrothed her unto his son, he shall deal with her after the manner of daughters. If he take him another wife; her food, her raiment, and her duty of marriage, shall he not diminish. And if he do not these three unto her, then shall she go out free. . . . *Exodus 21:7, 8, 9, 10, 11*

And ye shall . . . proclaim liberty throughout all the land all the inhabitants thereof . . . and ye shall return every man unto his possession, and ye shall return every man unto his family, (every fiftieth year . . . a jubilee shall the fiftieth year be unto you) *Leviticus 25:10, 11*

That every man should let his manservant, being . . . Hebrew . . . go free . . . (on their return from Babylon). *Jeremiah 34:9*

For they . . . which I brought forth out of the land of Egypt: they shall not be sold as bondsmen. *Leviticus 25:42*

. . . be not yet the servants of men. *1 Corinthians 7:23*

. . . be not entangled again with the yoke of bondage. *Galatians 5:1*

Thou shalt not deliver unto his master the servant which is escaped from his master unto thee; he shall dwell with thee, even among you, in that place which he shall choose in one of thy gates, where it liketh him best: thou shalt not oppress him. *Deuteronomy 23:15, 16*

Send him (Servant) to labor, that he be not idle; for idleness teacheth much evil. *Ecclesiasticus 33:27*

Masters, give unto your servants that which is just and equal. . . . *Colossians 4:1*

Let thy soul love a good servant, and defraud him not of liberty. *Ecclesiasticus 7:21*

And, ye masters forebear . . . threatening . . . *Ephesians 6:9*

And if a man smite his servant, or his maid, with a rod, and he die under his hand: he shall surely be punished. *Exodus 21:20*

And if a man smite the eye of his servant, or the eye of his maid, that it perish; he shall let him go free . . . and if he smite out his manservant's tooth, or his maidservant's tooth; he shall let him go free. . . . *Exodus 21:26, 27*

If thee ox shall push (injure) a manservant, or a maid-servant; (the owner of the ox) shall give unto their master thirty shekels of silver. . . . *Exodus 21:32*

A wise servant shall have rule over a son that causeth shame, and shall have part of the inheritance among the brethren. *Proverbs 17:2*

Servants be subject to your masters with all fear; not only to the good and gentle, but also to the froward. *1 Peter 2:18*

No man can serve two masters: for either he will hate the one, and love the other . . . ye cannot serve God and Mammon. *Matthew 6:24*

Masters, give unto your servants that which is just and equal. . . . *Colossians 4:1*

. . . Well done, thou good and faithful servant. *Matthew 25:21*

. . . There be many servants now a days that break away every man from his master. *1 Samuel 25:10*

MILITARY LAW

THERE IS "a time of war, and a time of peace." With this observation Ecclesiastes 3:8 has reviewed the history of warfare through the ages. It is futile to cry "peace, peace, when there is no peace." Thus Jeremiah 6:14 opened the way for the people of Israel to say in I Mac. 2:40 "If we all do as our brethren have done, and fight not for our lives and our laws against the heathen, they will now quickly root us out of the earth."

Whether the prophecy of Isaiah that "the nations shall beat their swords into ploughshares, and their spears into pruning hooks; nation shall not lift up sword against nation, neither shall they learn war any more," will ever be realized by man or not is still a matter of world argument.

There is no Biblical directive against war, in fact in Exodus 15 Moses says "The Lord is a man of war" and in Deuteronomy 20 "who goes with his people, to fight against their enemies."

All men during Biblical days who were from twenty years old and upward, if able to go to war, and not exempt from service had to go forth "armed to battle."

War was a necessity apparently for in Deuteronomy 23 stress is laid upon the need of maintaining sanitary conditions on the field of battle. Definite directions are given for the guidance of troops in the field.

Whether the Mosaic code concerning war was a necessity of the conquest of the Holy Land or whether the laws relative to the military come from primitive sources is of little consequence when it is observed that the laws in this regard today are in fact a re-enactment of those in Exodus, Numbers and Deuteronomy.

What man is there that has built a new house, and has not dedicated it? let him go and return to his house, lest he die in the battle, and another man dedicate it. And what man is he that hath planted a vineyard, and hath not yet eaten of it? let him also go and return unto his house, lest he die in the battle and another man eat of it. And what man is there that hath betrothed a wife, and hath not taken her? let him go and return unto his house, lest he die in the battle, and another man take her. What man is there that is fearful and faint-hearted? let him go and return unto his house, lest his brethren's heart faint as well as his heart. *Deuteronomy 20:5, 8*

When a man has taken a new wife, he shall not go out to war . . . but he shall be free at home one year . . .
Deuteronomy 24:5

. . . thou shalt save alive nothing that breatheth: but thou shalt utterly destroy them, namely the Hittites, and the Amorites, the Canaanites, and the Perizzites, the Hivites, and the Jebusites . . . *Deuteronomy 20:16, 17*

There is . . . a time of war, and a time of peace.
Ecclesiastes 3:8

When thou goest to war against thine enemies . . . and thou hast taken them captive, and seest among the captives a beautiful woman, and hast a desire unto her, that thou wouldest have her to thy wife: then thou shalt bring her home to thine house . . . and she shall put the raimant of her captivity from off her . . . and bewail her father and her mother a full month: and after that thou shalt go in unto her, and be her husband, and she shall be thy wife. And it shall be, if thou have no delight in her, then thou shall let her go whither she will; but thou shalt not sell her at all for money, thou shalt not make merchandise of her, because thou hast humbled her. *Deuteronomy 21:10, 14*

When the host goeth forth against thine enemies, then keep thee from every wicked thing. If there be among you any man, that is not clean by reason of uncleanness that chanceth him by night, then shall he go abroad out of the camp, he shall not come within the camp: But it shall be, when evening cometh on, he shall wash himself with water: and when the sun is down, he shall come into the camp again.

Deuteronomy 23:9, 10, 11

Thou shalt have a place also without the camp, whither thou shalt go forth abroad: and thou shalt have a paddle upon thy weapon; and it shall be, when thou wilt ease thyself abroad out of the camp, he shall not come within the camp: But it shall be, when evening cometh on, he shall wash himself with water: and when the sun is down, he shall come into the camp again.

Deuteronomy 23:9, 10, 11

Thou shalt have a place also without the camp, whither thou shalt go forth abroad: and thou shalt have a paddle upon thy weapon; and it shall be, when thou wilt ease thyself abroad, thou shalt dig therewith, and shalt turn back and cover that which cometh from thee: For the Lord thy God walketh in the midst of thy camp . . . therefore shall thy camp be holy: that he see no unclean thing in thee. . . .

Deuteronomy 23:12, 13, 14

. . . teach them war, at the least such as before knew nothing thereof. *Judges 3:2*

What king, going to make war against another king, sitteth not down first, and consulteth whether he be able with ten thousand to meet him that cometh against him with twenty thousand? *Luke 14:31*

When Thou comest nigh unto a city to fight against it, then proclaim peace into it. And it shall be, if it make thee answer of peace, and open unto thee, then it shall be, that all the people that is found therein shall be tributaries unto thee.

Deuteronomy 20:10, 11

And if it will make no peace with thee, but will make war against thee, then thou shalt besiege it: and when the Lord thy God hath delivered it into thine hands, thy shalt smite every male thereof with the edge of the sword: . . . thou shalt smite every male thereof with the edge of the sword: but the women, and the little ones, and the cattle, and all that is in the city, even all the spoil thereof, shalt thou take unto thyself. *Deuteronomy 20:13, 14*

League of Nations

And it came to pass, when all the kings which were on this side Jordan, in the hills, and in the valleys, and in all the coasts of the great sea over against Lebanon, the Hittite, and the Amovite, the Canaanite, the Perizziite, the Hivite, and the Jebusite, heard thereof; that they gathered themselves together, to fight with Joshua and with Israel, with one accord. *Joshua 9:1, 2*

OATHS

Possibly the first oath of record was taken by Abraham from his eldest servant as recorded in Genesis 24: "And Abraham said unto his eldest servant . . . I will make thee swear by the Lord . . . that thou shalt not take a wife unto my son of the daughters of the Canaanites, among whom I dwell: but thou shalt go unto my country, and to my kindred, and take a wife unto my son, Isaac . . . And the servant . . . sware to him concerning the matter."

It is universally understood that by taking an oath, the person so doing imprecates the vengeance of God upon him if the oath he takes is false. This is perhaps based on Deuteronomy 6:13 stating, "Thou shalt fear the Lord Thy God, and serve him, and shalt swear by his name."

An oath is a solemn declaration which is necessary as a condition to the filling of some office more or less public, such as becoming a witness and giving evidence in a court of law. There are assertory oaths, or those by which something is asserted as true, and promissory oaths, of those by which something is promised.

No oath was required under Biblical law. All testimony was received under the admonition of the Ninth Commandment: "Thou shalt not bear false witness against thy neighbor." Philo Judaeus wrote that "whosoever will not tell the truth without an oath, would not scruple to assert falsehood with an oath."

In place of an oath the solemn warning which was administered to each witness in the presence of the entire court admonished him to: "Forget not, O witness, that it is one thing to give evidence in a trial as to money and another in a trial for life. In a money suit, if thy witness-bearing shall do wrong, money may repair that wrong. But in this trial for life, if thou sinnest, the blood of the accused and the blood of his seed to the end of time shall be imputed unto thee. . . . For a man from one signet ring may strike off many impressions, and all of them shall be exactly alike. But He, the King of the kings, He the Holy and the Blessed, has struck off from His type of the first man the forms of all men that shall live, yet so that no one human being is wholly alike to any other. Wherefore let us think and believe that the whole world is created for a man such as he whose life hangs on thy words. But these ideas must not deter thee from testifying to what thou actually knowest. Scripture declares: "The witness who hath seen or known, and doth not tell, shall bear his iniquity." Nor must ye scruple about becoming the instrument of the alleged criminal's death. Remember the Scriptural maxim: 'When the wicked perish, there is shouting.' "

The elements of this preliminary caution were, first, a warning against injustice to the accused; second, a reminder of the retribution of Heaven upon the swearer; third, an admonition against timidity or fear in testifying.

Witnesses gave their testimony separately but always in the presence of the accused. Deuteronomy 19 provides that "the judges shall make diligent inquisition; and, behold, if the witness be a false witness and hath testified falsely against his brother, then shall ye do unto him as he had though to do unto his brother."

THE BIBLICAL LAW

And I will make thee swear by the Lord . . . that thou shalt not take a wife unto my son of the daughters of the Canaanites, among whom I dwell: but thouse shalt go unto my country, and to my kindred and take a wife unto my son Isaac . . . And the servant put his hand under the thigh of Abraham his master, and swore to him concerning that matter.

Genesis 24:2, 3, 4-9

. . . men verily swear by the greater; and an oath for confirmation is to them an end of all strife. *Hebrews 6:16*

Then shall an oath of the Lord be between them both, that he hath not put his hand unto his neighbor's goods; and the owner of it shall accept thereof . . . *Exodus 22:11*

And the time drew near that Israel must die: and he called his son Joseph, and said unto him . . . put . . . thy hand under my thigh, and deal kindly and truly with me; bury me not . . . in Egypt . . . and he said swear unto me. And he swore unto him. *Genesis 47:29-31*

Thou shalt fear the Lord thy God, and serve him and shalt swear by his name. *Deuteronomy 6:13*

Swear not at all; neither by heaven . . . nor by the earth . . .

Matthew 6:34, 35

. . . Swear not, neither by heaven, neither by the earth, neither by any other oath: but let your yea be yea; and your nay, nay. . . .

James 5:12

Lying lips are abomination to the Lord: but they that deal truly are his delight. *Proverbs 12:22*

. . . he that telleth lies shall not tarry in my sight.

Psalms 101:7

. . . ye shall not swear by my name falsely . . .

Leviticus 19:12

If a man vow a vow . . . or swear an oath to bind his soul with a bond; he shall not break his word, he shall do according to all that proceedeth out of his mouth.

Numbers 30:2

I will perform the oath which I swore. *Genesis 26:3*

OFFENSES AGAINST MORALS

UNDER BIBLICAL LAW the rape of a maiden is not a criminal offense in the strict sense of the word, since it may be expiated by a fine and forced marriage. "If a man find a damsel that is a virgin, that is not betrothed, and he lay hold of her, and lie with her, and they be found; then the man that lay with her shall give unto the damsel's father fifty shekels of silver, and she shall be his wife, because he hath humbled her; he may not put her away all his days."

In the case of seduction, the seducer must pay a dowry for the woman to be his wife: "If her father utterly refuse to give her to him, he shall pay money according to the dowry of virgins." Since the Bible does not specify the amount to be paid by the seducer, it must have been a fixed and accepted amount.

Insolent disregard of moral laws or restraint has been the way of some since the beginning of time. Biblical history cites many instances of sin concerning morals, and it is noteworthy that penalties then as now are generally the same.

The Old Testament unlike the New does not expressly condemn fornication. Many passages of the New Testament denounce this sin. No punishment was prescribed, and there is no evidence of any prosecution for this offense. Under Mosaic law, a virgin that is unbetrothed is guilty of no offense if she has sexual relations with a man; only the enticer is subject to punishment.

Incest is condemned. This sin consists in marriage or

sexual relationship between persons near of kin: "None of you shall approach to any that is near of kin to him, to uncover their nakedness." (Leviticus 18:6)

The punishment for incest was by "cutting off" or death. Leviticus 18:29 provides that whoever shall commit this abomination shall be cut off. It is further provided that death for both participants is the penalty if a man "lieth with his father's wife" and "If a man take a wife and her mother . . . they shall be burnt with fire, both he and they." (Leviticus 20:14)

Sodomy was named after the Sodomites, for which the cities of Sodom and Gomorrah were, according to biblical history, destroyed. Leviticus 18:22 defines the crime as "thou shalt not lie with mankind, as with womankind" and that the penalty is death.

In Romans 1, St. Paul observed that even women changed the natural use into that which is against nature, and that men burned in their lust one toward another.

Rape is committed when a man has sexual relations with a woman not his wife, against her will and without her consent. In Biblical law if committed against a "betrothed damself" the man is punished with death. If against a virgin, he must marry her, must pay her father fifty shekels of silver, and must mary her. He may never divorce her (Deuteronomy 22:25-29).

Adultery is the voluntary sexual intercourse of a married person with a person other than the offender's husband or wife. Open and notorious adultery is a criminal offense and punished as such.

Let all things be done decently and in order.

1 Corinthians 14:40

. . . in lewdness is decay and great want: for lewdness is the mother of famine. *Tobit 4:13*

Now the works of the flesh are manifest, which are these; adultery, fornication, uncleanness, lasciviousness.

Galatians 5:19

Adultery

Thou shalt not commit adultery. *Exodus 20:14*

. . . I will be a swift witness against . . . the adulterers . . .

Malachi 3:5

So he that goeth into his neighbor's wife; whosoever toucheth her shall not be innocent. *Proverbs 6:29*

But whoso committeth adultery with a woman lacketh understanding: he that doeth it destroyeth his own soul.

Proverbs 6:32

Moreover thou shalt not lie carnally with thy neighbor's wife, to defile thyself with her. *Leviticus 18:20*

Be ashamed . . . to gaze upon another man's wife: or to be overbusy with his maid, and come not near her bed.

Ecclesiasticus 41:17, 21, 22

. . . whosoever looketh on a woman to lust after her hath committed adultery with her already in his heart.

Matthew 5:28

Sit not at all with another man's wife, nor sit down with her in thine arms, and spend not thy money with her at the wine; lest thine heart incline unto her, and so through thy desire thou fall into destruction. *Ecclesiasticus 9:9*

[He that hath] defiled his neighbor's wife . . . shall surely die. *Ezekiel 18:11, 13*

And the man that committeth adultery with another man's wife, even he that committeth adultery with his neighbor's wife, the adulterer and the adulteress shall surely be put to death. *Leviticus 20:10*

If a man be found lying with a woman married to an husband, then they shall both of them die, both the man that lay with the woman, and the woman. *Deuteronomy 22:22*

And whosoever lieth carnally with a woman, that is a bondsmaid, betrothed to an husband, and not at all redeemed, nor freedom given her; she shall be scourged; they shall not be put to death, because she was not free. *Leviticus 19:20*

If a damsel that is a virgin be betrothed unto a husband; and a man find her in the city, and lie with her; then ye shall . . . stone them with stones that they die; the damsel, because she cried not, being in the city; and the man, because he hath humbled his neighbour's wife. . . . *Deuteronomy 22: 23, 24*

Bestiality

Neither shalt thou lie with any beast to defile thyself therewith: neither shall any woman stand before a beast to lie down thereto . . . *Leviticus 18:23*

And if a man lie with a beast, he shall surely be put to death: and ye shall slay the beast. *Leviticus 20:15*

And if a woman approach unto any beast, and lie down thereto, thou shalt kill the woman, and the beast. . . .
Leviticus 20:16

Whosoever lieth with a beast shall surely be put to death.
Exodus 22:19

Fornication

Flee fornication. Every sin that a man doeth is without the body; but he that committeth fornication sinneth against his own body. *1 Corinthians 6:18*

Neither let us commit fornication. . . . *1 Corinthians 10:8*

Incest

None of you shall approach to any that is near of kin to him, to uncover their nakedness. . . . *Leviticus 18:6*

For whosoever shall commit any . . . abomination [incest]. . . . shall be cut off from among their people. *Leviticus 18:29*

Menstruous Women

And if a woman have an issue, and her issue in her flesh be blood, she shall be put apart seven days: and whosoever toucheth her shall be unclean. *Leviticus 15:19*

And if a man shall lie with a woman having her sickness . . . both of them shall be cut off from their people.
Leviticus 20:18

Rape

And if a man entice a maid that is not betrothed, and lie with her, he shall surely endow her to be his wife.

If her father utterly refuse to give her unto him, he shall pay money according to the dowry of virgins.
Exodus 22:16, 17

If a damsel that is a virgin be betrothed unto an husband and a man find her in the city and lie with her . . . ye shall stone them . . . that they die; the damsel, because she cried not, being in the city; and the man, because he hath humbled his neighbor's wife . . . *Deuteronomy 22: 23, 24*

But if a man find a betrothed damsel in the field, and the man force her, and lie with her: then the man only . . . shall die. *Deuteronomy 22:25*

If a man find a damsel that is a virgin, which is not betrothed, and lay hold on her, and lie with her . . . then the man . . . shall give unto the damsel's father fifty shekels of silver, and she shall be his wife . . . he may not put her away all his days. *Deuteronomy 22:28, 29*

Sodomy

Thou shallt not lie with mankind, as with womankind: it is an abomination. *Leviticus 18:22*

If a man also lie with mankind, as he lieth with a woman, both of them have committed an abomination: they shall surely be put to death. *Leviticus 20:13*

PARENT AND CHILD

UNDER THE common law, children were of two sorts—legitimate and spurious, or bastards. A legitimate child is he that is born in lawful wedlock, or within a competent time afterwards. In this relationship the duty of parents to provide for the maintenance of their children is a principle of natural law; an obligation laid on them not only by natural duties, but by their own act, in bringing them into the world; for they would be in the highest manner injurious to their issue, if they only gave their children life, that they might afterwards see them perish. By begetting them, therefore, they have entered into a voluntary obligation, to endeavor as far as in them lies, that the life which they have bestowed shall be supported and preserved. Thus, the child has a perfect right of receiving maintenance from their parents.

Marriage in all civilized states is built on the natural obligation of the father to provide for his child; for that ascertains and makes known the person who is bound to fulfill this obligation; whereas, in promiscious and illicit conjunctions, the father is unknown, and the mother finds a thousand obstacles in her way—shame, remorse, the restrictions of her sex, and the rigor of laws that stifle her inclinations to perform this duty; and besides, she generally lacks ability.

The laws of all well regulated states have taken care to enforce the duty of parental support, though providence has done it more effectually than any law, by implanting in the breast of every parent that natural, or insuperable degree of affection, which not even the deformity of person or mind, not even the wickedness, ingratitude, or the rebellion of child, can totally suppress or extinguish.

It is common knowledge that those who are taught to respect parental authority in their early years also conform to the laws of the land and the conventions of society throughout their adult life.

Much consideration is given this subject in the Mosaic law, and one of the ten commandments is: "Thou shalt honor thy father and thy mother."

THE BIBLICAL LAW

Honor thy father and mother. . . . *Exodus 20:12*

A bastard shall not enter into the congregation of the Lord; even to his tenth generation shall he not enter into the congregation of the Lord. *Deuteronomy 23:2*

For better it is that thy children should seek to thee, than that thou shouldest stand to their courtesy.

Ecclesiasticus 33:21

Desire not a multitude of unprofitable children, neither delight in ungodly sons . . . and better it is to die without children, than to have them that are ungodly.

Ecclesiasticus 16:1, 3

He that begetteth a fool doeth it to his sorrow.

Proverbs 17:21

Thus shall it go also with the wife that leaveth her husband, and bringeth an heir by another . . . her children shall not take root, and her branches shall bring forth no fruit.

Ecclesiasticus 23:22, 25

And this one woman said, O my lord, I and this woman dwell in one house; and I was delivered of a child with her in the house.

And it came to pass the third day after that I was delivered, that this woman was delivered also; and we were together; there was no stranger with us in the house . . .

And this woman's child died in the night because she overlaid it. And she arose at midnight, and took my son from beside me, while thine handmaid slept, and laid it in her bosom, and laid her dead child in my bosom.

And when I rose in the morning to give my child suck, behold it was dead: but when I had considered it in the morning, behold, it was not my son, which I did bear.

And the other woman said, Nay . . . and the King said, bring me a sword, and they brought a sword before the King.

And the King said, divide the living child in two, and give half to one and half to the other. Then spake the woman whose the living child was unto the King, for her bowels yearned upon her son, and she said, O my Lord, give her the living child, and in no wise slay it. But the other said, Let it be neither mine nor thine, but divide it.

Then the King answered and said, Give her the living child, and in no wise slay it: she is the mother thereof.

1 Kings 3:16, 27

For the Lord hath given the father honor over the children, and hath confirmed the authority of the mother over the sons.

Ecclesiasticus 3:2

Chasten thy son while there is hope, and let not thy soul spare for his crying. *Proverbs 22:15*

Correct thy son, and he shall give thee rest; yea, he shall give delight unto thy soul. *Proverbs 29:17*

The rod and reproof give wisdom: but a child left to himself bringeth his mother to shame. *Proverbs 29:15*

. . . take wives for your sons, and give your daughters to husbands . . . that ye may be increased . . . *Jeremiah 29:6*

Hast thou daughters? . . . Marry thy daughter . . but give her to a man of understanding. *Ecclesiasticus 7:24, 25*

Ye shall fear every man his mother, and his father. . . .

Leviticus 19:3

He that feareth the Lord will honor his father, and will do service unto his parents . . . *Ecclesiasticus 3:7*

My son, keep thy father's commandment, and forsake not the law of thy mother. *Proverbs 6:20*

And he that curseth his father, or his mother, shall surely be put to death. *Exodus 21:17*

Whoso robbeth his father or his mother, and saith, it is no transgression; the same is the companion of a destroyer. *Proverbs 28:24*

. . . ye shall command your children to observe to do, all the words of this law. *Deuteronomy 32:46*

Train up a child in the way he should go: and when he is old, he will not depart from it. *Proverbs 22:6*

Fathers, provoke not your children to anger, lest they be discouraged. *Colossians 3:21*

. . . Thy servant my husband is dead . . . and the creditor is come to take unto him my two sons to be bondsmen. *Kings 4:1*

But forasmuch as he had not to pay, his lord commanded him to be sold, and his wife, and children, and all that he had, and payment to be made. *Matthew 18:25*

He that loveth his son causeth him oft to feel the rod, that he may have joy in him in the end. *Ecclesiasticus 30:1*

He that maketh too much of his son shall bind up his wounds . . . an horse not broken becometh headstrong: as a child left to himself will be willful. *Ecclesiasticus 30:7, 8*

Give him no liberty in his youth, and wink not at his follies. *Ecclesiasticus 30:11*

Chastise thy son, and hold him to labor, lest his lewd behavior be an offense unto thee. *Ecclesiasticus 7:24*

Keep a sure watch over a shameless daughter . . . *Ecclesiasticus 42:11*

. . . for the children ought not lay up (financial provision) for the parents, but the parents for the children.

2 Corinthians 12:14

Remember thy father and thy mother, when thy sittest among great men. Be not forgetful before (of) them.

Ecclesiasticus 23:14

Remember that thou wast begotten of them; and how canst thou recompense them the things that they have done for thee?

Ecclesiasticus 7:28

Help thy father in his age, and grieve him not as long as he liveth. And if his understanding fail, have patience with him . . . *Ecclesiasticus 3:12, 13*

He that forsaketh his father is as a blasphemer . . .

Ecclesiasticus 3:16

. . . the heir, as long as he is a child, differeth nothing from a servant, though he be lord of all. *Galatians 4:1*

Unto the woman [God] said, I will greatly multiply thy sorrow and thy conception; in sorrow thou wilt bring forth children. . . . *Genesis 3:16*

Chasten thy son while there is hope, and let not thy soul spare for his crying. *Proverbs 19:18*

. . . do not sin against the child . . . *Genesis 42:22*

If thy daughter be shameless, keep her in straitly, lest she abuse herself through overmuch liberty. *Ecclesiasticus 26:10*

Hast thou children? instruct them, and bow down their neck from their youth. *Ecclesiasticus 7:23*

Withhold not correction from the child: for if thou beatest him with the rod, he shall not die. *Proverbs 23:13*

An horse not broken becometh headstrong: and a child left to himself will be wilful. *Ecclesiasticus 30:8*

Children, obey your parents in all things: for this is well pleasing to the Lord. *Colossians 3:20*

PARTNERSHIP

GENERALLY, a partnership is an association of two or more persons for carrying on some business or undertaking. All history has recorded partnership arrangements and the Bible, not only refers to them, but advises the course of conduct to be followed by partners.

Wherever and whenever man creates an association of two or more people who contribute money or property to carry on a joint business and who share profits or losses in certain proportion, there will always be the necessity for rules of conduct.

In our laws today, partnership is one of mutual trust and fair dealing. The statutes are so many that thought must be given to the many weaknesses in this type of business arrangement. In Biblical times, as today, man is well advised to "be not ashamed of reckoning with thy partners."

THE BIBLICAL LAW

Be ashamed . . . of unjust dealing before thy partner. . . .
Ecclesiasticus 41:17, 18

Be not ashamed . . . of reckoning with thy partners.
Ecclesiasticus 42:1, 3

Whoso is partner with a thief hateth his own soul.
Proverbs 29:24

And so was also James and John, the sons of Zebedee, which were partners with Simon . . . *Luke 5:10*

Whether any do inquire of Titus, he is my partner and fellow-helper. . . . *II Corinthians 8:23*

If thou count me therefore a partner, receive him as myself. If he hath wronged thee, or oweth thee aught, put that on mine account. *Philemon 17, 18*

PENALTIES

OFFENSES COMMITTED against the person—murder, mayhem, assault, incest, and adultery, are considered not only sins against the Divinity but also crimes against organized society. These offenses brought either capital punishment or punishment by the lex talionis. By the lex talionis, the court inflicts upon the culprit the very injury which he has inflicted upon his victim: "Eye for eye, tooth for tooth, hand for hand, foot for foot, burning for burning, wound for wound, stripe for stripe."

The Scripture reads: "And if a man maim his neighbor, as he hath done, so shall it be done to him: breach for breach, eye for eye, tooth for tooth; as he hath maimed a man, so shall it be rendered unto him."

The lex talionis may seem barbarous and inhuman, but the principle of "life for life, eye for eye" established a fixed limit to retaliatory punishment. It substituted for the savage, primitive concept of limitless revenge and private resentment, a legal punishment as commensurate as possible with the injury inflicted. St. Augustine wrote that the lex talionis was a law of justice, not of hatred; one eye, not two eyes, for an eye; one tooth, not ten teeth, for a tooth; one life, not a whole family, for a life.

The Jews, however, from the earliest times, were dissatisfied with the literal interpretation of this Biblical directive. They held that the rule "eye for eye" had reference to the more humane law of compensation in money. Mayhem was thus made a fineable offense.

There was another offense, that of the false witness, which was considered a crime against the commonwealth and subject to the lex talionis. Of the false witness, the bible prescribes: "Then shall you do unto him as he purposed to do unto his neighbor . . . and ye shall have no pity: life for life, eye for eye, tooth for tooth, hand for hand, foot for foot."

In the Bible there is no mention of prisons—the closest was a ward which is described as a place of detention, where the law-breaker was held until he was brought to justice.

Cities of Refuge were established for the unintentional murderer. The primary object of these cities of refuge was to protect the unintentional murderer from the family avenger, who might otherwise slay him without due process of law. In Numbers we read: "Ye shall appoint you cities of refuge for you, that the manslayer that killeth any person through error may flee thither. And the cities shall be unto you for refuge from the avenger, that the manslayer die not, until he stand before the congregation for judgment." It would seem from such wording that the cities of refuge were non-penal in character.

However, Numbers also provides that the cities of refuge shall serve not only as a sanctuary for the manslayer, but also as a place of detention until the death of the high priest, and the text reads: "Then the congregation shall judge between the smiter and the avenger of blood according to these ordinances, and the congregation restore him to the city of refuge, whither he was fled; and he shall dwell therein until the death of the high priest, who was anointed with the holy oil."

Manslaughter was the only Biblical crime punishable by imprisonment and then only within a city of refuge. The character of the city of refuge, however, was an ordinary city and the manslayer was safe so long as he remained within its limits.

The latter Numbers text recognizes the right of the family avenger to kill the manslayer upon sight, if found outside the city during his period of confinement. The Biblical text reads: "But if the manslayer shall at any time go beyond the border of his city of refuge, and the avenger of blood slay the manslayer; there shall be no blood-guiltiness for him; because he must remain in his city of refuge until the death of the high priest; but after the death of the high priest, the manslayer may return into the land of his possession.

In Deuteronomy, the unintentional manslayer is likewise mentioned twice. Both texts re-state that the purpose of the cities of refuge is to protect the manslayer. The first reference reads: "That the manslayer might flee thither, that slayeth his neighbor unawares, and hated him not in time past; and that fleeing into one of these cities he may live."

The second Deuternomic text directs: "And this is the case of the manslayer, that shall flee thither and live. . . . He shall flee unto one of these cities and live; lest the avenger of blood pursue the manslayer, while his heart is hot, whereas he was not deserving of death, inasmuch as he hated him not in time past. Therefore I command thee saying: "Thou shalt separate three cities for thee."

There is an additional command that the roads leading to the cities of refuge be kept in perfect condition and be clearly designated, so that the manslayer may experience no difficulty in getting there. The second Deuteronomic text directs that "Thou shalt prepare thee the way, and divide the borders of the land, which the Lord thy God causeth thee to inherit, into three parts, that every manslayer may flee thither."

The procedure by which a manslayer is admitted into one of the cities of refuge is described in Joshua: "And the Lord spoke unto Joshua, saying 'Speak unto the children of Israel, saying: Assign you three cities of refuge, whereof I spoke unto you by the hand of Moses; that the manslayer that killeth any person through error and unawares may flee thither; and they shall be unto you for a refuge from the avenger of blood. And he shall flee unto one of those cities, and shall stand at the entrance of the gate of the city, and declare his cause in the ears of the elders of the city; and they shall take him into the city unto them, and give him a place, that he may dwell among them. And if the avenger of blood pursue after him, then shall they not deliver up the manslayer into his hand, because he smote his neighbor unawares, and hated him not before time. And he shall dwell in that city, until he stand before the congregation for judgment, until the death of the high priest that shall be in those days; then may the manslayer return, and come into his own city, and unto his own house, unto the city from whence he fled."

It appears therefore that the manslayer could not enter a city of refuge at will. Before being admitted, the manslayer must first state his case to a tribunal consisting of the elders of the city who first decide whether or not the case is one of manslaughter, and consequently whether it is one over which the city authorities have jurisdiction. If this tribunal finds him guilty of manslaughter, he may remain in the city of refuge.

THE BIBLICAL LAW

Mercy is seasonable in the time of affliction, as clouds of rain in the time of draught. *Ecclesiasticus 35:20*

Be not deceived . . . for whatsoever a man swoeth, that shall he also reap. *Galatians 6:7*

A good man obtaineth favor of the Lord: but a man of wicked devices will he condemn. *Proverbs 12:2*

For the upright shall dwell in the land, and the perfect shall remain in it. But the wicked shall be cut off from the earth, and the transgressors shall be rooted out of it. *Proverbs 2:21, 22*

I will destroy all the wicked of the land. *Psalms 101:8*

And the man that will do presumptuously, and will not hearken unto thee . . . judge, even that man shall die. . . . *Deuteronomy 17:12*

He that despised Moses' law died without mercy under two or three witnesses. *Hebrews 10:28*

For whosoever shall keep the whole law, and yet offend in one point, he is guilty of all. *James 2:10*

And whosoever shall trangress the law . . . shall be punished diligently, whether it be by death, or other punishment, by penalty of money, or by imprisonment. *1 Esdras 8:24*

For everyone that curseth his father or his mother shall be surely put to death. *Leviticus 20:9*

He that leadeth unto captivity shall go into captivity: he that killeth with the sword must be killed with the sword. *Revelation 13:10*

I, the Lord search the heart . . . even to give every man according to his ways, and according to the fruit of his doings. *Jeremiah 17:10*

And if a man cause a blemish in his neighbor; as he hath done, so shall it be done to him. Breach for breach, eye for eye, tooth for tooth. *Leviticus 24:19, 20*

Whoso sheddeth man's blood, by man shall his blood be shed . . . *Genesis 9:6*

And whosoever will not do the law of thy God, and the law of the king, let judgment be executed speedily upon him, whether it be unto death, or to banishment, or to confiscation of goods, or to imprisonment. *Ezra 7:26*

. . . they caught Paul & Silas . . . and brought them to the magistrates saying, These men being Jews, do exceedingly trouble our city, and teach customs, which are not lawful for us to receive . . . being Romans . . . and the magistrates rent off their clothes, and commanded to beat them . . . and they cast them into prison. *Acts 16:19, 20, 21, 22, 23*

. . . if the wicked man be worthy to be beaten, that the judge shall cause him to lie down, and to be beaten before his face, according to his fault . . . forty stripes he may give him, and not exceed. . . . *Deuteronomy 25:2, 3*

When the righteous turneth from his righteousness, and committeth iniquity, he shall even die thereby. *Ezekiel 33:18*

. . . the righteousness of the righteous shall not deliver him in the day of his transgression . . . neither shall the righteous be able to live for his righteousness in the day that he sinneth. *Ezekiel 33:12*

. . . if he [the righteous] trust to his own righteousness, and commit iniquity, all his righteousness shall not be remembered; but for his iniquity that he hath committed, he shall die for it. *Ezekiel 33:13*

And thine eye shall not pity; but life shall go for life, eye for eye, tooth for tooth, hand for hand, foot for foot. *Deuteronomy 19:21*

He [God] hath mercy on them . . . that diligently seek after his judgments. *Ecclesiasticus 18:14*

The Lord is slow to anger . . . and will not at all acquit the wicked . . . *Nahum 1:13*

For the Lord will not be slack . . . till he hath smitten in sunder the loins of the unmerciful and . . . till he have taken away the multitude of the proud, and broken the sceptre of the unrighteous. *Ecclesiasticus 35:18*

Till he [God] have rendered to every man according to his deeds, and to the works of men according to their devices; till he have judged the cause of his people, and made them to rejoice in his mercy. *Ecclesiasticus 35:19*

For he shall have judgment without mercy, that hath showed no mercy . . . *James 2:13*

If the wicked . . . give again that he had robbed, walk in the statutes of life, without committing iniquity . . he shall not die. *Ezekiel 33:15*

He that saith unto the wicked, thou art righteous; him shall the people curse . . . *Proverbs 24:24*

He that justifieth the wicked, and he that condemneth the just, even they both are abomination to the Lord.

Proverbs 17:15

They that forsake the law praise the wicked: but such as keep the law contend with them. *Proverbs 28:4*

Let favor be shewed to the wicked, yet will he not learn righteousness: in the land of uprighteness will he deal unjustly. . . . *Isaiah 26:10*

Who knowing the judgment of God, that they which commit such things are worthy of death, not only do the same, but have pleasure in them that do them. *Romans 1:32*

Woe unto them that call evil good, and good evil; that put darkness for light, and light for darkness; that put bitter for sweet and sweet for bitter. *Isaiah 5:20*

Moreover ye shall take no satisfaction for the life of a murderer, which is guilty of death: but he shall surely be put to death. And ye shall take no satisfaction for him that is fled to the city of his refuge. . . .

And if a man take a wife and her mother . . . they shall be burnt with fire, both he and they . . . *Leviticus 20:14*

And the daughter of any priest, if she profane herself by playing the whore . . . she shall be burnt with fire . . .

Leviticus 21:9

Cities of Refuge

. . . if the [the slayer] thrust him suddenly without enmity, or have cast upon him anything without laying of wait, or with

a stone . . . seeing him not, and cast it upon him, that he die, and was not his enemy, neither sought his harm. . . .

Numbers 35:22, 23

. . . . there shall be . . . cities for refuge, which ye shall appoint . . . that the slayer may flee thither, which killeth any person at unawares.

And they shall be . . . cities for refuge from the avenger; that the manslayer die not, until he stand before the congregation in judgment. *Numbers 35:6, 11, 12*

Then Moses severed three cities . . . that the slayer might flee thither, which should kill his neighbor unawares, and hated him not in times past; and that fleeing into one of these cities he might live. *Deuteronomy 4:41, 42*

Excusable Homicide

And this is the case of the slayer, which shall flee thither [City of refuge] that he may live; whoso killeth his neighbor ignorantly, whom he hated not in time past; as when goeth into the wood with his neighbor to hew wood, and his hand fetcheth a stroke with the axe to cut down the tree, and the head slippeth from the helve, and lighteth upon his neighbor, that he die; he shall flee unto one of those cities, and live: lest the avenger of the blood pursue the slayer, while his heart is hot, and overtake him . . . and slay him; whereas he was not worthy of death, inasmuch as he hated him not in time past.

Deuteronomy 19:4, 5, 6

And if the avenger of blood pursue after him, then they shall not deliver the slayer up into his hand; because he smote his neighbor unwittingly, and hated him not beforetime.

Joshua 20:5

Kidnaping

And he that stealeth a man, and selleth him . . . he shall surely be put to death. *Exodus 21:16*

If a man be found stealing any of his brethren of the children of Israel, and maketh merchandize of him, or selleth him; then that thief shall die. . . . *Deuteronomy 24:7*

Probation

But if the wicked will turn from all his sins that he hath committed . . . and do that which is lawful and right, he shall surely live, he shall not die. All his transgressions . . . they shall not be mentioned him. . . . *Ezekiel 18:21*

And [they] brought unto him a woman taken in adultery . . . they say unto him . . . Moses in the law commanded us, that such should be stoned: but what sayest thou? . . . but Jesus . . . said unto them, he that is without sin among you, let him first cast a stone at her . . . and Jesus said unto her . . . go and sin no more. *John 8:3, 11*

Reproach not a man that turneth from sin [crime], but remember that we are all worthy of punishment.

Ecclesiasticus 8:5

If we have no sin, we deceive ourselves, and the truth is not in us. *1 John 1:8*

PERJURY

PERJURY IS THE giving of false testimony under oath before any competent tribunal, officer or person by making a false statement, or by making a false affidavit before any person authorized to administer oaths. Any person who willfully and contrary to his oath states as true any material matter which he knows to be false has committed perjury.

In the law today the terms false swearing and perjury are used interchangeably. Perjury involves the making of a false statement oral or written. The statement must be as to a material pertinent fact. This type of statement is to be differentiated from a statement of opinion or belief, except that if a person willfully swears to a belief of fact which he knows does not exist, he is guilty of perjury.

In Biblical law the rule was that "thou shalt near bear false witness against thy neighbor." This one law if followed completely would obviate the necessity of legal and technical definitions of the offense of perjury. Whether man can morally and intellectually live within this Mosaic directive is a subject of philosophical conjecture, but Ecclesiasticus agrees that "the law shall be found perfect without lies" and that "a thief is better than a man that is accustomed to lie."

THE BIBLICAL LAW

Thou shalt not bear false witness against thy neighbor.
Exodus 20:16

And let none of you imagine evil in your hearts against his neighbor; and love no false oath . . . *Zechariah 8:17*

These . . . things doth the Lord hate: a false witness that speaketh lies, and he that soweth discord . . . *Proverbs 6:16, 19*

A false witness shall perish. . . . *Proverbs 21:28*

Be not a witness against thy neighbor without cause; and deceive not with thy lips. *Proverbs 24:28*

And ye shall not swear by my name falsely. . . .
Leviticus 19:12

Neither shalt thou bear false witness against thy neighbor.
Deuteronomy 5:20

. . . put not thine hand with the wicked to be an unrighteous witness. *Exodus 23:1*

The law shall be found perfect without lies: and wisdom is perfection to a faithful mouth. *Ecclesiasticus 34:8*

A false witness shall not be unpunished, and he that speaketh lies shall not escape. *Proverbs 18:5*

. . . if the witness be a false witness, and hath testified falsely against his brother; then shall ye do unto him, as he had thought to have done unto his brother. . . . *Deuteronomy 19:18, 19*

. . . he that telleth lies shall not tarry in my sight.
Psalms 101:7

Keep thee far from a false matter. *Exodus 23:7*

A thief is better than a man that is accustomed to lie.
Ecclesiasticus 20:25

PHYSICIANS AND MEDICINE

A PHYSICIAN is one who practices the art of healing, preserving and promoting health, and is one who prescribes remedies for the diseases of mankind. In the legal sense, he is, of course, required to be licensed to practice medicine.

Each state has certain requirements which must be met by one seeking to practice medicine. This was not the rule in Biblical days when medical knowledge was limited and it was not necessary for man to become specifically educated in the use of this science. Nor does the Bible provide for the physician and patient relationship, so that whatever is said between them is privileged and confidential and the patient's secrets in the keeping of his physician become inviolable.

There did exist in Biblical days the office of physician. According to many writings, Luke was a physician. The Bible is also inattentive to medicine itself, but refers in several places to the use of a physic. It does point out that God created medicines out of the earth and that such medicines should be used. Of course, we know today that many of the saving medicines which have been used to benefit mankind are produced from the earth. We must assume that the writers of the Bible had some understanding of the healing qualities of the earth on which we live.

It is interesting to speculate on the mention in the Bible of the first anaesthetic administered—"the Lord God caused a deep sleep to fall upon Adam, and he slept;

and he took one of his ribs and closed up the flesh instead thereof."

As early as Genesis 50:2 "Joseph commanded his servants, the physicians, to embalm his father."

Apothecaries, or druggists were known in biblical times. They compounded the incense and holy anointing oils used in religious ceremonies; also, flavoring extracts and medicinal herbs (Exodus 30:25). They were also the undertakers and prepared spices used in burials (2 Chronicles 16:14).

. . . use physic . . . even thou be sick. *Ecclesiasticus 18:19*

The Lord hath created medicines out of the earth; and he that is wise will not abhor them. *Ecclesiasticus 38:4*

And by the river upon the bank thereof . . . shall grow all trees . . . and the fruit thereof shall be for meat, and the leaf thereof for medicine. *Ezekiel 47:12*

Let them take a lump of figs, and lay it for a plaster upon the boil, and he shall recover. *Isaiah 38:21*

. . . in thy sickness be not negligent . . . then give place to the physician, for the Lord hath created him: let him not go from thee . . . there is a time when in their hands there is good success. *Ecclesiasticus 38:9, 12, 13*

A merry heart doth good like a medicine: but a broken spirit drieth the bones. *Proverbs 17:22*

. . . in his disease he sought not the Lord, but to the physicians. *2 Chronicles 16:12*

. . . ye are all physicians of no value. *Job 13:4*

Is there no balm in Gilead; is there no physician there? *Jeremiah 8:22*

The physician cutteth off a long disease; and he that is today a king tomorrow shall die. *Ecclesiasticus 10:10*

Honor a physician with the honor due unto him for the uses which ye may have of him. . . . *Ecclesiasticus 38:1*

. . . They that be whole need not a physician, but they that are sick. *Matthew 9:12*

Ye will surely say unto me this proverb, physician, heal thyself. . . . *Luke 4:23*

Apothecaries

Of such doth the apothecary make a confection; and of his works there is no end. . . . *Ecclesiasticus 37:8*

PROPERTY

UNDER BIBLICAL law the whole earth and all property belongs to God. The 49th Psalm philosophically evaluates man's ownership of property and possessions: ". . . wise men die, likewise the fool and the brutish person perish, and leave their wealth to others. Their inward thought is, that their houses shall continue forever, and their dwelling places to all generations: they call their lands after their own names. Nevertheless man . . . abideth not: he is like the beasts that perish . . . for when he dieth he shall carry nothing away."

As Sir William Blackstone in his Commentaries on the law wrote: "the earth and all things therein were the general property of mankind for the immediate gift of the Creator. . . . Thus the ground was in common, and no part was the permanent property of any man in particular; yet whoever was in the occupation of any determined spot of it, for rest, for shade, or the like, acquired for the time a sort of ownership, from which it would have been unjust and contrary to the law of nature to have driven him by force, but the instant that he quitted the use or occupation of it, another might seize it without injustice."

Property formerly owned, then sold may be redeemed under Biblical law. Redemption laws are not new to our jurisprudence, and are to be found applying in matters pertaining to mortgage foreclosures, particularly of homes when such foreclosures are made by the state. Mosaic law provides for redemption so that the tribal properties may remain intact.

THE BIBLICAL LAW

. . . I am God . . . every beast of the forest is mine, and the cattle upon a thousand hills . . . the wild beasts of the field are mine . . . the world is mine, and the fulness thereof.

Psalms 50:7, 10, 11, 12

. . . one born in my house is mine heir. *Genesis 15:3*

A good man leaveth an inheritance to his children's children . . .

Proverbs 13:22

. . . but he that shall come forth out of thine own bowels shall be thine heir. *Genesis 15:4*

If a man hath two wives, one beloved, and another hated . . . and if the first born son be hers that was hated: then . . . when he maketh his sons inherit that which he hath . . . he shall acknowledge the son of the hated for firstborn, by giving him a double portion of all that he hath.

Deuteronomy 21:15, 16, 17

And Esau said to Jacob, feed me . . . for I am faint: and Jacob said, sell me this day thy birthright . . . and he sold his birthright unto Jacob. *Genesis 25:30, 31, 32, 33*

. . . men . . . leave the rest of their substance to their babes.

Psalms 17:14

And Abraham gave all that he had unto Isaac. But unto the sons of the concubines, Abraham gave gifts . . .

Genesis 25:5, 6

Thou shalt not inherit in our father's house; for thou art the son of a strange woman. *Judges 11:2*

. . . if a man die, and have no son, then ye shall cause his inheritance to pass unto his daughter. And if he have no daughter, then ye shall give his inheritance unto his brethren. And if he have no brethren, then ye shall give his inheritance unto his father's brethren. And if his father have no brethren, then ye shall give his inheritance unto his kinsman that is next to him of his family, and he shall possess it.

Numbers 27:8, 9, 10, 11

. . . if the prince give a gift unto any of his sons, the inheritance thereof shall be his sons' . . . but if he give a gift of his inheritance to one of his servants, then it shall be his to the year of liberty; after it shall return to the prince; but his inheritance shall be his sons' for them. *Ezekiel 46:16, 17*

. . . let them marry to whom they think best; only to the family of the tribe of their father shall they marry. So shall not the inheritance of the children of Israel remove from tribe to tribe: for every one of the children of Israel shall keep himself to the inheritance of the tribe of his fathers. And every daughter, that possesseth an inheritance in any tribe of the children of Israel, shall be wife unto one of the family of the tribe of her father, that the children of Israel may enjoy every man the inheritance of his fathers. Neither shall the inheritance remove from one tribe to another tribe; but everyone of the tribes of the children of Israel shall keep himself to his own inheritance.
Numbers 36:6, 7, 8, 9

The land shall not be sold forever: for the land is mine . . .
Leviticus 25:23

Redemption of Sold Property

And in all the land of your possession ye shall grant a redemption for the land.

If thy brother be waxen poor, and hath sold away some of his possession, and if any of his kin come to redeem it, then shall he redeem that which his brother sold.

And if the man have none to redeem it, and himself be able to redeem it;

Then let him count the years of the sale thereof, and restore the overplus unto the man to whom he sold it; that he may return unto his possession. *Leviticus 25:24, 25, 26, 27, 28*

And if a man sell a dwellinghouse in a walled city, then he may redeem it within a whole year after it is sold. . . .

And if it be not redeemed within the space of a full year, then the house that is in the walled city shall be established for ever to him that bought it throughout his generations.

But the houses of the villages which have no wall round about them shall be counted as the fields of the country: they may be redeemed. . . . *Leviticus 25:29, 30, 31*

PROSTITUTION

PROSTITUTION is defined as promiscuous unchastity for gain. It was not an offense under the common law of England, nor is it synonymous with concubinage and other terms indicating a more restricted degree of abandonment. As ordinarily used in its application to lewd women, it does not refer to sexual intercourse with but one man. However illicit the relation may be, so long as the woman remains faithful to one lover, and is motivated only by affection or passion and not pecuniary gain, she is not, in the language of the law, termed a prostitute.

Prostitution is coeval with society. It stains the earliest mythological records. It is constantly assumed as an existing fact in biblical history, and rules of law were promulgated to curb this sin. There was no prohibition against possessing concubines in such number as man desired.

As early as the Bible of Genesis (38:16, 17) Tamar said to Judah: "what wilt thou give me, that thou mayest come in unto me? and he said, I will send thee a kid from the flock. And she said, wilt thou give me a pledge, till thou send it?"

Prostitution was recognized as an existing sin, biblical law providing that "there shall be no whore of the daughters of Israel."

THE BIBLICAL LAW

Whoredom and wine . . . take away the heart. *Hosea 4:11*

Beware of all whoredom. . . . *Tobit 4:12*

. . . the law is not made for a righteous man, but for the lawless . . . for whoremongers [and] for them that defile themselves with mankind . . . *1 Timothy 9, 10*

. . . no whoremonger . . . hath any inheritance in the kingdom of . . . God. *Ephesians 5:5*

Marriage is honorable in all, and the bed undefiled: but whoremongers . . . God will judge. *Hebrews 13:4*

What wilt thou give me, that thou mayest come in unto me? and he said, I will send thee a kid from the flock. And she said, wilt thou give me a pledge, till thou send it?
Genesis 38:16, 17, 18

But the . . . whoremongers . . . shall have their part in the lake which burneth with fire and brimstone . . .
Revelation 21:8

Do not prostitute thy daughter, to cause her to be a whore . . .
Leviticus 19:29

There shall be no whore of the daughters of Israel. . . .
Deuteronomy 23:17

. . . thou shalt not play the harlot . . . *Hosea 3:3*

She also lieth in wait as for a prey, and increaseth the transgressors among men. *Proverbs 23:28*

And the daughter of any priest, if she profane herself by playing the whore . . . she shall be burnt with fire.
Leviticus 21:9

An harlot shall be accounted as spittle . . .
Ecclesiasticus 26:22

Give not thy soul unto harlots, that thou lose not thine inheritance. *Ecclesiasticus 9:6*

Meet not with an harlot, lest thou fall into her snares. *Ecclesiasticus 9:3*

Be ashamed of whoredom . . . *Ecclesiasticus 41:17*

Wine and women will make men of understanding to fall away: and he that cleaveth to harlots will become impudent. Moths and worms shall have him to heritage. *Ecclesiasticus 19:2, 3*

For by means of a whorish woman a man is brought to a piece of bread . . . *Proverbs 6:26*

. . . many strong men have been slain by her. *Proverbs 7:26*

they give gifts to all whores. . . . *Ezekiel 16:33*

RELIGION

THE MONOTHEISM of the Hebrew tribes is based in the belief that there is only one God, who is worshipped as the righteous ruler of the world, who dispenses justice, and is the giver of the law. His power results from his being the creator, who directs his creatures in ethical responsibility and high moral consciousness.

In Hebrew and Christian thought, religion is man's recognition of his relation to God and his expression of that relation in faith, worship, and conduct. It must be thought of as embodying the means of attaining and expressing in conduct the values deemed characteristic of the ideal life.

Babylon greatly influenced and molded Hebrew life and religion. This impact of Babylon commenced when Abraham began his journey to Canaan from the City of Ur in Babylon, carrying with him the language and culture which influenced future Hebrew life, and again when the place of captivity of Judah was in Babylon. This long captivity exerted formative influences upon the thought and worship of the Hebrews.

The law of God against "graven images" was so firm in the thinking of the Hebrews that graven images were not permitted to be brought into Jerusalem; not even Roman standards, with their eagles, were permitted during the days of the Roman occupation. Condemnation by God and by him through his prophets held the Hebrews close to the stanchion of Monotheism.

The prophet in Israel did not claim to speak from human wisdom. He claimed knowledge which ordinary man could not possess, representing divine inspiration and direct instruction by God as a result of which he unveiled and foretold the course of human events. He expressed the pleasure or displeasure of God, and in his foresight discerned more than the future; declaring what man could hope for or must fear in the eyes of God.

The content of the prophets divine communication was not exclusively foretelling the future, but was often accompanied by instruction concerning actions to be performed by the Hebrews in their conduct toward God.

When the prophecy was one of doom, predictions of the future were accompanied by instruction to follow the way of God.

The Bible warns against false prophets, but does not direct how man can determine who is a true prophet and who an imposter. Jesus warned: "Beware of false prophets, which come to you in sheep's clothing, but inwardly they are ravening wolves."

Great discussions have gone on for innumerable years about the day of the Sabbath. Originally, the sect of Hebrews who followed Christ, and who became known as Christians, observed the Sabbath in accordance with Mosaic law, as well as the first day of the week—Sunday—in respect of the resurrection, but there is no command in the New Testament in this regard.

Sunday was a pagan day sacred to the sun god and derives from the Mithraic religion. The resurrection having occurred on Sunday seemed sufficient reason for transferring the Sabbath to Sunday. Some time during the 4th Century, A.D., church law required this observance and

Emperor Constantine confirmed it by law. It is entirely possible that the early Christians, in observing the first rather than the seventh day, desired to distinguish themselves from the Hebrews and afford some public evidence that Christianity was not a new Hebrew sect.

An interesting court decision on observing the Sabbath is found in Tennessee, where the playing of professional baseball was declared not to be against the law prohibiting persons to do or exercise any of the common avocations of life on Sunday. The Supreme Court of that state ruled that since the law concerning Sunday was passed in 1803, and baseball as a game, was not played formally until 1845, there could not have been any intention on the part of the legislature to prohibit baseball, and therefore there was no violation of the statute. The decision makes no reference to the mandate in the Bible.

It is important to understand the background of the Gospels and the early expansion of Christianity, which was the only movement of any kind in ancient times which arose in the masses. Jesus, like his first followers, belonged to the poor. They listened to him, because he was one of them, and when Christianity spread into the Roman Empire its appeal was only to the poor.

The United States Supreme Court has said that the "establishment of religion" clause of the First Amendment, made equally applicable to the states by the Fourteenth Amendment, means that neither a state nor the Federal government can set up a church. Neither can pass laws which aid one religion, aid all religions, or prefer one religion over another. Neither can force or influence a person to go to or remain away from church against his will or force him to profess a belief or disbelief in any religion.

No person can be punished for entertaining or professing religious beliefs or disbeliefs, or for church attendance or non-attendance. No tax in any amount, can be levied to support any religious activities or institutions, whatever they may be called, or whatever form they may adopt to teach or practice religion.

Neither a state nor the Federal government can, openly or secretly, participate in the affairs of any religious organization or group, and vice versa.

In Biblical times it was just the opposite. The Bible was the law, and the law was the Bible. Belief was mandatory, and disbelief carried certain fixed penalties. Any violation of the Holy Scriptures was a sign against God, and secondly, a crime against the state. There was only one religion and all others were forbidden—"I am the Lord thy God . . . thou shalt have no other Gods before me."

THE BIBLICAL LAW

Blasphemy

And he that blasphemeth the name of the Lord, he shall surely be put to death. . . . *Leviticus 24:16*

False Prophets

Beware of false prophets, which come to you in sheep's clothing, but inwardly they are ravening wolves.

Matthew 7:15

. . . Let not your prophets and your diviners . . . deceive you, neither harken to your dreams which ye cause to be dreamed. For they prophecy falsely unto you . . .

Jeremiah 29:8, 9

Holy Days

Six days shall work be done: but the seventh day is the sabbath of rest, an holy convocation; he shall do not work therein . . .

Leviticus 23:3

Three times thou shalt keep a feast unto me in the year. Thou shalt keep the feast of unleavened bread (passover) . . . and the feast of harvest, the first fruits of thy labors, which thou hast sown in the field: and the feast of ingathering, which is in the end of the year, when thou hast gathered thy labors out of the field. *Exodus 23:14, 15, 16*

. . . abide ye every man in his place, let no man go out of his place on the seventh day. *Exodus 16:29*

. . . bear no burden on the sabbath day, nor bring it in by the gates of Jerusalem; neither carry forth a burden out of your house on the sabbath, neither do ye any work . . .

Jeremiah 17:21, 22

Ye shall kindle no fire throughout your habitations upon the sabbath day. *Exodus 35:3*

And he (Jesus) came to Nazareth . . . and, as his custom was, he went into the synagogue on the sabbath day, and stood up for to read. *Luke 4:16*

Idolatry

Thou shalt not make unto thee any graven image . . . Thou shalt not bow down thyself to them, nor serve them. . . .
Exodus 20:4, 5

For the devising of idols was the beginning of spiritual fornication, and the invention of them the corruption of life.
Wisdom of Solomon 14:12

Turn yet not unto idols, nor make to yourselves molten gods . . .
Leviticus 19:4

Thy graven images also will I cut off . . . and thou shalt no more worship the work of thine hands. *Micah 5:13*

Ye shall make you no idols nor graven image, neither rear you up a standing image, neither shall ye set up any image of stone in your land, to bow down to it . . . *Leviticus 26:1*

Priests

Fear the Lord . . . and reverence his priests . . .
Ecclesiasticus 7:29

Fear the Lord and honor the priest; and give him his portion [of] the first fruits . . . *Ecclesiasticus 7:31*

And all the tithe of the land, whether of the seed of the land, or of the fruit of the tree, is the Lord's . . .
Leviticus 27:30

And, behold, I have given the children of Levi all the tenth in Israel for an inheritance, for their service which they serve, even the service of the tabernacle of the congregation.

Numbers 18:21

We will not hearken to the king's words, to go from our religion, either on the right hand, or the left. *1 Maccabees 2:22*

And he [Christ] went into the temple, and began to cast out them that sold therein, and them that bought; Saying unto them, it is written, my house is the house of prayer: but ye have made it a den of thieves. *Luke 19:45, 46*

ROBBERY

In robbery under Biblical law, no penalty was imposed upon the offender who was required, however, to make restitution to the victim, and if he had nothing with which to make restitution "he shall be sold for his theft." The thief was sold into slavery by court order for as long as was necessary for him to make restitution, but in no event was the term to exceed six years.

This Biblical law was actually followed by the Hebrews. Zedekiah, King of Judah, ordered the princes and other wealthy persons to free their slaves, which they did, but seized the slaves again. As a result, the prophet Jeremiah, foretold the people that they would be delivered into the hands of their enemies to be destroyed.

In latter Biblical times, a thief could be sold into slavery only if he was unable to repay the actual value of the property stolen by him. If he repaid the actual amount, but was unable to pay the penalty of twofold, as imposed by the Biblical law, he could not be sold into slavery for the purpose of enabling him to pay that indemnity. Strangely enough, no woman could under any circumstances be sold into penal slavery.

THE BIBLICAL LAW

Thou shalt not defraud thy neighbor, neither rob him.
Leviticus 19:13

Rob not the poor. . . . *Proverbs 22:22*

Whoso robbeth his father or his mother . . .. the same is the companion of a destroyer. *Proverbs 28:24*

. . . This is the portion of them that spoil us, and the lot of them that rob us. *Isaiah 17:14*

. . . and [they shall] rob those that robbed them . . .
Ezekiel 39:10

For they know not to do right, saith the Lord, who store up violence and robbery in their palaces. *Amos 3:10*

. . . But ye say, wherein have we robbed thee?. . . .
Malachi 3:8

. . . and the robber swalloweth up their substance *Job 5:5*
As the partridge that broodeth over young which she hath not brought forth, so is he that getteth riches, and not by right; in the midst of his days he shall leave them, and at his end he shall be a fool. *Jeremiah 17:11*

Then cried they all again, saying, not this man, but Barabbas. Now Barabbas was a robber. *John 18:40*

. . . He that entereth not by the door . . . but climbeth up some other way, the same is a thief and a robber. *John 10:1*
Woe unto them that . . . rob the fatherless. *Isaiah 10:1, 2*

If a soul sin . . . he shall restore that which he took violently (by robbery) away. . . . *Leviticus 6:2, 4*

SALES

Esau selling his birthright to Jacob is perhaps the first recorded sale in history of the right to inherit an estate. Potephar's buying of Joseph from the Ishmaelites in turn produced the first food administrator known to written history.

Biblical law prohibits dishonest sales of merchandise or the use of false weights and measures: "Thou shalt not have in thy bag divers weights, a great and a small. But thou shalt have a perfect and just weight, a perfect and just measure."

Sales of land "shall not be forever." This law preserved to each tribe the lands allotted them after the conquest of Canaan. There is no evidence of written documents of conveyance; the parties agreeing to the terms, the seller would give the buyer, before witnesses, some evidence or symbol of possession. The old English custom of "livery of seizin," or putting of a person in actual possession of land by performing some ceremony before witnesses which clearly placed the party in possession, was much the same as the Biblical manner of conveyance.

It appears that in later Biblical times, when writing came into usage, the methods of conveyance were much the same as in our law. When Jeremiah (32:9-14) purchased a field: "and I bought the field of Hanameel . . . and weighed him the money . . . and I subscribed the evidence and sealed it, and took witnesses . . . [and] I took the evidence of the purchase, both that which was sealed

. . . and that which was open: I gave the evidence unto Baruch . . in the sight of Hanameel and in the presence of witnesses that subscribed the book of the purchase, before all . . . that sat in the court . . . and I charged Baruch before them saying . . . take these evidences . . . both which is sealed . . . and this evidence which is open; and put them in an earthen vessel, that they may continue many days."

Under the law today the subject of sales is governed by statute.

THE BIBLICAL LAW

As a nail sticketh fast between the joinings of the stones; so doth sin stick close between buying and selling.

Ecclesiasticus 27:2

If thy brother be waxen poor, and hath sold away some of his possession, and if any of his kin come to redeem it, then shall he redeem that which his brother sold. *Leviticus 25:25*

The land shall not be sold forever: for the land is mine; for ye are strangers and sojourners with me. *Leviticus 25:23*

. . . in all land of your possession ye shall grant a redemption for the land. *Leviticus 25:24*

And I bought the field of Hanameel . . . and weighed him the money, even seventeen shekels of silver. And I subscribed the evidence (deed) and sealed it, and took witnesses, and weighed him the money in the balances. So I took the evidence of the purchase, both that which was sealed according to the law and custom . . . And I gave the evidence of the purchase unto Baruch . . . in the sight of Hanameel . . . and in the presence of the witnesses that subscribed the book of the purchase . . . and I charged Baruch before them saying . . . take these evidences . . . of the purchase, both which is sealed, and . . . which is open; and put them in an earthen vessel, that they may continue many days.

Jeremiah 32:9-14

He is a merchant, the balances of deceit are in his hand . . .

Hosea 12:7

. . . no devoted thing, that a man shall devote unto the Lord of all that he hath, both of man and beast, and of the field of his possession, shall be sold. . . . *Leviticus 27:28*

. . . Thy money perish with thee, because thou hast thought that the gift of God may be purchased with money. *Acts 8:20*

If thou buy an Hebrew servant, six years he shall serve: and in the seventh he shall go out free for nothing. *Exodus 21:2*

And if a man sell his daughter to be a maidservant, she shall not go out as the menservants do.

If she please not her master . . . then shall he let her be redeemed. *Exodus 21:7, 8*

He that withholdeth corn, the people shall curse him: but blessings shall be upon the head of him that selleth it.

Proverbs 11:26

And there was great famine in Samaria's and, behold . . . an ass's head was sold for fourscore pieces of silver and the fourth part of a cab of dove's dung for five pieces of silver.

2 Kings 6:25

. . . they were thy merchants: they traded the person of men and vessels of brass in thy market. *Ezekiel 27:13*

Esau came from the field and he was faint. And Esau said to Jacob, feed me . . . for I am faint. And Jacob said swear to me this day; and he swore unto him: and he sold his birthright to Jacob. Then Jacob gave Esau bread and pottage of lentils.

Genesis 25:29, 34

Solomon had a vineyard . . . he let out the vineyard unto keepers; every one for the fruit thereof was to bring a thousand pieces of silver. *Song of Solomon 8:11*

And if thou sell aught unto thy neighbor, or buyest aught of thy neighbor's hand, ye shall not oppress one another.

Leviticus 25:14

SURETY

MOST STATE LAWS define surety or guarantor as one who promises to answer for the debt, default, or miscarriage of another, or hypothecates property as security therefor. The obligation of a surety or guarantor arises only where there is a principal debtor. If there is no primary liability on the part of a third person, either express or implied, that is, if there is no debt, default or miscarriage, present or prospective, there is nothing to guarantee and there can be no contract of surety. Contracts of surety and contracts of guarantee were formerly separate and distinct matters but of late years they have been used as one synonymous term.

The laws of surety in the Bible are more than laws in the technical sense. They are philosophical directives pointing out the pitfalls when becoming surety, and at times justifying the act under specified conditions.

And Judah said unto Israel his father, send the lad with me . . . I will be surety for him; of my hand shalt thou require him: if I bring him not unto thee, and set him before thee, let me bear the blame forever. *Genesis 48:8, 9*

If he hath wronged thee, or oweth thee aught, put that on mine account . . . I will repay it. *Philemon 18, 19*

. . . if thou be surety for thy friend . . . thou art snared with the words of thy mouth. . . . *Proverbs 6:1, 2*

Be not one of them that . . . are sureties for debts.
Proverbs 22:26

Be not surety above thy power: for if thou be surety, take care to pay it. *Ecclesiasticus 8:13*

Forget not the friendship of thy surety, for he has given his life for thee: *Ecclesiasticus 29:15*

Suretyship hath undone many of good estate, and shaken them as a wave of the sea: mighty men hath it driven from their houses, so that they wandered among strange nations.
Ecclesiasticus 29:18

A man void of understanding striketh hands, and becometh surety in the presence of his friends. *Proverbs 17:18*

An honest man is surety for his neighbor: but he that is impudent will forsake him. *Ecclesiasticus 29:14*

A sinner will overthrow the good estate of his surety: and he that is of an unthankful mind will leave him [in danger] that delivered him. *Ecclesiasticus 29:16, 17*

THEFT

AMONG THE Babylonians, larceny, under certain circumstances, was a crime punishable by death. Among the Athenians, and until a comparatively recent date in England, theft was a capital crime. Sir William Blackstone in his Commentaries, writes: "Our ancient Saxon laws nominally punished theft with death, if above the value of twelve pence; but the criminal was permitted to redeem his life by a pecuniary ransom; as, among their ancestors the Germans, by a stated number of cattle. But in the ninth year of Henry the First, this power of redemption was taken away, and all persons guilty of larceny above the value of twelve pence were directed to be hanged; which law continues in force to this day." Only as recently as the reign of George IV was capital punishment abolished for larceny in England.

Under the Biblical law, offenses committed against property were punishable only by a fine. In the case of larceny, the offender had to pay double the amount stolen: "If the theft be found in his possession alive, whether it be an ox, or ass, or a sheep, and kill it, he shall pay five oxen for an ox and four sheep for a sheep."

THE BIBLICAL LAW

Thou shalt not steal. *Exodus 20:15*

Whoso is partner with a thief hateth his own soul. . . .
Proverbs 29:24

. . . for everyone that stealeth shall be cut off. . . .
Zechariah 5:3

. . . it is not lawful to eat anything that is stolen. *Tobit 2:13*

Men do not despise a thief, if he steal to satisfy his soul when he is hungry. *Proverbs 6:30*

Ye shall not steal, neither deal falsely. . . .
Leviticus 19:11

Then were there two thieves crucified with him . . .
Matthew 27:38

But if he [a thief] be found, he shall restore sevenfold . . .
Proverbs 6:31

If the theft be certainly found in his hand . . . he shall restore double. *Exodus 22:4*

If a man shall steal an ox, or a sheep, and kill it or sell it; he shall restore five oxen for an ox, and four sheep for a sheep.
Exodus 22:1

If a man shall deliver unto his neighbor money or stuff to keep, and it be stolen out of the man's house; if the thief be found, let him pay double. *Exodus 22:7*

. . . the day of the Lord so cometh as a thief in the night.
1 Thessalonians 5:2

TRESPASS

ANY UNLAWFUL interference with the property of another, or exercise of domain over it by which the owner is damnified is trespass. The basis of the offense is the injury to the complainant or to personal property in his possession.

In the common law trespass was limited to a direct invasion of property. In our law today, direct or indirect invasion of property is trespass, and may be committed by inconsequential and indirect injuries, as well as by direct and forcible injuries. The trespass must be intentional, or the result of recklessness or neglect, or the result of extra-hazardous activity.

Entry upon the lands of another, or into his house, may be a trespass. Entering a man's home without his permission, or the doing of any wilful act whether damaging or not is a violation of the law.

Trespass is an intentional harm, and for that reason there must be an intentional act done.

In the Bible a trespass is any transgression or offense against another. The trespass of today is a different offense than in Biblical days. Then trespass was committed if a man came "into the standing corn of thy neighbor, then thou mayest pluck the ears with thine hand; but thou shalt not move a sickle unto thy neighbor's standing corn."

In the early Biblical days one who felt he had been harmed sought vengeance on the cause of his harm, whether man or beast; often beasts such as cattle were killed because they injured a man or his property.

There is a form of trespass called malicious mischief by which another's property is damaged or destroyed. The Bible condemns all such acts, and cautions man not to trap his fellow but to be mindful of the danger of seeking another's downfall.

The Mosaic rule against unguarded excavations is the same as our law today. It provided then and it does now that it is negligence to leave open a pit wherein a person or animal may fall.

THE BIBLICAL LAW

For all manner of trespass, whether it be for ox, for ass, for sheep, for rainment, or for any manner of lost thing, which another challenges to be his, the cause of both parties shall come before the judges and whom the judges shall condemn, he shall pay double unto his neighbor. *Exodus 22:9*

Cursed be he that smiteth his neighbor secretly.
Deuteronomy 27:24

Lay hands suddenly on no man . . . *1 Timothy 6:22*

. . . if men strive together, and one smite another with a stone, or with his fist, and he die not, but keepeth his bed: if he rise again, and walk abroad upon his staff, then shall he that smote him be quit: only he shall pay for the loss of his time, and shall cause him to be thoroughly healed. *Exodus 21:18, 19*

If men strive and hurt a woman with child, so that her fruit depart from her, and yet no mischief follow; he shall . . . pay as the judges determine. *Exodus 21:22*

If fire break out, and catch in thorns, so that the stacks of corn, or the standing corn, or the field, be consumed therewith; he that kindled the fire shall surely make restitution. *Exodus 22:6*

Withdraw thy foot from thy neighbor's house lest he be weary of thee. . . , *Proverbs 25:17*

Remove not the old landmark; and enter not unto the fields of the fatherless. *Proverbs 23:10*

If a man shall cause a field or vineyard to be eaten, and shall put in his beast, and shall feed in another man's field; of the best of his own field, and of the best of his own vineyard, shall he make restitution. *Exodus 22:5*

When thou comest into thy neighbor's vineyard, then thou mayest eat grapes thy fill at thine own pleasure; but thou shalt not put any in thy vessel. When thou comest into the standing corn of thy neighbor, then thou mayest pluck the ears with thine hand; but thou shalt not move a sickle unto thy neighbor's standing corn. *Deuteronomy 23:24, 25*

Wicked man . . .. deviseth mischief continually.
Proverbs 6:12, 14

Thou shalt not . . . put a stumbling block before the blind . . .
Leviticus 19:14

And if a man shall open a pit, or . . . dig a pit, and not cover it, and an ox or an ass fall therein, the owner of the pit shall make it good. *Exodus 21:33, 34*

Woe to them that . . . take [fields] by violence . . .
Micah 22:1, 2

. . . forgive, I pray thee now, the trespass of thy brethren.
Genesis 50:17

. . . he shall recompense his trespass with the principal thereof, and add unto it the fifth part thereof . . . *Numbers 5:7*

. . . we have wronged no man, we have corrupted no man, we have defrauded no man. *2 Corinthians 7:2*

The wicked . . . deviseth mischief upon his bed . . .
Psalms 36:1, 4

. . . a wicked man . . . deviseth mischief continually . . .
Proverbs 6:12, 14

Whoso diggeth a pit shall fall therein: and he that setteth a trap shall be taken therein. *Ecclesiasticus 27:26*

WEIGHTS, MEASURES, TIME, AND MONEY

THE BIBLICAL DAY was reckoned from evening to evening (Leviticus 23:32), a custom arising from the use of the Lunar months. The day was divided into morning, noon and evening.

Later, time was indicated by hours, the day consisting of twelve hours from sunrise to sunset, while the night was divided into three watches, the first, from sunset to midnight, the second, from midnight to cock-crow, the third from cock-crow to sunrise. The Romans divided the night into four watches.

The week consisted of seven days which were numbered with the exception of the seventh which was named the Sabbath.

The month was lunar (Genesis 1:14), as seen from the observance of the day of the new moon by special offerings to the Lord (Numbers 10:10), the Passover season coinciding with the full moon.

The year began in the spring with the month Abib that answered to a part of our March and April. This was the sacred year, and the annual festivals were directly related to the agricultural seasons. Thus Pentecost or Feast of Weeks occurred in Sivan (May-June), the feast of Ingathering, first-fruits of wine and oil, in Ethanim (September-October).

There was also a civil year beginning in the autumn with the month of Ethanim, hence the Jewish civil New Year's day in the fall and the commemoration of the Feast of Trumpets, Day of Atonement, Feast of Tabernacles. It was useful for a people devoted to agriculture to commence the year with the season of ploughing and sowing, and to close it with the harvest.

Our knowledge of Biblical weights and measure is incomplete and authorities differ as to values and quantities. Gold and silver were used as standards of value, and weights were estimated according to the number of grains of barley, taken from the middle of the ear, to which they were equivalent.

In the Old Testament, shekels, mina, talent, etc., signify a certain weight of metal. After the captivity it was Simon Maccabees (about 139 B.C.) who minted the first Hebrew coins. These consisted of copper, silver, gold, and later foreign coins, Greek Persian and Roman were in use in the Holy Land.

The chief unit was the shekel—weight. This was the principal weight by which others were regulated, and was subdivided into the bekah, half shekel, or half weight. The talent, or kikkar, was the largest weight for metals used by the Hebrews, both of gold and silver.

The purchasing power of money in Biblical times was probably more than a hundred and fifty times as great as at present. A Roman penny (about 17 cents) was considered fair compensation for a day's labor. Authorities have computed that the gift of the Queen of Sheba to King Solomon amounted to over one million dollars, while Judas received thirty pieces of silver ($17.00) for the betrayal of Jesus.

The hand was used for determining measurements—finger, palm, span and forearm. The smallest measure among the Hebrews was the breadth of the human finger. The palm or handbreadth was the breadth of four fingers—from three to three and a half inches. The span signifies the distance from the point of the thumb to the point of the little finger when stretched as far as possible. The cubit was the distance from the elbow to the end of the middle finger—about eighteen inches. The measuring reed was the "sweet cane (Ezekiel 40:3, 5; 42:15, 16)." It was equal to six cubits, or about nine and a half to ten feet. Reference to these measuring methods is also to be found in Genesis 6, Exodus 25 and Acts 27.

Dry measure was divided into cab, omer, seah and ephah. The word cab occurs only in II Kings 6:25, and the word omer only in Exodus 16:16-36, while ephah of Egyptian origin occurs frequently and in capacity was equivalent to the liquid measure—bath. The cab was a little more than a quart, and the omer two quarts. The ephah equalled about three pecks.

In liquid measure the log is the smallest of the biblical series. Log originally meant a basin. The word hin, of Egyptian origin is the equal of twelve logs. The word bath is first mentioned in I Kings 7:26 and is the largest of the liquid measures. In quantity it is equal to the Ephah. The log was about two-thirds of a pint, and the bath about five gallons.

THE BIBLICAL LAW

Divers weights, and divers measures, both of them are alike abomination to the Lord. *Proverbs 20:10*

. . . the scant measure . . . is abominable. Shall I count them pure with the wicked balances, and with the bag of deceitful weights? *Micah 6:10, 11*

A false balance is abomination to the Lord; but a just weight is his delight. *Proverbs 11:1*

Ye shall do no unrighteousness in judgment, in meteyard, in weight, or in measure. Just balances [and] just weights shall ye have. *Leviticus 19:35, 36*

Of these things be not thou ashamed . . . of exactness of balances and weights. *Ecclesiasticus 42:1, 4*

Thou shalt not have in thy bag divers weights, a great and a small. But thou shalt have a perfect and just weight, a perfect and just measure shalt thou have. *Deuteronomy 25:13, 15*

. . . with what measure ye mete, it shall be measured to you again. *Matthew 7:2*

. . . Thou art weighed in the balances, and art found wanting. *Daniel 5:27*

WILLS

A WILL is an instrument for the disposition of one's property to take effect after death. It is the declaration of a man's intentions which he wills to be performed after his death concerning the disposition of his property, and the manner of handling such other matters as he may direct.

There is nothing which so generally strikes the imagination as the sole and despotic dominion which one man claims and exercises over the external things of the world, in total exclusion of the right of any other individual.

However, the most effectual way of abandoning property is by the death of the owner, when both the actual possession and intention of keeping possession ceasing, the property which is founded upon such possession and intention ought also to cease. But as governments are calculated for the peace of mankind, it is the universal law of almost every nation to give the dying person a power of continuing his property by disposing of his possessions by will.

Biblical law provides that the property possessed by man at the time of death should pass to his son or sons to the exclusion of daughters. In early American law, property was equally divided among the children; both sons and daughters.

The rules of succession are not overlooked in the law of Moses. Even as today, the succession follows rules which cannot be waived or altered.

There are Biblical deviations from the fixed rules. In one instance, a man left five daughters and no son, and the daughters petitioned Moses that their father's property be awarded to them. This Moses granted on the ground that the name of their father would otherwise be done away with (Numbers 27:4). Thereafter, the Elders of Gilead sought a ruling as to what should be done on the marriage of the five daughters so as to prevent their inheritance from passing to another tribe. Moses then ruled that the daughters could marry whomever they thought best, but such marriage must be only to the family of the tribe of their fathers (Numbers 36:6, 7, 8 and 9).

In Biblical times there was no knowledge or use of wills as we understand them today. Each person who had property would give it to the heirs before death whenever possible; otherwise, it descended according to the Mosaic laws of succession.

The oldest written will of which we have any knowledge was made in Egypt about 2,500 years B.C. There is no evidence of any written wills being used in Israel. Because each tribe controlled the assets of all its members, there was no necessity for documents of conveyance or inheritance.

THE BIBLICAL LAW

. . . where a testament is, there must also of necessity be the death of the testator. For a testament is of force after men are dead: otherwise it is of no strength at all while the testator liveth.

Hebrews 9:16, 17

Is it now lawful for me to do what I will with mine own?

Matthew 20:15

. . . set thine house in order: for thou shalt die. . . .

Isaiah 38:1

A good man leaveth an inheritance . . . *Proverbs 33:22*

. . . If a man die, and have no son then ye shall cause his inheritance to pass unto his daughter. And if he have no daughter, then ye shall give his inheritance unto his brethren. And if he have no brethren, then ye shall give his inheritance unto his father's brethren. And if his father have no brethren, then ye shall give his inheritance unto his kinsman that is next to him of his family, and he shall possess it. . . . *Numbers 27:8, 9, 10, 11*

And every daughter, that possesseth an inheritance in any tribe of the children of Israel, shall be wife unto one of the family of the tribe of her father, that the children of Israel may enjoy every man the inheritance of his father. Neither shall the inheritance remove from one tribe to another tribe; but every one of the tribes of the children of Israel shall keep himself to his own inheritance. *Numbers 36:8, 9*

A good man leaveth an inheritance to his children's children.

Proverbs 13:22

. . . but he that shall come forth out of thine own bowels shall be thine heir. *Genesis 15:4*

Thou shalt not inherit in our father's house; for thou art the son of a strange woman. *Judges 11:2*

At the time when thou shalt end thy days, and finish thy life, distribute thine inheritance. *Ecclesiasticus 33:23*

WOMAN

In a generic sense the word woman means the female part of the human race. In Biblical times women had little or no equality with man. She was under his supervision and control and from birth was taught her secondary position in the scheme of life. She could not own property nor could she inherit except by special dispensation of the tribal head, or as in Mosaic days, by special decree of Moses.

The word woman comes from the English Saxon word, wiman in the Saxon, i.e. wife, and sometimes it is by the Saxons derived from wamb, or wombe-man.

The Bible has a different reason for calling the female woman. As written in Genesis 2: "And the Lord caused a deep sleep to fall upon Adam and he slept: and he took one of his ribs and closed up the flesh instead thereof; and the rib which the Lord God had taken from man, made he a woman, and brought her into the man. And Adam said, This is now bone of my bones, and flesh of my flesh: she shall be called Woman, because she was taken out of man."

As late as the New Testament, St. Paul said: "Let your women keep silence in the churches; for it is not permitted unto them to speak; but they are commanded to be under obedience. . . ."

Hundreds of years would pass until woman would be recognized as man's equal. Wars and the economy of the world brought about the equality of the sexes, but at an awful price. The calm reserve of woman has been displaced by the anxiety of equal opportunity, and the respectful seclusion of the female sex has been displaced by the hardness of competitive existence.

In the history of the Hebrew people there have been but two women who governed their country: Jezebel's daughter Athalia who ruled Judea from 842 to 836 B.C., and Queen Salome Alexandra, who succeeded to the throne after the death of her husband in 76 B.C.

THE BIBLICAL LAW

Forego not a wise and good woman: for her grace is above gold. *Ecclesiasticus 7:19*

. . . that women adorn themselves in modest apparel, with shamefacedness and sobriety; not with braided hair, or gold, or pearls, or costly array; but (which becometh women professing godliness) with good works. *1 Timothy 2:9, 10*

Let women learn in silence with all subjection. *1 Timothy 2:11*

. . . let it not be that outward adorning of plaiting the hair, and of wearing of gold, or of putting on of apparel; but let be the hidden man of the heart . . . For after this manner in the old time the holy women also, who trusted in God, adorned themselves, being in subjection unto their own husbands. *1 Peter 3:3, 4, 5*

But I suffer not a woman to teach, nor to usurp authority over the man, but to be in silence. *1 Timothy 2:12*

Let your women keep silence in the churches; for it is not permitted unto them to speak; but they are commanded to be under obedience . . . *1 Corinthians 14:34*

And if they [women] will learn anything, let them ask their husbands at home: for it is a shame for women to speak in the church. *1 Corinthians 14:35*

The aged women likewise, that they be in behavior as becomes holiness, nor false accusers, not given to much wine, teachers of good things; that they may teach the young women to be sober, to love their husbands, to love their children, to be discreet, chaste, keepers at home, good, obedient to their own husbands . . . *Titus 2:2, 3, 4, 5*

All wickedness is but little to the wickedness of a women . . . *Ecclesiasticus 25:19*

As a jewel of gold in a swine's snout, so is a fair woman which is without discretion. *Proverbs 11:22*

An evil wife is a yoke shaken to and fro: he that hath hold of her is as though he held a scorpion. *Ecclesiasticus 26:7*

A drunken woman and a gadder abroad causeth great anger, and she will not cover her own shame. *Ecclesiasticus 26:8*

Give the water no passage; neither a wicked woman liberty to gad abroad. *Ecclesiasticus 25:25*

Thou shalt not approach unto a woman to uncover her nakedness, as long as she is put aside for her uncleanness (menstruation). *Leviticus 18:19*

And if a man shall lie with a woman having her sickness . . . both of them shall be cut off from among their people.
Leviticus 20:18

The woman also with whom man shall lie with seed of copulation, they shall both bathe themselves in water, and be unclean until the even. *Leviticus 15:18*

The woman shall not wear that which pertaineth unto man. . . .
Deuteronomy 22:5

The tender and delicate woman among you, which would not adventure to set the sole of her foot upon the ground for delicateness and tenderness, her eye shall be evil toward the husband of her bosom, and toward her son, and toward her daughter.
Deuteronomy 28:56

I will therefore that the younger women marry, bear children, guide the house, give none occasion to the adversary to speak reproachfully. *1 Timothy 5:14*

The whoredom of a woman may be known in her haughty looks and eyelids. *Ecclesiasticus 26:9*

acte étant nécessairement antérieur à l'autre est le vrai fondement de la société.

En effet, s'il n'y avait point de convention antérieure, où serait, à moins que l'élection ne fût unanime, l'obligation pour le petit nombre de se soumettre au choix du grand, et d'où cent qui veulent un maître ont-ils le droit de voter pour dix qui n'en veulent point ? La loi de la pluralité des suffrages est elle-même un établissement de convention, et suppose au moins une fois l'unanimité.

Chapitre VI
DU PACTE SOCIAL

Je suppose les hommes parvenus à ce point où les obstacles qui nuisent à leur conservation dans l'état de nature l'emportent par leur résistance sur les forces que chaque individu peut employer pour se maintenir dans cet état. Alors cet état primitif ne peut plus subsister, et le genre humain périrait s'il ne changeait sa manière d'être.

Or comme les hommes ne peuvent engendrer de nouvelles forces, mais seulement unir et diriger celles qui existent, ils n'ont plus d'autre moyen, pour se conserver, que de former par agrégation une somme de forces qui puisse l'emporter sur la résistance, de les mettre en jeu par un seul mobile et de les faire agir de concert.

Cette somme de forces ne peut naître que du concours de plusieurs ; mais la force et la liberté de chaque homme étant les premiers instruments de sa conservation, comment les engagera-t-il sans se nuire, et sans négliger les soins qu'il se doit ? Cette difficulté ramenée à mon sujet peut s'énoncer en ces termes :

« Trouver une forme d'association qui défende et protège de toute la force commune la personne et les

cessant d'être ennemis ou instruments de l'ennemi, ils redeviennent simplement hommes et l'on n'a plus de droit sur leur vie. Quelquefois on peut tuer l'État sans tuer un seul de ses membres. Or la guerre ne donne aucun droit qui ne soit nécessaire à sa fin. Ces principes ne sont pas ceux de Grotius ; ils ne sont pas fondés sur des autorités de poètes, mais ils dérivent de la nature des choses, et sont fondés sur la raison.

À l'égard du droit de conquête, il n'a d'autre fondement que la loi du plus fort. Si la guerre ne donne point au vainqueur le droit de massacrer les peuples vaincus, ce droit qu'il n'a pas ne peut fonder celui de les asservir. On n'a le droit de tuer l'ennemi que quand on ne peut le faire esclave ; le droit de le faire esclave ne vient donc pas du droit de le tuer. C'est donc un échange inique de lui faire acheter au prix de sa liberté sa vie sur laquelle on n'a aucun droit. En établissant le droit de vie et de mort sur le droit d'esclavage, et le droit d'esclavage sur le droit de vie et de mort, n'est-il pas clair qu'on tombe dans le cercle vicieux ?

En supposant même ce terrible droit de tout tuer, je dis qu'un esclave fait à la guerre ou un peuple conquis n'est tenu à rien du tout envers son maître, qu'à lui obéir autant qu'il y est forcé. En prenant un équivalent à sa vie, le vainqueur ne lui en a point fait grâce : au lieu de le tuer sans fruit, il l'a tué utilement. Loin donc qu'il ait acquis sur lui nulle autorité jointe à la force, l'état de guerre subsiste entre eux comme auparavant, leur relation même en est l'effet, et l'usage du droit de la guerre ne suppose aucun traité de paix. Ils ont fait une convention ; soit, mais cette convention, loin de détruire l'état de guerre, en suppose la continuité.

Ainsi, de quelque sens qu'on envisage les choses, le droit d'esclavage est nul, non seulement parce qu'il est illégitime, mais parce qu'il est absurde et ne signi-

biens de chaque associé, et par laquelle chacun s'unissant à tous n'obéisse pourtant qu'à lui-même et reste aussi libre qu'auparavant. » Tel est le problème fondamental dont le contrat social donne la solution.

Les clauses de ce contrat sont tellement déterminées par la nature de l'acte, que la moindre modification les rendrait vaines et de nul effet ; en sorte que, bien qu'elles n'aient peut-être jamais été formellement énoncées, elles sont partout les mêmes, partout tacitement admises et reconnues ; jusqu'à ce que, le pacte social étant violé, chacun rentre alors dans ses premiers droits et reprenne sa liberté naturelle, en perdant la liberté conventionnelle pour laquelle il y renonça.

Ces clauses bien entendues se réduisent toutes à une seule, savoir l'aliénation totale de chaque associé avec tous ses droits à toute la communauté : car, premièrement, chacun se donnant tout entier, la condition est égale pour tous, et la condition étant égale pour tous, nul n'a intérêt de la rendre onéreuse aux autres.

De plus, l'aliénation se faisant sans réserve, l'union est aussi parfaite qu'elle peut l'être et nul associé n'a plus rien à réclamer. Car s'il restait quelques droits aux particuliers, comme il n'y aurait aucun supérieur commun qui pût prononcer entre eux et le public, chacun étant en quelque point son propre juge prétendrait bientôt l'être en tous, l'état de nature subsisterait, et l'association deviendrait nécessairement tyrannique ou vaine.

Enfin chacun se donnant à tous ne se donne à personne, et comme il n'y a pas un associé sur lequel on n'acquière le même droit qu'on lui cède sur soi, on gagne l'équivalent de tout ce qu'on perd, et plus de force pour conserver ce qu'on a.

Si donc on écarte du pacte social ce qui n'est pas de son essence[15], on trouvera qu'il se réduit aux termes suivants. *Chacun de nous met en commun sa personne et toute sa puissance sous la suprême direction de la volonté générale; et nous recevons en corps chaque membre comme partie indivisible du tout*[16].

À l'instant, au lieu de la personne particulière de chaque contractant, cet acte d'association produit un corps moral et collectif composé d'autant de membres que l'assemblée a de voix, lequel reçoit de ce même acte son unité, son *moi* commun, sa vie et sa volonté[17]. Cette personne publique qui se forme ainsi par l'union de toutes les autres prenait autrefois le nom de *cité**, et prend maintenant celui de *république* ou de *corps politique*, lequel est appelé par ses membres *État* quand il est passif, *souverain* quand il est actif, *puissance* en le comparant à ses semblables. À l'égard des associés ils prennent collectivement le nom de *peuple*, et s'appellent en particulier *citoyens* comme participants à l'autorité souveraine, et *sujets* comme soumis aux lois de l'État.

---

* Le vrai sens de ce mot s'est presque entièrement effacé chez les modernes : la plupart prennent une ville pour une cité et un bourgeois pour un citoyen. Ils ne savent pas que les maisons font la ville mais que les citoyens font la cité. Cette même erreur coûta cher autrefois aux Carthaginois. Je n'ai pas lu que le titre de *cives* ait jamais été donné aux sujets d'aucun prince, pas même anciennement aux Macédoniens, ni de nos jours aux Anglais, quoique plus près de la liberté que tous les autres. Les seuls Français prennent tout familièrement ce nom de *citoyens*, parce qu'ils n'en ont aucune véritable idée, comme on peut le voir dans leurs dictionnaires, sans quoi ils tomberaient en l'usurpant dans le crime de lèse-majesté : ce nom chez eux exprime une vertu et non pas un droit. Quand Bodin a voulu parler de nos citoyens et bourgeois, il a fait une lourde bévue en prenant les uns pour les autres. M. d'Alembert ne s'y est pas trompé, et a bien distingué, dans son article *Genève*, les quatre ordres d'hommes (même cinq, en y comptant les simples étrangers) qui sont dans notre ville, et dont deux seulement composent la république. Nul autre auteur français, que je sache, n'a compris le vrai sens du mot *citoyen*.

Mais ces termes se confondent souvent et se prennent l'un pour l'autre; il suffit de les savoir distinguer quand ils sont employés dans toute leur précision.

Chapitre VII
DU SOUVERAIN

On voit par cette formule que l'acte d'association renferme un engagement réciproque du public avec les particuliers, et que chaque individu, contractant, pour ainsi dire, avec lui-même, se trouve engagé sous un double rapport : savoir, comme membre du souverain envers les particuliers, et comme membre de l'État envers le souverain[18]. Mais on ne peut appliquer ici la maxime du droit civil que nul n'est tenu aux engagements pris avec lui-même; car il y a bien de la différence entre s'obliger envers soi, ou envers un tout dont on fait partie.

Il faut remarquer encore que la délibération publique, qui peut obliger tous les sujets envers le souverain, à cause des deux différents rapports sous lesquels chacun d'eux est envisagé, ne peut, par la raison contraire, obliger le souverain envers lui-même, et que, par conséquent, il est contre la nature du corps politique que le souverain s'impose une loi qu'il ne puisse enfreindre. Ne pouvant se considérer que sous un seul et même rapport, il est alors dans le cas d'un particulier contractant avec soi-même; par où l'on voit qu'il n'y a ni ne peut y avoir nulle espèce de loi fondamentale obligatoire pour le corps du peuple, pas même le contrat social. Ce qui ne signifie pas que ce corps ne puisse fort bien s'engager envers autrui en ce qui ne déroge point à ce contrat; car, à l'égard de l'étranger, il devient un être simple, un individu.

Mais le corps politique ou le souverain ne tirant son être que de la sainteté du contrat ne peut jamais s'obliger, même envers autrui, à rien qui déroge à cet acte primitif, comme d'aliéner quelque portion de lui-même ou de se soumettre à un autre souverain. Violer l'acte par lequel il existe serait s'anéantir, et ce qui n'est rien ne produit rien.

Sitôt que cette multitude est ainsi réunie en un corps, on ne peut offenser un des membres sans attaquer le corps ; encore moins offenser le corps sans que les membres s'en ressentent. Ainsi le devoir et l'intérêt obligent également les deux parties contractantes à s'entraider mutuellement, et les mêmes hommes doivent chercher à réunir sous ce double rapport tous les avantages qui en dépendent.

Or, le souverain n'étant formé que des particuliers qui le composent n'a ni ne peut avoir d'intérêt contraire au leur ; par conséquent la puissance souveraine n'a nul besoin de garant envers les sujets, parce qu'il est impossible que le corps veuille nuire à tous ses membres ; et nous verrons ci-après qu'il ne peut nuire à aucun en particulier. Le souverain, par cela seul qu'il est, est toujours tout ce qu'il doit être.

Mais il n'en est pas ainsi des sujets envers le souverain, auquel malgré l'intérêt commun rien ne répondrait de leurs engagements s'il ne trouvait des moyens de s'assurer de leur fidélité.

En effet chaque individu peut comme homme avoir une volonté particulière contraire ou dissemblable à la volonté générale qu'il a comme citoyen. Son intérêt particulier peut lui parler tout autrement que l'intérêt commun ; son existence absolue et naturellement indépendante peut lui faire envisager ce qu'il doit à la cause commune comme une contribution gratuite, dont la perte sera moins nuisible aux autres que le payement n'en est onéreux pour lui, et regardant la personne morale qui constitue l'État comme un être de raison parce que ce n'est pas un homme, il jouirait des droits du citoyen sans vouloir remplir les devoirs du sujet, injustice dont le progrès causerait la ruine du corps politique.

Afin donc que le pacte social ne soit pas un vain formulaire, il renferme tacitement cet engagement qui seul peut donner de la force aux autres, que quiconque refusera d'obéir à la volonté générale y sera contraint par tout le corps : ce qui ne signifie autre chose sinon qu'on le forcera d'être libre; car telle est la condition qui donnant chaque citoyen à la patrie le garantit de toute dépendance personnelle; condition qui fait l'artifice et le jeu de la machine politique, et qui seule rend légitimes les engagements civils, lesquels sans cela seraient absurdes, tyranniques, et sujets aux plus énormes abus.

Chapitre VIII
DE L'ÉTAT CIVIL

Ce passage de l'état de nature à l'état civil produit dans l'homme un changement très remarquable, en substituant dans sa conduite la justice à l'instinct, et donnant à ses actions la moralité[19] qui leur manquait auparavant. C'est alors seulement que la voix du devoir succédant à l'impulsion physique et le droit à l'appétit, l'homme, qui jusque-là n'avait regardé que lui-même, se voit forcé d'agir sur d'autres principes, et de consulter sa raison avant d'écouter ses penchants. Quoiqu'il se prive dans cet état de plusieurs avantages qu'il tient de la nature, il en regagne de si grands, ses facultés s'exercent et se développent, ses idées s'étendent, ses sentiments s'ennoblissent, son âme tout entière s'élève à tel point, que si les abus de cette nouvelle condition ne le dégradaient souvent au-dessous de celle dont il est sorti, il devrait bénir sans cesse l'instant heureux qui l'en arracha pour jamais, et qui, d'un animal stupide et borné, fit un être intelligent et un homme.

Réduisons toute cette balance à des termes faciles à comparer. Ce que l'homme perd par le contrat social, c'est sa liberté naturelle et un droit illimité à tout ce qui le tente et qu'il peut atteindre ; ce qu'il gagne, c'est la liberté civile et la propriété de tout ce qu'il possède. Pour ne pas se tromper dans ces compensations, il faut bien distinguer la liberté naturelle qui n'a pour bornes que les forces de l'individu, de la liberté civile qui est limitée par la volonté générale, et la possession qui n'est que l'effet de la force ou le droit du premier occupant, de la propriété qui ne peut être fondée que sur un titre positif.

On pourrait sur ce qui précède ajouter à l'acquis de l'état civil la liberté morale, qui seule rend l'homme vraiment maître de lui ; car l'impulsion du seul appétit est esclavage, et l'obéissance à la loi qu'on s'est prescrite est liberté. Mais je n'en ai déjà que trop dit sur cet article, et le sens philosophique du mot *liberté* n'est pas ici de mon sujet.

Chapitre IX

DU DOMAINE RÉEL[20]

Chaque membre de la communauté se donne à elle au moment qu'elle se forme, tel qu'il se trouve actuellement, lui et toutes ses forces dont les biens qu'il possède font partie. Ce n'est pas que par cet acte la possession change de nature en changeant de mains, et devienne propriété dans celles du souverain ; mais comme les forces de la cité sont incomparablement plus grandes que celles d'un particulier, la possession publique est aussi dans le fait plus forte et plus irrévocable, sans être plus légitime, au moins pour les étrangers. Car l'État à l'égard de ses membres est maître de tous leurs biens par le contrat social, qui dans l'État sert de base à tous les droits ; mais il ne l'est à l'égard des autres puissances que par le droit de premier occupant qu'il tient des particuliers.

Le droit de premier occupant, quoique plus réel que celui du plus fort, ne devient un vrai droit qu'après l'établissement de celui de propriété. Tout homme a naturellement droit à tout ce qui lui est nécessaire ; mais l'acte positif qui le rend propriétaire de quelque bien l'exclut de tout le reste. Sa part étant faite, il doit s'y borner, et n'a plus aucun droit à la communauté. Voilà pourquoi le droit de premier occupant, si faible dans l'état de nature, est respectable à tout homme civil. On respecte moins dans ce droit ce qui est à autrui que ce qui n'est pas à soi.

En général, pour autoriser sur un terrain quelconque le droit de premier occupant, il faut les conditions suivantes. Premièrement que ce terrain ne soit encore habité par personne ; secondement qu'on n'en occupe que la quantité dont on a besoin pour subsister ; en troisième lieu qu'on en prenne possession, non par une vaine cérémonie, mais par le travail et la culture, seul signe de propriété qui à défaut de titres juridiques doive être respecté d'autrui.

En effet, accorder au besoin et au travail le droit de premier occupant, n'est-ce pas l'étendre aussi loin qu'il peut aller ? Peut-on ne pas donner des bornes à ce droit ? Suffira-t-il de mettre le pied sur un terrain commun pour s'en prétendre aussitôt le maître ?

Suffira-t-il d'avoir la force d'en écarter un moment les autres hommes pour leur ôter le droit d'y jamais revenir ? Comment un homme ou un peuple peut-il s'emparer d'un territoire immense et en priver tout le genre humain autrement que par une usurpation punissable, puisqu'elle ôte au reste des hommes le séjour et les aliments que la nature leur donne en commun ? Quand Nuñez Balboa prenait sur le rivage possession de la mer du Sud et de toute l'Amérique méridionale au nom de la couronne de Castille, était-ce assez pour en déposséder tous les habitants et en exclure tous les princes du monde ? Sur ce pied-là, ces cérémonies se multipliaient assez vainement, et le roi catholique n'avait tout d'un coup qu'à prendre de son cabinet possession de tout l'univers ; sauf à retrancher ensuite de son empire ce qui était auparavant possédé par les autres princes.

On conçoit comment les terres des particuliers réunies et contiguës deviennent le territoire public, et comment le droit de souveraineté s'étendant des sujets au terrain qu'ils occupent devient à la fois réel et personnel ; ce qui met les possesseurs dans une plus grande dépendance, et fait de leurs forces mêmes les garants de leur fidélité. Avantage qui ne paraît pas avoir été bien senti des anciens monarques, qui, ne s'appelant que rois des Perses, des Scythes, des Macédoniens, semblaient se regarder comme les chefs des hommes plutôt que comme les maîtres du pays. Ceux d'aujourd'hui s'appellent plus habituellement rois de France, d'Espagne, d'Angleterre, etc. En tenant ainsi le terrain, ils sont bien sûrs d'en tenir les habitants.

Ce qu'il y a de singulier dans cette aliénation, c'est que, loin qu'en acceptant les biens des particuliers la communauté les en dépouille, elle ne fait que leur en assurer la légitime possession, changer l'usurpation en un véritable droit, et la jouissance en propriété.

Alors les possesseurs étant considérés comme dépositaires du bien public, leurs droits étant respectés de tous les membres de l'État et maintenus de toutes ses forces contre l'étranger, par une cession avantageuse au public et plus encore à eux-mêmes, ils ont, pour ainsi dire, acquis tout ce qu'ils ont donné. Paradoxe qui s'explique aisément par la distinction des droits que le souverain et le propriétaire ont sur le même fonds, comme on verra ci-après.

Il peut arriver aussi que les hommes commencent à s'unir avant que de rien posséder, et que, s'emparant ensuite d'un terrain suffisant pour tous, ils en jouissent en commun, ou qu'ils le partagent entre eux, soit également soit selon des proportions établies par le souverain. De quelque manière que se fasse cette acquisition, le droit que chaque particulier a sur son propre fonds est toujours subordonné au droit que la communauté a sur tous, sans quoi il n'y aurait ni solidité dans le lien social, ni force réelle dans l'exercice de la souveraineté.

Je terminerai ce chapitre et ce livre par une remarque qui doit servir de base à tout le système social ; c'est qu'au lieu de détruire l'égalité naturelle, le pacte fondamental substitue au contraire une égalité morale et légitime à ce que la nature avait pu mettre d'inégalité physique entre les hommes, et que, pouvant être inégaux en force ou en génie, ils deviennent tous égaux par convention et de droit*.

---

* Sous les mauvais gouvernements cette égalité n'est qu'apparente et illusoire ; elle ne sert qu'à maintenir le pauvre dans sa misère, et le riche dans son usurpation. Dans le fait, les lois sont toujours utiles à ceux qui possèdent et nuisibles à ceux qui n'ont rien : d'où il suit que l'état social n'est avantageux aux hommes qu'autant qu'ils ont tous quelque chose et qu'aucun d'eux n'a rien de trop.

LIVRE II

Chapitre I

QUE LA SOUVERAINETÉ EST INALIÉNABLE

La première et la plus importante conséquence des principes ci-devant établis est que la volonté générale peut seule diriger les forces de l'État selon la fin de son institution, qui est le bien commun ; car si l'opposition des intérêts particuliers a rendu nécessaire l'établissement des sociétés, c'est l'accord de ces mêmes intérêts qui l'a rendu possible. C'est ce qu'il y a de commun dans ces différents intérêts qui forme le lien social, et s'il n'y avait pas quelque point dans lequel tous les intérêts s'accordent, nulle société ne saurait exister. Or c'est uniquement sur cet intérêt commun que la société doit être gouvernée.

Je dis donc que la souveraineté n'étant que l'exercice de la volonté générale ne peut jamais s'aliéner, et que le souverain, qui n'est qu'un être collectif, ne peut être représenté que par lui-même : le pouvoir peut bien se transmettre, mais non pas la volonté[21].

En effet, s'il n'est pas impossible qu'une volonté particulière s'accorde sur quelque point avec la volonté générale, il est impossible au moins que cet accord soit durable et constant ; car la volonté particulière tend par sa nature aux préférences, et la volonté générale à l'égalité. Il est plus impossible encore qu'on ait un garant de cet accord quand même il devrait toujours exister ; ce ne serait pas un effet de l'art mais du hasard. Le souverain peut bien dire, je veux actuellement ce que veut un tel homme ou du moins ce qu'il dit vouloir ; mais il ne peut pas dire : ce que cet homme voudra demain, je le voudrai encore ; puisqu'il est absurde que la volonté se donne des chaînes pour l'avenir, et puisqu'il ne dépend d'aucune volonté de consentir à rien de contraire au bien de l'être qui veut. Si donc le peuple promet simplement d'obéir, il se dissout par cet acte, il perd sa qualité de peuple ; à l'instant qu'il y a un maître il n'y a plus de souverain, et dès lors le corps politique est détruit.

Ce n'est point à dire que les ordres des chefs ne puissent passer pour des volontés générales, tant que le souverain libre de s'y opposer ne le fait pas. En pareil cas, du silence universel on doit présumer le consentement du peuple. Ceci s'expliquera plus au long.

Chapitre II

QUE LA SOUVERAINETÉ EST INDIVISIBLE

Par la même raison que la souveraineté est inaliénable, elle est indivisible. Car la volonté est générale*, ou elle ne l'est pas ; elle est celle du corps du peuple, ou seulement d'une partie. Dans le premier cas cette volonté déclarée est un acte de souveraineté et fait loi. Dans le second, ce n'est qu'une volonté particulière, ou un acte de magistrature ; c'est un décret tout au plus.

* Pour qu'une volonté soit générale il n'est pas toujours nécessaire qu'elle soit unanime, mais il est nécessaire que toutes les voix soient comptées ; toute exclusion formelle rompt la généralité.

Mais nos politiques ne pouvant diviser la souveraineté dans son principe, la divisent dans son objet : ils la divisent en force et en volonté, en puissance législative et en puissance exécutive, en droits d'impôts, de justice et de guerre ; en administration intérieure et en pouvoir de traiter avec l'étranger : tantôt ils confondent toutes ces parties et tantôt ils les séparent. Ils font du souverain un être fantastique et formé de pièces rapportées ; c'est comme s'ils composaient l'homme de plusieurs corps, dont l'un aurait des yeux, l'autre des bras, l'autre des pieds, et rien de plus. Les charlatans du Japon dépècent, dit-on, un enfant aux yeux des spectateurs ; puis, jetant en l'air tous ses membres l'un après l'autre, ils font retomber l'enfant vivant et tout rassemblé. Tels sont à peu près les tours de gobelets de nos politiques ; après avoir démembré le corps social par un prestige digne de la foire, ils rassemblent les pièces on ne sait comment.

Cette erreur vient de ne s'être pas fait des notions exactes de l'autorité souveraine, et d'avoir pris pour des parties de cette autorité ce qui n'en était que des émanations[22]. Ainsi, par exemple, on a regardé l'acte de déclarer la guerre et celui de faire la paix comme des actes de souveraineté ; ce qui n'est pas ; puisque chacun de ces actes n'est point une loi mais seulement une application de la loi, un acte particulier qui détermine le cas de la loi, comme on le verra clairement quand l'idée attachée au mot *loi* sera fixée.

En suivant de même les autres divisions on trouverait que toutes les fois qu'on croit voir la souveraineté partagée on se trompe, que les droits qu'on prend pour des parties de cette souveraineté lui sont tous subordonnés, et supposent toujours des volontés suprêmes dont ces droits ne donnent que l'exécution.

On ne saurait dire combien ce défaut d'exactitude a jeté d'obscurité sur les décisions des auteurs en matière de droit politique, quand ils ont voulu juger des droits respectifs des rois et des peuples, sur les principes qu'ils avaient établis. Chacun peut voir dans les chapitres III et IV du premier livre de Grotius comment ce savant homme et son traducteur Barbeyrac s'enchevêtrent, s'embarrassent dans leurs sophismes, crainte d'en dire trop ou de n'en pas dire assez selon leurs vues, et de choquer les intérêts qu'ils avaient à concilier. Grotius réfugié en France, mécontent de sa patrie, et voulant faire sa cour à Louis XIII, à qui son livre est dédié, n'épargne rien pour dépouiller les peuples de tous leurs droits et pour en revêtir les rois avec tout l'art possible. C'eût bien été aussi le goût de Barbeyrac, qui dédiait sa traduction au roi d'Angleterre George Ier. Mais malheureusement l'expulsion de Jacques II, qu'il appelle abdication, le forçait à se tenir sur la réserve, à gauchir, à tergiverser, pour ne pas faire de Guillaume un usurpateur. Si ces deux écrivains avaient adopté les vrais principes, toutes les difficultés étaient levées et ils eussent été toujours conséquents ; mais ils auraient tristement dit la vérité et n'auraient fait leur cour qu'au peuple. Or la vérité ne mène point à la fortune, et le peuple ne donne ni ambassades, ni chaires, ni pensions[23].

Chapitre III

SI LA VOLONTÉ GÉNÉRALE PEUT ERRER[24]

Il s'ensuit de ce qui précède que la volonté générale est toujours droite et tend toujours à l'utilité publique : mais il ne s'ensuit pas que les délibérations du peuple aient toujours la même rectitude. On veut toujours son bien, mais on ne le voit pas toujours. Jamais on ne corrompt le peuple, mais souvent on le trompe, et c'est alors seulement qu'il paraît vouloir ce qui est mal.

Il y a souvent bien de la différence entre la volonté de tous et la volonté générale; celle-ci ne regarde qu'à l'intérêt commun, l'autre regarde à l'intérêt privé, et ce n'est qu'une somme de volontés particulières : mais ôtez de ces mêmes volontés les plus et les moins qui s'entre-détruisent*, reste pour somme des différences la volonté générale.

Si, quand le peuple suffisamment informé délibère, les citoyens n'avaient aucune communication entre eux, du grand nombre de petites différences résulterait toujours la volonté générale, et la délibération serait toujours bonne. Mais quand il se fait des brigues, des associations partielles aux dépens de la grande, la volonté de chacune de ces associations devient générale par rapport à ses membres, et particulière par rapport à l'État : on peut dire alors qu'il n'y a plus autant de votants que d'hommes, mais seulement autant que d'associations. Les différences deviennent moins nombreuses et donnent un résultat moins général. Enfin quand une de ces associations est si grande qu'elle l'emporte sur toutes les autres, vous n'avez plus pour résultat une somme de petites différences, mais une différence unique; alors il n'y a plus de volonté générale, et l'avis qui l'emporte n'est qu'un avis particulier.

Il importe donc pour avoir bien l'énoncé de la volonté générale qu'il n'y ait pas de société partielle dans l'État,

* « Chaque intérêt, dit le M. d'A. [le marquis d'Argenson], a des principes différents. L'accord de deux intérêts particuliers se forme par opposition à celui d'un tiers. » Il eût pu ajouter que l'accord de tous les intérêts se forme par opposition à celui de chacun. S'il n'y avait point d'intérêts différents, à peine sentirait-on l'intérêt commun qui ne trouverait jamais d'obstacle; tout irait de lui-même, et la politique cesserait d'être un art.

et que chaque citoyen n'opine que d'après lui*. Telle fut l'unique et sublime institution du grand Lycurgue. Que s'il y a des sociétés partielles, il en faut multiplier le nombre et en prévenir l'inégalité, comme firent Solon, Numa, Servius. Ces précautions sont les seules bonnes pour que la volonté générale soit toujours éclairée, et que le peuple ne se trompe point.

Chapitre IV

DES BORNES DU POUVOIR SOUVERAIN

Si l'État ou la cité n'est qu'une personne morale[25] dont la vie consiste dans l'union de ses membres, et si le plus important de ses soins est celui de sa propre conservation, il lui faut une force universelle et compulsive pour mouvoir et disposer chaque partie de la manière la plus convenable au tout. Comme la nature donne à chaque homme un pouvoir absolu sur tous ses membres, le pacte social donne au corps politique un pouvoir absolu sur tous les siens, et c'est ce même pouvoir qui, dirigé par la volonté générale, porte, comme j'ai dit, le nom de souveraineté.

* « *Vera cosa è,* dit Machiavel, *che alcune divisioni nuocono alle republiche e alcune giovano : quelle nuocono che sono dalle sette e da partigiani accompagnate : quelle giovano che senza sette, senza partigiani si mantengono. Non potendo adunque provedere un fondatore d'una republica che non siano nimizicie in quella, hà da proveder almeno che non vi siano sette* » (*Hist. Florent.*, lib. VII.) – « *À la vérité, il y a des divisions qui nuisent à une république et d'autres qui lui profitent : celles-là lui nuisent, qui suscitent des sectes et des partis ; celles-ci lui profitent, que n'accompagnent ni sectes, ni partis. Puis donc que le fondateur d'une république ne peut empêcher qu'il n'y existe des inimitiés, il lui faut du moins empêcher qu'il n'y ait des sectes.* »

Mais, outre la personne publique, nous avons à considérer les personnes privées qui la composent, et dont la vie et la liberté sont naturellement indépendantes d'elle. Il s'agit donc de bien distinguer les droits respectifs des citoyens et du souverain*, et les devoirs qu'ont à remplir les premiers en qualité de sujets, du droit naturel dont ils doivent jouir en qualité d'hommes.

On convient que tout ce que chacun aliène, par le pacte social, de sa puissance, de ses biens, de sa liberté, c'est seulement la partie de tout cela dont l'usage importe à la communauté, mais il faut convenir aussi que le souverain seul est juge de cette importance.

Tous les services qu'un citoyen peut rendre à l'État, il les lui doit sitôt que le souverain les demande ; mais le souverain, de son côté, ne peut charger les sujets d'aucune chaîne inutile à la communauté ; il ne peut pas même le vouloir ; car sous la loi de raison rien ne se fait sans cause, non plus que sous la loi de nature.

Les engagements qui nous lient au corps social ne sont obligatoires que parce qu'ils sont mutuels, et leur nature est telle qu'en les remplissant on ne peut travailler pour autrui sans travailler aussi pour soi. Pourquoi la volonté générale est-elle toujours droite, et pourquoi tous veulent-ils constamment le bonheur de chacun d'eux, si ce n'est parce qu'il n'y a personne qui ne s'approprie ce mot, *chacun*, et qui ne songe à lui-même en votant pour tous ? Ce qui prouve que l'égalité de droit et la notion de justice qu'elle produit dérive de la préférence que chacun se donne et par conséquent de la nature de l'homme ; que la volonté générale pour être vraiment telle doit l'être dans son objet ainsi que dans

---

* Lecteurs attentifs, ne vous pressez pas, je vous prie, de m'accuser ici de contradiction. Je n'ai pu l'éviter dans les termes, vu la pauvreté de la langue : mais attendez.

son essence ; qu'elle doit partir de tous pour s'appliquer à tous, et qu'elle perd sa rectitude naturelle lorsqu'elle tend à quelque objet individuel et déterminé, parce qu'alors, jugeant de ce qui nous est étranger, nous n'avons aucun vrai principe d'équité qui nous guide.

En effet, sitôt qu'il s'agit d'un fait ou d'un droit particulier sur un point qui n'a pas été réglé par une convention générale et antérieure, l'affaire devient contentieuse. C'est un procès où les particuliers intéressés sont une des parties, et le public l'autre, mais où je ne vois ni la loi qu'il faut suivre, ni le juge qui doit prononcer. Il serait ridicule de vouloir alors s'en rapporter à une expresse décision de la volonté générale, qui ne peut être que la conclusion de l'une des parties, et qui par conséquent n'est pour l'autre qu'une volonté étrangère, particulière, portée en cette occasion à l'injustice et sujette à l'erreur. Ainsi, de même qu'une volonté particulière ne peut représenter la volonté générale, la volonté générale à son tour change de nature, ayant un objet particulier, et ne peut comme générale prononcer ni sur un homme ni sur un fait. Quand le peuple d'Athènes, par exemple, nommait ou cassait ses chefs, décernait des honneurs à l'un, imposait des peines à l'autre, et par des multitudes de décrets particuliers exerçait indistinctement tous les actes du gouvernement, le peuple alors n'avait plus de volonté générale proprement dite ; il n'agissait plus comme souverain, mais comme magistrat. Ceci paraîtra contraire aux idées communes, mais il faut me laisser le temps d'exposer les miennes.

On doit concevoir par là que ce qui généralise la volonté est moins le nombre des voix que l'intérêt commun qui les unit ; car, dans cette institution, chacun se soumet nécessairement aux conditions qu'il impose aux autres : accord admirable de l'intérêt et de la justice, qui donne aux délibérations communes un caractère d'équité qu'on voit évanouir dans la discussion de toute affaire particulière, faute d'un intérêt commun qui unisse et identifie la règle du juge avec celle de la partie.

Par quelque côté qu'on remonte au principe, on arrive toujours à la même conclusion ; savoir, que le pacte social établit entre les citoyens une telle égalité qu'ils s'engagent tous sous les mêmes conditions et doivent jouir tous des mêmes droits. Ainsi, par la nature du pacte, tout acte de souveraineté, c'est-à-dire tout acte authentique de la volonté générale, oblige ou favorise également tous les citoyens, en sorte que le souverain connaît seulement le corps de la nation, et ne distingue aucun de ceux qui la composent. Qu'est-ce donc proprement qu'un acte de souveraineté ? Ce n'est pas une convention du supérieur avec l'inférieur, mais une convention du corps avec chacun de ses membres. Convention légitime, parce qu'elle a pour base le contrat social, équitable, parce qu'elle est commune à tous, utile, parce qu'elle ne peut avoir d'autre objet que le bien général, et solide, parce qu'elle a pour garant la force publique et le pouvoir suprême. Tant que les sujets ne sont soumis qu'à de telles conventions, ils n'obéissent à personne, mais seulement à leur propre volonté : et demander jusqu'où s'étendent les droits respectifs du souverain et des citoyens, c'est demander jusqu'à quel point ceux-ci peuvent s'engager avec eux-mêmes, chacun envers tous et tous envers chacun d'eux.

On voit par là que le pouvoir souverain, tout absolu, tout sacré, tout inviolable qu'il est, ne passe ni ne peut passer les bornes des conventions générales, et que tout homme peut disposer pleinement de ce qui lui a été laissé de ses biens et de sa liberté par ces conventions ; de sorte que le souverain n'est jamais en droit de charger un sujet plus qu'un autre, parce qu'alors, l'affaire devenant particulière, son pouvoir n'est plus compétent.

Ces distinctions une fois admises, il est si faux que dans le contrat social il y ait de la part des particuliers aucune renonciation véritable, que leur situation, par l'effet de ce contrat, se trouve réellement préférable à ce qu'elle était auparavant, et qu'au lieu d'une aliénation ils n'ont fait qu'un échange avantageux d'une manière d'être incertaine et précaire contre une autre meilleure et plus sûre, de l'indépendance naturelle contre la liberté, du pouvoir de nuire à autrui contre leur propre sûreté, et de leur force que d'autres pouvaient surmonter contre un droit que l'union sociale rend invincible. Leur vie même qu'ils ont dévouée à l'État en est continuellement protégée, et lorsqu'ils l'exposent pour sa défense que font-ils alors que lui rendre ce qu'ils ont reçu de lui ? Que font-ils qu'ils ne fissent plus fréquemment et avec plus de danger dans l'état de nature, lorsque, livrant des combats inévitables, ils défendraient au péril de leur vie ce qui leur sert à la conserver ? Tous ont à combattre au besoin pour la patrie, il est vrai ; mais aussi nul n'a jamais à combattre pour soi. Ne gagne-t-on pas encore à courir pour ce qui fait notre sûreté une partie des risques qu'il faudrait courir pour nous-mêmes sitôt qu'elle nous serait ôtée ?

Chapitre V

DU DROIT DE VIE ET DE MORT[26]

On demande comment les particuliers n'ayant point droit de disposer de leur propre vie peuvent transmettre au souverain ce même droit qu'ils n'ont pas ? Cette question ne paraît difficile à résoudre que parce qu'elle est mal posée. Tout homme a droit de risquer sa propre vie pour la conserver. A-t-on jamais dit que celui qui se jette par une fenêtre pour échapper à un incendie soit coupable de suicide ? A-t-on même jamais imputé ce crime à celui qui périt dans une tempête dont en s'embarquant il n'ignorait pas le danger ?

Le traité social a pour fin la conservation des contractants. Qui veut la fin veut aussi les moyens, et ces moyens sont inséparables de quelques risques, même de quelques pertes. Qui veut conserver sa vie aux dépens des autres doit la donner aussi pour eux quand il faut. Or le citoyen n'est plus juge du péril auquel la loi veut qu'il s'expose ; et quand le prince lui a dit : « Il est expédient à l'État que tu meures », il doit mourir ; puisque ce n'est qu'à cette condition qu'il a vécu en sûreté jusqu'alors, et que sa vie n'est plus seulement un bienfait de la nature, mais un don conditionnel de l'État.

La peine de mort infligée aux criminels peut être envisagée à peu près sous le même point de vue : c'est pour n'être pas la victime d'un assassin que l'on consent à mourir si on le devient. Dans ce traité, loin de disposer de sa propre vie on ne songe qu'à la garantir, et il n'est pas à présumer qu'aucun des contractants prémédite alors de se faire pendre.

D'ailleurs tout malfaiteur, attaquant le droit social, devient par ses forfaits rebelle et traître à la patrie, il cesse d'en être membre en violant ses lois, et même il lui fait la guerre. Alors la conservation de l'État est incompatible avec la sienne, il faut qu'un des deux périsse, et quand on fait mourir le coupable, c'est moins comme citoyen que comme ennemi. Les procédures, le jugement, sont les preuves et la déclaration qu'il a rompu le traité social, et par conséquent qu'il n'est plus membre de l'État. Or comme il s'est reconnu tel, tout au moins par son séjour, il en doit être retranché par l'exil comme infracteur du pacte, ou par la mort comme ennemi public ; car un tel ennemi n'est pas une personne morale, c'est un homme, et c'est alors que le droit de la guerre est de tuer le vaincu.

Mais, dira-t-on, la condamnation d'un criminel est un acte particulier. D'accord : aussi cette condamnation n'appartient-elle point au souverain ; c'est un droit qu'il peut conférer sans pouvoir l'exercer lui-même. Toutes mes idées se tiennent, mais je ne saurais les exposer toutes à la fois.

Au reste la fréquence des supplices est toujours un signe de faiblesse ou de paresse dans le gouvernement. Il n'y a point de méchant qu'on ne pût rendre bon à quelque chose. On n'a droit de faire mourir, même pour l'exemple, que celui qu'on ne peut conserver sans danger.

À l'égard du droit de faire grâce ou d'exempter un coupable de la peine portée par la loi et prononcée par le juge, il n'appartient qu'à celui qui est au-dessus du juge et de la loi, c'est-à-dire au souverain ; encore son droit en ceci n'est-il pas bien net, et les cas d'en user sont-ils très rares. Dans un État bien gouverné il y a peu de punitions, non parce qu'on fait beaucoup de grâces, mais parce qu'il y a peu de criminels : la multitude des crimes en assure l'impunité lorsque l'État dépérit. Sous la République romaine jamais le Sénat ni les consuls ne tentèrent de faire grâce ; le peuple même n'en faisait pas, quoiqu'il révoquât quelquefois son propre jugement. Les fréquentes grâces annoncent que bientôt les forfaits n'en auront plus besoin, et chacun voit où cela mène. Mais je sens que mon cœur murmure et retient ma plume : laissons discuter ces questions à l'homme juste qui n'a point failli, et qui jamais n'eut lui-même besoin de grâce.

Chapitre VI
DE LA LOI

Par le pacte social nous avons donné l'existence et la vie au corps politique : il s'agit maintenant de lui donner le mouvement et la volonté par la législation. Car l'acte primitif par lequel ce corps se forme et s'unit ne détermine rien encore de ce qu'il doit faire pour se conserver[27].

Ce qui est bien et conforme à l'ordre est tel par la nature des choses et indépendamment des conventions humaines. Toute justice vient de Dieu, lui seul en est la source ; mais si nous savions la recevoir de si haut, nous n'aurions besoin ni de gouvernement ni de lois. Sans doute il est une justice universelle émanée de la raison seule ; mais cette justice, pour être admise entre nous, doit être réciproque. À considérer humainement les choses, faute de sanction naturelle les lois de la justice sont vaines parmi les hommes ; elles ne font que le bien du méchant et le mal du juste, quand celui-ci les observe avec tout le monde sans que personne les observe avec lui. Il faut donc des conventions et des lois pour unir les droits aux devoirs et ramener la justice à son objet. Dans l'état de nature, où tout est commun, je ne dois rien à ceux à qui je n'ai rien promis, je ne reconnais pour être à autrui que ce qui m'est inutile. Il n'en est pas ainsi dans l'état civil où tous les droits sont fixés par la loi.

Mais qu'est-ce donc enfin qu'une loi ? Tant qu'on se contentera de n'attacher à ce mot que des idées métaphysiques, on continuera de raisonner sans s'entendre et quand on aura dit ce que c'est qu'une loi de la nature on n'en saura pas mieux ce que c'est qu'une loi de l'État.

J'ai déjà dit qu'il n'y avait point de volonté générale sur un objet particulier. En effet cet objet particulier est dans l'État ou hors de l'État. S'il est hors de l'État, une volonté qui lui est étrangère n'est point générale par rapport à lui ; et si cet objet est dans l'État, il en fait partie : alors il se forme entre le tout et sa partie une relation qui en fait deux êtres séparés, dont la partie est l'un, et le tout, moins cette même partie, est l'autre. Mais le tout moins une partie n'est point le tout et tant que ce rapport subsiste il n'y a plus de tout mais deux parties inégales : d'où il suit que la volonté de l'une n'est point non plus générale par rapport à l'autre.

Mais quand tout le peuple statue sur tout le peuple il ne considère que lui-même ; et s'il se forme alors un rapport, c'est de l'objet entier sous un point de vue à l'objet entier sous un autre point de vue, sans aucune division du tout. Alors la matière sur laquelle on statue est générale comme la volonté qui statue. C'est cet acte que j'appelle une loi[28].

Quand je dis que l'objet des lois est toujours général, j'entends que la loi considère les sujets en corps et les actions comme abstraites, jamais un homme comme individu ni une action particulière. Ainsi la loi peut bien statuer qu'il y aura des privilèges, mais elle n'en peut donner nommément à personne ; la loi peut faire plusieurs classes de citoyens, assigner même les qualités qui donneront droit à ces classes, mais elle ne peut nommer tels et tels pour y être admis ; elle peut établir un gouvernement royal et une succession héréditaire, mais elle ne peut élire un roi, ni nommer une famille royale : en un mot, toute fonction qui se rapporte à un objet individuel n'appartient point à la puissance législative.

Sur cette idée, on voit à l'instant qu'il ne faut plus demander à qui il appartient de faire des lois, puisqu'elles sont des actes de la volonté générale ; ni si le prince est au-dessus des lois, puisqu'il est membre de l'État; ni si la loi peut être injuste, puisque nul n'est injuste envers lui-même; ni comment on est libre et soumis aux lois, puisqu'elles ne sont que des registres de nos volontés.

On voit encore que la loi réunissant l'universalité[29] de la volonté et celle de l'objet, ce qu'un homme, quel qu'il puisse être, ordonne de son chef n'est point une loi : ce qu'ordonne même le souverain sur un objet particulier n'est pas non plus une loi, mais un décret, ni un acte de souveraineté, mais de magistrature.

J'appelle donc république tout État régi par des lois, sous quelque forme d'administration que ce puisse être : car alors seulement l'intérêt public gouverne, et la chose publique est quelque chose. Tout gouvernement légitime est républicain* : j'expliquerai ci-après ce que c'est que gouvernement.

Les lois ne sont proprement que les conditions de l'association civile. Le peuple soumis aux lois en doit être l'auteur; il n'appartient qu'à ceux qui s'associent de régler les conditions de la société. Mais comment les régleront-ils ? Sera-ce d'un commun accord, par une inspiration subite ? Le corps politique a-t-il un organe pour énoncer ses volontés ? Qui lui donnera la prévoyance nécessaire pour en former les actes et les publier d'avance, ou comment les prononcera-t-il au moment du besoin ? Comment une multitude aveugle qui souvent ne sait ce qu'elle veut, parce qu'elle sait rarement

---

* Je n'entends pas seulement par ce mot une aristocratie ou une démocratie, mais en général tout gouvernement guidé par la volonté générale, qui est la loi. Pour être légitime il ne faut pas que le gouvernement se confonde avec le souverain, mais qu'il en soit le ministre : alors la monarchie elle-même est république. Ceci s'éclaircira dans le livre suivant.

ce qui lui est bon, exécuterait-elle d'elle-même une entreprise aussi grande, aussi difficile qu'un système de législation ? De lui-même le peuple veut toujours le bien, mais de lui-même il ne le voit pas toujours. La volonté générale est toujours droite, mais le jugement qui la guide n'est pas toujours éclairé. Il faut lui faire voir les objets tels qu'ils sont, quelquefois tels qu'ils doivent lui paraître, lui montrer le bon chemin qu'elle cherche, la garantir de la séduction des volontés particulières, rapprocher à ses yeux les lieux et les temps, balancer l'attrait des avantages présents et sensibles par le danger des maux éloignés et cachés. Les particuliers voient le bien qu'ils rejettent ; le public veut le bien qu'il ne voit pas. Tous ont également besoin de guides. Il faut obliger les uns à conformer leurs volontés à leur raison ; il faut apprendre à l'autre à connaître ce qu'il veut. Alors des lumières publiques résulte l'union de l'entendement et de la volonté dans le corps social, de là l'exact concours des parties, et enfin la plus grande force du tout. Voilà d'où naît la nécessité d'un législateur[30].

Chapitre VII

DU LÉGISLATEUR[31]

Pour découvrir les meilleures règles de société qui conviennent aux nations, il faudrait une intelligence supérieure qui vît toutes les passions des hommes et qui n'en éprouvât aucune ; qui n'eût aucun rapport avec notre nature et qui la connût à fond ; dont le bonheur fût indépendant de nous et qui pourtant voulût bien s'occuper du nôtre ; enfin, qui, dans le progrès des temps se ménageant une gloire éloignée, pût travailler dans un siècle et jouir dans un autre*. Il faudrait des dieux pour donner des lois aux hommes.

Le même raisonnement que faisait Caligula quant au fait, Platon le faisait quant au droit pour définir l'homme civil ou royal qu'il cherche dans son livre du règne[32]. Mais s'il est vrai qu'un grand prince est un homme rare, que sera-ce d'un grand législateur ? Le premier n'a qu'à suivre le modèle que l'autre doit proposer. Celui-ci est le mécanicien qui invente la machine, celui-là n'est que l'ouvrier qui la monte et la fait marcher. Dans la naissance des sociétés, dit Montesquieu, ce sont les chefs des républiques qui font l'institution, et c'est ensuite l'institution qui forme les chefs des républiques.

Celui qui ose entreprendre d'instituer un peuple doit se sentir en état de changer, pour ainsi dire, la nature humaine ; de transformer chaque individu, qui par lui-même est un tout parfait et solitaire, en partie d'un plus grand tout dont cet individu reçoive en quelque sorte sa vie et son être ; d'altérer la constitution de l'homme pour la renforcer ; de substituer une existence partielle et morale à l'existence physique et indépendante que nous avons tous reçue de la nature. Il faut, en un mot, qu'il ôte à l'homme ses forces propres pour lui en donner qui lui soient étrangères et dont il ne puisse faire usage sans le secours d'autrui. Plus ces forces naturelles sont mortes et anéanties, plus les acquises sont grandes et durables, plus aussi l'institution est solide et parfaite : en sorte que si chaque citoyen n'est rien, ne peut rien, que par tous les autres, et que la force acquise par le tout soit égale ou supérieure à la somme

---

* Un peuple ne devient célèbre que quand sa législation commence à décliner. On ignore combien de siècles l'institution de Lycurgue fit le bonheur des Spartiates avant qu'il fût question d'eux dans le reste de la Grèce.

des forces naturelles de tous les individus, on peut dire que la législation est au plus haut point de perfection qu'elle puisse atteindre.

Le législateur est à tous égards un homme extraordinaire dans l'État. S'il doit l'être par son génie, il ne l'est pas moins par son emploi. Ce n'est point magistrature, ce n'est point souveraineté. Cet emploi, qui constitue la république, n'entre point dans sa constitution; c'est une fonction particulière et supérieure qui n'a rien de commun avec l'empire humain; car si celui qui commande aux hommes ne doit pas commander aux lois, celui qui commande aux lois ne doit pas non plus commander aux hommes; autrement ses lois, ministres de ses passions, ne feraient souvent que perpétuer ses injustices, et jamais il ne pourrait éviter que des vues particulières n'altérassent la sainteté de son ouvrage.

Quand Lycurgue donna des lois à sa patrie, il commença par abdiquer la royauté. C'était la coutume de la plupart des villes grecques de confier à des étrangers l'établissement des leurs. Les républiques modernes de l'Italie imitèrent souvent cet usage; celle de Genève en fit autant et s'en trouva bien*. Rome, dans son plus bel âge, vit renaître en son sein tous les crimes de la tyrannie, et se vit prête à périr, pour avoir réuni sur les mêmes têtes l'autorité législative et le pouvoir souverain.

Cependant, les décemvirs eux-mêmes ne s'arrogèrent jamais le droit de faire passer aucune loi de leur

---

* Ceux qui ne considèrent Calvin que comme théologien connaissent mal l'étendue de son génie. La rédaction de nos sages édits, à laquelle il eut beaucoup de part, lui fait autant d'honneur que son *Institution.* Quelque révolution que le temps puisse amener dans notre culte, tant que l'amour de la patrie et de la liberté ne sera pas éteint parmi nous, jamais la mémoire de ce grand homme ne cessera d'y être en bénédiction.

seule autorité. « Rien de ce que nous vous proposons, disaient-ils au peuple, ne peut passer en loi sans votre consentement. Romains, soyez vous-mêmes les auteurs des lois qui doivent faire votre bonheur. »

Celui qui rédige les lois n'a donc ou ne doit avoir aucun droit législatif, et le peuple même ne peut, quand il le voudrait, se dépouiller de ce droit incommunicable, parce que selon le pacte fondamental il n'y a que la volonté générale qui oblige les particuliers, et qu'on ne peut jamais s'assurer qu'une volonté particulière est conforme à la volonté générale qu'après l'avoir soumise aux suffrages libres du peuple : j'ai déjà dit cela, mais il n'est pas inutile de le répéter.

Ainsi l'on trouve à la fois dans l'ouvrage de la législation deux choses qui semblent incompatibles : une entreprise au-dessus de la force humaine et, pour l'exécuter, une autorité qui n'est rien.

Autre difficulté qui mérite attention. Les sages qui veulent parler au vulgaire leur langage au lieu du sien n'en sauraient être entendus. Or, il y a mille sortes d'idées qu'il est impossible de traduire dans la langue du peuple. Les vues trop générales et les objets trop éloignés sont également hors de sa portée : chaque individu ne goûtant d'autre plan de gouvernement que celui qui se rapporte à son intérêt particulier, aperçoit difficilement les avantages qu'il doit retirer des privations continuelles qu'imposent les bonnes lois. Pour qu'un peuple naissant pût goûter les saines maximes de la politique et suivre les règles fondamentales de la raison d'État, il faudrait que l'effet pût devenir cause, que l'esprit social, qui doit être l'ouvrage de l'institution, présidât à l'institution même ; et que les hommes fussent avant les lois ce qu'ils doivent devenir par elles. Ainsi donc le législateur ne pouvant employer ni la force ni le raisonnement, c'est une nécessité qu'il recoure à une autorité d'un autre ordre, qui puisse entraîner sans violence et persuader sans convaincre.

Voilà ce qui força de tout temps les pères des nations de recourir à l'intervention du Ciel et d'honorer les dieux de leur propre sagesse, afin que les peuples, soumis aux lois de l'État comme à celles de la nature, et reconnaissant le même pouvoir dans la formation de l'homme et dans celle de la cité, obéissent avec liberté et portassent docilement le joug de la félicité publique.

Cette raison sublime qui s'élève au-dessus de la portée des hommes vulgaires est celle dont le législateur met les décisions dans la bouche des immortels, pour entraîner par l'autorité divine ceux que ne pourrait ébranler la prudence humaine*. Mais il n'appartient pas à tout homme de faire parler des dieux, ni d'en être cru quand il s'annonce pour être leur interprète. La grande âme du législateur est le vrai miracle qui doit prouver sa mission. Tout homme peut graver des tables de pierre, ou acheter un oracle, ou feindre un secret commerce avec quelque divinité, ou dresser un oiseau pour lui parler à l'oreille, ou trouver d'autres moyens grossiers d'en imposer au peuple. Celui qui ne saura que cela pourra même assembler par hasard une troupe d'insensés, mais il ne fondera jamais un empire, et son extravagant ouvrage périra bientôt avec lui. De vains prestiges

* « *E veramente,* dit Machiavel, *mai non fù alcuno ordinatore di leggi straordinarie in un popolo, che non ricorresse a Dio, perché altrimenti non sarebbero accettate ; perché sono molti beni conosciuti da uno prudente i quali non hanno in se raggioni evidenti da potergli persuadere ad altrui.* » (*Discorsi sopra Tito Livio*, lib. I, cap. XI.) – « *Il est bien vrai qu'il n'y eut jamais d'instituteur de lois extraordinaires chez un peuple qui ne se réclamât de Dieu, parce qu'autrement elles n'auraient pas été acceptées ; car bien des principes utiles, reconnus par le sage ne comportent point de preuves évidentes qui les fassent accepter par les autres esprits.* »

forment un lien passager, il n'y a que la sagesse qui le rende durable. La loi judaïque toujours subsistante, celle de l'enfant d'Ismaël qui depuis dix siècles régit la moitié du monde, annoncent encore aujourd'hui les grands hommes qui les ont dictées ; et tandis que l'orgueilleuse philosophie ou l'aveugle esprit de parti ne voit en eux que d'heureux imposteurs, le vrai politique admire dans leurs institutions ce grand et puissant génie qui préside aux établissements durables.

Il ne faut pas, de tout ceci, conclure avec Warburton que la politique et la religion aient parmi nous un objet commun, mais que, dans l'origine des nations, l'une sert d'instrument à l'autre.

Chapitre VIII
DU PEUPLE[33]

Comme avant d'élever un grand édifice l'architecte observe et sonde le sol pour voir s'il en peut soutenir le poids, le sage instituteur ne commence pas par rédiger de bonnes lois en elles-mêmes, mais il examine auparavant si le peuple auquel il les destine est propre à les supporter. C'est pour cela que Platon refusa de donner des lois aux Arcadiens et aux Cyréniens, sachant que ces deux peuples étaient riches et ne pouvaient souffrir l'égalité : c'est pour cela qu'on vit en Crète de bonnes lois et de méchants hommes, parce que Minos n'avait discipliné qu'un peuple chargé de vices.

Mille nations ont brillé sur la terre qui n'auraient jamais pu souffrir de bonnes lois ; et celles même qui l'auraient pu n'ont eu, dans toute leur durée, qu'un temps fort court pour cela. La plupart des peuples, ainsi que des hommes, ne sont dociles que dans leur jeunesse ; ils deviennent incorrigibles en vieillissant.

Quand une fois les coutumes sont établies et les préjugés enracinés, c'est une entreprise dangereuse et vaine de vouloir les réformer ; le peuple ne peut pas même souffrir qu'on touche à ses maux pour les détruire, semblable à ces malades stupides et sans courage qui frémissent à l'aspect du médecin.

Ce n'est pas que, comme quelques maladies bouleversent la tête des hommes et leur ôtent le souvenir du passé, il ne se trouve quelquefois dans la durée des États des époques violentes où les révolutions font sur les peuples ce que certaines crises font sur les individus, où l'horreur du passé tient lieu d'oubli, et où l'État, embrasé par les guerres civiles, renaît pour ainsi dire de sa cendre et reprend la vigueur de la jeunesse en sortant des bras de la mort. Telle fut Sparte au temps de Lycurgue, telle fut Rome après les Tarquins, et telles ont été parmi nous la Hollande et la Suisse après l'expulsion des tyrans.

Mais ces événements sont rares ; ce sont des exceptions dont la raison se trouve toujours dans la constitution particulière de l'État excepté. Elles ne sauraient même avoir lieu deux fois pour le même peuple, car il peut se rendre libre tant qu'il n'est que barbare, mais il ne le peut plus quand le ressort civil est usé. Alors les troubles peuvent le détruire sans que les révolutions puissent le rétablir, et sitôt que ses fers sont brisés, il tombe épars et n'existe plus. Il lui faut désormais un maître et non pas un libérateur. Peuples libres, souvenez-vous de cette maxime : « On peut acquérir la liberté, mais on ne la recouvre jamais. »

La jeunesse n'est pas l'enfance. Il est pour les nations comme pour les hommes un temps de jeunesse ou, si l'on veut, de maturité qu'il faut attendre avant de les soumettre à des lois : mais la maturité d'un peuple n'est pas toujours facile à connaître, et si on la prévient l'ouvrage est manqué. Tel peuple est disciplinable en naissant, tel autre ne l'est pas au bout de dix siècles. Les Russes ne seront jamais vraiment policés, parce qu'ils l'ont été trop tôt. Pierre avait le génie imitatif; il n'avait pas le vrai génie, celui qui crée et fait tout de rien. Quelques-unes des choses qu'il fit étaient bien, la plupart étaient déplacées. Il a vu que son peuple était barbare, il n'a point vu qu'il n'était pas mûr pour la police; il l'a voulu civiliser quand il ne fallait que l'aguerrir. Il a d'abord voulu faire des Allemands, des Anglais, quand il fallait commencer par faire des Russes : il a empêché ses sujets de devenir jamais ce qu'ils pourraient être, en leur persuadant qu'ils étaient ce qu'ils ne sont pas. C'est ainsi qu'un précepteur français forme son élève pour briller au moment de son enfance, et puis n'être jamais rien. L'empire de Russie voudra subjuguer l'Europe et sera subjugué lui-même. Les Tartares, ses sujets ou ses voisins, deviendront ses maîtres et les nôtres. Cette révolution me paraît infaillible. Tous les rois de l'Europe travaillent de concert à l'accélérer.

Chapitre IX

DU PEUPLE

(suite)

Comme la nature a donné des termes à la stature d'un homme bien conformé, passé lesquels elle ne fait plus que des géants ou des nains, il y a de même, eu égard à la meilleure constitution d'un État, des bornes à l'étendue qu'il peut avoir, afin qu'il ne soit ni trop grand pour pouvoir être bien gouverné, ni trop petit pour pouvoir se maintenir par lui-même. Il y a dans tout corps politique un *maximum* de force qu'il ne saurait passer, et duquel souvent il s'éloigne à force de s'agrandir. Plus le lien social s'étend, plus il se relâche ; et en général un petit État est proportionnellement plus fort qu'un grand.

Mille raisons démontrent cette maxime. Premièrement l'administration devient plus pénible dans les grandes distances, comme un poids devient plus lourd au bout d'un plus grand levier. Elle devient aussi plus onéreuse à mesure que les degrés se multiplient : car chaque ville a d'abord la sienne, que le peuple paye, chaque district la sienne encore payée par le peuple, ensuite chaque province, puis les grands gouvernements, les satrapies, les vice-royautés, qu'il faut toujours payer plus cher à mesure qu'on monte, et toujours aux dépens du malheureux peuple ; enfin vient l'administration suprême, qui écrase tout. Tant de surcharges épuisent continuellement les sujets : loin d'être mieux gouvernés par tous ces différents ordres, ils le sont moins bien que s'il n'y en avait qu'un seul au-dessus d'eux. Cependant à peine reste-t-il des ressources pour les cas extraordinaires ; et quand il y faut recourir, l'État est toujours à la veille de sa ruine.

Ce n'est pas tout ; non seulement le gouvernement a moins de vigueur et de célérité pour faire observer les lois, empêcher les vexations, corriger les abus, prévenir les entreprises séditieuses qui peuvent se faire dans des lieux éloignés ; mais le peuple a moins d'affection pour ses chefs qu'il ne voit jamais, pour la patrie qui est à ses yeux comme le monde, et pour ses concitoyens dont la plupart lui sont étrangers. Les mêmes lois ne peuvent convenir à tant de provinces diverses qui ont des mœurs différentes, qui vivent sous des climats opposés, et qui ne peuvent souffrir la même forme de gouvernement. Des lois différentes n'engendrent que trouble et confusion parmi des peuples qui, vivant sous les mêmes chefs et dans une communication continuelle, passent ou se marient les uns chez les autres et, soumis à d'autres coutumes, ne savent jamais si leur patrimoine est bien à eux. Les talents sont enfouis, les vertus ignorées, les vices impunis, dans cette multitude d'hommes inconnus les uns aux autres, que le siège de l'administration suprême rassemble dans un même lieu. Les chefs accablés d'affaires ne voient rien par eux-mêmes, des commis gouvernent l'État. Enfin les mesures qu'il faut prendre pour maintenir l'autorité générale, à laquelle tant d'officiers éloignés veulent se soustraire ou en imposer, absorbent tous les soins publics ; il n'en reste plus pour le bonheur du peuple, à peine en reste-t-il pour sa défense au besoin ; et c'est ainsi qu'un corps trop grand pour sa constitution s'affaisse et périt écrasé sous son propre poids.

D'un autre côté, l'État doit se donner une certaine base pour avoir de la solidité, pour résister aux secousses qu'il ne manquera pas d'éprouver et aux efforts qu'il sera contraint de faire pour se soutenir : car tous les peuples ont une espèce de force centrifuge, par laquelle ils agissent continuellement les uns contre les autres et tendent à s'agrandir aux dépens de leurs voisins, comme les tourbillons de Descartes. Ainsi les faibles risquent d'être bientôt engloutis et nul ne peut guère se conserver qu'en se mettant avec tous dans une espèce d'équilibre, qui rende la compression partout à peu près égale.

On voit par là qu'il y a des raisons de s'étendre et des raisons de se resserrer, et ce n'est pas le moindre talent du politique de trouver entre les unes et les autres la proportion la plus avantageuse à la conservation de l'État. On peut dire en général que les premières, n'étant qu'extérieures et relatives, doivent être subordonnées aux autres, qui sont internes et absolues ; une saine et forte constitution est la première chose qu'il faut rechercher, et l'on doit plus compter sur la vigueur qui naît d'un bon gouvernement que sur les ressources que fournit un grand territoire.

Au reste, on a vu des États tellement constitués, que la nécessité des conquêtes entrait dans leur constitution même, et que, pour se maintenir, ils étaient forcés de s'agrandir sans cesse. Peut-être se félicitaient-ils beaucoup de cette heureuse nécessité, qui leur montrait pourtant, avec le terme de leur grandeur, l'inévitable moment de leur chute.

Chapitre X
DU PEUPLE
(suite)

On peut mesurer un corps politique de deux manières ; savoir, par l'étendue du territoire, et par le nombre du peuple ; et il y a entre l'une et l'autre de ces mesures un rapport convenable pour donner à l'État sa véritable grandeur. Ce sont les hommes qui font l'État, et c'est le terrain qui nourrit les hommes : ce rapport est donc que la terre suffise à l'entretien de ses habitants, et qu'il y ait autant d'habitants que la terre en peut nourrir. C'est dans cette proportion que se trouve le *maximum* de force d'un nombre donné de peuple ; car s'il y a du terrain de trop, la garde en est onéreuse, la culture insuffisante, le produit superflu ; c'est la cause prochaine des guerres défensives : s'il n'y en a pas assez, l'État se trouve pour le supplément à la discrétion de ses voisins ; c'est la cause prochaine des guerres offensives. Tout peuple qui n'a par sa position que l'alternative entre le commerce ou la guerre, est faible en lui-même ; il dépend de ses voisins, il dépend des événements ; il n'a jamais qu'une existence incertaine et courte. Il subjugue et change de situation, ou il est subjugué et n'est rien. Il ne peut se conserver libre qu'à force de petitesse ou de grandeur.

On ne peut donner en calcul un rapport fixe entre l'étendue de terre et le nombre d'hommes qui se suffisent l'un à l'autre, tant à cause des différences qui se trouvent dans les qualités du terrain, dans ses degrés de fertilité, dans la nature de ses productions, dans l'influence des climats, que de celles qu'on remarque dans les tempéraments des hommes qui les habitent, dont les uns consomment peu dans un pays fertile, les autres beaucoup sur un sol ingrat. Il faut encore avoir égard à la plus grande ou moindre fécondité des femmes, à ce que le pays peut avoir de plus ou moins favorable à la population, à la quantité dont le législateur peut espérer d'y concourir par ses établissements ; de sorte qu'il ne doit pas fonder son jugement sur ce qu'il voit mais sur ce qu'il prévoit, ni s'arrêter autant à l'état actuel de la population qu'à celui où elle doit naturellement parvenir. Enfin il y a mille occasions où les accidents particuliers du lieu exigent ou permettent qu'on embrasse plus de terrain qu'il ne paraît nécessaire. Ainsi l'on s'étendra beaucoup dans un pays de montagnes, où les productions naturelles, savoir les bois, pâturages, demandent moins de travail, où l'expérience apprend que les femmes sont plus fécondes que dans les plaines, et où un grand sol incliné ne donne qu'une petite base horizontale, la seule qu'il faut compter pour la végétation. Au contraire, on peut se resserrer au bord de la mer, même dans des rochers et des sables presque stériles ; parce que la pêche y peut suppléer en grande partie aux productions de la terre, que les hommes doivent être plus rassemblés pour repousser les pirates, et qu'on a d'ailleurs plus de facilité pour délivrer le pays, par les colonies, des habitants dont il est surchargé.

À ces conditions pour instituer un peuple, il en faut ajouter une qui ne peut suppléer à nulle autre, mais sans laquelle elles sont toutes inutiles : c'est qu'on jouisse de l'abondance et de la paix ; car le temps où s'ordonne un État est, comme celui où se forme un bataillon, l'instant où le corps est le moins capable de résistance et le plus facile à détruire. On résisterait mieux dans un désordre absolu que dans un moment de fermentation, où chacun s'occupe de son rang et non du péril. Qu'une guerre, une famine, une sédition survienne en ce temps de crise, l'État est infailliblement renversé.

Ce n'est pas qu'il n'y ait beaucoup de gouvernements établis durant ces orages ; mais alors ce sont ces gouvernements mêmes qui détruisent l'État. Les usurpateurs amènent ou choisissent toujours ces temps de troubles pour faire passer, à la faveur de l'effroi public, les lois destructives que le peuple n'adopterait jamais de sang-froid. Le choix du moment de l'institution est un des caractères les plus sûrs par lesquels on peut distinguer l'œuvre du législateur d'avec celle du tyran.

Quel peuple est donc propre à la législation ? Celui qui, se trouvant déjà lié par quelque union d'origine, d'intérêt ou de convention, n'a point encore porté le vrai joug des lois ; celui qui n'a ni coutumes, ni superstitions bien enracinées ; celui qui ne craint pas d'être accablé par une invasion subite, qui, sans entrer dans les querelles de ses voisins, peut résister seul à chacun d'eux, ou s'aider de l'un pour repousser l'autre ; celui dont chaque membre peut être connu de tous, et où l'on n'est point forcé de charger un homme d'un plus grand fardeau qu'un homme ne peut porter ; celui qui peut se passer des autres peuples, et dont tout autre peuple peut se passer* ; celui qui n'est ni riche ni pauvre, et peut se

* Si de deux peuples voisins l'un ne pouvait se passer de l'autre, ce serait une situation très dure pour le premier, et très dangereuse pour le second. Toute nation sage, en pareil cas, s'efforcera bien vite de délivrer l'autre de cette dépendance. La république de Thlascala,

suffire à lui-même ; enfin celui qui réunit la consistance d'un ancien peuple avec la docilité d'un peuple nouveau. Ce qui rend pénible l'ouvrage de la législation, est moins ce qu'il faut établir que ce qu'il faut détruire ; et ce qui rend le succès si rare, c'est l'impossibilité de trouver la simplicité de la nature jointe aux besoins de la société. Toutes ces conditions, il est vrai, se trouvent difficilement rassemblées. Aussi voit-on peu d'États bien constitués.

Il est encore en Europe un pays capable de législation ; c'est l'île de Corse. La valeur et la constance avec laquelle ce brave peuple a su recouvrer et défendre sa liberté mériterait bien que quelque homme sage lui apprît à la conserver. J'ai quelque pressentiment qu'un jour cette petite île étonnera l'Europe.

Chapitre XI

DES DIVERS SYSTÈMES DE LÉGISLATION

Si l'on recherche en quoi consiste précisément le plus grand bien de tous, qui doit être la fin de tout système de législation, on trouvera qu'il se réduit à deux objets principaux, la *liberté*, et l'*égalité.* La liberté, parce que toute dépendance particulière est autant de force ôtée au corps de l'État ; l'égalité parce que la liberté ne peut subsister sans elle[34].

J'ai déjà dit ce que c'est que la liberté civile ; à l'égard de l'égalité, il ne faut pas entendre par ce mot que les

---

enclavée dans l'empire du Mexique, aima mieux se passer de sel que d'en acheter des Mexicains, et même que d'en accepter gratuitement. Les sages Thlascalans virent le piège caché sous cette libéralité. Ils se conservèrent libres ; et ce petit État, enfermé dans ce grand empire, fut enfin l'instrument de sa ruine.

degrés de puissance et de richesse soient absolument les mêmes, mais que, quant à la puissance, elle soit au-dessous de toute violence et ne s'exerce jamais qu'en vertu du rang et des lois et, quant à la richesse, que nul citoyen ne soit assez opulent pour en pouvoir acheter un autre, et nul assez pauvre pour être contraint de se vendre*. Ce qui suppose du côté des grands modération de biens et de crédit, et du côté des petits, modération d'avarice et de convoitise.

Cette égalité, disent-ils, est une chimère de spéculation qui ne peut exister dans la pratique. Mais si l'abus est inévitable, s'ensuit-il qu'il ne faille pas au moins le régler ? C'est précisément parce que la force des choses tend toujours à détruire l'égalité, que la force de la législation doit toujours tendre à la maintenir[35].

Mais ces objets généraux de toute bonne institution doivent être modifiés en chaque pays par les rapports qui naissent, tant de la situation locale, que du caractère des habitants, et c'est sur ces rapports qu'il faut assigner à chaque peuple un système particulier d'institution, qui soit le meilleur, non peut-être en lui-même, mais pour l'État auquel il est destiné. Par exemple le sol est-il ingrat et stérile, ou le pays trop serré pour les habitants ? Tournez-vous du côté de l'industrie et des arts, dont vous échangerez les productions contre les denrées qui vous manquent. Au contraire, occupez-vous de riches plaines et des coteaux fertiles ? Dans un bon terrain, manquez-vous d'habitants ? Donnez tous

* Voulez-vous donc donner à l'État de la consistance, rapprochez les degrés extrêmes autant qu'il est possible ; ne souffrez ni des gens opulents ni des gueux. Ces deux états, naturellement inséparables, sont également funestes au bien commun ; de l'un sortent les fauteurs de la tyrannie, et de l'autre les tyrans : c'est toujours entre eux que se fait le trafic de la liberté publique : l'un l'achète, et l'autre la vend.

vos soins à l'agriculture qui multiplie les hommes, et chassez les arts qui ne feraient qu'achever de dépeupler le pays en attroupant sur quelques points du territoire le peu d'habitants qu'il a*. Occupez-vous des rivages étendus et commodes? Couvrez la mer de vaisseaux, cultivez le commerce et la navigation; vous aurez une existence brillante et courte. La mer ne baigne-t-elle sur vos côtes que des rochers presque inaccessibles? Restez barbares et ichtyophages; vous en vivrez plus tranquilles, meilleurs peut-être, et sûrement plus heureux. En un mot, outre les maximes communes à tous, chaque peuple renferme en lui quelque cause qui les ordonne d'une manière particulière et rend sa législation propre à lui seul. C'est ainsi qu'autrefois les Hébreux et récemment les Arabes ont eu pour principal objet la religion, les Athéniens les lettres, Carthage et Tyr le commerce, Rhodes la marine, Sparte la guerre, et Rome la vertu. L'auteur de *L'Esprit des Lois* a montré dans des foules d'exemples par quel art le législateur dirige l'institution vers chacun de ces objets.

Ce qui rend la constitution d'un État véritablement solide et durable, c'est quand les convenances sont tellement observées que les rapports naturels et les lois tombent de concert sur les mêmes points, et que celles-ci ne font, pour ainsi dire, qu'assurer, accompagner, rectifier les autres. Mais si le législateur, se trompant dans son objet, prend un principe différent de celui qui naît de la nature des choses, que l'un tende à la servitude et l'autre à la liberté, l'un aux richesses l'autre à la population, l'un à la paix l'autre aux conquêtes, on verra

* Quelque branche de commerce extérieur, dit M. d'Argenson, ne répand guère qu'une fausse utilité pour un royaume en général : elle peut enrichir quelques particuliers, même quelques villes; mais la nation entière n'y gagne rien, et le peuple n'en est pas mieux.

les lois s'affaiblir insensiblement, la constitution s'altérer, et l'État ne cessera d'être agité jusqu'à ce qu'il soit détruit ou changé, et que l'invincible nature ait repris son empire.

Chapitre XII
DIVISION DES LOIS

Pour ordonner le tout, ou donner la meilleure forme possible à la chose publique, il y a diverses relations à considérer. Premièrement l'action du corps entier agissant sur lui-même, c'est-à-dire le rapport du tout au tout, ou du souverain à l'État, et ce rapport est composé de celui des termes intermédiaires, comme nous le verrons ci-après.

Les lois qui règlent ce rapport portent le nom de lois politiques, et s'appellent aussi lois fondamentales, non sans quelque raison si ces lois sont sages. Car s'il n'y a dans chaque État qu'une bonne manière de l'ordonner, le peuple qui l'a trouvée doit s'y tenir : mais si l'ordre établi est mauvais, pourquoi prendrait-on pour fondamentales des lois qui l'empêchent d'être bon ? D'ailleurs, en tout état de cause, un peuple est toujours le maître de changer ses lois, même les meilleures ; car s'il lui plaît de se faire mal à lui-même, qui est-ce qui a droit de l'en empêcher ?

La seconde relation est celle des membres entre eux ou avec le corps entier, et ce rapport doit être au premier égard aussi petit et au second aussi grand qu'il est possible : en sorte que chaque citoyen soit dans une parfaite indépendance de tous les autres, et dans une excessive dépendance de la cité ; ce qui se fait toujours par les mêmes moyens ; car il n'y a que la force de l'État qui fasse la liberté de ses membres. C'est de ce deuxième rapport que naissent les lois civiles.

On peut considérer une troisième sorte de relation entre l'homme et la loi, savoir celle de la désobéissance à la peine, et celle-ci donne lieu à l'établissement des lois criminelles, qui dans le fond sont moins une espèce particulière de lois que la sanction de toutes les autres.

À ces trois sortes de lois il s'en joint une quatrième, la plus importante de toutes ; qui ne se grave ni sur le marbre, ni sur l'airain, mais dans les cœurs des citoyens ; qui fait la véritable constitution de l'État ; qui prend tous les jours de nouvelles forces ; qui, lorsque les autres lois vieillissent ou s'éteignent, les ranime ou les supplée, conserve un peuple dans l'esprit de son institution, et substitue insensiblement la force de l'habitude à celle de l'autorité. Je parle des mœurs, des coutumes, et surtout de l'opinion ; partie inconnue à nos politiques mais de laquelle dépend le succès de toutes les autres : partie dont le grand législateur s'occupe en secret, tandis qu'il paraît se borner à des règlements particuliers qui ne sont que le cintre de la voûte, dont les mœurs, plus lentes à naître, forment enfin l'inébranlable clef.

Entre ces diverses classes, les lois politiques, qui constituent la forme du gouvernement, sont la seule relative à mon sujet.

LIVRE III[36]

Avant de parler des diverses formes de gouvernement, tâchons de fixer le sens précis de ce mot, qui n'a pas encore été fort bien expliqué.

Chapitre I
DU GOUVERNEMENT EN GÉNÉRAL

J'avertis le lecteur que ce chapitre doit être lu posément, et que je ne sais pas l'art d'être clair pour qui ne veut pas être attentif.

Toute action libre a deux causes qui concourent à la produire, l'une morale, savoir la volonté qui détermine l'acte ; l'autre physique, savoir la puissance qui l'exécute. Quand je marche vers un objet, il faut premièrement que j'y veuille aller ; en second lieu, que mes pieds m'y portent. Qu'un paralytique veuille courir, qu'un homme agile ne le veuille pas, tous deux resteront en place. Le corps politique a les mêmes mobiles : on y distingue de même la force et la volonté. Celle-ci sous le nom de *puissance législative*, l'autre sous le nom de *puissance exécutive.* Rien ne s'y fait ou ne doit s'y faire sans leur concours.

Nous avons vu que la puissance législative appartient au peuple, et ne peut appartenir qu'à lui. Il est aisé de voir, au contraire, par les principes ci-devant établis, que la puissance exécutive ne peut appartenir à la généralité comme législatrice ou souveraine ; parce que cette puissance ne consiste qu'en des actes particuliers qui ne sont point du ressort de la loi, ni par conséquent de celui du souverain, dont tous les actes ne peuvent être que des lois.

Il faut donc à la force publique un agent propre qui la réunisse et la mette en œuvre selon les directions de la volonté générale, qui serve à la communication de l'État et du souverain, qui fasse en quelque sorte dans la personne publique ce que fait dans l'homme l'union de l'âme et du corps. Voilà quelle est dans l'État la raison du gouvernement, confondu mal à propos avec le souverain, dont il n'est que le ministre.

Qu'est-ce donc que le gouvernement ? Un corps intermédiaire établi entre les sujets et le souverain pour leur mutuelle correspondance, chargé de l'exécution des lois, et du maintien de la liberté, tant civile que politique.

Les membres de ce corps s'appellent magistrats ou *rois*, c'est-à-dire *gouverneurs* ; et le corps entier porte le nom de *prince**. Ainsi ceux qui prétendent que l'acte par lequel un peuple se soumet à des chefs n'est point un contrat ont grande raison. Ce n'est absolument qu'une commission, un emploi dans lequel, simples officiers du souverain, ils exercent en son nom le pouvoir dont il les a faits dépositaires, et qu'il peut limiter, modifier et reprendre quand il lui plaît, l'aliénation d'un tel droit étant incompatible avec la nature du corps social, et contraire au but de l'association.

J'appelle donc *gouvernement* ou suprême administration l'exercice légitime de la puissance exécutive,

---

* C'est ainsi qu'à Venise on donne au collège le nom de *sérénissime prince*, même quand le doge n'y assiste pas.

et prince ou magistrat, l'homme ou le corps chargé de cette administration[37].

C'est dans le gouvernement que se trouvent les forces intermédiaires, dont les rapports composent celui du tout au tout ou du souverain à l'État. On peut représenter ce dernier rapport par celui des extrêmes d'une proportion continue, dont la moyenne proportionnelle est le gouvernement. Le gouvernement reçoit du souverain les ordres qu'il donne au peuple et, pour que l'État soit dans un bon équilibre il faut, tout compensé, qu'il y ait égalité entre le produit ou la puissance du gouvernement pris en lui-même et le produit ou la puissance des citoyens qui sont souverains d'un côté et sujets de l'autre[38].

De plus, on ne saurait altérer aucun des trois termes sans rompre à l'instant la proportion. Si le souverain veut gouverner, ou si le magistrat veut donner des lois, ou si les sujets refusent d'obéir, le désordre succède à la règle, la force et la volonté n'agissent plus de concert, et l'État dissous tombe ainsi dans le despotisme ou dans l'anarchie. Enfin, comme il n'y a qu'une moyenne proportionnelle entre chaque rapport, il n'y a non plus qu'un bon gouvernement possible dans un État. Mais, comme mille événements peuvent changer les rapports d'un peuple, non seulement différents gouvernements peuvent être bons à divers peuples, mais au même peuple en différents temps.

Pour tâcher de donner une idée des divers rapports qui peuvent régner entre ces deux extrêmes, je prendrai pour exemple le nombre du peuple, comme un rapport plus facile à exprimer.

Supposons que l'État soit composé de dix mille citoyens. Le souverain ne peut être considéré que collectivement et en corps. Mais chaque particulier en qualité de sujet est considéré comme individu. Ainsi le souverain est au sujet comme dix mille est à un ; c'est-à-dire que chaque membre de l'État n'a pour sa part que la dix millième partie de l'autorité souveraine, quoiqu'il lui soit soumis tout entier. Que le peuple soit composé de cent mille hommes, l'état des sujets ne change pas, et chacun porte également tout l'empire des lois, tandis que son suffrage, réduit à un cent millième, a dix fois moins d'influence dans leur rédaction. Alors, le sujet restant toujours un, le rapport du souverain augmente en raison du nombre des citoyens. D'où il suit que, plus l'État s'agrandit, plus la liberté diminue.

Quand je dis que le rapport augmente, j'entends qu'il s'éloigne de l'égalité. Ainsi, plus le rapport est grand dans l'acception des géomètres, moins il y a de rapport dans l'acception commune : dans la première, le rapport considéré selon la quantité se mesure par l'exposant, et dans l'autre, considéré selon l'identité, il s'estime par la similitude.

Or moins les volontés particulières se rapportent à la volonté générale, c'est-à-dire les mœurs aux lois, plus la force réprimante doit augmenter. Donc le gouvernement, pour être bon, doit être relativement plus fort à mesure que le peuple est plus nombreux.

D'un autre côté, l'agrandissement de l'État donnant aux dépositaires de l'autorité publique plus de tentations et de moyens d'abuser de leur pouvoir, plus le gouvernement doit avoir de force pour contenir le peuple, plus le souverain doit en avoir à son tour pour contenir le gouvernement. Je ne parle pas ici d'une force absolue, mais de la force relative des diverses parties de l'État.

Il suit de ce double rapport que la proportion continue entre le souverain, le prince et le peuple n'est point une idée arbitraire, mais une conséquence nécessaire de la nature du corps politique. Il suit encore que l'un des extrêmes, savoir le peuple comme sujet, étant fixe et représenté par l'unité, toutes les fois que la raison doublée augmente ou diminue, la raison simple augmente ou diminue semblablement, et que par conséquent le moyen terme est changé. Ce qui fait voir qu'il n'y a pas une constitution de gouvernement unique et absolue, mais qu'il peut y avoir autant de gouvernements différents en nature que d'États différents en grandeur.

Si, tournant ce système en ridicule, on disait que pour trouver cette moyenne proportionnelle et former le corps du gouvernement il ne faut, selon moi, que tirer la racine carrée du nombre du peuple ; je répondrais que je ne prends ici ce nombre que pour un exemple, que les rapports dont je parle ne se mesurent pas seulement par le nombre des hommes, mais en général par la quantité d'action, laquelle se combine par des multitudes de causes, qu'au reste si, pour m'exprimer en moins de paroles, j'emprunte un moment des termes de géométrie, je n'ignore pas, cependant, que la précision géométrique n'a point lieu dans les quantités morales.

Le gouvernement est en petit ce que le corps politique qui le renferme est en grand. C'est une personne morale douée de certaines facultés, active comme le souverain, passive comme l'État, et qu'on peut décomposer en d'autres rapports semblables, d'où naît par conséquent une nouvelle proportion, une autre encore dans celle-ci selon l'ordre des tribunaux, jusqu'à ce qu'on arrive à un moyen terme indivisible, c'est à dire à un seul chef ou magistrat suprême, qu'on peut se représenter, au milieu de cette progression, comme l'unité entre la série des fractions et celle des nombres.

Sans nous embarrasser dans cette multiplication de termes, contentons-nous de considérer le gouvernement comme un nouveau corps dans l'État, distinct du peuple et du souverain, et intermédiaire entre l'un et l'autre.

Il y a cette différence essentielle entre ces deux corps, que l'État existe par lui-même, et que le gouvernement n'existe que par le souverain. Ainsi la volonté dominante du prince n'est ou ne doit être que la volonté générale ou la loi ; sa force n'est que la force publique concentrée en lui : sitôt qu'il veut tirer de lui-même quelque acte absolu et indépendant, la liaison du tout commence à se relâcher. S'il arrivait enfin que le prince eût une volonté particulière plus active que celle du souverain, et qu'il usât, pour obéir à cette volonté particulière, de la force publique qui est dans ses mains, en sorte qu'on eût, pour ainsi dire, deux souverains, l'un de droit et l'autre de fait ; à l'instant l'union sociale s'évanouirait, et le corps politique serait dissous.

Cependant pour que le corps du gouvernement ait une existence, une vie réelle qui le distingue du corps de l'État, pour que tous ses membres puissent agir de concert et répondre à la fin pour laquelle il est institué, il lui faut un *moi* particulier, une sensibilité commune à ses membres, une force, une volonté propre qui tende à sa conservation. Cette existence particulière suppose des assemblées, des conseils, un pouvoir de délibérer, de résoudre, des droits, des titres, des privilèges qui appartiennent au prince exclusivement, et qui rendent la condition du magistrat plus honorable à proportion qu'elle est plus pénible. Les difficultés sont dans la manière d'ordonner dans le tout ce tout subalterne, de sorte qu'il n'altère point la constitution générale en affermissant la sienne, qu'il distingue toujours sa force particulière destinée à sa propre conservation de la force publique destinée à la conservation de l'État, et qu'en un mot il soit toujours prêt à sacrifier le gouvernement au peuple et non le peuple au gouvernement.

D'ailleurs, bien que le corps artificiel du gouvernement soit l'ouvrage d'un autre corps artificiel, et qu'il n'ait, en quelque sorte, qu'une vie empruntée et subordonnée, cela n'empêche pas qu'il ne puisse agir avec plus ou moins de vigueur ou de célérité, jouir, pour ainsi dire, d'une santé plus ou moins robuste. Enfin, sans s'éloigner directement du but de son institution, il peut s'en écarter plus ou moins, selon la manière dont il est constitué.

C'est de toutes ces différences que naissent les rapports divers que le gouvernement doit avoir avec le corps de l'État, selon les rapports accidentels et particuliers par lesquels ce même État est modifié. Car souvent le gouvernement le meilleur en soi deviendra le plus vicieux, si ses rapports ne sont altérés selon les défauts du corps politique auquel il appartient.

Chapitre II

DU PRINCIPE QUI CONSTITUE LES DIVERSES FORMES DE GOUVERNEMENT[39]

Pour exposer la cause générale de ces différences, il faut distinguer ici le prince et le gouvernement, comme j'ai distingué ci-devant l'État et le souverain.

Le corps du magistrat peut être composé d'un plus grand ou moindre nombre de membres. Nous avons dit que le rapport du souverain aux sujets était d'autant plus grand que le peuple était plus nombreux, et par une évidente analogie nous en pouvons dire autant du gouvernement à l'égard des magistrats.

Or la force totale du gouvernement, étant toujours celle de l'État, ne varie point : d'où il suit que plus il use de cette force sur ses propres membres, moins il lui en reste pour agir sur tout le peuple.

Donc plus les magistrats sont nombreux, plus le gouvernement est faible. Comme cette maxime est fondamentale, appliquons-nous à la mieux éclaircir.

Nous pouvons distinguer dans la personne du magistrat trois volontés essentiellement différentes. Premièrement la volonté propre de l'individu, qui ne tend qu'à son avantage particulier ; secondement la volonté commune des magistrats, qui se rapporte uniquement à l'avantage du prince, et qu'on peut appeler volonté de corps, laquelle est générale par rapport au gouvernement, et particulière par rapport à l'État, dont le gouvernement fait partie ; en troisième lieu la volonté du peuple ou la volonté souveraine, laquelle est générale, tant par rapport à l'État considéré comme le tout, que par rapport au gouvernement considéré comme partie du tout.

Dans une législation parfaite, la volonté particulière ou individuelle doit être nulle, la volonté de corps propre au gouvernement très subordonnée, et par conséquent la volonté générale ou souveraine toujours dominante et la règle unique de toutes les autres.

Selon l'ordre naturel, au contraire, ces différentes volontés deviennent plus actives à mesure qu'elles se concentrent. Ainsi la volonté générale est toujours la plus faible, la volonté de corps a le second rang, et la volonté particulière le premier de tous : de sorte que dans le gouvernement chaque membre est premièrement soi-même, et puis magistrat, et puis citoyen ; gradation directement opposée à celle qu'exige l'ordre social.

Cela posé : que tout le gouvernement soit entre les mains d'un seul homme. Voilà la volonté particulière et la volonté de corps parfaitement réunies, et par conséquent celle-ci au plus haut degré d'intensité qu'elle puisse avoir. Or comme c'est du degré de la volonté que dépend l'usage de la force, et que la force absolue du gouvernement ne varie point, il s'ensuit que le plus actif des gouvernements est celui d'un seul[40].

Au contraire, unissons le gouvernement à l'autorité législative ; faisons le prince du souverain et de tous les citoyens autant de magistrats. Alors la volonté de corps, confondue avec la volonté générale, n'aura pas plus d'activité qu'elle, et laissera la volonté particulière dans toute sa force. Ainsi le gouvernement, toujours avec la même force absolue, sera dans son *minimum* de force relative ou d'activité.

Ces rapports sont incontestables, et d'autres considérations servent encore à les confirmer. On voit par exemple, que chaque magistrat est plus actif dans son corps que chaque citoyen dans le sien, et que par conséquent la volonté particulière a beaucoup plus d'influence dans les actes du gouvernement, que dans ceux du souverain ; car chaque magistrat est presque toujours chargé de quelque fonction du gouvernement, au lieu que chaque citoyen pris à part n'a aucune fonction de la souveraineté. D'ailleurs, plus l'État s'étend, plus sa force réelle augmente, quoiqu'elle n'augmente pas en raison de son étendue : mais l'État restant le même, les magistrats ont beau se multiplier, le gouvernement n'en acquiert pas une plus grande force réelle, parce que cette force est celle de l'État, dont la mesure est toujours égale. Ainsi la force relative ou l'activité du gouvernement diminue, sans que sa force absolue ou réelle puisse augmenter.

Il est sûr encore que l'expédition des affaires devient plus lente à mesure que plus de gens en sont chargés, qu'en donnant trop à la prudence on ne donne pas assez à la fortune, qu'on laisse échapper l'occasion, et qu'à force de délibérer on perd souvent le fruit de la délibération.

Je viens de prouver que le gouvernement se relâche à mesure que les magistrats se multiplient, et j'ai prouvé ci-devant que plus le peuple est nombreux, plus la force réprimante doit augmenter. D'où il suit que le rapport des magistrats au gouvernement doit être inverse du rapport des sujets au souverain ; c'est-à-dire que, plus l'État s'agrandit, plus le gouvernement doit se resserrer ; tellement que le nombre des chefs diminue en raison de l'augmentation du peuple.

Au reste je ne parle ici que de la force relative du gouvernement, et non de sa rectitude : car, au contraire, plus le magistrat est nombreux, plus la volonté de corps se rapproche de la volonté générale ; au lieu que sous un magistrat unique cette même volonté de corps n'est, comme je l'ai dit, qu'une volonté particulière. Ainsi l'on perd d'un côté ce qu'on peut gagner de l'autre, et l'art du législateur est de savoir fixer le point où la force et la volonté du gouvernement, toujours en proportion réciproque, se combinent dans le rapport le plus avantageux à l'État.

Chapitre III

DIVISION DES GOUVERNEMENTS

On a vu dans le chapitre précédent pourquoi l'on distingue les diverses espèces ou formes de gouvernements par le nombre des membres qui les composent ; il reste à voir dans celui-ci comment se fait cette division.

Le souverain peut, en premier lieu, commettre le dépôt du gouvernement à tout le peuple ou à la plus grande partie du peuple, en sorte qu'il y ait plus de citoyens magistrats que de citoyens simples particuliers. On donne à cette forme de gouvernement le nom de *démocratie*.

Ou bien il peut resserrer le gouvernement entre les mains d'un petit nombre, en sorte qu'il y ait plus de simples citoyens que de magistrats ; et cette forme porte le nom d'*aristocratie.*

Enfin il peut concentrer tout le gouvernement dans les mains d'un magistrat unique dont tous les autres tiennent leur pouvoir. Cette troisième forme est la plus commune, et s'appelle *monarchie* ou gouvernement royal[41].

On doit remarquer que toutes ces formes ou du moins les deux premières sont susceptibles de plus ou de moins, et ont même une assez grande latitude ; car la démocratie peut embrasser tout le peuple ou se resserrer jusqu'à la moitié. L'aristocratie, à son tour, peut de la moitié du peuple se resserrer jusqu'au plus petit nombre indéterminément. La royauté même est susceptible de quelque partage. Sparte eut constamment deux rois par sa constitution ; et l'on a vu dans l'Empire romain jusqu'à huit empereurs à la fois sans qu'on pût dire que l'Empire fût divisé. Ainsi il y a un point où chaque forme de gouvernement se confond avec la suivante, et l'on voit que, sous trois seules dénominations, le gouvernement est réellement susceptible d'autant de formes diverses que l'État a de citoyens.

Il y a plus : ce même gouvernement pouvant à certains égards se subdiviser en d'autres parties, l'une administrée d'une manière et l'autre d'une autre, il peut résulter de ces trois formes combinées une multitude de formes mixtes, dont chacune est multipliable par toutes les formes simples.

On a, de tout temps, beaucoup disputé sur la meilleure forme de gouvernement, sans considérer que chacune d'elles est la meilleure en certains cas, et la pire en d'autres.

Si dans les différents États le nombre des magistrats suprêmes doit être en raison inverse de celui des citoyens, il s'ensuit qu'en général le gouvernement démocratique convient aux petits États, l'aristocratique aux médiocres, et le monarchique aux grands. Cette règle se tire immédiatement du principe, mais comment compter la multitude de circonstances qui peuvent fournir des exceptions ?

Chapitre IV
DE LA DÉMOCRATIE

Celui qui fait la loi sait mieux que personne comment elle doit être exécutée et interprétée. Il semble donc qu'on ne saurait avoir une meilleure constitution que celle où le pouvoir exécutif est joint au législatif. Mais c'est cela même qui rend ce gouvernement insuffisant à certains égards, parce que les choses qui doivent être distinguées[42] ne le sont pas, et que le prince et le souverain, n'étant que la même personne, ne forment, pour ainsi dire, qu'un gouvernement sans gouvernement.

Il n'est pas bon que celui qui fait des lois les exécute, ni que le corps du peuple détourne son attention des vues générales pour la donner aux objets particuliers. Rien n'est plus dangereux que l'influence des intérêts privés dans les affaires publiques, et l'abus des lois par le gouvernement est un mal moindre que la corruption du législateur, suite infaillible des vues particulières. Alors, l'État étant altéré dans sa substance, toute réforme devient impossible. Un peuple qui n'abuserait jamais du gouvernement n'abuserait pas non plus de l'indépendance ; un peuple qui gouvernerait toujours bien n'aurait pas besoin d'être gouverné.

À prendre le terme dans la rigueur de l'acception, il n'a jamais existé de véritable démocratie, et il n'en existera jamais. Il est contre l'ordre naturel que le grand nombre gouverne et que le petit soit gouverné. On ne peut imaginer que le peuple reste incessamment assemblé pour vaquer aux affaires publiques, et l'on voit aisément qu'il ne saurait établir pour cela des commissions sans que la forme de l'administration change[43].

En effet, je crois pouvoir poser en principe que quand les fonctions du gouvernement sont partagées entre plusieurs tribunaux, les moins nombreux acquièrent tôt ou tard la plus grande autorité, ne fût-ce qu'à cause de la facilité d'expédier les affaires, qui les y amène naturellement.

D'ailleurs, que de choses difficiles à réunir ne suppose pas ce gouvernement ! Premièrement un État très petit où le peuple soit facile à rassembler et où chaque citoyen puisse aisément connaître tous les autres ; secondement une grande simplicité de mœurs qui prévienne la multitude d'affaires et les discussions épineuses ; ensuite beaucoup d'égalité dans les rangs et dans les fortunes, sans quoi l'égalité ne saurait subsister longtemps dans les droits et l'autorité ; enfin peu ou point de luxe, car ou le luxe est l'effet des richesses, ou il les rend nécessaires ; il corrompt à la fois le riche et le pauvre, l'un par la possession, l'autre par la convoitise ; il vend la patrie à la mollesse, à la vanité ; il ôte à l'État tous ses citoyens pour les asservir les uns aux autres, et tous à l'opinion.

Voilà pourquoi un auteur célèbre a donné la vertu pour principe à la république[44], car toutes ces conditions ne sauraient subsister sans la vertu ; mais, faute d'avoir fait les distinctions nécessaires, ce beau génie a manqué souvent de justesse, quelquefois de clarté, et n'a pas vu que l'autorité souveraine étant partout la même, le même principe doit avoir lieu dans tout État bien constitué[45], plus ou moins, il est vrai, selon la forme du gouvernement.

Ajoutons qu'il n'y a pas de gouvernement si sujet aux guerres civiles et aux agitations intestines que le démocratique ou populaire, parce qu'il n'y en a aucun qui tende si fortement et si continuellement à changer de forme, ni qui demande plus de vigilance et de courage pour être maintenu dans la sienne. C'est surtout dans cette constitution que le citoyen doit s'armer de force et de constance, et dire chaque jour de sa vie au fond de son cœur ce que disait un vertueux palatin*, dans la Diète de Pologne : *Malo periculosam libertatem quam quietum servitium*[46].

S'il y avait un peuple de dieux, il se gouvernerait démocratiquement. Un gouvernement si parfait ne convient pas à des hommes.

Chapitre V
DE L'ARISTOCRATIE

Nous avons ici deux personnes morales très distinctes, savoir le gouvernement et le souverain, et par conséquent deux volontés générales, l'une par rapport à tous les citoyens, l'autre seulement pour les membres de l'administration. Ainsi, bien que le gouvernement puisse régler sa police intérieure comme il lui plaît, il ne peut jamais parler au peuple qu'au nom du souverain, c'est-à-dire au nom du peuple même ; ce qu'il ne faut jamais oublier.

Les premières sociétés se gouvernèrent aristocratiquement. Les chefs des familles délibéraient entre eux des affaires publiques. Les jeunes gens cédaient sans peine à l'autorité de l'expérience. De là les noms de

---

* Le palatin de Posnanie, père du roi de Pologne, duc de Lorraine.

prêtres, d'*anciens*, de *sénat*, de *gérontes*. Les sauvages de l'Amérique septentrionale se gouvernent encore ainsi de nos jours, et sont très bien gouvernés.

Mais, à mesure que l'inégalité d'institution l'emporta sur l'inégalité naturelle, la richesse ou la puissance* fut préférée à l'âge, et l'aristocratie devint élective. Enfin la puissance transmise avec les biens du père aux enfants rendant les familles patriciennes, rendit le gouvernement héréditaire, et l'on vit des sénateurs de vingt ans.

Il y a donc trois sortes d'aristocratie : naturelle, élective, héréditaire. La première ne convient qu'à des peuples simples : la troisième est le pire de tous les gouvernements. La deuxième est le meilleur : c'est l'aristocratie proprement dite.

Outre l'avantage de la distinction des deux pouvoirs, elle a celui du choix de ses membres ; car dans le gouvernement populaire tous les citoyens naissent magistrats ; mais celui-ci les borne à un petit nombre, et ils ne le deviennent que par élection** : moyen par lequel la probité, les lumières, l'expérience, et toutes les autres raisons de préférence et d'estime publique, sont autant de nouveaux garants qu'on sera sagement gouverné.

De plus, les assemblées se font plus commodément, les affaires se discutent mieux, s'expédient avec plus d'ordre et de diligence, le crédit de l'État est mieux soutenu chez l'étranger par de vénérables sénateurs que par une multitude inconnue ou méprisée.

---

* Il est clair que le mot *optimates*, chez les anciens, ne veut pas dire les meilleurs, mais les plus puissants. ** Il importe beaucoup de régler par des lois la forme de l'élection des magistrats, car, en l'abandonnant à la volonté du prince, on ne peut éviter de tomber dans l'aristocratie héréditaire, comme il est arrivé aux républiques de *Venise* et de *Berne*. Aussi la première est-elle depuis longtemps un État dissous ; mais la seconde se maintient par l'extrême sagesse de son Sénat : c'est une exception bien honorable et bien dangereuse.

En un mot, c'est l'ordre le meilleur et le plus naturel que les plus sages gouvernent la multitude, quand on est sûr qu'ils la gouverneront pour son profit et non pour le leur ; il ne faut point multiplier en vain les ressorts, ni faire avec vingt mille hommes ce que cent hommes choisis peuvent faire encore mieux. Mais il faut remarquer que l'intérêt de corps commence à moins diriger ici la force publique sur la règle de la volonté générale, et qu'une autre pente inévitable enlève aux lois une partie de la puissance exécutive.

À l'égard des convenances particulières, il ne faut ni un État si petit ni un peuple si simple et si droit que l'exécution des lois suive immédiatement de la volonté publique, comme dans une bonne démocratie. Il ne faut pas non plus une si grande nation que les chefs épars pour la gouverner puissent trancher du souverain chacun dans son département, et commencer par se rendre indépendants pour devenir enfin les maîtres.

Mais si l'aristocratie exige quelques vertus de moins que le gouvernement populaire, elle en exige aussi d'autres qui lui sont propres ; comme la modération dans les riches et le contentement dans les pauvres ; car il semble qu'une égalité rigoureuse y serait déplacée ; elle ne fut pas même observée à Sparte.

Au reste, si cette forme comporte une certaine inégalité de fortune, c'est bien pour qu'en général l'administration des affaires publiques soit confiée à ceux qui peuvent le mieux y donner tout leur temps, mais non pas, comme prétend Aristote, pour que les riches soient toujours préférés. Au contraire, il importe qu'un choix opposé apprenne quelquefois au peuple qu'il y a dans le mérite des hommes des raisons de préférence plus importantes que la richesse.

Chapitre VI
DE LA MONARCHIE

Jusqu'ici nous avons considéré le prince comme une personne morale et collective, unie par la force des lois, et dépositaire dans l'État de la puissance exécutive. Nous avons maintenant à considérer cette puissance réunie entre les mains d'une personne naturelle, d'un homme réel, qui seul ait droit d'en disposer selon les lois. C'est ce qu'on appelle un monarque ou un roi.

Tout au contraire des autres administrations où un être collectif représente un individu, dans celle-ci un individu représente un être collectif ; en sorte que l'unité morale qui constitue le prince est en même temps une unité physique, dans laquelle toutes les facultés que la loi réunit dans l'autre avec tant d'efforts se trouvent naturellement réunies.

Ainsi la volonté du peuple, et la volonté du prince, et la force publique de l'État, et la force particulière du gouvernement, tout répond au même mobile, tous les ressorts de la machine sont dans la même main, tout marche au même but ; il n'y a point de mouvements opposés qui s'entre-détruisent, et l'on ne peut imaginer aucune sorte de constitution dans laquelle un moindre effort produise une action plus considérable. Archimède assis tranquillement sur le rivage et tirant sans peine à flot un grand vaisseau, me représente un monarque habile gouvernant de son cabinet ses vastes États, et faisant tout mouvoir en paraissant immobile.

Mais s'il n'y a point de gouvernement qui ait plus de vigueur, il n'y en a point où la volonté particulière ait plus d'empire et domine plus aisément les autres ; tout marche au même but, il est vrai ; mais ce but n'est point celui de la félicité publique, et la force même de l'administration tourne sans cesse au préjudice de l'État.

Les rois veulent être absolus, et de loin on leur crie que le meilleur moyen de l'être est de se faire aimer de leurs peuples. Cette maxime est très belle, et même très vraie à certains égards. Malheureusement on s'en moquera toujours dans les cours. La puissance qui vient de l'amour des peuples est sans doute la plus grande ; mais elle est précaire et conditionnelle, jamais les princes ne s'en contenteront. Les meilleurs rois veulent pouvoir être méchants s'il leur plaît, sans cesser d'être les maîtres. Un sermonneur politique aura beau leur dire que la force du peuple étant la leur, leur plus grand intérêt est que le peuple soit florissant, nombreux, redoutable. Ils savent très bien que cela n'est pas vrai. Leur intérêt personnel est premièrement que le peuple soit faible, misérable, et qu'il ne puisse jamais leur résister. J'avoue que, supposant les sujets toujours parfaitement soumis, l'intérêt du prince serait alors que le peuple fût puissant, afin que cette puissance étant sienne le rendît redoutable à ses voisins ; mais comme cet intérêt n'est que secondaire et subordonné, et que les deux suppositions sont incompatibles, il est naturel que les princes donnent la préférence à la maxime qui leur est le plus immédiatement utile. C'est ce que Samuel représentait fortement aux Hébreux ; c'est ce que Machiavel a fait voir avec évidence. En feignant de donner des leçons aux rois il en a donné de grandes aux peuples. *Le Prince* de Machiavel est le livre des républicains*.

---

* Machiavel était un honnête homme et un bon citoyen ; mais, attaché à la maison de Médicis, il était forcé, dans l'oppression de sa patrie, de déguiser son amour pour la liberté. Le choix seul de son exécrable héros manifeste assez son intention secrète ; et l'opposition des maximes de son livre du *Prince* à celles de ses *Discours sur Tite-Live* et de son *Histoire de Florence*, démontre que ce profond politique n'a eu jusqu'ici que des lecteurs superficiels ou corrompus. La cour de Rome a sévèrement défendu son livre : je le

Nous avons trouvé, par les rapports généraux, que la monarchie n'est convenable qu'aux grands États, et nous le trouvons encore en l'examinant en elle-même. Plus l'administration publique est nombreuse, plus le rapport du prince aux sujets diminue et s'approche de l'égalité, en sorte que ce rapport est un ou l'égalité même dans la démocratie. Ce même rapport augmente à mesure que le gouvernement se resserre, et il est dans son *maximum* quand le gouvernement est dans les mains d'un seul. Alors il se trouve une trop grande distance entre le prince et le peuple, et l'État manque de liaison. Pour la former il faut donc des ordres intermédiaires. Il faut des princes, des grands, de la noblesse pour les remplir. Or rien de tout cela ne convient à un petit État, que ruinent tous ces degrés.

Mais s'il est difficile qu'un grand État soit bien gouverné, il l'est beaucoup plus qu'il soit bien gouverné par un seul homme et chacun sait ce qu'il arrive quand le roi se donne des substituts.

Un défaut essentiel et inévitable, qui mettra toujours le gouvernement monarchique au-dessous du républicain, est que dans celui-ci la voix publique n'élève presque jamais aux premières places que des hommes éclairés et capables, qui les remplissent avec honneur ; au lieu que ceux qui parviennent dans les monarchies ne sont le plus souvent que de petits brouillons, de petits fripons, de petits intrigants, à qui les petits talents qui font dans les cours parvenir aux grandes places, ne servent qu'à montrer au public leur ineptie aussitôt qu'ils y sont parvenus. Le peuple se trompe bien moins sur ce choix que le prince, et un homme d'un vrai mérite est presque aussi rare dans le ministère qu'un sot à la

---

crois bien ; c'est elle qu'il dépeint le plus clairement. *(Note de Rousseau à l'édition de 1782.)*

tête d'un gouvernement républicain. Aussi, quand par quelque heureux hasard un de ces hommes nés pour gouverner prend le timon des affaires dans une monarchie presque abîmée par ces tas de jolis régisseurs, on est tout surpris des ressources qu'il trouve, et cela fait époque dans un pays.

Pour qu'un État monarchique pût être bien gouverné, il faudrait que sa grandeur ou son étendue fût mesurée aux facultés de celui qui gouverne. Il est plus aisé de conquérir que de régir. Avec un levier suffisant, d'un doigt l'on peut ébranler le monde, mais pour le soutenir il faut les épaules d'Hercule. Pour peu qu'un État soit grand, le prince est presque toujours trop petit. Quand au contraire il arrive que l'État est trop petit pour son chef, ce qui est très rare, il est encore mal gouverné, parce que le chef, suivant toujours la grandeur de ses vues, oublie les intérêts des peuples, et ne les rend pas moins malheureux par l'abus des talents qu'il a de trop qu'un chef borné par le défaut de ceux qui lui manquent. Il faudrait, pour ainsi dire, qu'un royaume s'étendît ou se resserrât à chaque règne selon la portée du prince ; au lieu que, les talents d'un Sénat ayant des mesures plus fixes, l'État peut avoir des bornes constantes et l'administration n'aller pas moins bien.

Le plus sensible inconvénient du gouvernement d'un seul est le défaut de cette succession continuelle qui forme dans les deux autres une liaison non interrompue. Un roi mort, il en faut un autre ; les élections laissent des intervalles dangereux, elles sont orageuses, et à moins que les citoyens ne soient d'un désintéressement, d'une intégrité que ce gouvernement ne comporte guère, la brigue et la corruption s'en mêlent. Il est difficile que celui à qui l'État s'est vendu ne le vende pas à son tour, et ne se dédommage pas sur les faibles de l'argent que les puissants lui ont extorqué. Tôt ou tard tout devient vénal sous une pareille administration, et la paix dont on jouit sous les rois est pire que le désordre des interrègnes.

Qu'a-t-on fait pour prévenir ces maux ? On a rendu les couronnes héréditaires dans certaines familles, et l'on a établi un ordre de succession qui prévient toute dispute à la mort des rois. C'est-à-dire que, substituant l'inconvénient des régences à celui des élections, on a préféré une apparente tranquillité à une administration sage, et qu'on a mieux aimé risquer d'avoir pour chefs des enfants, des monstres, des imbéciles, que d'avoir à disputer sur le choix des bons rois ; on n'a pas considéré qu'en s'exposant ainsi aux risques de l'alternative on met presque toutes les chances contre soi. C'était un mot très sensé que celui du jeune Denis à qui son père en lui reprochant une action honteuse disait : « T'en ai-je donné l'exemple ? — Ah, répondit le fils, votre père n'était pas roi ! »

Tout concourt à priver de justice et de raison un homme élevé pour commander aux autres. On prend beaucoup de peine, à ce qu'on dit, pour enseigner aux jeunes princes l'art de régner : il ne paraît pas que cette éducation leur profite. On ferait mieux de commencer par leur enseigner l'art d'obéir. Les plus grands rois qu'ait célébrés l'histoire n'ont point été élevés pour régner ; c'est une science qu'on ne possède jamais moins qu'après l'avoir trop apprise, et qu'on acquiert mieux en obéissant qu'en commandant. *« Nam utilissimus idem ac brevissimus bonarum malarumque rerum delectus, cogitare quid aut nolueris sub alio principe, aut volueris**. »

---

* Tacite, *Histoires*[47].

Une suite de ce défaut de cohérence est l'inconstance du gouvernement royal, qui, se réglant tantôt sur un plan et tantôt sur un autre, selon le caractère du prince qui règne ou des gens qui règnent pour lui, ne peut avoir longtemps un objet fixe ni une conduite conséquente : variation qui rend toujours l'État flottant de maxime en maxime, de projet en projet, et qui n'a pas lieu dans les autres gouvernements où le prince est toujours le même. Aussi voit-on qu'en général, s'il y a plus de ruse dans une cour, il y a plus de sagesse dans un Sénat, et que les républiques vont à leurs fins par des vues plus constantes et mieux suivies, au lieu que chaque révolution dans le ministère en produit une dans l'État ; la maxime commune à tous les ministres, et presque à tous les rois, étant de prendre en toute chose le contre-pied de leur prédécesseur.

De cette même incohérence se tire encore la solution d'un sophisme très familier aux politiques royaux ; c'est non seulement de comparer le gouvernement civil au gouvernement domestique et le prince au père de famille, erreur déjà réfutée, mais encore de donner libéralement à ce magistrat toutes les vertus dont il aurait besoin, et de supposer toujours que le prince est ce qu'il devrait être ; supposition à l'aide de laquelle le gouvernement royal est évidemment préférable à tout autre, parce qu'il est incontestablement le plus fort, et que pour être aussi le meilleur il ne lui manque qu'une volonté de corps plus conforme à la volonté générale.

Mais si, selon Platon*, le roi par nature est un personnage si rare, combien de fois la nature et la fortune concourront-elles à le couronner, et si l'éducation royale

* *In Civili*[48].

corrompt nécessairement ceux qui la reçoivent, que doit-on espérer d'une suite d'hommes élevés pour régner? C'est donc bien vouloir s'abuser que de confondre le gouvernement royal avec celui d'un bon roi. Pour voir ce qu'est ce gouvernement en lui-même, il faut le considérer sous des princes bornés ou méchants; car ils arriveront tels au trône, ou le trône les rendra tels.

Ces difficultés n'ont pas échappé à nos auteurs, mais ils n'en sont point embarrassés. Le remède est, disent-ils, d'obéir sans murmure. Dieu donne les mauvais rois dans sa colère, et il faut les supporter comme des châtiments du Ciel. Ce discours est édifiant, sans doute; mais je ne sais s'il ne conviendrait pas mieux en chaire que dans un livre de politique. Que dire d'un médecin qui promet des miracles, et dont tout l'art est d'exhorter son malade à la patience? On sait bien qu'il faut souffrir un mauvais gouvernement quand on l'a; la question serait d'en trouver un bon.

Chapitre VII

DES GOUVERNEMENTS MIXTES

À proprement parler il n'y a point de gouvernement simple. Il faut qu'un chef unique ait des magistrats subalternes; il faut qu'un gouvernement populaire ait un chef. Ainsi, dans le partage de la puissance exécutive, il y a toujours gradation du grand nombre au moindre, avec cette différence que tantôt le grand nombre dépend du petit, et tantôt le petit du grand.

Quelquefois il y a partage égal, soit quand les parties constitutives sont dans une dépendance mutuelle, comme dans le gouvernement d'Angleterre; soit quand l'autorité de chaque partie est indépendante mais imparfaite, comme en Pologne. Cette dernière forme est mauvaise, parce qu'il n'y a point d'unité dans le gouvernement, et que l'État manque de liaison.

Lequel vaut le mieux, d'un gouvernement simple ou d'un gouvernement mixte ? Question fort agitée chez les politiques, et à laquelle il faut faire la même réponse que j'ai faite ci-devant sur toute forme de gouvernement.

Le gouvernement simple est le meilleur en soi, par cela seul qu'il est simple. Mais quand la puissance exécutive ne dépend pas assez de la législative, c'est-à-dire, quand il y a plus de rapport du prince au souverain que du peuple au prince, il faut remédier à ce défaut de proportion en divisant le gouvernement ; car alors toutes ses parties n'ont pas moins d'autorité sur les sujets, et leur division les rend toutes ensemble moins fortes contre le souverain.

On prévient encore le même inconvénient en établissant des magistrats intermédiaires qui, laissant le gouvernement en son entier, servent seulement à balancer les deux puissances et à maintenir leurs droits respectifs. Alors le gouvernement n'est pas mixte, il est tempéré.

On peut remédier par des moyens semblables à l'inconvénient opposé et, quand le gouvernement est trop lâche, ériger des tribunaux pour le concentrer : cela se pratique dans toutes les démocraties. Dans le premier cas, on divise le gouvernement pour l'affaiblir, et dans le second, pour le renforcer ; car les *maximum* de force et de faiblesse se trouvent également dans les gouvernements simples, au lieu que les formes mixtes donnent une force moyenne[49].

Chapitre VIII

QUE TOUTE FORME DE GOUVERNEMENT N'EST PAS PROPRE À TOUT PAYS

La liberté n'étant pas un fruit de tous les climats n'est pas à la portée de tous les peuples. Plus on médite ce principe établi par Montesquieu[50], plus on en sent la vérité. Plus on le conteste, plus on donne occasion de l'établir par de nouvelles preuves.

Dans tous les gouvernements du monde la personne publique consomme et ne produit rien. D'où lui vient donc la substance consommée? Du travail de ses membres. C'est le superflu des particuliers qui produit le nécessaire du public. D'où il suit que l'état civil ne peut subsister qu'autant que le travail des hommes rend au-delà de leurs besoins.

Or, cet excédent n'est pas le même dans tous les pays du monde. Dans plusieurs il est considérable, dans d'autres médiocre, dans d'autres nul, dans d'autres négatif. Ce rapport dépend de la fertilité du climat, de la sorte de travail que la terre exige, de la nature de ses productions, de la force de ses habitants, de la plus ou moins grande consommation qui leur est nécessaire, et de plusieurs autres rapports semblables desquels il est composé.

D'autre part, tous les gouvernements ne sont pas de même nature; il y en a de plus ou moins dévorants, et les différences sont fondées sur cet autre principe que, plus les contributions publiques s'éloignent de leur source, et plus elles sont onéreuses. Ce n'est pas sur la quantité des impositions qu'il faut mesurer cette charge, mais sur le chemin qu'elles ont à faire pour retourner dans les mains dont elles sont sorties; quand cette circulation est prompte et bien établie, qu'on paye peu ou beaucoup, il n'importe ; le peuple est toujours riche et les finances font toujours bien. Au contraire, quelque peu que le peuple donne, quand ce peu ne lui revient point, en donnant toujours bientôt il s'épuise ; l'État n'est jamais riche, et le peuple est toujours gueux.

Il suit de là que plus la distance du peuple au gouvernement augmente, et plus les tributs deviennent onéreux : ainsi dans la démocratie le peuple est le moins chargé, dans l'aristocratie il l'est davantage, dans la monarchie il porte le plus grand poids. La monarchie ne convient donc qu'aux nations opulentes ; l'aristocratie, aux États médiocres en richesse ainsi qu'en grandeur ; la démocratie, aux États petits et pauvres.

En effet, plus on y réfléchit, plus on trouve en ceci de différence entre les États libres et les monarchiques ; dans les premiers tout s'emploie à l'utilité commune ; dans les autres les forces publiques et particulières sont réciproques et l'une s'augmente par l'affaiblissement de l'autre. Enfin, au lieu de gouverner les sujets pour les rendre heureux, le despotisme les rend misérables pour les gouverner.

Voilà donc dans chaque climat des causes naturelles sur lesquelles on peut assigner la forme de gouvernement à laquelle la force du climat l'entraîne, et dire même quelle espèce d'habitants il doit avoir. Les lieux ingrats et stériles où le produit ne vaut pas le travail doivent rester incultes et déserts, ou seulement peuplés de sauvages. Les lieux où le travail des hommes ne rend exactement que le nécessaire doivent être habités par des peuples barbares, toute politie y serait impossible : les lieux où l'excès du produit sur le travail est médiocre conviennent aux peuples libres ; ceux où le terroir abondant et fertile donne beaucoup de produit pour peu de travail veulent être gouvernés monarchiquement, pour consumer par le luxe du prince l'excès du superflu des sujets ; car il vaut mieux que cet excès soit absorbé par le gouvernement que dissipé par les particuliers. Il y a des exceptions, je le sais : mais ces exceptions mêmes confirment la règle, en ce qu'elles produisent tôt ou tard des révolutions qui ramènent les choses dans l'ordre de la nature.

Distinguons toujours les lois générales des causes particulières qui peuvent en modifier l'effet. Quand tout le Midi serait couvert de républiques et tout le Nord d'États despotiques, il n'en serait pas moins vrai que par l'effet du climat le despotisme convient aux pays chauds, la barbarie aux pays froids, et la bonne politie aux régions intermédiaires. Je vois encore qu'en accordant le principe on pourra disputer sur l'application : on pourra dire qu'il y a des pays froids très fertiles et des méridionaux très ingrats. Mais cette difficulté n'en est une que pour ceux qui n'examinent pas la chose dans tous ses rapports. Il faut, comme je l'ai déjà dit, compter ceux des travaux, des forces, de la consommation, etc.

Supposons que de deux terrains égaux l'un rapporte cinq et l'autre dix. Si les habitants du premier consomment quatre et ceux du dernier neuf, l'excès du premier produit sera 1/5, et celui du second 1/10. Le rapport de ces deux excès étant donc inverse de celui des produits, le terrain qui ne produira que cinq donnera un superflu double de celui du terrain qui produit dix.

Mais il n'est pas question d'un produit double, et je ne crois pas que personne ose mettre en général la fertilité des pays froids en égalité même avec celle des pays chauds. Toutefois supposons cette égalité ; laissons, si l'on veut, en balance l'Angleterre avec la Sicile, et la Pologne avec l'Égypte. Plus au midi nous aurons l'Afrique et les Indes ; plus au nord nous n'aurons plus rien. Pour cette égalité de produit, quelle différence dans la culture ? En Sicile il ne faut que gratter la terre ; en Angleterre que de soins pour la labourer ! Or là où il faut plus de bras pour donner le même produit, le superflu doit être nécessairement moindre.

Considérez, outre cela, que la même quantité d'hommes consomme beaucoup moins dans les pays chauds. Le climat demande qu'on y soit sobre pour se porter bien : les Européens qui veulent y vivre comme chez eux périssent tous de dysenterie et d'indigestions. « Nous sommes, dit Chardin[51], des bêtes carnassières, des loups, en comparaison des Asiatiques. Quelques-uns attribuent la sobriété des Persans à ce que leur pays est moins cultivé, et moi je crois au contraire que leur pays abonde moins en denrées parce qu'il en faut moins aux habitants. Si leur frugalité, continue-t-il, était un effet de la disette du pays, il n'y aurait que les pauvres qui mangeraient peu, au lieu que c'est généralement tout le monde, et on mangerait plus ou moins en chaque province selon la fertilité du pays, au lieu que la même sobriété se trouve par tout le royaume. Ils se louent fort de leur manière de vivre, disant qu'il ne faut que regarder leur teint pour reconnaître combien elle est plus excellente que celle des chrétiens. En effet le teint des Persans est uni ; ils ont la peau belle, fine et polie, au lieu que le teint des Arméniens leurs sujets qui vivent à l'européenne, est rude, couperosé, et que leurs corps sont gros et pesants. »

Plus on approche de la ligne, plus les peuples vivent de peu. Ils ne mangent presque pas de viande ; le riz, le maïs, le couscous, le mil, la cassave, sont des aliments ordinaires. Il y a aux Indes des millions d'hommes dont la nourriture ne coûte pas un sol par jour. Nous voyons en Europe même des différences sensibles pour l'appétit entre les peuples du Nord et ceux du Midi. Un Espagnol vivra huit jours du dîner d'un Allemand. Dans les pays où les hommes sont plus voraces le luxe se tourne aussi vers les choses de consommation. En Angleterre, il se montre sur une table chargée de viandes ; en Italie on vous régale de sucre et de fleurs.

Le luxe des vêtements offre de semblables différences. Dans les climats où les changements de saisons sont prompts et violents, on a des habits meilleurs et plus simples, dans ceux où l'on ne s'habille que pour la parure on y cherche plus d'éclat que d'utilité, les habits eux-mêmes y sont un luxe. À Naples vous verrez tous les jours se promener au Pausilippe des hommes en veste dorée et point de bas. C'est la même chose pour les bâtiments : on donne tout à la magnificence quand on n'a rien à craindre des injures de l'air. À Paris, à Londres, on veut être logé chaudement et commodément. À Madrid on a des salons superbes, mais point de fenêtres qui ferment, et l'on couche dans des nids à rats.

Les aliments sont beaucoup plus substantiels et succulents dans les pays chauds ; c'est une troisième différence qui ne peut manquer d'influer sur la seconde. Pourquoi mange-t-on tant de légumes en Italie ? Parce qu'ils y sont bons, nourrissants, d'excellent goût. En France où ils ne sont nourris que d'eau ils ne nourrissent point, et sont presque comptés pour rien sur les tables. Ils n'occupent pourtant pas moins de terrain et coûtent du moins autant de peine à cultiver. C'est une expérience faite que les blés de Barbarie, d'ailleurs inférieurs à ceux de France, rendent beaucoup plus en farine, et que ceux de France à leur tour rendent plus que les blés du Nord. D'où l'on peut inférer qu'une gradation semblable s'observe généralement dans la même direction de la ligne au pôle. Or n'est-ce pas un désavantage visible d'avoir dans un produit égal une moindre quantité d'aliment ?

À toutes ces différentes considérations j'en puis ajouter une qui en découle et qui les fortifie : c'est que les pays chauds ont moins besoin d'habitants que les pays froids, et pourraient en nourrir davantage ; ce qui produit un double superflu toujours à l'avantage du despotisme. Plus le même nombre d'habitants occupe une grande surface, plus les révoltes deviennent difficiles ; parce qu'on ne peut se concerter ni promptement, ni secrètement, et qu'il est toujours facile au gouvernement d'éventer les projets et de couper les communications ; mais plus un peuple nombreux se rapproche, moins le gouvernement peut usurper sur le souverain : les chefs délibèrent aussi sûrement dans leurs chambres que le prince dans son conseil, et la foule s'assemble aussi tôt dans les places que les troupes dans leurs quartiers. L'avantage d'un gouvernement tyrannique est donc en ceci d'agir à grandes distances. À l'aide des points d'appui qu'il se donne sa force augmente au loin comme celle des leviers*. Celle du peuple au contraire n'agit que concentrée, elle s'évapore et se perd en s'étendant, comme l'effet de la poudre éparse à terre et qui ne prend feu que grain à grain. Les pays les moins peuplés sont ainsi les plus propres à la tyrannie : les bêtes féroces ne règnent que dans les déserts.

---

* Ceci ne contredit pas ce que j'ai dit ci-devant, liv. II, chap. IX, sur les inconvénients des grands États ; car il s'agissait là de l'autorité du gouvernement sur ses membres, et il s'agit ici de sa force contre les sujets. Ses membres épars lui servent de points d'appui pour agir au loin sur le peuple, mais il n'a nul point d'appui pour agir directement sur ces membres mêmes. Ainsi, dans l'un des cas, la longueur du levier en fait la faiblesse, et la force dans l'autre cas.

Chapitre IX

DES SIGNES D'UN BON GOUVERNEMENT

Quand donc on demande absolument quel est le meilleur gouvernement, on fait une question insoluble comme indéterminée ; ou si l'on veut, elle a autant de bonnes solutions qu'il y a de combinaisons possibles dans les positions absolues et relatives des peuples.

Mais si l'on demandait à quel signe on peut connaître qu'un peuple donné est bien ou mal gouverné, ce serait autre chose, et la question de fait pourrait se résoudre.

Cependant on ne la résout point, parce que chacun veut la résoudre à sa manière. Les sujets vantent la tranquillité publique, les citoyens la liberté des particuliers ; l'un préfère la sûreté des possessions, et l'autre celle des personnes ; l'un veut que le meilleur gouvernement soit le plus sévère, l'autre soutient que c'est le plus doux ; celui-ci veut qu'on punisse les crimes, et celui-là qu'on les prévienne ; l'un trouve beau qu'on soit craint des voisins, l'autre aime mieux qu'on en soit ignoré ; l'un est content quand l'argent circule, l'autre exige que le peuple ait du pain. Quand même on conviendrait sur ces points et d'autres semblables, en serait-on plus avancé ? Les quantités morales manquant de mesure précise, fût-on d'accord sur le signe, comment l'être sur l'estimation ?

Pour moi, je m'étonne toujours qu'on méconnaisse un signe aussi simple, ou qu'on ait la mauvaise foi de n'en pas convenir. Quelle est la fin de l'association politique ? C'est la conservation et la prospérité de ses membres. Et quel est le signe le plus sûr qu'ils se conservent et prospèrent ? C'est leur nombre et leur population. N'allez donc pas chercher ailleurs ce signe si disputé. Toute chose d'ailleurs égale, le gouvernement sous lequel, sans moyens étrangers, sans naturalisations, sans colonies, les citoyens peuplent et multiplient davantage, est infailliblement le meilleur : celui sous lequel un peuple diminue et dépérit est le pire. Calculateurs, c'est maintenant votre affaire ; comptez, mesurez, comparez*.

---

* On doit juger sur le même principe des siècles qui méritent la préférence pour la prospérité du genre humain. On a trop admiré ceux où l'on a vu fleurir les lettres et les arts, sans pénétrer l'objet secret de leur culture, sans en considérer le funeste effet, *idque apud imperitos humanitas vocabatur, cum pars servitutis esset*[52]. Ne verrons-nous jamais dans les maximes des livres l'intérêt grossier qui fait parler les auteurs ? Non, quoi qu'ils en puissent dire, quand, malgré son éclat, un pays se dépeuple, il n'est pas vrai que tout aille bien, et il ne suffit pas qu'un poète ait cent mille livres de rente pour que son siècle soit le meilleur de tous. Il faut moins regarder au repos apparent et à la tranquillité des chefs qu'au bien-être des nations entières et surtout des États les plus nombreux. La grêle désole quelques cantons, mais elle fait rarement disette. Les émeutes, les guerres civiles effarouchent beaucoup les chefs, mais elles ne font pas les vrais malheurs des peuples, qui peuvent même avoir du relâche tandis qu'on dispute à qui les tyrannisera. C'est de leur état permanent que naissent leurs prospérités ou leurs calamités réelles : quand tout reste écrasé sous le joug, c'est alors que tout dépérit ; c'est alors que les chefs les détruisant à leur aise, *ubi solitudinem faciunt pacem appellant*[53]. Quand les tracasseries des grands agitaient le royaume de France, et que le coadjuteur de Paris portait au Parlement un poignard dans sa poche, cela n'empêchait pas que le peuple français ne vécût heureux et nombreux dans une honnête et libre aisance. Autrefois la Grèce fleurissait au sein des plus cruelles guerres ; le sang y coulait à flots, et tout le pays était couvert d'hommes. Il semblait, dit Machiavel, qu'au milieu des meurtres, des proscriptions, des guerres civiles, notre république en devînt plus puissante ; la vertu de ses citoyens, leurs mœurs, leur indépendance, avaient plus d'effet pour la renforcer que toutes ses dissensions n'en avaient pour l'affaiblir. Un peu d'agitation donne du ressort aux âmes, et ce qui fait vraiment prospérer l'espèce est moins la paix que la liberté.

Chapitre X

DE L'ABUS DU GOUVERNEMENT ET DE SA PENTE À DÉGÉNÉRER[54]

Comme la volonté particulière agit sans cesse contre la volonté générale, ainsi le gouvernement fait un effort continuel contre la souveraineté. Plus cet effort augmente, plus la constitution s'altère, et comme il n'y a point ici d'autre volonté de corps qui résistant à celle du prince, fasse équilibre avec elle il doit arriver tôt ou tard que le prince opprime enfin le souverain et rompe le traité social. C'est là le vice inhérent et inévitable qui dès la naissance du corps politique tend sans relâche à le détruire, de même que la vieillesse et la mort détruisent enfin le corps de l'homme.

Il y a deux voies générales par lesquelles un gouvernement dégénère : savoir, quand il se resserre, ou quand l'État se dissout.

Le gouvernement se resserre quand il passe du grand nombre au petit, c'est-à-dire de la démocratie à l'aristocratie, et de l'aristocratie à la royauté. C'est là son inclinaison naturelle*. S'il rétrogradait du petit nombre au

* La formation lente et le progrès de la république de Venise dans ses lagunes offrent un exemple notable de cette succession ; et il est bien étonnant que, depuis plus de douze cents ans, les Vénitiens semblent n'en être encore qu'au second terme, lequel commença au *Serrar di consiglio*, en 1198. Quant aux anciens ducs qu'on leur reproche, quoi qu'en puisse dire le *Squittinio della libertà veneta*, il est prouvé qu'ils n'ont point été leurs souverains.

On ne manquera pas de m'objecter la République romaine, qui suivit, dira-t-on, un progrès tout contraire, passant de la monarchie à l'aristocratie, et de l'aristocratie à la démocratie. Je suis bien éloigné d'en penser ainsi.

Le premier établissement de Romulus fut un gouvernement mixte qui dégénéra promptement en despotisme. Par des causes particulières, l'État périt avant le temps, comme on voit mourir un

grand, on pourrait dire qu'il se relâche, mais ce progrès inverse est impossible.

En effet, jamais le gouvernement ne change de forme que quand son ressort usé le laisse trop affaibli pour pouvoir conserver la sienne. Or, s'il se relâchait encore en s'étendant, sa force deviendrait tout à fait nulle, et il subsisterait encore moins. Il faut donc remonter et serrer le ressort à mesure qu'il cède, autrement l'État qu'il soutient tomberait en ruine.

Le cas de la dissolution de l'État peut arriver de deux manières.

---

nouveau-né avant d'avoir atteint l'âge d'homme. L'expulsion des Tarquins fut la véritable époque de la naissance de la république. Mais elle ne prit pas d'abord une forme constante, parce qu'on ne fit que la moitié de l'ouvrage en n'abolissant pas le patriciat. Car, de cette manière, l'aristocratie héréditaire, qui est la pire des administrations légitimes, restant en conflit avec la démocratie, la forme de gouvernement, toujours incertaine et flottante, ne fut fixée, comme l'a prouvé Machiavel, qu'à l'établissement des tribuns ; alors seulement il y eut un vrai gouvernement et une véritable démocratie. En effet, le peuple alors n'était pas seulement souverain, mais aussi magistrat et juge : le sénat n'était qu'un tribunal en sous-ordre, pour tempérer ou concentrer le gouvernement ; et les consuls eux-mêmes, bien que patriciens, bien que premiers magistrats, bien que généraux absolus à la guerre, n'étaient à Rome que les présidents du peuple.

Dès lors on vit aussi le gouvernement prendre sa pente naturelle et tendre fortement à l'aristocratie. Le patriciat s'abolissant comme de lui-même, l'aristocratie n'était plus dans le corps des patriciens comme elle est à Venise et à Gênes, mais dans le corps du Sénat composé de patriciens et de plébéiens, même dans le corps des tribuns quand ils commencèrent d'usurper une puissance active : car les mots ne font rien aux choses ; et quand le peuple a des chefs qui gouvernent pour lui, quelque nom que portent ces chefs, c'est toujours une aristocratie.

De l'abus de l'aristocratie naquirent les guerres civiles et le triumvirat. Sylla, Jules César, Auguste, devinrent dans le fait de véritables monarques : et enfin, sous le despotisme de Tibère, l'État fut dissous. L'histoire romaine ne dément donc pas mon principe : elle le confirme.

Premièrement quand le prince n'administre plus l'État selon les lois et qu'il usurpe le pouvoir souverain. Alors il se fait un changement remarquable ; c'est que, non pas le gouvernement, mais l'État se resserre : je veux dire que le grand État se dissout et qu'il s'en forme un autre dans celui-là, composé seulement des membres du gouvernement, et qui n'est plus rien au reste du peuple que son maître et son tyran. De sorte qu'à l'instant que le gouvernement usurpe la souveraineté, le pacte social est rompu ; et tous les simples citoyens, rentrés de droit dans leur liberté naturelle, sont forcés mais non pas obligés d'obéir.

Le même cas arrive aussi quand les membres du gouvernement usurpent séparément le pouvoir qu'ils ne doivent exercer qu'en corps ; ce qui n'est pas une moindre infraction des lois, et produit encore un plus grand désordre. Alors on a, pour ainsi dire, autant de princes que de magistrats ; et l'État, non moins divisé que le gouvernement, périt ou change de forme.

Quand l'État se dissout, l'abus du gouvernement quel qu'il soit prend le nom commun d'*anarchie.* En distinguant, la démocratie dégénère en *ochlocratie*, l'aristocratie en *oligarchie* : j'ajouterais que la royauté dégénère en *tyrannie*, mais ce dernier mot est équivoque et demande explication.

Dans le sens vulgaire un tyran est un roi qui gouverne avec violence et sans égard à la justice et aux lois. Dans le sens précis un tyran est un particulier qui s'arroge l'autorité royale sans y avoir droit. C'est ainsi que les Grecs entendaient ce mot de tyran : ils le donnaient indifféremment aux bons et aux mauvais princes dont l'autorité n'était pas légitime*. Ainsi

* *« Omnes enim et habentur et dicuntur tyranni, qui potestate utuntur perpetua in ea civitate quæ libertate usa est »* (Corn.

tyran et *usurpateur* sont deux mots parfaitement synonymes.

Pour donner différents noms à différentes choses, j'appelle *tyran* l'usurpateur de l'autorité royale, et *despote* l'usurpateur du pouvoir souverain. Le tyran est celui qui s'ingère contre les lois à gouverner selon les lois ; le despote est celui qui se met au-dessus des lois mêmes. Ainsi le tyran peut n'être pas despote mais le despote est toujours tyran.

Chapitre XI
DE LA MORT DU CORPS POLITIQUE

Telle est la pente naturelle[56] et inévitable des gouvernements les mieux constitués. Si Sparte et Rome ont péri, quel État peut espérer de durer toujours ? Si nous voulons former un établissement durable, ne songeons donc point à le rendre éternel. Pour réussir il ne faut pas tenter l'impossible, ni se flatter de donner à l'ouvrage des hommes une solidité que les choses humaines ne comportent pas.

Le corps politique, aussi bien que le corps de l'homme, commence à mourir dès sa naissance et porte en lui-même les causes de sa destruction. Mais l'un et l'autre peuvent avoir une constitution plus ou moins robuste et propre à le conserver plus ou moins

---

Nep., *In Miltiad.*, cap. VIII)[55]. Il est vrai qu'Aristote (*Mor. Nicom.*, lib. VIII, cap. X) distingue le tyran du roi, en ce que le premier gouverne pour sa propre utilité, et le second seulement pour l'utilité de ses sujets ; mais, outre que généralement tous les auteurs grecs ont pris le mot *tyran* dans un autre sens, comme il paraît surtout par le Hiéron de Xénophon, il s'ensuivrait de la distinction d'Aristote que depuis le commencement du monde il n'aurait pas encore existé un seul roi.

longtemps. La constitution de l'homme est l'ouvrage de la nature ; celle de l'État est l'ouvrage de l'art. Il ne dépend pas des hommes de prolonger leur vie, il dépend d'eux de prolonger celle de l'État aussi loin qu'il est possible, en lui donnant la meilleure constitution qu'il puisse avoir. Le mieux constitué finira, mais plus tard qu'un autre, si nul accident imprévu n'amène sa perte avant le temps.

Le principe de la vie politique est dans l'autorité souveraine. La puissance législative est le cœur de l'État, la puissance exécutive en est le cerveau, qui donne le mouvement à toutes les parties. Le cerveau peut tomber en paralysie et l'individu vivre encore. Un homme reste imbécile et vit ; mais sitôt que le cœur a cessé ses fonctions, l'animal est mort[57].

Ce n'est point par les lois que l'État subsiste, c'est par le pouvoir législatif. La loi d'hier n'oblige pas aujourd'hui, mais le consentement tacite est présumé du silence, et le souverain est censé confirmer incessamment les lois qu'il n'abroge pas, pouvant le faire. Tout ce qu'il a déclaré vouloir une fois il le veut toujours, à moins qu'il ne le révoque[58].

Pourquoi donc porte-t-on tant de respect aux anciennes lois ? C'est pour cela même. On doit croire qu'il n'y a que l'excellence des volontés antiques qui les ait pu conserver si longtemps : si le souverain ne les eût reconnues constamment salutaires, il les eût mille fois révoquées. Voilà pourquoi, loin de s'affaiblir, les lois acquièrent sans cesse une force nouvelle dans tout État bien constitué ; le préjugé de l'antiquité les rend chaque jour plus vénérables : au lieu que partout où les lois s'affaiblissent en vieillissant, cela prouve qu'il n'y a plus de pouvoir législatif, et que l'État ne vit plus.

Chapitre XII
COMMENT SE MAINTIENT L'AUTORITÉ SOUVERAINE[59]

Le souverain n'ayant d'autre force que la puissance législative n'agit que par des lois ; et les lois n'étant que des actes authentiques de la volonté générale, le souverain ne saurait agir que quand le peuple est assemblé[60]. Le peuple assemblé, dira-t-on ! Quelle chimère ! C'est une chimère aujourd'hui, mais ce n'en était pas une il y a deux mille ans. Les hommes ont-ils changé de nature ?

Les bornes du possible dans les choses morales sont moins étroites que nous ne pensons. Ce sont nos faiblesses, nos vices, nos préjugés, qui les rétrécissent. Les âmes basses ne croient point aux grands hommes : de vils esclaves sourient d'un air moqueur à ce mot de liberté.

Par ce qui s'est fait, considérons ce qui se peut faire. Je ne parlerai pas des anciennes républiques de la Grèce ; mais la République romaine était, ce me semble, un grand État, et la ville de Rome une grande ville. Le dernier cens donna dans Rome quatre cent mille citoyens portant armes, et le dernier dénombrement de l'Empire plus de quatre millions de citoyens sans compter les sujets, les étrangers, les femmes, les enfants, les esclaves.

Quelle difficulté n'imaginerait-on pas d'assembler fréquemment le peuple immense de cette capitale et de ses environs ! Cependant, il se passait peu de semaines que le peuple romain ne fût assemblé, et même plusieurs fois. Non seulement il exerçait les droits de la souveraineté, mais une partie de ceux du gouvernement. Il traitait certaines affaires, il jugeait certaines causes, et tout ce peuple était sur la place publique presque aussi souvent magistrat que citoyen.

En remontant aux premiers temps des nations on trouverait que la plupart des anciens gouvernements, même monarchiques tels que ceux des Macédoniens et des Francs, avaient de semblables conseils. Quoi qu'il en soit, ce seul fait contestable répond à toutes les difficultés. De l'existant au possible la conséquence me paraît bonne.

Chapitre XIII
COMMENT SE MAINTIENT L'AUTORITÉ SOUVERAINE
(suite)

Il ne suffit pas que le peuple assemblé ait une fois fixé la constitution de l'État en donnant la sanction à un corps de lois ; il ne suffit pas qu'il ait établi un gouvernement perpétuel, ou qu'il ait pourvu une fois pour toutes à l'élection des magistrats. Outre les assemblées extraordinaires que des cas imprévus peuvent exiger, il faut qu'il y en ait de fixes et de périodiques que rien ne puisse abolir ni proroger, tellement qu'au jour marqué le peuple soit légitimement convoqué par la loi, sans qu'il soit besoin pour cela d'aucune convocation formelle.

Mais hors de ces assemblées juridiques par leur seule date, toute assemblée du peuple qui n'aura pas été convoquée par les magistrats préposés à cet effet et selon les formes prescrites doit être tenue pour illégitime, et tout ce qui s'y fait pour nul ; parce que l'ordre même de s'assembler doit émaner de la loi.

Quant aux retours plus ou moins fréquents des assemblées légitimes, ils dépendent de tant de considérations qu'on ne saurait donner là-dessus de règles précises. Seulement on peut dire en général que plus le gouvernement a de force, plus le souverain doit se montrer fréquemment.

Ceci, me dira-t-on, peut être bon pour une seule ville; mais que faire quand l'État en comprend plusieurs? Partagera-t-on l'autorité souveraine? ou bien doit-on la concentrer dans une seule ville et assujettir tout le reste?

Je réponds qu'on ne doit faire ni l'un ni l'autre. Premièrement l'autorité souveraine est simple et une, et l'on ne peut la diviser sans la détruire. En second lieu, une ville, non plus qu'une nation, ne peut être légitimement sujette d'une autre, parce que l'essence du corps politique est dans l'accord de l'obéissance et de la liberté, et que ces mots de *sujet* et de *souverain* sont des corrélations identiques dont l'idée se réunit sous le seul mot de citoyen[61].

Je réponds encore que c'est toujours un mal d'unir plusieurs villes en une seule cité, et que, voulant faire cette union, l'on ne doit pas se flatter d'en éviter les inconvénients naturels. Il ne faut point objecter l'abus des grands États à celui qui n'en veut que de petits; mais comment donner aux petits États assez de force pour résister aux grands? Comme jadis les villes grecques résistèrent au grand roi, et comme plus récemment la Hollande et la Suisse ont résisté à la maison d'Autriche.

Toutefois, si l'on ne peut réduire l'État à de justes bornes, il reste encore une ressource; c'est de n'y point souffrir de capitale, de faire siéger le gouvernement alternativement dans chaque ville, et d'y rassembler aussi tour à tour les États du pays.

Peuplez également le territoire, étendez-y partout les mêmes droits, portez-y partout l'abondance et la vie;

c'est ainsi que l'État deviendra tout à la fois le plus fort et le mieux gouverné qu'il soit possible. Souvenez-vous que les murs des villes ne se forment que du débris des maisons des champs. À chaque palais que je vois élever dans la capitale, je crois voir mettre en masures tout un pays.

Chapitre XIV
COMMENT SE MAINTIENT L'AUTORITÉ SOUVERAINE
(suite)

À l'instant que le peuple est légitimement assemblé en corps souverain, toute juridiction du gouvernement cesse ; la puissance exécutive est suspendue, et la personne du dernier citoyen est aussi sacrée et inviolable que celle du premier magistrat, parce qu'où se trouve le représenté, il n'y a plus de représentant[62]. La plupart des tumultes qui s'élevèrent à Rome dans les comices vinrent d'avoir ignoré ou négligé cette règle. Les consuls alors n'étaient que les présidents du peuple, les tribuns de simples orateurs*, le Sénat n'était rien du tout.

Ces intervalles de suspension où le prince reconnaît ou doit reconnaître un supérieur actuel, lui ont toujours été redoutables ; et ces assemblées du peuple, qui sont l'égide du corps politique et le frein du gouvernement, ont été de tout temps l'horreur des chefs : aussi n'épargnent-ils jamais ni soins, ni objections, ni

* À peu près selon le sens qu'on donne à ce mot dans le Parlement d'Angleterre. La ressemblance de ces emplois eût mis en conflit les consuls et les tribuns, quand même toute juridiction eût été suspendue.

difficultés, ni promesses, pour en rebuter les citoyens. Quand ceux-ci sont avares, lâches, pusillanimes, plus amoureux du repos que de la liberté, ils ne tiennent pas longtemps contre les efforts redoublés du gouvernement : c'est ainsi que, la force résistante augmentant sans cesse, l'autorité souveraine s'évanouit à la fin, et que la plupart des cités tombent et périssent avant le temps.

Mais entre l'autorité souveraine et le gouvernement arbitraire, il s'introduit quelquefois un pouvoir moyen dont il faut parler.

Chapitre XV
DES DÉPUTÉS OU REPRÉSENTANTS

Sitôt que le service public cesse d'être la principale affaire des citoyens, et qu'ils aiment mieux servir de leur bourse que de leur personne, l'État est déjà près de sa ruine. Faut-il marcher au combat? ils payent des troupes et restent chez eux; faut-il aller au Conseil? ils nomment des députés et restent chez eux. À force de paresse et d'argent ils ont enfin des soldats pour asservir la patrie et des représentants pour la vendre[63].

C'est le tracas du commerce et des arts, c'est l'avide intérêt du gain, c'est la mollesse et l'amour des commodités, qui changent les services personnels en argent. On cède une partie de son profit pour l'augmenter à son aise. Donnez de l'argent, et bientôt vous aurez des fers. Ce mot de *finance* est un mot d'esclave; il est inconnu dans la cité. Dans un État vraiment libre les citoyens font tout avec leurs bras et rien avec de l'argent. Loin de payer pour s'exempter de leurs devoirs, ils paieront pour les remplir eux-mêmes. Je suis bien loin des idées communes ; je crois les corvées moins contraires à la liberté que les taxes.

Mieux l'État est constitué, plus les affaires publiques l'emportent sur les privées dans l'esprit des citoyens. Il y a même beaucoup moins d'affaires privées, parce que la somme du bonheur commun fournissant une portion plus considérable à celui de chaque individu, il lui en reste moins à chercher dans les soins particuliers. Dans une cité bien conduite chacun vole aux assemblées ; sous un mauvais gouvernement nul n'aime à faire un pas pour s'y rendre, parce que nul ne prend intérêt à ce qui s'y fait, qu'on prévoit que la volonté générale n'y dominera pas, et qu'enfin les soins domestiques absorbent tout. Les bonnes lois en font faire de meilleures, les mauvaises en amènent de pires. Sitôt que quelqu'un dit des affaires de l'État, *que m'importe ?* on doit compter que l'État est perdu.

L'attiédissement de l'amour de la patrie, l'activité de l'intérêt privé, l'immensité des États, les conquêtes, l'abus du gouvernement ont fait imaginer la voie de députés ou représentants du peuple dans les assemblées de la nation. C'est ce qu'en certains pays on ose appeler le tiers état. Ainsi l'intérêt particulier de deux ordres est mis au premier et second rang ; l'intérêt public n'est qu'au troisième.

La souveraineté ne peut être représentée par la même raison qu'elle ne peut être aliénée ; elle consiste essentiellement dans la volonté générale, et la volonté ne se représente point ; elle est la même, ou elle est autre ; il n'y a point de milieu[64]. Les députés du peuple ne sont donc ni ne peuvent être ses représentants, ils ne sont que ses commissaires ; ils ne peuvent rien conclure définitivement. Toute loi que le peuple en personne n'a pas ratifiée est nulle ; ce n'est point une loi. Le peuple anglais pense être libre, il se trompe fort; il ne l'est que durant l'élection des membres du Parlement: sitôt qu'ils sont élus, il est esclave, il n'est rien. Dans les courts moments de sa liberté, l'usage qu'il en fait mérite bien qu'il la perde.

L'idée des représentants est moderne : elle nous vient du gouvernement féodal, de cet inique et absurde gouvernement dans lequel l'espèce humaine est dégradée, et où le nom d'homme est en déshonneur. Dans les anciennes républiques et même dans les monarchies, jamais le peuple n'eut des représentants; on ne connaissait pas ce mot-là. Il est très singulier qu'à Rome où les tribuns étaient si sacrés on n'ait pas même imaginé qu'ils pussent usurper les fonctions du peuple, et qu'au milieu d'une si grande multitude, ils n'aient jamais tenté de passer de leur chef un seul plébiscite. Qu'on juge cependant de l'embarras que causait quelquefois la foule par ce qui arriva du temps des Gracques, où une partie des citoyens donnait son suffrage de dessus les toits.

Où le droit et la liberté sont toutes choses, les inconvénients ne sont rien. Chez ce sage peuple tout était mis à sa juste mesure : il laissait faire à ses licteurs ce que ses tribuns n'eussent osé faire; il ne craignait pas que ses licteurs voulussent le représenter.

Pour expliquer cependant comment les tribuns le représentaient quelquefois, il suffit de concevoir comment le gouvernement représente le souverain. La loi n'étant que la déclaration de la volonté générale, il est clair que, dans la puissance législative, le peuple ne peut être représenté; mais il peut et doit l'être dans la puissance exécutive, qui n'est que la force appliquée à la loi[65]. Ceci fait voir qu'en examinant bien les choses on trouverait que très peu de nations ont des lois. Quoi qu'il en soit, il est sûr que les tribuns, n'ayant aucune partie du pouvoir exécutif, ne purent jamais représenter le peuple romain par les droits de leurs charges, mais seulement en usurpant sur ceux du Sénat.

Chez les Grecs tout ce que le peuple avait à faire il le faisait par lui-même : il était sans cesse assemblé sur la place. Il habitait un climat doux ; il n'était point avide ; des esclaves faisaient ses travaux ; sa grande affaire était sa liberté. N'ayant plus les mêmes avantages, comment conserver les mêmes droits ? Vos climats plus durs vous donnent plus de besoins*, six mois de l'année la place publique n'est pas tenable, vos langues sourdes ne peuvent se faire entendre en plein air ; vous donnez plus à votre gain qu'à votre liberté, et vous craignez bien moins l'esclavage que la misère.

Quoi ! la liberté ne se maintient qu'à l'appui de la servitude ? Peut-être. Les deux excès se touchent. Tout ce qui n'est point dans la nature a ses inconvénients, et la société civile plus que tout le reste. Il y a telles positions malheureuses où l'on ne peut conserver sa liberté qu'aux dépens de celle d'autrui et où le citoyen ne peut être parfaitement libre que l'esclave ne soit extrêmement esclave. Telle était la position de Sparte. Pour vous, peuples modernes, vous n'avez point d'esclaves, mais vous l'êtes ; vous payez leur liberté de la vôtre. Vous avez beau vanter cette préférence, j'y trouve plus de lâcheté que d'humanité.

Je n'entends point par tout cela qu'il faille avoir des esclaves ni que le droit d'esclavage soit légitime, puisque j'ai prouvé le contraire : je dis seulement les raisons pourquoi les peuples modernes qui se croient libres ont des représentants, et pourquoi les peuples

* Adopter dans les pays froids le luxe et la mollesse des Orientaux, c'est vouloir se donner leurs chaînes ; c'est s'y soumettre encore plus nécessairement qu'eux.

anciens n'en avaient pas. Quoi qu'il en soit, à l'instant qu'un peuple se donne des représentants, il n'est plus libre ; il n'est plus.

Tout bien examiné, je ne vois pas qu'il soit désormais possible au souverain de conserver parmi nous l'exercice de ses droits si la cité n'est très petite. Mais si elle est très petite, elle sera subjuguée ? Non. Je ferai voir ci-après* comment on peut réunir la puissance extérieure d'un grand peuple avec la police aisée et le bon ordre d'un petit État.

Chapitre XVI

QUE L'INSTITUTION DU GOUVERNEMENT N'EST POINT UN CONTRAT[66]

Le pouvoir législatif une fois bien établi, il s'agit d'établir de même le pouvoir exécutif ; car ce dernier, qui n'opère que par des actes particuliers, n'étant pas de l'essence de l'autre, en est naturellement séparé. S'il était possible que le souverain, considéré comme tel, eût la puissance exécutive, le droit et le fait seraient tellement confondus qu'on ne saurait plus ce qui est loi et ce qui ne l'est pas, et le corps politique ainsi dénaturé serait bientôt en proie à la violence contre laquelle il fut institué.

Les citoyens étant tous égaux par le contrat social, ce que tous doivent faire tous peuvent le prescrire, au lieu que nul n'a droit d'exiger qu'un autre fasse ce qu'il ne fait pas lui-même. Or c'est proprement ce droit, indis-

* C'est ce que je m'étais proposé de faire dans la suite de cet ouvrage, lorsqu'en traitant des relations externes j'en serais venu aux confédérations. Matière toute neuve et où les principes sont encore à établir.

pensable pour faire vivre et mouvoir le corps politique, que le souverain donne au prince en instituant le gouvernement.

Plusieurs ont prétendu que l'acte de cet établissement était un contrat entre le peuple et les chefs qu'il se donne ; contrat par lequel on stipulait entre les deux parties les conditions sous lesquelles l'une s'obligeait à commander et l'autre à obéir. On conviendra, je m'assure, que voilà une étrange manière de contracter. Mais voyons si cette opinion est soutenable.

Premièrement, l'autorité suprême ne peut pas plus se modifier que s'aliéner ; la limiter, c'est la détruire. Il est absurde et contradictoire que le souverain se donne un supérieur ; s'obliger d'obéir à un maître, c'est se remettre en pleine liberté.

De plus, il est évident que ce contrat du peuple avec telles ou telles personnes serait un acte particulier. D'où il suit que ce contrat ne saurait être une loi ni un acte de souveraineté, et que par conséquent il serait illégitime.

On voit encore que les parties contractantes seraient entre elles sous la seule loi de nature et sans aucun garant de leurs engagements réciproques, ce qui répugne de toutes manières à l'état civil. Celui qui a la force en main étant toujours le maître de l'exécution, autant vaudrait donner le nom de contrat à l'acte d'un homme qui dirait à un autre : « Je vous donne tout mon bien, à condition que vous m'en rendrez ce qu'il vous plaira. »

Il n'y a qu'un contrat dans l'État, c'est celui de l'association ; et celui-là seul en exclut tout autre. On ne saurait imaginer aucun contrat public qui ne fût une violation du premier.

Chapitre XVII

DE L'INSTITUTION DU GOUVERNEMENT

Sous quelle idée faut-il donc concevoir l'acte par lequel le gouvernement est institué? Je remarquerai d'abord que cet acte est complexe ou composé de deux autres, savoir : l'établissement de la loi et l'exécution de la loi.

Par le premier, le souverain statue qu'il y aura un corps de gouvernement établi sous telle ou telle forme; et il est clair que cet acte est une loi.

Par le second, le peuple nomme les chefs qui seront chargés du gouvernement établi. Or cette nomination étant un acte particulier n'est pas une seconde loi, mais seulement une suite de la première et une fonction du gouvernement[67].

La difficulté est d'entendre comment on peut avoir un acte de gouvernement avant que le gouvernement existe, et comment le peuple, qui n'est que souverain ou sujet, peut devenir prince ou magistrat dans certaines circonstances.

C'est encore ici que se découvre une de ces étonnantes propriétés du corps politique, par lesquelles il concilie des opérations contradictoires en apparence. Car celle-ci se fait par une conversion subite de la souveraineté en démocratie; en sorte que, sans aucun changement sensible, et seulement par une nouvelle relation de tous à tous, les citoyens devenus magistrats passent des actes généraux aux actes particuliers, et de la loi à l'exécution.

Ce changement de relation n'est point une subtilité de spéculation sans exemple dans la pratique : il a lieu tous les jours dans le Parlement d'Angleterre, où la Chambre basse en certaines occasions se tourne en grand comité, pour mieux discuter les affaires, et devient ainsi simple commission, de cour souveraine qu'elle était l'instant précédent ; en telle sorte qu'elle se fait ensuite rapport à elle-même, comme chambre des Communes, de ce qu'elle vient de régler en grand comité, et délibère de nouveau sous un titre de ce qu'elle a déjà résolu sous un autre.

Tel est l'avantage propre au gouvernement démocratique de pouvoir être établi dans le fait par un simple acte de la volonté générale. Après quoi, ce gouvernement provisionnel reste en possession, si telle est la forme adoptée, ou établit au nom du souverain le gouvernement prescrit par la loi, et tout se trouve ainsi dans la règle. Il n'est pas possible d'instituer le gouvernement d'aucune autre manière légitime et sans renoncer aux principes ci-devant établis.

Chapitre XVIII

MOYEN DE PRÉVENIR LES USURPATIONS DU GOUVERNEMENT

De ces éclaircissements il résulte, en confirmation du chapitre XVI, que l'acte qui institue le gouvernement n'est point un contrat, mais une loi, que les dépositaires de la puissance exécutive ne sont point les maîtres du peuple mais ses officiers, qu'il peut les établir et les destituer quand il lui plaît, qu'il n'est point question pour eux de contracter mais d'obéir, et qu'en se chargeant des fonctions que l'État leur impose ils ne font que remplir leur devoir de citoyens, sans avoir en aucune sorte le droit de disputer sur les conditions.

Quand donc il arrive que le peuple institue un gouvernement héréditaire, soit monarchique dans une famille, soit aristocratique dans un ordre de citoyens, ce n'est point un engagement qu'il prend : c'est une forme provisionnelle qu'il donne à l'administration, jusqu'à ce qu'il lui plaise d'en ordonner autrement.

Il est vrai que ces changements sont toujours dangereux, et qu'il ne faut jamais toucher au gouvernement établi que lorsqu'il devient incompatible avec le bien public ; mais cette circonspection est une maxime de politique et non pas une règle de droit, et l'État n'est pas plus tenu de laisser l'autorité civile à ses chefs, que l'autorité militaire à ses généraux.

Il est vrai encore qu'on ne saurait en pareil cas observer avec trop de soin toutes les formalités requises pour distinguer un acte régulier et légitime d'un tumulte séditieux, et la volonté de tout un peuple des clameurs d'une faction. C'est ici surtout qu'il ne faut donner au cas odieux que ce qu'on ne peut lui refuser dans toute la rigueur du droit, et c'est aussi de cette obligation que le prince tire un grand avantage pour conserver sa puissance malgré le peuple, sans qu'on puisse dire qu'il l'ait usurpée. Car en paraissant n'user que de ses droits il lui est fort aisé de les étendre, et d'empêcher sous le prétexte du repos public les assemblées destinées à rétablir le bon ordre ; de sorte qu'il se prévaut d'un silence qu'il empêche de rompre, ou des irrégularités qu'il fait commettre, pour supposer en sa faveur l'aveu de ceux que la crainte fait taire, et pour punir ceux qui osent parler. C'est ainsi que les décemvirs, ayant d'abord été élus pour un an, puis continués pour une autre année, tentèrent de retenir à perpétuité leur pouvoir, en ne permettant plus aux comices de s'assembler ; et c'est par ce facile moyen que tous les gouvernements du monde, une fois revêtus de la force publique, usurpent tôt ou tard l'autorité souveraine.

Les assemblées périodiques dont j'ai parlé ci-devant sont propres à prévenir ou différer ce malheur, surtout quand elles n'ont pas besoin de convocation formelle ; car alors le prince ne saurait les empêcher sans se déclarer ouvertement infracteur des lois et ennemi de l'État.

L'ouverture de ces assemblées qui n'ont pour objet que le maintien du traité social, doit toujours se faire par deux propositions qu'on ne puisse jamais supprimer, et qui passent séparément par les suffrages.

La première : « S'il plaît au souverain de conserver la présente forme de gouvernement. »

La seconde : « S'il plaît au peuple d'en laisser l'administration à ceux qui en sont actuellement chargés. »

Je suppose ici ce que je crois avoir démontré, savoir qu'il n'y a dans l'État aucune loi fondamentale qui ne se puisse révoquer, non pas même le pacte social ; car si tous les citoyens s'assemblaient pour rompre ce pacte d'un commun accord, on ne peut douter qu'il ne fût très légitimement rompu. Grotius pense même que chacun peut renoncer à l'État dont il est membre, et reprendre sa liberté naturelle et ses biens en sortant du pays*. Or il serait absurde que tous les citoyens réunis ne pussent pas ce que peut séparément chacun d'eux[68].

---

* Bien entendu qu'on ne quitte pas pour éluder son devoir et se dispenser de servir la patrie au moment qu'elle a besoin de nous. La fuite alors serait criminelle et punissable ; ce ne serait plus retraite, mais désertion.

LIVRE IV

Chapitre I

QUE LA VOLONTÉ GÉNÉRALE EST INDESTRUCTIBLE

Tant que plusieurs hommes réunis se considèrent comme un seul corps, ils n'ont qu'une seule volonté qui se rapporte à la commune conservation, et au bien-être général. Alors tous les ressorts de l'État sont vigoureux et simples, ses maximes sont claires et lumineuses, il n'a point d'intérêts embrouillés, contradictoires, le bien commun se montre partout avec évidence, et ne demande que du bon sens pour être aperçu. La paix, l'union, l'égalité, sont ennemies des subtilités politiques. Les hommes droits et simples sont difficiles à tromper à cause de leur simplicité, les leurres, les prétextes raffinés ne leur en imposent point ; ils ne sont pas même assez fins pour être dupes. Quand on voit chez le plus heureux peuple du monde des troupes de paysans régler les affaires de l'État sous un chêne et se conduire toujours sagement, peut-on s'empêcher de mépriser les raffinements des autres nations, qui se rendent illustres et misérables avec tant d'art et de mystères ?

Un État ainsi gouverné a besoin de très peu de lois, et à mesure qu'il devient nécessaire d'en promulguer de nouvelles, cette nécessité se voit universellement. Le premier qui les propose ne fait que dire ce que tous ont déjà senti, et il n'est question ni de brigues ni d'éloquence pour faire passer en loi ce que chacun a déjà résolu de faire, sitôt qu'il sera sûr que les autres le feront comme lui.

Ce qui trompe les raisonneurs c'est que ne voyant que des États mal constitués dès leur origine, ils sont frappés de l'impossibilité d'y maintenir une semblable police. Ils rient d'imaginer toutes les sottises qu'un fourbe adroit, un parleur insinuant pourrait persuader au peuple de Paris ou de Londres. Ils ne savent pas que Cromwell eût été mis aux sonnettes par le peuple de Berne, et le duc de Beaufort à la discipline par les Genevois.

Mais quand le nœud social commence à se relâcher et l'État à s'affaiblir; quand les intérêts particuliers commencent à se faire sentir et les petites sociétés à influer sur la grande, l'intérêt commun s'altère et trouve des opposants : l'unanimité ne règne plus dans les voix, la volonté générale n'est plus la volonté de tous, il s'élève des contradictions, des débats, et le meilleur avis ne passe point sans disputes.

Enfin quand l'État près de sa ruine ne subsiste plus que par une forme illusoire et vaine, que le lien social est rompu dans tous les cœurs, que le plus vil intérêt se pare effrontément du nom sacré du bien public, alors la volonté générale devient muette; tous guidés par des motifs secrets n'opinent pas plus comme citoyens que si l'État n'eût jamais existé; et l'on fait passer faussement sous le nom de lois des décrets iniques qui n'ont pour but que l'intérêt particulier.

S'ensuit-il de là que la volonté générale soit anéantie ou corrompue ? Non, elle est toujours constante, inaltérable et pure; mais elle est subordonnée à d'autres qui l'emportent sur elle. Chacun, détachant son intérêt de l'intérêt commun, voit bien qu'il ne peut l'en séparer tout à fait, mais sa part du mal public ne lui paraît rien auprès du bien exclusif qu'il prétend s'approprier. Ce bien particulier excepté, il veut le bien général pour son propre intérêt tout aussi fortement qu'aucun autre. Même en vendant son suffrage à prix d'argent il n'éteint pas en lui la volonté générale, il l'élude. La faute qu'il commet est de changer l'état de la question et de répondre autre chose que ce qu'on lui demande ; en sorte qu'au lieu de dire par son suffrage, « il est avantageux à l'État », il dit, « il est avantageux à tel homme ou à tel parti que tel ou tel avis passe ». Ainsi la loi de l'ordre public dans les assemblées n'est pas tant d'y maintenir la volonté générale que de faire qu'elle soit toujours interrogée et qu'elle réponde toujours.

J'aurais ici bien des réflexions à faire sur le simple droit de voter dans tout acte de souveraineté ; droit que rien ne peut ôter aux citoyens ; et sur celui d'opiner, de proposer, de diviser, de discuter, que le gouvernement a toujours grand soin de ne laisser qu'à ses membres ; mais cette importante matière demanderait un traité à part, et je ne puis tout dire dans celui-ci.

Chapitre II
DES SUFFRAGES

On voit par le chapitre précédent que la manière dont se traitent les affaires générales peut donner un indice assez sûr de l'état actuel des mœurs, et de la santé du corps politique. Plus le concert règne dans les assemblées, c'est-à-dire plus les avis approchent de l'unanimité, plus aussi la volonté générale est dominante ; mais les longs débats, les dissensions, le tumulte, annoncent l'ascendant des intérêts particuliers et le déclin de l'État.

Ceci paraît moins évident quand deux ou plusieurs ordres entrent dans sa constitution, comme à Rome les patriciens et les plébéiens, dont les querelles troublèrent souvent les comices, même dans les plus beaux temps de la République : mais cette exception est plus apparente que réelle ; car alors, par le vice inhérent au corps politique, on a, pour ainsi dire, deux États en un : ce qui n'est pas vrai des deux ensemble est vrai de chacun séparément. Et en effet dans les temps même les plus orageux les plébiscites du peuple, quand le sénat ne s'en mêlait pas, passaient toujours tranquillement et à la grande pluralité des suffrages : les citoyens n'ayant qu'un intérêt, le peuple n'avait qu'une volonté.

À l'autre extrémité du cercle l'unanimité revient. C'est quand les citoyens tombés dans la servitude n'ont plus ni liberté ni volonté. Alors la crainte et la flatterie changent en acclamations les suffrages ; on ne délibère plus, on adore ou l'on maudit. Telle était la vile manière d'opiner du Sénat sous les empereurs. Quelquefois cela se faisait avec des précautions ridicules. Tacite observe que sous Othon les sénateurs, accablant Vitellius d'exécrations, affectaient de faire en même temps un bruit épouvantable afin que, si par hasard il devenait le maître, il ne pût savoir ce que chacun d'eux avait dit.

De ces diverses considérations naissent les maximes sur lesquelles on doit régler la manière de compter les voix et de comparer les avis, selon que la volonté générale est plus ou moins facile à connaître, et l'État plus ou moins déclinant.

Il n'y a qu'une seule loi qui par sa nature exige un consentement unanime. C'est le pacte social : car l'association civile est l'acte du monde le plus volontaire ; tout homme étant né libre et maître de lui-même, nul ne peut, sous quelque prétexte que ce puisse être, l'assujettir sans son aveu. Décider que le fils d'une esclave naît esclave, c'est décider qu'il ne naît pas homme.

Si donc lors du pacte social il s'y trouve des opposants, leur opposition n'invalide pas le contrat, elle empêche seulement qu'ils n'y soient compris ; ce sont des étrangers parmi les citoyens. Quand l'État est institué le consentement est dans la résidence ; habiter le territoire, c'est se soumettre à la souveraineté*.

Hors ce contrat primitif, la voix du plus grand nombre oblige toujours tous les autres ; c'est une suite du contrat même. Mais on demande comment un homme peut être libre et forcé de se conformer à des volontés qui ne sont pas les siennes. Comment les opposants sont-ils libres et soumis à des lois auxquelles ils n'ont pas consenti ?

Je réponds que la question est mal posée. Le citoyen consent à toutes les lois, même à celles qu'on passe malgré lui, et même à celles qui le punissent quand il ose en violer quelqu'une. La volonté constante de tous les membres de l'État est la volonté générale : c'est par elle qu'ils sont citoyens et libres**. Quand on pro-

* Ceci doit toujours s'entendre d'un État libre ; car d'ailleurs la famille, les biens, le défaut d'asile, la nécessité, la violence, peuvent retenir un habitant dans le pays malgré lui ; et alors son séjour seul ne suppose plus son consentement au contrat ou à la violation du contrat. ** À Gênes, on lit au-devant des prisons et sur les fers des galériens ce mot *Libertas.* Cette application de la devise est belle et juste. En effet il n'y a que les malfaiteurs de tous états qui empêchent le citoyen d'être libre. Dans un pays où tous ces gens-là seraient aux galères, on jouirait de la plus parfaite liberté.

pose une loi dans l'assemblée du peuple, ce qu'on leur demande n'est pas précisément s'ils approuvent la proposition ou s'ils la rejettent, mais si elle est conforme ou non à la volonté générale qui est la leur : chacun en donnant son suffrage dit son avis là-dessus, et du calcul des voix se tire la déclaration de la volonté générale. Quand donc l'avis contraire au mien l'emporte, cela ne prouve autre chose sinon que je m'étais trompé, et que ce que j'estimais être la volonté générale ne l'était pas. Si mon avis particulier l'eût emporté, j'aurais fait autre chose que ce que j'avais voulu, c'est alors que je n'aurais pas été libre.

Ceci suppose, il est vrai, que tous les caractères de la volonté générale sont encore dans la pluralité ; quand ils cessent d'y être, quelque parti qu'on prenne il n'y a plus de liberté.

En montrant ci-devant comme on substituait des volontés particulières à la volonté générale dans les délibérations publiques, j'ai suffisamment indiqué les moyens praticables de prévenir cet abus ; j'en parlerai encore ci-après. À l'égard du nombre proportionnel des suffrages pour déclarer cette volonté, j'ai aussi donné les principes sur lesquels on peut le déterminer. La différence d'une seule voix rompt l'égalité, un seul opposant rompt l'unanimité : mais entre l'unanimité et l'égalité il y a plusieurs partages inégaux, à chacun desquels on peut fixer ce nombre selon l'état et les besoins du corps politique.

Deux maximes générales peuvent servir à régler ces rapports : l'une, que, plus les délibérations sont importantes et graves, plus l'avis qui l'emporte doit approcher de l'unanimité ; l'autre, que, plus l'affaire agitée exige de célérité, plus on doit resserrer la différence prescrite dans le partage des avis : dans les délibérations qu'il faut terminer sur-le-champ, l'excédent d'une seule voix doit suffire. La première de ces maximes paraît plus convenable aux lois, et la seconde aux affaires. Quoi qu'il en soit, c'est sur leur combinaison que s'établissent les meilleurs rapports qu'on peut donner à la pluralité pour prononcer.

Chapitre III
DES ÉLECTIONS

À l'égard des élections du prince et des magistrats, qui sont, comme je l'ai dit, des actes complexes, il y a deux voies pour y procéder ; savoir, le choix et le sort. L'une et l'autre ont été employées en diverses républiques, et l'on voit encore actuellement un mélange très compliqué des deux dans l'élection du doge de Venise.

« Le suffrage par le sort, dit Montesquieu, est de la nature de la démocratie. » J'en conviens, mais comment cela ? « Le sort, continue-t-il, est une façon d'élire qui n'afflige personne : il laisse à chaque citoyen une espérance raisonnable de servir la patrie. » Ce ne sont pas là des raisons.

Si l'on fait attention que l'élection des chefs est une fonction du gouvernement et non de la souveraineté, on verra pourquoi la voie du sort est plus dans la nature de la démocratie, où l'administration est d'autant meilleure que les actes en sont moins multipliés.

Dans toute véritable démocratie la magistrature n'est pas un avantage, mais une charge onéreuse qu'on ne peut justement imposer à un particulier plutôt qu'à un autre. La loi seule peut imposer cette charge à celui sur qui le sort tombera. Car alors, la condition étant égale pour tous, et le choix ne dépendant d'aucune volonté humaine, il n'y a point d'application particulière qui altère l'universalité de la loi.

Dans l'aristocratie le prince choisit le prince, le gouvernement se conserve par lui-même, et c'est là que les suffrages sont bien placés.

L'exemple de l'élection du doge de Venise confirme cette distinction loin de la détruire : cette forme mêlée convient dans un gouvernement mixte. Car c'est une erreur de prendre le gouvernement de Venise pour une véritable aristocratie. Si le peuple n'y a nulle part au gouvernement, la noblesse y est peuple elle-même. Une multitude de pauvres Barnabotes n'approcha jamais d'aucune magistrature, et n'a de sa noblesse que le vain titre d'excellence et le droit d'assister au grand conseil. Ce grand conseil étant aussi nombreux que notre Conseil général à Genève, ses illustres membres n'ont pas plus de privilèges que nos simples citoyens. Il est certain qu'ôtant l'extrême disparité des deux républiques, la bourgeoisie de Genève représente exactement le patriciat vénitien ; nos natifs et habitants représentent les citadins et le peuple de Venise ; nos paysans représentent les sujets de terre ferme : enfin de quelque manière que l'on considère cette république, abstraction faite de sa grandeur, son gouvernement n'est pas plus aristocratique que le nôtre. Toute la différence est que, n'ayant aucun chef à vie, nous n'avons pas le même besoin du sort.

Les élections par sort auraient peu d'inconvénient dans une véritable démocratie où tout étant égal, aussi bien par les mœurs et par les talents que par les maximes et par la fortune, le choix deviendrait presque indifférent. Mais j'ai déjà dit qu'il n'y avait point de véritable démocratie.

Quand le choix et le sort se trouvent mêlés, le premier doit remplir les places qui demandent des talents propres, telles que les emplois militaires : l'autre convient à celles où suffisent le bon sens, la justice, l'intégrité, telles que les charges de judicature ; parce que dans un État bien constitué ces qualités sont communes à tous les citoyens.

Le sort ni les suffrages n'ont aucun lieu dans le gouvernement monarchique. Le monarque étant de droit seul prince et magistrat unique, le choix de ses lieutenants n'appartient qu'à lui. Quand l'abbé de Saint-Pierre proposait de multiplier les Conseils du roi de France, et d'en élire les membres par scrutin, il ne voyait pas qu'il proposait de changer la forme du gouvernement.

Il me resterait à parler de la manière de donner et de recueillir les voix dans l'assemblée du peuple ; mais peut-être l'historique de la police romaine à cet égard expliquera-t-il plus sensiblement toutes les maximes que je pourrais établir. Il n'est pas indigne d'un lecteur judicieux de voir un peu en détail comment se traitaient les affaires publiques et particulières dans un Conseil de deux cent mille hommes.

Chapitre IV

DES COMICES ROMAINS

Nous n'avons nuls monuments bien assurés des premiers temps de Rome ; il y a même grande apparence que la plupart des choses qu'on en débite sont des fables* ; et en général la partie la plus instructive des

---

* Le nom de *Rome*, qu'on prétend venir de *Romulus* est grec, et signifie *force* ; le nom de *Numa* est grec aussi, et signifie *loi*.

annales des peuples, qui est l'histoire de leur établissement, est celle qui nous manque le plus. L'expérience nous apprend tous les jours de quelles causes naissent les révolutions des empires : mais comme il ne se forme plus de peuples, nous n'avons guère que des conjectures pour expliquer comment ils se sont formés.

Les usages qu'on trouve établis attestent au moins qu'il y eut une origine à ces usages. Des traditions qui remontent à ces origines, celles qu'appuient les plus grandes autorités et que de plus fortes raisons confirment doivent passer pour les plus certaines. Voilà les maximes que j'ai tâché de suivre en recherchant comment le plus libre et le plus puissant peuple de la terre exerçait son pouvoir suprême.

Après la fondation de Rome, la République naissante, c'est-à-dire l'armée du fondateur, composée d'Albains, de Sabins et d'étrangers, fut divisée en trois classes qui de cette division prirent le nom de *tribus.* Chacune de ces tribus fut subdivisée en dix curies, et chaque curie en décuries, à la tête desquelles on mit des chefs appelés *curions* et *décurions.*

Outre cela, on tira de chaque tribu un corps de cent cavaliers ou chevaliers, appelé centurie, par où l'on voit que ces divisions, peu nécessaires dans un bourg, n'étaient d'abord que militaires. Mais il semble qu'un instinct de grandeur portait la petite ville de Rome à se donner d'avance une police convenable à la capitale du monde.

De ce premier partage, résulta bientôt un inconvénient. C'est que la tribu des Albains* et celle des Sabins**

Quelle apparence que les deux premiers rois de cette ville aient porté d'avance des noms si bien relatifs à ce qu'ils ont fait ? * *Ramnenses.* ** *Tacienses.*

restant toujours au même état, tandis que celle des étrangers* croissant sans cesse par le concours perpétuel de ceux-ci, cette dernière ne tarda pas à surpasser les deux autres. Le remède que Servius trouva à ce dangereux abus fut de changer la division, et à celle des races, qu'il abolit, d'en substituer une autre tirée des lieux de la ville occupés par chaque tribu. Au lieu de trois tribus il en fit quatre, chacune desquelles occupait une des collines de Rome et en portait le nom. Ainsi, remédiant à l'inégalité présente, il la prévint encore pour l'avenir ; et afin que cette division ne fût pas seulement de lieux mais d'hommes, il défendit aux habitants d'un quartier de passer dans un autre ; ce qui empêcha les races de se confondre.

Il doubla aussi les trois anciennes centuries de cavalerie, et y en ajouta douze autres, mais toujours sous les anciens noms ; moyen simple et judicieux, par lequel il acheva de distinguer le corps des chevaliers de celui du peuple, sans faire murmurer ce dernier.

À ces quatre tribus urbaines, Servius en ajouta quinze autres appelées tribus rustiques ; parce qu'elles étaient formées des habitants de la campagne, partagés en autant de cantons. Dans la suite on en fit autant de nouvelles, et le peuple romain se trouva enfin divisé en trente-cinq tribus, nombre auquel elles restèrent fixées jusqu'à la fin de la République.

De cette distinction des tribus de la ville et des tribus de la campagne résulta un effet digne d'être observé, parce qu'il n'y en a point d'autre exemple, et que Rome lui dut à la fois la conservation de ses mœurs et l'accroissement de son empire. On croirait que les tribus urbaines s'arrogèrent bientôt la puissance et les hon-

---

* *Luceres.*

neurs, et ne tardèrent pas d'avilir les tribus rustiques : ce fut tout le contraire. On connaît le goût des premiers Romains pour la vie champêtre. Ce goût leur venait du sage instituteur qui unit à la liberté les travaux rustiques et militaires, et relégua pour ainsi dire à la ville les arts, les métiers, l'intrigue, la fortune et l'esclavage.

Ainsi, tout ce que Rome avait d'illustre vivant aux champs et cultivant les terres, on s'accoutuma à ne chercher que là les soutiens de la République. Cet état, étant celui des plus dignes patriciens, fut honoré de tout le monde ; la vie simple et laborieuse des villageois fut préférée à la vie oisive et lâche des bourgeois de Rome, et tel n'eût été qu'un malheureux prolétaire à la ville, qui, laboureur aux champs, devint un citoyen respecté. Ce n'est pas sans raison, disait Varron, que nos magnanimes ancêtres établirent au village la pépinière de ces robustes et vaillants hommes qui les défendaient en temps de guerre et les nourrissaient en temps de paix. Pline dit positivement que les tribus des champs étaient honorées à cause des hommes qui les composaient ; au lieu qu'on transférait par ignominie dans celles de la ville les lâches qu'on voulait avilir. Le Sabin Appius Claudius, étant venu s'établir à Rome, y fut comblé d'honneurs et inscrit dans une tribu rustique qui prit dans la suite le nom de sa famille. Enfin les affranchis entraient tous dans les tribus urbaines, jamais dans les rurales, et il n'y a pas durant toute la République un seul exemple d'aucun de ces affranchis parvenu à aucune magistrature, quoique devenu citoyen.

Cette maxime était excellente ; mais elle fut poussée si loin, qu'il en résulta enfin un changement et certainement un abus dans la police.

Premièrement, les censeurs, après s'être arrogé longtemps le droit de transférer arbitrairement les citoyens d'une tribu à l'autre, permirent à la plupart de se faire inscrire dans celle qui leur plaisait ; permission qui sûrement n'était bonne à rien, et ôtait un des grands ressorts de la censure. De plus, les grands et les puissants se faisant tous inscrire dans les tribus de la campagne, et les affranchis devenus citoyens restant avec la populace dans celles de la ville, les tribus en général n'eurent plus de lieu ni de territoire ; mais toutes se trouvèrent tellement mêlées, qu'on ne pouvait plus discerner les membres de chacune que par les registres, en sorte que l'idée du mot *tribu* passa ainsi du réel au personnel, ou plutôt devint presque une chimère.

Il arriva encore que les tribus de la ville, étant plus à portée, se trouvèrent souvent les plus fortes dans les comices, et vendirent l'État à ceux qui daignaient acheter les suffrages de la canaille qui les composait.

À l'égard des curies, l'instituteur en ayant fait dix en chaque tribu, tout le peuple romain alors renfermé dans les murs de la ville se trouva composé de trente curies, dont chacune avait ses temples, ses dieux, ses officiers, ses prêtres et ses fêtes appelées *compitalia*, semblables aux *paganalia* qu'eurent dans la suite les tribus rustiques.

Au nouveau partage de Servius, ce nombre de trente ne pouvant se répartir également dans ses quatre tribus, il n'y voulut point toucher ; et les curies indépendantes des tribus devinrent une autre division des habitants de Rome. Mais il ne fut point question de curies ni dans les tribus rustiques ni dans le peuple qui les composait, parce que les tribus étant devenues un établissement purement civil, et une autre police ayant été introduite pour la levée des troupes, les divisions militaires de Romulus se trouvèrent superflues. Ainsi, quoique tout citoyen fût inscrit dans une tribu, il s'en fallait beaucoup que chacun ne le fût dans une curie.

Servius fit encore une troisième division, qui n'avait aucun rapport aux deux précédentes, et devint par ses effets la plus importante de toutes. Il distribua tout le peuple romain en six classes, qu'il ne distingua ni par le lieu ni par les hommes, mais par les biens. En sorte que les premières classes étaient remplies par les riches, les dernières par les pauvres, et les moyennes par ceux qui jouissaient d'une fortune médiocre. Ces six classes étaient subdivisées en cent quatre-vingt-treize autres corps, appelés centuries ; et ces corps étaient tellement distribués que la première classe en comprenait seule plus de la moitié, et la dernière n'en formait qu'un seul. Il se trouva ainsi que la classe la moins nombreuse en hommes l'était le plus en centuries, et que la dernière classe entière n'était comptée que pour une subdivision, bien qu'elle contînt seule plus de la moitié des habitants de Rome.

Afin que le peuple pénétrât moins les conséquences de cette dernière forme, Servius affecta de lui donner un air militaire : il inséra dans la seconde classe deux centuries d'armuriers, et deux d'instruments de guerre dans la quatrième. Dans chaque classe, excepté la dernière, il distingua les jeunes et les vieux, c'est-à-dire ceux qui étaient obligés de porter les armes, et ceux que leur âge en exemptait par les lois ; distinction qui plus que celle des biens produisit la nécessité de recommencer souvent le cens ou dénombrement. Enfin, il voulut que l'assemblée se tînt au champ de Mars, et que tous ceux qui étaient en âge de servir y vinssent avec leurs armes.

La raison pour laquelle il ne suivit pas dans la dernière classe cette même division des jeunes et des vieux, c'est qu'on n'accordait point à la populace dont elle était composée l'honneur de porter les armes pour la patrie ; il fallait avoir des foyers pour obtenir le droit de les défendre : et de ces innombrables troupes de gueux dont brillent aujourd'hui les armées des rois, il n'y en a pas un, peut-être, qui n'eût été chassé avec dédain d'une cohorte romaine, quand les soldats étaient les défenseurs de la liberté.

On distingua pourtant encore, dans la dernière classe, les *prolétaires* de ceux qu'on appelait *capite censi*. Les premiers, non tout à fait réduits à rien, donnaient au moins des citoyens à l'État, quelquefois même des soldats dans les besoins pressants. Pour ceux qui n'avaient rien du tout et qu'on ne pouvait dénombrer que par leurs têtes, ils étaient tout à fait regardés comme nuls, et Marius fut le premier qui daigna les enrôler.

Sans décider ici si ce troisième dénombrement était bon ou mauvais en lui-même, je crois pouvoir affirmer qu'il n'y avait que les mœurs simples des premiers Romains, leur désintéressement, leur goût pour l'agriculture, leur mépris pour le commerce et pour l'ardeur du gain, qui pussent le rendre praticable. Où est le peuple moderne chez lequel la dévorante avidité, l'esprit inquiet, l'intrigue, les déplacements continuels, les perpétuelles révolutions des fortunes, pussent laisser durer vingt ans un pareil établissement sans bouleverser tout l'État ? Il faut même bien remarquer que les mœurs et la censure plus fortes que cette institution en corrigèrent le vice à Rome, et que tel riche se vit relégué dans la classe des pauvres pour avoir trop étalé sa richesse.

De tout ceci l'on peut comprendre aisément pourquoi il n'est presque jamais fait mention que de cinq classes, quoiqu'il y en eût réellement six. La sixième, ne fournissant ni soldats à l'armée, ni votants au champ de Mars*, et n'étant presque d'aucun usage dans la République, était rarement comptée pour quelque chose.

Telles furent les différentes divisions du peuple romain. Voyons à présent l'effet qu'elles produisaient dans les assemblées. Ces assemblées légitimement convoquées s'appelaient *comices* : elles se tenaient ordinairement dans la place de Rome ou au champ de Mars, et se distinguaient en comices par curies, comices par centuries, et comices par tribus, selon celle de ces trois formes sur laquelle elles étaient ordonnées : les comices par curies étaient de l'institution de Romulus ; ceux par centuries de Servius ; ceux par tribus des tribuns du peuple. Aucune loi ne recevait la sanction, aucun magistrat n'était élu que dans les comices ; et comme il n'y avait aucun citoyen qui ne fût inscrit dans une curie, dans une centurie, ou dans une tribu, il s'ensuit qu'aucun citoyen n'était exclu du droit de suffrage, et que le peuple romain était véritablement souverain de droit et de fait.

Pour que les comices fussent légitimement assemblés et que ce qui s'y faisait eût force de loi il fallait trois conditions : la première que le corps ou le magistrat qui les convoquait fût revêtu pour cela de l'autorité nécessaire ; la seconde que l'assemblée se fît un des jours permis par la loi ; la troisième que les augures fussent favorables.

La raison du premier règlement n'a pas besoin d'être expliquée. Le second est une affaire de police : ainsi

---

* Je dis au *champ de Mars*, parce que c'était là que s'assemblaient les comices par centuries : dans les deux autres formes, le peuple s'assemblait au *forum* ou ailleurs ; et alors les *capite censi* avaient autant d'influence et d'autorité que les premiers citoyens.

il n'était pas permis de tenir les comices les jours de férie et de marché, où les gens de la campagne venant à Rome pour leurs affaires n'avaient pas le temps de passer la journée dans la place publique. Par le troisième, le sénat tenait en bride un peuple fier et remuant, et tempérait à propos l'ardeur des tribuns séditieux ; mais ceux-ci trouvèrent plus d'un moyen de se délivrer de cette gêne.

Les lois et l'élection des chefs n'étaient pas les seuls points soumis au jugement des comices : le peuple romain ayant usurpé les plus importantes fonctions du gouvernement, on peut dire que le sort de l'Europe était réglé dans ses assemblées. Cette variété d'objets donnait lieu aux diverses formes que prenaient ces assemblées selon les matières sur lesquelles il avait à prononcer.

Pour juger de ces diverses formes, il suffit de les comparer. Romulus, en instituant les curies, avait en vue de contenir le sénat par le peuple et le peuple par le sénat, en dominant également sur tous. Il donna donc au peuple par cette forme toute l'autorité du nombre pour balancer celle de la puissance et des richesses qu'il laissait aux patriciens. Mais, selon l'esprit de la monarchie, il laissa cependant plus d'avantage aux patriciens par l'influence de leurs clients sur la pluralité des suffrages. Cette admirable institution des patrons et des clients fut un chef-d'œuvre de politique et d'humanité sans lequel le patriciat, si contraire à l'esprit de la République, n'eût pu subsister. Rome seule a eu l'honneur de donner au monde ce bel exemple, duquel il ne résulta jamais d'abus, et qui pourtant n'a jamais été suivi.

Cette même forme des curies ayant subsisté sous les rois jusqu'à Servius, et le règne du dernier Tarquin n'étant point compté pour légitime, cela fit distinguer généralement les lois royales par le nom de *leges curiatæ.*

Sous la République les curies, toujours bornées aux quatre tribus urbaines, et ne contenant plus que la populace de Rome, ne pouvaient convenir ni au sénat, qui était à la tête des patriciens, ni aux tribuns qui, quoique plébéiens, étaient à la tête des citoyens aisés. Elles tombèrent donc dans le discrédit, et leur avilissement fut tel, que leurs trente licteurs assemblés faisaient ce que les comices par curies auraient dû faire.

La division par centuries était si favorable à l'aristocratie, qu'on ne voit pas d'abord comment le sénat ne l'emportait pas toujours dans les comices qui portaient ce nom, et par lesquels étaient élus les consuls, les censeurs et les autres magistrats curules. En effet des cent quatre-vingt-treize centuries qui formaient les six classes de tout le peuple romain, la première classe en comprenant quatre-vingt-dix-huit, et les voix ne se comptant que par centuries, cette seule première classe l'emportait en nombre de voix sur toutes les autres. Quand toutes ses centuries étaient d'accord, on ne continuait pas même à recueillir les suffrages ; ce qu'avait décidé le plus petit nombre passait pour une décision de la multitude, et l'on peut dire que dans les comices par centuries les affaires se réglaient à la pluralité des écus bien plus qu'à celle des voix.

Mais cette extrême autorité se tempérait par deux moyens : premièrement les tribuns pour l'ordinaire, et toujours un grand nombre de plébéiens, étant dans la classe des riches, balançaient le crédit des patriciens dans cette première classe.

Le second moyen consistait en ceci, qu'au lieu de faire d'abord voter les centuries selon leur ordre, ce qui aurait toujours fait commencer par la première, on en tirait une au sort, et celle-là* procédait seule à l'élection ; après quoi toutes les centuries, appelées un autre jour selon leur rang, répétaient la même élection et la confirmaient ordinairement. On ôtait ainsi l'autorité de l'exemple au rang pour la donner au sort, selon le principe de la démocratie.

Il résultait de cet usage un autre avantage encore ; c'est que les citoyens de la campagne avaient le temps, entre les deux élections, de s'informer du mérite du candidat provisionnellement nommé, afin de ne donner leur voix qu'avec connaissance de cause. Mais, sous prétexte de célérité, l'on vint à bout d'abolir cet usage, et les deux élections se firent le même jour.

Les comices par tribus étaient proprement le Conseil du peuple romain. Ils ne se convoquaient que par les tribuns ; les tribuns y étaient élus et y passaient leurs plébiscites. Non seulement le sénat n'y avait point de rang, il n'avait pas même le droit d'y assister ; et, forcés d'obéir à des lois sur lesquelles ils n'avaient pu voter, les sénateurs, à cet égard, étaient moins libres que les derniers citoyens. Cette injustice était tout à fait mal entendue, et suffisait seule pour invalider les décrets d'un corps où tous ses membres n'étaient pas admis. Quand tous les patriciens eussent assisté à ces comices selon le droit qu'ils en avaient comme citoyens, devenus alors simples particuliers ils n'eussent guère influé sur une forme de suffrages qui se recueillaient par tête, et où le moindre prolétaire pouvait autant que le prince du sénat.

---

* Cette centurie, ainsi tirée au sort, s'appelait *prœrogativa*, à cause qu'elle était la première à qui l'on demandait son suffrage, et c'est de là qu'est venu le mot de prérogative.

On voit donc qu'outre l'ordre qui résultait de ces diverses distributions pour le recueillement des suffrages d'un si grand peuple, ces distributions ne se réduisaient pas à des formes indifférentes en elles-mêmes, mais que chacune avait des effets relatifs aux vues qui la faisaient préférer.

Sans entrer là-dessus en de plus longs détails, il résulte des éclaircissements précédents que les comices par tribus étaient plus favorables au gouvernement populaire, et les comices par centuries à l'aristocratie. À l'égard des comices par curies où la seule populace de Rome formait la pluralité, comme ils n'étaient bons qu'à favoriser la tyrannie et les mauvais desseins, ils durent tomber dans le décri, les séditieux eux-mêmes s'abstenant d'un moyen qui mettait trop à découvert leurs projets. Il est certain que toute la majesté du peuple romain ne se trouvait que dans les comices par centuries qui seuls étaient complets ; attendu que dans les comices par curies manquaient les tribus rustiques, et dans les comices par tribus le sénat et les patriciens.

Quant à la manière de recueillir les suffrages, elle était chez les premiers Romains aussi simple que leurs mœurs, quoique moins simple encore qu'à Sparte. Chacun donnait son suffrage à haute voix, un greffier les écrivait à mesure : pluralité de voix dans chaque tribu déterminait le suffrage de la tribu, pluralité de voix entre les tribus déterminait le suffrage du peuple, et ainsi des curies et des centuries. Cet usage était bon tant que l'honnêteté régnait entre les citoyens, et que chacun avait honte de donner publiquement son suffrage à un avis injuste ou à un sujet indigne ; mais, quand le peuple se corrompit et qu'on acheta les voix, il convint qu'elles se donnassent en secret pour contenir les acheteurs par la défiance, et fournir aux fripons le moyen de n'être pas des traîtres.

Je sais que Cicéron blâme ce changement et lui attribue en partie la ruine de la République. Mais, quoique je sente le poids que doit avoir ici l'autorité de Cicéron, je ne puis être de son avis. Je pense au contraire que, pour n'avoir pas fait assez de changements semblables, on accéléra la perte de l'État. Comme le régime des gens sains n'est pas propre aux malades, il ne faut pas vouloir gouverner un peuple corrompu par les mêmes lois qui conviennent à un bon peuple. Rien ne prouve mieux cette maxime que la durée de la République de Venise, dont le simulacre existe encore, uniquement parce que ses lois ne conviennent qu'à de méchants hommes.

On distribua donc aux citoyens des tablettes par lesquelles chacun pouvait voter sans qu'on sût quel était son avis. On établit aussi de nouvelles formalités pour le recueillement des tablettes, le compte des voix, la comparaison des nombres, etc. Ce qui n'empêcha pas que la fidélité des officiers chargés de ces fonctions* ne fût souvent suspectée. On fit enfin, pour empêcher la brigue et le trafic des suffrages, des édits dont la multitude montre l'inutilité.

Vers les derniers temps on était souvent contraint de recourir à des expédients extraordinaires pour suppléer à l'insuffisance des lois. Tantôt on supposait des prodiges ; mais ce moyen, qui pouvait en imposer au peuple, n'en imposait pas à ceux qui le gouvernaient ; tantôt on convoquait brusquement une assemblée avant que les candidats eussent eu le temps de faire leurs

* *Custodes, diribitores, rogatores suffragiorum*[69]. *(Note de Rousseau à l'éd. de 1762.)*

brigues ; tantôt on consumait toute une séance à parler quand on voyait le peuple gagné prêt à prendre un mauvais parti. Mais enfin l'ambition éluda tout ; et ce qu'il y a d'incroyable, c'est qu'au milieu de tant d'abus, ce peuple immense, à la faveur de ses anciens règlements, ne laissait pas d'élire les magistrats, de passer les lois, de juger les causes, d'expédier les affaires particulières et publiques, presque avec autant de facilité qu'eût pu faire le Sénat lui-même.

Chapitre V

DU TRIBUNAT

Quand on ne peut établir une exacte proportion entre les parties constitutives de l'État, ou que des causes indestructibles en altèrent sans cesse les rapports, alors on institue une magistrature particulière qui ne fait point corps avec les autres, qui replace chaque terme dans son vrai rapport, et qui fait une liaison ou un moyen terme soit entre le prince et le peuple, soit entre le prince et le souverain, soit à la fois des deux côtés s'il est nécessaire.

Ce corps, que j'appellerai *tribunat*, est le conservateur des lois et du pouvoir législatif. Il sert quelquefois à protéger le souverain contre le gouvernement, comme faisaient à Rome les tribuns du peuple ; quelquefois à soutenir le gouvernement contre le peuple, comme fait maintenant à Venise le conseil des Dix ; et quelquefois à maintenir l'équilibre de part et d'autre, comme faisaient les éphores à Sparte.

Le tribunat n'est point une partie constitutive de la cité, et ne doit avoir aucune portion de la puissance législative ni de l'exécutive, mais c'est en cela même que la sienne est plus grande : car ne pouvant rien faire il peut tout empêcher. Il est plus sacré et plus révéré, comme défenseur des lois, que le prince qui les exécute et que le souverain qui les donne. C'est ce qu'on vit bien clairement à Rome quand ces fiers patriciens, qui méprisèrent toujours le peuple entier, furent forcés de fléchir devant un simple officier du peuple, qui n'avait ni auspices ni juridiction.

Le tribunat sagement tempéré est le plus ferme appui d'une bonne constitution ; mais pour peu de force qu'il ait de trop, il renverse tout : à l'égard de la faiblesse, elle n'est pas dans sa nature ; et pourvu qu'il soit quelque chose, il n'est jamais moins qu'il ne faut.

Il dégénère en tyrannie quand il usurpe la puissance exécutive dont il n'est que le modérateur, et qu'il veut dispenser les lois qu'il ne doit que protéger. L'énorme pouvoir des éphores, qui fut sans danger tant que Sparte conserva ses mœurs, en accéléra la corruption commencée. Le sang d'Agis, égorgé par ces tyrans, fut vengé par son successeur : le crime et le châtiment des éphores hâtèrent également la perte de la République ; et après Cléomène, Sparte ne fut plus rien. Rome périt encore par la même voie et le pouvoir excessif des tribuns, usurpé par décret, servit enfin, à l'aide des lois faites pour la liberté, de sauvegarde aux empereurs qui la détruisirent. Quant au conseil des Dix à Venise, c'est un tribunal de sang, horrible également aux patriciens et au peuple, et qui, loin de protéger hautement les lois, ne sert plus, après leur avilissement, qu'à porter dans les ténèbres des coups qu'on n'ose apercevoir.

Le tribunat s'affaiblit, comme le gouvernement, par la multiplication de ses membres. Quand les tribuns du peuple romain, d'abord au nombre de deux, puis de cinq, voulurent doubler ce nombre, le Sénat les laissa faire, bien sûr de contenir les uns par les autres ; ce qui ne manqua pas d'arriver.

Le meilleur moyen de prévenir les usurpations d'un si redoutable corps, moyen dont nul gouvernement ne s'est avisé jusqu'ici, serait de ne pas rendre ce corps permanent, mais de régler les intervalles durant lesquels il resterait supprimé. Ces intervalles, qui ne doivent pas être assez grands pour laisser aux abus le temps de s'affermir, peuvent être fixés par la loi, de manière qu'il soit aisé de les abréger au besoin par des commissions extraordinaires.

Ce moyen me paraît sans inconvénient, parce que, comme je l'ai dit, le tribunat ne faisant point partie de la constitution peut être ôté sans qu'elle en souffre ; et il me paraît efficace, parce qu'un magistrat nouvellement rétabli ne part point du pouvoir qu'avait son prédécesseur, mais de celui que la loi lui donne.

Chapitre VI
DE LA DICTATURE

L'inflexibilité des lois, qui les empêche de se plier aux événements, peut en certains cas les rendre pernicieuses et causer par elles la perte de l'État dans sa crise. L'ordre et la lenteur des formes demandent un espace de temps que les circonstances refusent quelquefois. Il peut se présenter mille cas auxquels le législateur n'a point pourvu, et c'est une prévoyance très nécessaire de sentir qu'on ne peut tout prévoir.

Il ne faut donc pas vouloir affermir les institutions politiques jusqu'à s'ôter le pouvoir d'en suspendre l'effet. Sparte elle-même a laissé dormir ses lois.

Mais il n'y a que les plus grands dangers qui puissent balancer celui d'altérer l'ordre public, et l'on ne doit jamais arrêter le pouvoir sacré des lois que quand il s'agit du salut de la patrie. Dans ces cas rares et manifestes, on pourvoit à la sûreté publique par un acte particulier qui en remet la charge au plus digne. Cette commission peut se donner de deux manières selon l'espèce du danger.

Si, pour y remédier, il suffit d'augmenter l'activité du gouvernement, on le concentre dans un ou deux de ses membres. Ainsi ce n'est pas l'autorité des lois qu'on altère, mais seulement la forme de leur administration. Que si le péril est tel que l'appareil des lois soit un obstacle à s'en garantir, alors on nomme un chef suprême qui fasse taire toutes les lois et suspende un moment l'autorité souveraine ; en pareil cas, la volonté générale n'est pas douteuse, et il est évident que la première intention du peuple est que l'État ne périsse pas. De cette manière la suspension de l'autorité législative ne l'abolit point : le magistrat qui la fait taire ne peut la faire parler, il la domine sans pouvoir la représenter ; il peut tout faire, excepté des lois.

Le premier moyen s'employait par le sénat romain quand il chargeait les consuls par une formule consacrée de pourvoir au salut de la République. Le second avait lieu quand un des deux consuls nommait un dictateur* ; usage dont Albe avait donné l'exemple à Rome.

Dans les commencements de la République on eut très souvent recours à la dictature, parce que l'État n'avait pas encore une assiette assez fixe pour pouvoir se soutenir par la seule force de sa constitution.

* Cette nomination se faisait de nuit et en secret, comme si l'on avait eu honte de mettre un homme au-dessus des lois.

Les mœurs rendant alors superflues bien des précautions qui eussent été nécessaires dans un autre temps, on ne craignait ni qu'un dictateur abusât de son autorité, ni qu'il tentât de la garder au-delà du terme. Il semblait, au contraire, qu'un si grand pouvoir fût à charge à celui qui en était revêtu, tant il se hâtait de s'en défaire ; comme si c'eût été un poste trop pénible et trop périlleux de tenir la place des lois !

Aussi n'est-ce pas le danger de l'abus, mais celui de l'avilissement qui me fait blâmer l'usage indiscret de cette suprême magistrature dans les premiers temps. Car tandis qu'on la prodiguait à des élections, à des dédicaces, à des choses de pure formalité, il était à craindre qu'elle ne devînt moins redoutable au besoin, et qu'on ne s'accoutumât à regarder comme un vain titre celui qu'on n'employait qu'à de vaines cérémonies.

Vers la fin de la République, les Romains devenus plus circonspects, ménagèrent la dictature avec aussi peu de raison qu'ils l'avaient prodiguée autrefois. Il était aisé de voir que leur crainte était mal fondée, que la faiblesse de la capitale faisait alors sa sûreté contre les magistrats qu'elle avait dans son sein, qu'un dictateur pouvait, en certains cas, défendre la liberté publique sans jamais y pouvoir attenter, et que les fers de Rome ne seraient point forgés dans Rome même, mais dans ses armées : le peu de résistance que firent Marius à Sylla, et Pompée à César, montra bien ce qu'on pouvait attendre de l'autorité du dedans contre la force du dehors.

Cette erreur leur fit faire de grandes fautes. Telle, par exemple, fut celle de n'avoir pas nommé un dictateur dans l'affaire de Catilina : car comme il n'était question que du dedans de la ville et, tout au plus, de quelque province d'Italie, avec l'autorité sans bornes que les lois donnaient au dictateur il eût facilement dissipé la conjuration, qui ne fut étouffée que par un concours d'heureux hasards que jamais la prudence humaine ne devait attendre.

Au lieu de cela, le sénat se contenta de remettre tout son pouvoir aux consuls ; d'où il arriva que Cicéron, pour agir efficacement, fut contraint de passer ce pouvoir dans un point capital et que, si les premiers transports de joie firent approuver sa conduite, ce fut avec justice que dans la suite on lui demanda compte du sang des citoyens versé contre les lois ; reproche qu'on n'eût pu faire à un dictateur. Mais l'éloquence du consul entraîna tout ; et lui-même, quoique Romain, aimant mieux sa gloire que sa patrie, ne cherchait pas tant le moyen le plus légitime et le plus sûr de sauver l'État, que celui d'avoir tout l'honneur de cette affaire*. Aussi fut-il honoré justement comme libérateur de Rome, et justement puni comme infracteur des lois. Quelque brillant qu'ait été son rappel, il est certain que ce fut une grâce.

Au reste, de quelque manière que cette importante commission soit conférée, il importe d'en fixer la durée à un terme très court qui jamais ne puisse être prolongé. Dans les crises qui la font établir, l'État est bientôt détruit ou sauvé, et, passé le besoin pressant, la dictature devient tyrannique ou vaine. À Rome les dictateurs ne l'étant que pour six mois, la plupart abdiquèrent avant ce terme. Si le terme eût été plus long, peut-être eussent-ils été tentés de le prolonger encore, comme firent les décemvirs celui d'une année. Le dictateur n'avait que

---

* C'est ce dont il ne pouvait se répondre en proposant un dictateur, n'osant se nommer lui-même et ne pouvant s'assurer que son collègue le nommerait.

le temps de pourvoir au besoin qui l'avait fait élire, il n'avait pas celui de songer à d'autres projets.

Chapitre VII

DE LA CENSURE

De même que la déclaration de la volonté générale se fait par la loi, la déclaration du jugement public se fait par la censure ; l'opinion publique est l'espèce de loi dont le censeur est le ministre, et qu'il ne fait qu'appliquer aux cas particuliers, à l'exemple du prince.

Loin donc que le tribunal censorial soit l'arbitre de l'opinion du peuple, il n'en est que le déclarateur, et sitôt qu'il s'en écarte, ses décisions sont vaines et sans effet.

Il est inutile de distinguer les mœurs d'une nation des objets de son estime ; car tout cela tient au même principe et se confond nécessairement. Chez tous les peuples du monde, ce n'est point la nature mais l'opinion qui décide du choix de leurs plaisirs. Redressez les opinions des hommes et leurs mœurs s'épureront d'elles-mêmes. On aime toujours ce qui est beau ou ce qu'on trouve tel, mais c'est sur ce jugement qu'on se trompe : c'est donc ce jugement qu'il s'agit de régler. Qui juge des mœurs juge de l'honneur, et qui juge de l'honneur prend sa loi de l'opinion.

Les opinions d'un peuple naissent de sa constitution ; quoique la loi ne règle pas les mœurs, c'est la législation qui les fait naître : quand la législation s'affaiblit les mœurs dégénèrent, mais alors le jugement des censeurs ne fera pas ce que la force des lois n'aura pas fait.

Il suit de là que la censure peut être utile pour conserver les mœurs, jamais pour les rétablir. Établissez des censeurs durant la vigueur des lois ; sitôt qu'elles l'ont perdue, tout est désespéré ; rien de légitime n'a plus de force lorsque les lois n'en ont plus.

La censure maintient les mœurs en empêchant les opinions de se corrompre, en conservant leur droiture par de sages applications, quelquefois même en les fixant lorsqu'elles sont encore incertaines. L'usage des seconds dans les duels, porté jusqu'à la fureur dans le royaume de France, y fut aboli par ces seuls mots d'un édit du roi : « Quant à ceux qui ont la lâcheté d'appeler des seconds. » Ce jugement, prévenant celui du public, le détermina tout d'un coup. Mais quand les mêmes édits voulurent prononcer que c'était aussi une lâcheté de se battre en duel, ce qui est très vrai, mais contraire à l'opinion commune, le public se moqua de cette décision, sur laquelle son jugement était déjà porté.

J'ai dit ailleurs* que l'opinion publique n'étant point soumise à la contrainte, il n'en fallait aucun vestige dans le tribunal établi pour la représenter. On ne peut trop admirer avec quel art ce ressort, entièrement perdu chez les modernes, était mis en œuvre chez les Romains et mieux chez les Lacédémoniens.

Un homme de mauvaises mœurs ayant ouvert un bon avis dans le Conseil de Sparte, les éphores, sans en tenir compte, firent proposer le même avis par un citoyen vertueux. Quel honneur pour l'un, quelle honte pour l'autre, sans avoir donné ni louange ni blâme à aucun

---

* Je ne fais qu'indiquer dans ce chapitre ce que j'ai traité plus au long dans la *Lettre à M. d'Alembert.*

des deux ! Certains ivrognes de Samos* souillèrent le tribunal des éphores : le lendemain par édit public il fut permis aux Samiens d'être des vilains. Un vrai châtiment eût été moins sévère qu'une pareille impunité. Quand Sparte a prononcé sur ce qui est ou n'est pas honnête, la Grèce n'appelle pas de ses jugements.

Chapitre VIII

DE LA RELIGION CIVILE[70]

Les hommes n'eurent point d'abord d'autres rois que les dieux, ni d'autre gouvernement que le théocratique. Ils firent le raisonnement de Caligula ; et alors ils raisonnaient juste. Il faut une longue altération de sentiments et d'idées pour qu'on puisse se résoudre à prendre son semblable pour maître, et se flatter qu'on s'en trouvera bien.

De cela seul qu'on mettait Dieu à la tête de chaque société politique, il s'ensuivit qu'il y eut autant de dieux que de peuples. Deux peuples étrangers l'un à l'autre, et presque toujours ennemis, ne purent longtemps reconnaître un même maître. Deux armées se livrant bataille ne sauraient obéir au même chef. Ainsi des divisions nationales résulta le polythéisme, et de là l'intolérance théologique et civile qui naturellement est la même, comme il sera dit ci-après.

La fantaisie qu'eurent les Grecs de retrouver leurs dieux chez les peuples barbares, vint de celle qu'ils avaient aussi de se regarder comme les souverains natu-

* Ils étaient d'une autre île, que la délicatesse de notre langue défend de nommer dans cette occasion. *(Note de Rousseau à l'éd. de 1782.)*

rels de ces peuples. Mais c'est de nos jours une érudition bien ridicule que celle qui roule sur l'identité des dieux de diverses nations : comme si Moloch, Saturne et Cronos pouvaient être le même Dieu ; comme si le Baal des Phéniciens, le Zeus des Grecs et le Jupiter des Latins pouvaient être le même ; comme s'il pouvait rester quelque chose commune à des êtres chimériques portant des noms différents !

Que si l'on demande comment dans le paganisme où chaque État avait son culte et ses dieux il n'y avait point de guerre de religion ? Je réponds que c'était par cela même que chaque État, ayant son culte propre aussi bien que son gouvernement, ne distinguait point ses dieux de ses lois. La guerre politique était aussi théologique ; les départements des dieux étaient pour ainsi dire fixés par les bornes des nations. Le dieu d'un peuple n'avait aucun droit sur les autres peuples. Les dieux des païens n'étaient point des dieux jaloux ; ils partageaient entre eux l'empire du monde : Moïse même et le peuple hébreu se prêtaient quelquefois à cette idée en parlant du Dieu d'Israël. Ils regardaient, il est vrai, comme nuls les dieux des Cananéens, peuples proscrits, voués à la destruction, et dont ils devaient occuper la place ; mais voyez comment ils parlaient des divinités des peuples voisins qu'il leur était défendu d'attaquer : « La possession de ce qui appartient à Chamos, votre dieu, disait Jephté aux Ammonites, ne vous est-elle pas légitimement due ? Nous possédons au même titre les terres que notre Dieu vainqueur s'est acquises*. » C'était là, ce me semble, une parité bien

---

* *Nonne ea quœ possidet Chamos deus tuus, tibi jure debentur?* Tel est le texte de la *Vulgate.* Le P. de Carrières a traduit : « Ne croyez-vous pas avoir droit de posséder ce qui appartient à Chamos

reconnue entre les droits de Chamos et ceux du Dieu d'Israël.

Mais quand les Juifs, soumis aux rois de Babylone et dans la suite aux rois de Syrie, voulurent s'obstiner à ne reconnaître aucun autre Dieu que le leur, ce refus, regardé comme une rébellion contre le vainqueur, leur attira les persécutions qu'on lit dans leur histoire et dont on ne voit aucun autre exemple avant le christianisme*.

Chaque religion étant donc uniquement attachée aux lois de l'État qui la prescrivait, il n'y avait point d'autre manière de convertir un peuple que de l'asservir ni d'autres missionnaires que les conquérants, et l'obligation de changer de culte étant la loi des vaincus, il fallait commencer par vaincre avant d'en parler. Loin que les hommes combattissent pour les dieux, c'étaient, comme dans Homère, les dieux qui combattaient pour les hommes ; chacun demandait au sien la victoire, et la payait par de nouveaux autels. Les Romains, avant de prendre une place, sommaient ses dieux de l'abandonner, et quand ils laissaient aux Tarentins leurs dieux irrités, c'est qu'ils regardaient alors ces dieux comme soumis aux leurs et forcés de leur faire hommage. Ils laissaient aux vaincus leurs dieux comme ils leur laissaient leurs lois. Une couronne au Jupiter du Capitole était souvent le seul tribut qu'ils imposaient.

---

votre dieu ? » J'ignore la force du texte hébreu ; mais je vois que, dans la *Vulgate*, Jephté reconnaît positivement le droit du dieu Chamos, et que le traducteur français affaiblit cette reconnaissance par un *selon vous* qui n'est pas dans le latin.

* Il est de la dernière évidence que la guerre des Phocéens, appelée guerre sacrée, n'était pas une guerre de religion. Elle avait pour objet de punir des sacrilèges, et non de soumettre des mécréants.

Enfin les Romains ayant étendu avec leur empire leur culte et leurs dieux, et ayant souvent eux-mêmes adopté ceux des vaincus en accordant aux uns et aux autres le droit de cité, les peuples de ce vaste empire se trouvèrent insensiblement avoir des multitudes de dieux et de cultes, à peu près les mêmes partout : et voilà comment le paganisme ne fut enfin dans le monde connu qu'une seule et même religion.

Ce fut dans ces circonstances que Jésus vint établir sur la terre un royaume spirituel ; ce qui, séparant le système théologique du système politique, fit que l'État cessa d'être un, et causa les divisions intestines qui n'ont jamais cessé d'agiter les peuples chrétiens. Or, cette idée nouvelle d'un royaume de l'autre monde n'ayant pu jamais entrer dans la tête des païens, ils regardèrent toujours les chrétiens comme de vrais rebelles qui, sous une hypocrite soumission, ne cherchaient que le moment de se rendre indépendants et maîtres, et d'usurper adroitement l'autorité qu'ils feignaient de respecter dans leur faiblesse. Telle fut la cause des persécutions.

Ce que les païens avaient craint est arrivé ; alors tout a changé de face, les humbles chrétiens ont changé de langage, et bientôt on a vu ce prétendu royaume de l'autre monde devenir sous un chef visible le plus violent despotisme dans celui-ci.

Cependant comme il y a toujours eu un prince et des lois civiles, il a résulté de cette double puissance un perpétuel conflit de juridiction qui a rendu toute bonne politique impossible dans les États chrétiens ; et l'on n'a jamais pu venir à bout de savoir auquel du maître ou du prêtre on était obligé d'obéir.

Plusieurs peuples cependant, même dans l'Europe ou à son voisinage, ont voulu conserver ou rétablir l'ancien système, mais sans succès; l'esprit du christianisme a tout gagné. Le culte sacré est toujours resté ou redevenu indépendant du souverain, et sans liaison nécessaire avec le corps de l'État. Mahomet eut des vues très saines, il lia bien son système politique, et tant que la forme de son gouvernement subsista sous les califes ses successeurs, ce gouvernement fut exactement un, et bon en cela. Mais les Arabes devenus florissants, lettrés, polis, mous et lâches, furent subjugués par des barbares; alors la division entre les deux puissances recommença; quoiqu'elle soit moins apparente chez les mahométans que chez les chrétiens, elle y est pourtant, surtout dans la secte d'Ali, et il y a des États, tels que la Perse, où elle ne cesse de se faire sentir.

Parmi nous, les rois d'Angleterre se sont établis chefs de l'Église, autant en ont fait les czars : mais, par ce titre, ils s'en sont moins rendus les maîtres que les ministres; ils ont moins acquis le droit de la changer que le pouvoir de la maintenir; ils n'y sont pas législateurs, ils n'y sont que princes. Partout où le clergé fait un corps*, il est maître et législateur dans sa partie. Il y a donc deux puissances, deux souverains, en Angleterre et en Russie, tout comme ailleurs.

De tous les auteurs chrétiens le philosophe Hobbes est le seul qui ait bien vu le mal et le remède, qui ait

* Il faut bien remarquer que ce ne sont pas tant des assemblées formelles, comme celles de France, qui lient le clergé en un corps, que la communion des Églises. La communion et l'excommunication sont le pacte social du clergé, pacte avec lequel il sera toujours le maître des peuples et des rois. Tous les prêtres qui communiquent ensemble sont concitoyens, fussent-ils des deux bouts du monde. Cette invention est un chef-d'œuvre en politique. Il n'y avait rien de semblable parmi les prêtres païens; aussi n'ont-ils jamais fait un corps de clergé.

osé proposer de réunir les deux têtes de l'aigle, et de tout ramener à l'unité politique, sans laquelle jamais État ni gouvernement ne seront bien constitués. Mais il a dû voir que l'esprit dominateur du christianisme était incompatible avec son système, et que l'intérêt du prêtre serait toujours plus fort que celui de l'État. Ce n'est pas tant ce qu'il y a d'horrible et de faux dans sa politique que ce qu'il y a de juste et de vrai qui l'a rendue odieuse*.

Je crois qu'en développant sous ce point de vue les faits historiques, on réfuterait aisément les sentiments opposés de Bayle et de Warburton, dont l'un prétend que nulle religion n'est utile au corps politique, et dont l'autre soutient au contraire que le christianisme en est le plus ferme appui. On prouverait au premier que jamais État ne fut fondé que la religion ne lui servît de base, et au second que la loi chrétienne est au fond plus nuisible qu'utile à la forte constitution de l'État. Pour achever de me faire entendre, il ne faut que donner un peu plus de précision aux idées trop vagues de religion relatives à mon sujet.

La religion considérée par rapport à la société, qui est ou générale ou particulière, peut aussi se diviser en deux espèces, savoir, la religion de l'homme et celle du citoyen. La première, sans temples, sans autels, sans rites, bornée au culte purement intérieur du Dieu suprême et aux devoirs éternels de la morale, est la pure et simple religion de l'Évangile, le vrai théisme, et ce qu'on peut appeler le droit divin naturel. L'autre ins-

---

* Voyez, entre autres, dans une lettre de Grotius à son frère du 11 avril 1643, ce que ce savant homme approuve et ce qu'il blâme dans le livre *De cive.* Il est vrai que, porté à l'indulgence, il paraît pardonner à l'auteur le bien en faveur du mal ; mais tout le monde n'est pas si clément.

crite dans un seul pays, lui donne ses dieux, ses patrons propres et tutélaires; elle a ses dogmes, ses rites, son culte extérieur prescrit par des lois : hors la seule nation qui la suit, tout est pour elle infidèle, étranger, barbare; elle n'étend les devoirs et les droits de l'homme qu'aussi loin que ses autels. Telles furent toutes les religions des premiers peuples, auxquelles on peut donner le nom de droit divin civil ou positif.

Il y a une troisième sorte de religion plus bizarre, qui donnant aux hommes deux législations, deux chefs, deux patries, les soumet à des devoirs contradictoires et les empêche de pouvoir être à la fois dévots et citoyens. Telle est la religion des Lamas, telle est celle des Japonais, tel est le christianisme romain. On peut appeler celle-ci la religion du prêtre. Il en résulte une sorte de droit mixte et insociable qui n'a point de nom.

À considérer politiquement ces trois sortes de religions, elles ont toutes leurs défauts. La troisième est si évidemment mauvaise, que c'est perdre le temps de s'amuser à le démontrer. Tout ce qui rompt l'unité sociale ne vaut rien. Toutes les institutions qui mettent l'homme en contradiction avec lui-même ne valent rien.

La seconde est bonne en ce qu'elle réunit le culte divin et l'amour des lois, et que, faisant de la patrie l'objet de l'adoration des citoyens, elle leur apprend que servir l'État, c'est en servir le Dieu tutélaire. C'est une espèce de théocratie, dans laquelle on ne doit point avoir d'autre pontife que le prince, ni d'autres prêtres que les magistrats. Alors mourir pour son pays c'est aller au martyre, violer les lois, c'est être impie, et soumettre un coupable à l'exécration publique, c'est le dévouer au courroux des dieux; *sacer esto.*

Mais elle est mauvaise en ce qu'étant fondée sur l'erreur et sur le mensonge elle trompe les hommes, les rend crédules, superstitieux, et noie le vrai culte de la divinité dans un vain cérémonial. Elle est mauvaise encore quand, devenant exclusive et tyrannique, elle rend un peuple sanguinaire et intolérant, en sorte qu'il ne respire que meurtre et massacre, et croit faire une action sainte en tuant quiconque n'admet pas ses dieux. Cela met un tel peuple dans un état naturel de guerre avec tous les autres, très nuisible à sa propre sécurité.

Reste donc la religion de l'homme ou le christianisme, non pas celui d'aujourd'hui, mais celui de l'Évangile, qui en est tout à fait différent. Par cette religion sainte, sublime, véritable, les hommes, enfants du même Dieu, se reconnaissent tous pour frères, et la société qui les unit ne se dissout pas même à la mort.

Mais cette religion n'ayant nulle relation particulière avec le corps politique laisse aux lois la seule force qu'elles tirent d'elles-mêmes sans leur en ajouter aucune autre, et par là un des grands liens de la société particulière reste sans effet. Bien plus ; loin d'attacher les cœurs des citoyens à l'État, elle les en détache comme de toutes les choses de la terre : je ne connais rien de plus contraire à l'esprit social.

On nous dit qu'un peuple de vrais chrétiens formerait la plus parfaite société que l'on puisse imaginer. Je ne vois à cette supposition qu'une grande difficulté ; c'est qu'une société de vrais chrétiens ne serait plus une société d'hommes.

Je dis même que cette société supposée ne serait avec toute sa perfection ni la plus forte ni la plus durable. À force d'être parfaite, elle manquerait de liaison ; son vice destructeur serait dans sa perfection même.

Chacun remplirait son devoir ; le peuple serait soumis aux lois, les chefs seraient justes et modérés, les magistrats intègres, incorruptibles, les soldats mépriseraient la mort, il n'y aurait ni vanité ni luxe : tout cela est fort bien, mais voyons plus loin.

Le christianisme est une religion toute spirituelle, occupée uniquement des choses du ciel ; la patrie du chrétien n'est pas de ce monde. Il fait son devoir, il est vrai, mais il le fait avec une profonde indifférence sur le bon ou mauvais succès de ses soins. Pourvu qu'il n'ait rien à se reprocher, peu lui importe que tout aille bien ou mal ici-bas. Si l'État est florissant, à peine ose-t-il jouir de la félicité publique, il craint de s'enorgueillir de la gloire de son pays ; si l'État dépérit, il bénit la main de Dieu qui s'appesantit sur son peuple.

Pour que la société fût paisible et que l'harmonie se maintînt, il faudrait que tous les citoyens sans exception fussent également bons chrétiens. Mais si malheureusement il s'y trouve un seul ambitieux, un seul hypocrite, un Catilina, par exemple, un Cromwell, celui-là très certainement aura bon marché de ses pieux compatriotes. La charité chrétienne ne permet pas aisément de penser mal de son prochain. Dès qu'il aura trouvé par quelque ruse l'art de leur en imposer et de s'emparer d'une partie de l'autorité publique, voilà un homme constitué en dignité ; Dieu veut qu'on le respecte ; bientôt voilà une puissance ; Dieu veut qu'on lui obéisse ; le dépositaire de cette puissance en abuse-t il ? C'est la verge dont Dieu punit ses enfants. On se ferait conscience de chasser l'usurpateur : il faudrait troubler le repos public, user de violence, verser du sang : tout cela s'accorde mal avec la douceur du chrétien ; et après tout, qu'importe qu'on soit libre ou serf dans cette vallée de misères ? L'essentiel est d'aller en paradis, et la résignation n'est qu'un moyen de plus pour cela.

Survient-il quelque guerre étrangère ? Les citoyens marchent sans peine au combat ; nul d'entre eux ne songe à fuir ; ils font leur devoir, mais sans passion pour la victoire ; ils savent plutôt mourir que vaincre. Qu'ils soient vainqueurs ou vaincus, qu'importe ? La Providence ne sait-elle pas mieux qu'eux ce qu'il leur faut ? Qu'on imagine quel parti un ennemi fier, impétueux, passionné, peut tirer de leur stoïcisme. Mettez vis-à-vis d'eux ces peuples généreux que dévorait l'ardent amour de la gloire et de la patrie, supposez votre république chrétienne vis-à-vis de Sparte ou de Rome : les pieux chrétiens seront battus, écrasés, détruits, avant d'avoir eu le temps de se reconnaître, ou ne devront leur salut qu'au mépris que leur ennemi concevra pour eux. C'était un beau serment à mon gré que celui des soldats de Fabius ; ils ne jurèrent pas de mourir ou de vaincre, ils jurèrent de revenir vainqueurs, et tinrent leur serment. Jamais des chrétiens n'en eussent fait un pareil ; ils auraient cru tenter Dieu.

Mais je me trompe en disant une république chrétienne ; chacun de ces deux mots exclut l'autre. Le christianisme ne prêche que servitude et dépendance. Son esprit est trop favorable à la tyrannie pour qu'elle n'en profite pas toujours. Les vrais chrétiens sont faits pour être esclaves ; ils le savent et ne s'en émeuvent guère ; cette courte vie a trop peu de prix à leurs yeux.

Les troupes chrétiennes sont excellentes, nous dit-on. Je le nie. Qu'on m'en montre de telles. Quant à moi, je ne connais point de troupes chrétiennes. On me citera les croisades. Sans disputer sur la valeur des croisés, je remarquerai que, bien loin d'être des chrétiens, c'étaient des soldats du prêtre, c'étaient des citoyens de l'Église : ils se battaient pour son pays spirituel, qu'elle avait rendu temporel on ne sait comment. À le bien prendre, ceci rentre sous le paganisme : comme l'Évangile n'établit point une religion nationale, toute guerre sacrée est impossible parmi les chrétiens.

Sous les empereurs païens les soldats chrétiens étaient braves ; tous les auteurs chrétiens l'assurent, et je le crois : c'était une émulation d'honneur contre les troupes païennes. Dès que les empereurs furent chrétiens cette émulation ne subsista plus ; et quand la croix eut chassé l'aigle, toute la valeur romaine disparut.

Mais, laissant à part les considérations politiques, revenons au droit, et fixons les principes sur ce point important. Le droit que le pacte social donne au souverain sur les sujets ne passe point, comme je l'ai dit, les bornes de l'utilité publique*. Les sujets ne doivent donc compte au souverain de leurs opinions qu'autant que ces opinions importent à la communauté. Or il importe bien à l'État que chaque citoyen ait une religion qui lui fasse aimer ses devoirs ; mais les dogmes de cette religion n'intéressent ni l'État ni ses membres qu'autant que ces dogmes se rapportent à la morale et aux devoirs que celui qui la professe est tenu de remplir envers autrui. Chacun peut avoir au surplus telles opinions qu'il lui plaît, sans qu'il appartienne au souverain d'en connaître. Car comme il n'a point de compétence dans l'autre monde, quel que soit le sort des sujets dans

* « Dans la république, dit le marquis d'Argenson, chacun est parfaitement libre en ce qui ne nuit pas aux autres. » Voilà la borne invariable ; on ne peut la poser plus exactement. Je n'ai pu me refuser au plaisir de citer quelquefois ce manuscrit quoique non connu du public, pour rendre honneur à la mémoire d'un homme illustre et respectable, qui avait conservé jusque dans le ministère le cœur d'un vrai citoyen, et des vues droites et saines sur le gouvernement de son pays.

la vie à venir ce n'est pas son affaire, pourvu qu'ils soient bons citoyens dans celle-ci.

Il y a donc une profession de foi purement civile dont il appartient au souverain de fixer les articles, non pas précisément comme dogmes de religion, mais comme sentiments de sociabilité, sans lesquels il est impossible d'être bon citoyen ni sujet fidèle*. Sans pouvoir obliger personne à les croire, il peut bannir de l'État quiconque ne les croit pas ; il peut le bannir, non comme impie, mais comme insociable, comme incapable d'aimer sincèrement les lois, la justice, et d'immoler au besoin sa vie à son devoir. Que si quelqu'un, après avoir reconnu publiquement ces mêmes dogmes, se conduit comme ne les croyant pas, qu'il soit puni de mort ; il a commis le plus grand des crimes, il a menti devant les lois.

Les dogmes de la religion civile doivent être simples, en petit nombre, énoncés avec précision sans explications ni commentaires. L'existence de la divinité puissante, intelligente, bienfaisante, prévoyante et pourvoyante, la vie à venir, le bonheur des justes, le châtiment des méchants, la sainteté du contrat social et des lois : voilà les dogmes positifs. Quant aux dogmes négatifs, je les borne à un seul, c'est l'intolérance : elle rentre dans les cultes que nous avons exclus.

Ceux qui distinguent l'intolérance civile et l'intolérance théologique se trompent, à mon avis. Ces deux intolérances sont inséparables. Il est impossible de vivre en paix avec des gens qu'on croit damnés ; les

---

* César, plaidant pour Catilina, tâchait d'établir le dogme de la mortalité de l'âme : Caton et Cicéron, pour le réfuter, ne s'amusèrent point à philosopher ; ils se contentèrent de montrer que César parlait en mauvais citoyen et avançait une doctrine pernicieuse à l'État. En effet voilà de quoi devait juger le Sénat de Rome et non d'une question de théologie.

aimer serait haïr Dieu qui les punit : il faut absolument qu'on les ramène ou qu'on les tourmente. Partout où l'intolérance théologique est admise, il est impossible qu'elle n'ait pas quelque effet civil*, et sitôt qu'elle en a, le souverain n'est plus souverain, même au temporel ; dès lors les prêtres sont les vrais maîtres ; les rois ne sont que leurs officiers.

Maintenant qu'il n'y a plus et qu'il ne peut plus y avoir de religion nationale exclusive, on doit tolérer toutes celles qui tolèrent les autres, autant que leurs dogmes n'ont rien de contraire aux devoirs du citoyen. Mais quiconque ose dire : *hors de l'Église, point de salut*, doit être chassé de l'État, à moins que l'État ne soit l'Église, et que le prince ne soit le pontife. Un tel dogme n'est bon que dans un gouvernement théocratique ; dans tout autre il est pernicieux. La raison sur laquelle on dit qu'Henri IV embrassa la religion

* Le mariage, par exemple, étant un contrat civil, a des effets civils sans lesquels il est même impossible que la société subsiste. Supposons donc qu'un clergé vienne à bout de s'attribuer à lui seul le droit de passer cet acte, droit qu'il doit nécessairement usurper dans toute religion intolérante ; alors n'est-il pas clair qu'en faisant valoir à propos l'autorité de l'Église il rendra vaine celle du prince, qui n'aura plus de sujets que ceux que le clergé voudra bien lui donner ? Maître de marier ou de ne pas marier les gens, selon qu'ils auront ou n'auront pas telle ou telle doctrine, selon qu'ils admettront ou rejetteront tel ou tel formulaire, selon qu'ils lui seront plus ou moins dévoués, en se conduisant prudemment et tenant ferme, n'est-il pas clair qu'il disposera seul des héritages, des charges, des citoyens, de l'État même, qui ne saurait subsister, n'étant plus composé que de bâtards ? Mais, dira-t-on, l'on appellera comme d'abus, on ajournera, décrétera, saisira le temporel. Quelle pitié ! Le clergé, pour peu qu'il ait, je ne dis pas de courage, mais de bon sens, laissera faire et ira son train ; il laissera tranquillement appeler, ajourner, décréter, saisir, et finira par rester le maître. Ce n'est pas, ce me semble, un grand sacrifice d'abandonner une partie quand on est sûr de s'emparer du tout.

romaine la devrait faire quitter à tout honnête homme, et surtout à tout prince qui saurait raisonner.

Chapitre IX
CONCLUSION

Après avoir posé les vrais principes du droit politique et tâché de fonder l'État sur sa base, il resterait à l'appuyer par ses relations externes ; ce qui comprendrait le droit des gens, le commerce, le droit de la guerre et les conquêtes, le droit public, les ligues, les négociations, les traités, etc. Mais tout cela forme un nouvel objet trop vaste pour ma courte vue ; j'aurais dû la fixer toujours plus près de moi.

Annexes

I

DU CONTRAT SOCIAL
Première version

ou

ESSAI SUR LA FORME DE LA RÉPUBLIQUE
[dit « Manuscrit de Genève »]

(Livre I, chapitre 2)

DE LA SOCIÉTÉ GÉNÉRALE DU GENRE HUMAIN

Commençons par rechercher d'où naît la nécessité des institutions politiques.

La force de l'homme est tellement proportionnée à ses besoins naturels et à son état primitif que, pour peu que cet état change et que ses besoins augmentent, l'assistance de ses semblables lui devient nécessaire ; et quand enfin ses désirs embrassent toute la nature, le concours de tout le genre humain suffit à peine pour les assouvir. C'est ainsi que les mêmes causes qui nous rendent méchants nous rendent encore esclaves, et nous asservissent en nous dépravant. Le sentiment de notre faiblesse vient moins de notre nature que de notre cupidité : nos besoins nous rapprochent à mesure que nos passions nous divisent ; et plus nous devenons ennemis de nos semblables, moins nous pouvons nous passer d'eux. Tels sont les premiers liens de la société générale ; tels sont les fondements de cette bienveillance universelle dont la nécessité reconnue semble étouffer le sentiment, et dont chacun voudrait recueillir le fruit sans être obligé de la cultiver. Car, quant à l'identité de nature, son effet est nul en cela ; parce qu'elle est autant pour les hommes un sujet de querelle que d'union, et met aussi souvent entre eux la concurrence et la jalousie que la bonne intelligence et l'accord.

De ce nouvel ordre de choses naissent des multitudes de rapports sans mesure, sans règle, sans consistance, que les hommes altèrent et changent continuellement, cent travaillant à les détruire pour un qui travaille à les fixer. Et comme l'existence relative d'un homme dans l'état de nature dépend de mille autres rapports qui sont dans un flux continuel, il ne peut jamais s'assurer d'être le même durant deux instants de sa vie ; la paix et le bonheur ne sont pour lui qu'un éclair ; rien n'est permanent que la misère qui résulte de toutes ces vicissitudes. Quand ses sentiments et ses idées pourraient s'élever jusqu'à l'amour de l'ordre et aux notions sublimes de la vertu, il lui serait impossible de faire jamais une application sûre de ses principes dans un état de choses qui ne lui laisserait discerner ni le bien ni le mal, ni l'honnête homme ni le méchant.

La société générale, telle que nos besoins mutuels peuvent l'engendrer, n'offre donc point une assistance efficace à l'homme devenu misérable ; ou du moins elle ne donne de nouvelles forces qu'à celui qui en a déjà trop, tandis que le faible, perdu, étouffé, écrasé dans la multitude, ne trouve nul asile où se réfugier, nul support à sa faiblesse, et périt enfin victime de cette union trompeuse, dont il attendait son bonheur.

Si l'on est une fois convaincu que, dans les motifs qui portent les hommes à s'unir entre eux par des liens volontaires, il n'y a rien qui se rapporte au point de réunion ; que, loin de se proposer un objet de félicité commune d'où chacun pût tirer la sienne, le bonheur de l'un fait le malheur d'un autre ; si l'on voit enfin qu'au lieu de tendre tous au bien général ils ne se rapprochent entre eux que parce que tous s'en éloignent ; on doit sentir aussi que, quand même un tel état pourrait subsister, il ne serait qu'une source de crimes et de misères pour des hommes dont chacun ne verrait que son intérêt, ne suivrait que ses penchants et n'écouterait que ses passions.

Ainsi, la douce voix de la nature n'est plus pour nous un guide infaillible, ni l'indépendance, que nous avons reçue d'elle, un état désirable ; la paix et l'innocence nous ont échappé pour jamais, avant que nous en eussions goûté les délices. Insensible aux stupides hommes des premiers temps, échappée aux hommes éclairés des temps postérieurs, l'heureuse vie de l'âge d'or fut toujours un état étranger à la race humaine, ou pour l'avoir méconnu quand elle en pouvait jouir, ou pour l'avoir perdu quand elle aurait pu le connaître.

Il y a plus encore : cette parfaite indépendance et cette liberté sans règle, fût-elle même demeurée jointe à l'antique innocence, aurait eu toujours un vice essentiel, et nuisible au progrès de nos plus excellentes facultés : savoir, le défaut de cette liaison des parties qui constitue le tout. La terre serait couverte d'hommes, entre lesquels il n'y aurait presque aucune communication ; nous nous toucherions par quelques points, sans être unis par aucun ; chacun resterait isolé parmi les autres, chacun ne songerait qu'à soi ; notre entendement ne saurait se développer ; nous vivrions sans rien sentir, nous mourrions sans avoir vécu ; tout notre bonheur consisterait à ne pas connaître notre misère ; il n'y aurait ni bonté dans nos cœurs ni moralité dans nos actions, et nous n'aurions jamais goûté le plus délicieux sentiment de l'âme, qui est l'amour de la vertu.

Il est certain que le mot de *genre humain* n'offre à l'esprit qu'une idée purement collective, qui ne suppose aucune union réelle entre les individus qui le constituent. Ajoutons-y, si l'on veut, cette supposition : concevons le genre humain comme une personne morale ayant, avec un sentiment d'existence commune qui lui donne l'individualité et la constitue une, un mobile universel qui fasse agir chaque partie pour une fin générale et relative au tout. Concevons que ce sentiment commun soit celui de l'humanité, et que la loi naturelle soit le principe actif de toute la machine. Observons ensuite ce qui résulte de la constitution de l'homme dans ses rapports avec ses semblables : et, tout au contraire de ce que nous avons supposé, nous trouverons que le progrès de la société étouffe l'humanité dans les cœurs, en éveillant l'intérêt personnel, et que les notions de la loi naturelle, qu'il faudrait plutôt appeler la loi de raison, ne commencent à se développer que quand le développement antérieur des passions rend impuissants tous ses préceptes. Par où l'on voit que ce prétendu traité social, dicté par la nature, est une véritable chimère ; puisque les conditions en sont toujours inconnues ou impraticables, et qu'il faut nécessairement les ignorer ou les enfreindre.

Si la société générale existait ailleurs que dans les systèmes des philosophes, elle serait, comme je l'ai dit, un être moral qui aurait des qualités propres, et distinctes de celles des êtres particuliers qui la constituent ; à peu près comme les composés chimiques ont des propriétés qu'ils ne tiennent d'aucun des mixtes qui les composent. Il y aurait une langue universelle que la nature apprendrait à tous les hommes, et qui serait le premier instrument de leur mutuelle communication. Il y aurait une sorte de sensorium commun qui servirait à la correspondance de toutes les parties. Le bien ou le mal public ne serait pas seulement la somme des biens ou des maux particuliers, comme dans une simple agrégation, mais il résiderait dans la liaison qui les unit ; il serait plus grand que cette somme ; et, loin que la félicité publique fût établie sur le bonheur des particuliers, c'est elle qui en serait la source.

Il est faux que, dans l'état d'indépendance, la raison nous porte à concourir au bien commun par la vue de notre propre intérêt. Loin que l'intérêt particulier s'allie au bien général, ils s'excluent l'un l'autre dans l'ordre naturel des choses ; et les lois sociales sont un joug que chacun veut bien imposer aux autres, mais non pas s'en charger lui-même. « Je sens que je porte l'épouvante et le trouble au milieu de l'espèce humaine », dit l'homme indépendant que le sage étouffe ; « mais il faut que je sois malheureux, ou que je fasse le malheur des autres, et personne ne m'est plus cher que moi. C'est vainement », pourra-t-il ajouter, « que je voudrais concilier mon intérêt avec celui d'autrui ; tout ce que vous me dites des avantages de la loi sociale pourrait être bon, si, tandis que je l'observerais scrupuleusement envers les autres, j'étais sûr qu'ils l'observeraient tous envers moi. Mais quelle sûreté pouvez-vous me donner là-dessus ? et ma situation peut-elle être pire que de me voir exposé à tous les maux que les plus forts voudront me faire, sans oser me dédommager sur les faibles ? Ou donnez-moi des garants contre toute entreprise injuste, ou n'espérez pas que je m'en abstienne à mon tour. Vous avez beau me dire qu'en renonçant aux devoirs que m'impose la loi naturelle je me prive en même temps de ses droits, et que mes violences autoriseront toutes celles dont on voudra user envers moi. J'y consens d'autant plus volontiers que je ne vois point comment ma modération pourrait m'en garantir. Au surplus, ce sera mon affaire de mettre les forts dans mes intérêts, en partageant avec eux les dépouilles des faibles ; cela vaudra mieux que la justice pour mon avantage et pour ma sûreté. » La preuve que c'est ainsi qu'eût raisonné l'homme éclairé et indépendant est que c'est ainsi que raisonne toute société souveraine qui ne rend compte de sa conduite qu'à elle-même.

Que répondre de solide à de pareils discours, si l'on ne veut amener la religion à l'aide de la morale, et faire intervenir immédiatement la volonté de Dieu pour lier la société des hommes ? Mais les notions sublimes du Dieu des sages, les douces lois de la fraternité qu'il nous impose, les vertus sociales des âmes pures, qui sont le vrai culte qu'il veut de nous, échapperont toujours à la multitude. On lui fera toujours des dieux insensés comme elle, auxquels elle sacrifiera de légères commodités pour se livrer en leur honneur à mille passions horribles et destructives. La terre entière regorgerait de sang, et le genre humain périrait bientôt, si la philosophie et les lois ne retenaient les fureurs du fanatisme, et si la voix des hommes n'était plus forte que celle des dieux.

En effet, si les notions du grand Être et de la loi naturelle étaient innées dans tous les cœurs, ce fut un soin bien superflu d'enseigner expressément l'une et l'autre. C'était nous apprendre ce que nous savions déjà, et la manière dont on s'y est pris eût été bien plus propre à nous le faire oublier. Si elles ne l'étaient pas, tous ceux à qui Dieu ne les a point données sont dispensés de les savoir. Dès qu'il a fallu pour cela des instructions particulières, chaque peuple a les siennes qu'on lui prouve être les seules bonnes, et d'où dérivent plus souvent le carnage et les meurtres que la concorde et la paix.

Laissons donc à part les préceptes sacrés des religions diverses, dont l'abus cause autant de crimes que leur usage en peut épargner ; et rendons au philosophe l'examen d'une question que le théologien n'a jamais traitée qu'au préjudice du genre humain.

Mais le premier me renverra par-devant le genre humain même, à qui seul il appartient de décider, parce que le plus grand bien de tous est la seule passion qu'il ait. C'est, me dira-t-il, à la volonté générale que l'individu doit s'adresser pour savoir jusqu'où il doit être homme, citoyen, sujet, père, enfant, et quand il lui convient de vivre et de mourir. « Je vois bien là, je l'avoue, la règle que je puis consulter ; mais je ne vois pas encore », dira notre homme indépendant, « la raison qui doit m'assujettir à cette règle. Il ne s'agit pas de m'apprendre ce que c'est que justice ; il s'agit de me montrer quel intérêt j'ai d'être juste. » En effet, que la volonté générale soit dans chaque individu un acte pur de l'entendement qui raisonne dans le silence des passions sur ce que l'homme peut exiger de son semblable, et sur ce que son semblable est en droit d'exiger de lui, nul n'en disconviendra. Mais où est l'homme qui puisse ainsi se séparer de lui-même ? et, si le soin de sa propre conservation est le premier précepte de la nature, peut-on le forcer de regarder ainsi l'espèce en général pour s'imposer, à lui, des devoirs dont il ne voit point la liaison avec sa constitution particulière ? Les objections précédentes ne subsistent-elles pas toujours ? et ne reste-t-il pas encore à voir comment son intérêt personnel exige qu'il se soumette à la volonté générale ?

De plus; comme l'art de généraliser ainsi ses idées est un des exercices les plus difficiles et les plus tardifs de l'entendement humain, le commun des hommes sera-t-il jamais en état de tirer de cette manière de raisonner les règles de sa conduite? et quand il faudrait consulter la volonté générale sur un acte particulier, combien de fois n'arriverait-il pas à un homme bien intentionné de se tromper sur la règle ou sur l'application, et de ne suivre que son penchant en pensant obéir à la loi? Que ferait-il donc pour se garantir de l'erreur? Écoutera-t-il la voix intérieure? Mais cette voix n'est, dit-on, formée que par l'habitude de juger et de sentir dans le sein de la société, et selon ses lois; elle ne peut donc servir à les établir. Et puis il faudrait qu'il ne se fût élevé dans son cœur aucune de ces passions qui parlent plus haut que la conscience, couvrent sa timide voix, et font soutenir aux philosophes que cette voix n'existe pas. Consultera-t-il les principes du droit écrit, les actions sociales de tous les peuples, les conventions tacites des ennemis mêmes du genre humain? La première difficulté revient toujours, et ce n'est que de l'ordre social, établi parmi nous, que nous tirons les idées de celui que nous imaginons. Nous concevons la société générale d'après nos sociétés particulières; l'établissement des petites républiques nous fait songer à la grande; et nous ne commençons proprement à devenir hommes qu'après avoir été citoyens. Par où l'on voit ce qu'il faut penser de ces prétendus cosmopolites qui, justifiant leur amour pour la patrie par leur amour pour le genre humain, se vantent d'aimer tout le monde, pour avoir droit de n'aimer personne.

Ce que le raisonnement nous démontre à cet égard est parfaitement confirmé par les faits; et pour peu qu'on remonte dans les hautes antiquités, on voit aisément que les saines idées du droit naturel et de la fraternité commune de tous les hommes se sont répandues assez tard, et ont fait des progrès si lents dans le monde qu'il n'y a que le christianisme qui les ait suffisamment généralisées. Encore trouve-t-on dans les lois mêmes de Justinien les anciennes violences autorisées à bien des égards, non seulement sur les ennemis déclarés, mais sur tout ce qui n'était pas sujet de l'Empire ; en sorte que l'humanité des Romains ne s'étendait pas plus loin que leur domination.

En effet, on a cru longtemps, comme l'observe Grotius, qu'il était permis de voler, piller, maltraiter les étrangers et surtout les barbares, jusqu'à les réduire en esclavage. De là vient qu'on demandait à des inconnus, sans les choquer, s'ils étaient brigands ou pirates ; parce que le métier, loin d'être ignominieux, passait alors pour honorable. Les premiers héros, comme Hercule et Thésée, qui faisaient la guerre aux brigands ne laissaient pas d'exercer le brigandage eux-mêmes ; et les Grecs appelaient souvent traités de paix ceux qui se faisaient entre des peuples qui n'étaient point en guerre. Les mots d'étrangers et d'ennemis ont été longtemps synonymes chez plusieurs anciens peuples, même chez les Latins. *Hostis enim*, dit Cicéron, *apud majores nostros dicebatur, quem nunc peregrinum dicimus.* L'erreur de Hobbes n'est donc pas d'avoir établi l'état de guerre entre les hommes indépendants et devenus sociables ; mais d'avoir supposé cet état naturel à l'espèce, et de l'avoir donné pour cause aux vices dont il est l'effet.

Mais quoiqu'il n'y ait point de société naturelle et générale entre les hommes, quoiqu'ils deviennent malheureux et méchants en devenant sociables, quoique les lois de la justice et de l'égalité ne soient rien pour ceux qui vivent à la fois dans la liberté de l'état de nature et soumis aux besoins de l'état social ; loin de penser qu'il n'y ait ni vertu ni bonheur pour nous, et que le Ciel nous ait abandonnés sans ressource à la dépravation de l'espèce, efforçons-nous de tirer du mal même le remède qui doit le guérir. Par de nouvelles associations, corrigeons, s'il se peut, le défaut de l'association générale. Que notre violent interlocuteur juge lui-même du succès. Montrons-lui, dans l'art perfectionné, la réparation des maux que l'art commencé fit à la nature; montrons-lui toute la misère de l'état qu'il croyait heureux, tout le faux du raisonnement qu'il croyait solide. Qu'il voie dans une meilleure constitution de choses le prix des bonnes actions, le châtiment des mauvaises et l'accord aimable de la justice et du bonheur. Éclairons sa raison de nouvelles lumières, échauffons son cœur de nouveaux sentiments, et qu'il apprenne à multiplier son être et sa félicité, en les partageant avec ses semblables. Si mon zèle ne m'aveugle pas dans cette entreprise, ne doutons point qu'avec une âme forte et un sens droit cet ennemi du genre humain n'abjure enfin sa haine, avec ses erreurs; que la raison qui l'égarait ne le ramène à l'humanité; qu'il n'apprenne à préférer à son intérêt apparent son intérêt bien entendu; qu'il ne devienne bon, vertueux, sensible, et pour tout dire enfin, d'un brigand féroce, qu'il voulait être, le plus ferme appui d'une société bien ordonnée.

II

ÉMILE

ou

DE L'ÉDUCATION

(Extrait du livre V)

Le droit politique est encore à naître, et il est à présumer qu'il ne naîtra jamais. Grotius, le maître de tous nos savants en cette partie, n'est qu'un enfant, et, qui pis est, un enfant de mauvaise foi. Quand j'entends élever Grotius jusqu'aux nues et couvrir Hobbes d'exécration, je vois combien d'hommes sensés lisent ou comprennent ces deux auteurs. La vérité est que leurs principes sont exactement semblables ; ils ne diffèrent que par les expressions. Ils diffèrent aussi par la méthode. Hobbes s'appuie sur des sophismes, et Grotius sur des poètes ; tout le reste leur est commun.

Le seul moderne en état de créer cette grande et inutile science eût été l'illustre Montesquieu. Mais il n'eut garde de traiter des principes du droit politique ; il se contenta de traiter du droit positif des gouvernements établis ; et rien au monde n'est plus différent que ces deux études.

Celui pourtant qui veut juger sainement des gouvernements tels qu'ils existent est obligé de les réunir toutes deux : il faut savoir ce qui doit être pour bien juger de ce qui est. La plus grande difficulté pour éclaircir ces importantes matières est d'intéresser un particulier à les discuter, de répondre à ces deux questions : Que m'importe ? et : Qu'y puis-je faire ? Nous avons mis notre Émile en état de répondre à toutes deux.

La deuxième difficulté vient des préjugés de l'enfance, des maximes dans lesquelles on a été nourri, surtout de la partialité des auteurs, qui, parlant toujours de la vérité dont ils ne se soucient guère, ne songent qu'à leur intérêt dont ils ne parlent point. Or le peuple ne donne ni chaires, ni pensions, ni places d'académies : qu'on juge comment ses droits doivent être établis par ces gens-là ! J'ai fait en sorte que cette difficulté fût encore nulle pour Émile. À peine sait-il ce que c'est que gouvernement ; la seule chose qui lui importe est de trouver le meilleur. Son projet n'est point de faire des livres ; et si jamais il en fait, ce ne sera point pour faire sa cour aux puissances, mais pour établir les droits de l'humanité.

Il reste une troisième difficulté, plus spécieuse que solide, et que je ne veux ni résoudre ni proposer : il me suffit qu'elle n'effraye point mon zèle ; bien sûr qu'en des recherches de cette espèce, de grands talents sont moins nécessaires qu'un sincère amour de la justice et un vrai respect pour la vérité. Si donc les matières de gouvernement peuvent être équitablement traitées, en voici, selon moi, le cas ou jamais.

Avant d'observer, il faut se faire des règles pour ses observations : il faut se faire une échelle pour y rapporter les mesures qu'on prend. Nos principes de droit politique sont cette échelle. Nos mesures sont les lois politiques de chaque pays.

Nos éléments seront clairs, simples, pris immédiatement dans la nature des choses. Ils se formeront des questions discutées entre nous, et que nous ne convertirons en principes que quand elles seront suffisamment résolues.

Par exemple, remontant d'abord à l'état de nature, nous examinerons si les hommes naissent esclaves ou libres, associés ou indépendants ; s'ils se réunissent volontairement ou par force ; si jamais la force qui les réunit peut former un droit permanent, par lequel cette force antérieure oblige, même quand elle est surmontée par une autre, en sorte que, depuis la force du roi Nemrod, qui, dit-on, lui soumit les premiers peuples, toutes les autres forces qui ont détruit celle-là soient devenues iniques et usurpatoircs, et qu'il n'y ait plus de légitimes rois que les descendants de Nemrod ou ses ayants cause ; ou bien si cette première force venant à cesser, la force qui lui succède oblige à son tour, et détruit l'obligation de l'autre, en sorte qu'on ne soit obligé d'obéir qu'autant qu'on y est forcé, et qu'on en soit dispensé sitôt qu'on peut faire résistance : droit qui, ce semble, n'ajouterait pas grand-chose à la force, et ne serait guère qu'un jeu de mots.

Nous examinerons si l'on ne peut pas dire que toute maladie vient de Dieu, et s'il s'ensuit pour cela que ce soit un crime d'appeler le médecin.

Nous examinerons encore si l'on est obligé en conscience de donner sa bourse à un bandit qui nous la demande sur le grand chemin, quand même on pourrait la lui cacher ; car enfin le pistolet qu'il tient est aussi une puissance.

Si ce mot de puissance en cette occasion veut dire autre chose qu'une puissance légitime, et par conséquent soumise aux lois dont elle tient son être.

Supposé qu'on rejette ce droit de force, et qu'on admette celui de la nature ou l'autorité paternelle comme principe des sociétés, nous rechercherons la mesure de cette autorité, comment elle est fondée dans la nature, si elle a d'autre raison que l'utilité de l'enfant, sa faiblesse et l'amour naturel que le père a pour lui ; si donc, la faiblesse de l'enfant venant à cesser, et sa raison à mûrir, il ne devient pas seul juge naturel de ce qui convient à sa conservation, par conséquent son propre maître, et indépendant de tout autre homme, même de son père ; car il est encore plus sûr que le fils s'aime lui-même, qu'il n'est sûr que le père aime le fils.

Si, le père mort, les enfants sont tenus d'obéir à leur aîné ou à quelque autre qui n'aura pas pour eux l'attachement naturel d'un père ; et si de race en race, il y aura toujours un chef unique, auquel toute la famille soit tenue d'obéir. Auquel cas on chercherait comment l'autorité pourrait jamais être partagée, et de quel droit il y aurait sur la terre entière plus d'un chef qui gouvernât le genre humain.

Supposé que les peuples se fussent formés par choix, nous distinguerons alors le droit du fait ; et nous demanderons si, s'étant ainsi soumis à leurs frères, oncles ou parents, non qu'ils y fussent obligés, mais parce qu'ils l'ont bien voulu, cette sorte de société ne rentre pas toujours dans l'association libre et volontaire.

Passant ensuite au droit d'esclavage, nous examinerons si un homme peut légitimement s'aliéner à un autre, sans restriction, sans réserve, sans aucune espèce de condition ; c'est-à-dire s'il peut renoncer à sa personne, à sa vie, à sa raison, à *son moi*, à toute moralité dans ses actions, et cesser en un mot d'exister avant sa mort, malgré la nature qui le charge immédiatement de sa propre conservation, et malgré sa conscience et sa raison qui lui prescrivent ce qu'il doit faire et ce dont il doit s'abstenir.

Que s'il y a quelque réserve, quelque restriction dans l'acte d'esclavage, nous discuterons si cet acte ne devient pas alors un vrai contrat, dans lequel chacun des deux contractants, n'ayant point en cette qualité de supérieur commun*, restent leurs propres juges quant aux conditions du contrat, par conséquent libres chacun dans cette partie, et maîtres de le rompre sitôt qu'ils s'estiment lésés.

Que si donc un esclave ne peut s'aliéner sans réserve à son maître, comment un peuple peut-il s'aliéner sans réserve à son chef? et si l'esclave reste juge de l'observation du contrat par son maître, comment le peuple ne restera-t-il pas juge de l'observation du contrat par son chef?

Forcés de revenir ainsi sur nos pas, et considérant le sens de ce mot collectif de peuple, nous chercherons si, pour l'établir, il ne faut pas un contrat, au moins tacite, antérieur à celui que nous supposons.

Puisque avant de s'élire un roi le peuple est un peuple, qu'est-ce qui l'a fait tel sinon le contrat social? Le contrat social est donc la base de toute société civile, et c'est dans la nature de cet acte qu'il faut chercher celle de la société qu'il forme.

Nous rechercherons quelle est la teneur de ce contrat, et si l'on ne peut pas à peu près l'énoncer par cette formule : « Chacun de nous met en commun ses biens, sa personne, sa vie, et toute sa puissance, sous la suprême direction de la volonté générale, et nous recevons en corps chaque membre comme partie indivisible du tout. »

Ceci supposé, pour définir les termes dont nous avons besoin, nous remarquerons qu'au lieu de la personne

---

* S'ils en avaient un, ce supérieur commun ne serait autre que le souverain; et alors le droit d'esclavage, fondé sur le droit de souveraineté, n'en serait pas le principe.

particulière de chaque contractant, cet acte d'association produit un corps moral et collectif, composé d'autant de membres que l'assemblée a de voix. Cette personne publique prend en général le nom de *corps politique*, lequel est appelé par ses membres *État* quand il est passif, *souverain* quand il est actif, *puissance* en le comparant à ses semblables. À l'égard des membres eux-mêmes, ils prennent le nom de *peuple* collectivement, et s'appellent en particulier *citoyen*, comme membres de la *cité* ou participants à l'autorité souveraine, et *sujets*, comme soumis à la même autorité.

Nous remarquons que cet acte d'association renferme un engagement réciproque du public et des particuliers, et que chaque individu, contractant pour ainsi dire avec lui-même, se trouve engagé sous un double rapport, savoir comme membre du souverain envers les particuliers, et comme membre de l'État envers le souverain.

Nous remarquerons encore que nul n'étant tenu aux engagements qu'on n'a pris qu'avec soi, la délibération publique qui peut obliger tous les sujets envers le souverain, à cause des deux différents rapports sous lesquels chacun d'eux est envisagé, ne peut obliger l'État envers lui-même. Par où l'on voit qu'il n'y a ni ne peut y avoir d'autre loi fondamentale proprement dite que le seul pacte social. Ce qui ne signifie pas que le corps politique ne puisse, à certains égards, s'engager envers autrui ; car, par rapport à l'étranger, il devient un être simple, un individu.

Les deux parties contractantes, savoir chaque particulier et le public, n'ayant aucun supérieur commun qui puisse juger leurs différends, nous examinerons si chacun des deux reste le maître de rompre le contrat quand il lui plaît, c'est-à-dire d'y renoncer pour sa part sitôt qu'il se croit lésé.

Pour éclaircir cette question, nous observons que, selon le pacte social, le souverain ne pouvant agir que par des volontés communes et générales, ses actes ne doivent de même avoir que des objets généraux et communs ; d'où il suit qu'un particulier ne saurait être lésé directement par le souverain qu'ils ne le soient tous, ce qui ne se peut, puisque ce serait vouloir se faire du mal à soi-même. Ainsi le contrat social n'a jamais besoin d'autre garant que la force publique, parce que la lésion ne peut jamais venir que des particuliers ; et alors ils ne sont pas pour cela libres de leur engagement, mais punis de l'avoir violé.

Pour bien décider toutes les questions semblables, nous aurons soin de nous rappeler toujours que le pacte social est d'une nature particulière, et propre à lui seul, en ce que le peuple ne contracte qu'avec lui-même, c'est-à-dire le peuple en corps comme souverain, avec les particuliers comme sujets : condition qui fait tout l'artifice et le jeu de la machine politique, et qui seule rend légitimes, raisonnables et sans danger des engagements qui sans cela seraient absurdes, tyranniques et sujets aux plus énormes abus.

Les particuliers ne s'étant soumis qu'au souverain, et l'autorité souveraine n'étant autre chose que la volonté générale, nous verrons comment chaque homme, obéissant au souverain, n'obéit qu'à lui-même, et comment on est plus libre dans le pacte social que dans l'état de nature.

Après avoir fait la comparaison de la liberté naturelle avec la liberté civile quant aux personnes, nous ferons, quant aux biens, celle du droit de propriété avec le droit de souveraineté, du domaine particulier avec le domaine éminent. Si c'est sur le droit de propriété qu'est fondée l'autorité souveraine, ce droit est celui qu'elle doit le plus respecter ; il est inviolable et sacré pour elle tant qu'il demeure un droit particulier et individuel ; sitôt qu'il est considéré comme commun à tous les citoyens, il est soumis à la volonté générale, et cette volonté peut l'anéantir. Ainsi le souverain n'a nul droit de toucher au bien d'un particulier, ni de plusieurs : mais il peut légitimement s'emparer du bien de tous, comme cela se fit à Sparte au temps de Lycurgue, au lieu que l'abolition des dettes par Solon fut un acte illégitime.

Puisque rien n'oblige les sujets que la volonté générale, nous rechercherons comment se manifeste cette volonté, à quels signes on est sûr de la reconnaître, ce que c'est qu'une loi, et quels sont les vrais caractères de la loi. Ce sujet est tout neuf : la définition de la loi est encore à faire.

À l'instant que le peuple considère en particulier un ou plusieurs de ses membres, le peuple se divise. Il se forme entre le tout et sa partie une relation qui en fait deux êtres séparés, dont la partie est l'un, et le tout, moins cette partie, est l'autre. Mais le tout moins une partie n'est pas le tout ; tant que ce rapport subsiste, il n'y a donc plus de tout, mais deux parties inégales.

Au contraire, quand tout le peuple statue sur tout le peuple, il ne considère que lui-même ; et s'il se forme un rapport, c'est de l'objet entier sous un point de vue à l'objet entier sous un autre point de vue, sans aucune division du tout. Alors l'objet sur lequel on statue est général, et la volonté qui statue est aussi générale. Nous examinerons s'il y a quelque autre espèce d'acte qui puisse porter le nom de loi.

Si le souverain ne peut parler que par des lois, et si la loi ne peut jamais avoir qu'un objet général et relatif également à tous les membres de l'État, il s'ensuit que le souverain n'a jamais le pouvoir de rien statuer sur un objet particulier ; et, comme il importe cependant à la conservation de l'État qu'il soit aussi décidé des choses particulières, nous rechercherons comment cela peut se faire.

Les actes du souverain ne peuvent être que des actes de volonté générale, des lois ; il faut ensuite des actes déterminants, des actes de force ou de gouvernement pour l'exécution de ces mêmes lois ; et ceux-ci, au contraire, ne peuvent avoir que des objets particuliers. Ainsi l'acte par lequel le souverain statue qu'on élira un chef est une loi, et l'acte par lequel on élit ce chef en exécution de la loi n'est qu'un acte de gouvernement.

Voici donc un troisième rapport sous lequel le peuple assemblé peut être considéré, savoir comme magistrat ou exécuteur de la loi qu'il a portée comme souverain*.

Nous examinerons s'il est possible que le peuple se dépouille de son droit de souveraineté pour en revêtir un homme ou plusieurs ; car l'acte d'élection n'étant pas une loi, et dans cet acte le peuple n'étant pas souverain lui-même, on ne voit point comment alors il peut transférer un droit qu'il n'a pas.

L'essence de la souveraineté consistant dans la volonté générale, on ne voit point non plus comment on peut s'assurer qu'une volonté particulière sera toujours d'accord avec cette volonté générale. On doit bien plutôt présumer qu'elle y sera souvent contraire ; car l'intérêt privé tend toujours aux préférences, et l'intérêt public à l'égalité ; et, quand cet accord serait possible, il suffirait qu'il ne fût pas nécessaire et indestructible pour que le droit souverain n'en pût résulter.

---

* Ces questions et propositions sont la plupart extraites du *Traité du Contrat social*, extrait lui-même d'un plus grand ouvrage, entrepris sans consulter mes forces, et abandonné depuis longtemps. Le petit traité que j'en ai détaché, et dont c'est ici le sommaire, sera publié à part.

Nous rechercherons si, sans violer le pacte social, les chefs du peuple, sous quelque nom qu'ils soient élus, peuvent jamais être autre chose que les officiers du peuple, auxquels il ordonne de faire exécuter les lois ; si ces chefs ne lui doivent pas compte de leur administration, et ne sont pas soumis eux-mêmes aux lois qu'ils sont chargés de faire observer.

Si le peuple ne peut aliéner son droit suprême, peut-il le confier pour un temps ? s'il ne peut se donner un maître, peut-il se donner des représentants ? cette question est importante et mérite discussion.

Si le peuple ne peut avoir ni souverain ni représentants, nous examinerons comment il peut porter ses lois lui-même ; s'il doit avoir beaucoup de lois ; s'il doit les changer souvent ; s'il est aisé qu'un grand peuple soit son propre législateur ;

Si le peuple romain n'était pas un grand peuple ;

S'il est bon qu'il y ait de grands peuples.

Il suit des considérations précédentes qu'il y a dans l'État un corps intermédiaire entre les sujets et le souverain ; et ce corps intermédiaire, formé d'un ou de plusieurs membres, est chargé de l'administration publique, de l'exécution des lois, et du maintien de la liberté civile et politique.

Les membres de ce corps s'appellent *magistrats* ou *rois*, c'est-à-dire gouverneurs. Le corps entier, considéré par les hommes qui le composent, s'appelle *prince*, et, considéré par son action, il s'appelle *gouvernement.*

Si nous considérons l'action du corps entier agissant sur lui-même, c'est-à-dire le rapport du tout au tout, ou du souverain à l'État, nous pouvons comparer ce rapport à celui des extrêmes d'une proportion continue, dont le gouvernement donne le moyen terme. Le magistrat reçoit du souverain les ordres qu'il donne au peuple ; et, tout compensé, son produit ou sa puissance est au même degré que le produit ou la puissance des citoyens, qui sont sujets d'un côté et souverains de l'autre. On ne saurait altérer aucun des trois termes sans rompre à l'instant la proportion. Si le souverain veut gouverner, ou si le prince veut donner des lois, ou si le sujet refuse d'obéir, le désordre succède à la règle, et l'État dissous tombe dans le despotisme ou dans l'anarchie.

Supposons que l'État soit composé de dix mille citoyens. Le souverain ne peut être considéré que collectivement et en corps ; mais chaque particulier a, comme sujet, une existence individuelle et indépendante. Ainsi le souverain est au sujet comme dix mille à un ; c'est-à-dire que chaque membre de l'État n'a pour sa part que la dix millième partie de l'autorité souveraine, quoiqu'il lui soit soumis tout entier. Que le peuple soit composé de cent mille hommes, l'état des sujets ne change pas et chacun porte toujours tout l'empire des lois, tandis que son suffrage, réduit à un cent millième, a dix fois moins d'influence dans leur rédaction. Ainsi, le sujet restant toujours un, le rapport du souverain augmente en raison du nombre des citoyens. D'où il suit que plus l'État s'agrandit, plus la liberté diminue.

Or, moins les volontés particulières se rapportent à la volonté générale, c'est-à-dire les mœurs aux lois, plus la force réprimante doit augmenter. D'un autre côté, la grandeur de l'État donnant aux dépositaires de l'autorité publique plus de tentations et de moyens d'en abuser, plus le gouvernement a de force pour contenir le peuple, plus le souverain doit en avoir à son tour pour contenir le gouvernement.

Il suit de ce double rapport que la proportion continue entre le souverain, le prince et le peuple n'est point une idée arbitraire, mais une conséquence de la nature de l'État. Il suit encore que l'un des extrêmes, savoir le peuple, étant fixe, toutes les fois que la raison doublée augmente ou diminue, la raison simple augmente ou diminue à son tour; ce qui ne peut se faire sans que le moyen terme change autant de fois. D'où nous pouvons tirer cette conséquence, qu'il n'y a pas une constitution de gouvernement unique et absolue, mais qu'il doit y avoir autant de gouvernements différents en nature qu'il y a d'États différents en grandeur.

Si plus le peuple est nombreux, moins les mœurs se rapportent aux lois, nous examinerons si, par une analogie assez évidente, on ne peut pas dire aussi que plus les magistrats sont nombreux, plus le gouvernement est faible.

Pour éclaircir cette maxime, nous distinguerons dans la personne de chaque magistrat trois volontés essentiellement différentes : premièrement, la volonté propre de l'individu, qui ne tend qu'à son avantage particulier; secondement, la volonté commune des magistrats, qui se rapporte uniquement au profit du prince; volonté qu'on peut appeler volonté de corps, laquelle est générale par rapport au gouvernement, et particulière par rapport à l'État dont le gouvernement fait partie; en troisième lieu, la volonté du peuple ou la volonté souveraine, laquelle est générale, tant par rapport à l'État considéré comme le tout, que par rapport au gouvernement considéré comme partie du tout. Dans une législation parfaite, la volonté particulière et individuelle doit être presque nulle; la volonté de corps propre au gouvernement très subordonnée; et par conséquent la volonté générale et souveraine est la règle de toutes les autres. Au contraire, selon l'ordre naturel, ces différentes volontés deviennent plus actives à mesure qu'elles se concentrent; la volonté générale est toujours la plus faible, la volonté du corps a le second rang, et la volonté particulière est préférée à tout; en sorte que chacun est premièrement soi-même, et puis magistrat, et puis citoyen : gradation directement opposée à celle qu'exige l'ordre social.

Cela posé, nous supposerons le gouvernement entre les mains d'un seul homme. Voilà la volonté particulière et la volonté de corps parfaitement réunies, et par conséquent celle-ci au plus haut degré d'intensité qu'elle puisse avoir. Or, comme c'est de ce degré que dépend l'usage de la force, et que la force absolue du gouvernement, étant toujours celle du peuple, ne varie point, il s'ensuit que le plus actif des gouvernements est celui d'un seul.

Au contraire, unissons le gouvernement à l'autorité suprême, faisons le prince du souverain, et des citoyens autant de magistrats : alors la volonté de corps, parfaitement confondue avec la volonté générale, n'aura pas plus d'activité qu'elle, et laissera la volonté particulière dans toute sa force. Ainsi le gouvernement, toujours avec la même force absolue, sera dans son *minimum* d'activité.

Ces règles sont incontestables, et d'autres considérations servent à les confirmer. On voit, par exemple, que les magistrats sont plus actifs dans leur corps que le citoyen n'est dans le sien, et que par conséquent la volonté particulière y a beaucoup plus d'influence. Car chaque magistrat est presque toujours chargé de quelque fonction particulière du gouvernement ; au lieu que chaque citoyen pris à part n'a aucune fonction de la souveraineté. D'ailleurs, plus l'État s'étend, plus sa force réelle augmente, quoiqu'elle n'augmente pas en raison de son étendue ; mais, l'État restant le même, les magistrats ont beau se multiplier, le gouvernement n'en acquiert pas une plus grande force réelle, parce qu'il est dépositaire de celle de l'État, que nous supposons toujours égale. Ainsi, par cette pluralité, l'activité du gouvernement diminue sans que sa force puisse augmenter.

Après avoir trouvé que le gouvernement se relâche à mesure que les magistrats se multiplient, et que, plus le peuple est nombreux, plus la force réprimante du gouvernement doit augmenter, nous conclurons que le rapport des magistrats au gouvernement doit être inverse de celui des sujets au souverain; c'est-à-dire que plus l'État s'agrandit, plus le gouvernement doit se resserrer, tellement que le nombre des chefs diminue en raison de l'augmentation du peuple.

Pour fixer ensuite cette diversité de formes sous des dénominations plus précises, nous remarquerons en premier lieu que le souverain peut commettre le dépôt du gouvernement à tout le peuple ou à la plus grande partie du peuple, en sorte qu'il y ait plus de citoyens magistrats que de citoyens simples particuliers. On donne le nom de *démocratie* à cette forme de gouvernement.

Ou bien il peut resserrer le gouvernement entre les mains d'un nombre moindre, en sorte qu'il y ait plus de simples citoyens que de magistrats; et cette forme porte le nom d'*aristocratie*.

Enfin il peut concentrer tout le gouvernement entre les mains d'un magistrat unique. Cette troisième forme est la plus commune, et s'appelle *monarchie* ou gouvernement royal.

Nous remarquerons que toutes ces formes, ou du moins les deux premières, sont susceptibles de plus et de moins, et ont même une assez grande latitude. Car la démocratie peut embrasser tout le peuple ou se resserrer jusqu'à la moitié. L'aristocratie, à son tour, peut de la moitié du peuple se resserrer indéterminément jusqu'aux plus petits nombres. La royauté même admet quelquefois un partage, soit entre le père et le fils, soit entre deux frères, soit autrement. Il y avait toujours deux rois à Sparte, et l'on a vu dans l'Empire romain jusqu'à huit empereurs à la fois, sans qu'on pût dire que l'Empire fût divisé. Il y a un point où chaque forme de gouvernement se confond avec la suivante ; et, sous trois dénominations spécifiques, le gouvernement est réellement capable d'autant de formes que l'État a de citoyens.

Il y a plus : chacun de ces gouvernements pouvant à certains égards se subdiviser en diverses parties, l'une administrée d'une manière et l'autre d'une autre, il peut résulter de ces trois formes combinées une multitude de formes mixtes, dont chacune est multipliable par toutes les formes simples.

On a de tout temps beaucoup disputé sur la meilleure forme de gouvernement, sans considérer que chacune est la meilleure en certains cas, et la pire en d'autres. Pour nous, si, dans les différents États, le nombre des magistrats* doit être inverse de celui des citoyens, nous conclurons qu'en général le gouvernement démocratique convient aux petits États, l'aristocratique aux médiocres, et le monarchique aux grands.

C'est par le fil de ces recherches que nous parviendrons à savoir quels sont les devoirs et les droits des citoyens, et si l'on peut séparer les uns des autres ; ce que c'est que la patrie, en quoi précisément elle consiste, et à quoi chacun peut connaître s'il a une patrie ou s'il n'en a point.

Après avoir ainsi considéré chaque espèce de société civile en elle-même, nous les comparerons pour en observer les divers rapports : les unes grandes, les autres petites ; les unes fortes, les autres faibles ; s'attaquant,

---

* On se souviendra que je n'entends parler ici que de magistrats suprêmes ou chefs de la nation, les autres n'étant que leurs substituts en telle ou telle partie.

s'offensant, s'entre-détruisant ; et, dans cette action et réaction continuelle, faisant plus de misérables et coûtant la vie à plus d'hommes que s'ils avaient tous gardé leur première liberté. Nous examinerons si l'on n'en a pas fait trop ou trop peu dans l'institution sociale ; si les individus soumis aux lois et aux hommes, tandis que les sociétés gardent entre elles l'indépendance de la nature, ne restent pas exposés aux maux des deux États, sans en avoir les avantages, et s'il ne vaudrait pas mieux qu'il n'y eût point de société civile au monde que d'y en avoir plusieurs. N'est-ce pas cet État mixte qui participe à tous les deux et n'assure ni l'un ni l'autre, *per quem neutrum licet, nec tanquam in bello paratum esse, nec tanquam in pace securum* ? N'est-ce pas cette association partielle et imparfaite qui produit la tyrannie et la guerre ? et la tyrannie et la guerre ne sont-elles pas les plus grands fléaux de l'humanité ?

Nous examinerons enfin l'espèce de remèdes qu'on a cherchés à ces inconvénients par les ligues et confédérations, qui, laissant chaque État son maître au-dedans, l'arment au-dehors contre tout agresseur injuste. Nous rechercherons comment on peut établir une bonne association fédérative, ce qui peut la rendre durable, et jusqu'à quel point on peut étendre le droit de la confédération sans nuire à celui de la souveraineté.

L'abbé de Saint-Pierre avait proposé une association de tous les États de l'Europe pour maintenir entre eux une paix perpétuelle. Cette association était-elle praticable ? et, supposant qu'elle eût été établie, était-il à présumer qu'elle eût duré ?* Ces recherches nous mènent

* Depuis que j'écrivais ceci, les raisons *pour* ont été exposées dans l'extrait de ce projet ; les raisons *contre*, du moins celles qui m'ont paru solides, se trouveront dans le recueil de mes écrits, à la suite de ce même extrait.

directement à toutes les questions de droit public qui peuvent achever d'éclaircir celles du droit politique.

Enfin nous poserons les vrais principes du droit de la guerre, et nous examinerons pourquoi Grotius et les autres n'en ont donné que de faux.

Je ne serais pas étonné qu'au milieu de tous nos raisonnements, mon jeune homme, qui a du bon sens, me dît en m'interrompant : On dirait que nous bâtissons notre édifice avec du bois, et non pas avec des hommes, tant nous alignons exactement chaque pièce à la règle ! Il est vrai, mon ami ; mais songez que le droit ne se plie point aux passions des hommes, et qu'il s'agissait entre nous d'établir les vrais principes du droit politique. À présent que nos fondements sont posés, venez examiner ce que les hommes ont bâti dessus, et vous verrez de belles choses !

III

LETTRES ÉCRITES DE LA MONTAGNE

(Sixième Lettre)

Encore une lettre, Monsieur, et vous êtes délivré de moi. Mais je me trouve en la commençant dans une situation bizarre ; obligé de l'écrire, et ne sachant de quoi la remplir. Concevez-vous qu'on ait à se justifier d'un crime qu'on ignore, et qu'il faille se défendre sans savoir de quoi l'on est accusé ? C'est pourtant ce que j'ai à faire au sujet des gouvernements. Je suis, non pas accusé, mais jugé, mais flétri pour avoir publié deux ouvrages téméraires, scandaleux, impies, tendant à détruire la religion chrétienne et tous les gouvernements. Quant à la religion, nous avons eu du moins quelque prise pour trouver ce qu'on a voulu dire, et nous l'avons examiné. Mais quant aux gouvernements, rien ne peut nous fournir le moindre indice. On a toujours évité toute espèce d'explication sur ce point : on n'a jamais voulu dire en quel lieu j'entreprenais ainsi de les détruire, ni comment, ni pourquoi, ni rien de ce qui peut constater que le délit n'est pas imaginaire. C'est comme si l'on jugeait quelqu'un pour avoir tué un homme sans dire ni où, ni qui, ni quand ; pour un meurtre abstrait. À l'inquisition l'on force bien l'accusé de deviner de quoi on l'accuse, mais on ne le juge pas sans dire de quoi.

L'auteur des *Lettres écrites de la campagne* évite avec le même soin de s'expliquer sur ce prétendu délit : il joint également la religion et les gouvernements dans la même accusation générale : puis, entrant en matière sur la religion, il déclare vouloir s'y borner, et il tient parole. Comment parviendrons-nous à vérifier l'accusation qui regarde les gouvernements, si ceux qui l'intentent refusent de dire sur quoi elle porte ?

Remarquez même comment d'un trait de plume, cet auteur change l'état de la question. Le Conseil prononce que mes livres tendent à détruire tous les gouvernements. L'auteur des *Lettres* dit seulement que les gouvernements y sont livrés à la plus audacieuse critique. Cela est fort différent. Une critique, quelque audacieuse qu'elle puisse être, n'est point une conspiration. Critiquer ou blâmer quelques lois n'est pas renverser toutes les lois. Autant vaudrait accuser quelqu'un d'assassiner les malades lorsqu'il montre les fautes des médecins.

Encore une fois, que répondre à des raisons qu'on ne veut pas dire ? Comment se justifier contre un jugement qu'on porte sans motifs ? Que, sans preuve de part et d'autre, ces Messieurs disent que je veux renverser tous les gouvernements, et que je dise, moi, que je ne veux pas renverser tous les gouvernements, il y a dans ces assertions parité exacte, excepté que le préjugé est pour moi ; car il est à présumer que je sais mieux que personne ce que je veux faire.

Mais où la parité manque, c'est dans l'effet de l'assertion. Sur la leur mon livre est brûlé, ma personne est décrétée ; et ce que j'affirme ne rétablit rien. Seulement, si je prouve que l'accusation est fausse et le jugement inique, l'affront qu'ils m'ont fait retourne à eux-mêmes : le décret, le bourreau, tout y devrait retourner ; puisque nul ne détruit si radicalement le gouvernement, que celui qui en tire un usage directement contraire à la fin pour laquelle il est institué.

Il ne suffit pas que j'affirme, il faut que je prouve ; et c'est ici qu'on voit combien est déplorable le sort d'un particulier soumis à d'injustes magistrats, quand ils n'ont rien à craindre du souverain, et qu'ils se mettent au-dessus des lois. D'une affirmation sans preuve, ils font une démonstration ; voilà l'innocent puni. Bien plus, de sa défense même ils lui font un nouveau crime, et il ne tiendrait pas à eux de le punir encore d'avoir prouvé qu'il était innocent.

Comment m'y prendre pour montrer qu'ils n'ont pas dit vrai ; pour prouver que je ne détruis point les gouvernements ? Quelque endroit de mes écrits que je défende, ils diront que ce n'est pas celui-là qu'ils ont condamné ; quoiqu'ils aient condamné tout, le bon comme le mauvais, sans nulle distinction. Pour ne leur laisser aucune défaite, il faudrait donc tout reprendre, tout suivre d'un bout à l'autre, livre à livre, page à page, ligne à ligne, et presque enfin, mot à mot. Il faudrait de plus, examiner tous les gouvernements du monde, puisqu'ils disent que je les détruis tous. Quelle entreprise ! que d'années y faudrait-il employer ? Que d'*in-folios* faudrait-il écrire ; et après cela qui les lirait ?

Exigez de moi ce qui est faisable. Tout homme sensé doit se contenter de ce que j'ai à vous dire : vous ne voulez sûrement rien de plus.

De mes deux livres brûlés à la fois sous des imputations communes, il n'y en a qu'un qui traite du droit politique et des matières de gouvernement. Si l'autre en traite, ce n'est que dans un extrait du premier. Ainsi je suppose que c'est sur celui-ci seulement que tombe l'accusation. Si cette accusation portait sur quelque passage particulier, on l'aurait cité, sans doute ; on en aurait au moins extrait quelque maxime, fidèle ou infidèle, comme on a fait sur les points concernant la religion.

C'est donc le système établi dans le corps de l'ouvrage qui détruit les gouvernements ; il ne s'agit donc que d'exposer ce système ou de faire une analyse du livre ; et si nous n'y voyons évidemment les principes destructifs dont il s'agit, nous saurons du moins où les chercher dans l'ouvrage, en suivant la méthode de l'auteur.

Mais, Monsieur, si durant cette analyse, qui sera courte, vous trouvez quelque conséquence à tirer, de grâce ne vous pressez pas. Attendez que nous en raisonnions ensemble. Après cela vous y reviendrez si vous voulez.

Qu'est-ce qui fait que l'État est un ? C'est l'union de ses membres. Et d'où naît l'union de ses membres ? De l'obligation qui les lie. Tout est d'accord jusqu'ici.

Mais quel est le fondement de cette obligation ? Voilà où les auteurs se divisent. Selon les uns, c'est la force ; selon d'autres, l'autorité paternelle ; selon d'autres, la volonté de Dieu. Chacun établit son principe et attaque celui des autres : je n'ai pas moi-même fait autrement, et, suivant la plus saine partie de ceux qui ont discuté ces matières, j'ai posé pour fondement du corps politique la convention de ses membres, j'ai réfuté les principes différents du mien.

Indépendamment de la vérité de ce principe, il l'emporte sur tous les autres par la solidité du fondement qu'il établit ; car quel fondement plus sûr peut avoir l'obligation parmi les hommes que le libre engagement de celui qui s'oblige ? On peut disputer tout autre principe* ; on ne saurait disputer celui-là.

* Même celui de la volonté de Dieu, du moins quant à l'application. Car bien qu'il soit clair que ce que Dieu veut l'homme doit le vouloir, il n'est pas clair que Dieu veuille qu'on préfère tel

Mais par cette condition de la liberté, qui en renferme d'autres, toutes sortes d'engagements ne sont pas valides, même devant les tribunaux humains. Ainsi pour déterminer celui-ci l'on doit en expliquer la nature, on doit en trouver l'usage et la fin, on doit prouver qu'il est convenable à des hommes, et qu'il n'a rien de contraire aux lois naturelles : car il n'est pas plus permis d'enfreindre les lois naturelles par le contrat social, qu'il n'est permis d'enfreindre les lois positives par les contrats des particuliers, et ce n'est que par ces lois mêmes qu'existe la liberté qui donne force à l'engagement.

J'ai pour résultat de cet examen que l'établissement du contrat social est un pacte d'une espèce particulière, par lequel chacun s'engage envers tous, d'où s'ensuit l'engagement réciproque de tous envers chacun, qui est l'objet immédiat de l'union.

Je dis que cet engagement est d'une espèce particulière, en ce qu'étant absolu, sans condition, sans réserve, il ne peut toutefois être injuste ni susceptible d'abus; puisqu'il n'est pas possible que le corps se veuille nuire à lui-même, tant que le tout ne veut que par tous.

Il est encore d'une espèce particulière en ce qu'il lie les contractants sans les assujettir à personne, et qu'en leur donnant leur seule volonté pour règle, il les laisse aussi libres qu'auparavant.

La volonté de tous est donc l'ordre, la règle suprême, et cette règle générale et personnifiée est ce que j'appelle le souverain.

Il suit de là que la souveraineté est indivisible, inaliénable, et qu'elle réside essentiellement dans tous les membres du corps.

---

gouvernement à tel autre, ni qu'on obéisse à Jacques plutôt qu'à Guillaume. Or voilà de quoi il s'agit.

Mais comment agit cet être abstrait et collectif? Il agit par des lois, et il ne saurait agir autrement.

Et qu'est-ce qu'une loi? C'est une déclaration publique et solennelle de la volonté générale, sur un objet d'intérêt commun.

Je dis sur un objet d'intérêt commun; parce que la loi perdrait sa force et cesserait d'être légitime, si l'objet n'en importait à tous.

La loi ne peut par sa nature avoir un objet particulier et individuel; mais l'application de la loi tombe sur des objets particuliers et individuels.

Le pouvoir législatif qui est le souverain a donc besoin d'un autre pouvoir qui exécute, c'est-à-dire qui réduise la loi en actes particuliers. Ce second pouvoir doit être établi de manière qu'il exécute toujours la loi, et qu'il n'exécute jamais que la loi. Ici vient l'institution du gouvernement.

Qu'est-ce que le gouvernement? C'est un corps intermédiaire établi entre les sujets et le souverain pour leur mutuelle correspondance, chargé de l'exécution des lois et du maintien de la liberté tant civile que politique.

Le gouvernement comme partie intégrante du corps politique participe à la volonté générale qui le constitue; comme corps lui-même il a sa volonté propre. Ces deux volontés quelquefois s'accordent et quelquefois se combattent. C'est de l'effet combiné de ce concours et de ce conflit que résulte le jeu de toute la machine.

Le principe qui constitue les diverses formes du gouvernement consiste dans le nombre des membres qui le composent. Plus ce nombre est petit, plus le gouvernement a de force; plus le nombre est grand, plus le gouvernement est faible; et comme la souveraineté tend toujours au relâchement, le gouvernement tend toujours à se renforcer. Ainsi le corps exécutif doit l'emporter à la longue sur le corps législatif, et quand la loi est enfin soumise aux hommes, il ne reste que des esclaves et des maîtres ; l'État est détruit.

Avant cette destruction, le gouvernement doit par son progrès naturel changer de forme et passer par degrés du grand nombre au moindre.

Les diverses formes dont le gouvernement est susceptible se réduisent à trois principales. Après les avoir comparées par leurs avantages et par leurs inconvénients, je donne la préférence à celle qui est intermédiaire entre les deux extrêmes et qui porte le nom d'aristocratie. On doit se souvenir ici que la constitution de l'État et celle du gouvernement sont deux choses très distinctes, et que je ne les ai pas confondues. Le meilleur des gouvernements est l'aristocratique ; la pire des souverainetés est l'aristocratique.

Ces discussions en amènent d'autres sur la manière dont le gouvernement dégénère et sur les moyens de retarder la destruction du corps politique.

Enfin, dans le dernier livre j'examine par voie de comparaison avec le meilleur gouvernement qui ait existé, savoir celui de Rome, la police la plus favorable à la bonne constitution de l'État ; puis je termine ce livre et tout l'ouvrage par des recherches sur la manière dont la religion peut et doit entrer comme partie constitutive dans la composition du corps politique.

Que pensiez-vous, Monsieur, en lisant cette analyse courte et fidèle de mon livre ? Je le devine. Vous disiez en vous-même ; voilà l'histoire du gouvernement de Genève. C'est ce qu'ont dit à la lecture du même ouvrage tous ceux qui connaissent votre constitution.

Et en effet, ce contrat primitif, cette essence de la souveraineté, cet empire des lois, cette institution du gouvernement, cette manière de le resserrer à divers degrés pour compenser l'autorité par la force, cette tendance à l'usurpation, ces assemblées périodiques, cette adresse à les ôter, cette destruction prochaine, enfin, qui vous menace et que je voulais prévenir ; n'est-ce pas trait pour trait l'image de votre république, depuis sa naissance jusqu'à ce jour ?

J'ai donc pris votre constitution, que je trouvais belle, pour modèle des institutions politiques, et vous proposant en exemple à l'Europe, loin de chercher à vous détruire j'exposais les moyens de vous conserver. Cette constitution, toute bonne qu'elle est, n'est pas sans défaut ; on pouvait prévenir les altérations qu'elle a souffertes, la garantir du danger qu'elle court aujourd'hui. J'ai prévu ce danger, je l'ai fait entendre, j'indiquais des préservatifs ; était-ce la vouloir détruire que de montrer ce qu'il fallait faire pour la maintenir ? C'était par mon attachement pour elle que j'aurais voulu que rien ne pût l'altérer. Voilà tout mon crime ; j'avais tort, peut-être ; mais si l'amour de la patrie m'aveugla sur cet article, était-ce à elle de m'en punir ?

Comment pouvais-je tendre à renverser tous les gouvernements, en posant en principes tous ceux du vôtre ? Le fait seul détruit l'accusation. Puisqu'il y avait un gouvernement existant sur mon modèle, je ne tendais donc pas à détruire tous ceux qui existaient. Eh ! Monsieur ; si je n'avais fait qu'un système, vous êtes bien sûr qu'on n'aurait rien dit. On se fût contenté de reléguer le *Contrat social* avec la *République* de Platon, l'*Utopie* et les *Sévarambes* dans le pays des chimères. Mais je peignais un objet existant, et l'on voulait que cet objet changeât de face. Mon livre portait témoignage contre l'attentat qu'on allait faire. Voilà ce qu'on ne m'a pas pardonné.

Mais voici qui vous paraîtra bizarre. Mon livre attaque tous les gouvernements, il n'est proscrit dans aucun ! Il en établit un seul, il le propose en exemple, et c'est dans celui-là qu'il est brûlé ! N'est-il pas singulier que les gouvernements attaqués se taisent, et que le gouvernement respecté sévisse ? Quoi ! Le magistrat de Genève se fait le protecteur des autres gouvernements contre le sien même ! Il punit son propre citoyen d'avoir préféré les lois de son pays à toutes les autres ! Cela est-il concevable, et le croiriez-vous si vous ne l'eussiez vu ? Dans tout le reste de l'Europe, quelqu'un s'est-il avisé de flétrir l'ouvrage ? Non ; pas même l'État où il a été imprimé*. Pas même la France où les magistrats sont là-dessus si sévères. Y a-t-on défendu le livre ? Rien de semblable ; on n'a pas laissé d'abord entrer l'édition de Hollande, mais on l'a contrefaite en France, et l'ouvrage y court sans difficulté. C'était donc une affaire de commerce et non de police : on préférait le profit du libraire de France au profit du libraire étranger. Voilà tout.

Le *Contrat social* n'a été brûlé nulle part qu'à Genève où il n'a pas été imprimé ; le seul magistrat de Genève y a trouvé des principes destructifs de tous les gouvernements. À la vérité, ce magistrat n'a point dit quels étaient ces principes ; en cela je crois qu'il a fort prudemment fait.

L'effet des défenses indiscrètes est de n'être point observées et d'énerver la force de l'autorité. Mon livre est dans les mains de tout le monde à Genève, et que n'est-il également dans tous les cœurs ! Lisez-le, Monsieur, ce livre si décrié, mais si nécessaire ; vous y verrez partout la loi mise au-dessus des hommes ; vous y verrez partout la liberté réclamée, mais toujours sous

* Dans le fort des premières clameurs causées par les procédures de Paris et de Genève, le magistrat surpris défendit les deux livres : mais sur son propre examen ce sage magistrat a bien changé de sentiment, surtout quant au *Contrat social*.

l'autorité des lois, sans lesquelles la liberté ne peut exister, et sous lesquelles on est toujours libre, de quelque façon qu'on soit gouverné. Par là je ne fais pas, dit-on, ma cour aux puissances; tant pis pour elles; car je sais leurs vrais intérêts, si elles savaient les voir et les suivre. Mais les passions aveuglent les hommes sur leur propre bien. Ceux qui soumettent les lois aux passions humaines sont les vrais destructeurs des gouvernements; voilà les gens qu'il faudrait punir.

Les fondements de l'État sont les mêmes dans tous les gouvernements, et ces fondements sont mieux posés dans mon livre que dans aucun autre. Quand il s'agit ensuite de comparer les diverses formes de gouvernement, on ne peut éviter de peser séparément les avantages et les inconvénients de chacun : c'est ce que je crois avoir fait avec impartialité. Tout balancé, j'ai donné la préférence au gouvernement de mon pays. Cela était naturel et raisonnable; on m'aurait blâmé si je ne l'eusse pas fait. Mais je n'ai point donné d'exclusion aux autres gouvernements; au contraire : j'ai montré que chacun avait sa raison qui pouvait le rendre préférable à tout autre, selon les hommes, les temps et les lieux. Ainsi loin de détruire tous les gouvernements, je les ai tous établis.

En parlant du gouvernement monarchique en particulier, j'en ai bien fait valoir l'avantage, et je n'en ai pas non plus déguisé les défauts. Cela est, je pense, du droit d'un homme qui raisonne; et quand je lui aurais donné l'exclusion, ce qu'assurément je n'ai pas fait, s'ensuivrait-il qu'on dût m'en punir à Genève? Hobbes a-t-il été décrété dans quelque monarchie parce que ses principes sont destructifs de tout gouvernement républicain, et fait-on le procès chez les rois aux auteurs qui rejettent et dépriment les républiques? Le droit n'est-il pas réciproque, et les républicains ne sont-ils pas souverains dans leur pays comme les rois le sont dans le leur ? Pour moi, je n'ai rejeté aucun gouvernement, je n'en ai méprisé aucun. En les examinant, en les comparant j'ai tenu la balance et j'ai calculé les poids : je n'ai rien fait de plus.

On ne doit punir la raison nulle part, ni même le raisonnement ; cette punition prouverait trop contre ceux qui l'imposeraient. Les représentants ont très bien établi que mon livre, où je ne sors pas de la thèse générale, n'attaquant point le gouvernement de Genève et imprimé hors de son territoire, ne peut être considéré que dans le nombre de ceux qui traitent du droit naturel et politique, sur lesquels les lois ne donnent au Conseil aucun pouvoir, et qui se sont toujours vendus publiquement dans la ville, quelque principe qu'on y avance et quelque sentiment qu'on y soutienne. Je ne suis pas le seul qui discutant par abstraction des questions de politique ait pu les traiter avec quelque hardiesse ; chacun ne le fait pas, mais tout homme a droit de le faire ; plusieurs usent de ce droit, et je suis le seul qu'on punisse pour en avoir usé. L'infortuné Sidney pensait comme moi, mais il agissait ; c'est pour son fait et non pour son livre qu'il eut l'honneur de verser son sang. Althusius en Allemagne s'attira des ennemis, mais on ne s'avisa pas de le poursuivre criminellement. Locke, Montesquieu, l'abbé de Saint-Pierre ont traité les mêmes matières, et souvent avec la même liberté tout au moins. Locke en particulier les a traitées exactement dans les mêmes principes que moi. Tous trois sont nés sous des rois, ont vécu tranquilles et sont morts honorés dans leurs pays. Vous savez comment j'ai été traité dans le mien.

Aussi soyez sûr que loin de rougir de ces flétrissures je m'en glorifie, puisqu'elles ne servent qu'à mettre en évidence le motif qui me les attire, et que ce motif n'est que d'avoir bien mérité de mon pays. La conduite du

Conseil envers moi m'afflige, sans doute, en rompant des nœuds qui m'étaient si chers ; mais peut-elle m'avilir ? Non, elle m'élève, elle me met au rang de ceux qui ont souffert pour la liberté. Mes livres, quoi qu'on fasse, porteront toujours témoignage d'eux-mêmes, et le traitement qu'ils ont reçu ne fera que sauver de l'opprobre ceux qui auront l'honneur d'être brûlés après eux.

PROJET DE CONSTITUTION POUR LA CORSE

AVANT-PROPOS

On demande un plan de gouvernement bon pour la Corse[1]. C'est demander plus que l'on ne croit. Il y a des peuples qui de quelque manière qu'on s'y prenne ne sauraient être bien gouvernés parce que chez eux la loi manque de prise et qu'un gouvernement sans loi ne peut être un bon gouvernement. Tout au contraire, il [le peuple corse] me paraît le plus heureusement disposé par la nature pour recevoir une bonne administration. Mais ce n'est pas assez encore. Toutes choses ont leurs abus souvent nécessaires et ceux des établissements politiques sont si voisins de leur institution que ce n'est presque pas la peine de la faire pour la voir si vite dégénérer.

On veut parer à cet inconvénient par des machines qui maintiennent le gouvernement dans son état primitif, on lui donne mille chaînes, mille entraves pour le retenir sur sa pente, et on l'embarrasse tellement, qu'affaissé sous le poids de ses fers il demeure inactif, immobile et s'il ne décline pas vers sa chute, il ne va pas non plus à sa fin.

Tout cela vient de ce qu'on sépare trop deux choses inséparables, savoir le corps qui gouverne et le corps qui est gouverné. Ces deux corps n'en font qu'un par l'institution primitive, ils ne se séparent que par l'abus de l'institution[2].

Les plus sages en pareil cas observant des rapports de convenance forment le gouvernement pour la nation. Il y a pourtant beaucoup mieux à faire, c'est de former la nation pour le gouvernement. Dans le premier cas à mesure que le gouvernement décline, la nation restant la même, la convenance s'évanouit; dans le second, tout change de pas égal et la nation entraînant le gouvernement par sa force, le maintient quand elle se maintient et le fait décliner quand elle décline. L'un convient à l'autre dans tous les temps.

Le peuple corse est dans l'heureux état qui rend une bonne institution possible, il peut partir du premier point et prendre des mesures pour ne pas dégénérer. Plein de vigueur et de santé il peut se donner un gouvernement qui le maintienne vigoureux et sain. Cependant cet établissement doit trouver déjà des obstacles. Les Corses n'ont pas pris encore les vices des autres nations mais ils ont déjà pris leurs préjugés; ce sont ces préjugés qu'il faut combattre et détruire pour former un bon établissement.

PROJET

La situation avantageuse de l'île de Corse et l'heureux naturel de ses habitants semblent leur offrir un espoir raisonnable de pouvoir devenir un peuple florissant et figurer un jour dans l'Europe si, dans l'institution qu'ils méditent ils tournent leurs vues de ce côté-là mais l'extrême épuisement où les ont jetés quarante années de guerres continuelles, la pauvreté présente de leur île et l'état de dépopulation et de dévastation où elle est ne leur permettent pas de se donner sitôt une administration dispendieuse, telle qu'il la faudrait pour les policer dans cet objet.

D'ailleurs mille obstacles invincibles s'opposeraient à l'exécution de ce plan. Gênes maîtresse encore d'une partie de la côte et de presque toutes les places maritimes écraserait mille fois leur marine naissante sans cesse exposée au double danger des Génois et des barbaresques*. Ils ne pourraient tenir la mer qu'avec des bâtiments armés qui leur coûteraient dix fois plus que le trafic ne leur pourrait rendre. Exposés sur terre et sur mer, forcés de se garder de toutes parts, que deviendraient-ils ?

* Les barbaresques n'inquiètent guère à présent les Corses parce qu'ils savent qu'il n'y a rien à gagner avec eux mais sitôt que ceux-ci commenceront à faire le commerce et à échanger des marchandises ils séviront. Vous les auriez sur les bras.

à la discrétion de tout le monde, ne pouvant dans leur faiblesse faire aucun traité de commerce avantageux, ils recevraient la loi de tous ; ils n'auraient au milieu de tant de risques que les profits que personne autre ne daignerait faire et qui se réduiraient à rien. Que si par un bonheur difficile à comprendre ils surmontaient toutes ces difficultés, leur prospérité même attirant sur eux les yeux de leurs voisins serait un nouveau péril pour leur liberté mal établie. Objet continuel de convoitise pour les grandes puissances et de jalousie pour les petites, leur île serait menacée à chaque instant d'une nouvelle servitude dont elle ne pourrait plus se tirer.

Dans quelque vue que la nation corse veuille se policer la première chose qu'elle doit faire est de se donner par elle-même toute la consistance qu'elle peut avoir. Quiconque dépend d'autrui et n'a pas ses ressources en lui-même, ne saurait être libre[3]. Des alliances, des traités, la foi des hommes, tout cela peut lier le faible au fort et ne lie jamais le fort au faible. Ainsi laissez les négociations aux puissances et ne comptez que sur vous. Braves Corses, qui sait mieux que vous tout ce qu'on peut tirer de soi-même ? Sans amis, sans appuis, sans argent, sans armée, asservis à des maîtres terribles, seuls vous avez secoué leur joug. Vous les avez vus liguer contre vous, tour à tour, les plus redoutables potentats de l'Europe, inonder votre île d'armées étrangères[4] ; vous avez tout surmonté. Votre seule constance a fait ce que l'argent n'aurait pu faire ; pour vouloir conserver vos richesses vous auriez perdu votre liberté. Il ne faut point conclure des autres nations à la vôtre. Les maximes tirées de votre propre expérience sont les meilleures sur lesquelles vous puissiez vous gouverner.

Il s'agit moins de devenir autres que vous n'êtes, que de savoir vous conserver tels. Les Corses ont beaucoup gagné depuis qu'ils sont libres, ils ont joint la prudence au courage, ils ont appris à obéir à leurs égaux, ils ont acquis des vertus et des mœurs, et ils n'avaient point de lois, s'ils pouvaient d'eux-mêmes rester ainsi, je ne verrais presque rien à faire. Mais quand le péril qui les a réunis s'éloignera, les factions qu'il écarte renaîtront parmi eux et, au lieu de réunir leurs forces pour le maintien de leur indépendance, ils les useront les uns contre les autres et n'en auront plus pour se défendre, si l'on vient encore à les attaquer. Voilà déjà ce qu'il faut prévenir. Les divisions des Corses ont été de tout temps un artifice de leurs maîtres pour les rendre faibles et dépendants, mais cet artifice employé sans cesse a produit enfin l'inclination et les a rendus naturellement inquiets, remuants, difficiles à gouverner même par leurs propres chefs. Il faut de bonnes lois, il faut une institution nouvelle pour rétablir la concorde dont la tyrannie a détruit jusqu'au désir. La Corse assujettie à des maîtres étrangers dont jamais elle n'a porté patiemment le dur joug, fut toujours agitée. Il faut maintenant que son peuple fasse une étude nouvelle ; et qu'il cherche la paix dans la liberté.

Voici donc les principes qui selon moi doivent servir de base à leur législation : tirer parti de leur peuple et de leur pays toujours autant qu'il sera possible ; cultiver et rassembler leurs propres forces, ne s'appuyer que sur elles, et ne songer pas plus aux puissances étrangères que s'il n'en existait aucune[5].

Partons de là pour établir les maximes de notre institution.

L'île de Corse ne pouvant s'enrichir en argent doit tâcher de s'enrichir en hommes. La puissance qui vient de la population est plus réelle que celle qui vient des finances et produit plus sûrement son effet. L'emploi des bras des hommes ne pouvant se cacher va toujours à la destination publique, il n'en est pas ainsi de l'emploi de l'argent ; il s'écoule et se fond dans des destinations particulières ; on l'amasse pour une fin, on le répand pour une autre ; le peuple paye pour qu'on le protège et ce qu'il donne sert à l'opprimer. De là vient qu'un État riche en argent est toujours faible, et qu'un État riche en hommes est toujours fort*.

Pour multiplier les hommes il faut multiplier leur subsistance, de là l'agriculture. Je n'entends pas par ce mot l'art de raffiner sur l'agriculture, d'établir des académies qui en parlent, de faire des livres qui en traitent. J'entends une constitution qui porte un peuple à s'étendre sur toute la surface de son territoire, à s'y fixer, à le cultiver dans tous ses points, à aimer la vie champêtre, les travaux qui s'y rapportent, à y trouver si bien le nécessaire et les agréments de la vie qu'il ne désire point d'en sortir.

Le goût de l'agriculture n'est pas seulement avantageux à la population en multipliant la subsistance des hommes mais en donnant au corps de la nation un tempérament et des mœurs qui les font naître en plus grand nombre. Par tout pays les habitants des campagnes peuplent plus que ceux des villes, soit par la simplicité de la vie rustique qui forme des corps mieux constitués,

---

* La plupart des usurpateurs ont employé l'un de ces deux moyens pour affermir leur puissance. Le premier d'appauvrir les peuples subjugués et de les rendre barbares, l'autre au contraire de les efféminer sous prétexte de les instruire et de les enrichir. La première de ces voies a constamment produit un effet contraire à son objet, et il en a toujours résulté de la part des peuples vexés des actes de vigueur, des révolutions, des républiques. L'autre voie a toujours eu son effet, et les peuples amollis, corrompus, délicats, raisonneurs, tenant dans l'ignominie de la servitude de beaux discours sur la liberté, ont été tous écrasés sous leurs maîtres puis détruits par des conquérants.

soit par l'assiduité au travail qui prévient le désordre et les vices, car toute chose égale les femmes les plus chastes, celles dont les sens sont moins enflammés par l'usage des plaisirs font plus d'enfants que les autres, et il n'est pas moins sûr que des hommes énervés par la débauche, fruit certain de l'oisiveté, sont moins propres à la génération que ceux qu'un état laborieux rend plus tempérants.

Les paysans sont attachés à leur sol beaucoup plus que les citadins à leurs villes. L'égalité, la simplicité de la vie rustique a pour ceux qui n'en connaissent point d'autre un attrait qui ne leur fait pas désirer d'en changer. De là le contentement de son état qui rend l'homme paisible, de là l'amour de la patrie qui l'attache à sa constitution.

La culture de la terre forme des hommes patients et robustes tels qu'il les faut pour devenir bons soldats. Ceux qu'on tire des villes sont mutins et mous, ils ne peuvent supporter les fatigues de la guerre, ils se fondent dans les marches, les maladies les consument, ils se battent entre eux et fuient devant l'ennemi. Les milices exercées sont les troupes les plus sûres et les meilleures ; la véritable éducation du soldat est d'être laboureur.

Le seul moyen de maintenir un État dans l'indépendance des autres est l'agriculture. Eussiez-vous toutes les richesses du monde si vous n'avez de quoi vous nourrir vous dépendez d'autrui. Vos voisins peuvent donner à votre argent le prix qu'il leur plaît parce qu'ils peuvent attendre ; mais le pain qui nous est nécessaire a pour nous un prix dont nous ne saurions disputer et dans toute espèce de commerce c'est toujours le moins pressé qui fait la loi à l'autre. J'avoue que dans un système de finance, il faudrait opérer selon d'autres vues ; tout dépend du dernier but auquel on tend. Le commerce produit la richesse mais l'agriculture assure la liberté[6].

On dira qu'il vaudrait mieux avoir l'une et l'autre à la fois mais elles sont incompatibles comme il sera montré ci-après. Par tout pays, ajoutera-t-on, l'on cultive la terre. J'en conviens ; comme par tout pays on a du commerce, partout on trafique peu ou beaucoup mais ce n'est pas à dire que partout l'agriculture et le commerce fleurissent. Je n'examine pas ici ce qui se fait par la nécessité des choses mais ce qui résulte de l'espèce du gouvernement et de l'esprit général[7] de la nation.

Quoique la forme de gouvernement que se donne un peuple soit plus souvent l'ouvrage du hasard et de la fortune que celui d'un vrai choix, il y a pourtant dans la nature et le sol de chaque pays des qualités qui lui rendent un gouvernement plus propre qu'un autre, et chaque forme de gouvernement a une force particulière qui porte les peuples vers telle ou telle occupation.

La forme de gouvernement que nous avons à choisir est d'un côté la moins coûteuse parce que la Corse est pauvre, et de l'autre la plus favorable à l'agriculture parce que l'agriculture est quant à présent la seule occupation qui puisse conserver au peuple corse l'indépendance qu'il s'est acquise et lui donner la consistance dont il a besoin.

L'administration la moins coûteuse est celle qui passe par le moins de degrés et demande le moins de différents ordres, tel est en général l'état républicain et en particulier le démocratique.

L'administration la plus favorable à l'agriculture est celle dont la force n'étant point réunie en quelque point n'emporte pas l'inégale distribution du peuple mais le laisse également dispersé sur le territoire, telle est la démocratie.

On voit dans la Suisse une application bien frappante de ces principes. La Suisse en général est un pays pauvre et stérile. Son gouvernement est partout républicain. Mais dans les cantons plus fertiles que les autres tels que ceux de Berne, de Soleure et de Fribourg le gouvernement est aristocratique. Dans les plus pauvres, dans ceux où la culture est plus ingrate et demande un plus grand travail le gouvernement est démocratique. L'État n'a que ce qu'il faut pour subsister sous la plus simple administration. Il s'épuiserait et périrait sous toute autre.

On dira que la Corse plus fertile et sous un climat plus doux peut supporter un gouvernement plus onéreux. Cela serait vrai dans un autre temps, mais maintenant, accablée par un long esclavage, désolée par de longues guerres, la nation a premièrement besoin de se rétablir. Quand elle aura mis en valeur son sol fertile elle pourra songer à devenir florissante et se donner une plus brillante administration. Je dirai plus. Le succès de la première institution en rendra dans la suite le changement nécessaire. La culture des champs cultive l'esprit ; tout peuple cultivateur multiplie ; il multiplie à proportion du produit de sa terre et quand cette terre est féconde il multiplie à la fin si fort qu'elle ne peut plus lui suffire ; alors il est forcé d'établir des colonies, ou de changer son gouvernement.

Quand le pays est saturé d'habitants on n'en peut plus employer l'excédent à la culture, il faut occuper cet excédent à l'industrie, au commerce, aux arts, et ce nouveau système demande une autre administration. Puisse l'établissement que la Corse va faire, la mettre bientôt dans la nécessité d'en changer ainsi. Mais tant qu'elle n'aura pas plus d'hommes qu'elle n'en peut nourrir, tant qu'il restera dans l'île un pouce de terre en friche, elle doit s'en tenir au système rustique et n'en changer que quand l'île ne lui suffira plus.

Le système rustique tient comme j'ai dit à l'état démocratique. Ainsi la forme que nous avons à choisir est donnée. Il est vrai qu'il y a dans son application quelques modifications à faire à cause de la grandeur de l'île; car un gouvernement purement démocratique convient à une petite ville plutôt qu'à une nation. On ne saurait assembler tout le peuple d'un pays comme celui d'une cité et quand l'autorité suprême est confiée à des députés le gouvernement change et devient aristocratique. Celui qui convient à la Corse est un gouvernement mixte[8] où le peuple ne s'assemble que par parties et où les dépositaires de son pouvoir sont souvent changés. C'est ce qu'a très bien vu l'auteur du mémoire fait en 1764 à Vescovato[9], mémoire excellent et qu'on peut consulter avec confiance sur tout ce qui n'est pas expliqué dans celui-ci.

De cette forme bien établie il résultera deux grands avantages. L'un, de ne confier l'administration qu'au petit nombre, ce qui permet le choix des gens éclairés. L'autre, de faire concourir tous les membres de l'État à l'autorité suprême, ce qui mettant tout le peuple dans un niveau parfait, lui permet de s'épandre sur toute la surface de l'île et de la peupler partout également. C'est ici la maxime fondamentale de notre institution. Rendons-la telle qu'elle maintienne la population partout en équilibre et par cela seul nous l'aurons rendue aussi parfaite qu'elle puisse être. Si cette maxime est bonne, nos règles deviennent claires et notre ouvrage se simplifie à un point étonnant.

Une partie de cet ouvrage est déjà faite : nous avons moins d'établissements que de préjugés à détruire, il s'agit moins de changer que d'achever. Les Génois eux-mêmes ont préparé votre institution et par un soin digne de la Providence, en croyant affermir la tyrannie ils ont fondé la liberté. Ils vous ont ôté presque tout commerce et en effet ce n'est pas maintenant le temps d'en avoir. S'il était ouvert au-dehors il faudrait l'interdire jusqu'à ce que votre constitution eût pris son assiette et que le dedans vous fournît tout ce que vous pouvez en tirer. Ils ont gêné l'exportation de vos denrées. Votre avantage n'est point qu'elles soient exportées, mais qu'il naisse dans l'île assez d'hommes pour les consommer.

Les pièves[10] et juridictions particulières qu'ils ont formées ou conservées pour faciliter les recouvrements des impôts et l'exécution des ordres sont le seul moyen possible d'établir la démocratie dans tout un peuple qui ne peut s'assembler à la fois dans un même lieu ; elles sont aussi le seul moyen de maintenir le pays indépendant des villes qu'il est plus aisé de tenir sous le joug. Ils se sont encore appliqués à détruire la noblesse, à la priver de ses dignités, de ses titres, à éteindre les grands fiefs ; il est heureux pour vous qu'ils se soient chargés de ce qu'il y avait d'odieux dans cette entreprise que vous n'auriez peut-être pu faire s'ils ne l'avaient faite avant vous. N'hésitez point d'achever leur ouvrage ; en croyant travailler pour eux ils travaillaient pour vous. La fin seule est bien différente, car celle des Génois était dans la chose même et la vôtre est dans son effet. Ils ne voulaient qu'avilir la noblesse et vous voulez anoblir la nation.

Ceci est un point sur lequel je vois que les Corses n'ont pas encore des idées saines. Dans tous leurs mémoires justificatifs, dans leur protestation d'Aix-la-Chapelle ils se sont plaints que Gênes avait déprimé ou plutôt détruit leur noblesse. C'était un grief sans doute, mais ce n'était pas un malheur, c'est au contraire un avantage, sans lequel il leur serait impossible de rester libres.

C'est prendre l'ombre pour le corps de mettre la dignité d'un État dans les titres de quelques-uns de ses membres. Quand le royaume de Corse appartenait à Gênes il pouvait lui être utile d'avoir des marquis, des comtes, des nobles titrés qui servissent pour ainsi dire de médiateurs au peuple corse auprès de la République. Mais contre qui lui seraient maintenant utiles de pareils protecteurs moins propres à le garantir de la tyrannie qu'à l'usurper eux-mêmes, qui le désoleraient par leurs vexations et par leurs débats, jusqu'à ce qu'un d'eux ayant asservi les autres fît ses sujets de tous ses concitoyens ?

Distinguons deux sortes de noblesse. La noblesse féodale qui appartient à la monarchie et la noblesse politique qui appartient à l'aristocratie. La première a plusieurs ordres ou degrés, les uns titrés, les autres non titrés, depuis les grands vassaux jusqu'aux simples gentilshommes ; ses droits bien que héréditaires sont pour ainsi dire individuels, particuliers, attachés à chaque famille et tellement indépendants les uns des autres qu'ils le sont même de la constitution de l'État et de la souveraineté. La seconde, au contraire, unie en un seul corps indivisible dont tous les droits sont dans le corps, non dans ses membres, forme une partie tellement essentielle du corps politique qu'elle ne peut subsister sans lui ni lui sans elle, et tous les individus qui la composent, égaux par leur naissance en titres, en privilèges, en autorité, se confondent sous le nom commun de patriciens.

Il est clair par les titres que portait l'ancienne noblesse corse et par les fiefs qu'elle possédait avec des droits approchant de la souveraineté même, qu'elle était dans la première classe et qu'elle devait son origine soit aux conquérants, maures ou français, soit aux princes que les papes avaient investis de l'île de Corse. Or cette espèce de noblesse peut si peu entrer dans une république démocratique ou mixte qu'elle ne peut pas même entrer dans une aristocratie, car l'aristocratie n'admet que des droits de corps et non des droits individuels. La démocratie ne connaît d'autre noblesse après la vertu que la liberté et l'aristocratie ne connaît de même d'autre noblesse que l'autorité. Tout ce qui est étranger à la constitution doit être soigneusement banni du corps politique. Laissez donc aux autres États tous ces titres de marquis et de comtes avilissants pour les simples citoyens. La loi fondamentale de votre institution doit être l'égalité. Tout doit s'y rapporter jusqu'à l'autorité même, qui n'est établie que pour la défendre, tout doit être égal par droit de naissance. L'État ne doit accorder des distinctions qu'au mérite, aux vertus, aux services rendus à la patrie et ces distinctions ne doivent pas être plus héréditaires que ne le sont les qualités sur lesquelles elles sont fondées. Nous verrons bientôt comment on peut graduer chez un peuple différents ordres sans que la naissance et la noblesse y entrent pour rien.

Tous fiefs, hommages, cens et droits féodaux, ci-devant abolis le seront donc pour toujours, et l'État rachètera ceux qui subsistent encore en sorte que tous titres et droits seigneuriaux demeurent éteints et supprimés dans toute l'île.

Pour que toutes les parties de l'État gardent entre elles autant qu'il est possible le même niveau que nous tâchons d'établir entre les individus, on réglera les bornes des districts, piéves et juridictions de manière à diminuer l'extrême inégalité qui s'y fait sentir. La seule province de Bastia et de Nebbio contient autant d'habitants que les sept provinces de Capo Corso, d'Aleria, de Porto-Vecchio, de Sartène, de Vico, de Calvi et d'Algagliola. Celle d'Ajaccio en contient plus que les quatre qui l'avoisinent. Sans ôter entièrement les limites et bouleverser les ressorts on peut par quelques légers changements modérer ces disproportions énormes. Par exemple l'abolition des fiefs donne la facilité de former de ceux de Canari, de Brando et de Nonza une nouvelle juridiction qui, renforcée de la piève de Pietra-bugno se trouvera à peu près égale à la juridiction de Capo Corso. Le fief d'Istria réuni à la province de Sartène ne la rendra pas encore égale à celle de Corte et celle de Bastia et Nebbio quoique diminuée d'une piève peut être partagée en deux juridictions encore très fortes dont le Guolo fera la séparation. Ceci n'est qu'un exemple pour me faire entendre ; car je ne connais pas assez le local pour pouvoir rien déterminer.

Par ces légers changements l'île de Corse que je suppose entièrement libre se trouverait divisée en douze juridictions qui ne seront pas entièrement disproportionnées, surtout lorsque ayant resserré comme on le doit les droits municipaux des villes, on aura laissé par ces villes moins de poids à leur juridiction.

Les villes sont utiles dans un pays à proportion de ce qu'on y cultive le commerce et les arts mais elles sont nuisibles au système que nous avons adopté. Leurs habitants sont cultivateurs ou oisifs. Or, la culture se fait toujours mieux par les colons que par les urbains, et c'est de l'oisiveté que viennent tous les vices qui jusqu'à ce moment ont désolé la Corse. Le sot orgueil des bourgeois ne fait qu'avilir et décourager le laboureur. Livrés à la mollesse, aux passions qu'elle excite, ils se plongent dans la débauche et se vendent pour y satisfaire ; l'intérêt les rend serviles et la fainéantise les rend inquiets, ils sont esclaves ou mutins, jamais libres. Cette différence s'est bien fait sentir durant toute la présente guerre, et depuis que la nation a brisé ses fers. C'est la vigueur de vos pièves qui a fait la révolution, c'est leur fermeté qui l'a soutenue ; cet inébranlable courage que nul revers ne peut abattre vous vient d'elles. Les villes peuplées d'hommes mercenaires ont vendu leur nation pour se conserver quelques petits privilèges que les Génois savaient avec art leur faire valoir et, justement punies de leur lâcheté, elles demeurent les nids de la tyrannie, tandis que déjà le peuple corse jouit avec gloire de la liberté qu'il s'est acquise au prix de son sang.

Il ne faut point qu'un peuple cultivateur regarde avec convoitise le séjour des villes et envie le sort des fainéants qui les peuplent ; par conséquent il n'en faut point favoriser l'habitation par des avantages nuisibles à la population générale et à la liberté de la nation. Il faut qu'un laboureur ne soit par la naissance inférieur à personne, qu'il ne voie au-dessus de lui que les lois et les magistrats et qu'il puisse devenir magistrat lui-même s'il en est digne par ses lumières et par sa probité. En un mot les villes et leurs habitants non plus que les fiefs et leurs possesseurs ne doivent garder aucun privilège exclusif ; toute l'île doit jouir des mêmes droits, supporter les mêmes charges, et devenir indistinctement ce qu'on appelle en termes du pays : *terra di commune*[11].

Or si les villes sont nuisibles, les capitales le sont encore plus. Une capitale est un gouffre où la nation presque entière va perdre ses mœurs, ses lois, son courage et sa liberté. On s'imagine que les grandes villes favorisent l'agriculture parce qu'elles consomment beaucoup de denrées mais elles consomment encore plus de cultivateurs, soit par le désir de prendre un meilleur métier qui les attire, soit par le dépérissement naturel des races bourgeoises que la campagne recrute toujours. Les environs des capitales ont un air de vie, mais plus on s'éloigne plus tout est désert. De la capitale s'exhale une peste continuelle qui mine et détruit enfin la nation.

Cependant, il faut au gouvernement un centre, un point de réunion auquel tout se rapporte : il y aurait trop d'inconvénient à rendre errante l'administration suprême. Pour la faire circuler de province en province il faudrait diviser l'île en plusieurs petits États confédérés dont chacun aurait à son tour la présidence ; mais ce système compliquerait le jeu de la machine, les pièces en seraient moins liées. L'île n'étant pas assez grande pour rendre cette division nécessaire l'est trop pour pouvoir se passer d'une capitale. Mais il faut que cette capitale forme la correspondance de toutes les juridictions sans en attirer les peuples ; que tout y communique, et que chaque chose reste à sa place. En un mot il faut que le siège du gouvernement suprême soit moins une capitale qu'un chef-lieu.

La seule nécessité a là-dessus dirigé le choix de la nation comme l'eût fait la raison même. Les Génois restés maîtres des places maritimes ne vous ont laissé que la ville de Corte non moins heureusement située pour l'administration corse que l'était Bastia pour l'administration génoise. Corte placée au milieu de l'île voit tous ces rivages presque à égales distances. Elle est précisément entre les deux grandes parties *di quà e di là dai monti*[12] également à portée de tout. Elle est loin de la mer ce qui conservera plus longtemps à ses habitants leurs mœurs, leur simplicité, leur droiture, leur caractère national que si elle était sujette à l'affluence des étrangers. Elle est dans la partie la plus élevée de l'île, dans un air très sain mais dans un sol peu fertile et presque à la source des rivières, ce qui, rendant l'abord des denrées plus difficile, ne lui permet point de trop s'agrandir. Que si l'on ajoute à tout cela la précaution de ne rendre aucune des grandes charges de l'État héréditaire ni même à vie, il est à présumer que les hommes publics n'y formant que des habitations passagères ne lui donneront de longtemps cette splendeur funeste qui fait le lustre et la perte des États.

Voici les premières réflexions que m'a suggérées l'examen rapide du local de l'île. Avant de parler maintenant plus en détail du gouvernement il faut commencer par voir ce qu'il doit faire et sur quelles maximes il doit se conduire. C'est là ce qui doit achever de décider de sa forme, car chaque forme de gouvernement a son esprit qui lui est naturel, propre et duquel elle ne s'écartera jamais.

Nous avons égalisé jusqu'ici le sol national autant qu'il nous a été possible ; tâchons maintenant d'y tracer le plan de l'édifice qu'il faut élever. La première règle que nous avons à suivre est le caractère national. Tout peuple a ou doit avoir un caractère national et s'il en manquait il faudrait commencer par le lui donner[13]. Les insulaires surtout moins mêlés, moins confondus avec les autres peuples en ont d'ordinaire un plus marqué. Les Corses en particulier en ont un naturellement très sensible ; et si défiguré par l'esclavage et la tyrannie il est devenu difficile à connaître, en revanche il est aussi par leur position isolée facile à rétablir et conserver.

L'île de Corse, dit Diodore, est montagneuse, pleine de bois, et arrosée par de grands fleuves. Ses habitants se nourrissent de lait, de miel et de viande, que le pays leur fournit largement. Ils observent entre eux les règles de la justice et de l'humanité avec plus d'exactitude que les autres barbares ; celui qui le premier trouve du miel dans les montagnes et dans les creux des arbres est assuré que personne ne le lui disputera. Ils sont toujours certains de retrouver leurs brebis sur lesquelles chacun met sa marque et qu'ils laissent paître ensuite dans les campagnes sans que personne les garde : le même esprit d'équité paraît les conduire dans toutes les rencontres de la vie.

Les grands historiens savent dans les plus simples narrations et sans raisonner eux-mêmes rendre sensible au lecteur la raison de chaque fait qu'ils rapportent.

Quand un pays n'est pas peuplé par des colonies, c'est de la nature du sol que naît le caractère primitif des habitants. Un terrain rude, inégal, difficile à cultiver, doit plus fournir à la nourriture des bêtes qu'à celle des hommes, les champs y doivent être rares et les pâturages abondants. De là la multiplication du bétail et la vie pastorale. Les troupeaux des particuliers errant dans les montagnes s'y mêlent, s'y confondent. Le miel n'a d'autre clef que la marque du premier occupant ; la propriété ne peut s'établir ni se conserver que sous la foi publique et il faut bien que tout le monde soit juste sans quoi personne n'aurait rien et la nation périrait.

Des montagnes, des bois, des rivières, des pâturages. Ne croirait-on pas lire la description de la Suisse ? Aussi retrouvait-on jadis dans les Suisses le même caractère que Diodore donne aux Corses : l'équité, l'humanité, la bonne foi. Toute la différence était qu'habitant un climat plus rude ils étaient plus laborieux. Ensevelis durant six mois sous les neiges ils étaient forcés de faire des provisions pour l'hiver, épars sur leurs rochers ils les cultivaient avec une fatigue qui les rendait robustes ; un travail continuel leur ôtait le temps de connaître les passions ; les communications étant toujours pénibles, quand les neiges et les glaces achevaient de les fermer, chacun dans sa cabane, était forcé de se suffire à lui-même et à sa famille : de là l'heureuse et grossière industrie ; chacun exerçait dans sa maison tous les arts nécessaires ; tous étaient maçons, charpentiers, menuisiers, charrons. Les rivières et les torrents qui les séparaient les uns des autres donnaient en revanche à chacun d'eux les moyens de se passer de ses voisins ; les scies, les forges, les moulins se multipliant, ils apprirent à ménager le cours des eaux tant pour le jeu des rouages que pour multiplier les arrosements. C'est ainsi qu'au milieu de leurs précipices et de leurs vallons chacun vivant sur son sol parvint à en tirer tout son nécessaire, à s'y trouver au large, à ne désirer rien au-delà. Les intérêts, les besoins ne se croisant point et nul ne dépendant d'un autre, tous n'avaient entre eux que des liaisons de bienveillance et d'amitié ; la concorde et la paix régnaient sans effort dans leurs nombreuses familles, ils n'avaient presque autre chose à traiter entre eux que des mariages où l'inclination seule était consultée, que l'ambition ne formait point, que l'intérêt et l'inégalité n'arrêtaient jamais. Ce peuple pauvre mais sans besoins dans la plus parfaite indépendance multipliait ainsi dans une union que rien ne pouvait altérer ; il n'avait pas de vertus puisque, n'ayant point de vices à vaincre, bien faire ne lui coûtait rien, et il était bon et juste sans savoir même ce que c'était que justice et que vertu. De la force avec laquelle cette vie laborieuse et indépendante attachait les Suisses à leur patrie résultaient deux plus grands moyens de la défendre, savoir le concert dans les résolutions et le courage dans les combats. Quand on considère l'union constante qui régnait entre des hommes sans maîtres, presque sans lois et que les princes qui les entouraient s'efforçaient de diviser par toutes les manœuvres de la politique ; quand on voit l'inébranlable fermeté, la constance, l'acharnement même que ces hommes terribles portaient dans les combats, résolus de mourir ou de vaincre et n'ayant pas même l'idée de séparer leur vie de leur liberté, l'on n'a plus de peine à concevoir les prodiges qu'ils ont faits pour la défense de leur pays et de leur indépendance, on n'est plus surpris de voir les trois plus grandes puissances et les troupes les plus belliqueuses de l'Europe échouer successivement dans leur entreprise contre cette héroïque nation que sa simplicité rendait aussi invincible à la ruse que son courage à la valeur. Corses, voilà le modèle que vous devez suivre pour revenir à votre état primitif.

Mais ces hommes rustiques qui d'abord ne connaissaient qu'eux-mêmes, leurs montagnes et leurs bestiaux, en se défendant contre les autres nations apprirent à les connaître. Leurs victoires leur ouvrirent les frontières de leur voisinage, la réputation de leur bravoure fit naître aux princes l'idée de les employer. Ils commencèrent à solder ces troupes qu'ils n'avaient pu vaincre. Ces braves gens qui avaient si bien défendu leur liberté devinrent les oppresseurs de celle d'autrui. On s'étonnait de leur voir porter au service des princes la même valeur qu'ils avaient mise à leur résister, la même fidélité qu'ils avaient gardée à la patrie ; vendre à prix d'argent les vertus qui se paient le moins et que l'argent corrompt le plus vite. Mais dans ces premiers temps ils portaient au service des princes la même fierté qu'ils avaient mise à leur résister ; ils s'en regardaient moins comme les satellites que comme les défenseurs et croyaient moins leur avoir vendu leurs services que leur protection.

Insensiblement ils s'avilirent et ne furent plus que des mercenaires. Le goût de l'argent leur fit sentir qu'ils étaient pauvres ; le mépris de leur état a détruit insensiblement les vertus qui en étaient l'ouvrage et les Suisses sont devenus des hommes à cinq sols, comme les Français à quatre. Une autre cause plus cachée a corrompu cette vigoureuse nation. Leur vie isolée et simple les rendait indépendants ainsi que robustes ; chacun ne connaissait de maître que lui ; mais tous ayant le même intérêt et les mêmes goûts, s'unissaient sans peine pour vouloir faire les mêmes choses ; l'uniformité de leur vie leur tenait lieu de loi. Mais quand la fréquentation des autres peuples leur eut fait aimer ce qu'ils devaient craindre et admirer ce qu'ils devaient mépriser, l'ambition des principaux leur fit changer de maxime ; ils sentirent que pour mieux dominer le peuple il fallait lui donner des goûts plus dépendants. De là l'introduction du commerce, de l'industrie et du luxe, qui liant les particuliers à l'autorité publique par leurs métiers et par leurs besoins les fait dépendre de ceux qui gouvernent beaucoup plus qu'ils n'en dépendaient dans leur état primitif.

La pauvreté ne s'est fait sentir dans la Suisse que quand l'argent a commencé d'y circuler. Il a mis la même inégalité dans les ressources que dans les fortunes ; il est devenu un grand moyen d'acquérir ôté à ceux qui n'avaient rien. Les établissements de commerce et de manufacture se sont multipliés. Les arts ont ôté une multitude de mains à l'agriculture. Les hommes en se divisant inégalement se sont multipliés et se sont répandus dans les pays plus favorablement situés et où les ressources étaient encore plus faciles. Les uns ont déserté leur patrie, les autres lui sont devenus inutiles en consommant et ne produisant rien. La multitude des enfants est devenue à charge. Le peuplement a sensiblement diminué, et tandis que l'on se multipliait dans les villes, la culture des terres plus négligée, les besoins de la vie plus onéreux en rendant les denrées étrangères plus nécessaires ont mis le pays dans une plus grande dépendance de ses voisins. La vie oiseuse a introduit la corruption et multiplié les pensionnaires des puissances ; l'amour de la patrie éteint dans tous les cœurs y a fait place au seul amour de l'argent ; tous les sentiments qui donnent du ressort à l'âme étant étouffés, on n'a plus vu ni fermeté dans la conduite ni vigueur dans les résolutions. Jadis la Suisse pauvre faisait la loi à la France, maintenant la Suisse riche tremble au sourcil froncé d'un ministre français.

Voilà de grandes leçons pour le peuple corse ; voyons de quelle manière il doit se les appliquer. Le peuple corse conserve un grand nombre de ses vertus primitives qui faciliteront beaucoup notre constitution. Il a aussi contracté dans la servitude beaucoup de vices auxquels il doit remédier ; de ces vices quelques-uns disparaîtront d'eux-mêmes avec la cause qui les fit naître, d'autres ont besoin qu'une cause contraire déracine la passion qui les produit*.

Je mets dans la première classe l'humeur indomptable et féroce qu'on leur attribue. On les accuse d'être mutins ; comment le sait-on, puisqu'ils n'ont jamais été gouvernés justement ? En les animant sans cesse les uns contre les autres, on devait prévoir que cette animosité tournerait souvent contre ceux dont elle était l'ouvrage.

Je mets dans la seconde classe le penchant au vol et au meurtre qui les a rendus odieux. La source de ces deux vices est la paresse et l'impunité ; cela est clair, quant au premier, et facile à prouver quant au second puisque les haines de famille et les projets de vengeance qu'ils étaient sans cesse occupés à satisfaire naissent dans des entretiens oiseux et prennent de la consistance

* Il y a dans tous les États (peuples) un progrès, un développement naturel et nécessaire depuis leur naissance jusqu'à leur destruction. Pour rendre leur durée aussi longue et aussi belle qu'il est possible, il faut mieux en marquer (reculer) le premier terme avant qu'après ce point de vigueur (et de force). (Il vaut mieux que l'État ait encore à croître en force depuis le moment de l'institution que de n'avoir plus qu'à décliner.) Il ne faut pas vouloir que la Corse soit tout d'un coup ce qu'elle peut être (car elle ne se maintiendrait point dans un état), il vaut mieux qu'elle y parvienne et qu'elle monte que d'y être à l'instant même et ne faire que décliner. Le dépérissement où elle est ferait de son état de vigueur un état très faible, au lieu qu'en la disposant pour y atteindre cet état sera dans la suite un état très bon.

dans de sombres méditations et s'exécutent sans peine par l'assurance de l'impunité.

Qui pourrait n'être pas saisi d'horreur contre un gouvernement barbare qui pour voir ces infortunés s'entr'égorger les uns les autres n'épargnait aucun soin pour les y exciter? Le meurtre n'était pas puni; que dis-je, il était récompensé; le prix du sang était un des revenus de la République; il fallut que les malheureux Corses pour éviter une destruction totale achetassent par un tribut la grâce d'être désarmés.

Les Génois se vantent d'avoir favorisé l'agriculture dans l'île, les Corses paraissent en convenir. Je n'en conviendrai pas de même; le mauvais succès prouve qu'ils avaient pris de mauvais moyens. Dans cette conduite, la République n'avait pas pour but de multiplier les habitants de l'île puisqu'elle favorisait si ouvertement les assassinats, ni de les faire vivre dans l'aisance puisqu'elle les ruinait par les exactions, ni même de faciliter le recouvrement des tailles puisqu'elle chargeait de droits la vente et le transport des denrées et en défendait l'exportation. Elle avait pour but au contraire de rendre plus onéreuses ces mêmes tailles qu'elle n'osait augmenter, de tenir toujours les Corses dans l'abaissement en les attachant pour ainsi dire à leur glèbe, en les détournant du commerce, des arts, de toutes les professions lucratives, en les empêchant de s'élever, de s'instruire, de s'enrichir, elle avait pour but d'avoir toutes les denrées à vil prix par les monopoles de ses officiers. Elle prenait toutes les mesures pour épuiser l'île d'argent, pour l'y rendre nécessaire et pour l'empêcher toutefois d'y rentrer. La tyrannie ne pouvait employer de manœuvre plus raffinée, en paraissant favoriser la culture, elle achevait d'écraser la nation; elle voulait la réduire à un tas de vils paysans vivant dans la plus déplorable misère.

Qu'arrivait-il de là ? Les Corses découragés abandonnaient un travail qui n'était animé d'aucun espoir. Ils aimaient mieux ne rien faire que de se fatiguer à pure perte. La vie laborieuse et simple fit place à la paresse, au désœuvrement, à toutes sortes de vices, le vol leur procurait l'argent dont ils avaient besoin pour payer leur taille, et qu'ils ne trouvaient point avec leurs denrées ; ils quittaient leurs champs pour travailler sur les grands chemins.

Que les Corses, ramenés à une vie laborieuse perdent l'habitude d'errer dans l'île comme des bandits, que leurs occupations égales et simples les tenant concentrés dans leurs familles leur laisse peu d'intérêts à démêler entre eux ! Que leur travail leur fournisse aisément de quoi subsister, eux et leur famille ! Que ceux qui ont toutes les choses nécessaires à la vie ne soient pas encore obligés d'avoir de l'argent en espèces, soit pour payer les tailles et autres impositions, soit pour fournir à des besoins de fantaisie ou de luxe qui sans contribuer au bien-être de celui qui l'étale ne fait qu'exciter l'envie et la haine d'autrui !

On voit aisément comment le système auquel nous avons donné la préférence conduit à ces avantages mais cela ne suffit pas. Il s'agit de faire adopter au peuple la pratique de ce système, de lui faire aimer l'occupation que nous voulons lui donner, d'y fixer ses plaisirs, ses désirs, ses goûts, d'en faire généralement le bonheur de la vie, et d'y borner les projets de l'ambition.

Je ne vois nuls moyens plus prompts et plus sûrs pour en venir là que les deux suivants : l'un d'attacher pour ainsi dire les hommes à la terre en tirant d'elle leurs distinctions et leurs droits, et l'autre, d'affermir ce lien par celui de la famille en la rendant nécessaire à l'état des pères.

J'ai pensé que dans cette vue, posant la loi fondamentale sur les distinctions tirées de la nature de la chose[14], on pouvait diviser toute la nation corse en trois classes dont l'inégalité toujours personnelle pouvait être heureusement substituée à l'inégalité de race ou d'habitation qui résulte du système féodal municipal que nous abolissons.

La première classe sera celle des citoyens.

La seconde celle des patriotes.

La troisième celle des aspirants.

Il sera dit ci-après à quels titres on sera inscrit dans chaque classe et de quels privilèges on y jouira.

Cette distinction par classes ne doit point se faire par un cens ou dénombrement au moment de l'institution, mais elle doit s'établir successivement d'elle-même par le simple progrès du temps. Le premier acte de l'établissement projeté doit être un serment solennel[15] prêté par tous les Corses âgés de vingt ans et au-dessus, et tous ceux qui prêteront ce serment doivent être indistinctement inscrits au nombre des citoyens. Il est bien juste que tous ces vaillants hommes qui ont délivré leur nation au prix de leur sang entrent en possession de tous ces avantages et jouissent au premier rang de la liberté qu'ils lui ont acquise.

Mais dès le jour de l'union[16] formée et du serment solennellement prêté tous ceux qui nés dans l'île n'auraient pas atteint l'âge resteront dans la classe des aspirants jusqu'à ce qu'aux conditions suivantes ils puissent monter aux deux autres classes.

Tout aspirant marié selon la loi, qui aura quelque fonds en propre indépendamment de la dot de sa femme sera inscrit dans la classe des patriotes.

Tout patriote marié ou veuf qui aura deux enfants vivants, une habitation à lui et un fonds de terre suffisant pour sa subsistance sera inscrit dans la classe des citoyens.

Ce premier pas, suffisant pour mettre les terres en crédit, ne l'est pas pour les mettre en culture si l'on n'ôte la nécessité d'argent qui a fait la pauvreté de l'île sous le gouvernement génois. Il faut établir pour maxime certaine que partout où l'argent est de première nécessité la nation se détache de l'agriculture pour se jeter dans les professions plus lucratives; l'état de laboureur est alors ou un objet de commerce et une espèce de manufacture pour les grands fermiers, ou le pis-aller de la misère pour la foule des paysans. Ceux qui s'enrichissent par le commerce et l'industrie placent, quand ils ont assez gagné, leur argent en fonds de terre que d'autres cultivent pour eux; toute la nation se trouve ainsi divisée en riches fainéants qui possèdent des terres et en malheureux paysans qui n'ont pas de quoi vivre en les cultivant.

Plus l'argent est nécessaire aux particuliers, plus il l'est au gouvernement; d'où il suit que, plus le commerce fleurit, plus les taxes sont fortes, et pour payer ces taxes il ne sert de rien que le paysan cultive sa terre s'il n'en vend pas le produit. Il a beau avoir du blé, du vin, de l'huile, il lui faut absolument de l'argent, il faut qu'il porte çà et là sa denrée dans les villes, qu'il se fasse petit marchand, petit vendeur, petit fripon. Ses enfants élevés dans le courtage se débauchent, s'attachent aux villes, perdent le goût de leur état et se font matelots ou soldats plutôt que de prendre l'état de leur père. Bientôt la campagne se dépeuple et la ville regorge de vagabonds, peu à peu le pain manque, la misère publique augmente avec l'opulence des particuliers et l'une et l'autre de concert amènent tous les vices qui causent enfin la ruine d'une nation.

Je regarde si bien tout système de commerce comme destructif de l'agriculture, que je n'en excepte pas même le commerce des denrées qui sont le produit de l'agriculture. Pour qu'elle pût se soutenir dans ce système il faudrait que le profit pût se partager également entre le marchand et le cultivateur. Mais c'est ce qui est impossible parce que le négoce de l'un étant libre et celui de l'autre forcé le premier fera toujours la loi au second, rapport qui rompant l'équilibre ne peut faire un état solide et permanent.

Il ne faut pas s'imaginer que l'île en sera plus riche lorsqu'elle aura beaucoup d'argent. Cela est vrai vis-à-vis des autres peuples, et par ses rapports extérieurs, mais en elle-même une nation n'en est ni plus riche ni plus pauvre pour avoir plus ou moins d'argent ou ce qui revient à la même chose parce que la même quantité d'argent y circule avec plus ou moins d'activité. Non seulement l'argent est un signe mais c'est un signe relatif qui n'a d'effet véritable que par l'inégalité de sa distribution. Car supposé que dans l'île de Corse chaque particulier n'ait que dix écus ou qu'il ait cent mille écus, l'état respectif de tous est dans ces deux cas absolument le même ; ils n'en sont entre eux ni plus riches ni plus pauvres, et la seule différence est que la seconde supposition rend le négoce plus embarrassant. Si la Corse avait besoin des étrangers elle aurait besoin d'argent, mais pouvant se suffire à elle-même elle n'en a pas besoin ; et puisqu'il n'est utile que comme signe d'inégalité, moins il en circulera dans l'île, plus l'abondance réelle y régnera.

Il faut voir si ce qu'on fait avec de l'argent ne peut se faire sans argent ; et supposant qu'il se puisse il faut comparer les deux moyens relativement à notre objet.

Il est prouvé par les faits que l'île de Corse même dans l'état de friche et d'épuisement où elle est suffit à la subsistance de ses habitants, puisque durant trente-six ans de guerre qu'ils ont plus manié les armes que la charrue il n'y est cependant pas entré pour leur usage un seul bâtiment de denrées et de vivres d'aucune espèce. Elle a même tout ce qu'il faut outre les vivres pour les mettre et les maintenir dans un état florissant sans rien emprunter du dehors. Elle a des laines pour ses étoffes, du chanvre et du lin pour des toiles et des cordages, des cuirs pour des chaussures, des bois de construction pour la marine, du fer pour des forges, du cuivre pour des ustensiles et pour de la petite monnaie. Elle a du sel pour son usage; elle en aura beaucoup au-delà en rétablissant les salines d'Aleria que les Génois maintenaient avec tant de peine et de dépense dans un état de destruction, et qui donnaient du sel encore en dépit d'eux. Les Corses quand ils le voudraient ne pourraient commercer en dehors par échange à moins qu'ils n'achetassent des superfluités; ainsi l'argent même en pareil cas ne leur serait pas nécessaire pour le commerce, puisqu'il est la seule marchandise qu'ils iraient chercher. Il suit de là que dans ces rapports de nation à nation la Corse n'a aucun besoin d'argent.

Au-dedans l'île est assez grande et coupée par des montagnes; ses grandes et nombreuses rivières sont peu navigables; ses parties ne communiquent pas naturellement entre elles; mais la différence de leurs productions les tient dans une dépendance mutuelle par le besoin qu'elles ont les unes des autres. La province de Cap Corse qui ne produit presque que du vin a besoin de blés et d'huiles que lui fournit la Balagne. Corte sur la hauteur donne de même des grains et manque de tout le reste; Bonifacio au pied des rochers et à l'autre extrémité de l'île a besoin de tout et ne fournit rien. Le projet d'une égale population demande donc une circulation de denrées, un versement facile d'une juridiction dans une autre et par conséquent un commerce intérieur.

Mais je dis à cela deux choses. L'une qu'avec le concours du gouvernement ce commerce peut se faire en grande partie par des échanges ; l'autre, qu'avec le même concours et par une suite naturelle de notre établissement, ce commerce et ces échanges doivent diminuer de jour en jour et se réduire enfin à très peu de chose.

On sait que dans l'épuisement où les Génois avaient mis la Corse l'argent sortant toujours et ne rentrant point devint à la fin si rare que dans quelques cantons de l'île la monnaie n'était plus connue et qu'on n'y faisait de ventes ni d'achats que par des échanges.

Les Corses dans leurs mémoires ont cité ce fait parmi leurs griefs ; ils avaient raison, puisque, l'argent étant nécessaire pour payer les tailles, ces pauvres gens qui n'en avaient plus, saisis et exécutés dans leurs maisons, se voyaient dépouillés de leurs ustensiles les plus nécessaires, de leurs meubles, de leurs hardes, de leurs guenilles qu'il fallait transporter d'un lieu à l'autre et dont la vente ne rendait pas la dixième partie de leur prix. De sorte que faute d'argent ils payaient l'imposition dix fois pour une.

Mais, comme dans notre système on ne sera plus forcé de payer la taille en espèces, le défaut d'argent n'étant point un signe de misère ne servira point à l'augmenter ; les échanges pourront donc se faire en nature et sans valeurs intermédiaires, et l'on pourra vivre dans l'abondance sans jamais manier un sou.

Je vois que sous les gouverneurs génois qui défendaient et gênaient de mille façons la traite des denrées d'une province à l'autre, les communes faisaient des magasins de blés, de vins, d'huile, pour attendre le moment favorable et permis pour la traite, et que ces magasins servaient aux officiers génois de prétexte à mille odieux monopoles. L'idée de ces magasins n'étant pas nouvelle en sera d'autant plus facile à exécuter et fournira pour les échanges un moyen commode et simple pour le public et pour les particuliers sans risque des inconvénients qui le rendaient onéreux au peuple.

Même sans avoir recours à des magasins ou entrepôts réels, on pourrait établir dans chaque paroisse ou chef-lieu un registre public à partie double où les particuliers feraient inscrire chaque année, d'un côté l'espèce et la quantité des denrées qu'ils ont de trop et de l'autre celles qui leur manquent. De la balance et comparaison de ces registres faites de province à province on pourrait tellement régler le prix des denrées et la mesure des traites que chaque piève ferait la consommation de son superflu et l'acquisition de son nécessaire, sans qu'il y eût ni défaut ni excédent dans la quantité et presque aussi commodément que si la récolte se mesurait sur ses besoins.

Ces opérations peuvent se faire avec la plus grande justesse et sans monnaie réelle, soit par la voie d'échanges ou à l'aide d'une simple monnaie idéale qui servirait de terme de comparaison telle par exemple que sont les pistoles en France, soit en prenant pour monnaie quelque bien réel qui se nombre comme était le bœuf chez les Grecs ou la brebis chez les Romains, et qu'on fixe dans sa valeur moyenne, car alors un bœuf peut valoir plus ou moins d'un bœuf et une brebis plus ou moins d'une brebis, différence qui rend la monnaie idéale préférable, parce qu'elle est toujours exacte n'étant prise que pour nombre abstrait.

Tant qu'on s'en tiendra là les traites se maintiendront en équilibre et les échanges se réglant uniquement sur l'abondance ou la rareté relatives des denrées et sur la plus ou moins grande facilité des transports resteront toujours et partout en rapports compensés, et toutes les productions de l'île également dispersées y prendront d'elles-mêmes le niveau de la population. J'ajoute que l'administration publique pourra sans inconvénient présider à ces traites, à ces échanges, en tenir la balance, en régler la mesure, en faire la distribution parce que tant qu'ils se feront en nature les officiers publics n'en pourront abuser et n'en auront pas même la tentation au lieu que la conversion des denrées en argent ouvre la porte à toutes les exactions, à tous les monopoles, à toutes les friponneries ordinaires aux gens en place en pareil cas.

On doit s'attendre à beaucoup d'embarras en commençant, mais ces embarras sont inévitables dans tout établissement qui commence et qui contrarie un usage établi. J'ajoute que cette régie une fois établie acquerra chaque année une nouvelle facilité non seulement par la pratique et l'expérience, mais par la diminution successive des traites qui doit nécessairement en résulter jusqu'à ce qu'elles se réduisent d'elles-mêmes à la plus petite quantité possible, ce qui est le but final que l'on doit se proposer.

Il faut que tout le monde vive et que personne ne s'enrichisse. C'est là le principe fondamental de la prospérité de la nation, et la police que je propose va pour sa partie à ce but aussi directement qu'il est possible.

Les denrées superflues n'étant point un objet de commerce et ne se débitant point en argent ne seront cultivées qu'en proportion du besoin qu'on aura du nécessaire, et quiconque pourra se procurer immédiatement celles qui lui manquent sera sans intérêt d'en avoir de trop.

Sitôt que les productions de la terre ne seront point marchandise, leur cultivation se proportionnera peu à peu dans chaque province et même dans chaque héritage au besoin général de la province et au besoin particulier du cultivateur. Chacun s'efforcera d'avoir en nature et par sa propre culture, toutes les choses qui lui sont nécessaires plutôt que par des échanges qui seront toujours moins sûrs et moins commodes, à quelque point qu'ils soient facilités.

C'est un avantage sans contredit de donner à chaque terrain ce qu'il est le plus propre à produire ; par cette disposition l'on tire d'un pays plus et plus aisément que par aucune autre. Mais cette considération tout importante qu'elle est n'est que secondaire. Il vaut mieux que la terre produise un peu moins et que les habitants soient mieux ordonnés. Parmi tous ces mouvements de trafic et d'échanges il est impossible que les vices destructeurs ne se glissent pas dans une nation. Le défaut de quelques convenances dans le choix du terrain peut se compenser par le travail et il vaut mieux mal employer les champs que les hommes. Du reste tout cultivateur peut et doit faire ce choix dans ses terres, et chaque paroisse ou communauté dans ses biens communaux, comme il se dit ci-après.

On craindra je le sens, que cette économie ne produise un effet contraire à celui que j'en attends, qu'au lieu d'exciter la culture elle ne la décourage, que les colons n'ayant aucun débit de leurs denrées ne négligent leurs travaux, qu'ils ne se bornent à la subsistance sans chercher l'abondance, et que contents de recueillir pour eux l'absolu nécessaire, ils ne laissent au surplus leurs terres en friche. On paraîtra même fondé sur l'expérience du gouvernement génois sous lequel la défense d'exporter les denrées hors de l'île avait exactement produit cet effet.

Mais il faut considérer que sous cette administration l'argent étant de première nécessité formait l'objet immédiat du travail, que par conséquent tout travail qui ne pouvait en produire était nécessairement négligé, que le cultivateur accablé de mépris, de vexations, de misères regardait son état comme le comble du malheur, que voyant qu'il n'y pouvait trouver ses besoins il en cherchait un autre ou tombait dans le découragement. Au lieu qu'ici toutes les vues de l'institution tendent à rendre cet état heureux dans sa médiocrité, respectable dans sa simplicité. Fournissant tous les besoins de la vie, tous les tributs publics sans ventes et sans trafic, tous les moyens de la considération, il n'en laissera pas même imaginer un meilleur ou plus noble. Ceux qui le rempliront ne voyant rien au-dessus d'eux en feront leur gloire, et s'en frayant une route aux plus grands emplois ils le rempliront comme les premiers Romains. Ne pouvant sortir de cet état on voudra s'y distinguer, on voudra le remplir mieux que d'autres, faire de plus grandes récoltes, fournir un plus fort contingent à l'État, mériter dans les élections les suffrages du peuple. De nombreuses familles bien nourries et bien vêtues en feront honorer les chefs, et l'abondance réelle étant l'unique objet de luxe chacun voudra se distinguer par ce luxe-là. Tant que le cœur humain demeurera ce qu'il est de pareils établissements ne produiront pas la paresse.

Ce que les magistrats particuliers et les pères de famille doivent faire dans chaque juridiction, dans chaque piève, dans chaque héritage pour n'avoir pas besoin des autres, le gouvernement général de l'île doit le faire pour n'avoir pas besoin des peuples voisins.

Un registre exact des marchandises qui sont entrées dans l'île durant un certain nombre d'années donnera un état sûr et fidèle de celles dont elle ne peut se passer ; car ce n'est pas dans la situation présente que le luxe et le superflu y peuvent avoir lieu. Avec d'attentives observations tant sur ce que l'île produit que sur ce qu'elle peut produire on trouvera que le nécessaire étranger se réduit à très peu de chose, et c'est ce qui se confirme parfaitement par les faits, puisque dans les années 1735 et 1736 que l'île bloquée par la marine génoise n'avait aucune communication avec la terre ferme, non seulement rien n'y manqua pour le comestible, mais les besoins d'aucune espèce n'y furent insupportables. Ceux qui s'y firent sentir le plus furent les munitions de guerre, les cuirs, les cotons pour les mèches ; encore suppléa-t-on à ce dernier par la moelle de certains roseaux.

De ce petit nombre d'importations nécessaires il faut retrancher encore tout ce que l'île ne fournit pas maintenant mais qu'elle peut fournir mieux cultivée et vivifiée par l'industrie. Plus on doit écarter avec soin les arts oiseux, les arts d'agrément et de mollesse, plus on doit favoriser ceux qui sont utiles à l'agriculture et avantageux à la vie humaine. Il ne nous faut ni sculpteurs ni orfèvres mais il nous faut des charpentiers et des forgerons, il nous faut des tisserands, de bons ouvriers en laine et non pas des brodeurs ni des tireurs d'or[17].

On commencera par s'assurer des matières premières les plus nécessaires, savoir le bois, le fer, la laine, le cuir, le chanvre et le lin. L'île abondait en bois tant pour la construction que pour le chauffage, mais il ne faut pas se fier à cette abondance et abandonner l'usage et la coupe des forêts à la seule discrétion des propriétaires. À mesure que la population de l'île augmentera et que les défrichements se multiplieront il se fera dans les bois un dégât rapide qui ne pourra se réparer que très lentement. Là-dessus on peut tirer du pays où je vis des leçons de prévoyance. La Suisse était jadis couverte de bois en telle abondance qu'elle en était incommodée. Mais tant pour la multiplication des pâturages que pour l'établissement des manufactures on les a coupés sans mesure et sans règle ; maintenant ces forêts immenses ne montrent que des rochers presque nus. Heureusement, avertis par l'exemple de la France les Suisses ont vu le danger et y ont mis ordre autant qu'il a dépendu d'eux. Il reste à voir si leurs précautions ne sont pas trop tardives ; car si malgré ces précautions leurs bois diminuent journellement il est clair qu'ils doivent enfin se détruire.

La Corse en s'y prenant de plus loin n'aura pas le même danger à craindre. Il faut établir de bonne heure une exacte police sur les forêts et en régler tellement les coupes que la reproduction égale la consommation. Il ne faudra pas faire comme en France où les maîtres des eaux et forêts ayant un droit sur la coupe des arbres ont intérêt de tout détruire, soin dont ils s'acquittent aussi de leur mieux. Il faut de loin prévoir l'avenir : quoiqu'il ne soit pas à propos d'établir à présent une marine le temps viendra où cet établissement doit avoir lieu et alors on sentira l'avantage de n'avoir pas livré aux marines étrangères les belles forêts qui sont proches de la mer. On doit exploiter ou vendre les bois vieux et qui ne profitent plus mais il faut laisser sur pied tous ceux qui sont dans leur force ; ils auront dans leur temps leur emploi.

On a trouvé, dit-on, dans l'île une mine de cuivre, cela est bon, mais les mines de fer valent encore mieux. Il y en a sûrement dans l'île ; la situation des montagnes, la nature du terrain, les eaux thermales qu'on trouve dans la province de Cap Corse et ailleurs, tout me fait croire qu'on trouvera beaucoup de ces mines si l'on cherche bien et qu'on emploie à ces recherches des gens entendus. Cela supposé, l'on n'en permettra pas indifféremment l'exploitation mais on choisira les emplacements les plus favorables, les plus à portée des bois et des rivières pour établir des forges, et où l'on pourra ouvrir les routes les plus commodes pour le transport.

On aura les mêmes attentions pour les manufactures de toute espèce, chacune dans les choses qui les regardent, afin de faciliter autant qu'il se peut le travail et la distribution. L'on se gardera pourtant bien de former ces sortes d'établissements dans les quartiers de l'île les plus peuplés et les plus fertiles. Au contraire on choisira, toute chose égale, les terrains les plus arides et qui s'ils n'étaient peuplés par l'industrie resteraient déserts. On aura par là quelque embarras de plus pour les approvisionnements nécessaires ; mais les avantages qu'on y trouvera et les inconvénients qu'on évitera doivent l'emporter infiniment sur cette considération.

D'abord nous suivons ainsi notre grand et premier principe qui est non seulement d'étendre et multiplier la population mais de l'égaliser dans toute l'île autant qu'il est possible[18]. Car si les endroits stériles n'étaient pas peuplés par l'industrie ils resteraient déserts et ce serait autant de perdu pour l'agrandissement possible de la nation.

Si l'on formait de pareils établissements dans les lieux fertiles, l'abondance des vivres et le profit du travail nécessairement plus grand dans les arts que dans l'agriculture détournant les cultivateurs ou leurs familles des soins rustiques et dépeuplant insensiblement la campagne forceraient d'attirer de loin de nouveaux colons pour la cultiver. Ainsi surchargeant d'habitants quelques points du territoire nous en dépeuplerions d'autres et rompant ainsi l'équilibre nous irions directement contre l'esprit de notre institution.

Le transport des denrées les rendant plus coûteuses dans les fabriques diminuera par là le profit des ouvriers et tenant leur état plus rapproché de celui de cultivateur maintiendra mieux entre eux l'équilibre. Cet équilibre ne peut cependant être tel que l'avantage ne soit toujours pour l'industrie, soit parce que l'argent qui est dans l'État s'y porte en plus grande abondance, soit par les moyens de fortune par qui la puissance et l'inégalité font leur jeu, soit par la plus grande force qu'ont plus d'hommes rassemblés et que les ambitieux savent réunir à leur avantage. Il importe donc que cette partie trop favorisée demeure dans la dépendance du reste de la nation pour sa subsistance ; en cas de divisions intestines il est dans la nature de notre institution que ce soit le colon qui fasse la loi à l'ouvrier.

Avec des précautions on peut sans danger favoriser dans l'île l'établissement des arts utiles et je doute si ces établissements bien conduits ne peuvent pas pourvoir à tout le nécessaire, sans avoir besoin de rien tirer du dehors si ce n'est quelques bagatelles pour lesquelles on permettra une exportation proportionnelle toujours balancée avec soin par l'administration.

J'ai montré jusqu'ici comment le peuple corse pouvait subsister dans l'aisance et l'indépendance avec très peu de trafic, comment de ce peu qui lui sera nécessaire la plus grande partie se peut faire aisément par des échanges, et comment il peut réduire presque à rien les nécessités des importations du dehors de l'île[19]. On voit par là que si l'usage de l'argent et de la monnaie ne peut être absolument anéanti dans les affaires des particuliers, il se peut réduire au moins à si peu de chose qu'il en naîtra difficilement des abus, qu'il ne se fera point de fortunes par cette voie, et que quand il s'en pourrait faire elles deviendraient presque inutiles et donneraient peu d'avantage à leurs possesseurs.

Mais les finances publiques comment les gouvernerons-nous ? Quels revenus assignerons-nous à l'administration ? L'établirons-nous gratuite ou comment réglerons-nous son entretien ? C'est ce qu'il faut maintenant considérer.

Les systèmes de finances sont des inventions modernes. Ce mot de finance n'était pas plus connu des anciens que ceux de taille et de capitation. Le mot *vectigal*[20] se prenait dans un autre sens comme il sera dit ci-après. Le souverain mettait des impositions sur les peuples conquis ou vaincus, jamais sur ses sujets immédiats surtout dans les républiques. Bien loin que le peuple d'Athènes fût chargé d'impôts le gouvernement le payait au contraire ; et Rome à qui ses guerres devaient tant coûter faisait souvent des distributions de blés et même de terres au peuple. L'État subsistait cependant, entretenait de grandes armées sur mer et sur terre, et faisait des ouvrages publics considérables et d'aussi grandes dépenses tout au moins qu'en font proportionnellement les États modernes. Comment cela se faisait-il ?

Il faut distinguer dans les États deux époques, leur commencement et leur accroissement. Dans le commencement d'un État il n'avait d'autre revenu que le domaine public et ce domaine était considérable. Romulus le fit du tiers de toutes les terres. Il assigna le second tiers pour l'entretien des prêtres et des choses sacrées, le troisième tiers seulement fut partagé entre les citoyens. C'était peu mais ce peu était franc. Croit-on que le laboureur français ne se réduirait pas volontiers au tiers de ce qu'il cultive à condition d'avoir ce tiers franc de toute taille, de tout cens, de toute dîme et de ne payer aucune espèce d'impôt ?

Ainsi le revenu public ne se tirait point en argent mais en denrées et autres productions. La dépense était de même nature que la recette. On ne payait ni les magistrats ni les troupes, on les nourrissait, on leur fournissait des habits, et dans les besoins pressants les charges extraordinaires du peuple étaient en corvées et point en argent. Ces superbes travaux publics ne coûtaient presque rien à l'État ; c'était l'ouvrage de ces redoutables légions qui travaillaient comme elles se battaient et qui n'étaient pas composées de canaille mais de citoyens.

Quand les Romains commencèrent à s'agrandir et devinrent conquérants ils prirent sur les peuples vaincus l'entretien de leurs troupes, quand ils les payèrent, les sujets furent imposés, jamais les Romains. Dans les dangers pressants le Sénat se cotisait, il faisait des emprunts qu'il rendait fidèlement et durant toute la durée de la République je ne sache pas que jamais le peuple romain ait payé l'imposition pécuniaire ni par tête ni sur les terres.

Corses, voilà un beau modèle ! Ne vous étonnez pas qu'il y eût plus de vertu chez les Romains qu'ailleurs, l'argent y était moins nécessaire. L'État avait de petits revenus et faisait de grandes choses. Son trésor était dans les bras des citoyens. Je pourrais dire que par la situation de la Corse et par la forme de son gouvernement il n'y en aura point au monde de moins dispendieux, puisqu'étant une île et une république elle n'aura nul besoin de troupes réglées et que les chefs de l'État rentrant tous dans l'égalité ne pourront rien tirer de la masse commune qui n'y retourne en très peu de temps.

Mais ce n'est pas ainsi que j'envisage le nerf de la force publique. Au contraire je veux qu'on dépense beaucoup pour le service de l'État ; je ne dispute pour dire mieux que sur le choix des espèces. Je regarde les finances comme la graisse du corps politique, qui s'engorgeant dans certains réseaux musculaires, surcharge le corps d'un embonpoint inutile et le rend plutôt lourd que fort. Je veux nourrir l'État d'un aliment plus salutaire qui s'unisse soi-même avec sa substance, qui se change en fibres, en muscles, sans engorger les vaisseaux, qui donne de la vigueur et non de la grosseur aux membres et qui renforce le corps sans l'appesantir.

Loin de vouloir que l'État soit pauvre, je voudrais, au contraire, qu'il eût tout et que chacun n'eût sa part aux biens communs qu'en proportion de ses services. L'acquisition de tous les biens des Égyptiens faite au roi par Joseph eût été bonne s'il n'eût fait trop ou trop peu. Mais sans entrer dans ces spéculations qui m'éloignent de mon objet il suffit de faire entendre ici ma pensée qui n'est pas de détruire absolument la propriété particulière, parce que cela est impossible, mais de la renfermer dans les plus étroites bornes, de lui donner une mesure, une règle, un frein qui la contienne, qui la dirige, qui la subjugue et la tienne toujours subordonnée au bien public. Je veux en un mot que la propriété de l'État soit aussi grande, aussi forte et celle des citoyens aussi petite, aussi faible qu'il est possible[21]. Voilà pourquoi j'évite de la mettre en choses dont le possesseur particulier est trop le maître telles que la monnaie et l'argent que l'on cache aisément à l'inspection publique.

L'établissement d'un domaine public n'est pas, j'en conviens, une chose aussi facile à faire aujourd'hui dans la Corse déjà partagée à ses habitants, qu'elle le fut dans Rome naissante avant que son territoire conquis appartînt encore à personne. Cependant je sais qu'il reste dans l'île une grande quantité d'excellente terre en friche dont il est très facile au gouvernement de tirer parti soit en les aliénant pour un certain nombre d'années à ceux qui les mettront en culture soit en les faisant défricher par corvées chacune dans sa communauté. Il faudrait avoir été sur les lieux pour juger de la distribution qu'on peut faire de ces terres et du parti qu'on en peut tirer, mais je ne doute point qu'au moyen de quelques échanges et de certains arrangements peu difficiles on ne puisse dans chaque juridiction et même dans chaque piève se procurer des fonds communaux qui pourront même augmenter en peu d'années par l'ordre dont il sera parlé dans la loi des successions.

Un autre moyen plus facile encore et qui doit fournir un revenu plus net, plus sûr et beaucoup plus considérable est de suivre un exemple que j'ai sous les yeux dans les cantons protestants. Lors de la réformation de ces cantons, ils s'emparèrent des dîmes ecclésiastiques et ces dîmes sur lesquelles ils entretiennent honnêtement leur clergé ont fait le principal revenu de l'État. Je ne dis pas que les Corses doivent toucher aux revenus de l'Église, à Dieu ne plaise ! mais je crois que le peuple ne sera pas fort vexé quand l'État lui demandera autant que lui demande le clergé, déjà suffisamment renté en fonds de terre. L'assiette de cette taxe sera établie sans peine, sans embarras et presque sans frais puisqu'on n'aura qu'à doubler la dîme ecclésiastique et en prendre la moitié.

Je tire une troisième sorte de revenu, la plus sûre et la meilleure, des hommes mêmes, en employant leur travail, leurs bras et leur cœur plutôt que leur bourse au service de la patrie, soit pour sa défense, dans les milices, soit pour ses commodités par des corvées dans les travaux publics.

Que ce mot de corvée n'effarouche point des républicains ! Je sais qu'il est en abomination en France mais l'est-il en Suisse ? Les chemins s'y font aussi par corvées et personne ne se plaint. L'apparente commodité du paiement ne peut séduire que des esprits superficiels et c'est une maxime certaine que moins il y a d'intermédiaires entre le besoin et le service, moins le service doit être onéreux.

Sans oser déployer tout à fait ma pensée, sans donner ici les corvées et tous les travaux personnels des citoyens pour un bien absolu je conviendrai si l'on veut qu'il serait mieux que tout cela se fît en payant, si les moyens de payer n'introduisaient une infinité d'abus sans mesure et de maux plus grands, plus illimités que ceux qui peuvent résulter de cette contrainte, surtout quand celui qui l'impose est du même état que ceux qui sont imposés.

Au reste pour que la contribution soit répartie avec égalité il est juste que celui qui n'ayant point de terres ne peut payer la dîme sur leur produit, la paie du travail de ses bras, ainsi les corvées doivent tomber spécialement sur l'ordre des aspirants. Mais des citoyens et des patriotes doivent les conduire au travail et leur en donner l'exemple. Que tout ce qui se fait pour le bien public soit toujours honorable ! Que le magistrat même, occupé d'autres soins, montre que ceux-là ne sont pas au-dessous de lui comme ces consuls romains qui pour donner l'exemple à leurs troupes mettaient les premiers la main aux travaux du camp !

Quant aux amendes et confiscations qui font dans les républiques une quatrième sorte de recette, j'espère au moyen du présent établissement qu'elle sera nulle à peu près dans la nôtre, ainsi je ne la mets pas en ligne de compte.

Tous ces revenus publics étant en nature de choses plutôt qu'en monnaie paraissent embarrassants dans leur recouvrement, dans leur garde et dans leur emploi ; et cela est vrai en partie, mais il s'agit moins ici de l'administration la plus facile que de la plus saine, et il vaut mieux qu'elle donne un peu plus d'embarras et qu'elle engendre moins d'abus. Le meilleur système économique pour la Corse et pour une république n'est assurément pas le meilleur pour une monarchie et pour un grand État. Celui que je propose ne réussirait ni en France ni en Angleterre et ne pourrait pas même s'y établir mais il a le plus grand succès dans la Suisse où il est établi depuis des siècles et il est le seul qu'elle eût pu supporter.

On donne à ferme les recettes dans chaque juridiction; elles se font en nature ou en argent au choix des contribuables; le paiement des magistrats et officiers se fait aussi pour la plus grande partie en blé, en vin, en fourrage, en bois. De cette manière le recouvrement n'est ni embarrassant au public ni onéreux aux particuliers mais l'inconvénient que j'y vois est qu'il y a des hommes dont le métier est de gagner sur le prince et de vexer les sujets.

Il importe extrêmement de ne souffrir dans la république aucun financier par état : moins à cause de leurs gains malhonnêtes qu'à cause de leurs principes et de leurs exemples, qui trop prompts à se répandre dans la nation détruisent tous les bons sentiments par l'estime de l'abondance illicite et de ses avantages, couvrent de mépris et d'opprobre le désintéressement, la simplicité, les mœurs et toutes les vertus.

Gardons-nous d'augmenter le trésor pécuniaire aux dépens du trésor moral; c'est ce dernier qui nous met vraiment en possession des hommes et de toute leur puissance, au lieu que par l'autre on n'obtient que l'apparence des services mais on n'achète point la volonté. Il vaut mieux que l'administration du fisc soit celle d'un père de famille et perde quelque chose que de gagner davantage et être celle d'un usurier.

Laissons donc la recette en régie, dût-elle rapporter beaucoup moins. Évitons même de faire de cette régie un métier, car ce serait presque le même inconvénient que de la mettre en ferme. Ce qui rend le plus pernicieux un système de finance est l'emploi de financier. À nul prix que ce puisse être il ne faut point de publicains dans l'État. Au lieu de faire des recettes de la régie et des revenus publics un métier lucratif, il en faut faire au contraire l'épreuve du mérite et de l'intégrité des jeunes citoyens; il faut que cette régie soit pour ainsi dire le noviciat des emplois publics et le premier pas pour parvenir aux magistratures. Ce qui m'a suggéré cette idée est la comparaison de l'administration de l'Hôtel-Dieu de Paris, dont chacun connaît les déprédations et les brigandages, avec celle de l'Hôtel-Dieu de Lyon qui offre un exemple d'ordre et de désintéressement qui n'a peut-être rien d'égal sur la terre. D'où vient cette différence ? Les Lyonnais en eux-mêmes valent-ils mieux que les Parisiens ? Non. Mais à Lyon cet office d'administration est un état de passage. Il faut commencer par le bien remplir pour pouvoir devenir échevin et prévôt des marchands, au lieu qu'à Paris les administrateurs sont tels par état pour toute leur vie ; ils s'arrangent pour tirer le meilleur parti possible d'un emploi qui n'est point pour eux une épreuve mais un métier, une récompense, un état attaché pour ainsi dire à d'autres états. Il y a certaines places dont il est convenu que les revenus seront augmentés par le droit de voler les pauvres.

Et qu'on ne pense pas que ce travail demande plus d'expérience et de lumières que n'en peuvent avoir de jeunes gens, il ne demande qu'une activité à laquelle ils sont singulièrement propres, et comme ils sont d'ordinaire moins avares, moins durs dans l'exaction que les gens âgés, sensibles d'une part aux misères du pauvre et de l'autre intéressés fortement à bien remplir un emploi qui leur sert d'épreuve ils s'y conduisent précisément comme il convient à la chose.

Le receveur de chaque paroisse rendra ses comptes à la piève, celui de chaque piève à sa juridiction et celui de chaque juridiction à la chambre des comptes qui sera composée d'un certain nombre de conseillers d'État et présidée par le doge. Le trésor public consistera de cette manière pour la plus grande partie en denrées et autres productions réparties en petits magasins dans tout le royaume et pour quelque partie en argent qui sera remis dans la caisse générale après avoir prélevé les menues dépenses à faire sur les lieux.

Comme les particuliers seront toujours libres de payer leur contingent en argent ou en denrées au taux qui sera fait tous les ans dans chaque juridiction, le gouvernement ayant une fois calculé la meilleure proportion qui doit se trouver entre ces deux espèces de contribution, sitôt que cette proportion s'altérera, sera en état d'apercevoir sur-le-champ cette altération, d'en chercher la cause et d'y remédier.

C'est ici la clef de notre gouvernement politique, la seule partie qui demande de l'art, des calculs, de la méditation. C'est pourquoi la chambre des comptes qui partout ailleurs n'est qu'un tribunal très subordonné aura ici le centre des affaires, donnera le branle à toute l'administration et sera composée des premières têtes de l'État.

Quand les recouvrements en denrées passeront leur mesure et que ceux en argent n'atteindront pas à la leur ce sera un signe que l'agriculture et la population vont bien mais que l'industrie utile se néglige ; il conviendra de la ranimer un peu de peur que les particuliers, devenus aussi trop isolés, trop indépendants, trop sauvages, ne tiennent plus assez au gouvernement.

Mais ce défaut de proportion, signe infaillible de prospérité, sera toujours peu à craindre et facile à remédier. Il n'en sera pas de même du défaut contraire lequel sitôt qu'il se fait sentir est déjà de la plus grande conséquence et ne peut être trop tôt corrigé, car quand les contribuants fourniront plus d'argent que de denrées ce sera une marque assurée qu'il y a trop d'exportation chez l'étranger, que le commerce devient trop facile, que les arts lucratifs s'étendent dans l'île aux dépens de l'agriculture et conséquemment que la simplicité et toutes les vertus qui lui sont attachées commencent à dégénérer. Les abus qui produisent cette altération indiquent les remèdes qu'il y faut apporter, mais ces remèdes demandent une grande sagesse dans la manière de les administrer ; car il est ici bien plus aisé de prévenir le mal que de le détruire.

Si l'on ne fait que mettre des impôts sur les objets de luxe, fermer ses ports au commerce étranger, supprimer les manufactures, arrêter la circulation des espèces, on ne ferait que jeter le peuple dans la paresse, la misère, le découragement ; on fera disparaître l'argent sans multiplier les denrées ; on ôtera la ressource de la fortune sans rétablir celle du travail. Toucher au prix des monnaies est encore une mauvaise opération dans une république, premièrement parce que c'est alors le public qui se vole lui-même ce qui ne signifie rien du tout, en second lieu parce qu'il y a entre la quantité des signes et celle des choses une proportion qui en règle toujours de même la valeur respective et que quand le prince veut changer les signes il ne fait que changer les noms puisque alors la valeur des choses change nécessairement en même rapport. Chez les rois c'est autre chose et quand le prince hausse les monnaies il en retire l'avantage réel de voler ses créanciers : mais pour peu que cette opération se répète cet avantage se compense et s'efface par la perte du crédit public.

Établissez alors des lois somptuaires, mais rendez-les toujours plus sévères pour les premiers de l'État, relâchez-les pour les degrés inférieurs ; faites qu'il y ait de la vanité à être simple, et qu'un riche ne sache en quoi se faire honneur de son argent. Ce ne sont point là des spéculations impraticables : c'est ainsi que les Vénitiens n'accordent qu'à leurs nobles le droit de porter leur gros vilain drap noir de Padoue, pour que les meilleurs citadins tiennent à honneur d'avoir la même permission.

Quand il y a de la simplicité dans les mœurs, les lois agraires sont nécessaires, parce qu'alors le riche ne pouvant placer sa richesse en autre chose accumule ses possessions : mais ni les lois agraires ni aucunes lois ne peuvent jamais avoir d'effet rétroactif et l'on ne peut confisquer nulles terres acquises légitimement en quelque quantité qu'elles puissent être en vertu d'une loi postérieure qui défende d'en avoir tant.

Aucune loi ne peut dépouiller aucun particulier d'aucune portion de son bien. La loi peut seulement l'empêcher d'en acquérir davantage ; alors s'il enfreint la loi il mérite le châtiment et le surplus illégitimement acquis peut et doit être confisqué. Les Romains virent la nécessité des lois agraires quand il n'était plus temps de les établir, et faute de la distinction que je viens de faire ils détruisirent enfin la République par un moyen qui l'eût dû conserver : les Gracques voulurent ôter aux patriciens leurs terres ; il eût fallu les empêcher de les acquérir. Il est bien vrai que dans la suite ces mêmes patriciens en acquirent encore malgré la loi mais c'est que le mal était invétéré quand elle fut portée et qu'il n'était plus temps d'y remédier.

La crainte et l'espoir sont les deux instruments avec lesquels on gouverne les hommes ; mais au lieu d'employer l'un et l'autre indifféremment il faut en user selon leur nature. La crainte n'excite pas, elle retient ; et son usage dans les lois pénales n'est pas de porter à bien faire mais d'empêcher de faire le mal. Nous ne voyons pas même que la crainte de la misère rende les fainéants laborieux. Ainsi pour exciter parmi les hommes une véritable émulation au travail il ne faut pas le leur montrer comme un moyen d'éviter la faim mais comme un moyen d'aller au bien-être. Ainsi posons cette règle générale que nul ne doit être châtié pour s'être abstenu mais pour avoir fait.

Pour éveiller donc l'activité d'une nation il faut lui présenter de grands désirs, de grandes espérances, de grands motifs positifs d'agir. Les grands mobiles qui font agir les hommes bien examinés se réduisent à deux, la volupté et la vanité, encore si vous ôtez de la première tout ce qui appartient à l'autre vous trouverez en dernière analyse que tout se réduit à la presque seule vanité. Il est aisé de voir que tous les voluptueux de parade ne sont que vains. Leur volupté prétendue n'est qu'ostentation, elle consiste plus à la montrer ou à la décrire qu'à la goûter. Le vrai plaisir est simple et paisible, il aime le silence et le recueillement; celui qui le goûte est tout à la chose, il ne s'amuse pas à dire : j'ai du plaisir. Or la vanité est le fruit de l'opinion; elle en naît et s'en nourrit. D'où il suit que les arbitres de l'opinion d'un peuple le sont de ses actions. Il recherche les choses à proportion du prix qu'il leur donne; lui montrer ce qu'il doit estimer, c'est lui dire ce qu'il doit faire.

Ce nom de vanité n'est pas bien choisi parce qu'elle n'est qu'une des deux branches de l'amour-propre. Il faut m'expliquer. L'opinion qui met un grand prix aux objets frivoles produit la vanité; mais celle qui tombe sur des objets grands et beaux par eux-mêmes produit l'orgueil. On peut donc rendre un peuple orgueilleux ou vain selon le choix des objets sur lesquels on dirige ses jugements.

L'orgueil est plus naturel que la vanité puisqu'il consiste à s'estimer par des biens vraiment estimables; au lieu que la vanité, donnant un prix à ce qui n'en a point est l'ouvrage des préjugés lents à naître. Il faut du temps pour fasciner les yeux d'une nation. Comme il n'y a rien de plus réellement beau que l'indépendance et la puissance tout peuple qui se forme est d'abord orgueilleux. Mais, jamais peuple nouveau ne fut vain car la vanité par sa nature est individuelle; elle ne peut être l'instrument d'une aussi grande chose que de former un corps de nation.

Deux états contraires jettent les hommes dans l'engourdissement de la paresse. L'un est cette paix de l'âme qui fait qu'on est content de ce qu'on possède, l'autre est une convoitise insatiable qui fait sentir l'impossibilité de la contenter. Celui qui vit sans désirs et celui qui sait ne pouvoir obtenir ce qu'il désire restent également dans l'inaction. Il faut pour agir et qu'on aspire à quelque chose et qu'on puisse espérer d'y parvenir. Tout gouvernement qui veut jeter de l'activité parmi le peuple doit avoir pris soin de mettre à sa portée des objets capables de le tenter. Faites que le travail offre aux citoyens de grands avantages, non seulement selon votre estimation mais selon la leur, infailliblement vous les rendrez laborieux*. Entre ces avantages, non seulement les plus attrayants ne sont pas toujours les richesses, mais elles peuvent l'être moins qu'aucun autre, tant qu'elles ne servent pas de moyen pour parvenir à ceux dont on est tenté.

La voie la plus générale et la plus sûre qu'on puisse avoir pour satisfaire ses désirs quels qu'ils puissent être est la puissance. Ainsi à quelque passion qu'un homme ou qu'un peuple soit enclin, s'il en a de vives il aspire vivement à la puissance, soit comme fin s'il est orgueilleux ou vain, soit comme moyen s'il est vindicatif ou voluptueux.

* C'est alors qu'il faudra employer l'excédent à l'industrie et aux arts pour attirer de l'étranger ce qui manque à un peuple si nombreux pour sa subsistance. Alors naîtront aussi peu à peu les vices inséparables de ces établissements et qui corrompant par degrés la nation dans ses goûts et dans ses principes, altéreront et détruiront enfin le gouvernement. Ce mal est inévitable et puisqu'il faut que toutes les choses humaines finissent, il est beau qu'après une longue et vigoureuse existence un État finisse par l'excès de la population.

C'est donc dans l'économie bien entendue de la puissance civile que consiste le grand art du gouvernement non seulement pour se maintenir lui-même mais pour répandre dans tout l'État l'activité, la vie ; pour rendre le peuple actif et laborieux.

La puissance civile s'exerce de deux manières : l'une légitime par l'autorité, l'autre abusive par les richesses. Partout où les richesses dominent, la puissance et l'autorité sont ordinairement séparées, parce que les moyens d'acquérir la richesse et les moyens de parvenir à l'autorité n'étant pas les mêmes sont rarement employés par les mêmes gens. Alors la puissance apparente est dans les mains des magistrats et la puissance réelle est dans celles des riches. Dans un tel gouvernement tout marche au gré des passions des hommes, rien ne tend au but de l'institution.

Il arrive alors que l'objet de la convoitise se partage : les uns aspirent à l'autorité pour en vendre l'usage aux riches et s'enrichir eux-mêmes par ce moyen ; les autres et le plus grand nombre vont directement aux richesses, avec lesquelles ils sont sûrs d'avoir un jour la puissance en achetant soit l'autorité soit ceux qui en sont les dépositaires.

Supposez que dans un État ainsi constitué les honneurs et l'autorité d'un côté soient héréditaires, et que de l'autre les moyens d'acquérir les richesses ne soient à la portée que d'un petit nombre et dépendent du crédit, de la faveur, des amis. Il est impossible alors que tandis que quelques aventuriers iront à la fortune et de là par degrés aux emplois, un découragement universel ne gagne pas le gros de la nation et ne la jette pas dans la langueur.

CONSIDÉRATIONS SUR LE GOUVERNEMENT DE POLOGNE

ET SUR SA RÉFORMATION PROJETÉE

(Chapitres 6-9, 13)

[6.] QUESTION DES TROIS ORDRES

Je n'entends guère parler de gouvernement sans trouver qu'on remonte à des principes qui me paraissent faux ou louches. La république de Pologne[1], a-t-on souvent dit et répété, est composée de trois ordres : l'ordre équestre, le Sénat et le roi. J'aimerais mieux dire que la nation polonaise est composée de trois ordres : les nobles, qui sont tout ; les bourgeois, qui ne sont rien ; et les paysans, qui sont moins que rien[2]. Si l'on compte le Sénat pour un ordre dans l'État, pourquoi ne compte-t-on pas aussi pour tel la chambre des Nonces, qui n'est pas moins distincte et qui n'a pas moins d'autorité. Bien plus, cette division, dans le sens même qu'on la donne, est évidemment incomplète ; car il y fallait ajouter les ministres, qui ne sont ni rois, ni sénateurs, ni nonces et qui, dans la plus grande indépendance, n'en sont pas moins dépositaires de tout le pouvoir exécutif. Comment me fera-t-on jamais comprendre que la partie qui n'existe que par le tout, forme pourtant, par rapport au tout, un ordre indépendant de lui. La pairie en Angleterre, attendu qu'elle est héréditaire, forme, je l'avoue, un ordre existant par lui-même. Mais en Pologne, ôtez l'ordre équestre, il n'y a plus de Sénat, puisque nul ne peut être sénateur s'il n'est premièrement noble polonais. De même il n'y a plus de roi, puisque c'est l'ordre équestre qui le nomme, et que le roi ne peut rien sans lui : mais ôtez le Sénat et le roi, l'ordre équestre et par lui l'État et le souverain demeurent en leur entier ; et dès demain, s'il lui plaît, il aura un Sénat et un roi comme auparavant.

Mais pour n'être pas un ordre dans l'État, il ne s'ensuit pas que le Sénat n'y soit rien ; et quand il n'aurait pas en corps le dépôt des lois, ses membres, indépendamment de l'autorité du corps, ne le seraient pas moins de la puissance législative, et ce serait leur ôter le droit qu'ils tiennent de leur naissance que de les empêcher d'y voter en pleine Diète toutes les fois qu'il s'agit de faire ou de révoquer des lois ; mais ce n'est plus alors comme sénateurs qu'ils votent, c'est simplement comme citoyens. Sitôt que la puissance législative parle, tout rentre dans l'égalité ; toute autre autorité se tait devant elle, sa voix est la voix de Dieu sur la terre[3]. Le roi même, qui préside à la Diète, n'a pas alors, je le soutiens, le droit d'y voter, s'il n'est noble polonais.

On me dira sans doute ici que je prouve trop et que, si les sénateurs n'ont pas voix comme tels à la Diète, ils ne doivent pas non plus l'avoir comme citoyens, puisque les membres de l'ordre équestre n'y votent pas par eux-mêmes, mais seulement par leurs représentants, au nombre desquels les sénateurs ne sont pas. Et pourquoi voteraient-ils comme particuliers dans la Diète, puisque aucun autre noble, s'il n'est nonce, n'y peut voter ? Cette objection me paraît solide dans l'état présent des choses ; mais quand les changements projetés seront faits, elle ne le sera plus ; parce qu'alors les sénateurs eux-mêmes seront des représentants perpétuels de la nation, mais qui ne pourront agir en matière de législation qu'avec le concours de leurs collègues.

Qu'on ne dise donc pas que le concours du roi, du Sénat et de l'ordre équestre est nécessaire pour former une loi. Ce droit n'appartient qu'au seul ordre équestre, dont les sénateurs sont membres comme les nonces, mais où le Sénat en corps n'entre pour rien. Telle est ou doit être en Pologne la loi de l'État : mais la loi de la nature, cette loi sainte, imprescriptible, qui parle au cœur de l'homme et à sa raison, ne permet pas qu'on resserre ainsi l'autorité législative, et que les lois obligent quiconque n'y a pas voté personnellement comme les nonces, ou du moins par ses représentants comme le corps de la noblesse. On ne viole point impunément cette loi sacrée, et l'état de faiblesse, où une si grande nation se trouve réduite, est l'ouvrage de cette barbarie féodale qui fait retrancher du corps de l'État sa partie la plus nombreuse, et quelquefois la plus saine.

À Dieu ne plaise que je croie avoir besoin de prouver ici ce qu'un peu de bon sens et d'entrailles suffisent pour faire sentir à tout le monde ! Et d'où la Pologne prétend-elle tirer la puissance et les forces qu'elle étouffe à plaisir dans son sein ? Nobles polonais, soyez plus, soyez hommes. Alors seulement vous serez heureux et libres ; mais ne vous flattez jamais de l'être tant que vous tiendrez vos frères dans les fers.

Je sens la difficulté du projet d'affranchir vos peuples. Ce que je crains n'est pas seulement l'intérêt mal entendu, l'amour propre et les préjugés des maîtres. Cet obstacle vaincu, je craindrais les vices et la lâcheté des serfs. La liberté est un aliment de bon suc, mais de forte digestion ; il faut des estomacs bien sains pour le supporter. Je ris de ces peuples avilis qui, se laissant ameuter par des ligueurs, osent parler de liberté sans même en avoir l'idée et, le cœur plein de tous les vices des esclaves, s'imaginent que, pour être libres il suffit d'être des mutins. Fière et sainte liberté ! si ces pauvres gens pouvaient te connaître, s'ils savaient à quel prix on t'acquiert et te conserve, s'ils sentaient combien tes lois sont plus austères que n'est dur le joug des tyrans ; leurs faibles âmes, esclaves de passions qu'il faudrait étouffer, te craindraient plus cent fois que la servitude ; ils te fuiraient avec effroi comme un fardeau prêt à les écraser.

Affranchir les peuples de Pologne est une grande et belle opération, mais hardie, périlleuse, et qu'il ne faut pas tenter inconsidérément. Parmi les précautions à prendre, il en est une indispensable et qui demande du temps. C'est, avant toute chose, de rendre dignes de la liberté et capables de la supporter les serfs qu'on veut affranchir[4]. J'exposerai ci-après un des moyens qu'on peut employer pour cela. Il serait téméraire à moi d'en garantir le succès, quoique je n'en doute pas. S'il est quelque meilleur moyen, qu'on le prenne. Mais quel qu'il soit, songez que vos serfs sont des hommes comme vous, qu'ils ont en eux l'étoffe pour devenir tout ce que vous êtes : travaillez d'abord à la mettre en œuvre, et n'affranchissez leurs corps qu'après avoir affranchi leurs âmes[5]. Sans ce préliminaire, comptez que votre opération réussira mal.

[7.] MOYENS DE MAINTENIR LA CONSTITUTION

La législation de Pologne a été faite successivement de pièces et de morceaux, comme toutes celles de l'Europe. À mesure qu'on voyait un abus, on faisait une loi pour y remédier. De cette loi naissaient d'autres abus qu'il fallait corriger encore. Cette manière d'opérer n'a point de fin, et mène au plus terrible de tous les abus, qui est d'énerver toutes les lois à force de les multiplier.

L'affaiblissement de la législation s'est fait en Pologne d'une manière bien particulière, et peut-être unique. C'est qu'elle a perdu sa force sans avoir été subjuguée par la puissance exécutive[6]. En ce moment encore la puissance législative conserve toute son autorité : elle est dans l'inaction, mais sans rien voir au-dessus d'elle. La Diète est aussi souveraine qu'elle l'était lors de son établissement. Cependant elle est sans force ; rien ne la domine, mais rien ne lui obéit. Cet état est remarquable et mérite réflexion.

Qu'est-ce qui a conservé jusqu'ici l'autorité législative ? C'est la présence continuelle du législateur. C'est la fréquence des Diètes, c'est le fréquent renouvellement des nonces, qui ont maintenu la République. L'Angleterre, qui jouit du premier de ces avantages, a perdu sa liberté pour avoir négligé l'autre. Le même Parlement dure si longtemps, que la Cour, qui s'épuiserait à l'acheter tous les ans, trouve son compte à l'acheter pour sept, et n'y manque pas. Première leçon pour vous.

Un second moyen, par lequel la puissance législative s'est conservée en Pologne, est premièrement le partage de la puissance exécutive, qui a empêché ses dépositaires d'agir de concert pour l'opprimer, et en second lieu le passage fréquent de cette même puissance exécutive par différentes mains : ce qui a empêché tout système suivi d'usurpation. Chaque roi faisait dans le cours de son règne quelques pas vers la puissance arbitraire. Mais l'élection de son successeur forçait celui-ci de rétrograder au lieu de poursuivre ; et les rois au commencement de chaque règne étaient contraints par les *pacta conventa*[7] de partir tous du même point. De sorte que, malgré la pente habituelle vers le despotisme, il n'y avait aucun progrès réel.

Il en était de même des ministres et grands officiers. Tous indépendants et du Sénat et les uns des autres avaient dans leurs départements respectifs, une autorité sans bornes ; mais outre que ces places se balançaient mutuellement, en ne se perpétuant pas dans les mêmes familles elles n'y portaient aucune force absolue ; et tout le pouvoir, même usurpé, retournait toujours à sa source. Il n'en eût pas été de même si toute la puissance exécutive eût été, soit dans un seul corps comme le Sénat, soit dans une famille par l'hérédité de la couronne. Cette famille ou ce corps auraient probablement opprimé tôt ou tard la puissance législative, et par là mis les Polonais sous le joug que portent toutes les nations, et dont eux seuls sont encore exempts ; car je ne compte déjà plus la Suède. Deuxième leçon.

Voilà l'avantage ; il est grand sans doute, mais voici l'inconvénient, qui n'est guère moindre. La puissance exécutive partagée entre plusieurs individus manque d'harmonie entre ses parties, et cause un tiraillement continuel incompatible avec le bon ordre. Chaque dépositaire d'une partie de cette puissance se met, en vertu de cette partie, à tous égards au-dessus des magistrats et des lois. Il reconnaît à la vérité l'autorité de la Diète ; mais ne reconnaissant que celle-là, quand la Diète est dissoute il n'en reconnaît plus du tout ; il méprise les tribunaux et brave leurs jugements. Ce sont autant de petits despotes qui, sans usurper précisément l'autorité souveraine, ne laissent pas d'opprimer en détail les citoyens, et donnent l'exemple funeste et trop suivi de violer sans scrupule et sans crainte les droits et la liberté des particuliers.

Je crois que voilà la première et principale cause de l'anarchie qui règne dans l'État. Pour ôter cette cause, je ne vois qu'un moyen. Ce n'est pas d'armer les tribunaux particuliers de la force publique contre ces petits tyrans ; car cette force, tantôt mal administrée et tantôt surmontée par une force supérieure pourrait exciter des troubles et des désordres capables d'aller par degrés jusqu'aux guerres civiles : mais c'est d'armer de toute la force exécutive un corps respectable et permanent, tel que le Sénat, capable par sa consistance et par son autorité, de contenir dans leur devoir les magnats tentés de s'en écarter. Ce moyen me paraît efficace, et le serait certainement ; mais le danger en serait terrible et très difficile à éviter. Car comme on peut voir dans le *Contrat social*[8], tout corps dépositaire de la puissance exécutive tend fortement et continuellement à subjuguer la puissance législative, et y parvient tôt ou tard.

Pour parer à cet inconvénient, on vous propose de partager le Sénat en plusieurs conseils ou départements présidés chacun par le ministre chargé de ce département lequel ministre ainsi que les membres de chaque Conseil changerait au bout d'un temps fixé et roulerait avec ceux des autres départements. Cette idée peut être bonne : c'était celle de l'abbé de Saint-Pierre, et il l'a bien développée dans sa *Polysynodie.* La puissance exécutive ainsi divisée et passagère sera plus subordonnée à la législative, et les diverses parties de l'administration seront plus approfondies et mieux traitées séparément. Ne comptez pourtant pas trop sur ce moyen : si elles sont toujours séparées, elles manqueront de concert, et bientôt, se contrecarrant mutuellement, elles useront presque toutes leurs forces les unes contre les autres, jusqu'à ce qu'une d'entre elles ait pris l'ascendant et les domine toutes : ou bien si elles s'accordent et se concertent, elles ne feront réellement qu'un même corps et n'auront qu'un même esprit, comme les chambres d'un parlement ; et de toutes manières je tiens pour impossible que l'indépendance et l'équilibre se maintiennent si bien entre elles, qu'il n'en résulte pas toujours un centre ou foyer d'administration où toutes les forces particulières se réuniront toujours pour opprimer le souverain. Dans presque toutes nos républiques les Conseils sont ainsi distribués en départements qui dans leur origine étaient indépendants les uns des autres, et qui bientôt ont cessé de l'être.

L'invention de cette division par chambres ou départements est moderne. Les anciens qui savaient mieux que nous comment se maintient la liberté ne connurent point cet expédient. Le Sénat de Rome gouvernait la moitié du monde connu, et n'avait pas même l'idée de ces partages. Ce Sénat, cependant, ne parvint jamais à opprimer la puissance législative, quoique les sénateurs fussent à vie. Mais les lois avaient des censeurs, le peuple avait des tribuns, et le Sénat n'élisait pas les consuls.

Pour que l'administration soit forte, bonne et marche bien à son but, toute la puissance exécutive doit être dans les mêmes mains : mais il ne suffit pas que ces mains changent ; il faut qu'elles n'agissent, s'il est possible, que sous les yeux du législateur, et que ce soit lui qui les guide. Voilà le vrai secret pour qu'elles n'usurpent pas son autorité.

Tant que les États s'assembleront et que les nonces changeront fréquemment, il sera difficile que le Sénat ou le roi oppriment ou usurpent l'autorité législative. Il est remarquable que jusqu'ici les rois n'aient pas tenté de rendre les Diètes plus rares, quoiqu'ils ne fussent pas forcés, comme ceux d'Angleterre, à les assembler fréquemment sous peine de manquer d'argent. Il faut ou que les choses se soient toujours trouvées dans un état de crise qui ait rendu l'autorité royale insuffisante pour y pourvoir, ou que les rois se soient assurés par leurs brigues dans les Diétines d'avoir toujours la pluralité des nonces à leur disposition, ou qu'à la faveur du *liberum veto*[9] ils aient été sûrs d'arrêter toujours les délibérations qui pouvaient leur déplaire et de dissoudre les Diètes à leur volonté. Quand tous ces motifs ne subsisteront plus, on doit s'attendre que le roi, ou le Sénat, ou tous les deux ensemble, feront de grands efforts pour se délivrer des Diètes et les rendre aussi rares qu'il se pourra. Voilà ce qu'il faut surtout prévenir et empêcher. Le moyen proposé est le seul, il est simple et ne peut manquer d'être efficace. Il est bien singulier qu'avant le *Contrat social*[10], où je le donne, personne ne s'en fût avisé.

Un des plus grands inconvénients des grands États, celui de tous qui y rend la liberté le plus difficile à conserver, est que la puissance législative ne peut s'y montrer elle-même, et ne peut agir que par députation. Cela a son mal et son bien, mais le mal l'emporte. Le législateur[11] en corps est impossible à corrompre, mais facile à tromper. Ses représentants sont difficilement trompés, mais aisément corrompus, et il arrive rarement qu'ils ne le soient pas. Vous avez sous les yeux l'exemple du Parlement d'Angleterre, et par le *liberum veto* celui de votre propre nation. Or on peut éclairer celui qui s'abuse, mais comment retenir celui qui se vend. Sans être instruit des affaires de Pologne, je parierais tout au monde qu'il y a plus de lumières dans la Diète et plus de vertu dans les Diétines.

Je vois deux moyens de prévenir ce mal terrible de la corruption, qui de l'organe de la liberté fait l'instrument de la servitude.

Le premier est, comme je l'ai déjà dit, la fréquence des Diètes qui, changeant souvent les représentants, rend leur séduction plus coûteuse et plus difficile. Sur ce point votre constitution vaut mieux que celle de la Grande-Bretagne, et quand on aura ôté ou modifié le *liberum veto*, je n'y vois aucun autre changement à faire, si ce n'est d'ajouter quelques difficultés à l'envoi des mêmes nonces à deux Diètes consécutives, et d'empêcher qu'ils ne soient élus un grand nombre de fois. Je reviendrai ci-après sur cet article.

Le second moyen est d'assujettir les représentants à suivre exactement leurs instructions et à rendre un compte sévère à leurs constituants de leur conduite à la Diète. Là-dessus je ne puis qu'admirer la négligence, l'incurie, et j'ose dire la stupidité de la nation anglaise, qui, après avoir armé ses députés de la suprême puissance, n'y ajoute aucun frein pour régler l'usage qu'ils en pourront faire pendant sept ans entiers que dure leur commission.

Je vois que les Polonais ne sentent pas assez l'importance de leurs Diétines, ni tout ce qu'ils leur doivent, ni tout ce qu'ils peuvent en obtenir en étendant leur autorité et leur donnant une forme plus régulière. Pour moi, je suis convaincu que si les Confédérations ont sauvé la patrie, ce sont les Diétines qui l'ont conservée, et que c'est là qu'est le vrai palladium de la liberté.

Les instructions des nonces doivent être dressées avec grand soin, tant sur les articles annoncés dans les universaux[12], que sur les autres besoins présents de l'État ou de la province, et cela par une commission présidée, si l'on veut, par le maréchal de la Diétine, mais composée au reste de membres choisis à la pluralité des voix ; et la noblesse ne doit point se séparer que ces instructions n'aient été lues, discutées et consenties en pleine assemblée. Outre l'original de ces instructions, remis aux nonces avec leurs pouvoirs, il en doit rester un double signé d'eux dans les registres de la Diétine. C'est sur ces instructions qu'ils doivent à leur retour rendre compte de leur conduite aux Diétines de relation qu'il faut absolument rétablir, et c'est sur ce compte rendu qu'ils doivent être ou exclus de toute autre nonciature subséquente, ou déclarés derechef admissibles, quand ils auront suivi leurs instructions à la satisfaction de leurs constituants. Cet examen est de la dernière importance. On n'y saurait donner trop d'attention ni en marquer l'effet avec trop de soin. Il faut qu'à chaque mot que le nonce dit à la Diète, à chaque démarche qu'il fait, il se voie d'avance sous les yeux de ses constituants, et qu'il sente l'influence qu'aura leur jugement tant sur ses projets d'avancement que sur l'estime de ses compatriotes, indispensable pour leur exécution : car enfin ce n'est pas pour y dire leur sentiment particulier, mais pour y déclarer les volontés de la nation qu'elle envoie des nonces à la Diète. Ce frein est absolument nécessaire pour les contenir dans leur devoir et prévenir toute corruption, de quelque part qu'elle vienne. Quoi qu'on en puisse dire, je ne vois aucun inconvénient à cette gêne, puisque la chambre des nonces n'ayant ou ne devant avoir aucune part au détail de l'administration, ne peut jamais avoir à traiter aucune matière imprévue : d'ailleurs pourvu qu'un nonce ne fasse rien de contraire à l'expresse volonté de ses constituants, ils ne lui feraient pas un crime d'avoir opiné en bon citoyen sur une matière qu'ils n'auraient pas prévue, et sur laquelle ils n'auraient rien déterminé. J'ajoute enfin que, quand il y aurait en effet quelque inconvénient à tenir ainsi les nonces asservis à leurs instructions, il n'y aurait point encore à balancer vis-à-vis l'avantage immense que la loi ne soit jamais que l'expression réelle des volontés de la nation.

Mais aussi, ces précautions prises, il ne doit jamais y avoir conflit de juridiction entre la Diète et les Diétines, et quand une loi a été portée en pleine Diète je n'accorde pas même à celles-ci droit de protestation. Qu'elles punissent leurs nonces, que s'il le faut elles leur fassent même couper la tête quand ils ont prévariqué : mais qu'elles obéissent pleinement, toujours, sans exception, sans protestation, qu'elles portent comme il est juste la peine de leur mauvais choix ; sauf à faire à la prochaine Diète, si elles le jugent à propos, des représentations aussi vives qu'il leur plaira.

Les Diètes étant fréquentes ont moins besoin d'être longues, et six semaines de durée me paraissent bien suffisantes pour les besoins ordinaires de l'État. Mais il est contradictoire que l'autorité souveraine se donne des entraves à elle-même, surtout quand elle est immédiatement entre les mains de la nation. Que cette durée des Diètes ordinaires continue d'être fixée à six semaines, à la bonne heure ; mais il dépendra toujours de l'assemblée de prolonger ce terme par une délibération expresse lorsque les affaires le demanderont. Car enfin, si la Diète qui par sa nature est au-dessus de la loi dit, *Je veux rester*, qui est-ce qui lui dira, *Je ne veux pas que tu restes.* Il n'y a que le seul cas qu'une Diète voulût durer plus de deux ans, qu'elle ne le pourrait pas : ses pouvoirs alors finiraient et ceux d'une autre Diète commenceraient avec la troisième année. La Diète, qui peut tout, peut sans contredit prescrire un plus long intervalle entre les Diètes : mais cette nouvelle loi ne pourrait regarder que les Diètes subséquentes, et celle qui la porte n'en peut profiter. Les principes dont ces règles se déduisent sont établis dans le *Contrat social*[13].

À l'égard des Diètes extraordinaires, le bon ordre exige en effet qu'elles soient rares, et convoquées uniquement pour d'urgentes nécessités. Quand le roi les juge telles, il doit je l'avoue en être cru : mais ces nécessités pourraient exister et qu'il n'en convînt pas ; faut-il alors que le Sénat en juge ? Dans un État libre on doit prévoir tout ce qui peut attaquer la liberté. Si les Confédérations restent, elles peuvent en certains cas suppléer les Diètes extraordinaires : mais si vous abolissez les Confédérations, il faut un règlement pour ces Diètes nécessairement.

Il me paraît impossible que la loi puisse fixer raisonnablement la durée des Diètes extraordinaires, puisqu'elle dépend absolument de la nature des affaires qui les font convoquer. Pour l'ordinaire la célérité y est nécessaire ; mais cette célérité étant relative aux matières à traiter qui ne sont pas dans l'ordre des affaires courantes, on ne peut rien statuer là-dessus d'avance, et l'on pourrait se trouver en tel état qu'il importerait que la Diète restât assemblée jusqu'à ce que cet état eût changé, ou que le temps des Diètes ordinaires fît tomber les pouvoirs de celle-là.

Pour ménager le temps si précieux dans les Diètes, il faudrait tâcher d'ôter de ces assemblées les vaines discussions qui ne servent qu'à le faire perdre. Sans doute il y faut, non seulement de la règle et de l'ordre, mais du cérémonial et de la majesté. Je voudrais même qu'on donnât un soin particulier à cet article, et qu'on sentît, par exemple, la barbarie et l'horrible indécence de voir l'appareil des armes profaner le sanctuaire des lois. Polonais, êtes-vous plus guerriers que n'étaient les Romains ? et jamais dans les plus grands troubles de leur république, l'aspect d'un glaive ne souilla les comices ni le Sénat. Mais je voudrais aussi qu'en s'attachant aux choses importantes et nécessaires on évitât tout ce qui peut se faire ailleurs également bien. Le Rugi, par exemple, c'est-à-dire l'examen de la légitimité des nonces, est un temps perdu dans la Diète : non que cet examen ne soit en lui-même une chose importante, mais parce qu'il peut se faire aussi bien et mieux dans le lieu même où ils ont été élus, où ils sont le plus connus et où ils ont tous leurs concurrents. C'est dans leur palatinat même, c'est dans la Diétine qui les député que la validité de leur élection peut être mieux constatée et en moins de temps, comme cela se pratique pour les commissaires de Radom et les députés au Tribunal. Cela fait, la Diète doit les admettre sans discussion sur le laudum dont ils sont porteurs, et cela non seulement pour prévenir les obstacles qui peuvent retarder l'élection du maréchal, mais surtout les intrigues par lesquelles le Sénat ou le roi pourraient gêner les élections et chicaner les sujets qui leur seraient désagréables. Ce qui vient de se passer à Londres est une leçon pour les Polonais. Je sais bien que ce Wilkes[14] n'est qu'un brouillon; mais par l'exemple de sa réjection la planche est faite, et désormais on n'admettra plus dans la chambre des Communes que des sujets qui conviennent à la Cour.

Il faudrait commencer par donner plus d'attention au choix des membres qui ont voix dans les Diétines. On discernerait par là plus aisément ceux qui sont éligibles pour la nonciature. Le livre d'or de Venise est un modèle à suivre à cause des facilités qu'il donne. Il serait commode et très aisé de tenir dans chaque grod[15] un registre exact de tous les nobles qui auraient aux conditions requises entrée et voix aux Diétines. On les inscrirait dans le registre de leur district à mesure qu'ils atteindraient l'âge requis par les lois, et l'on rayerait ceux qui devraient en être exclus dès qu'ils tomberaient dans ce cas, en marquant la raison de leur exclusion. Par ces registres auxquels il faudrait donner une forme bien authentique, on distinguerait aisément, tant les membres légitimes des Diétines, que les sujets éligibles pour la nonciature, et la longueur des discussions serait fort abrégée sur cet article.

Une meilleure police dans les Diètes et Diétines serait assurément une chose fort utile ; mais, je ne le redirai jamais trop, il ne faut pas vouloir à la fois deux choses contradictoires. La police est bonne, mais la liberté vaut mieux, et plus vous gênerez la liberté par des formes, plus ces formes fourniront de moyens à l'usurpation. Tous ceux dont vous userez pour empêcher la licence dans l'ordre législatif, quoique bons en eux-mêmes, seront tôt ou tard employés pour l'opprimer. C'est un grand mal que les longues et vaines harangues qui font perdre un temps si précieux, mais c'en est un bien plus grand qu'un bon citoyen n'ose parler quand il a des choses utiles à dire. Dès qu'il n'y aura dans les Diètes que certaines bouches qui s'ouvrent, et qu'il leur sera défendu de tout dire, elles ne diront plus que ce qui peut plaire aux puissants.

Après les changements indispensables dans la nomination des emplois et dans la distribution des grâces, il y aura vraisemblablement moins de vaines harangues et moins de flagorneries adressées au roi sous cette forme. On pourrait cependant pour élaguer un peu les tortillages et les amphigouris obliger tout harangueur à énoncer au commencement de son discours la proposition qu'il veut faire, et, après avoir déduit ses raisons, de donner ses conclusions sommaires, comme font les gens du roi dans les tribunaux. Si cela n'abrégeait pas les discours, cela contiendrait du moins ceux qui ne veulent parler que pour ne rien dire, et faire consumer le temps à ne rien faire.

Je ne sais pas bien quelle est la forme établie dans les Diètes pour donner la sanction aux lois ; mais je sais que pour des raisons dites ci-devant, cette forme ne doit pas être la même que dans le Parlement de la Grande-Bretagne ; que le Sénat de Pologne doit avoir l'autorité d'administration, non de législation[16], que dans toute cause législative, les sénateurs doivent voter seulement comme membres de la Diète, non comme membres du Sénat, et que les voix doivent être comptées par tête également dans les deux chambres. Peut-être l'usage du *liberum veto* a-t-il empêché de faire cette distinction, mais elle sera très nécessaire quand le *liberum veto* sera ôté, et cela d'autant plus que ce sera un avantage immense de moins dans la chambre des Nonces, car je ne suppose pas que les sénateurs, bien moins les ministres, aient jamais eu part à ce droit. Le *veto* des nonces polonais représente celui des tribuns du peuple à Rome. Or ils n'exerçaient pas ce droit comme citoyens, mais comme représentants du peuple romain. La perte du *liberum veto* n'est donc que pour la chambre des Nonces, et le corps du Sénat n'y perdant rien y gagne par conséquent.

Ceci posé, je vois un défaut à corriger dans la Diète ; c'est que le nombre des sénateurs égalant presque celui des nonces, le Sénat a une trop grande influence dans les délibérations, et peut aisément, par son crédit dans l'ordre équestre, gagner le petit nombre de voix dont il a besoin pour être toujours prépondérant.

Je dis que c'est un défaut ; parce que le Sénat, étant un corps particulier dans l'État a nécessairement des intérêts de corps différents de ceux de la nation, et qui même à certains égards y peuvent être contraires. Or la loi, qui n'est que l'expression de la volonté générale, est bien le résultat de tous les intérêts particuliers combinés et balancés par leur multitude. Mais les intérêts de corps faisant un poids trop considérable rompraient l'équilibre et ne doivent pas y entrer collectivement. Chaque individu doit avoir sa voix, nul corps quel qu'il soit n'en doit avoir une[17]. Or si le Sénat avait trop de poids dans la Diète, non seulement il y porterait son intérêt, mais il le rendrait prépondérant.

Un remède naturel à ce défaut se présente de lui-même ; c'est d'augmenter le nombre des nonces ; mais je craindrais que cela ne fît trop de mouvement dans l'État et n'approchât trop du tumulte démocratique. S'il fallait absolument changer la proportion, au lieu d'augmenter le nombre des nonces, j'aimerais mieux diminuer le nombre des sénateurs. Et dans le fond je ne vois pas trop pourquoi, y ayant déjà un palatin à la tête de chaque province, il y faut encore de grands castellans. Mais ne perdons jamais de vue l'importante maxime de ne rien changer sans nécessité, ni pour retrancher ni pour ajouter.

Il vaut mieux à mon avis avoir un Conseil moins nombreux et laisser plus de liberté à ceux qui le composent, que d'en augmenter le nombre et de gêner la liberté dans les délibérations, comme on est toujours forcé de faire quand ce nombre devient trop grand : à quoi j'ajouterai, s'il est permis de prévoir le bien ainsi que le mal, qu'il faut éviter de rendre la Diète aussi nombreuse qu'elle peut l'être pour ne pas s'ôter le moyen d'y admettre un jour sans confusion de nouveaux députés, si jamais on en vient à l'anoblissement des villes et à l'affranchissement des serfs, comme il est à désirer pour la force et le bonheur de la nation.

Cherchons donc un moyen de remédier à ce défaut, d'une autre manière et avec le moins de changement qu'il se pourra.

Tous les sénateurs sont nommés par le roi, et conséquemment sont ses créatures. De plus, ils sont à vie, et à ce titre ils forment un corps indépendant et du roi et de l'ordre équestre qui comme je l'ai dit a son intérêt à part et doit tendre à l'usurpation. Et l'on ne doit pas ici m'accuser de contradiction parce que j'admets le Sénat comme un corps distinct dans la République, quoique je ne l'admette pas comme un ordre composant de la République ; car cela est fort différent.

Premièrement, il faut ôter au roi la nomination du Sénat, non pas tant à cause du pouvoir qu'il conserve par là sur les sénateurs et qui peut n'être pas grand, que par celui qu'il a sur tous ceux qui aspirent à l'être, et par eux sur le corps entier de la nation. Outre l'effet de ce changement dans la constitution, il en résultera l'avantage inestimable d'amortir, parmi la noblesse l'esprit courtisan, et d'y substituer l'esprit patriotique. Je ne vois aucun inconvénient que les sénateurs soient nommés par la Diète, et j'y vois de grands biens trop clairs pour avoir besoin d'être détaillés. Cette nomination peut se faire tout d'un coup dans la Diète, ou premièrement dans les Diétines par la présentation d'un certain nombre de sujets pour chaque place vacante dans leurs palatinats respectifs. Entre ces élus la Diète ferait son choix, ou bien elle en élirait un moindre nombre parmi lesquels on pourrait laisser encore au roi le droit de choisir. Mais pour aller tout d'un coup au plus simple, pourquoi chaque palatin ne serait-il pas élu définitivement dans la Diétine de sa province ? Quel inconvénient a-t-on vu naître de cette élection pour les palatins de Polock, de Witebsk, et pour le staroste[18] de Samogitie, et quel mal y aurait-il que le privilège de ces trois provinces devînt un droit commun pour toutes ? Ne perdons pas de vue l'importance dont il est pour la Pologne de tourner sa constitution vers la forme fédérative, pour écarter autant qu'il est possible les maux attachés à la grandeur ou plutôt à l'étendue de l'État.

En second lieu, si vous faites que les sénateurs ne soient plus à vie vous affaiblirez considérablement l'intérêt de corps qui tend à l'usurpation. Mais cette opération a ses difficultés : premièrement, parce qu'il est dur à des hommes accoutumés à manier les affaires publiques de se voir réduits tout d'un coup à l'état privé sans avoir démérité ; secondement, parce que les places de sénateurs sont unies à des titres de palatins et de castellans et à l'autorité locale qui y est attachée, et qu'il résulterait du désordre et des mécontentements du passage perpétuel de ces titres et de cette autorité d'un individu à un autre. Enfin cette amovibilité ne peut pas s'étendre aux évêques, et ne doit peut-être pas s'étendre aux ministres, dont les places exigeant des talents particuliers ne sont pas toujours faciles à bien remplir. Si les évêques seuls étaient à vie, l'autorité du clergé, déjà trop grande, augmenterait considérablement, et il est important que cette autorité soit balancée par des sénateurs qui soient à vie ainsi que les évêques, et qui ne craignent pas plus qu'eux d'être déplacés.

Voici ce que j'imaginerais pour remédier à ces divers inconvénients. Je voudrais que les places de sénateurs du premier rang continuassent d'être à vie. Cela ferait, en y comprenant outre les évêques et les palatins tous les castellans du premier rang, quatre-vingt-neuf sénateurs inamovibles.

Quant aux castellans du second rang, je les voudrais tous à temps, soit pour deux ans, en faisant à chaque Diète une nouvelle élection, soit pour plus longtemps s'il était jugé à propos ; mais toujours sortant de place à chaque terme, sauf à élire de nouveau ceux que la Diète voudrait continuer, ce que je permettrais un certain nombre de fois seulement selon le projet qu'on trouvera ci-après.

L'obstacle des titres serait faible, parce que ces titres ne donnant presque d'autre fonction que de siéger au Sénat pourraient être supprimés sans inconvénient, et qu'au lieu du titre de castellans à bancs, ils pourraient porter simplement celui de sénateurs députés. Comme par la réforme, le Sénat revêtu de la puissance exécutive, serait perpétuellement assemblé dans un certain nombre de ses membres, un nombre proportionné de sénateurs députés seraient de même tenus d'y assister toujours à tour de rôle. Mais il ne s'agit pas ici de ces sortes de détails.

Par ce changement à peine sensible, ces castellans ou sénateurs députés deviendraient réellement autant de représentants de la Diète qui feraient contrepoids au corps du Sénat et renforceraient l'ordre équestre dans les assemblées de la nation ; en sorte que les sénateurs à vie quoique devenus plus puissants, tant par l'abolition du *veto* que par la diminution de la puissance royale et de celle des ministres fondue en partie dans leurs corps, n'y pourraient pourtant faire dominer l'esprit de ce corps, et le Sénat, ainsi mi-parti de membres à temps et de membres à vie, serait aussi bien constitué qu'il est possible pour faire un pouvoir intermédiaire entre la chambre des Nonces et le roi, ayant à la fois assez de consistance pour régler l'administration et assez de dépendance pour être soumis aux lois. Cette opération me paraît bonne, parce qu'elle est simple et cependant d'un grand effet.

On propose pour modérer les abus du *veto*, de ne plus compter les voix par tête de nonce mais de les compter par palatinats. On ne saurait trop réfléchir sur ce changement avant que de l'adopter, quoiqu'il ait ses avantages et qu'il soit favorable à la forme fédérative. Les voix prises par masse et collectivement vont toujours moins directement à l'intérêt commun que prises ségrégativement par individu. Il arrivera très souvent que parmi les nonces d'un palatinat un d'entre eux, dans leurs délibérations particulières, prendra l'ascendant sur les autres, et déterminera pour son avis la pluralité, qu'il n'aurait pas si chaque voix demeurait indépendante. Ainsi les corrupteurs auront moins à faire et sauront mieux à qui s'adresser ; de plus, il vaut mieux que chaque nonce ait à répondre pour lui seul à sa Diétine, afin que nul ne s'excuse sur les autres, que l'innocent et le coupable ne soient pas confondus, et que la justice distributive soit mieux observée. Il se présente bien des raisons contre cette forme qui relâcherait beaucoup le lien commun, et pourrait à chaque Diète exposer l'État à se diviser. En rendant les nonces plus dépendants de leurs instructions et de leurs constituants on gagne à peu près le même avantage sans aucun inconvénient. Ceci suppose il est vrai que les suffrages ne se donnent point par scrutin, mais à haute voix, afin que la conduite et l'opinion de chaque nonce à la Diète soient connues, et qu'il en réponde en son propre et privé nom. Mais cette matière des suffrages étant une de celles que j'ai discutées avec le plus de soin dans le *Contrat social*[19], il est superflu de me répéter ici.

Quant aux élections, on trouvera peut-être d'abord quelque embarras à nommer à la fois dans chaque Diète tant de sénateurs députés et en général aux élections d'un grand nombre sur un plus grand nombre qui reviendront quelquefois dans le projet que j'ai à proposer : mais en recourant pour cet article au scrutin l'on ôterait aisément cet embarras au moyen de cartons imprimés et numérotés qu'on distribuerait aux électeurs la veille de l'élection, et qui contiendraient les noms de tous les candidats entre lesquels cette élection doit être faite. Le lendemain les électeurs viendraient à la file rapporter dans une corbeille tous leurs cartons, après avoir marqué chacun dans le sien ceux qu'il élit ou ceux qu'il exclut selon l'avis qui serait en tête des cartons. Le déchiffrement de ces mêmes cartons se ferait tout de suite en présence de l'assemblée par le secrétaire de la Diète assisté de deux autres secrétaires *ad actum*[20] nommés sur-le-champ par le maréchal dans le nombre des nonces présents. Par cette méthode l'opération deviendrait si courte et si simple que sans dispute et sans bruit tout le Sénat se remplirait aisément dans une séance. Il est vrai qu'il faudrait encore une règle pour déterminer la liste des candidats ; mais cet article aura sa place et ne sera pas oublié.

Reste à parler du roi, qui préside à la Diète, et qui doit être par sa place le suprême administrateur des lois.

[8.] DU ROI

C'est un grand mal que le chef d'une nation soit l'ennemi-né de la liberté dont il devrait être le défenseur. Ce mal, à mon avis, n'est pas tellement inhérent à cette place qu'on ne pût l'en détacher, ou du moins l'amoindrir considérablement. Il n'y a point de tentation sans espoir. Rendez l'usurpation impossible à vos rois, vous leur en ôterez la fantaisie ; et ils mettront à vous bien gouverner et à vous défendre tous les efforts qu'ils font maintenant pour vous asservir. Les instituteurs[21] de la Pologne comme l'a remarqué M. le comte Wielhorski, ont bien songé à ôter aux rois les moyens de nuire mais non pas celui de corrompre, et les grâces dont ils sont les distributeurs leur donnent abondamment ce moyen. La difficulté est qu'en leur ôtant cette distribution l'on paraît leur tout ôter : c'est pourtant ce qu'il ne faut pas faire ; car autant vaudrait n'avoir point de roi, et je crois impossible à un aussi grand État que la Pologne de s'en passer; c'est-à-dire d'un chef suprême qui soit à vie. Or à moins que le chef d'une nation ne soit tout à fait nul, et par conséquent inutile, il faut bien qu'il puisse faire quelque chose, et si peu qu'il fasse[22], il faut nécessairement que ce soit du bien ou du mal.

Maintenant tout le Sénat est à la nomination du roi : c'est trop. S'il n'a aucune part à cette nomination, ce n'est pas assez. Quoique la pairie en Angleterre soit aussi à la nomination du roi, elle en est bien moins dépendante, parce que cette pairie une fois donnée est héréditaire, au lieu que les évêchés, palatinats et castellanies n'étant qu'à vie retournent à la mort de chaque titulaire à la nomination du roi.

J'ai dit comment il me paraît que cette nomination devrait se faire, savoir les palatins et grands castellans à vie par leurs Diétines respectives; les castellans du second rang à temps et par la Diète. À l'égard des évêques il me paraît difficile, à moins qu'on ne les fasse élire par leurs chapitres, d'en ôter la nomination au roi, et je crois qu'on peut la lui laisser, excepté toutefois celle de l'archevêque de Gnesne qui appartient naturellement à la Diète, à moins qu'on n'en sépare la primatie, dont elle seule doit disposer. Quant aux ministres, surtout les grands généraux et grands trésoriers, quoique leur puissance qui fait contrepoids à celle du roi doive être diminuée en proportion de la sienne, il ne me paraît pas prudent de laisser au roi le droit de remplir ces places par ses créatures, et je voudrais au moins qu'il n'eût que le choix sur un petit nombre de sujets présentés par la Diète. Je conviens que, ne pouvant plus ôter ces places après les avoir données, il ne peut plus compter absolument sur ceux qui les remplissent : mais c'est assez du pouvoir qu'elles lui donnent sur les aspirants, sinon pour le mettre en état de changer la face du gouvernement du moins pour lui en laisser l'espérance, et c'est surtout cette espérance qu'il importe de lui ôter à tout prix.

Pour le grand chancelier, il doit ce me semble, être de nomination royale. Les rois sont les juges-nés de leurs peuples ; c'est pour cette fonction quoiqu'ils l'aient tous abandonnée, qu'ils ont été établis : elle ne peut leur être ôtée ; et quand ils ne veulent pas la remplir eux-mêmes, la nomination de leurs substituts en cette partie est de leur droit, parce que c'est toujours à eux de répondre des jugements qui se rendent en leur nom. La nation peut, il est vrai, leur donner des assesseurs, et le doit lorsqu'ils ne jugent pas eux-mêmes : ainsi le tribunal de la couronne où préside non le roi, mais le grand chancelier est sous l'inspection de la nation, et c'est avec raison que les Diétines en nomment les autres membres. Si le roi jugeait en personne, j'estime qu'il aurait le droit de juger seul. En tout état de cause son intérêt serait toujours d'être juste, et jamais des jugements iniques ne furent une bonne voie pour parvenir à l'usurpation.

À l'égard des autres dignités, tant de la couronne que des palatinats, qui ne sont que des titres honorifiques et donnent plus d'éclat que de crédit, on ne peut mieux faire que de lui en laisser la pleine disposition : qu'il puisse honorer le mérite et flatter la vanité, mais qu'il ne puisse conférer la puissance.

La majesté du trône doit être entretenue avec splendeur, mais il importe que de toute la dépense nécessaire à cet effet on en laisse faire au roi le moins qu'il est possible. Il serait à désirer que tous les officiers du roi fussent aux gages de la République et non pas aux siens, et qu'on réduisît en même rapport tous les revenus royaux, afin de diminuer autant qu'il se peut le maniement des deniers par les mains du roi.

On a proposé de rendre la couronne héréditaire. Assurez-vous qu'au moment que cette loi sera portée la Pologne peut dire adieu pour jamais à sa liberté[23]. On pense y pourvoir suffisamment en bornant la puissance royale. On ne voit pas que ces bornes posées par les lois seront franchies à trait de temps par des usurpations graduelles, et qu'un système adopté et suivi sans interruption par une famille royale doit l'emporter à la longue sur une législation qui par sa nature tend sans cesse au relâchement. Si le roi ne peut corrompre les grands par des grâces, il peut toujours les corrompre par des promesses dont ses successeurs sont garants, et comme les plans formés par la famille royale se perpétuent avec elle on prendra bien plus de confiance en ses engagements, et l'on comptera bien plus sur leur accomplissement, que quand la couronne élective montre la fin des projets du monarque avec celle de sa vie. La Pologne est libre parce que chaque règne est précédé d'un intervalle où la nation rentrée dans tous ses droits et reprenant une vigueur nouvelle coupe le progrès des abus et des usurpations, où la législation se remonte et reprend son premier ressort. Que deviendront les *pacta conventa*, l'égide de la Pologne, quand une famille établie sur le trône à perpétuité le remplira sans intervalle, et ne laissera à la nation, entre la mort du père et le couronnement du fils qu'une vaine ombre de liberté sans effet, qu'anéantira bientôt la simagrée du serment fait par tous les rois à leur sacre, et par tous oublié pour jamais l'instant d'après ? Vous avez vu le Danemark, vous voyez l'Angleterre, et vous allez voir la Suède. Profitez de ces exemples pour apprendre une fois pour toutes que, quelques précautions qu'on puisse entasser, hérédité dans le trône et liberté dans la nation seront à jamais des choses incompatibles.

Les Polonais ont toujours eu du penchant à transmettre la couronne du père au fils, ou aux plus proches par voie d'héritage quoique toujours par droit d'élection. Cette inclination, s'ils continuent à la suivre les mènera tôt ou tard au malheur de rendre la couronne héréditaire, et il ne faut pas qu'ils espèrent lutter aussi longtemps de cette manière contre la puissance royale que les membres de l'Empire germanique ont lutté contre celle de l'empereur, parce que la Pologne n'a point en elle-même de contrepoids suffisant pour maintenir un roi héréditaire dans la subordination légale. Malgré la puissance de plusieurs membres de l'Empire, sans l'élection accidentelle de Charles VII les capitulations impériales ne seraient déjà plus qu'un vain formulaire, comme elles l'étaient au commencement de ce siècle ; et les *pacta conventa* deviendront bien plus vains encore, quand la famille royale aura eu le temps de s'affermir et de mettre toutes les autres au-dessous d'elle. Pour dire en un mot mon sentiment sur cet article, je pense qu'une couronne élective avec le plus absolu pouvoir vaudrait encore mieux pour la Pologne, qu'une couronne héréditaire avec un pouvoir presque nul.

Au lieu de cette fatale loi qui rendrait la couronne héréditaire j'en proposerais une bien contraire, qui si elle était admise, maintiendrait la liberté de la Pologne. Ce serait d'ordonner par une loi fondamentale que jamais la couronne ne passerait du père au fils et que tout fils d'un roi de Pologne serait pour toujours exclu du trône. Je dis que je proposerais cette loi si elle était nécessaire : mais occupé d'un projet qui ferait le même effet sans elle, je renvoie à sa place l'explication de ce projet, et supposant que par son effet les fils seront exclus du trône de leur père, au moins immédiatement, je crois voir que la liberté bien assurée ne sera pas le seul avantage qui résultera de cette exclusion. Il en naîtra un autre encore très considérable ; c'est en ôtant tout espoir aux rois d'usurper et transmettre à leurs enfants un pouvoir arbitraire, de porter toute leur activité vers la gloire et la prospérité de l'État, la seule vue qui reste ouverte à leur ambition. C'est ainsi que le chef de la nation en deviendra, non plus l'ennemi-né, mais le premier citoyen. C'est ainsi qu'il fera sa grande affaire d'illustrer son règne par des établissements utiles qui le rendent cher à son peuple, respectable à ses voisins, qui fassent bénir avec lui sa mémoire, et c'est ainsi que, hors les moyens de nuire et de séduire qu'il ne faut jamais lui laisser, il conviendra d'augmenter sa puissance en tout ce qui peut concourir au bien public. Il aura peu de force immédiate et directe pour agir par lui-même, mais il aura beaucoup d'autorité, de surveillance et d'inspection pour contenir chacun dans son devoir et pour diriger le gouvernement à son véritable but. La présidence de la Diète, du Sénat et de tous les corps, un sévère examen de la conduite de tous les gens en place, un grand soin de maintenir la justice et l'intégrité dans tous les tribunaux, de conserver l'ordre et la tranquillité dans l'État, de lui donner une bonne assiette au-dehors, le commandement des armées en temps de guerre, les établissements utiles en temps de paix, sont des devoirs qui tiennent particulièrement à son office de roi, et qui l'occuperont assez s'il veut les remplir par lui-même ; car les détails de l'administration étant confiés à des ministres établis pour cela, ce doit être un crime à un roi de Pologne de confier aucune partie de la sienne à des favoris. Qu'il fasse son métier en personne, ou qu'il y renonce. Article important sur lequel la nation ne doit jamais se relâcher.

C'est sur de semblables principes qu'il faut établir l'équilibre et la pondération des pouvoirs qui composent la législation et l'administration. Ces pouvoirs, dans les mains de leurs dépositaires et dans la meilleure proportion possible devraient être en raison directe de leur nombre et inverse du temps qu'ils restent en place. Les parties composantes de la Diète suivront d'assez près ce meilleur rapport. La chambre des Nonces, la plus nombreuse sera aussi la plus puissante, mais tous ses membres changeront fréquemment. Le Sénat moins nombreux aura une moindre part à la législation, mais une plus grande à la puissance exécutive, et ses membres participant à la constitution des deux extrêmes seront partie à temps et partie à vie comme il convient à un corps intermédiaire. Le roi, qui préside à tout continuera d'être à vie, et son pouvoir toujours très grand pour l'inspection, sera borné par la chambre des Nonces quant à la législation et par le Sénat quant à l'administration. Mais pour maintenir l'égalité, principe de la constitution, rien n'y doit être héréditaire que la noblesse. Si la couronne était héréditaire, il faudrait pour conserver l'équilibre que la pairie ou l'ordre sénatorial le fût aussi comme en Angleterre. Alors l'ordre équestre abaissé perdrait son pouvoir, la chambre des Nonces n'ayant pas, comme celle des Communes, celui d'ouvrir et fermer tous les ans le trésor public, et la constitution polonaise serait renversée de fond en comble.

[9.] CAUSES PARTICULIÈRES DE L'ANARCHIE

La Diète bien proportionnée et bien pondérée ainsi dans toutes ses parties sera la source d'une bonne législation et d'un bon gouvernement. Mais il faut pour cela que ses ordres soient respectés et suivis. Le mépris des lois et l'anarchie où la Pologne a vécu jusqu'ici ont des causes faciles à voir. J'en ai déjà ci-devant marqué la principale et j'en ai indiqué le remède. Les autres causes concourantes sont, 1° le *liberum veto*, 2° les confédérations, 3° et l'abus qu'ont fait les particuliers du droit qu'on leur a laissé d'avoir des gens de guerre à leur service.

Ce dernier abus est tel, que si l'on ne commence pas par l'ôter, toutes les autres réformes sont inutiles. Tant que les particuliers auront le pouvoir de résister à la force exécutive, ils croiront en avoir le droit, et tant qu'ils auront entre eux de petites guerres, comment veut-on que l'État soit en paix ? J'avoue que les places fortes ont besoin de gardes ; mais pourquoi faut-il des places qui sont fortes seulement contre les citoyens et faibles contre l'ennemi ? J'ai peur que cette réforme ne souffre des difficultés ; cependant je ne crois pas impossible de les vaincre, et pour peu qu'un citoyen puissant soit raisonnable, il consentira sans peine à n'avoir plus à lui de gens de guerre quand aucun autre n'en aura.

J'ai dessein de parler ci-après des établissements militaires ; ainsi je renvoie à cet article ce que j'aurais à dire dans celui-ci.

Le *liberum veto* n'est pas un droit vicieux en lui-même, mais sitôt qu'il passe sa borne il devient le plus dangereux des abus : il était le garant de la liberté publique ; il n'est plus que l'instrument de l'oppression. Il ne reste, pour ôter cet abus funeste que d'en détruire la cause tout à fait. Mais il est dans le cœur de l'homme de tenir aux privilèges individuels plus qu'à des avantages plus grands et plus généraux. Il n'y a qu'un patriotisme éclairé par l'expérience qui puisse apprendre à sacrifier à de plus grands biens un droit brillant devenu pernicieux par son abus, et dont cet abus est désormais inséparable. Tous les Polonais doivent sentir vivement les maux que leur a fait souffrir ce malheureux droit. S'ils aiment l'ordre et la paix, ils n'ont aucun moyen d'établir chez eux l'un et l'autre, tant qu'ils y laisseront subsister ce droit, bon dans la formation du corps politique ou quand il a toute sa perfection, mais absurde et funeste tant qu'il reste des changements à faire et il est impossible qu'il n'en reste pas toujours, surtout dans un grand État entouré de voisins puissants et ambitieux.

Le *liberum veto* serait moins déraisonnable s'il tombait uniquement sur les points fondamentaux de la constitution : mais qu'il ait lieu généralement dans toutes les délibérations des Diètes, c'est ce qui ne peut s'admettre en aucune façon. C'est un vice dans la constitution polonaise que la législation et l'administration n'y soient pas assez distinguées, et que la Diète exerçant le pouvoir législatif y mêle des parties d'administration, fasse indifféremment des actes de souveraineté et de gouvernement, souvent même des actes mixtes par lesquels ses membres sont magistrats et législateurs tout à la fois[24].

Les changements proposés tendent à mieux distinguer ces deux pouvoirs, et par là même à mieux marquer les bornes du *liberum veto*. Car je ne crois pas qu'il soit jamais tombé dans l'esprit de personne de l'étendre aux matières de pure administration, ce qui serait anéantir l'autorité civile et tout le gouvernement.

Par le droit naturel des sociétés l'unanimité a été requise pour la formation du corps politique et pour les lois fondamentales qui tiennent à son existence[25], telles, par exemple, que la première corrigée, la cinquième, la neuvième, et l'onzième, marquées dans la Pseudo-Diète de 1768. Or, l'unanimité requise pour l'établissement de ces lois doit l'être de même pour leur abrogation. Ainsi voilà des points sur lesquels le *liberum veto* peut continuer de subsister et puisqu'il ne s'agit pas de le détruire totalement, les Polonais qui sans beaucoup de murmure ont vu resserrer ce droit par la Diète illégale de 1768, devront sans peine le voir réduire et limiter dans une Diète plus libre et plus légitime.

Il faut bien peser et bien méditer les points capitaux qu'on établira comme lois fondamentales, et l'on fera porter sur ces points seulement la force du *liberum veto.* De cette manière on rendra la constitution solide et ses lois irrévocables autant qu'elles peuvent l'être : car il est contre la nature du corps politique de s'imposer des lois qu'il ne puisse révoquer[26] ; mais il n'est ni contre la nature ni contre la raison qu'il ne puisse révoquer ces lois qu'avec la même solennité qu'il mit à les établir. Voilà toute la chaîne qu'il peut se donner pour l'avenir. C'en est assez et pour affermir la constitution et pour contenter l'amour des Polonais pour le *liberum veto*, sans s'exposer dans la suite aux abus qu'il a fait naître.

Quant à ces multitudes d'articles qu'on a mis ridiculement au nombre des lois fondamentales, et qui font seulement le corps de la législation, de même que tous ceux qu'on range sous le titre de matières d'État, ils sont sujets par la vicissitude des choses à des variations indispensables qui ne permettent pas d'y requérir l'unanimité. Il est encore absurde que dans quelque cas que ce puisse être un membre de la Diète en puisse arrêter l'activité, et que la retraite ou la protestation d'un nonce ou de plusieurs puisse dissoudre l'assemblée et casser ainsi l'autorité souveraine. Il faut abolir ce droit barbare et décerner peine capitale contre quiconque serait tenté de s'en prévaloir. S'il y avait des cas de protestation contre la Diète, ce qui ne peut être tant qu'elle sera libre et complète, ce serait aux palatinats et Diétines que ce droit pourrait être conféré, mais jamais à des nonces qui comme membres de la Diète ne doivent avoir sur elle aucun degré d'autorité ni récuser ses décisions.

Entre le *veto* qui est la plus grande force individuelle que puissent avoir les membres de la souveraine puissance et qui ne doit avoir lieu que pour les lois véritablement fondamentales, et la pluralité, qui est la moindre et qui se rapporte aux matières de simple administration, il y a différentes proportions sur lesquelles on peut déterminer la prépondérance des avis en raison de l'importance des matières. Par exemple quand il s'agira de législation, l'on peut exiger les trois quarts au moins des suffrages, les deux tiers dans les matières d'État, la pluralité seulement pour les élections et autres affaires courantes et momentanées. Ceci n'est qu'un exemple pour expliquer mon idée et non une proportion que je détermine.

Dans un État tel que la Pologne où les âmes ont encore un grand ressort, peut-être eût-on pu conserver dans son entier ce beau droit du *liberum veto* sans beaucoup de risque, et peut-être même avec avantage, pourvu qu'on eût rendu ce droit dangereux à exercer, et qu'on y eût attaché de grandes conséquences pour celui qui s'en serait prévalu. Car il est, j'ose le dire, extravagant que celui qui rompt ainsi l'activité de la Diète et laisse l'État sans ressource, s'en aille jouir chez lui tranquillement et impunément de la désolation publique qu'il a causée.

Si donc dans une résolution presque unanime un seul opposant conservait le droit de l'annuler, je voudrais qu'il répondît de son opposition sur sa tête, non seulement à ses constituants dans la Diétine post-comitiale, mais ensuite à toute la nation dont il a fait le malheur.

Je voudrais qu'il fût ordonné par la loi que six mois après son opposition, il serait jugé solennellement par un tribunal extraordinaire établi pour cela seul, composé de tout ce que la nation a de plus sage, de plus illustre et de plus respecté, et qui ne pourrait le renvoyer simplement absous, mais serait obligé de le condamner à mort, sans aucune grâce, ou de lui décerner une récompense et des honneurs publics pour toute sa vie, sans pouvoir jamais prendre aucun milieu entre ces deux alternatives.

Des établissements de cette espèce, si favorables à l'énergie du courage et à l'amour de la liberté, sont trop éloignés de l'esprit moderne pour qu'on puisse espérer qu'ils soient adoptés ni goûtés, mais ils n'étaient pas inconnus aux anciens et c'est par là que leurs instituteurs savaient élever les âmes et les enflammer au besoin d'un zèle vraiment héroïque. On a vu, dans des républiques où régnaient des lois plus dures encore, de généreux citoyens se dévouer à la mort dans le péril de la patrie pour ouvrir un avis qui pût la sauver. Un *veto* suivi du même danger peut sauver l'État dans l'occasion, et n'y sera jamais fort à craindre.

Oserais-je parler ici des confédérations et n'être pas de l'avis des savants. Ils ne voient que le mal qu'elles font ; il faudrait voir aussi celui qu'elles empêchent. Sans contredit la confédération est un état violent dans la République ; mais il est des maux extrêmes qui rendent les remèdes violents nécessaires, et dont il faut tâcher de guérir à tout prix. La confédération est en Pologne ce qu'était la dictature chez les Romains : l'une et l'autre font taire les lois dans un péril pressant, mais avec cette grande différence que la dictature, directement contraire à la législation romaine et à l'esprit du gouvernement a fini par le détruire, et que les confédérations au contraire n'étant qu'un moyen de raffermir et rétablir la constitution ébranlée par de grands efforts, peuvent tendre et renforcer le ressort relâché de l'État sans pouvoir jamais le briser. Cette forme fédérative, qui peut-être dans son origine eut une cause fortuite, me paraît être un chef-d'œuvre de politique. Partout où la liberté règne elle est incessamment attaquée et très souvent en péril. Tout État libre où les grandes crises n'ont pas été prévues est à chaque orage en danger de périr. Il n'y a que les Polonais qui de ces crises mêmes aient su tirer un nouveau moyen de maintenir la constitution. Sans les confédérations il y a longtemps que la République de Pologne ne serait plus, et j'ai grand-peur qu'elle ne dure pas longtemps après elles, si l'on prend le parti de les abolir. Jetez les yeux sur ce qui vient de se passer. Sans les confédérations l'État était subjugué ; la liberté était pour jamais anéantie. Voulez-vous ôter à la République la ressource qui vient de la sauver[27] ?

Et qu'on ne pense pas que quand le *liberum veto* sera aboli et la pluralité rétablie, les confédérations deviendront inutiles, comme si tout leur avantage consistait dans cette pluralité. Ce n'est pas la même chose. La puissance exécutive attachée aux confédérations leur donnera toujours dans les besoins extrêmes une vigueur, une activité, une célérité que ne peut avoir la Diète, forcée à marcher à pas plus lents, avec plus de formalités, et qui ne peut faire un seul mouvement irrégulier sans renverser la constitution.

Non, les confédérations sont le bouclier, l'asile, le sanctuaire de cette constitution. Tant qu'elles subsisteront il me paraît impossible qu'elle se détruise. Il faut les laisser, mais il faut les régler. Si tous les abus étaient ôtés, les confédérations deviendraient presque inutiles. La réforme de votre gouvernement doit opérer cet effet. Il n'y aura plus que les entreprises violentes qui mettent dans la nécessité d'y recourir ; mais ces entreprises sont dans l'ordre des choses qu'il faut prévoir. Au lieu donc d'abolir les confédérations, déterminez les cas où elles peuvent légitimement avoir lieu, et puis réglez-en bien la forme et l'effet, pour leur donner une sanction légale autant qu'il est possible sans gêner leur formation ni leur activité. Il y a même de ces cas où par le seul fait toute la Pologne doit être à l'instant confédérée ; comme par exemple au moment où sous quelque prétexte que ce soit et hors le cas d'une guerre ouverte, des troupes étrangères mettent le pied dans l'État[28] ; parce qu'enfin, quel que soit le sujet de cette entrée et le gouvernement même y eût-il consenti, confédération chez soi n'est pas hostilité chez les autres. Lorsque, par quelque obstacle que ce puisse être la Diète est empêchée de s'assembler au temps marqué par la loi, lorsqu'à l'instigation de qui que ce soit on fait trouver des gens de guerre au temps et au lieu de son assemblée, ou que sa forme est altérée, ou que son activité est suspendue, ou que sa liberté est gênée en quelque façon que ce soit ; dans tous ces cas la confédération générale doit exister par le seul fait ; les assemblées et signatures particulières n'en sont que des branches, et tous les maréchaux en doivent être subordonnés à celui qui aura été nommé le premier.

[13.] PROJET POUR ASSUJETTIR À UNE MARCHE GRADUELLE TOUS LES MEMBRES DU GOUVERNEMENT

Voici pour graduer cette marche un projet que j'ai tâché d'adapter aussi bien qu'il était possible à la forme du gouvernement établi, réformé seulement quant à la nomination des sénateurs de la manière et par les raisons ci-devant déduites.

Tous les membres actifs de la République, j'entends ceux qui auront part à l'administration, seront partagés en trois classes marquées par autant de signes distinctifs que ceux qui composeront ces classes porteront sur leurs personnes. Les ordres de chevalerie qui jadis étaient des preuves de vertu, ne sont maintenant que des signes de la faveur des rois. Les rubans et bijoux qui en sont la marque ont un air de colifichet et de parure féminine qu'il faut éviter dans notre institution. Je voudrais que les marques des trois ordres que je propose fussent des plaques de divers métaux, dont le prix matériel serait en raison inverse du grade de ceux qui les porteraient.

Le premier pas dans les affaires publiques sera précédé d'une épreuve pour la jeunesse dans les places d'avocats, d'assesseurs, de juges même dans les tribunaux subalternes, de régisseurs de quelque portion des deniers publics, et en général dans tous les postes inférieurs qui donnent à ceux qui les remplissent occasion de montrer leur mérite, leur capacité, leur exactitude, et surtout leur intégrité. Cet état d'épreuve doit durer au moins trois ans, au bout desquels, munis des certificats de leurs supérieurs, et du témoignage de la voix publique, ils se présenteront à la Diétine de leur province, où, après un examen sévère de leur conduite, on honorera ceux qui en seront jugés dignes d'une plaque d'or portant leur nom, celui de leur province, la date de leur réception et au-dessous cette inscription en plus gros caractères : *Spes patriae*[29]. Ceux qui auront reçu cette plaque la porteront toujours attachée à leur bras droit ou sur leur cœur ; ils prendront le titre de *Servants d'État*, et jamais dans l'ordre équestre il n'y aura que des servants d'État qui puissent être élus nonces à la Diète, députés au Tribunal, commissaires à la chambre des comptes, ni chargés d'aucune fonction publique qui appartienne à la souveraineté.

Pour arriver au second grade il sera nécessaire d'avoir été trois fois nonce à la Diète et d'avoir obtenu chaque fois aux Diétines de relation l'approbation de ses constituants, et nul ne pourra être élu nonce une seconde ou troisième fois s'il n'est muni de cet acte pour sa précédente nonciature. Le service au Tribunal ou à Radom en qualité de commissaire ou de député équivaudra à une nonciature, et il suffira d'avoir siégé trois fois dans ces assemblées indifféremment mais toujours avec approbation pour arriver de droit au second grade. En sorte que sur les trois certificats présentés à la Diète, le servant d'État qui les aura obtenus sera honoré de la seconde plaque et du titre dont elle est la marque.

Cette plaque sera d'argent de même forme et grandeur que la précédente, elle portera les mêmes inscriptions, excepté qu'au lieu des deux mots *Spes patriae*, on y gravera ces deux-ci : *Civis electus*[30]. Ceux qui porteront ces plaques seront appelés *citoyens de choix*, ou simplement *élus*, et ne pourront plus être simples nonces, députés au Tribunal, ni commissaires à la Chambre : mais ils seront autant de candidats pour les places de sénateurs. Nul ne pourra entrer au Sénat qu'il n'ait passé par ce second grade, qu'il n'en ait porté la marque, et tous les sénateurs députés qui selon le projet, en seront immédiatement tirés, continueront de la porter jusqu'à ce qu'ils parviennent au troisième grade.

C'est parmi ceux qui auront atteint le second que je voudrais choisir les principaux des collèges et inspecteurs de l'éducation des enfants. Ils pourraient être obligés de remplir un certain temps cet emploi avant que d'être admis au Sénat, et seraient tenus de présenter à la Diète l'approbation du collège des administrateurs de l'éducation : sans oublier que cette approbation comme toutes les autres doit toujours être visée par la voix publique, qu'on a mille moyens de consulter.

L'élection des sénateurs députés se fera dans la chambre des Nonces à chaque Diète ordinaire, en sorte qu'ils ne resteront que deux ans en place ; mais ils pourront être continués ou élus derechef deux autres fois, pourvu que chaque fois en sortant de place, ils aient préalablement obtenu de la même chambre un acte d'approbation semblable à celui qu'il est nécessaire d'obtenir des Diétines pour être élu nonce une seconde et troisième fois : car sans un acte pareil obtenu à chaque gestion l'on ne parviendra plus à rien, et l'on n'aura, pour n'être pas exclu du gouvernement que la ressource de recommencer par les grades inférieurs, ce qui doit être permis pour ne pas ôter à un citoyen zélé, quelque faute qu'il puisse avoir commise, tout espoir de l'effacer et de parvenir. Au reste, on ne doit jamais charger aucun comité particulier d'expédier ou refuser ces certificats ou approbations ; il faut toujours que ces jugements soient portés par toute la chambre, ce qui se fera sans embarras ni perte de temps si l'on suit pour le jugement des sénateurs députés sortant de place la même méthode des cartons que j'ai proposée pour leur élection.

On dira peut-être ici que tous ces actes d'approbation donnés d'abord par des corps particuliers, ensuite par les Diétines et enfin par la Diète, seront moins accordés au mérite, à la justice et à la vérité, qu'extorqués par la brigue et le crédit. À cela je n'ai qu'une chose à répondre. J'ai cru parler à un peuple qui sans être exempt de vices avait encore du ressort et des vertus, et cela supposé, mon projet est bon. Mais si déjà la Pologne en est à ce point que tout y soit vénal et corrompu jusqu'à la racine, c'est en vain qu'elle cherche à réformer ses lois et à conserver sa liberté, il faut qu'elle y renonce et qu'elle plie sa tête au joug. Mais revenons.

Tout sénateur député qui l'aura été trois fois avec approbation passera de droit au troisième grade le plus élevé dans l'État, et la marque lui en sera conférée par le roi sur la nomination de la Diète. Cette marque sera une plaque d'acier bleu semblable aux précédentes et portera cette inscription *Custos legum*[31]. Ceux qui l'auront reçue la porteront tout le reste de leur vie à quelque poste éminent qu'ils parviennent, et même sur le trône quand il leur arrivera d'y monter.

Les palatins et grands castellans ne pourront être tirés que du corps des gardiens des lois, de la même manière que ceux-ci l'ont été des citoyens élus, c'est-à-dire par le choix de la Diète, et comme ces palatins occupent les postes les plus éminents de la République et qu'ils les occupent à vie, afin que leur émulation ne s'endorme pas dans les places où ils ne voient plus que le trône au-dessus d'eux, l'accès leur en sera ouvert, mais de manière à n'y pouvoir arriver encore que par la voix publique et à force de vertu.

Remarquons, avant que d'aller plus loin que la carrière que je donne à parcourir aux citoyens pour arriver graduellement à la tête de la République, paraît assez bien proportionnée aux mesures de la vie humaine pour que ceux qui tiennent les rênes du gouvernement ayant passé la fougue de la jeunesse puissent néanmoins être encore dans la vigueur de l'âge, et qu'après quinze ou vingt ans d'épreuve continuellement sous les yeux du public il leur reste encore un assez grand nombre d'années à faire jouir la patrie de leurs talents, de leur expérience et de leurs vertus, et à jouir eux-mêmes dans les premières places de l'État du respect et des honneurs qu'ils auront si bien mérités. En supposant qu'un homme commence à vingt ans d'entrer dans les affaires, il est possible qu'à trente-cinq il soit déjà palatin ; mais comme il est bien difficile et qu'il n'est pas même à propos que cette marche graduelle se fasse si rapidement, on n'arrivera guère à ce poste éminent avant la quarantaine, et c'est l'âge, à mon avis, le plus convenable pour réunir toutes les qualités qu'on doit rechercher dans un homme d'État. Ajoutons ici que cette marche paraît appropriée autant qu'il est possible aux besoins du gouvernement. Dans le calcul des probabilités, j'estime qu'on aura tous les deux ans au moins cinquante citoyens élus et vingt gardiens des lois : nombres plus que suffisants pour recruter les deux parties du Sénat auxquelles mènent respectivement ces deux grades. Car on voit aisément que quoique le premier rang du Sénat soit le plus nombreux, étant à vie il aura moins souvent des places à remplir que le second, qui dans mon projet, se renouvelle à chaque Diète ordinaire.

On a déjà vu et l'on verra bientôt encore que je ne laisse pas oisifs les *élus* surnuméraires en attendant qu'ils entrent au Sénat comme députés ; pour ne pas laisser oisifs non plus les gardiens des lois, en attendant qu'ils y rentrent comme palatins ou castellans, c'est de leur corps que je formerais le collège des administrateurs de l'éducation dont j'ai parlé ci-devant. On pourrait donner pour président à ce collège le primat ou un autre évêque, en statuant au surplus qu'aucun autre ecclésiastique, fût-il évêque et sénateur, ne pourrait y être admis.

Voilà, ce me semble, une marche assez bien graduée pour la partie essentielle et intermédiaire du tout, savoir la noblesse et les magistrats ; mais il nous manque encore les deux extrêmes, savoir le peuple et le roi. Commençons par le premier jusqu'ici compté pour rien, mais qu'il importe enfin de compter pour quelque chose, si l'on veut donner une certaine force, une certaine consistance à la Pologne. Rien de plus délicat que l'opération dont il s'agit, car enfin, bien que chacun sente quel grand mal c'est pour la République que la nation soit en quelque façon renfermée dans l'ordre équestre, et que tout le reste, paysans et bourgeois, soit nul tant dans le gouvernement que dans la législation, telle est l'antique constitution[32]. Il ne serait en ce moment ni prudent ni possible de la changer tout d'un coup ; mais il peut l'être d'amener par degrés ce changement, de faire sans révolution sensible, que la partie la plus nombreuse de la nation s'attache d'affection à la patrie et même au gouvernement. Cela s'obtiendra par deux moyens : le premier, une exacte observation de la justice, en sorte que le serf et le roturier n'ayant jamais à craindre d'être injustement vexés par le noble, se guérissent de l'aversion qu'ils doivent naturellement avoir pour lui. Ceci demande une grande réforme dans les tribunaux et un soin particulier pour la formation du corps des avocats.

Le second moyen, sans lequel le premier n'est rien est d'ouvrir une porte aux serfs pour acquérir la liberté et aux bourgeois pour acquérir la noblesse. Quand la chose dans le fait ne serait pas praticable, il faudrait au moins qu'on la vît telle en possibilité ; mais on peut faire plus, ce me semble, et cela sans courir aucun risque. Voici par exemple un moyen qui me paraît mener de cette manière au but proposé.

Tous les deux ans dans l'intervalle d'une Diète à l'autre, on choisirait dans chaque province un temps et un lieu convenables où les *élus* de la même province qui ne seraient pas encore sénateurs députés s'assembleraient, sous la présidence d'un *custos legum* qui ne serait pas encore sénateur à vie, dans un comité censorial ou de bienfaisance auquel on inviterait, non tous les curés, mais seulement ceux qu'on jugerait les plus dignes de cet honneur : je crois même que cette préférence, formant un jugement tacite aux yeux du peuple pourrait jeter aussi quelque émulation parmi les curés de village, et en garantir un grand nombre des mœurs crapuleuses auxquelles ils ne sont que trop sujets.

Dans cette assemblée, où l'on pourrait encore appeler des vieillards et notables de tous les états, on s'occuperait à l'examen des projets d'établissements utiles pour la province; on entendrait les rapports des curés sur l'état de leurs paroisses et des paroisses voisines, celui des notables sur l'état de la culture, sur celui des familles de leur canton; on vérifierait soigneusement ces rapports; chaque membre du comité ajouterait ses propres observations, et l'on tiendrait de tout cela un fidèle registre dont on tirerait des mémoires succincts pour les Diétines.

On examinerait en détail les besoins des familles surchargées, des infirmes, des veuves, des orphelins, et l'on y pourvoirait proportionnellement sur un fonds formé par les contributions gratuites des aisés de la province. Ces contributions seraient d'autant moins onéreuses qu'elles deviendraient le seul tribut de charité, attendu qu'on ne doit souffrir dans toute la Pologne ni mendiants ni hôpitaux. Les prêtres, sans doute, crieront beaucoup pour la conservation des hôpitaux, et ces cris ne sont qu'une raison de plus pour les détruire.

Dans ce même comité, qui ne s'occuperait jamais de punitions ni de réprimandes, mais seulement de bienfaits, de louanges et d'encouragements, on ferait sur de bonnes informations des listes exactes des particuliers de tous états dont la conduite serait digne d'honneur et de récompense*. Ces listes seraient envoyées au Sénat et au roi pour y avoir égard dans l'occasion et placer toujours bien leurs choix et leurs préférences, et c'est sur les indications des mêmes assemblées que seraient données dans les collèges par les administrateurs de l'éducation les places gratuites dont j'ai parlé ci-devant.

Mais la principale et la plus importante occupation de ce comité serait de dresser sur de fidèles mémoires, et sur le rapport de la voix publique bien vérifié, un rôle des paysans qui se distingueraient par une bonne conduite, une bonne culture, de bonnes mœurs, par le soin de leur famille, par tous les devoirs de leur état bien remplis. Ce rôle serait ensuite présenté à la Diétine qui y choisirait un nombre fixé par la loi pour être affranchi, et qui pourvoirait par des moyens convenus au dédommagement des patrons, en les faisant jouir d'exemptions, de prérogatives, d'avantages enfin proportionnés au nombre de leurs paysans qui auraient été trouvés dignes de la liberté. Car il faudrait absolument faire en sorte qu'au lieu d'être onéreux au maître l'affranchissement du serf lui devînt honorable et avantageux. Bien entendu que pour éviter l'abus ces affran-

---

* Il faut, dans ces estimations, avoir beaucoup plus d'égard aux personnes qu'à quelques actions isolées. Le vrai bien se fait avec peu d'éclat. C'est par une conduite uniforme et soutenue, par des vertus privées et domestiques, par tous les devoirs de son état bien remplis, par des actions enfin qui découlent de son caractère et de ses principes qu'un homme peut mériter des honneurs, plutôt que par quelques grands coups de théâtre qui trouvent déjà leur récompense dans l'admiration publique. L'ostentation philosophique aime beaucoup les actions d'éclat ; mais tel, avec cinq ou six actions de cette espèce, bien brillantes, bien bruyantes et bien prônées, n'a pour but que de donner le change sur son compte et d'être toute sa vie injuste et dur impunément. *Donnez-nous la monnaie des grandes actions.* Ce mot de femme est un mot très judicieux.

chissements ne se feraient point par les maîtres, mais dans les Diétines, par jugement, et seulement jusqu'au nombre fixé par la loi.

Quand on aurait affranchi successivement un certain nombre de familles dans un canton, l'on pourrait affranchir des villages entiers, y former peu à peu des communes, leur assigner quelques biens-fonds, quelques terres communales comme en Suisse, y établir des officiers communaux, et lorsqu'on aurait amené par degrés les choses jusqu'à pouvoir sans révolution sensible achever l'opération en grand, leur rendre enfin le droit que leur donna la nature de participer à l'administration de leur pays en envoyant des députés aux Diétines.

Tout cela fait, on armerait tous ces paysans devenus hommes libres et citoyens, on les enrégimenterait, on les exercerait, et l'on finirait par avoir une milice vraiment excellente, plus que suffisante pour la défense de l'État.

On pourrait suivre une méthode semblable pour l'anoblissement d'un certain nombre de bourgeois, et même sans les anoblir leur destiner certains postes brillants qu'ils rempliraient seuls à l'exclusion des nobles, et cela à l'imitation des Vénitiens si jaloux de leur noblesse, qui néanmoins outre d'autres emplois subalternes donnent toujours à un citadin la seconde place de l'État, savoir celle de grand chancelier, sans qu'aucun patricien puisse jamais y prétendre. De cette manière, ouvrant à la bourgeoisie la porte de la noblesse et des honneurs, on l'attacherait d'affection à la patrie et au maintien de la constitution. On pourrait encore sans anoblir les individus, anoblir collectivement certaines villes, en préférant celles où fleuriraient davantage le commerce, l'industrie et les arts et où par conséquent l'administration municipale serait la meilleure. Ces villes anoblies pourraient, à l'instar des villes impériales envoyer des nonces à la Diète, et leur exemple ne manquerait pas d'exciter dans toutes les autres un vif désir d'obtenir le même honneur.

Les comités censoriaux chargés de ce département de bienfaisance, qui jamais à la honte des rois et des peuples n'a encore existé nulle part, seraient, quoique sans élection, composés de la manière la plus propre à remplir leurs fonctions avec zèle et intégrité, attendu que leurs membres, aspirant aux places sénatoriales où mènent leurs grades respectifs, porteraient une grande attention à mériter par l'approbation publique les suffrages de la Diète ; et ce serait une occupation suffisante pour tenir ces aspirants en haleine et sous les yeux du public dans les intervalles qui pourraient séparer leurs élections successives. Remarquez que cela se ferait cependant sans les tirer pour ces intervalles de l'état de simples citoyens gradués, puisque cette espèce de tribunal, si utile et si respectable, n'ayant jamais que du bien à faire, ne serait revêtu d'aucune puissance coactive : ainsi je ne multiplie point ici les magistratures, mais je me sers chemin faisant du passage de l'une à l'autre pour tirer parti de ceux qui les doivent remplir.

Sur ce plan, gradué dans son exécution par une marche successive qu'on pourrait précipiter, ralentir, ou même arrêter selon son bon ou mauvais succès, on n'avancerait qu'à volonté, guidé par l'expérience, on allumerait dans tous les états inférieurs un zèle ardent pour contribuer au bien public, on parviendrait enfin à vivifier toutes les parties de la Pologne, et à les lier de manière à ne faire plus qu'un même corps dont la vigueur et les forces seraient au moins décuplées de ce qu'elles peuvent être aujourd'hui, et cela avec l'avantage inestimable d'avoir évité tout changement vif et brusque et le danger des révolutions.

Vous avez une belle occasion de commencer cette opération d'une manière éclatante et noble qui doit faire le plus grand effet. Il n'est pas possible que, dans les malheurs que vient d'essuyer la Pologne les confédérés n'aient reçu des assistances et des marques d'attachement de quelques bourgeois et même de quelques paysans. Imitez la magnanimité des Romains, si soigneux après les grandes calamités de leur république, de combler des témoignages de leur gratitude les étrangers, les sujets, les esclaves, et même jusqu'aux animaux qui durant leurs disgrâces leur avaient rendu quelques services signalés. Ô le beau début à mon gré que de donner solennellement la noblesse à ces bourgeois et la franchise à ces paysans, et cela avec toute la pompe et tout l'appareil qui peuvent rendre cette cérémonie auguste, touchante et mémorable ! Et ne vous en tenez pas à ce début. Ces hommes ainsi distingués doivent demeurer toujours les enfants de choix de la patrie. Il faut veiller sur eux, les protéger, les aider, les soutenir, fussent-ils même de mauvais sujets. Il faut à tout prix les faire prospérer toute leur vie, afin que, par cet exemple mis sous les yeux du public, la Pologne montre à l'Europe entière ce que doit attendre d'elle dans ses succès quiconque osa l'assister dans sa détresse.

Voilà quelque idée grossière et seulement par forme d'exemple de la manière dont on peut procéder pour que chacun voie devant lui la route libre pour arriver à tout, que tout tende graduellement en bien servant la patrie aux rangs les plus honorables, et que la vertu puisse ouvrir toutes les portes que la fortune se plaît à fermer.

Mais tout n'est pas fait encore, et la partie de ce projet qui me reste à exposer est sans contredit la plus embarrassante et la plus difficile ; elle offre à surmonter des obstacles contre lesquels la prudence et l'expérience des politiques les plus consommés ont toujours échoué. Cependant il me semble qu'en supposant mon projet adopté, avec le moyen très simple que j'ai à proposer, toutes les difficultés sont levées, tous les abus sont prévenus, et ce qui semblait faire un nouvel obstacle se tourne en avantage dans l'exécution.

COMMENTAIRES ET NOTES

Discours sur les sciences et les arts

Notes

1. En octobre 1749, sur le chemin qui le mène à la forteresse de Vincennes où Diderot est enfermé pour délit d'opinion, Rousseau découvre dans le *Mercure de France* le sujet mis au concours par l'académie de Dijon : « Si le rétablissement des sciences et des arts a contribué à épurer les mœurs ». Il dira (*Confessions*, VIII) combien cette lecture le bouleversa : « À l'instant de cette lecture je vis un autre univers et je devins un autre homme. » En juillet 1750, l'académie couronne le *Discours* de Rousseau. L'ouvrage est publié au début de l'année 1751. Le succès est immédiat et Rousseau, qui cherchait la célébrité, enfin la trouve. Le *Discours* fait l'objet de nombreuses réfutations, auxquelles il répond jusqu'au printemps 1752.

Première partie

2. Il peut s'agir de Diderot. La citation de Montaigne est au livre III des *Essais*, chapitre 8.

3. Avec le *Discours sur les sciences et les arts*, la notion de « progrès » fait son entrée en politique, de la façon la plus paradoxale qui soit : en tant que preuve de la régression du genre humain ! Dans la *Dernière Réponse* (texte dans lequel Rousseau

réfute un certain Bordes, rhéteur de Lyon qui lui a adressé des objections) il écrit : « Le progrès des lettres est toujours en proportion avec la grandeur des empires. Soit. Je vois qu'on me parle toujours de fortune et de grandeur. Je parlais *moi* de mœurs et de vertu[1]. » Rousseau parle, lui, de vérité et de vertu, les autres parlent de profit et de bénéfice. Si donc le *Discours* fait le procès du progrès matériel, c'est parce que celui-ci n'est pas accompagné d'un progrès moral. Et plus encore, il y a régression morale parce qu'il y a progrès matériel. Arts, lettres et spectacles sont les signes d'une dépravation du genre humain – en tout cas de l'homme européen.

En fait, la clef de ce premier *Discours* est dans l'idée que Rousseau exploite avec ostentation : *on* nous dit (les rhéteurs mondains tels que Bordes) que les arts et les lettres sont les manifestations du degré de civilisation[2] auxquels les Européens sont parvenus, mais *moi* je vous dis que cela n'est que dangereux artifices. Rousseau oppose *moi* à *on*, c'est-à-dire à la société. Tout au long du *Discours*, les apparences sont opposées à la « vérité ». Le vrai sera le discours de *moi* et l'apparence sera le discours de la société. À la facticité du social il opposera – c'est très sensible à la fin du *Discours* – l'authenticité de la « conscience » et de son contenu : la vérité. Tout se passe comme si, pour Rousseau, la société mettait la conscience hors d'elle-même en réduisant vérité et vertu à leurs manifestations extérieures, mondaines. Ainsi, l'opposition *de l'être et de l'apparaître* est-elle l'instrument rhétorique permettant l'énoncé du paradoxe du progrès. L'apparaître du progrès – arts, lettres, sciences – est tout le contraire de son être : l'avilissement moral du genre humain.

C'est pourquoi Rousseau se *singularise*[3] par rapport à ses contemporains, ceux qui aiment le progrès, les manières et les mœurs du monde. Il se singularise en disant : je vous parle, moi,

1. *Œuvres complètes*, III, Gallimard, « Bibliothèque de la Pléiade », p. 79. 2. Mot que n'emploie pas Rousseau. 3. Rousseau est moins solitaire que singulier.

de vertu et de vérité, alors que l'on ne fait que parler profits et intérêts. On me parle de bien matériel, je vous parle, moi, de bien moral. Tout le *Discours* est organisé autour de ce procédé consistant à découvrir, au-delà des apparences – au-delà des *paraîtres* – une vérité dont Rousseau vient d'avoir la révélation : l'être social en sa vérité.

4. Rousseau n'hésite pas ici à donner dans le grand style : c'est le Rousseau « romain ». La prosopopée de Fabricius est inspirée de Plutarque (que Rousseau père fit lire à Jean-Jacques de très bonne heure) : *Vie des hommes illustres*, XLV.

5. La condition personnelle de Rousseau le fait se sentir proche de Socrate : incompris (ou trop bien compris) de la cité d'Athéna, Socrate fut condamné à mort et but la ciguë. Rousseau, qui se sent victime du « mépris », est lui aussi mû par le désir socratique de vertu et de vérité.

6. Rousseau se pose ici comme l'interprète du genre humain.

Seconde partie

7. Paradoxe central du *Discours*.

8. À n'en pas douter, Rousseau lui-même. Mais au-delà de sa personne, la *recherche de la vérité* – qui est la philosophie même – est le programme que Rousseau propose aux bonnes volontés de son temps, s'il en existe à part Diderot. Le projet philosophique reste en tout cas le sens dernier du *Discours*, car la philosophie peut détourner les hommes des chemins funestes de l'erreur, du faux semblant, de l'apparaître et leur faire retrouver les voies de la vérité.

Le programme du *Discours sur les sciences et les arts*, défini seulement dans son esprit, non dans ses méthodes ni même dans ses objets, sera entrepris et mené à bien, dans le *Discours sur l'inégalité*, d'abord, puis dans le *Contrat social* : il s'agit de penser l'homme civil tel qu'il peut être compte tenu de l'homme tel qu'il est; car on ne reviendra ni à l'état de pure nature ni à l'ignorance des origines.

9. Dans la préface à *Narcisse*, Rousseau écrira : « Étrange et funeste constitution où les richesses accumulées facilitent toujours les moyens d'en accumuler de plus grandes, et où il est impossible à celui qui n'a rien d'acquérir quelque chose : où l'homme de bien n'a nul moyen de sortir de la misère; où les fripons sont les plus honorés, et où il faut nécessairement renoncer à la vertu pour devenir un honnête homme ! » (Cité par J. Roger dans son *Introduction* au *Discours*, GF-Flammarion, Paris, 1971, p. 20.)

10. Ce thème de la « dépravation » arrive ici, pour ainsi dire, au fil de l'écriture, mais sera thématisé de façon réfléchie dans le *Discours sur l'inégalité.* Par dépravation, Rousseau entend la régression morale.

11. Rousseau ici s'en prend à la rhétorique formelle des nouveaux sophistes qu'il oppose à la philosophie qui démêle l'erreur de la vérité.

12. Ouvrage de Diderot : *Pensées philosophiques.* « Il y a des gens dont il ne faut pas dire qu'ils craignent Dieu, mais bien qu'ils en ont peur » (d'après François Bouchardy, Gallimard, « Bibliothèque de la Pléiade », p. 1253).

13. Rousseau manifestement ne connaît pas Spinoza, qu'il assimile à Hobbes sans autre forme de procès : il est de bon ton, à l'époque, de soupçonner Hobbes de vouloir asservir la multitude et Spinoza de propager l'athéisme. Les deux auteurs sont d'accord sur l'idée que le désir est l'essence de l'homme, et que mon droit est égal à ma puissance – mais en tirent des conclusions *politiques* diamétralement opposées.

14. Francis Bacon de Verulam, (1561-1656), auteur du *Novum Organum* (1620), où il expose la théorie de la méthode expérimentale.

15. Cicéron.

16. Il s'agit de Bacon (*cf. supra*, note 14).

DISCOURS SUR L'ORIGINE DE L'INÉGALITÉ

Commentaire

I. Tout comme le premier *Discours* répondait à une question de l'académie de Dijon, le second – que Rousseau publie en 1755 – est une réponse à une question de la même académie, mise au concours dans le *Mercure de France* en 1753 : « Quelle est la source de l'inégalité parmi les hommes, et si elle est autorisée par la loi naturelle. » Il suffit de prendre connaissance de la note portée sur le registre de l'académie pour avoir une idée de l'enthousiasme que la réponse de Rousseau provoqua chez ses juges : « Elle n'a pas été achevée de lire à cause de sa longueur et de sa *mauvaise tradition*[1], etc. » C'est cette « mauvaise tradition » qui nous intéresse car, si le *Discours sur les sciences et les arts* est une sorte de préface à l'œuvre future du penseur politique, le *Discours sur l'origine et les fondements de l'inégalité parmi les hommes* en est véritablement le premier chapitre.

L'auteur s'interroge en effet, ici, en philosophe sur un point fondamental – l'inégalité morale et matérielle des hommes ; en philosophe et non en simple amateur d'idées, si l'on peut dire. Rousseau d'emblée rectifie l'énoncé de la question posée maladroitement par l'académie pour lui donner une formulation théorique pertinente ; le problème, en effet, n'est pas de savoir si la loi naturelle autorise ou n'autorise pas l'inégalité, car c'est là suggérer que tout le monde est d'accord sur le sens qu'il faut donner à l'expression « loi naturelle ». Et non seulement à l'expression, mais à la chose elle-même.

Rousseau n'accepte pas ce point de départ de la discussion, il entend formuler lui-même la question de l'inégalité en formulant

1. Cité par Jean Starobinski dans son Introduction au *Discours*, Gallimard, « Bibliothèque de la Pléiade », p. XLIII (souligné par moi).

le point de vue original à partir duquel il entreprendra de répondre. Et ce nouveau point de vue est philosophique. Il s'agira de traiter de l'inégalité du double point de vue de son *origine* et de ses *fondements*. Certes, les académiciens avaient demandé que la thématique de l'origine fût prise en compte (« Quelle est la source de l'inégalité… »). Mais pas celle des « fondements ». En substituant « origine » à « source » et en associant origine et fondements, Rousseau intervient dans le débat en philosophe. Il demandera : Qu'est-ce qui *fonde* l'inégalité ? Cette formulation est une question philosophique. Car justement elle ne présuppose pas la réponse : l'académie demandait de considérer si la loi naturelle autorisait l'inégalité, et plus encore elle suggérait d'examiner si cette autorisation de l'inégalité par la loi naturelle était précisément son origine.

Cette façon d'envisager le problème porte en elle deux présupposés. Le premier est que c'est dans la « loi naturelle » (comme si cette notion allait de soi) que se trouve la clef de l'inégalité ; le deuxième est qu'il n'est pas besoin de définir l'inégalité (puisqu'il s'agit plutôt d'en rechercher l'origine). Il y a donc deux notions communes dans la question académique : loi naturelle et inégalité. Autrement dit, la question contient déjà la réponse.

À vrai dire, les académiciens ont eu raison de déclarer que le *Discours* de Rousseau était de « mauvaise tradition » car Rousseau ne répondra pas à la question posée, mais à une autre que l'on peut formuler ainsi : *L'inégalité, de quel droit ?* Posant la question du fondement (Qu'est-ce qui fonde ?), il pose la question de droit : *Quid juris ?* Et non pas une question de fait : au commencement, la loi naturelle autorisa-t-elle l'inégalité ? C'est là une question historique, et même événementielle.

Mais cette formulation ne convient pas à Rousseau. Pourquoi ? Parce que cette origine-là – le commencement – n'est pas connaissable. Et, par conséquent, il n'est pas possible d'expliquer quoi que ce soit de la vie sociale des hommes, ici et maintenant, à partir d'un commencement dont nul ne sait et ne peut savoir si la nature (et même Dieu) avait organisé l'égalité des hommes ou la soumission de la multitude à une poignée de maîtres.

C'est dans cette perspective qu'il convient de lire le *Discours sur l'origine et les fondements de l'inégalité parmi les hommes*; non pas comme réponse à une question qui n'en est pas une, mais au contraire comme formulation d'une question et découverte d'un problème théorique. Qu'est-ce qui fonde l'inégalité? Voilà la question. Y a-t-il un fondement à l'inégalité? Voilà l'étonnement philosophique. Dès lors, Rousseau oublie pour ainsi dire les académiciens et leurs notions communes. Il répond à la question qu'il a lui-même posée, en deux temps.

La première partie du *Discours* est une remontée théorique vers les principes du droit naturel; au cours de cette *remontée au principe* (sans rapport avec l'imagerie d'un commencement pastoral de l'épopée humaine!), Rousseau rencontre les théoriciens du droit naturel (il les imite, d'ailleurs; il les pille et les critique aussi avec la même conviction faite à la fois de respect et d'irrespect) : Grotius, Hobbes, Locke, Pufendorf, Burlamaqui, etc. La seconde partie du *Discours* décrit, véritable antithèse de la première partie, la chute sociale de l'homme, l'entrée historique dans le mal – et dans le malheur. C'est pourquoi le *Discours*, où de ligne en ligne, de page en page, une pensée se découvre et s'énonce, manifeste une « ferveur intellectuelle » rare dans un texte théorique. « Peu importe, écrit J. Starobinski, que Rousseau ait pris son bien chez les philosophes, chez les jurisconsultes, chez les naturalistes, chez les voyageurs : en intégrant à son œuvre le matériau que lui fournissent ses prédécesseurs, il les fait disparaître et nous dispense d'y recourir. Le *Discours sur l'inégalité* peut avoir tant de sources qu'il plaira aux érudits d'apercevoir; cette œuvre est en elle-même une œuvre-source, à partir de laquelle on peut faire commencer toute la réflexion moderne sur la nature de la société[1]. »

II. Comprenons donc que ce *Discours* est une allégorie, un mythe comparable à ceux dont Platon parsème ses *Dialogues* afin de permettre au lecteur d'accéder aux Formes. C'est, ici, le mythe

1. *Ibid.*, p. LI.

de l'état de nature ou plutôt, c'est « l'état de nature » comme mythe. L'origine à laquelle nous accédons n'est pas un commencement et l'enquête à laquelle nous participons n'est pas une histoire ; en revanche, le mythe de l'état de nature (récit de la *chute* hors de la nature) permet à la fois de comprendre et le principe de notre histoire et le fondement de notre servitude.

Nous pouvons donc, guidés par Rousseau, examiner en philosophes cette étrange mésaventure qui attendait le « genre humain » au tournant d'une histoire tragique : la nôtre. C'est Rousseau lui-même qui le dit, dans un style imité de l'antique, mais qui convient bien pour l'occasion : « Ô homme, de quelque contrée que tu sois, quelles que soient tes opinions, écoute. Voici ton histoire [...] »

L'histoire, donc, commence ainsi : elle commence dans la non-histoire, précisément. L'état de nature est une étendue, un espace, il n'est pas un temps. Il est repos. L'histoire, elle, sera durée, c'est-à-dire inquiétude, travail. Le *Discours* fait le récit édifiant d'une histoire conjecturée et développe ainsi une authentique philosophie de l'histoire. Il retrace le passage du non-historique à l'historique, l'avènement de l'homme et du temps humain. Il condense dans ce roman vrai d'une histoire possible, sinon probable, les éléments d'une *anthropologie philosophique* propre aux modernes que Rousseau, bien entendu, n'invente pas de toutes pièces, mais qu'il structure en un discours cohérent. Il montre comment l'homme (ou plutôt l'animal humain) est un être de besoin qui, au sein de la nature – l'étendue extérieure –, vit d'abord en harmonie avec elle. Puis, à la faveur d'un glissement progressif insensible mais certain, il est doucement confronté à la nécessité et, alors que ses besoins étaient toujours déjà satisfaits, il lui est maintenant de plus en plus nécessaire de travailler. La nature se fait rare, si l'on peut dire ; de mère nourricière, prodigue de ses biens, elle devient avare. Ainsi, l'animal humain devient-il homme : être de besoin, étranger à la nature. L'homme est l'autre de la nature, il s'écarte de l'animalité primitive. Et c'est ici que le *mal* passe : l'homme entre en société à la faveur du travail auquel la nature le contraint. Car la nature ne donne plus rien à l'homme sans travail. Les besoins ne peuvent être satisfaits sans labeur : il semble que la nature se retire et laisse l'homme dans une autre solitude. Avant cette dérive du « besoin », l'individu était solitaire et heureux; son bonheur venait de son appartenance à la nature. Avec le besoin – cette espèce d'accident cosmique – c'est le *genre humain* qui est solitaire car séparé de la nature pour lui résister, ou mieux pour subsister. L'homme est seul avec lui-même et c'est cette toute nouvelle solitude, née d'une inimitié contingente et imprévisible entre homme et nature, qui signe le malheur métaphysique de l'homme.

Homme et nature sont les deux divinités philosophiques forgées par Rousseau dans son *Discours*; ce sont les personnages d'un vaste psychodrame métaphysique qui se déploie pour donner corps à une fiction historique et morale. Homme et nature se substituent opportunément à la Providence et le *Discours* de Rousseau remplace désormais celui de Bossuet sur « l'Histoire universelle ». Il s'agit de pister l'avènement *humain* du malheur : la chute – trop humaine – de l'homme hors de la nature.

On peut suivre Rousseau dans sa généalogie du malheur – cette sorte d'histoire laïque de la chute. La métaphore biblique ici n'est pas forcée : le paradis terrestre des origines mythiques cède la place à un devenir – l'histoire – qui est celui d'un rachat. Il faudra recourir à un *artifice* (le contrat social) pour retrouver les bienfaits de la nature – la béatitude de l'animal naturel –; un artifice et un paradoxe car le salut de l'homme sera dans la société alors même que la généalogie du malheur nous montre par le détail combien la société est fautive[1]. Car, selon Rousseau, le mal n'est pas dans l'homme

1. Car c'est un contresens encore répandu qui court depuis Voltaire – qui fait de Rousseau l'apôtre d'un retour à la nature. Il n'en est rien : la *nature est perdue* à jamais, et c'est cette perte qui est le commencement du *destin* de l'homme : sa chute dans l'histoire du mal. (On se souvient de Voltaire : « J'ay reçu, Monsieur, votre nouveau livre contre le genre humain… On n'a jamais tant employé d'esprit à vouloir nous rendre bêtes. Il prend envie de marcher à quatre pattes quand on lit votre ouvrage… »; lettre de Voltaire à Rousseau du 30 août 1755).

en tant que tel (qui n'est ni bon ni méchant, parce qu'il est l'un et l'autre) ; il n'est pas non plus en Dieu[1], le mal est social. L'*essence sociale* du mal, telle est l'originalité de ce *Discours sur l'inégalité*. L'origine de l'inégalité est dans la société, elle ne procède donc ni des dispositions de la nature, ni des facéties méchantes d'un dieu qui aurait des leçons à donner aux hommes. Quant au *mal* lui-même, il n'est pas une fatalité de la nature humaine. L'homme n'est ni bon ni méchant par nature. On voit que le mal métaphysique qui pèse sur l'homme n'a pas sa solution dans la métaphysique elle-même (et moins encore dans la théologie), mais dans la *politique*. C'est sur le terrain politique (et bien entendu social) que se trouve la solution.

Mais la solution ne saurait procéder des faits. Ou plutôt, ayant « écarté les faits » pour comprendre les causes du mal, on ne saurait y recourir pour trouver les remèdes à ce même mal. Il faut donc recourir au droit. On retrouve ici le *sens philosophique* de la démarche du *Discours*. Rousseau posait la question de droit, c'est-à-dire une question de principe afin d'ordonner son enquête. C'est donc pour lui une conséquence nécessaire que de nous inviter à découvrir le principe d'une solution à la condition malheureuse des hommes. Ce principe est celui-là même du droit : la question de droit – opposée à la question de fait – permet d'atteindre le Droit

1. On a pu dire que le *Discours sur l'inégalité* était une théodicée, *cf.* Cassirer : *Le Problème Jean-Jacques Rousseau* (1932), trad., Paris, 1987, p. 55-57. Mais ce n'est pas assez, aux yeux de Rousseau, de justifier Dieu, il lui importe encore de justifier la nature elle-même : « Un auteur célèbre [Maupertuis] calculant les biens et les maux de la vie humaine et comparant les deux sommes, a trouvé que la dernière surpassait l'autre de beaucoup, et qu'à tout prendre la vie était pour l'homme un assez mauvais présent. Je ne suis point surpris de sa conclusion ; il a tiré tous ses raisonnements de la constitution de l'homme civil : s'il fût remonté jusqu'à l'homme naturel, on peut juger qu'il eût trouvé des résultats très différents, qu'il eût aperçu que l'homme n'a guère de maux que ceux qu'il s'est donnés lui-même, et que la nature eût été justifiée » (note IX ajoutée par Rousseau à son *Discours*).

comme solution au problème politique du mal. Et cette question de droit – *qui institue le règne du droit* – est celle qui rend possible la critique des faits eux-mêmes, qui permet aussi de s'élever à une mise en question de la *légitimité* de l'ordre et des traditions établis[1].

III. Rousseau en ce point joue avec nos nerfs ! En effet, le *Discours* conduit à une sorte d'impasse : d'une part, il administre la preuve de la béatitude du sauvage, mais c'est pour nous avertir, immédiatement, que ce paradis-là est bel et bien perdu : on ne retournera point au paradis. D'autre part – et peut-être corrélativement – la vie civilisée est peinte comme l'avènement d'un terrible malheur. Nous voici donc dans une impasse qui se double en quelque sorte d'un paradoxe : alors même que les hommes ne peuvent pas retourner aux joies sensibles de la vie bucolique, ils sont contraints de rester dans les filets corrompus de la vie civilisée.

À vrai dire, Rousseau donnera le détail de la solution à ce difficile problème dans le *Contrat social.* Solution d'ailleurs, on le verra[2], purement théorique. Bien qu'il esquisse la théorie dans le *Discours sur l'inégalité*, c'est cependant dans le *Contrat* que sera construit le système. Et l'on verra alors que le *Discours* était en somme une introduction générale au système : il y annonce l'obligation de recourir à la philosophie des principes. Le *Discours* est le chemin – une sorte de « long détour » platonicien en dehors de la caverne permettant d'accéder aux lumières de la raison et à l'Idée. Mais il est vrai que le *Discours* ne construit pas l'Idée, il l'annonce, il en brosse l'esquisse, il indique les voies qu'il y a lieu de suivre pour parvenir jusqu'à elle.

1. D'où l'étonnante sagacité de l'académie… 2. Solution entièrement et délibérément *spéculative*, c'est-à-dire qui ne porte que sur le principe lui-même, d'où le sous-titre du *Contrat social* : « Principes du droit politique ». (*Cf. infra.*, notre commentaire du *Contrat.*)

La solution au problème – problème qui, désormais, dépasse de loin la seule question de l'inégalité en ouvrant celle, combien plus ample, de l'homme social, de l'animal civil –, Rousseau la trouvera dans la volonté ; c'est volontairement que les hommes entrent en société. Du coup, ils sont responsables, ils sont libres en se soumettant à une loi qu'ils se sont librement et volontairement donnée. Le *Contrat social* examinera dans le détail l'avènement social et politique de cet animal dénaturé qu'est l'homme. L'anthropologie philosophique élaborée dans le *Discours* livrera de la sorte sa raison d'être. L'homme dé-naturé retrouvera, grâce au *détour philosophique*, les raisons de sa chute et les moyens de reconstituer par un artifice, tout entier réglé par la volonté, le bonheur des origines. La philosophie permet ainsi de recréer dans la société la sensualité perdue de la nature.

N'est-ce pas là donner prise à un immense paradoxe qui plane sur l'ensemble de la réflexion de Rousseau puisque la philosophie – la pensée – assume une lourde responsabilité dans la « dépravation » de l'homme naturel[1] ? On peut le penser. Il reste que par sa véhémence le *Discours sur l'inégalité* se donne comme une violente conversion à la vraie philosophie politique, à une philosophie de la liberté à laquelle, ultime paradoxe, Rousseau nous force et nous contraint. Quiconque se préoccupe de *politique* – parce qu'il la pense ou parce qu'il en fait – a subi ou subira la conversion philosophique du *Discours*. Car, plus encore que dans le *Contrat social*, la philosophie du *Discours* convertit parce qu'elle est rhétorique ; elle persuade plus qu'elle ne démontre. Et c'est précisément cette démonstration qu'entreprendra le *Contrat*.

1. « [...] j'ose presque assurer, écrit Rousseau dans la première partie de son *Discours*, que l'état de réflexion est un état contre nature, et que l'homme qui médite est un animal dépravé. »

Notes

1. « C'est plutôt chez les êtres conformes à la nature que chez ceux qui sont dégradés qu'il faut examiner ce qui est "par nature" » (Aristote, *Politique,* I, 5, 1254-a, traduction P. Pellegrin). Rousseau place en exergue cette affirmation d'Aristote en manière d'hommage certainement, mais surtout parce que cette affirmation du philosophe grec prend son sens au sein d'une philosophie de la nature *(phusis)* qu'il s'agit de réfuter. L'homme *n'est pas*, chez Rousseau comme chez les modernes en général, ce qu'il est chez les anciens et chez Aristote en particulier : un « vivant politique par nature ». L'homme est être social par accident et par volonté. La Cité elle-même n'est pas une réalité existant par nature, ce qu'elle est chez les anciens, mais le fruit d'une convention. Notons encore que, plaçant Aristote en tête de son ouvrage, Rousseau signifie ainsi qu'il ne craint pas de se mesurer aux plus grands.

En fait, c'est la notion de « nature » qui n'a pas le même sens chez un ancien et chez un moderne. Les premiers entendaient par là la totalité de l'être en général en tant qu'il est ordonné à une fin qui lui est propre; cette nature est jaillissement et harmonie des êtres singuliers. Au sein de cette nature, qui est *cosmos*, l'homme est pensé lui-même comme naturel, c'est-à-dire comme nature : son être, la réalité de ce qu'il est, est sa fin même. Cela est vrai également de la cité *(polis)*; réalité existant par nature, la *polis* en procède et doit être réglée selon la nature – et non contre elle. Quant aux modernes, ils entendent par nature, l'étendue extérieure, qui s'oppose et se distingue de la pensée, la matière opposée à l'esprit; la nature est *objet*, l'homme est *sujet*. Une distinction privée de sens pour un Grec.

Dédicace

2. Le « bon sens ou raison », disait Descartes, et cela vaut également pour Rousseau. Rousseau ici marque son intention philosophique : c'est par une analyse de la raison qui interroge les faits

en leur posant la question de droit que Rousseau entend s'occuper de la question politique. Ce ne sont pas des considérations d'intérêt ou d'opportunité qui peuvent rendre compte de la chose publique ; il faut remonter aux principes, par un détour de la raison, afin de découvrir les justes maximes d'un bon gouvernement. Et ces « maximes » sont à la fois des préceptes de la raison et des principes qu'elle seule découvre.

Préface

3. Glaucus, dieu marin dont Platon (*République*, X, 611) figure l'âme humaine : sa face reste visible malgré les outrages du temps et des éléments.

4. *Raisonnements* et *conjectures* sont les deux armes théoriques du *Discours*. Puisque faits et événements permettant de reconstituer la nature humaine originaire, telle qu'elle était avant le temps et l'histoire, sont inconnaissables, il convient de contourner cette difficulté par la raison et non par l'imagination, par exemple, ni même en se donnant un postulat. Conjecturer, c'est raisonner.

5. Passage extrêmement célèbre dans lequel Rousseau écarte tout malentendu possible sur ses intentions. Le *Discours* n'est pas la description d'un « état de nature » historique. Il ne s'agit pas d'enquêter sur une époque historique de l'humanité, alors que celle-ci vivait de pêche et de cueillette. Il s'agit au contraire de reconstruire par un raisonnement le processus contradictoire et malheureux par lequel l'homme en est arrivé à ce qu'il est aujourd'hui, ici et maintenant : soumis, esclave, lui qui jadis était libre et heureux. L'état de nature n'est donc pas un moment de l'histoire humaine, c'est un modèle théorique utile et même « nécessaire » à la compréhension de l'histoire présente. Car, à la différence de l'histoire passée – les premiers commencements – dont nul ne sait ce qu'elle est, l'histoire présente, elle, est connaissable. Et, à vrai dire, réformable. Mais, pour la réformer, c'est-à-dire substituer ce qui doit être à ce qui est, il faut établir ce qui fut. Or, ce qui fut jadis est inconnaissable si l'on s'en tient à la seule observation. Rousseau entreprend donc de

construire un *modèle théorique* de l'évolution-régression du passé au présent.

L'effet produit est extrêmement dangereux. Le modèle théorique de l'état de nature s'applique alors, une fois bien construit, à une réalité historique dont il rend compte adéquatement : le présent lui-même. Aussi, quand Rousseau dit que cet état de nature n'existera probablement jamais, il a raison de le dire, si l'on entend par là la paix et la félicité de la vie pastorale. Mais il sait bien que l'autre côté de l'état de nature (alors qu'un état civil digne de ce nom n'est pas encore établi), l'état de nature que décrit Hobbes, véritable état de guerre entre les hommes existe, lui, bel et bien, non pas dans le passé des origines, mais dans les temps historiques présents.

La *fiction* de l'état de nature permet ainsi de poser à l'histoire, celle-là même que Rousseau a sous les yeux, la question éminemment philosophique : *de quel droit ?* C'est à cela que s'emploie le *Discours sur l'inégalité.*

6. Burlamaqui, jurisconsulte de Genève, auteur d'un traité dont Rousseau était familier : *Principes du droit naturel* (1747).

7. « Il serait bien difficile de convenir d'une bonne définition de la loi naturelle ». Ce jugement sert de conclusion à la discussion précédente dans laquelle Rousseau distingue et oppose les anciens aux modernes (*cf. supra*, note 1). Il est clair que dans ce passage Rousseau discute (et met en cause) la pertinence de la question posée par l'académie de Dijon ; la « loi naturelle », semble-t-il dire, n'est pas définissable, on ne peut donc en partir comme si sa définition allait de soi.

Il importe donc de définir la loi naturelle chez les modernes. Elle doit être distinguée du droit naturel. Chez les modernes, le droit naturel d'un être quelconque est égal à sa puissance : c'est ce que je peux faire, c'est ce que je suis libre de faire ; c'est ce qu'il est en mon pouvoir de faire. Le droit énonce ainsi une *liberté.* Hobbes (*Léviathan*, livres I et II), Spinoza (*Traité théologico-politique*, chap. XVI), Locke (*Second traité du gouvernement civil*, chap. II, III) sont les meilleurs représentants philosophes du droit naturel moderne. Quant aux jurisconsultes modernes, outre Burlamaqui déjà cité, il y a notamment Pufendorf, professeur de droit naturel à Heidelberg en 1661, auteur d'un traité latin en 1672, traduit en français par Barbeyrac en 1706 et que Rousseau a étudié : *Le Droit de la nature et des gens.* Quant à ce que les modernes nomment loi (naturelle ou civile), elle est dans son principe général un commandement emportant l'obéissance[1]. Commandement de la nature (loi naturelle) de me conserver dans l'être, commandement du souverain (loi positive) de régler ma conduite conformément à la volonté commune.

En ce sens, la relation qu'entretiennent la loi et le droit est, chez les modernes, l'inverse de ce qu'elle était chez les anciens, et chez Aristote en particulier. Le droit naturel des anciens est ce droit – *jus* – qui procède de la nature. On le connaît en observant la nature et son ordre. C'est la constitution même de la *phusis.* Dans l'ordre politique, la loi sera donc l'expression du droit naturel ainsi entendu : la loi de la cité ne fera qu'exprimer le *juste par nature.* Cela signifie que la loi est l'expression du droit (du juste); elle l'énonce. Chez les modernes cette relation sera inversée radicalement : c'est la loi (volonté) qui, en s'énonçant, énoncera le juste – le droit.

8. Amour de soi et pitié sont les deux piliers de cette morale naturelle que Rousseau préfère à la loi et au droit naturels. Puisqu'il n'y a pas d'homme naturel – il n'y a que des civilisés –, on ne peut en effet que supposer chez l'homme l'existence de ces deux sentiments « antérieurs à la raison ».

Dans la note XV qu'il ajoute au *Discours sur l'inégalité*, Rousseau distingue entre « amour de soi » et « amour-propre » : « Il ne

1. En ce sens, la loi-rapport de Montesquieu est également un commandement emportant l'obéissance : « Les lois, dans la signification la plus étendue, sont les rapports nécessaires qui dérivent de la nature des choses » (*De l'esprit des lois*, I, 1). Tous les êtres, en effet, sont contraints d'exister et donc d'obéir et de se soumettre aux lois de leur nature et de la nature.

faut pas confondre l'amour-propre et l'amour de soi-même, écrit-il ; deux passions très différentes par leur nature et par leurs effets. L'amour de soi-même est un sentiment naturel qui porte tout animal à veiller à sa propre conservation[1] et qui, dirigé dans l'homme par la raison et modifié par la pitié, produit l'humanité et la vertu. L'amour-propre n'est qu'un sentiment relatif, factice et né dans la société, qui porte chaque individu à faire plus de cas de soi que de tout autre, qui inspire aux hommes tous les maux qu'ils se font mutuellement et qui est la véritable source de l'honneur. Ceci bien entendu, je dis que dans notre état primitif, dans le véritable état de nature, l'amour-propre n'existe pas. »

9. Traduction : « Apprends ce que Dieu a ordonné que tu sois, et où est ta place dans le monde humain » (Perse, *Satires*, III, 71-73).

Préambule

10. Célèbre précepte de méthode aux allures de provocation. En fait, Rousseau s'affirme ici philosophe – non parce que le philosophe mépriserait les faits ! mais au contraire, parce qu'il entend les expliquer. On ne saurait donc en partir en tant que principes et normes de l'explication, puisqu'il s'agit précisément de les comprendre. Plus haut il vient de dire, critiquant les philosophes qui se sont succédé dans l'étude de l'homme : « Ils parlaient de l'homme sauvage, et ils peignaient l'homme civil. » C'est la confusion du fait et du droit qui rend possible une telle confusion. « Commençons donc par écarter tous les faits » signifie : posons aux faits la question de droit.

Première partie

11. Ce « philosophe illustre » est Montesquieu (*De l'esprit des lois*, I, 2). Quant à Thomas Hobbes, il expose dans le *Léviathan*

1. C'est donc ce que philosophes et jurisconsultes appellent « loi naturelle ».

(1651) la théorie la plus complète de l'état de nature comme état de guerre (I, 13). La condition naturelle des hommes, déterminés qu'ils sont par le désir, est une immense contradiction opposant la *loi* naturelle au *droit* naturel : la loi naturelle leur enjoint de faire tout ce qu'il est en leur pouvoir de faire pour se conserver dans l'être ; le droit naturel leur enseigne que tout est permis pour obéir à la loi de nature. De cette antinomie de la loi et du droit de nature naît la lutte à mort de chacun contre chacun et de tous contre tous. C'est l'état de guerre. Cette théorie hobbesienne de l'état de guerre est critiquée par Richard Cumberland, auteur, en 1672, d'un *Traité philosophique des lois naturelles* et par Pufendorf *(Droit de la nature et des gens)*.

12. De cette critique de la médecine surgit brusquement un chef-d'œuvre de l'art rhétorique de Rousseau : « L'homme qui médite est un animal dépravé. » La pensée (et donc la philosophie), en permettant à l'homme de s'écarter, de s'éloigner et enfin de quitter la nature, est un instrument de la chute hors de la nature. Par là, le philosophe et le médecin ont ensemble une même responsabilité dans la dépravation de l'homme, celui-ci parce qu'il diminue le corps, celui-là parce qu'il substitue l'idée au sentiment. (*Cf.* note suivante).

13. Rousseau vient d'affirmer, au détour d'une phrase : « l'esprit déprave les sens ». Ce thème de la dépravation – issue de la pensée (« esprit », dit ici Rousseau ; « réflexion », disait-il tout à l'heure) est à mettre en contrepoint de celui de la perfectibilité (*cf.* note suivante) : il le prépare et l'annonce.

On saisit ainsi la dialectique de Rousseau : l'homme, qui est un animal, échappe à la bestialité franche par sa capacité à devenir meilleur. Car, si une telle capacité lui manquait, il ne serait pas différent des bêtes. Rousseau se tient donc en ce point du *Discours* sur une ligne de crête extrêmement périlleuse. Périlleuse du point de vue de la démonstration. Mais il ne démontre pas, il affirme et il persuade : si l'homme qui pense et réfléchit est un animal dépravé, c'est cependant à sa capacité de produire des idées que l'homme doit d'échapper virtuellement à la bestialité. Mieux, c'est dans sa capacité à prendre conscience de ses idées que l'homme est un peu plus qu'une simple bête. « Tout animal a des idées puisqu'il a des sens » semble être une proposition issue tout droit du sensualisme de Condillac. Mais Rousseau s'en démarque très vite quelques lignes plus bas ; il accorde alors que, chez l'homme, ce qu'il appelle la « puissance de vouloir ou plutôt de choisir » est de nature spirituelle. On passe donc de l'animal à l'esprit en écartant la bête.

Il y a donc bel et bien de l'esprit dans cet animal dépravé et c'est cet esprit qui le rend perfectible.

14. Nous voici arrivés à la notion de « perfectibilité ». Elle renvoie à l'idée de *progrès moral* chère au XVIIIe et chère à Rousseau en particulier. Rousseau, on le voit, s'efforce donc de montrer la *possibilité* du progrès moral et intellectuel à partir de l'affirmation de la régression sociale et de la dépravation de l'homme naturel. Du coup, l'histoire n'est pas seulement celle de la chute, elle devient en même temps la préhistoire du progrès. Et le *Discours* n'est pas seulement la généalogie du mal, il est l'archéologie des conditions du progrès. C'est entre ces deux durées, l'une qui engendre la réalité du mal actuel, l'autre la possibilité du bien futur que se situe le destin de l'homme. Et son choix. On voit déjà que l'homme est terriblement libre : le choix lui appartient. Plus que jamais, Rousseau met l'homme en face de ses responsabilités. C'est de ton histoire qu'il s'agit ! s'exclame-t-il au début du *Discours*. C'est un appel à la volonté, au choix d'un destin qui le fera retrouver sa qualité d'homme ou bien le fera irrémédiablement retourner chez les animaux… et régresser jusqu'aux bêtes (*cf. supra* notre commentaire).

15. Condillac, dans son *Essai sur l'origine des connaissances humaines* (1746) fait le récit allégorique de l'invention des langues par deux enfants. En général, la critique que Rousseau adresse aux spéculations sur l'origine des langues par le moyen d'une convention est, dit-il, que « la parole paraît avoir été fort nécessaire, pour établir l'usage de la parole ». Et Rousseau un peu plus loin mettra un terme à cette discussion sur l'origine des langues en formulant ainsi le problème qui, en effet, se pose et qui, ainsi posé, est sans

solution : « lequel a été le plus nécessaire, de la société déjà liée, à l'institution des langues, ou des langues déjà inventées à l'établissement de la société ». C'est un cercle logique.

16. Traduction : « Chez eux l'ignorance des vices est plus efficace que chez d'autres la connaissance de la vertu. »

17. Bernard de Mandeville, écrivain politique anglais est l'auteur en 1723 de *The Fable of the Bees, or private Vices public Benefits. La Fable des abeilles : vices privés et prospérité publique* défendait la théorie selon laquelle la vertu est incapable de produire des richesses. Au contraire, les séductions du vice et le goût du luxe sont les véritables moteurs de l'économie ; eux seuls permettent l'opulence : « Quittez donc vos plaintes, mortels insensés ! En vain vous cherchez à associer la grandeur d'une nation avec la probité. »

18. *Cf. supra*, note 8.

19. Rousseau examine ici le *désir* comme essence de l'homme. En cela il continue une tradition inaugurée par Hobbes et surtout Spinoza : le désir est pulsion de la nature, un « besoin » qui, dès lors qu'il est satisfait, disparaît de lui-même. Et Rousseau prendra soin dans les lignes suivantes de « distinguer le moral du physique dans le sentiment de l'amour ». Alors que le physique de l'amour est une pulsion de la nature, au contraire, le « moral de l'amour » est un sentiment factice issu de la société. Il permet d'élucider la relation homme-femme en tant que relation sociale de domination : « Il est facile de voir que le moral de l'amour est un sentiment factice ; né de la société, et célébré par les femmes avec beaucoup d'habileté et de soin pour établir leur empire, et rendre dominant le sexe qui devrait obéir. »

20. Ce paragraphe explicite le résultat auquel la première partie du *Discours* nous a permis de parvenir. C'est la notion de perfectibilité qui est mise en avant. Elle signifie que l'homme est virtuellement capable du meilleur : les « vertus sociales » sont en puissance, dit-il, dans l'homme naturel, mais elles ne peuvent d'elles-mêmes provoquer le passage à la vie civile. Il faut pour cela des « causes étrangères ». « C'est la faiblesse de l'homme qui le rend sociable, écrit

Rousseau dans l'*Émile* (livre IV) ; ce sont nos misères communes qui portent nos cœurs à l'humanité : nous ne lui devrions rien si nous n'étions pas hommes. » Ainsi que l'indique J. Starobinski (ouvr. cité), Rousseau affirme la nécessité de comprendre simultanément histoire morale et histoire politique du « genre humain ».

Seconde partie

21. Le *temps* ou, plutôt, la conscience du temps (et conséquemment sa mesure) est le moteur de l'engagement mutuel. C'est à partir de l'appropriation du temps que toute autre appropriation est possible et que la société elle-même est possible. En effet, Rousseau montre que l'idée de *contrat* – les « engagements mutuels » – suppose une représentation des trois moments du temps, et, en tout cas, une *anticipation de l'avenir.* Ce que quitte l'homme à l'état de nature, c'est donc le présent, pour entrer dans l'avenir. Le temps – qui sera le temps de l'histoire – est l'avenir. Chez les modernes, dont Rousseau contribue ici même avec ce *Discours* à élaborer l'anthropologie philosophique, le temps de l'histoire est le temps de l'avenir. Le projet historique des hommes – et c'est en cela qu'il doit être dit « historique » – est une conquête de l'avenir. Le présent, au contraire, correspond à une non-histoire, il est l'instant de la jouissance naturelle, il est l'élément de l'immédiateté sensible. Avec l'appropriation du temps – dans la forme du contrat, contrat d'échange des biens, et bientôt contrat social et politique – l'homme cesse définitivement, pour son malheur selon Rousseau, d'être naturel. Histoire (temps humain de l'*avenir*) s'oppose ici à nature (durée organique du *présent*). On trouvera l'exposé conceptuel le plus général de cette conception spécifiquement moderne de l'homme et de son histoire dans Hegel dont la *Phénoménologie de l'esprit* (1807) retrace le parcours de l'esprit hors de la nature.

Cette conception du temps est au service d'une conception de la liberté propre aux modernes et ne peut s'entendre qu'en référence à l'opposition homme-nature.

22. La première ligne de cette seconde partie était écrite pour réfuter le *droit* de propriété – qui n'est pas, selon Rousseau, un droit de nature car c'est plutôt un droit de la société civile : « Le premier qui, ayant enclos un terrain, s'avisa de dire : *Ceci est à moi*, et trouva des gens assez simples pour le croire, fut le vrai fondateur de la société civile. » Mais il est vrai que les choses étant ordonnées à la propriété et par elle, Rousseau reste fidèle à son inspiration et ne peut que constater et comprendre cet état de fait. Et la généalogie du mal – genèse de la société civile – doit donc partir de la propriété. Or, l'effet le plus marquant et le plus décisif de la propriété est la division du travail avec ses deux pôles essentiels : l'agriculture et la métallurgie. Rousseau n'a alors pas de mal à « imaginer le reste » comme il dit.

À vrai dire la propriété, véritable calamité des origines, s'avère cependant avoir été le moteur permettant aux hommes de développer leurs facultés latentes : grâce à elle ils peuvent « porter leurs vues dans l'avenir », la raison est « rendue active » et l'esprit « arrivé presque au terme de la perfection, dont il est susceptible ».

23. Traduction : « Épouvanté d'un mal si nouveau, riche et misérable tout ensemble, il désire échapper à ses richesses, et ce qu'il avait souhaité naguère, il le hait », Ovide, *Métamorphoses*, XI, 127 (*in* Starobinski, ouvr. cité, p. 1350), Rousseau ici fait sienne la théorie hobbesienne de l'état de nature : l'homme y est un loup pour l'homme. L'état de nature est un état de guerre. Mais cette acceptation provisoire des thèses de Hobbes est pour ainsi dire une ruse. Car Rousseau s'empressera de ridiculiser le pacte de soumission que Hobbes propose dans *Léviathan* pour sortir de l'état de guerre. La formule hobbesienne de la soumission au souverain à laquelle Rousseau fait allusion (deux paragraphes plus bas à la suite de la citation d'Ovide) est celle-ci : « J'autorise cet homme ou cette assemblée, et je lui abandonne mon droit de me gouverner moi-même, à cette condition que tu lui abandonnes ton droit et tu autorises toutes ses actions de la même manière » (*Léviathan*, XVII).

24. C'est donc la propriété qui cause l'inégalité, et l'on sait que la propriété est d'institution humaine. Ici Rousseau critique à la fois

Hobbes (*cf.* note précédente) et Locke. Le premier pour avoir fait de la force un droit par un pacte honteux du fort sur le faible. Le second pour faire de la propriété le fondement de tout lien civil. En effet, on lit dans Locke, *Second Traité du gouvernement civil*, § 124 : « La fin capitale et principale, en vue de laquelle les hommes s'associent dans des républiques et se soumettent à des gouvernements, c'est la conservation de leur propriété. »

Au fond le *Discours sur l'inégalité* est tout entier dirigé à la fois contre Hobbes et Locke reconnus ensemble coupables de donner à la société des fondements faux et, pire encore, illégitimes : Hobbes fonde la société et l'État sur la soumission et la force déguisée en droit ; Locke fonde la société sur la propriété.

Rousseau, qui partait dans le *Discours sur l'inégalité* à la recherche d'un fondement vrai à la société, récuse donc ces deux fondements (qui n'en sont pas) et propose, lui, un *fondement moral.*

25. La soumission au souverain, chez Hobbes, est définitive.

26. Cette « maxime du droit politique » fait écho à l'affirmation de Spinoza, qui traverse toute son œuvre politique, selon laquelle la fin de l'État est la liberté de l'individu. Du coup, ce dernier conserve son droit naturel, une conséquence que se garde bien de tirer Rousseau quand il s'agit, dans le *Contrat social*, de déterminer les clauses du contrat (*cf. infra*, notre commentaire du *Contrat*).

27. Traduction : « C'est une affreuse servitude qu'ils appellent la paix », Tacite, *Histoires*, IV, 17.

28. Cette description rapide du « vrai contrat » afin de contrebalancer le faux contrat de Hobbes (et de Locke) est une version très rudimentaire et surtout très différente de ce que sera le contrat définitif, tel que l'exposera le *Contrat social.* Ici, il s'agit peut-on dire d'une version libéralisée du pacte de soumission de Hobbes. Rousseau parle ici d'un « vrai contrat entre le peuple et ses chefs ». Il y a chez Hobbes un faux contrat entre les individus de la multitude (qui n'est pas encore peuple) s'engageant entre eux à se soumettre au souverain qui les représente. Dans les deux cas le

pacte a pour effet la soumission verticale de la multitude au maître. Dans le *Discours*, Rousseau confond encore souveraineté et gouvernement, d'où l'idée d'un contrat entre gouvernés et gouvernants (« le peuple et ses chefs »). Rousseau pense ainsi – à l'époque du *Discours* – s'opposer à l'absolutisme de Hobbes pour qui le pacte liant les gouvernés *entre eux* les soumet au souverain qui, lui, *n'est pas* partie au contrat. L'originalité du *Contrat social* sera de présenter la formule inédite d'un contrat horizontal, liant les individus entre eux pour les lier en commun à la volonté générale, c'est-à-dire en fait à eux-mêmes comme « peuple » et d'affirmer simultanément que la relation gouvernés/gouvernants n'est pas, elle, un contrat.

En fait, on verra (*cf. infra*, notre commentaire du *Contrat*) que la théorie rousseauiste du contrat social est une traduction stricte, en termes contractualistes propres à l'école du droit naturel, de la théorie bodinienne de la souveraineté. Pour l'heure, constatons que, lorsqu'il écrit le *Discours sur l'inégalité*, Rousseau n'est pas en complète possession de son concept fondateur de volonté générale.

29. Traduction (J. Starobinski, *in* ouvr. cité, p. 1358). « Si tu m'ordonnes d'enfoncer le glaive dans la poitrine de mon frère et dans la gorge de mon père ou encore dans les entrailles de mon épouse enceinte, fût-ce à contrecœur, j'accomplirai tout. » (Lucain, *Pharsale*, I, 36.)

30. Traduction : « Qui ne met aucun espoir dans l'honnêteté » (d'après Tacite, *Histoires*, I, 21, selon J. Starobinski).

31. Ce paragraphe est une véritable charge contre ce qui est déjà l'Ancien Régime. Il décrit tout simplement l'inégalité sociale comme « état de nature ». Ce texte appelle de fait[1] à une refondation car, ayant diagnostiqué le mal, on ne voit pas que la philosophie dans laquelle s'est engagé Rousseau reculerait à proposer un

---

1. Bien que Rousseau n'ait jamais eu le projet politique réel de recourir à une transformation révolutionnaire des choses ou d'y contribuer explicitement.

remède. Tout ici en effet est à recommencer : « C'est ici que tous les particuliers redeviennent égaux parce qu'ils ne sont rien ». Ce jugement semble déjà anticiper les paroles révolutionnaires, car il n'est pas loin de proclamer le droit du peuple – qui n'est rien – à devenir quelque chose.

Discours sur l'économie politique

Notes

1. Rédigé par Rousseau vraisemblablement fin 1754, le *Discours sur l'économie politique* est un article pour l'*Encyclopédie* de Diderot et d'Alembert ; il fut publié dans le tome V en novembre 1755.

La notion d'économie politique n'est pas prise dans le sens que nous lui connaissons aujourd'hui[1]. Rousseau l'entend dans un sens étymologique dont il s'explique dès les premières lignes de son article : il s'agit en fait de la théorie du gouvernement, c'est-à-dire de l'application de la loi à l'administration des choses. Le dernier tiers de l'article sera d'ailleurs consacré à l'administration des finances publiques. La problématique fondamentale du *Discours sur l'économie politique* consiste à distinguer « *souveraineté* » (qui est le principe de l'État) et « *gouvernement* » (qui est la forme de l'administration de l'État).

Dans cet article, Rousseau manifeste un extrême souci de pragmatisme ; c'est sa première incursion dans le domaine de la « poli-

---

1. C'est à Adam Smith que l'on doit notre conception de la science économique comme science de la *nature et des causes de la richesse.* L'ouvrage d'Adam Smith, *Recherches sur la nature et les causes de la richesse des nations*, fut publié en 1776. A. Smith était l'ami de David Hume.

tique appliquée », selon l'expression de Barbara de Negroni. Il y en aura deux autres à propos de la Corse et de la Pologne[1].

2. Rousseau vient de procéder à l'élimination de tout ce qui n'est pas de son sujet : principalement l'homologie traditionnelle entre le pouvoir du père de famille et celui du chef politique. Cette thèse (illustrée par le théoricien de l'absolutisme monarchique Filmer[2]) avait déjà été réfutée par Locke dans son premier *Traité du gouvernement civil* (1690). Comme Rousseau l'écrit un peu plus bas dans le texte : « l'État n'a rien de commun avec la famille ».

3. Aristote, *Politique*, I, 1, 1252-a. : « Quant à ceux qui pensent qu'être homme politique, roi, chef de famille, maître d'esclave, c'est la même chose, ils n'ont pas raison. C'est, en effet, selon le grand ou le petit nombre, pensent-ils que chacune de ces fonctions diffère des autres, et non pas selon une différence spécifique : ainsi, quand on commanderait à peu de gens on serait maître, à plus de gens chef de famille, et à encore plus homme politique ou roi, comme s'il n'y avait aucune différence entre une grande famille et une petite cité. » Traduction P. Pellegrin, GF-Flammarion, Paris, 1990.

4. Il s'agit de la distinction établie par Bodin dans les *Six Livres de la République* (1576), et que Rousseau fait sienne, entre État ou souveraineté, et gouvernement ou magistrats. Le *Contrat social* est entièrement construit sur cette distinction fondamentale. *Cf. infra* notre commentaire du *Contrat social.*

5. Dans l'*Encyclopédie*, à l'article *Droit naturel*, Diderot écrit : « La soumission à la volonté générale est le lien de toutes les sociétés, sans en excepter celles qui sont formées par le crime. Hélas, la vertu est si belle, que les voleurs en respectent l'image dans le fond même de leurs cavernes ! » (cité par Barbara de Negroni, ouvr. cité, p. 266).

---

1. Sur la « politique appliquée » de Rousseau, *cf.* l'Introduction et les commentaires de B. de Negroni à son édition des textes de Rousseau (*cf. infra*, bibliographie). 2. *Patriarcha*, l'ouvrage de Filmer que réfute Locke, a été publié après la mort de Filmer en 1680.

6. Hommage à Machiavel que l'on retrouvera dans le *Contrat social* (III, 6).

7. Sans la loi, issue de la volonté générale, les hommes retourneraient à la servitude issue de la force. Le *Contrat social* (I, III) réduira à néant le sophisme – sémantique et moral – du droit du plus fort. Dans ce paragraphe, Rousseau se laisse aller au lyrisme : « prodiges », « voix céleste ».

8. Telle est bien la thèse centrale de ce *Discours sur l'économie politique* : le gouvernement a pour tâche d'administrer la volonté générale, c'est-à-dire qu'il doit se borner à faire passer la généralité de la loi dans la particularité des choses. Cette affirmation est corrélative de cette autre : que le souverain seul est l'auteur de la volonté générale. Le « gouvernement », lui, n'est qu'un exécutant, mandaté pour un temps par le souverain, de sa volonté. Le problème théorique – et pratique – est de faire en sorte que le gouvernement ne se substitue pas de fait au souverain, autrement dit que sa volonté particulière ne supplante pas la volonté générale.

9. Apparaît ici, comme en filigrane, l'idée qui sera développée dans le *Contrat* de la liberté comme autonomie : « l'obéissance à la loi qu'on s'est prescrite est liberté » (*Contrat social*, I, VIII).

10. Il s'agit ici de la vertu civique, c'est-à-dire de la moralité publique, fondée objectivement sur la volonté générale, telle qu'elle existe dans la conscience individuelle. C'est la vertu du citoyen, dont Rousseau dit qu'elle réside dans l'accord de sa volonté propre, particulière, avec la volonté générale. Rousseau inaugure la théorie de la moralité sur laquelle se fonde le système « républicain » de la citoyenneté. C'est l'idée de *devoir* qui structure ici sa pensée ; il évoquera, dans les paragraphes suivants, l'amour du devoir. Le *Contrat social* développe cette thématique dans la forme plus rigoureuse de la déduction *a priori* des principes.

11. Ce principe – l'État protège jusqu'au « dernier de ses membres » avec la même – détermination qu'il veille au salut de la communauté elle-même est le corrélat nécessaire de l'accord existant entre la volonté individuelle et la volonté générale, entre le particulier et l'universel.

12. Ce dernier paragraphe est à lui seul un véritable résumé de la finalité morale et politique de « l'éducation publique » républicaine : faire de l'homme un *citoyen.* L'éducation du citoyen, Rousseau l'entend comme équilibre des droits et des devoirs : « [...] comme on participe en naissant aux droits des citoyens, l'instant de notre naissance doit être le commencement de l'exercice de nos devoirs. » C'est donc en développant très tôt chez l'enfant « l'amour de la patrie » que le citoyen intégrera en sa conscience individuelle le sens du bien commun.

13. D'après R. Derathé (« Bibliothèque de la Pléiade », p. 1403), voir Pufendorf, *Droit de la nature et des gens* (IV, 10, § 4).

14. « L'instituteur d'une république », c'est-à-dire le législateur (*cf. Contrat social*, II, VII).

15. « Il nourrit et il enrichit » (B. de Negroni).

16. Contrat de dupes, qu'on ose à peine appeler « contrat ». Le contrat suppose l'égalité formelle des deux contractants : or, il n'y a pas, par définition, d'*égalité* de quelque sorte que ce soit entre le riche et le pauvre. Cependant, ce faux contrat que ridiculise Rousseau montre *a contrario* que la servitude politique a pour cause l'inégalité économique.

Écrits sur l'abbé de Saint-Pierre

Notes

Jugement sur le projet de paix perpétuelle

1. Charles Irénée Castel, abbé de Saint-Pierre (1658-1743) est l'auteur d'un *Projet de paix perpétuelle* en 3 volumes, publié de 1713 à 1717. Mme Dupin demanda à Rousseau (qui était alors son secrétaire) de lui faire un résumé de l'œuvre ; Rousseau s'acquitta de sa tâche entre 1756 et 1759. Rousseau disait de l'abbé : « C'eût

été un homme très sage s'il n'eût eu la folie de la raison. » Outre le résumé de l'œuvre, Rousseau rédigea un « *Jugement* » que nous donnons ici et un texte sur « *L'état de guerre* ». Ces deux textes se complètent par leur objet qui est d'examiner la possibilité de la paix dans une Europe orientée plutôt à la guerre, et, par conséquent, de définir la guerre elle-même. L'« utopie » de l'abbé ne rencontra aucun écho en son temps ; l'ouvrage était inspiré par un plan de fédération du monde chrétien dont Sully fait état dans ses *Économies royales* (1638-1662) et attribué à Henri IV. D'où la longue évocation du rôle pacifique du « bon roi » dans le *Jugement* de Rousseau.

Mais l'intérêt du *Jugement*, rédigé à la manière d'un compte rendu, réside principalement dans la charge extrêmement virulente contre la monarchie rendue responsable de la guerre des nations – d'où, aux yeux de Rousseau, l'intérêt du projet d'Henri IV, roi fédérateur.

2. Principe méthodologique général chez Rousseau : les faits ne sont jamais juges de ce qui est vrai *a priori*, c'est-à-dire selon la raison ; l'événement n'est pas juge des principes.

3. Cette distinction de l'apparence et du réel est déjà celle qui fonde la rhétorique du *Discours sur les sciences et les arts* (*cf.* notre commentaire, note 2). Le réel – ici l'intérêt réel, autrement dit, le véritable intérêt – est opposé aux données historiques observables (« l'apparent ») : les monarchies. Il faut donc induire de cette opposition de l'apparent et du réel que *la monarchie s'oppose à l'intérêt véritable des peuples et des nations.* Et Rousseau nomme ensuite cet intérêt véritable ou, mieux, cet intérêt général ; c'est, dit-il, le *bien public*, le *bonheur des sujets*, la *gloire de la nation* : toutes choses qui sont mises en échec par l'intérêt particulier des rois. C'est pourquoi Rousseau souligne avec force l'incapacité des rois (des « princes ») de se soumettre au droit. Or, une union fédérative serait une union juridique, fondée sur la souveraineté du droit[1].

1. Observons que ce thème sera repris et conceptualisé par Kant dans un texte fondateur reprenant d'ailleurs le titre du livre de l'abbé : *Vers la paix perpétuelle* (1795). Une traduction française

4. Après ce préambule Rousseau se livre à la critique radicale de la monarchie comme système politique d'assujettissement des peuples à la guerre.

5. Réalisme de Rousseau. Le projet de Saint-Pierre n'est pas faux parce qu'irréalisable – puisqu'il est vrai selon la raison –; mais il faut savoir que sa mise en œuvre suppose une révolution. Rousseau semble demander : peut-on *vouloir* une révolution « qui ferait peut-être plus de mal tout d'un coup qu'elle n'en préviendrait pour des siècles »? En méditant sur l'abbé de Saint-Pierre, Rousseau écrivait déjà pour la révolution *sans le savoir et sans le vouloir.*

L'état de guerre

6. Dans *Léviathan* (1651), Hobbes énonce la théorie de l'état de nature comme état de guerre de chacun contre tous (*cf.* notre commentaire du *Discours sur l'inégalité*, note 11).

7. Par définition la loi est un commandement auquel tout homme est soumis. La loi *naturelle* est donc un commandement de la nature. Déjà au début du *Discours sur l'inégalité*, Rousseau écartait l'idée d'une connaissance de la loi naturelle par la seule raison : « Il est impossible d'entendre la loi de nature et par conséquent d'y obéir, sans être ùn très grand raisonneur et un profond métaphysicien. Ce qui signifie précisément que les hommes ont dû employer pour l'établissement de la société des lumières qui ne se développent qu'avec beaucoup de peine et pour fort peu de gens dans le sein de la société même. » Il revient donc à cette idée ici même, dans ce texte sur *l'état de guerre* et précise que la loi de nature est une loi qui parle au « cœur » de tout homme, plutôt qu'à la raison (sur le problème de la définition de la « loi naturelle » *cf.* notre commentaire du *Discours sur l'inégalité*, note 7).

---

anonyme, datant de 1796, a été immédiatement transmise à Sieyès; *cf.* l'intéressante mise au point de Heinz Wismann, éditeur dans la « Pléiade » du texte de Kant, *Œuvres philosophiques*, III, p. 329-331.

En fait, Rousseau reproche au « sophiste » Hobbes d'avoir brossé le portrait féroce de l'homme à l'état de nature en lui prêtant les caractères de l'homme civil assujetti à une autorité politique illégitime. On voit que, du point de vue de Rousseau, une loi « naturelle » qui serait, comme chez Hobbes, connue par la raison, ne serait en vérité qu'une simple loi de l'état de société.

8. *Cf. Contrat social*, I, IV.

9. Ici comme ailleurs, Rousseau entend parler du point de vue de la vérité, c'est-à-dire du point de vue de la raison : il pense les *principes*.

10. C'est-à-dire de l'état civil ou politique. La guerre est donc pour Rousseau le produit de la souveraineté, non de l'état de nature (c'est ce qu'il écrit explicitement quelques lignes plus bas). Observons que c'est dans cette perspective – il n'est de guerre qu'entre les États, non entre les hommes – que la théorie de la guerre moderne a été élaborée par Clausewitz qui observait, lui, les guerres napoléoniennes : « Nous disons donc, écrit Clausewitz, que la guerre n'appartient pas au domaine des arts et des sciences, mais à celui de l'existence sociale. Elle est un conflit des grands intérêts réglé par le sang, et c'est seulement en cela qu'elle diffère des autres conflits. Il vaudrait mieux la comparer, plutôt qu'à un art quelconque, au commerce, qui est aussi un conflit d'intérêts et d'activités humaines ; elle ressemble *encore plus* à la politique… De plus la politique est la matrice dans laquelle la guerre se développe ; ses linéaments formés rudimentairement s'y cachent comme les propriétés des créatures vivantes[1]. »

11. Sur la théorie de l'État comme « être moral », *cf. Contrat social*, II, IV, et note 25.

12. Rousseau a raison de dire « comme j'ai toujours fait » (ci-dessus note 9) ; il entend élaborer les fondements (*cf. infra* notre commentaire I et II du *Contrat social*).

---

1. Carl von Clausewitz, *De la guerre* (1834), trad. P. Naville, Paris, Minuit, 1955, p. 145.

13. La crainte du système de Hobbes n'empêche pas Rousseau d'admirer le philosophe, à la fois « sophiste » et « beau génie ».

14. Voir *supra*, note 7.

Du contrat social

Commentaire

I. Le projet théorique de Rousseau dans le *Contrat social*

On lit dans les *Confessions* : « J'étais assez magnifique en projets… Des divers ouvrages que j'avais sur le chantier, celui que je méditais depuis plus longtemps, dont je m'occupais avec le plus de goût, auquel je voulais travailler toute ma vie, et qui devait selon moi mettre le sceau à ma réputation était mes *Institutions politiques*. Il y avait treize à quatorze ans que j'en avais conçu la première idée, lorsqu'étant à Venise j'avais eu quelqu'occasion de remarquer les défauts de ce gouvernement si vanté. Depuis lors, mes vues s'étaient beaucoup étendues par l'étude historique de la morale. J'avais vu que tout tenait radicalement à la politique, et que, de quelque façon qu'on s'y prît, aucun peuple ne serait jamais que ce que la nature de son Gouvernement le ferait être[1]. »

Le projet des *Institutions*… demeura ce qu'il n'a jamais cessé d'être : un projet de jeunesse. Et Rousseau se contenta de rédiger deux fois[2] un traité politique de moindre volume, mais de plus grande envergure, qui devint *Du contrat social ou Principes du*

---

1. *Œuvres complètes*, Gallimard, « Bibliothèque de la Pléiade », I, p. 84. 2. La première version du *Contrat* est connue sous le titre de « Manuscrit de Genève ». Nous en donnons un extrait ici en Annexe au *Contrat social* (*cf. supra*, p. 395).

droit politique. Publié en 1762 chez Rey à Amsterdam, le livre passa pratiquement inaperçu du grand public de son temps. Et ce n'est que sous la Révolution que sa carrière commença ; c'est ainsi que Lakanal en septembre 1794, dans son *Rapport sur Jean-Jacques Rousseau*, déclare : « C'est la Révolution qui nous a expliqué le *Contrat social*[1]. » Si la Révolution fut une façon d'expliquer le *Contrat*, c'est peut-être parce que son concept central – la volonté générale – demeurait obscur. Cela vient aussi de ce que, paradoxalement, le public intellectuel en France n'était pas habitué à une réflexion philosophique abstraite sur la politique du type de celle que Rousseau expose dans le *Contrat social.* Paradoxalement, car nous étions à l'époque des « Philosophes ».

Aussi, si la Révolution « explique » le *Contrat*, c'est parce qu'elle lui emprunte une partie de son vocabulaire et donc de ses principes (une partie seulement). L'idée selon laquelle la loi est l'expression de la volonté générale, et l'affirmation que le principe de toute souveraineté réside dans la nation, voilà deux propositions de la Révolution qui sont incontestablement issues du *Contrat.* Cependant, l'idée que la souveraineté réside dans la nation n'est pas, *sous cette forme*, nouvelle, ni même révolutionnaire. Elle n'est pas absolument rejetée par Louis XV, lors de la séance dite de la Flagellation, en mars 1766 ; il affirme, certes, que la souveraineté réside en sa personne, mais que sa personne incarne la nation : son corps de monarque *est* le corps même de la nation, son corps visible.

Si donc, la Révolution « explique » le *Contrat social* – au point d'être elle-même comme un contrat social historique, événement fondateur réel –, c'est parce que, désormais, le corps visible de la nation est le « peuple » à la place du roi. C'est, comme dit Rousseau, le « peuple en corps ». Là où le monarque disait et exprimait la volonté de la nation qu'il incarnait, c'est désormais le « peuple » qui l'énonce. On voit que la Révolution, en ce qu'elle est le

1. Les cendres du philosophe furent alors transférées au Panthéon…

commentaire explicatif d'un livre de philosophie politique, donne son sens à des notions aussi abstraites et difficiles – car proprement métaphysiques – que celles de « peuple », « Souveraineté », « volonté ».

Du *contrat social ou Principes du droit politique* donne un sens nouveau à ces notions. Il le fait en appliquant la théorie philosophique et juridique du « droit naturel » moderne à la théorie générale de la souveraineté élaborée par Bodin en 1576. C'est cela qui confère au *Contrat* son caractère difficile car uniquement préoccupé de questionner les « principes ». Aller droit au *principe* des choses civiles et politiques – et non au fait qu'il s'agit ici comme ailleurs[1] d'écarter –, telle est l'ambition de Rousseau, au fur et à mesure qu'il croit avancer dans la réflexion, l'étude et la recherche pour venir à bout de son grand projet : doter son siècle d'*Institutions politiques.* Il aperçoit par ses lectures qu'il s'agit toujours de remonter au principe des choses, à leur concept comme nous dirions aujourd'hui. C'est pourquoi le projet d'*Institutions* est abandonné. D'ailleurs, Montesquieu a déjà fait ce travail : construire la théorie des « gouvernements établis ». Faut-il donc réécrire *De l'esprit des lois* ? Non. En fait, quand Rousseau découvre la politique ou plutôt quand il découvre que « tout tient à la politique », il semble penser et réfléchir son projet par rapport à Montesquieu – ce « beau génie ». C'est au cours de sa réalisation que le projet devient autre : il s'agit de fonder le droit politique. *Fonder le droit politique*, telle est la forme que prend au fur et à mesure des années d'étude le projet de jeunesse. Les *Institutions* ne sont plus alors qu'un souvenir. Si l'on en juge sur les résultats – et non sur les intentions déclarées, sincères ou calculées –, c'est-à-dire si l'on en juge sur les œuvres – les textes –, il faut convenir qu'il ne reste rien, dans le *Contrat social*, du projet des *Institutions politiques.* Ni la méthode ni le programme. Cela semble pouvoir être admis si l'on considère simultanément

1. C'est ce qu'il fait dans le *Discours sur l'inégalité. Cf. supra*, notre commentaire du *Discours.*

les deux ambitions, contradictoires entre elles, qui sont celles de Rousseau philosophe : fonder le droit politique et donner un nouvel *Esprit des lois*.

Le rapport à Montesquieu est extrêmement significatif du projet théorique de Rousseau. Il s'en explique notamment dans *Émile*. Dans ce texte (extrait du livre V), trois données sont considérées simultanément par Rousseau, ou mieux, Rousseau évoque leurs relations réciproques : le droit politique, l'œuvre de « l'illustre Montesquieu » et, en filigrane puisqu'il s'apprête à la résumer, la théorie développée dans le *Contrat social*. Lisons ce texte, au demeurant justement célèbre, qui fait écho à celui que nous citions en ouvrant ce commentaire :

« Le droit politique est encore à naître, et il est à présumer qu'il ne naîtra jamais. Grotius, le maître de tous nos savants en cette partie, n'est qu'un enfant, et, qui pis est, un enfant de mauvaise foi. Quand j'entends élever Grotius jusqu'aux nues et couvrir Hobbes d'exécration, je vois combien d'hommes sensés lisent ou comprennent ces deux auteurs. La vérité est que leurs principes sont exactement semblables. Ils ne diffèrent que par les expressions. Ils diffèrent aussi par la méthode. Hobbes s'appuie sur des sophismes, et Grotius sur des poètes ; tout le reste leur est commun.

« Le seul moderne en état de créer cette grande et inutile science eût été l'illustre Montesquieu. Mais il n'eut garde de traiter des principes du droit politique ; il se contenta de traiter du droit positif des gouvernements établis ; et rien au monde n'est plus différent que ces deux études[1]. »

En dehors de la rhétorique et de l'irrésistible séduction que les formules bien faites exercent toujours sur Rousseau, ce texte montre que, contrairement à ce qu'en dit son auteur, le *Contrat social* ne doit plus guère, et même plus rien, aux projets de jeunesse et ne peut s'entendre par rapport à eux. C'est un livre qui vise à fonder le droit politique en fondant l'État sur de vraies bases. C'est là explici-

1. Nous donnons le texte extrait de l'*Émile* en Annexe au *Contrat* ; *cf.* p. 405.

tement ce que déclare Rousseau dans la « Conclusion » jetée là en quelques lignes à la fin de l'ouvrage : « *Après avoir posé les vrais principes du droit politique et tâché de fonder l'État sur sa base*, il resterait à l'appuyer par ses relations externes [...][1]. »

À vrai dire, le mot important de ce passage est la conjonction de coordination *et* : poser les vrais principes du droit politique ET fonder l'État sont une seule et même chose. L'ouvrage s'emploiera donc à récuser les faux principes (Hobbes surtout, parce que le penseur est d'envergure et ne se réduit pas à n'être qu'un vil sophiste payé). Mais réfuter l'adversaire n'est possible qu'à une condition théorique et une seule : que soit substitué le vrai au faux, la liberté à la servitude. Cela veut dire que Rousseau n'entreprend pas de s'*opposer* aux théoriciens du passé parce qu'ils ont tort de vouloir la servitude, il entreprend de *poser* les « vrais principes » parce qu'il n'y a pas de liberté sans vérité. Puisque les principes adverses sont ceux qui justifient la servitude, ils sont faux. Par conséquent, les principes vrais établiront la liberté. Si les hommes sont asservis, c'est parce qu'ils sont dans l'erreur, c'est-à-dire dans l'ignorance du vrai.

Rousseau établit d'emblée la liaison de la vérité et de la liberté[2]. Et c'est cette liaison – absente chez Hobbes et chez Montesquieu comme des jurisconsultes – qui donne son statut unique au texte du *Contrat.* Unique et inintelligible pour la plupart des contemporains. C'est cette liaison vérité/liberté qui délibérément et consciemment organise la déduction des concepts *(genèse du droit politique)* et le plan de leur exposition *(structure du droit politique).*

Dès lors, on comprend d'abord que Rousseau reproche à l'illustre Montesquieu de se limiter au droit positif des gouvernements établis – alors qu'il s'agit, selon Rousseau, d'établir *des vérités*, autrement dit, d'énoncer les « principes ». On comprend ensuite que l'ouvrage reste sans écho jusqu'à la Révolution en rai-

---

1. *Du contrat social*, IV, IX. Souligné par moi (G. M.). 2. En cela il renoue avec l'inspiration de Platon qui entendait démontrer la possibilité et la nécessité d'un discours *vrai* en politique, seul capable, selon lui, de fonder la Cité juste.

son de son statut de texte philosophique dont l'objet est de juger ce qui est par ce qui doit être, en posant aux faits la question de fond : *Quid juris ?* Enfin, on comprend que la Révolution, pour reprendre le mot de Lakanal, « explique » le *Contrat* car elle établit le monde sur d'autres bases, en énonçant d'autres principes – les « vrais principes » ; bases et principes qui, précisément, se trouvaient définis et développés dans le *Contrat social.*

II. LA QUESTION DU « DROIT POLITIQUE ».

S'il faut faire une révolution pour comprendre une philosophie (parce que, fût-ce contre les intentions du philosophe lui-même, une révolution *peut* se réclamer de lui), il reste que Rousseau, comme tout autre penseur, n'élabore sa théorie que par rapport à d'autres théories. En ce sens, quand il déclare que le « droit politique est encore à naître », c'est là une assertion polémique qui lui permet de fonder doublement son propre discours : d'abord en réfutant à l'avance les théories qui précèdent la sienne, leur déniant la qualité d'être vraies ; ensuite en affectant, *ipso facto*, à son propre système une valeur de vérité qui lui confère le statut de fondation : *Du contrat social ou Principes du droit politique* est clairement dans l'esprit de son auteur la présentation systématique du « droit politique » que l'on attend depuis longtemps et dont les hommes ont un urgent besoin. En ce sens l'ouvrage est l'avènement du « droit politique » constitué (systématique). C'est là, en tout cas, ce que Rousseau veut faire comprendre à ses contemporains, comme à ses lecteurs de l'avenir[1], en donnant à son livre le sous-titre de « Principes du droit politique ».

1. Dans une lettre à son éditeur Rey, du 7 novembre 1761, parlant du *Contrat* dont il achève la rédaction, Rousseau écrit : « Quoiqu'il ne soit pas de nature à se répandre aussi promptement qu'un roman, j'espère qu'il ne s'usera pas de même et que ce sera un livre pour tous les temps. »

On peut donc, avec Rousseau, faire naître le droit politique du *Contrat social.* Mais cette naissance n'est pas, à vrai dire, un commencement. Ce qui commence avec le *Contrat*, c'est une certaine conception de la souveraineté, non la souveraineté elle-même. C'est donc plutôt d'un recommencement qu'il s'agit, recommencement que la Révolution inscrit dans les choses. En ce sens, le contrat social, entendu comme théorie aussi bien que comme pratique, permet de passer d'une souveraineté à une autre : du monarque au peuple.

Jusqu'à Rousseau inclusivement, on peut donner à la notion de « droit politique » plusieurs définitions. Une définition que l'on peut dire « académique » (ou « reçue »). C'est à cette tradition académique que Rousseau s'adresse et s'oppose ; avant lui, les traités de politique (philosophiques ou juridiques) se présentent souvent comme des traités du droit naturel. Les ouvrages (bien connus de Rousseau) de Pufendorf, Grotius, Burlamaqui, Barbeyrac sont des ouvrages représentatifs de l'école du droit naturel ; on y expose le droit *politique*, en tant que droit des sociétés civiles. En ce sens, « droit politique » se distingue de « droit naturel », comme l'état civil se distingue de l'état de nature, bien qu'on ne puisse penser celui-là sans recourir à celui-ci. Cette conception est celle des jurisconsultes.

On peut distinguer ensuite un sens « étroit » de la notion de droit politique, étroit car technique. On le trouve dans Montesquieu, penseur qui n'appartient pas à l'école du droit naturel ; ce sens restreint permet à l'auteur de *L'Esprit des lois* de distinguer des domaines d'investigation, de classer des matières dont la science politique doit produire la connaissance. Le « droit politique » a, chez Montesquieu, le sens de notre actuel « droit public interne » : il règle les relations gouvernants/gouvernés. Il le distingue ainsi du « droit des gens », équivalent de notre moderne « droit international public ». C'est pourquoi il écrit : « Considérés comme vivant dans une société qui doit être maintenue, ils [les hommes] ont des lois dans le rapport qu'ont ceux qui gouvernent avec ceux qui sont gouvernés ; et c'est le droit politique[1]. » On voit que par « droit politique » Montesquieu entend finalement le corps des règles (et généralement des normes juridiques) permettant non la fondation de l'État, mais son maintien ; non l'avènement de la souveraineté, mais sa conservation.

Il n'en est pas de même pour l'auteur du *Contrat*, d'où la troisième définition du « droit politique » qu'il lègue, en son principe, à l'avenir. La notion a ici un sens plus philosophique et pourrait être l'équivalent de « philosophie de l'État » si l'on entend par là l'exposé conceptuel du système de la liberté politique propre aux modernes, liberté qui est tout entière pensée à partir de la notion de *souveraineté.* Ainsi, et de façon plus précise, par « Droit politique » faut-il entendre, à la suite de Rousseau, le *système de l'éthique* ; l'éthique – avec ses trois moments : moral, politique et juridique – y est présentée selon l'agencement de ses concepts, selon leur système. C'est là un point de vue proprement philosophique car il présente l'*idée* de l'État et l'État comme Idée. C'est là ce que fait Rousseau, d'où la distance qu'il prend avec Montesquieu, lequel s'occupe des « gouvernements établis ». Rousseau, lui, a en vue l'*idée*, non l'histoire. Et le *Contrat social* est l'exposé rigoureux de l'idée de l'État selon ce qu'il est en sa vérité[2]. C'est la raison pour laquelle Rousseau prend soin de toujours affirmer, quand l'occasion se présente, qu'il est question dans le *Contrat social* d'établir les « vrais principes » ; il ne s'agit pas là d'une figure de style, mais d'un projet théorique. C'est Rousseau qui le premier chez les modernes tente de penser l'État selon son idée propre, selon son concept.

Il faut donc bien parler d'un recommencement du « droit politique » avec Rousseau. Et, puisque le *Contrat social* introduit un nouveau point de vue (éminemment philosophique) pour penser la politique, il était nécessaire de renouveler la définition que nous

1. *De l'esprit des lois*, 1, 3. 2. C'est pourquoi l'idéalisme allemand (de Kant à Hegel) est redevable à Rousseau d'avoir le premier entrepris de comprendre l'État comme Idée.

avions des concepts et des notions ayant permis jusqu'alors sa compréhension. C'est en effet ce qui se passe et Rousseau redéfinit radicalement la notion qui organise toutes les autres – la *souveraineté* – en forgeant l'équation « Peuple = Souverain ». Mais, on va le voir, il ne touche pas à l'idée de souveraineté. L'effet de cette redéfinition du droit politique – à partir de sa notion première, la souveraineté – est de redéfinir la « république » elle-même comme « démocratie ». C'est pourquoi l'on est fondé – en suivant en cela Rousseau lui-même – à dire que le « droit politique » qui était à naître au moment de l'*Émile* est né au moment du *Contrat social*[1].

L'idée de souveraineté est centrale chez les modernes : c'est à partir d'elle que s'organisent la compréhension de la liberté politique et l'idée même de « république ». La redéfinition du droit politique à partir de Rousseau ne modifiera pas cette donnée constante de l'entendement politique des modernes ; au contraire, Rousseau est tributaire de cette notion : l'ensemble de son système consiste à la redéfinir en vérité – c'est-à-dire selon ce qu'elle est conformément à son concept. Or, la souveraineté chez Rousseau est ce qu'elle est chez son inventeur, Jean Bodin ; elle est le principe même de la république, l'âme de l'État. Il s'agit donc pour Rousseau – comme, du reste, pour tous les penseurs de la politique depuis Bodin – non de mettre en cause le principe de souveraineté comme idée de la république en général, mais de savoir en quoi elle consiste et, surtout,

1. On peut penser que si le *Contrat social* a été assez peu lu avant la Révolution, cela vient précisément de la nouveauté de son point de vue et, corrélativement, de la mutation radicale des définitions de notions reçues. Et c'est bien entendu la notion du « Souverain » qui est la plus bouleversée, bouleversement qui ne facilitait pas, c'est le moins qu'on puisse dire, la compréhension de l'ouvrage entier. C'est cet étonnement mêlé d'effroi que le jésuite Berthier manifeste dans ses *Observations sur le « Contrat social »* (ouvrage publié seulement après sa mort, en 1789) en s'émouvant qu'un écrivain politique ait eu l'audace de « retirer la souveraineté au roi »…

quel est le *sujet* de la souveraineté – ou, si l'on préfère, quel est le souverain. La souveraineté – sa définition et son titulaire, deux choses qui vont ensemble – reste donc chez Rousseau ce qu'elle était avant lui et ce qu'elle est après lui : l'essence de l'État permettant de *penser l'État comme Idée.* Ainsi, penser l'État, c'est penser la souveraineté. Le *Contrat* conservera donc la souveraineté, mais sans maintenir le souverain.

Dans son ouvrage publié en français en 1576 – *Les Six Livres de la République* – Bodin fait pour la première fois la théorie générale de la souveraineté. Si Machiavel avait la notion, il n'en fait pas la théorie ; Machiavel pense l'exercice de la souveraineté, notamment dans *Le Prince* ; Bodin, lui, reconstruit l'ensemble de la politique à partir de l'idée de souveraineté. Reconstruction immense, faisant appel au droit, à la jurisprudence, à la philosophie, à l'histoire, aux récits ethnographiques de voyages, à la géographie, à la linguistique, à la théologie, à la mathématique aussi et, Montesquieu s'en souviendra, à la climatologie. Bodin fonde une science universelle de l'État. Toutes les sciences de son temps sont mobilisées par lui pour établir au cours de mille pages ce qu'il en est de la « république bien ordonnée », autrement dit, de l'État de droit. Or, cet État de droit repose sur un principe et un seul, la souveraineté. Et c'est parce que la souveraineté est, dit-il, la « définition » de la république qu'il y a lieu de faire le détour par Bodin pour lire le *Contrat social.*

Nous disions, en effet, que Rousseau renouvelle le droit politique, c'est dire qu'il renouvelle la souveraineté : avec lui elle passe, on le sait, du monarque au peuple, passage d'un titulaire à un autre. Mais ce passage est déjà prévu dans la définition que donne Bodin de la souveraineté au moment où, dans *Les Six Livres de la République*, il invente la « puissance souveraine ». Dès lors, il apparaît que si le *Contrat social* opère une rupture au sein de la conceptualité politique moderne (au point de transformer le système du droit politique), c'est parce qu'il applique la théorie du droit naturel à la conception bodinienne de la souveraineté. Pourtant, une telle application a déjà été opérée par Hobbes, mais l'auteur de *Léviathan* en arrive aux conclusions *politiques* de Bodin lui-même, qui construisit le concept de souveraineté afin d'établir en droit comme en fait la monarchie. Hobbes, peut-on dire, donne raison à Bodin à l'intérieur de la problématique contractualiste propre à la tradition du droit naturel.

La nouveauté de Rousseau vient, quant à elle, de ce qu'il conserve le principe bodinien de souveraineté en fondant le « peuple » comme souverain. Or, cette figure où le peuple est « en puissance de souveraineté », pour parler comme Bodin, est déjà énoncée dans *Les Six Livres de la République*, mais, et cela est capital, elle ne l'est pas en termes de contrat ou de pacte. C'est pourquoi nous disons que Rousseau adapte Bodin (tout en réfutant Hobbes) aux exigences de la théorie du Droit naturel, adaptation ou interprétation qui vise, on va le voir, non à révolutionner la souveraineté en tant qu'idée, mais seulement son titulaire : *non la souveraineté, mais le souverain.*

Qu'est-ce donc que la souveraineté ? Voilà la question qui se pose si l'on veut comprendre le souverain tel que le met en scène le *Contrat social* – le « peuple ». La réponse, donc, se trouve chez Bodin[1] qu'il faut brièvement interroger maintenant. *Les Six Livres* commencent ainsi : « République est un droit gouvernement de plusieurs ménages, et de ce qui leur est commun, avec puissance souveraine[2]. » Cette affirmation de Bodin – qui fait de la souveraineté le principe ou l'idée de la « République » (État) – ne sera jamais mise en cause par ses successeurs, non plus que la définition qu'il donne de la souveraineté elle-même. « La souveraineté, écrit-il, est puissance absolue et perpétuelle d'une république... Il est ici besoin de former la définition de la souveraineté, parce qu'il n'y a ni jurisconsulte ni philosophe politique qui l'ait définie, bien que ce soit le point principal et le plus nécessaire d'être entendu au traité de la République. Et d'autant que nous avons dit

1. Nous citons *Les Six Livres de la République* dans l'édition *reprint* procurée par Scientia Verlag Aalen, Darmstadt, 1977, qui reproduit le texte de 1583. 2. *Ibid.*, p. 1.

que République est un droit gouvernement de plusieurs familles, et de ce qui leur est commun, avec puissance souveraine. J'ai dit que cette puissance est *perpétuelle* parce qu'il se peut faire qu'*on donne puissance absolue à un ou à plusieurs à certain temps*, lequel expiré, ils ne sont plus rien que sujets. Et tant qu'ils sont en puissance, ils ne se peuvent appeler princes souverains, vu qu'ils ne sont que *dépositaires et gardes* de cette puissance, jusqu'à ce qu'il plaise *au peuple* ou *au prince* la révoquer : qui en demeure toujours saisi[1]. »

Retenons de ce texte trois éléments essentiels pour la compréhension de la souveraineté : d'abord, elle est la « *définition* » de l'État[2] (et non simplement la qualité du pouvoir dont disposerait un individu ou un groupe); ensuite, elle est « *perpétuelle* », autrement dit, la puissance est dite « souveraine » si, et seulement si, elle n'est pas soumise au temps, c'est-à-dire limitée en durée; enfin, elle, et elle seule, permet de désigner ceux qui, pour une durée déterminée et finie, auront la charge d'exécuter ce qu'elle aura décidé de faire passer dans les choses; ceux-là, Bodin les appelle « *magistrats* » ou « *gouvernement* ». Si l'on exprime ces trois données dans la forme d'un *système*, qui est le système de la souveraineté tel que l'énonce le droit politique, on obtient la compréhension suivante de la souveraineté : elle est un système politique qui distingue État et gouvernement[3], c'est-à-dire volonté et pouvoir. Et Bodin nomme « souveraineté » la puissance de poser le pouvoir, puissance qui est, elle, non limitée dans le temps.

C'est pourquoi la souveraineté est indivisible et incommunicable chez Bodin comme chez Rousseau pour la raison que si le roi ou le peuple communique la souveraineté qu'il a en sa puissance,

1. *Ibid.*, p. 122 (orthographe et ponctuation modernisées). 2. La souveraineté est « l'âme de l'État », dira Hobbes au début de *Léviathan.* 3. Une distinction dont Bodin revendique avec raison la radicale nouveauté et dont il observe que le plus grand des « anciens et des modernes », Aristote, s'est rendu coupable de l'avoir ignorée : « Aristote a pris la forme de gouvernement pour l'état d'une république » (*ibid.*, p. 338).

il cesse par le fait même d'être le souverain. En revanche, étant la *puissance* de désigner le corps des magistrats (« gouvernement ») disposant pour un temps du *pouvoir* de mettre en œuvre la politique du souverain, la souveraineté reste, elle, « perpétuelle » comme le veut sa définition. Et cela quel que soit le souverain qui l'incarne : roi ou peuple.

La souveraineté existe donc en elle-même (c'est-à-dire comme *idée* de l'État ou République), mais elle s'incarne ou bien dans le roi[1] ou bien dans le peuple. Dans les deux cas, le souverain, qu'il soit roi ou qu'il soit peuple – *un seul ou tous en un* –, désigne un « gouvernement », distinct de lui et dont le pouvoir ne peut jamais être défini comme « puissance souveraine »[2].

Telle est, brièvement présentée, la théorie de la souveraineté, pensée par Bodin en 1576 et telle qu'on la retrouve en 1762, développée par Rousseau à l'intérieur de la problématique contractualiste du droit naturel moderne.

Il y aurait lieu de lire, ou relire, le *Contrat* à la lumière des *Six Livres* ; ce qu'on vient à peine d'esquisser. On verrait que pour avoir

---

1. Bodin dit également le « Prince ». Il y a donc chez lui deux souverains qui se complètent si l'on peut dire : un seul et tous. Et, quand Bodin examine la souveraineté du peuple (quand le peuple est « en puissance de souveraineté »), il constate que, dans ce cas, chaque individu du peuple est « petit roi ». À l'inverse de Bodin, on sait que Rousseau réserve le nom de « prince » au *gouvernement*, c'est-à-dire au corps de magistrats non souverain, mais désigné par le souverain – le « peuple » – pour exercer le pouvoir exécutif.

2. Bodin admettait explicitement la possibilité de la souveraineté du peuple – autrement dit, que le peuple soit le sujet incarnant la souveraineté de l'État ou République. Il est remarquable d'observer que, ce faisant, il trouvait la formule de nos républiques démocratiques et présidentielles modernes. En effet, selon lui, le peuple en souveraineté peut parfaitement désigner *un seul homme* – « roi » selon le vocabulaire bodinien, « président » selon notre sémantique moderne – pour le gouverner ; et cela *pour un temps* seulement, pendant lequel le premier magistrat de la république est comptable de ses actions devant le « peuple souverain » qui lui renouvelle sa confiance ou la lui retire…

réformé le souverain, Rousseau n'a pas réformé la souveraineté, mais au contraire lui a conféré les marques d'une dignité populaire que Bodin en son temps lui avait finalement refusée car, selon son inventeur, la souveraineté ne sied adéquatement qu'à la monarchie. En vertu même de sa définition, « la souveraineté ne peut être ni subsister, écrit Bodin, à parler proprement, sinon en monarchie : car nul ne peut être souverain en une république qu'un seul : s'ils sont deux ou trois ou plusieurs, pas un n'est souverain, d'autant que pas un seul ne peut donner ni recevoir loi de son compagnon, ou d'un peuple tenir la souveraineté, si est-ce qu'elle n'a point de vrai sujet, s'il n'y a un chef avec puissance souveraine[1]. »

Le *Contrat social* est dépendant des *Six Livres de la République* pour ce qui est de son concept central, la souveraineté. C'est pourquoi ce qu'on accorde souvent à Rousseau – l'originalité de sa distinction souveraineté/gouvernement – est en fait la structure conceptuelle de la souveraineté telle que l'établit Bodin. C'est elle qui commande le plan du *Contrat.*

III. LE PLAN DU *CONTRAT SOCIAL*.

Déterminé par la conception de la souveraineté, héritée de Bodin, l'ouvrage est divisé en quatre « livres ». Il obéit en fait à une exposition en deux temps. D'abord, Rousseau expose la théorie de la souveraineté (livres I et II) ; ensuite il expose la théorie du gouvernement (livres III et IV).

Cette distinction est cohérente car elle reproduit à la fois la définition de la souveraineté élaborée par Bodin et la théorie rousseauiste du droit politique. Chez Rousseau, le « souverain » étant le peuple, il importe donc de concevoir philosophiquement ce « peuple » – c'est le penser comme sujet d'une volonté qui lui est propre – la volonté générale. Cela correspond à la *fondation de la souveraineté* – à la fois dans son *sujet* et dans son *principe.* Quand

1. *Ibid.*, p. 961.

la fondation est achevée – qui est la fondation de l'État –, il faut passer à l'exposé de la conservation de l'État : autrement dit, à son « gouvernement ».

D'abord fonder, ensuite maintenir (conserver), tels sont les deux moments de la *séquence historique* de la vie de l'État moderne. Ce sont ces deux moments que le *Contrat social* expose du point de vue philosophique propre au « droit politique » – c'est la *séquence théorique* de l'État.

C'est pourquoi le passage du premier moment de l'ouvrage (livres I et II) au deuxième moment (livres III et IV) est défini par Rousseau à l'intérieur d'un vocabulaire et d'une problématique strictement bodiniens. Il s'agit pour lui de passer du « souverain » au « gouvernement » : « Qu'est-ce donc que le gouvernement ? demande Rousseau. Un corps intermédiaire établi entre les sujets et le souverain [...]. Les membres de ce corps s'appellent magistrats ou *rois*, c'est-à-dire *gouverneurs* ; et le corps entier porte le nom de *prince*. Ainsi ceux qui prétendent que l'acte par lequel un peuple se soumet à des chefs n'est point un contrat ont grande raison. Ce n'est *absolument qu'une commission, un emploi dans lequel, simples officiers du souverain, ils exercent en son nom le pouvoir dont il les a faits dépositaires, et qu'il peut limiter, modifier et reprendre quand il lui plaît* [...].[1] »

On voit que Rousseau ordonne son exposé systématique du droit politique conformément à la distinction bodinienne constitutive de la souveraineté : ce qui fonde et ce qui est fondé, la volonté qui pose et le pouvoir qui est posé. D'abord, le *fondement* de l'État, ensuite, le *gouvernement* de l'État.

Le plan du *Contrat social* reproduit cet ordre des raisons, qui n'est pas simplement le plan d'un livre mais, peut-on dire, *le plan de l'État* :

1. *Du contrat social*, III, I : « Du gouvernement en général » (souligné par moi, G. M.).

I. Du fondement de l'État ou De la souveraineté

Chap. I. 1 : Du fondement comme objet du droit politique.
Chap. I. 2 à I. 5 : Réfutation des prétendus fondements.
Chap. I. 6 à I. 9 : Fondation du principe de souveraineté.
Chap. II. 1 à II. 3 : Définition du principe de souveraineté.
Chap. II. 4 et 5 : De la souveraineté comme puissance.
Chap. II. 6 et 7 : De la loi comme manifestation de la souveraineté.
Chap. II. 8 à II. 10 : Du souverain ou théorie du « peuple ».
Chap. II. 11 et 12 : Liberté et égalité comme effets d'un fondement légitime.

II. Du gouvernement de l'État ou Du prince

Chap. III. 1 à III. 3 : De l'exercice de la souveraineté.
Chap. III. 4 à III. 7 : Des diverses formes de l'exercice de la souveraineté.
Chap. III. 8 et 9 : De l'adéquation des gouvernements aux circonstances.
Chap. III. 10 à III. 15 : De l'évolution et de la destruction des États historiques.
Chap. III. 16 à III. 18 : De la distinction souverain/prince (État/gouvernement).
Chap. IV. 1 à IV. 3 : Questions diverses I : La règle de majorité.
Chap. IV. 4 à IV. 7 : Questions diverses II : Le modèle antique, Rome.
Chap. IV. 8 : Questions diverses III : Politique et religion.
Chap. IV. 9 : Conclusion.

Laissons à Rousseau[1] le dernier mot : « *Je cherche le droit et la raison et ne dispute pas des faits.* » C'est ce que montre l'exposé des matières du « droit politique ».

1. Première version du *Contrat*, I, v : « Fausses notions du lien social ».

Notes

Dédicace

1. Traduction : « Proposons un traité dont les clauses soient justes » (Virgile, *Énéide*, XI, 321-322).

Livre I

Chap. I

2. L'article 1 de la *Déclaration des droits de l'homme et du citoyen* proclamera : « Les hommes naissent libres et égaux en droits. » Ce qui est une adaptation de la formule de Rousseau visant à affirmer que les hommes ont des droits égaux. R. Derathé indique (Pléiade, III, p. 1433) que la formule de Rousseau pourrait bien être une vive réplique à Bossuet qui affirme dans sa *Politique tirée des propres paroles de l'Écriture sainte* : « Les hommes naissent tous sujets. »

Chap. II

3. La formule par laquelle s'ouvre le livre I du *Contrat* trouve ici son commentaire : la liberté de l'homme est une donnée issue de sa nature et de la nature. Et Rousseau retient, comme première loi naturelle, la loi – c'est-à-dire l'obligation – que nous fait la nature de nous conserver dans l'être. Dès lors, si la nature fait les hommes libres, il est clair que c'est la société qui les asservit. Une proposition connue depuis le *Discours sur l'inégalité.* On voit que le problème théorique du *Contrat social* devient, de ce fait même, celui de déterminer *en droit* les conditions d'une liberté retrouvée, artificielle. Dès les premières lignes il ne subsiste aucun doute sur les intentions de Rousseau : la société civile, telle qu'elle est devenue, est mauvaise car ses lois sont mauvaises, il s'agit donc de fonder un ordre légitime afin de reconstituer la liberté naturelle perdue.

4. Jurisconsulte hollandais du droit naturel, Hugo Grotius est l'auteur d'un grand traité (*De jure belli ac pacis*, 1625) : *Du droit de la guerre et de la paix*, traduit par Barbeyrac en 1724, que Rousseau étudia – et dont il s'emploie dans le *Contrat* à réfuter la doctrine. Grotius, dont l'influence au XVIIe siècle est très grande dans le développement de l'école du droit naturel, est aux yeux de Rousseau un « sophiste payé ». Lui reprochant « d'établir le droit par le fait », Rousseau voit en Grotius l'adversaire en personne (*cf. infra*, note 23).

5. Thomas Hobbes, philosophe anglais, publie en 1651 *Leviathan*, son ouvrage principal (traduction G. Mairet, Gallimard, « Folio », 2001); auteur également, en 1642, d'un *De cive (Du citoyen)*. Le mot de « hobbisme », forgé à partir du nom de Hobbes, est, dans le courant du XVIIIe siècle, synonyme d'absolutisme. Sur Hobbes, auteur fondamental, on peut se reporter à : M. Malherbe, *Thomas Hobbes ou l'œuvre de la raison* (Vrin, 1984) et P.-F. Moreau, *Hobbes. Philosophie, science et religion* (P.U.F., 1989).

6. *Cf.* Aristote, *Politique* (I, 2, 1252a).

Chap. III

7. Rousseau, qui recherche un fondement légitime à l'obéissance, ne saurait bien entendu le trouver dans la force. Si la force fondait le droit, ce mot de droit serait privé de sens. La notion de « force » doit être distinguée de celle de « puissance » (ou « pouvoir ») : la première est pure violence physique et, comme telle, non légitime ; la seconde est une autorité légitime, c'est-à-dire fondée en droit. C'est pourquoi ce chapitre III explique simplement que ces deux mots « force » et « droit », mis ensemble, produisent une *contradiction dans les termes*, C'est-à-dire sémantique : les mots y perdent leur sens ; c'est pourquoi Rousseau dit que le « mot de droit », dans ce contexte de la force, « ne signifie ici rien du tout ».

Dans la mesure où la norme de droit sera issue d'une convention passée *verbalement* entre les hommes – convention qui sera le pacte fondateur lui-même –, il s'agit de préserver le sens des mots. C'est pourquoi Rousseau, au cours de ce chapitre III, s'emploie à établir ce que parler veut dire.

8. En effet, Rousseau n'a de cesse que la question fondamentale – qui est la question du fondement de l'autorité légitime – soit bien posée. Ayant écarté le prétendu fondement de l'autorité dans la force, il s'apprête (chapitre IV) à réfuter le prétendu droit d'esclavage.

Chap. IV

9. Le problème est remarquablement bien posé par Rousseau : il est posé en termes de *liberté* et d'« *aliénation* » de cette liberté. D'une part, l'homme est libre par nature, on ne peut donc dériver sa servitude de la nature sans se contredire ; d'autre part, la servitude ne saurait trouver un fondement légitime dans la force – puisque la force ne fait pas droit ; par conséquent, il n'y a pas d'aliénation possible de la liberté.

Mais surtout ce quatrième chapitre met fin à ce qu'on peut appeler la *réduction du problème politique à ses propres termes*. Il s'agit de fonder *la liberté*, or il est manifeste que, pour Rousseau, les théoriciens ont plutôt fondé la servitude. Cela vient de ce qu'ils confondent le droit et le fait. Cette confusion du droit et du fait, Rousseau la décèle et la dénonce au cours des chapitres I à IV.

Mais il est remarquable que sa découverte du problème : la liberté (et non la servitude !) procède moins de la négation des sophismes de l'adversaire que d'une affirmation *a priori*. D'où la proposition centrale de ce chapitre – véritable commencement théorique du Contrat : « Renoncer à sa liberté c'est renoncer à sa qualité d'homme, aux droits de l'humanité, même à ses devoirs. » Jusqu'à présent (chap. I à III) Rousseau avait nié que la philosophie (Aristote, Hobbes) et le droit naturel (Grotius) aient trouvé le fondement recherché. Rousseau, maintenant, établit que le fondement légitime est dans *l'affirmation* a priori *de la liberté* – c'est-à-dire dans l'impossibilité de l'aliéner.

Rechercher un fondement légitime et sûr à l'autorité, c'est d'abord affirmer *a priori* la liberté ; *a priori*, c'est-à-dire comme exigence pure de la raison. Rousseau a donc ramené le problème politique à son centre : la liberté.

10. *Cf.* note précédente.

11. Une fois encore, il s'agit de savoir *ce que parler veut dire.* Rousseau prépare le sens des mots afin que nous sachions ce que nous dirons au moment d'énoncer les clauses du contrat. On voit que la question des mots est la question même des choses.

12. Francisation du grec *politéia*, constitution politique ; la *polis* était la cité, la *politéia* était la constitution de la cité.

13. Rousseau recourt, ici encore, à la critique sémantique : les mots « esclavage » et « droit » sont contradictoires ; c'est une nouvelle *contradiction dans les termes*. Du coup, le mot *droit* n'a plus de signification. Vidé de son sens, parce que la double tradition philosophique et juridique du droit naturel le rapporte à des antithèses, « force », « esclavage », il était nécessaire de le restituer dans sa pureté. Telle a été la fonction des quatre premiers chapitres : extraire l'idée vraie du droit des sédiments déposés par des générations de sophistes et de rhéteurs, par l'histoire elle-même, excaver la notion pure du droit afin de la brandir comme fondement.

Chap. V

14. Le chapitre V achève la réfutation. Et Rousseau confirme qu'il s'agissait bien, jusqu'à présent, d'une *réduction* du problème à son propre terme. En effet, il s'agit, dit Rousseau, de « remonter à une première convention ». Cette remontée à l'origine est une remontée au principe, corrélative de la réduction opérée jusqu'alors ; on peut dire que, débarrassé des scories, le droit politique que Rousseau expose pose ici sa première pierre : la convention originaire. Celle-ci, en tant que fondement légitime, fait l'objet d'une déduc-

tion *a priori*, c'est-à-dire purement rationnelle. En ce sens le pacte social apparaît bien pour ce qu'il est : une construction purement théorique, un modèle formel d'association dont les propriétés seront déduites *a priori*.

Ce chapitre v est donc stratégique : il donne sens à la volonté de Rousseau, constante chez lui, de déterminer *a priori* les conditions de la liberté – c'est-à-dire, comme il dit, selon « le droit et la raison », au lieu de « disputer des faits ».

Chap. VI

15. La volonté d'écarter les sédiments et les scories est ici évidente : il s'agit bien de déduire *a priori* la forme de la civilité.

16. Il s'agit ici (comme c'était le cas chez Hobbes, par exemple) d'une formule : le contrat s'exprime dans une *clause*, c'est-à-dire une suite verbale, une suite de « termes », dit Rousseau. Et l'on voit d'ailleurs, dans la suite immédiate du texte, comment Rousseau prend soin de déterminer avec précision le sens des mots. C'est la mise en place du vocabulaire du droit politique.

La clef ou plutôt le moteur de l'association est le legs que chacun fait à tous de sa puissance. Par puissance, il faut entendre le droit naturel que j'ai de me gouverner moi-même, c'est-à-dire ma liberté naturelle.

C'est la raison pour laquelle Rousseau explique que la fin empirique du pacte d'association est de doter les individus, en tant que « citoyens », d'une liberté conventionnelle en remplacement de cette liberté naturelle dont ils viennent de consentir l'abandon.

17. La formule ici est capitale – et difficile. Elle montre que le pacte social, instaurateur de la civilité parmi les hommes, consiste en la *transmutation volontaire de la multitude en l'unité d'un peuple.* Ce qui consiste à fonder le corps politique, autrement dit, l'État. Ce qui se crée, par l'accord des volontés individuelles, c'est une volonté nouvelle commune, non réductible à l'addition des volontés individuelles qui la posent.

Chez Rousseau le pacte social, comme chez Hobbes, consiste à réduire la multitude au peuple, c'est-à-dire le multiple à l'un.

Il faut donc comprendre que la volonté est dite « générale » par Rousseau parce qu'elle est la volonté d'une personne une – le peuple –, sachant que cette personne est elle-même l'unité d'une multiplicité. Tout comme le corps politique issu de l'association civile, le « peuple » est un corps moral, un moi collectif. Il est un *sujet commun*, doué d'une volonté propre. Or, et cela est capital pour bien entendre la notion rousseauiste de « volonté générale », ce sujet commun – personne morale une – possède une volonté une. Et si Rousseau la qualifie de « générale », c'est que le vouloir du peuple est vouloir de l'universel.

La volonté générale est donc bien générale car elle est celle d'une personne une – à savoir le peuple. Au contraire, la volonté de tous serait une volonté émanant du multiple – à savoir la juxtaposition des volontés singulières de tous les individus de la multitude. Ce qui distingue la volonté générale de la volonté de tous est ce qui distingue, respectivement, l'un du multiple. (*Cf. infra*, note 24.)

Ainsi, le contrat originaire a-t-il pour effet de produire, 1) un *corps politique* (État) lequel est doté, 2) d'une *volonté* (« volonté générale ») qui est celle, 3) d'une *personne* (« moi commun »), le « *peuple* » qui est, 4) le *souverain.*

Chap. VII

18. L'engagement que chacun prend est un engagement envers soi-même : chacun fait à soi-même la promesse d'obéir à la volonté générale. C'est pourquoi chaque individu – et donc tous – se retrouve lié en commun à une volonté commune. Chaque individu – et donc tous – est à la fois homme, en tant qu'il se fait cette promesse, et citoyen en tant qu'il s'engage à se soumettre aux décrets de la volonté générale.

Il suit de cette promesse individuelle, mais collective, l'avènement d'un *moi* – une subjectivité commune – qui est un peuple et, plutôt, qui est « le peuple », autrement dit, le corps vivant de l'État. C'est ce peuple, en tant que corps moral collectif, doté de volonté, que Rousseau appelle le « souverain ».

On voit que l'essence du pacte est d'instaurer le souverain. Par conséquent les individus ne passent pas un contrat avec le souverain, puisque celui-ci n'existe pas encore. Il n'existe que dans l'acte collectif des individus de se faire promesse à eux-mêmes. Rousseau a donc formellement raison de dire que par cet acte les individus – devenus citoyens – n'aliènent aucune parcelle de leur volonté propre (leur liberté) puisque la part qu'ils consentent à léguer au souverain est exactement celle dont ils sont pourvus comme citoyens.

La différence avec Hobbes, de ce point de vue, est totale : chez Hobbes, les individus pactisent entre eux afin de se soumettre ensemble et simultanément au souverain. Or, le souverain chez Hobbes – monarque ou assemblée – n'est pas partie au contrat. C'est donc un contrat de soumission à autrui que les individus font *avec eux-mêmes*, pacte de sujétion car ils abdiquent leur volonté pour s'en remettre à la volonté d'un autre :

« Le seul moyen d'ériger pareille puissance commune […] est de rassembler tout leur pouvoir et toute leur force sur un seul homme ou sur une assemblée d'hommes qui peut, à la majorité des voix, ramener toutes leurs volontés à une seule volonté ; ce qui revient à dire : désigner un homme, ou une assemblée d'hommes, pour prendre en charge leur personne. […]. C'est plus qu'un consentement ou un accord ; il s'agit d'une véritable unité de tous les hommes en une seule et même personne, réalisée par convention de chacun avec chacun, de telle manière que c'est comme si chaque homme devait dire à tout homme : *J'autorise cet homme ou cette assemblée d'hommes, et je lui abandonne mon droit de me gouverner moi-même, à la condition que tu lui abandonnes ton droit et autorises toutes ses actions de la même manière.* Cela fait, la multitude ainsi unie en une seule personne, est appelée un État, en latin *Civitas.* Telle est la génération de ce grand Léviathan, ou plutôt (pour parler avec plus de déférence) de ce *dieu mortel*, auquel nous devons, sous le *dieu immortel*, notre paix et notre protection. En effet, en vertu du pouvoir que lui a conféré chaque individu singulier dans l'État, il dispose de tant de puissance et de force assemblées en lui que la terreur qu'elles inspirent lui permet de modeler les volontés de tous les hommes afin de pacifier l'intérieur, et de s'entraider face aux ennemis de l'extérieur[1]. »

Chez Hobbes, le souverain est donc extérieur au contrat. Chez Rousseau, il est le résultat du contrat. C'est pourquoi Rousseau a formellement raison de dire que l'abandon par chacun de sa puissance (liberté) est totale et sans condition – car, en somme, *il s'abandonne à lui-même.* Il ne saurait donc s'asservir lui-même.

Notons que si cette clause est formellement irréprochable, elle reste hautement rhétorique : car il faut admettre en effet que l'unité postulée du corps social, exprimée par l'unité de la volonté, repose sur la scission de l'individu qui est tantôt homme, tantôt citoyen : « Chaque individu, écrit Rousseau, peut comme homme avoir une volonté particulière contraire ou dissemblable à la volonté générale qu'il a comme citoyen. » C'est sans doute pourquoi, Rousseau, à la fin de ce chapitre VII, annonce que ce conflit peut être – et même doit être – résolu par la force : « On le forcera d'être libre ».

Il est vrai que dans l'esprit de Rousseau il s'agit ici non de donner droit à la force, mais de donner force au droit. C'est ce *renversement d'état* que cause le contrat originaire.

Chap. VIII

19. L'avènement de la société civile est l'avènement de la moralité, moralité *objective*, car indépendante des subjectivités particulières. C'est un résultat auquel était déjà parvenu le *Discours sur l'inégalité.* La moralité peut être dite « objective » parce qu'elle

1. *Léviathan*, II, 7 (traduction G. Mairet). C'est Hobbes qui souligne.

procède de la généralité de la loi – son critère est l'universalité. Elle se distingue ainsi de l'appréciation subjective (et donc arbitraire) de la moralité quand, à l'état de nature, les hommes ne disposent que de leur seul jugement particulier. C'est pourquoi Rousseau dit, plus bas dans ce chapitre, qu'il y a lieu de distinguer entre *liberté naturelle* qui relève de l'individu et *liberté civile* qui procède de la volonté générale.

D'où la célèbre formule qui termine ce chapitre sur l'obéissance à la loi qu'on s'est prescrite. Formule qui, à ce stade du *Contrat*, est doublement significative du projet de Rousseau qui est de constituer le droit politique. Ce dernier est, pour ainsi dire, la science de la liberté civile. Et l'on a vu (*supra*, note 9) que Rousseau, ayant écarté dans les premiers chapitres les scories empêchant de penser le fondement vrai de la liberté civile, optait finalement pour une déduction entièrement *a priori* de la liberté comme droit (chap. v), déduction pure de la raison.

La première signification de cette formule – « l'obéissance à la loi qu'on s'est prescrite est liberté » – est de signaler que la *déduction* a priori *du principe de la liberté* est désormais achevée : la liberté de l'individu réside dans la relation qu'entretiennent chez lui l'homme et le citoyen, dans leur cohabitation. Autrement dit, l'individu est libre – sa liberté étant garantie – dans le cadre juridique et moral de l'État, c'est-à-dire s'il est « membre du souverain », citoyen de l'État. La liberté vraie de l'individu, ou plutôt de la personne, n'est pas celle de Robinson. La deuxième signification est dans l'indication que la liberté réside dans l'*autonomie* de la volonté car, à la faveur du pacte, j'ai volontairement posé une loi à laquelle je me suis fait la promesse d'obéir : la liberté est liée au devoir. Or – et c'est le point capital – cette loi n'est pas subjective, elle est objective car liée à la volonté générale.

Le projet fondamental de Rousseau prend ainsi corps : unifier, dans l'individu, le particulier et l'universel (*cf. infra*, notes 54 et 61).

Chap. IX

20. Expression juridique signifiant littéralement *domination sur les choses*; autrement dit, il s'agira ici d'examiner quelle est la nature du droit de propriété. Rousseau, à l'inverse de Locke (déjà réfuté sur ce point dans le *Discours sur l'inégalité*) nie que la propriété soit un droit naturel. Locke y voyait d'ailleurs l'unique vraie raison qu'ont les hommes de former des sociétés civiles : celles-ci ont pour but de sauvegarder la propriété. Rousseau pense, au contraire, que la propriété et par conséquent le droit de propriété sont une conséquence de la fondation des sociétés politiques par lesquelles les hommes échappent à l'état de nature.

Toutefois, si Rousseau et Locke s'opposent quant à l'origine de la propriété, ils sont en accord quant aux obligations qu'elle entraîne dans la société civile. C'est pourquoi Rousseau lui consacre un chapitre après avoir traité de la fondation de la société civile. Notons en tout cas que la propriété est la première chose qui doit être réglée une fois conçue *a priori* l'origine de l'état civil. Voici le texte de Locke, à mettre en parallèle avec le chapitre sur le « Domaine réel » : « Il serait contradictoire de supposer qu'un individu s'associe avec d'autres, pour que sa propriété soit protégée et réglementée, mais que ses terres dont les lois de la société doivent régir le titre échappent à la juridiction du gouvernement dont il est, lui-même, le sujet en sa qualité de propriétaire. C'est donc par un seul et même acte qu'il associe la république à sa personne, qui était libre, et ses terres, qui étaient libres aussi; les personnes et possessions sont assujetties l'une et l'autre au gouvernement et à la souveraineté de la société politique tant que celle-ci dure[1]. »

1. *Deuxième Traité du gouvernement civil* (1690), § 120, Vrin, Paris, 1967 (traduction Gilson).

Livre II

Chap. I

21. Affirmation fondamentale au moment même où Rousseau, ayant achevé la déduction *a priori* des fondements de la liberté civile, entreprend maintenant avec ce livre II d'énoncer les caractères essentiels de la souveraineté.

La *volonté* ne se transmet pas. Seul le *pouvoir* se transmet. Nous voici d'emblée renvoyés à la théorie bodinienne de la souveraineté. La volonté est puissance, elle est principe de souveraineté. Par conséquent le souverain ne saurait, sauf à renoncer à lui-même, aliéner ou « transmettre » son propre principe : la volonté générale. La volonté générale est la pensée du souverain. Elle est la *souveraineté en tant que pensée.* Autrement dit, quand le souverain pense, il *veut.* Il pense l'universel, raison pourquoi sa volonté est générale ou bien n'est pas. « Le souverain, dit Rousseau, par cela seul qu'il est, est toujours tout ce qu'il doit être » (I, VII). Or, son *être* étant manifesté dans et par sa volonté, il ne saurait transmettre celle-ci sans se détruire. Le peuple (le souverain en personne) ne transmet pas sa volonté, mais, en revanche, il peut transmettre le *pouvoir d'exécuter ses volontés.* Et c'est la transmission de ce pouvoir – non de la volonté – qui cause le « gouvernement ».

Mais nous n'en sommes pas encore au gouvernement. Et si Rousseau prend soin ici de faire cette précision capitale, c'est qu'il entend qu'il n'y ait aucun doute sur l'essence de la souveraineté : elle est absolue, indivisible, non transmissible. Ce qui veut dire – et l'on retrouvera ce thème plus tard – que la souveraineté ne se représente pas. Les gouvernants ou magistrats (que Rousseau appellera « le prince ») ne représentent pas le souverain – ils exécutent sa volonté. (*Cf. supra*, notre commentaire, II, et *infra*, notes 62-65.)

Observons que la théorie bodinienne de la souveraineté sert adéquatement les intérêts de Rousseau ; en effet, conformément à sa définition, la souveraineté est perpétuelle et ne peut donc être transmise : le souverain est perpétuellement souverain, il est perpétuellement ce qu'il est. C'est là très exactement ce que Rousseau établit *a priori* de la liberté elle-même, dans son concept : nul ne saurait s'en défaire.

Il y a coïncidence ou plutôt identité entre la liberté en tant que telle et la souveraineté dans son concept. On peut donc dire que la souveraineté est la forme *a posteriori* d'une liberté découverte *a priori.* Elle lui donne corps ; c'est en prenant forme dans la souveraineté que la liberté devient vraie. Ou, ce qui est la même chose : l'état social – c'est-à-dire l'État – est l'élément de la liberté, laquelle n'est, à l'état de nature, qu'une simple virtualité, un simple possible.

Chap. II

22. Tout ce passage n'est intelligible que s'il est rapporté à la théorie de la souveraineté, telle que l'énonce Jean Bodin dans *Les Six Livres de la République* et que Rousseau a faite sienne (*cf. supra*, notre commentaire, II). Rousseau en effet distingue, à la suite de Bodin, le souverain et le gouvernement, c'est-à-dire le principe de l'autorité des formes en lesquelles cette autorité s'exerce. Il distingue donc la *volonté* qui est puissance souveraine, du *pouvoir* qui est l'exécution de la puissance. Autrement dit, le « gouvernement » ou les « magistrats » ou encore, comme dit Rousseau, le « prince ».

Aussi, au sens propre, un acte de la volonté (acte du souverain) est-il une *loi* ; un acte du pouvoir (acte du gouvernement) est un *décret.* Et si l'on nomme « loi » ce qui n'est qu'un décret, c'est que l'on confond volonté et pouvoir, l'État (souveraineté) et le gouvernement.

Cela signifie d'une part qu'il ne saurait y avoir de parties de la souveraineté, car la souveraineté est *une* – elle est simple, non composée. D'autre part, tout pouvoir est une commission – une « émanation » –, dit Rousseau, de la puissance. Autrement dit, le gouvernement est une émanation du souverain. Les magistrats (le « prince ») sont commis par le peuple (le souverain).

Si la souveraineté pouvait être morcelée en « parties » – ce qui, soit dit au passage, est une contradiction dans les termes –, il y aurait destruction de la souveraineté : non pas une volonté une, mais des volontés multiples[1]. C'est-à-dire non pas la volonté générale, mais des volontés particulières ; et c'est ce point précisément qu'examine Rousseau au chapitre suivant.

23. Ce dernier alinéa est une remarquable charge contre les « sophistes payés ». Remarquons que la charge commence par une référence au « droit politique » : Rousseau, dans le *Contrat*, ne perd jamais de vue son projet : fonder le « droit politique » sur des bases vraies. Or, précisément, si les Grotius, les Barbeyrac sont des sophistes payés – payés par les rois... –, c'est parce qu'ils ont le souci non de la vérité des principes, mais de leur fortune personnelle. Aussi la charge se conclut-elle sur ce thème : « la vérité ne mène point à la fortune ».

Chap. III

24. « Errer », c'est-à-dire être dans l'erreur. Le peuple peut-il se tromper et vouloir autre chose que son bien, qui est le bien commun ? Telle est la question qui est posée ici. Il est impossible, par définition, que le peuple se trompe si c'est bien la volonté générale qui est exprimée.

En revanche, la volonté générale, qui ne se trompe pas, peut être trompée. En premier lieu, elle peut être trompée par les sophistes, c'était là le sens de la fin du chapitre précédent. Mais surtout, elle peut être trompée par l'esprit de parti. Partis, groupes d'intérêt et de pression, « sectes », dit encore Rousseau citant Machiavel, etc.,

---

1. Ce qui ne signifie pas, comme le dit Rousseau dans une note, que la volonté générale doive être assimilée à une volonté exprimée à l'unanimité. Si la volonté générale est une, c'est qu'elle est la volonté d'une personne une – le peuple comme moi collectif ; elle est donc la volonté de l'un.

tout cela concourt à tromper le peuple, à le détourner de ses buts. Pour Rousseau, les partis ne concourent pas à l'expression de la volonté générale pour la raison qu'ils sont, par définition même, l'expression de la particularité. Or, la volonté générale est la pensée de l'universel : c'est en ce sens qu'elle exprime la moralité objective.

Sur la différence – essentielle – entre volonté générale et volonté de tous, explicitement énoncée ici, au deuxième paragraphe de ce chapitre III, *cf. supra*, note 17.

Chap. IV

25. Ce premier paragraphe est essentiel car il désigne la théorie qui permet de rendre compte du passage de la théorie bodinienne de la souveraineté à la théorie rousseauiste du souverain. Nous avons observé en temps utile (*supra* dans notre commentaire, II) que Rousseau adapte Bodin à la théorie du droit naturel moderne. Cette adaptation s'opère grâce à la théorie des « êtres moraux ». Et, précisément, grâce à la conception, propre à l'école du droit naturel, de l'État comme personne morale. La première ligne de ce chapitre IV fait explicitement référence à cette conception.

Il est probable que Rousseau a trouvé dans Pufendorf cette conception qui lui convient de l'État « personne morale ». Cet auteur, héritier de Grotius et véritable fondateur de l'école du droit naturel moderne, développe dans son traité *Droit de la nature et des gens*[1] une théorie complète des « *êtres moraux* » ; pour lui l'État est une personne morale parce qu'il soutient les autres : « Les substances corporelles, écrit Pufendorf, supposent nécessairement un Espace où elles puissent placer, pour ainsi dire, leur existence, et exercer leurs mouvements physiques : on dit aussi que les *Personnes* morales sont dans un certain *État*, où l'on les conçoit

1. 1672, traduit par Barbeyrac (1706) ; le texte que nous citons est extrait du livre I, chap. I : « De l'origine des États moraux et de leurs différentes sortes en général », § 3 (c'est Pufendorf qui souligne).

comme renfermées pour déployer leurs actions et y produire leurs effets. *On peut donc définir l'État, un Être moral qui est le soutien des autres.* »

Cette conception convient à Rousseau car elle lui permet de concevoir le peuple comme moi moral collectif, siège de l'unité du vouloir et de l'agir au sein de l'État. Chez Rousseau, l'État est, peut-on dire, la demeure du peuple : sans l'État – qui est une sorte d'*espace*, dit Pufendorf – il n'y aurait pas de peuple. Pourquoi ? Parce que, nous l'avons vu aussi bien chez Bodin que chez Rousseau, la souveraineté est la définition de l'État, elle est l'âme de la république. En tant que telle, elle est passive, parce qu'elle est l'*idée* de l'État ; mais en tant que volonté, elle est active : volonté qui existe dans le peuple ou dans le roi. Rousseau, on le sait, la fait exister dans le peuple. Il n'y aurait pas de « peuple », s'il n'y avait pas de souveraineté, pas d'État. Le peuple est donc le souverain, et sa volonté est souveraine si, et seulement si, elle prend corps au sein de l'État.

On voit que la théorie de la souveraineté du peuple chez Rousseau relève à la fois de la théorie bodinienne de la souveraineté et de la théorie de la personnalité morale de l'État propre à l'école du droit naturel.

Chap. v

26. Ces chapitres iv et v « Des bornes du pouvoir souverain » et « Du droit de vie et de mort » tirent en quelque sorte les conséquences de la définition de la souveraineté (chap. i à iii) du point de vue de l'étendue de la puissance souveraine. Étant absolue – jusqu'au droit de donner la mort –, la puissance souveraine n'est pas par cela même totalitaire. L'absolutisme de la puissance – déjà conçu par Hobbes – découle de sa définition : étant suprême et non soumise au temps (limitée en durée), la puissance souveraine est absolue car « perpétuelle », dit Bodin. Mais elle n'est pas, ainsi pensée, totalitaire (quand bien même elle pourrait dégénérer, comme le sait bien Rousseau). Le totalitarisme pro-

cède d'une volonté particulière – un parti – qui s'érige en universel : c'est la partie qui se prend pour le tout. Autrement dit, c'est quand une partie du peuple se prend pour le peuple parce qu'elle prétend le représenter en parlant en son nom, qu'il y a danger de totalitarisme. Or, selon sa définition, la volonté générale *est* l'universel. Sur ces questions du totalitarisme supposé de la volonté générale illustré notamment par l'infaillibilité de celle-ci, *cf.* Pierre Manent, *Naissances de la politique moderne*, p. 171 *sq.*, Payot, Paris, 1977.

Ayant procédé à la définition de la souveraineté comme principe de l'État (chap. I à III), puis à l'examen de sa puissance (chap. IV et V), Rousseau entreprend ensuite d'exposer en quoi et comment la souveraineté se manifeste; c'est la théorie de la loi (chap. VI et VII).

Chap. VI

27. Il y a ici l'amorce d'une distinction essentielle, qui n'est pas propre à Rousseau, et qui a son origine chez Machiavel : il ne suffit pas de fonder la souveraineté, il faut aussi la conserver. Ce sont là les deux composantes de la politique correspondant aux deux moments de l'action comme de la pensée : fondation et conservation. Montesquieu distinguait déjà entre *lois civiles* qui ont rapport à la fondation de l'État et *lois politiques* qui ont rapport à sa conservation.

Rousseau appelle « loi » un acte de souveraineté; c'est dire que la loi n'exprime que la volonté générale et la volonté générale n'exprime que la loi. Toute autre manifestation de la volonté n'est donc pas une loi.

28. La définition de Montesquieu de la loi comme « rapport » est ici utilisée par Rousseau pour expliquer que la loi exprime une double généralité, dans sa *forme* (volonté) et dans son *objet* (la matière de la loi). Ces précisions et distinctions que fait Rousseau ont pour but de distinguer radicalement les actes de souveraineté ou lois des actes de gouvernement ou décrets.

Rousseau vient d'écrire : « Quand tout le peuple statue sur tout le peuple, il ne considère que lui-même ». Il s'agit non seulement de l'acte fondateur, l'acte par lequel un peuple est un peuple, mais encore de celui par lequel la loi s'exprime chaque fois qu'elle s'exprime, autrement dit, quand le citoyen se manifeste en tant que citoyen, « membre du souverain ». La loi est ce qui donne vie à l'État, au corps social ; en ce sens, elle est *la pensée du souverain* : quand le peuple pense, sa pensée est loi.

29. La loi est une pensée : c'est la pensée de l'universel (*cf.* la note précédente). Seul le « peuple » est capable de se représenter les choses selon le *point de vue de l'universel.* Le roi – personne singulière – ne peut se représenter que la particularité ; son point de vue est la singularité. Il en est de même, selon Rousseau, du corps des magistrats (le « gouvernement » ou « prince ») qui ne peut accéder à l'universel en raison de la particularité de sa volonté et de la singularité de son être.

Le critère de l'*universalité* est le critère unique et décisif de la loi au sens propre. C'est là une découverte capitale de Rousseau dont Kant se souviendra.

30. Rousseau, évoquant la « multitude aveugle qui souvent ne sait ce qu'elle veut » appartient-il ici à ceux auxquels Machiavel reproche de méconnaître la nature des peuples ? Non. Au contraire, Rousseau suit plutôt ici la leçon du grand Florentin. En effet Machiavel, qui étudie le naturel des peuples dans les *Discours sur la première décade de Tite-Live*, et celui des princes dans *Le Prince*, affirme lui aussi que les peuples ont besoin d'un guide qui leur donne des lois. Cependant, le « législateur » de Rousseau ne gouverne pas – à l'inverse du prince de Machiavel – ; il ne fait que rédiger les lois, c'est-à-dire que manifester dans la forme de l'écrit la pensée du souverain.

Quoi qu'il en soit, Rousseau est ici proche de Machiavel, ce « républicain », qui pense que la *république*, où le peuple gouverne, est supérieure au gouvernement d'un prince. « Je dis d'abord, écrit-il, que cette légèreté dont les écrivains accusent la multitude est aussi le défaut des hommes pris individuellement, et plus particulièrement celui des princes; car quiconque n'est pas retenu par le frein des lois commettra les mêmes fautes qu'une multitude déchaînée; il y a des milliers de princes, on compte le nombre des bons et des sages... Je conclus donc contre l'opinion commune qui veut que le peuple, lorsqu'il domine, soit léger, inconstant, ingrat, et je soutiens que ces défauts ne sont pas plus le fait des peuples que celui des princes... Ajoutons que les villes où les peuples gouvernent font d'étonnants progrès en peu de temps... cette différence ne peut naître que de la supériorité du gouvernement d'un peuple sur celui d'un prince[1]. » Sur le rapport Machiavel/Rousseau au sujet de la question du législateur (prince-législateur chez le premier, législateur seulement chez le second), voir l'utile mise au point de Robert Derathé, « Bibliothèque de la Pléiade », p. 1461-1462.

Chap. VII

31. Rousseau, en brossant le portrait du sage législateur, du philosophe appelé à donner des lois aux peuples, brosse son propre portrait quand il aura à travailler aux constitutions de Corse et de Pologne (*cf. infra*, p. 435 et suiv.).

32. Platon, *Le Politique.*

Chap. VIII

33. Les historiens se sont parfois étonnés avec raison de ce que Rousseau ait cru devoir placer ici un exposé en trois temps de sociologie des peuples qui ne « cadre » pas avec le ton abstrait des exposés précédents. Rousseau, en effet, choisit de revenir au fait, lui qui se plaçait au point de vue du droit, c'est-à-dire de la raison. Pourtant, ce choix ne devrait pas surprendre absolument : il s'agit ici d'esquisser une théorie du peuple *du point de vue du législateur* – sous l'influence évidente de Montesquieu. Rousseau écrit un

1. *Discours...*, I, 58.

court traité du naturel des peuples : car le législateur doit connaître les peuples, leur esprit et leur histoire, pour rédiger leurs lois. Il s'agit donc de préparer la théorie de la législation que Rousseau s'apprête à exposer au chapitre suivant (chap. XI). On lit d'ailleurs dans l'*Émile* « qu'il n'y a pas une constitution de gouvernement unique et absolue, mais qu'il doit y avoir autant de gouvernements différents en nature qu'il y a d'États différents en grandeur[1] ».

Observons enfin que ces trois chapitres, qui n'en font qu'un, font la transition entre « l'esprit général » de Montesquieu[2] et « l'esprit d'un peuple » de Hegel. C'est le peuple comme *sujet* de l'histoire et unique *sujet* de toute constitution politique.

Chap. XI

34. *Liberté* et *égalité* sont des objets généraux ; à ce titre ils sont les objets que le peuple souverain pense, ils sont donc la matière de la volonté générale. La fin de la loi (son but) étant de déterminer les principes de liberté et d'égalité, on peut dire que la loi énonce l'universel. C'est pourquoi la difficulté théorique de toute législation vient de ce que le législateur doit concilier l'*universalité* de la loi avec la *particularité* d'un peuple. Particularité que Rousseau vient de montrer dans les chapitres précédents.

Égalité et liberté sont des idées de la raison, connues *a priori* – elles sont les idées du droit. Penser la politique, c'est donc concilier l'universalité du droit avec la particularité de l'histoire.

35. « Force des choses » et « force de la législation » : ce rapport de force est constitutif de la pensée politique, c'est l'opposition de la force et du droit, de l'histoire et de la raison. Penser les prin-

---

1. *Cf. supra*, le résumé du « droit politique » en Annexe II au *Contrat social*. 2. « Plusieurs choses gouvernent les hommes : le climat, la religion, les lois, les maximes du gouvernement, les exemples des choses passées, les mœurs, les manières ; d'où il se forme un esprit général qui en résulte » (*De l'esprit des lois*, XIX, 4).

cipes du droit politique, c'est équilibrer ces deux forces : le *Contrat social* est une tentative pour faire la part des choses du point de vue de la raison (*cf.* note précédente).

Livre III

36. On en arrive, avec ce livre III, au deuxième moment de l'exposé théorique des principes du droit politique. Cette division correspond à la distinction fondamentale établie par Bodin et suivie par Rousseau entre l'État et le gouvernement. Par État, il faut entendre, aussi bien chez Bodin que chez Rousseau, le corps politique (ou république) considéré dans son principe qui est la souveraineté. S'il n'y a pas de souveraineté, il n'y a pas de république, pas de corps politique. Et s'il y a souveraineté, il y a le souverain. Or, le souverain est le corps politique lui-même considéré non comme pur principe, mais comme volonté d'un sujet. Et ce sujet – le « souverain » – est le peuple. La volonté souveraine est volonté du peuple ; en tant que telle, elle est la *puissance d'État* ou « souveraineté ». Autrement dit : l'État est l'unité souveraineté/souverain. Son principe, Bodin l'appelle « puissance souveraine », Rousseau la nomme « volonté générale ».

Cette définition de l'État comme souveraineté contient une seconde distinction, la distinction souverain/sujets. C'est-à-dire la distinction peuple/individus d'un peuple, distinction entre l'unicité du souverain et la multiplicité des sujets. C'est cette même distinction que Rousseau retrouve au sein même de l'individu, à l'état civil, entre « citoyen » et « sujet ».

Il s'agit donc ici, au cours de ce livre III, d'entreprendre la théorie du gouvernement en tant qu'il est conceptuellement distinct de l'État ou souveraineté, mais aussi uni à lui comme le sont les deux faces d'une médaille : la puissance de vouloir et la force d'exécuter ce qui est voulu. La volonté et l'exécution de cette volonté : volonté et pouvoir. Il est nécessaire en effet, selon le concept de souveraineté lui-même que la loi (volonté) soit énoncée et ensuite exécutée (pouvoir). Ce sont deux moments différents de la volonté, différents, mais coexistant ensemble dans l'unité de l'État. La puissance de dire la loi – *énonciation* – est puissance souveraine et gît dans le peuple; le pouvoir de diriger selon la loi – *exécution* – est un simple pouvoir et gît dans le « prince ».

La distinction réelle État/gouvernement (peuple/prince, souverain/magistrats) correspond donc à la distinction conceptuelle fondement/gouvernement, volonté/pouvoir, énonciation/exécution.

Ayant donc jusqu'a présent examiné le fondement, Rousseau entreprend l'étude du gouvernement, respectivement la puissance de fonder un ordre politique et le pouvoir de le gouverner.

Chap. I

37. On a souvent observé qu'il y avait ici deux définitions du gouvernement. À vrai dire il n'y en a qu'une que Rousseau prend soin d'exposer en deux temps : le gouvernement est la *médiation* permettant au peuple en tant que souverain de diriger la multitude des individus en tant que sujette. C'est la médiation permettant à la multiplicité des individus d'être ordonnée à l'unité d'un peuple.

En un premier temps, Rousseau énonce son idée d'un « corps intermédiaire »; en un second temps, il rappelle que ce corps intermédiaire – intermédiaire entre l'auteur du vouloir et les sujets soumis au vouloir – n'est qu'une commission, un office et en aucun cas une « aliénation ». C'est un dépôt. En d'autres termes, le gouvernement – ensemble des ministres – est dépositaire pour une durée déterminée et finie d'une autorisation (ou « pouvoir ») d'agir conformément aux directives du souverain. Autrement dit encore, *la volonté ne s'aliène pas* car ce serait aliéner la liberté, ce qui est contradictoire avec l'idée de liberté comme idée de la raison (*cf. supra*, note 9).

Gouverner, c'est administrer la volonté dans les choses. Il est donc évident qu'il faut y être autorisé; qu'il faut être commis à cette fonction par une autorité habilitée à déterminer qui gouvernera, comment et combien de temps.

On aperçoit clairement que le peuple souverain peut désigner un homme, roi ou président, quel que soit son nom, pour faire passer sa volonté dans les choses. Cet homme peut s'entourer d'un conseil nombreux ou restreint ; quoi qu'il en soit, il reste soumis au souverain. Cette idée, que l'on trouve énoncée la première fois chez Bodin, se retrouve également chez Locke : « Chaque fois qu'un pouvoir, écrit Locke, est conféré comme l'instrument d'une certaine mission, en vue d'une certaine fin, il a cette fin pour limite et, dès lors qu'il est manifeste qu'elle a été négligée ou contrariée, cela entraîne nécessairement la déchéance de l'habilitation, qui se fondait sur la confiance ; le pouvoir fait donc retour à ceux qui l'avaient conféré… La communauté reste donc perpétuellement investie du pouvoir suprême d'assurer son propre salut[1]. »

38. Rapport « du tout au tout ou du souverain à l'État », les « citoyens qui sont souverains d'un côté et sujets de l'autre ». Ce sont là autant de formulations complexes que Rousseau aura le tort d'obscurcir plus encore en les développant à l'intérieur d'un tissu rhétorique de métaphores mathématisantes[2].

Il est vrai que Rousseau doit résoudre ici un problème considérable : une véritable énigme devant laquelle Bodin, lui-même, avait reculé. Il s'agit de savoir comment le peuple-souverain peut soumettre le peuple-sujet. Le problème en effet se pose car, s'il ne se posait pas, on se demande ce que serait l'utilité de la volonté générale, c'est-à-dire de la loi. Il faut bien que la loi soit exécutée une fois qu'elle est énoncée. Et c'est d'ailleurs de cette distinction que

---

1. *Deuxième Traité du gouvernement civil*, ouvr. cité, p. 161, § 149. 2. Rousseau cependant reconnaît un peu plus bas dans ce même chapitre I « que la précision géométrique n'a point lieu dans les quantités morales ». Jean Roussel, dans sa belle édition des *Œuvres politiques*, donne les indications bibliographiques et les explications utiles permettant de déchiffrer le langage de Rousseau dans ce passage, Classiques Garnier, Bordas, Paris, 1989 (p. 641-642). Voir également l'étude magistrale d'Alexis Philonenko sur le *Contrat social* dans *Dictionnaire des œuvres politiques*, P.U.F., 1986.

se déduit nécessairement la distinction de la puissance souveraine et du pouvoir d'exécuter. Autrement dit, Rousseau doit expliquer comment le peuple *peut* se gouverner lui-même : c'est-à-dire se soumettre à sa propre loi (dans les deux sens du verbe pouvoir : en droit et en fait). La théorie du gouvernement comme « corps intermédiaire » vise à élaborer la théorie politique de l'autonomie du peuple : se gouverner soi-même selon sa propre loi. C'est donc la réflexion du peuple allant de soi sur soi-même que Rousseau désigne ici par la notion d'un rapport « du tout au tout ou du souverain à l'État » et par l'idée selon laquelle les citoyens « sont souverains d'un côté et sujets de l'autre ».

La solution à cette énigme – celle d'un peuple qui s'assujettit lui-même à sa propre loi et qui, donc, est à la fois peuple-souverain et peuple-sujet – se trouve dans *Les Six Livres de la République* de Jean Bodin. Cet auteur que Rousseau adapte à la lumière de l'école du droit naturel construit la souveraineté à partir de l'idée de « division » du corps politique, c'est-à-dire chez lui de la séparation souverain/sujets. Or, cette séparation ou « division », Bodin explique qu'elle est essentielle à la souveraineté – elle appartient à son essence. Supprimez la division et vous supprimez la souveraineté, donc l'État. Ce point semble capital pour le bon entendement de Rousseau ; Bodin affirme en effet que, dans *l'État populaire* (qui est très proche de la démocratie de Rousseau), la « division » souverain/sujets disparaît. C'est d'ailleurs, entre autres, une raison pour laquelle Bodin condamne ce type de république. Dans une république bien ordonnée, pense-t-il, il doit y avoir autorité du souverain sur les sujets. Mais selon Bodin une telle autorité disparaît dans « l'estat populaire ». « Le Monarque est divisé du Peuple, écrit Bodin ; et en l'état Aristocratique les Seigneurs sont divisés du menu Peuple : de sorte qu'*en l'une et l'autre République il y a deux parties : à savoir celui ou ceux qui tiennent la souveraineté, d'une part, et le peuple de l'autre*, qui cause les difficultés qui sont entre eux pour les droits de souveraineté, et qui cessent en l'état populaire. » Et Bodin de conclure que ces difficultés quant au droit de souveraineté ne peuvent « avoir lieu en l'État populaire vu que *le peuple ne fait qu'un corps, et ne se peut obliger soi-même* »[1].

Il importe donc à Rousseau de reconstituer la « division » bodinienne afin de préserver le principe de souveraineté – la volonté générale. C'est pourquoi le peuple souverain aura autorité sur la multitude sujette et l'individu d'un État est à la fois citoyen et sujet. Un dédoublement que peut concevoir Rousseau qui dispose de la théorie des êtres moraux – que Bodin ignore. Il y a « deux parties », comme le voulait Bodin, dans la république de Rousseau : d'une part le *peuple* et d'autre part les *sujets*. Or, ces deux parties sont un seul et même corps physique – ce qui effrayait Bodin –, mais ils sont deux corps moraux philosophiquement distincts – deux *êtres moraux*, ce qui satisfait Rousseau (*cf. supra*, note 25 sur les « êtres moraux »).

Le « gouvernement » ou « prince » est donc bien l'intermédiaire entre deux parties qui n'en font qu'une : la partie gouvernante et la partie gouvernée, le peuple-souverain et le peuple-sujet, autrement dit le peuple et… lui-même. Les individus, écrivait Rousseau (I, VI), « prennent collectivement le nom de *peuple*, et s'appellent en particulier *citoyens* comme participants à l'autorité souveraine, et *sujets* comme soumis aux lois de l'État[2]. »

Chap. II

39. Il s'agit bien des formes de gouvernement – et non d'État. Il n'y a en effet qu'une république : celle où la souveraineté est

1. *Les Six Livres de la République*, *op. cit.*, p. 143. (C'est moi qui souligne G. M.) 2. Chez Rousseau le peuple est une personne morale (comme l'est l'État lui-même) ; voici la formation de la personne morale « peuple » selon Pufendorf : « Les Personnes morales composées se forment lors que plusieurs Individus humains s'unissent ensemble de telle manière, que ce qu'ils veulent ou qu'ils font en vertu de cette union n'est censé être qu'une seule volonté et qu'une seule action » (*Le Droit de la nature et des gens*, ouvr. cité, I, 1, § 3).

dans le peuple, où le peuple est « le souverain ». Dès lors la question de la déduction des types de gouvernement est simple en son principe : sachant que le souverain *est* le peuple, il s'agit de savoir si le peuple doit faire dépôt, pour une durée dont il est le seul juge, de l'exécution de sa volonté à un seul magistrat (roi = monarchie), à quelques-uns (aristocratie), à un grand nombre (démocratie).

Il apparaît clairement que la réponse à cette question dépend des circonstances et de l'esprit d'un peuple. Et c'est ce que Rousseau examine dans les chapitres qui suivent.

40. Le principe du choix d'un gouvernement est celui du « degré d'intensité ». Rousseau, qui utilisait tout à l'heure des métaphores mathématiques, utilise maintenant des métaphores relevant de la physique des forces.

Quand il s'agira – ce qui est la tâche du législateur – de constituer un peuple en lui donnant ses lois fondamentales, il faudra déterminer au plus juste quel est le degré d'intensité que la volonté doit atteindre dans le gouvernement de ce peuple. Ce qui ne dépend pas du législateur, mais du peuple lui-même.

Chap. III

41. *Cf. supra*, note 39.

Chap. IV

42. Cette distinction est celle, canonique en droit politique, entre État et gouvernement, c'est-à-dire entre la puissance qui fonde le corps politique et le pouvoir qui est fondé, pour quelque temps, à l'administrer.

43. Il s'agit dans ce chapitre de la théorie pure de la démocratie – et non d'une utopie démocratique qui s'avouerait telle ; *pure* parce que déduite *a priori* du concept de souveraineté.

44. Montesquieu, *De l'esprit*…, III, 3.

45. Montesquieu n'a pas vu, dit Rousseau, que l'État est partout le même : en effet, il n'y a pas de formes différentes d'État, mais

seulement un même gouvernement sous différentes formes possibles (*cf. supra*, note 39).

46. Traduction : « Je préfère les dangers de la liberté à la paix de la servitude. » Maxime que Rousseau affectionne. Jean Roussel observe justement : « Les maximes et les hymnes de la Révolution reprendront souvent le même thème. Dans ce chapitre, l'appel à la constance et à la force morale a quelque chose de désabusé, dans la mesure où l'homme en paraît incapable » (*Œuvres politiques*, p. 646).

Chap. VI

47. Traduction (J. Roussel) : « Car le moyen le plus commode et le plus rapide de discerner le bien du mal, c'est de te demander ce que tu aurais ou n'aurais pas voulu si un autre que toi avait été roi » (Tacite, *Histoires*, I, 16).

48. Platon, *Le Politique.*

Chap. VII

49. Le gouvernement « mixte » est une forme impure : il participe à la fois du maximum d'intensité de force et du minimum, d'où l'image de Rousseau concluant son exposé en disant qu'il s'agit d'une « force moyenne ». Mais il faut ajouter que le souci de Rousseau est de penser la théorie du gouvernement dans le cadre d'une proportion juste. Observons que le thème de la juste proportion constitue le couronnement de l'œuvre de Bodin, attaché à la fin des *Six Livres* à exprimer mathématiquement ce qu'il appelle, en se référant à Platon notamment, la « justice harmonique ».

Chap. VIII

50. Rousseau s'inscrit ici dans la lignée de la « théorie des climats » déjà énoncée par Bodin dans *Les Six Livres* et développée par Montesquieu dans *De l'esprit des lois.*

Ce chapitre fait pendant à ceux concernant le peuple (livre II). Rousseau expliquait alors les conditions particulières auxquelles le législateur devait prêter attention pour connaître un peuple ; il explique ici les particularités à prendre en compte pour connaître le pays. De bonnes lois et un bon gouvernement sont adéquats au peuple et au pays.

51. Jean Chardin dont le *Voyage en Perse* (1711) fut plusieurs fois réédité.

Chap. IX

52. Traduction (J. Roussel) : « Les sots appelaient culture ce qui était déjà un commencement de servitude » (Tacite, *Agricola*, XXI).

53. « Ils font un désert, et ils appellent cela la paix », *ibid.*, XXXI.

Chap. X

54. Commence ici une longue réflexion s'étendant jusqu'au chapitre XV, et se proposant d'exposer les causes de l'évolution et de la destruction des États historiques. On voit que cette étude est menée par Rousseau à l'intérieur de la théorie du gouvernement. C'est que le gouvernement – et non la souveraineté en tant que telle – est la cause possible de la mort des corps politiques.

Rousseau se livre donc à une théorie politique de l'histoire puisque l'État est considéré ici comme réalité historique. Or, la principale cause de dégénérescence des États (en dehors de l'inadéquation des lois au peuple (livre II, VIII-X) ou au pays (livre III, VIII-IX), est fondamentalement le conflit toujours mortel pour le corps politique entre la volonté générale et les volontés particulières.

On peut dire que le fil d'Ariane du *Contrat social* est pour ainsi dire dévoilé ici : *le droit politique vise à unifier dans une même unité éthique – politique, juridique et morale – le particulier et l'universel.* Cela est vrai des individus eux-mêmes, à la fois sujets et citoyens, et des peuples particuliers, mais capables de vouloir le général en pensant l'universel. C'est fondamentalement la rupture de ce lien capital – universel/particulier – qui cause la fin des corps politiques. Corrélativement, c'est la découverte de ce lien qui fait le grand législateur.

Les gouvernements étant chargés d'administrer la particularité, il est essentiel qu'ils n'usurpent pas ce devoir en excédant ses limites. Si un gouvernement confond la particularité de sa volonté et de son action avec la volonté générale, ce qui sur le plan de l'action revient à confondre l'intérêt particulier et l'intérêt général, c'est l'État qui est en péril. Or, Rousseau constate qu'une telle confusion (confusion du particulier et de l'universel) est, à vrai dire, la « pente naturelle » de tout gouvernement…

55. Traduction (J. Roussel) : « Sont en effet tenus pour des tyrans, et désignés comme tels, tous ceux qui disposent à vie du pouvoir dans une cité qui a été libre. »

Chap. XI

56. *Cf. supra*, note 54.

57. Remarquable résumé, par sa concision, sa force rhétorique (« l'animal est mort ») et sa précision théorique à la fois. « *Le principe de la vie politique est dans l'autorité souveraine* » ; c'est la réaffirmation de l'axiome fondamental du droit politique. Il était bon de le rappeler ici après avoir montré comment disparaissent les corps politiques.

58. Ce sont moins les lois elles-mêmes qui maintiennent l'État que le pouvoir de les énoncer, autrement dit, le pouvoir souverain entendu ici comme pouvoir législatif. Le pouvoir de faire les lois peut signifier pouvoir de donner force aux lois anciennes, c'est-à-dire aux lois coutumières. Rousseau applique ici au souverain le dicton « Qui ne dit mot consent » : si le souverain ne révoque pas la coutume explicitement, la coutume a force de loi. C'est là ce que disait Bodin pour qui, la « puissance de donner loi » étant la première « marque » de souveraineté, il revient au souverain (qu'il soit monarque ou peuple) de donner force aux lois anciennes. « Toute la force des lois civiles et coutumes, dit Bodin, gît au pouvoir du Prince

souverain. Voilà donc quant à la première marque de souveraineté, qui est pouvoir de donner loi ou commander à tous en général, et à chacun en particulier : qui est incommunicable aux sujets[1]. » Rousseau, ici encore, suit Bodin puisqu'il affirme que « dans tout État bien constitué », c'est le souverain et lui seul qui est juge de l'opportunité de conférer aux lois anciennes « une force nouvelle ».

Chap. XII

59. Ces trois courts chapitres, qui n'en font qu'un, abordent le problème de la conservation de l'État sous l'angle du « maintien de l'autorité souveraine ». Pour Rousseau, il n'est pas d'autorité souveraine en dehors du peuple, aussi, la question du « maintien » de cette autorité revient-elle à établir *comment le peuple pourrait se trouver déposséder de sa souveraineté.* La réponse est : par les représentants. Ces trois chapitres sont en fait une préparation à l'affirmation catégorique du chapitre XV auquel ils sont unis : « À l'instant qu'un peuple se donne des représentants, il n'est plus libre ; il n'est plus. »

60. « Le souverain ne saurait agir que quand le peuple est assemblé. » Voilà une proposition théorique centrale du droit politique.

Chap. XIII

61. En tant qu'il énonce la loi, l'individu est citoyen-souverain ; en tant qu'il s'y soumet, il est citoyen-sujet : liaison, dans l'individu civil, du particulier à l'universel. C'est cette corrélation particulier/universel que Rousseau, dans le *Contrat social*, met pour la première fois en lumière en tant que principe du droit politique (*cf. supra*, note 54). En ce sens le *Contrat social* doit être regardé comme la théorie du citoyen[2] telle que l'établiront la Révolution et

1. Bodin, *Les Six Livres de la République*, ouvr. cité, p. 222. 2. « Citoyen, c'est-à-dire petit roi », dit Bodin, *ibid.*, p. 943.

le XIXe siècle. Observons que c'est en ce point précis – le statut du citoyen – que se joue aujourd'hui l'avenir du « droit politique » tel que l'a conçu Rousseau.

Chap. XIV

62. La suspension du pouvoir exécutif (« gouvernement » ou « magistrat ») a lieu du seul fait que le peuple s'assemble, dit Rousseau. Or, il envisage ce cas de figure en terme de représentation : « Où se trouve le représenté, il n'y a plus de représentant. » Aussi, on peut en conclure que les « magistrats » formant le gouvernement peuvent être considérés comme des « représentants » du souverain. Mais ils ne représentent pas la volonté, ils ne représentent que le pouvoir d'exécuter qui, originairement, n'est que la puissance souveraine en tant qu'elle s'exerce. Ce qui serait assez conforme à l'idée que se faisait Bodin du gouvernement qui est, selon lui, « *garde* de la puissance souveraine[1] ».

Au reste, si Rousseau s'oppose à toute idée de représentation, c'est parce que le représentant peut usurper la souveraineté ; c'est là l'objet du prochain chapitre et c'est déjà cette « pente naturelle » du prince à « abuser » de son pouvoir qui est analysée dans le chapitre X.

Chap. XV

63. À vrai dire, c'est moins en raison de la corruption possible ou réelle des représentants (« députés ») que pour une raison de principe touchant la souveraineté elle-même, son concept, que Rousseau s'oppose à toute idée de représentation. La *volonté* ne saurait se transmettre, ni se représenter. Rousseau, en effet, a parfaitement vu que représenter la volonté, c'est en perdre le contrôle, si l'on peut dire. Autrement dit, c'est s'exposer à perdre le principe même de sa souveraineté, donc de sa liberté. Il est probable que la théo-

1. *Ibid.*, p. 122.

rie de la représentation chez Hobbes est ici dans la visée critique de Rousseau : le monarque hobbesien est le « représentant » des volontés multiples (*cf. supra*, note 18). Remarquons cependant que, au cours de ses études de politique appliquée, Rousseau admet la représentation (*cf. infra*, note 11 de notre commentaire des *Considérations sur le gouvernement de Pologne*).

64. *Cf.* note précédente.

65. Explicitement pensé ici comme « représentant » (*cf. supra*, note 62), le gouvernement ne représente que le *pouvoir* du souverain ; au contraire, les députés prétendent représenter sa *volonté* (*cf. supra*, note 21).

Chap. XVI

66. Les commentateurs s'accordent à penser que l'argumentation de ce chapitre est une réfutation de Pufendorf et des théoriciens qui l'ont suivi dans l'élaboration de sa théorie de la soumission du peuple au souverain. Ajoutons que, conformément à la distinction propre à la souveraineté – distinction souverain/gouvernement (volonté/pouvoir) –, il est exclu que le gouvernement résulte d'un contrat puisqu'il est institué, pour un temps, par la volonté elle-même. Rousseau réfute donc Pufendorf par… Bodin.

On voit bien ici, d'ailleurs, en quoi Rousseau se sépare de Bodin : ce n'est pas sur le principe de souveraineté lui-même, comme principe de l'État, ce n'est pas non plus sur le fait que le « peuple » soit souverain (une idée connue de Bodin), c'est sur le fait que Rousseau interprète la *fondation* de la souveraineté comme contrat social. Du coup on aperçoit toute la force polémique et révolutionnaire de l'idée de contrat : elle permet d'exclure de la souveraineté toute autre « personne » que le peuple, d'une part ; d'autre part, le contrat permet de ramener le roi au rang de simple ministre… du souverain.

Chap. XVII

67. L'institution du gouvernement est un acte en deux temps ; cela est absolument conforme à la définition de la souveraineté. Deux temps qui correspondent respectivement aux deux ordres constitutifs de la souveraineté : volonté et pouvoir. Le premier temps est une *loi* : le peuple (souverain) déclare sa volonté ; le second est un *effet de la loi* et consiste à confier le pouvoir de l'exécuter à tels ou tels : c'est déjà la loi qui s'exécute dès lors que le « prince » est désigné par le souverain.

Il n'y a aucune espèce de contrat de gouvernement, il y a seulement la souveraineté qui s'exécute conformément à son concept. À vrai dire, supposer un contrat de souveraineté, c'est ou bien vouloir asservir le peuple en l'assujettissant à un maître, ou bien méconnaître la structure de la souveraineté – ou les deux à la fois. Il est clair que ce dernier point est l'avis même de Rousseau.

Chap. XVIII

68. Ici s'achève, à proprement parler, l'exposé rousseauiste des *principes théoriques* du « droit politique ». Et ce dernier paragraphe peut être lu comme une invite à refaire le contrat, selon les principes que Rousseau vient d'établir : les lois fondamentales étant issues de la volonté des hommes, il est apparent que les hommes qui les ont faites peuvent, par cette raison même, aussi bien les défaire.

Le livre IV sera consacré à des questions diverses : le problème du vote, les exemples historiques, et la question des rapports de la politique et de la religion. Ces questions, rejetées à la suite de la déduction abstraite des principes, ne relèvent pas de l'étude de ces mêmes principes. L'exposé qu'il fera de ces questions diverses n'apporte rien, en effet, de nouveau et n'ajoute pas à la compréhension du *Contrat social* qui avait pour ambition « *de fonder l'État sur sa base* ».

Livre IV

Chap. IV

69. Traduction : « Ceux qui gardent les suffrages, les distribuent, les recueillent. »

Chap. VIII

70. Ce chapitre du *Contrat social* (ajouté *in extremis* par Rousseau) fut le plus controversé de l'ouvrage. C'est dire l'incompréhension à laquelle se heurta l'élaboration théorique de Rousseau, car cette longue dissertation sur la religion civile est en fait une attaque superficielle du christianisme. Rousseau est ici très provocateur ; il n'est pas philosophe. Sa critique du christianisme (« je ne connais rien de plus contraire à l'esprit social »), qui est plutôt une critique du pouvoir des prêtres, n'atteint pas les sommets de la critique politique de la religion atteints près d'un siècle plus tôt par Spinoza dans le *Traité théologico-politique* (1670)[1], pour qui la révélation est un auxiliaire de l'obéissance.

À vrai dire, la critique du christianisme, incapable selon Rousseau de fonder le lien social parce que le chrétien est porté à regarder le ciel plutôt que la terre, étonne, car Rousseau ici est en retrait par rapport aux audaces de sa propre pensée quand il élabore les principes du droit politique.

1. « La foi, écrit Spinoza, n'exige pas tant la vérité que la piété et elle n'est pieuse et productrice de salut qu'à proportion de son obéissance ».

Projet de constitution pour la Corse

Notes

1. Dans le *Contrat social*, Rousseau écrit : « Il est encore en Europe un pays capable de législation ; c'est l'île de Corse. La valeur et la constance avec laquelle ce brave peuple a su recouvrer et défendre sa liberté mériterait bien que quelque homme sage lui apprît à la conserver. J'ai quelque pressentiment qu'un jour cette petite île étonnera l'Europe[1] » (livre II, chap. x). Ce passage détermina Mathieu Buttafoco, officier en France du Royal Italien, à contacter Rousseau et à lui demander d'étudier un plan constitutionnel pour la Corse. Dans sa lettre du 31 août 1764, présentant sa requête auprès du philosophe, Buttafoco écrit : « Il est à souhaiter que vous voulussiez être cet homme sage qui pourrait procurer les moyens de conserver cette liberté qui a coûté tant de sang à acquérir[2]. » La lettre de Buttafoco est très adroite : elle désigne explicitement le philosophe comme ce « sage » qu'il appelait lui-même de ses vœux. Rousseau accepte et demande une documentation très abondante.

L'histoire de la Corse, de ses luttes contre Gênes (puissance coloniale qui exerçait sa tyrannie sur l'île), la résistance armée, tout cela, qui avait ému l'Europe, avait suscité l'intérêt moral et poli-

---

1. Le pressentiment de Rousseau ne devait pas se réaliser, car la Corse n'étonna pas l'Europe. Rousseau, en effet, ne songeait pas alors à un Bonaparte, qui, sorti de Corse, allait mettre l'Europe à feu et à sang, mais tout au contraire, il espérait un miracle qui n'eut pas lieu, celui de la fondation, en Corse, d'un gouvernement légitime qui eût été un exemple pour l'Europe. Rapprocher cette parole du *Contrat* de l'avènement, tant redouté par Rousseau, d'un despote armé, est un contresens. 2. Cité par J. Roussel dans son édition des *Œuvres politiques*, p. 362 (*cf. infra*, bibliographie).

tique de Rousseau. C'est pourquoi il jugeait que la Corse était le seul pays en Europe « capable de législation ». « Dans l'Europe des Lumières, la Corse était en passe de devenir un pays mythique, écrit Jean Roussel. Par leur lutte contre les Génois, les Corses attiraient depuis longtemps l'admiration des esprits éclairés. Ils s'étaient soulevés en 1729 et au terme de trois années de guerre (1732-1735), avaient expulsé l'oppresseur. Mais la guerre de Succession d'Autriche et le traité d'Aix-la-Chapelle les avaient remis, en principe, sous la domination génoise, en 1749. Deux ans plus tard, c'est contre ce traité que s'organise le soulèvement dont Pascal Paoli prend la tête. La révolte des Corses connaît le succès, et Paoli organise son pouvoir. Cette victoire de la liberté a un grand retentissement. Il est exagéré d'y voir la première des révolutions qui conduiront le siècle jusqu'à 1789. Elle n'en brille pas moins du plus vif éclat, en Angleterre, en Italie, en France[1]. »

En mars 1765, Rousseau cependant renonce à travailler au projet de constitution pour la Corse, ses idées étant, dit-il, trop différentes de celles des Corses. Il continuera néanmoins d'étudier le problème corse jusqu'en septembre 1765. Le *Projet* resta inachevé et ne fut publié qu'en 1861.

2. Rousseau se place ici, dans le *Projet*, du point de vue de la fondation du corps politique plutôt que du point de vue de sa conservation. Fondation et conservation sont les deux moments constitutifs de la vie politique d'un peuple. Il s'agit pour Rousseau de se représenter comment fonder la souveraineté, ce qui revient à instituer le *principe* de l'État (la souveraineté en tant que telle) et la *forme* en laquelle la souveraineté s'exerce et passe dans les choses (c'est-à-dire le « gouvernement »). Dans ses *Considérations sur le gouvernement de Pologne*, Rousseau envisage plutôt le problème politique sous l'angle de la conservation : réforme du gouvernement, non pas fondation du corps politique (*cf.* notre commentaire de ce texte). En ce sens, le *Projet* et les *Considérations* sont remarquablement complémentaires.

---

1. J. Roussel, *ibid.*, p. 361.

3. Formule rappelant le fondement de toute idée de liberté chez Rousseau : l'*autonomie* ou obéissance à soi-même. Il en déduira le nécessaire recours à l'autarcie (voir plus bas).

4. Barbara de Negroni, dans son édition du *Projet* (*cf. infra*, bibliographie), fournit les indications historiques : « Gênes, pour réprimer les mouvements d'insurrection contre son autorité, appela des armées étrangères à son secours. De 1730 à 1733, Charles VI d'Autriche envoya 8 000 hommes en Corse ; en 1738 eut lieu la première intervention française sous le commandement du comte de Boissieux ; en 1745 et 1746, les Anglais, les Sardes et les Français s'affrontent en Corse où ils constituent un front d'hostilités secondaires dans la guerre de Succession d'Autriche ; cela conduira la France à organiser en 1748 une seconde intervention, sous la direction du marquis de Cursay, pour empêcher une mainmise anglaise ou sarde sur la Corse. Les Corses, de leur côté, essayèrent également de provoquer une internationalisation du conflit en intéressant les Espagnols à leur cause » (p. 274).

5. Rousseau conseille le recours à une politique autarcique.

6. Rousseau ici est physiocrate : seule l'agriculture satisfait les besoins en produisant le nécessaire de façon autarcique ; il est également mercantiliste – le commerce enrichit. Rousseau écrit ces pages en 1764 ou 1765 ; un peu plus de dix ans plus tard, Adam Smith fondera l'économie politique avec ses *Recherches sur la nature et les causes de la richesse des nations*. Il démontrera que le travail industriel est source de richesse.

7. Cette notion – l'esprit général – est introduite par Montesquieu, *cf. De l'esprit des lois*, à qui Rousseau l'emprunte : « Plusieurs choses gouvernent les hommes : le climat, la religion, les lois, les maximes du gouvernement, les exemples des choses passées, les mœurs, les manières : d'où il se forme un esprit général qui en résulte » (XIX, 4).

8. Sur le « gouvernement mixte », *cf. Contrat social*, III, VII.

9. Mémoire rédigé par Buttafoco, qu'il adressa sur sa demande à Rousseau.

10. Unité administrative ecclésiastique.

11. La *Terre de la commune* se définit par opposition à la *Terre des seigneurs* (B. de Negroni).

12. En deçà et au-delà des monts (B. de Negroni).

13. C'est la règle fondamentale que doit observer le législateur : donner des lois au peuple, conformément à son esprit.

14. La loi fondamentale, c'est-à-dire le pacte civil lui-même, est donc une clause de la volonté qui reproduit, par un artifice, les dispositions de la nature. Le *Contrat social* est tout entier destiné, dans l'esprit de Rousseau, à exposer les principes généraux de la fondation du corps politique entendue comme acte de substitution de la liberté artificielle à la liberté naturelle.

15. Nous sommes bien au moment où se produit l'événement fondateur du corps politique : le contrat. Le « serment » que chacun doit prononcer est le même pour tous, c'est la formule de fondation.

16. Le corps politique est une personne une, un « moi commun », c'est une personne morale, possédant une volonté une, la volonté générale (*cf. Contrat social*, I, VI et notre commentaire de ce passage). On lit au livre I de l'*Émile* : « Les bonnes institutions sociales sont celles qui savent le mieux dénaturer l'homme, lui ôter son existence absolue pour lui en donner une relative, et transporter le *moi* dans l'unité commune ; en sorte que chaque particulier ne se croie plus un, mais partie de l'unité, et ne soit plus sensible que dans le tout. »

17. Les arts sont cause de « mollesse » : Rousseau n'a pas varié, en ce domaine, depuis le *Discours sur les sciences et les arts*.

18. « Égaliser la population », c'est-à-dire la répartir également. Remarquons au passage l'affirmation constante de Rousseau concernant la nécessité de toujours « multiplier » la population, autrement dit, l'accroître (*cf. Contrat social*, III, III).

19. Rousseau a donc lié la fondation du corps politique à une économie rustique, autarcique et nataliste.

20. Impôts indirects, redevances qu'un particulier doit à l'État.

21. Rousseau, on le voit, n'est pas disposé à interdire toute propriété privée, mais seulement à la limiter considérablement, probablement aux seuls biens de consommation ou de subsistance immédiate, la grosse propriété étant, elle, du domaine public. C'est pourquoi il suggère, quelques lignes plus bas, que l'État, s'étant approprié les terres en friche, les fasse cultiver par corvées.

Considérations sur le gouvernement de Pologne

Notes

1. Les *Considérations sur le gouvernement de Pologne* ont été demandées à Rousseau par Wielhorski. Le comte Michel Wielhorski était l'envoyé de la Confédération de Bar auprès de la cour de France. Choiseul menait une politique de soutien à la Confédération de Bar alors en résistance armée contre le roi Stanislas, créature de Catherine II de Russie et de la Diète polonaise. Les « confédérations » étaient des ligues de noblesse autorisées par la constitution. Créée par la noblesse polonaise en février 1768, la Confédération de Bar débordait largement le cadre politique strictement polonais pour devenir un problème de politique internationale à l'échelle européenne.

Rousseau accepta de travailler pour la Confédération et, en juin 1771, il remit le texte des *Considérations* à Wielhorski. Les *Considérations* furent publiées après la mort de Rousseau, en 1782.

Alors que dans son *Projet pour la Corse* Rousseau étudie les conditions d'application des principes du droit politique à la question de la *fondation* réelle d'un ordre républicain légitime, ici, dans les *Considérations*, il s'attache principalement à la question de la réforme pratique d'une république et de son nouveau *gouvernement*.

2. Au lieu du titre définitif – « Question des trois ordres » –, Rousseau avait songé intituler ce chapitre : « Souveraineté, où réside-t-elle ? » Le problème est de savoir, en effet, quelle est la personne morale qui, en Pologne, est le souverain. Les premières lignes de ce chapitre font plutôt penser que, au sens propre, il n'y a pas de souveraineté et, par suite, il n'y a pas même de « république » : il y a une « nation ». Quant à la première phrase du chapitre, elle récuse le sens que l'on donne habituellement à « gouvernement » – car ce mot est employé ordinairement dans un contexte où les principes sont « faux ou louches ». En résumé, ces trois premières phrases sont une réfutation des lieux communs.

Les trois ordres – qui sont les ordres de la « nation », non de la « république », précise Rousseau – sont la noblesse, la bourgeoisie et les serfs. L'*ordre équestre* se compose des seuls citoyens : nobles, ils possèdent une parcelle de la souveraineté. Quant au gouvernement de Pologne – que Rousseau est invité à réformer –, il est constitué par l'ordre équestre, le Sénat et un roi électif. La *Diète* est l'assemblée législative constituée de l'ordre équestre ; elle est réunie tous les deux ans par le roi. Les *nonces* sont les élus de la noblesse qui siègent à la *Diète.* Le collège électoral des nobles (élisant les nonces) est la *Diétine.* (Sur la question complexe des institutions polonaises, voir les explications de B. de Negroni, que nous suivons ici, dans son excellente édition de la « politique appliquée » de Rousseau, *cf. infra*, bibliographie.)

3. Ce passage fait écho au *Contrat social* (III, XIV) : « À l'instant que le peuple est légitimement assemblé en corps souverain, toute juridiction du gouvernement cesse ; la puissance exécutive est suspendue, et la personne du dernier citoyen est aussi sacrée et inviolable que celle du premier magistrat, parce qu'où se trouve le représenté, il n'y a plus de représentant. » L'expression « la voix de Dieu » est évidemment ici une métaphore pour exprimer le caractère transcendant de la volonté générale sur toute volonté particulière – notamment celle des exécutants.

4. Rousseau recommande la prudence. Et, s'il s'agit de libérer les serfs de leur servitude, cela ne peut se faire du jour au lendemain : ce serait créer des citoyens qui ne sauraient jouir de leur liberté civile tant l'habitude de la servitude est une seconde nature. La Pologne comptait huit millions de serfs.

5. « Affranchir leurs âmes » : Rousseau compte sur l'éducation. En effet, l'homme n'est pas citoyen par nature ; il doit donc être amené à la cité (*cf. Discours sur l'économie politique* et notre commentaire, note 12).

6. C'est là un des problèmes centraux que Rousseau a voulu résoudre dans ses principes du droit politique : puisque la « pente naturelle » du gouvernement est de dégénérer en prenant le pas sur la souveraineté (*cf. Contrat social*, III, x), qu'il ne devrait cependant que *servir*, il faut trouver les moyens d'écarter ce danger. Résoudre ce problème, c'est résoudre l'énigme politique.

7. Les *pacta conventa* sont un recueil de lois fondamentales de la Pologne que tout roi doit jurer de respecter le jour de son sacre (B. de Negroni).

8. III, x.

9. C'est-à-dire le *veto* dont disposait tout membre de la Diète depuis 1650.

10. III, XIII.

11. Apparemment, Rousseau n'est pas fidèle aux principes du droit politique tels qu'il les expose dans le *Contrat.* Cependant, il s'agit ici de politique appliquée ; il importe donc à Rousseau, puisqu'il s'agit de l'histoire réelle, non de renoncer à ses principes, ou de les appliquer à toute force, mais de tenir compte de la résistance de la nécessité, des contraintes de la matière historique (*cf. Contrat social*, III, xv, sur l'impossibilité de représenter la volonté, et nos commentaires, notes 21 et 62 65).

12. Les « universaux » : convocation spécifiant les points de délibération des Diétines et de la Diète (B. de Negroni).

13. III, XIII, XIV.

14. Homme politique anglais (1727-1797), membre des Communes, auteur de satires politiques.

15. Greffe ayant fonction d'enregistrement.

16. Distinction capitale du droit politique : la puissance souveraine (ou « législative », comme dit encore Rousseau) est spécifiquement différente, dans son concept et dans la chose, du pouvoir d'administrer (ou « gouvernement »).

17. C'est la crainte constante de Rousseau vis-à-vis des corps et des partis : ceux-ci développent une *volonté de corps* qui ne manque jamais d'entrer en conflit avec la volonté générale et de la « subjuguer ».

18. Palatin, castellan, staroste sont des charges héréditaires de noblesse terrienne.

19. IV, II et IV.

20. Pour cette fonction.

21. « Instituteur », c'est-à-dire *législateur* dans le sens que Rousseau donne à ce terme dans le *Contrat.*

22. Dans ses *Principes de la philosophie du droit* (1821), Hegel explique que le monarque d'une monarchie constitutionnelle *ne fait rien*; il se borne, dit-il, « à dire oui et à mettre les points sur les i » (§ 273, trad. Derathé, Paris, Vrin, 1975).

23. Le pouvoir exécutif, par définition même de la souveraineté, ne saurait être qu'un dépôt, une commission consentie *pour un temps* (*cf. Contrat social*, commentaire II). Seule la souveraineté est « perpétuelle », non le gouvernement (Bodin, suivi par Rousseau).

24. Ce paragraphe est l'application parfaitement orthodoxe du principe pur de souveraineté : distinction des deux « pouvoirs » – de souveraineté et de gouvernement. La confusion des deux est cause d'anarchie.

25. *Cf. Contrat social*, IV, II. Les « lois fondamentales » sont les clauses du pacte social lui-même.

26. Le corps social étant l'effet de la volonté, ce que la volonté pose, la volonté peut également le défaire. C'est là une conséquence suivant nécessairement de la définition même de la « souveraineté » : le souverain n'est *pas* soumis à sa propre volonté (les lois), attendu qu'il *est* la volonté même. Ce que le souverain veut, il peut

cesser souverainement de le vouloir. En revanche, le gouvernement – qui n'est *pas* souverain – est soumis à la loi.

27. Le souci de Rousseau législateur est ici évident : il s'agit de préserver la liberté en mesurant toujours comment, dans les choses, les principes généraux qui les expliquent sont vérifiés : ainsi le droit de *veto* est contraire à la liberté s'il en est fait un usage abusif. Quant aux *confédérations* – Rousseau a sous les yeux la confédération de Bar, et c'est à la demande de celle-ci qu'il rédige les *Considérations* –, un point de vue hâtif serait de les supprimer parce qu'elles forment un corps particulier dans l'État. Pourtant, un examen attentif et nuancé des circonstances historiques montre qu'elles sont plutôt un levier de la liberté : il faut savoir ménager sa place à la volonté de corps.

28. Il s'agit bien entendu des troupes de Catherine II, protectrice de Stanislas.

29. Espoir de la patrie.

30. Citoyen choisi.

31. Gardien des lois (pour ces trois notes : B. de Negroni).

32. Rousseau ici prend les choses telles qu'elles sont, non telles qu'elles devraient être selon les principes du droit politique. Cela vient, dit-il, qu'« il ne serait en ce moment ni prudent ni possible de la changer [la constitution] tout d'un coup ». Prudence du philosophe.

Remarquons enfin que, à la lumière des *Considérations* comme du *Projet*, c'est un contresens de voir dans le *Contrat social* une « utopie » ou même la description d'une république « idéale ». Le *Contrat* énonce des principes : il pense l'idée de l'État ou l'État comme *Idée*. Or, l'idée n'est pas opposée à l'histoire réelle, seul l'idéal s'y oppose.

CHRONOLOGIE

1712, *28 juin.* — Naissance à Genève de Jean-Jacques Rousseau. Suzanne Bernard, sa mère, meurt le 7 juillet.

1715. — Mort de Louis XIV.

1717-1722. — Le père de Rousseau lui fait lire Plutarque.

1722-1724. — Jean-Jacques est en pension chez le pasteur Lambercier.

1723. — Sacre de Louis XV.

1725. — Rousseau apprenti graveur chez Ducommun.

1726. — Exil forcé de Voltaire à Londres.

1728. — Rousseau quitte Genève ; on le convertit, à Turin, au catholicisme.

1729. — Émeutes en Corse contre le gouvernement génois.

1730. — Rousseau est professeur de musique à Lausanne.

1731. — À Paris, où il occupe un emploi de précepteur.

1734. — Voltaire, retour de Londres, publie les *Lettres philosophiques.*

1738. — Traité de Vienne, fin de la guerre de Succession de Pologne.

1739. — Hume : *Traité de la nature humaine.*

1740-1741. — Il occupe l'emploi de précepteur chez M. de Mably à Lyon.

1743. — Rousseau secrétaire de l'ambassadeur de France, Montaigu, à Venise.

1745. — Amitié avec Diderot à Paris.

1746. — Condillac : *Essai sur l'origine des connaissances humaines.*

1747. — Burlamaqui, professeur à Genève, publie ses *Principes du droit naturel.*

1748. — Montesquieu : *De l'esprit des lois.*

1749. — Rousseau collabore à l'*Encyclopédie*. Diderot : *Lettre sur les aveugles.*

Juillet. — Diderot enfermé à Vincennes.

Octobre. — Rousseau visite Diderot à Vincennes; il a alors une « inspiration subite » en découvrant dans le *Mercure de France* la question mise au concours par l'Académie de Dijon : « Si le rétablissement des sciences et des arts a contribué à épurer les mœurs. »

1750. *9 juillet.* — Rousseau est couronné pour son *Discours sur les sciences et les arts.* Vives polémiques. Rousseau répond.

1752. — Première condamnation de l'*Encyclopédie.*

1753. — Nouvelle question de l'Académie de Dijon : « Quelle est la source de l'inégalité parmi les hommes, et si elle est autorisée par la loi naturelle. » Conflit de souveraineté entre le roi et les parlements.

1754. — Voyage de Rousseau à Genève où il est réintégré à l'Église calviniste; il recouvre sa citoyenneté.

1755. — Rousseau publie : *Discours sur l'origine et les fondements de l'inégalité parmi les hommes.* (Le discours n'a pas été couronné par l'Académie.) Mort de Montesquieu. Tremblement de terre de Lisbonne : émotion de Voltaire. Rousseau rédige l'article « Économie politique » pour l'*Encyclopédie*. Il étudie les textes de l'abbé de Saint-Pierre que lui a remis son éditeur Rey.

1756. — *Lettre sur la Providence*, adressée à Voltaire. Début de la guerre de Sept Ans.

1757. — D'Alembert publie son article « Genève » dans l'*Encyclopédie*. L'article porte la marque de Voltaire.

1758. — *Lettre à d'Alembert sur les spectacles.*

1759. — Voltaire : *Candide*. Rousseau rédige l'*Émile*.

1760. — Rousseau transmet à Rey un « brouillon » du *Contrat social* : le « Manuscrit de Genève » (première version du *Contrat social*).

1761. — Publication de *La Nouvelle Héloïse* et des *Extraits du « projet » de l'abbé de Saint-Pierre.*

1762. *Avril et mai.* — Publication du *Contrat social* puis de l'*Émile*.

Juin. — Le *Contrat* et l'*Émile* sont brûlés par le bourreau à Genève. En France, début de l'affaire Calas.

7 juin. — La Sorbonne dénonce l'*Émile*.

9 juin. — Condamnation de l'*Émile* par le parlement de Paris. Rousseau, décrété de prise de corps, prend la fuite dans la principauté de Neuchâtel.

Août. — Mandement contre l'*Émile* de l'archevêque de Paris Christophe de Beaumont.

1763. — Rousseau publie sa *Lettre à Christophe de Beaumont*. Fin de la guerre de Sept Ans. Tronchin de Genève justifie la condamnation des œuvres de Rousseau dans des *Lettres* anonymes.

1764. — Réponse de Rousseau à Tronchin dans ses *Lettres écrites de la montagne*. Buttafoco demande à Rousseau d'être le législateur de la Corse.

Décembre. — Voltaire lance contre Rousseau un pamphlet anonyme : *Le Sentiment des citoyens.*

1765. — Voltaire obtient la réhabilitation de Calas. On brûle le *Contrat social* dans les capitales d'Europe; Rousseau écrit à Guyenet le 6 février 1765 : « Le 22 janvier on a brûlé mon livre à La Haye; on doit aujourd'hui le brûler à Genève; on le brûlera, j'espère, encore ailleurs. Voilà par le froid qu'il fait des gens bien brûlants. Que de feux de joie brillent à mon honneur dans l'Europe! »

Mars. — Rousseau renonce à être le législateur des Corses, mais il continue de travailler au *Projet de constitution pour la Corse.*

1766. — Séance de la « Flagellation » au parlement de Paris : Louis XV réaffirme sa souveraineté. Rousseau part en Angleterre avec Hume.

1767. — Brouillé avec Hume, Rousseau s'établit en France chez le prince de Conti, à Trye.

1768. — Confédération de Bar en Pologne. La France achète la Corse à Gênes.

1770. — Rousseau part pour Paris.

Octobre. — Rencontre avec Wielhorski qui le persuade d'étudier la question du gouvernement de Pologne.

Décembre. — Disgrâce de Choiseul.

1771. — Rousseau remet à Wielhorski, en *juin*, le manuscrit des *Considérations sur le gouvernement de Pologne.* La police interdit à Rousseau de faire des lectures publiques de ses *Confessions.*

1772-1776. — Rédaction de *Rousseau, juge de Jean-Jacques* et des *Rêveries du promeneur solitaire.*

1774. — Mort de Louis XV; Louis XVI lui succède.

1776. — Au printemps, il distribue lui-même dans les rues de Paris un tract qu'il vient d'écrire : *À tout Français aimant encore la justice et la vérité.* Adam Smith publie ses *Recherches sur la nature et les causes de la richesse des nations.*

Début de la Révolution américaine.

1778. — Achèvement des *Rêveries*.
20 mai. — Rousseau s'installe à Ermenonville.
2 juillet. — Mort de Rousseau à Ermenonville.
1791. — La rue Plâtrière à Paris devient rue Jean-Jacques Rousseau.
1794. — Transfert des restes de Rousseau au Panthéon.

Bibliographie sommaire

La bibliographie rousseauiste est immense. Nous nous limitons ici aux ouvrages ayant proposé une interprétation décisive de l'œuvre de Rousseau et, particulièrement, de sa politique.

I. Éditions des écrits politiques

Œuvres complètes, tome III. *Du contrat social – Écrits politiques*, Paris, Gallimard, « Bibliothèque de la Pléiade », 1964. Édition de référence sous la direction de Bernard Gagnebin et Marcel Raymond. Introductions et notes de François Bouchardy (*Discours sur les sciences et les arts*), Jean Starobinski (*Discours sur l'inégalité*), Robert Derathé (*Du contrat social, Discours sur l'économie politique, Manuscrit de Genève*), Sven Stelling Michaud (*Écrits sur l'abbé de Saint-Pierre* et *Projet de constitution pour la Corse*), Jean-Daniel Candaux (*Lettres écrites de la montagne* et *Dépêches de Venise*), Jean Fabre (*Considérations sur le gouvernement de Pologne*).

Œuvres politiques, édition de Jean Roussel. Introduction générale, bibliographie, repères chronologiques, choix de textes, notes, variantes, appendice établis par Jean Roussel, Paris, Bordas, « Classiques Garnier », 1989. Ce volume contient : *Discours sur l'inégalité, Discours sur l'économie politique, Écrits sur l'abbé de Saint-Pierre, Du contrat social, Projet de constitution pour la Corse, Considérations sur le gouvernement de Pologne* et, en appendice, la première version du *Contrat social.*

Du contrat social :

– Introduction, notes et commentaires par Maurice Halbwachs, Paris, Aubier-Montaigne, 1943 (rééd. 1967).
– Version définitive précédée de la première version. Édition critique par Simone Goyard-Fabre, Paris, Honoré Champion, 2010.

Discours sur l'économique politique, Projet de constitution pour la Corse, Considérations sur le gouvernement de Pologne, édition, notes, bibliographie et chronologie par Barbara de Negroni, Paris, GF-Flammarion, 1990.

II. Études sur Rousseau

BACZKO (B.), *Rousseau, solitude et communauté*, Paris, Mouton, 1974.

BRUNEL (P.), *L'État et le souverain*, Paris, PUF, 1978.

BURGELIN (P.), *La Philosophie de l'existence de Jean-Jacques Rousseau*, Paris, PUF, 1982.

CASSIRER (E.), *La Philosophie des Lumières*, Paris, Fayard, 1966.

—, *Le Problème Jean-Jacques Rousseau*, Paris, Hachette, 1987.

Derathé (R.), *Jean-Jacques Rousseau et la science politique de son temps*, 2e éd., Paris, Vrin, 1992.

Études sur le Contrat social, Paris, Les Belles Lettres, 1964.

Goldschmidt (V.), *Anthropologie et politique. Les principes du système de Rousseau*, Paris, Vrin, 1974.

Goyard-Fabre (S.), *Politique et philosophie dans l'œuvre de Jean-Jacques Rousseau*, Paris, PUF, 2001.

Groethuysen (B.), *Jean-Jacques Rousseau*, Paris, Gallimard, 1949.

Lafrance (G.), dir., *Études sur le* Contrat social, Ottawa, Pensée libre, 1989.

L'Aminot (T.), *Bibliographie mondiale de Rousseau*, http ://rousseaustudies.free.fr

Leduc-Fayette (D.), *Jean-Jacques Rousseau et le mythe de l'Antiquité*, Paris, Vrin, 1974.

Mairet (G.), *Le Principe de souveraineté. Histoires et fondements du pouvoir moderne*, Paris, Gallimard, « Folio », 1997.

Manent (P.), *Naissances de la politique moderne. Machiavel, Hobbes, Rousseau*, Paris, Payot, 1984.

Masters (R. D.), *La Philosophie politique de Rousseau*, Paris, ENS-LSH Éditions, 2002.

Pensée de Rousseau, Paris, Le Seuil, 1984.

Philonenko (A.), *Jean-Jacques Rousseau et la pensée du malheur*, 3 vol., Paris, Vrin, 1984.

Spitz (J. F.), *La Liberté politique*, Paris, PUF, 1995.

Starobinski (J.), *Jean-Jacques Rousseau, la transparence et l'obstacle*, suivi de *Sept essais sur Rousseau*, Paris, Gallimard (1976), « Tel », 1987.

Terrel (J.), *Les Théories du contrat social*, Paris, Le Seuil, 2001.

Trousson (R.), *Jean-Jacques Rousseau*, Paris, Tallandier, 2003.

Trousson (R.), Eigeldinger (F. S.), *Dictionnaire de Jean-Jacques Rousseau*, Paris, Champion, 2006.
Vincenti (L.), *Jean-Jacques Rousseau, l'individu et la république*, Paris, Kimé, 2000.

Table

Commentaires et notes

Composition réalisée par DATAGRAFIX

Achevé d'imprimer en mars 2012 en France par
CPI BRODARD ET TAUPIN
La Flèche (Sarthe)
N° d'impression : 67709
Dépôt légal 1re publication : janvier 1992
Édition 02 – mars 2012
LIBRAIRIE GÉNÉRALE FRANÇAISE
31, rue de Fleurus – 75278 Paris Cedex 06